Reframing
Organizations

Reframing Organizations

Artistry, Choice, and Leadership

THIRD EDITION

LEE G. BOLMAN

TERRENCE E. DEAL

JOSSEY-BASS
A Wiley Imprint
www.josseybass.com

Published by Jossey-Bass
A Wiley Imprint
989 Market Street, San Francisco, CA 94103-1741   www.josseybass.com

Jossey-Bass books and products are available through most bookstores. To contact Jossey-Bass directly call our Customer Care Department within the U.S. at 800-956-7739, outside the U.S. at 317-572-3986 or fax 317-572-4002.

Jossey-Bass also publishes its books in a variety of electronic formats. Some content that appears in print may not be available in electronic books.

Credits are on p. 484.

Library of Congress Cataloging-in-Publication Data

Bolman, Lee G.
   Reframing organizations : artistry, choice, and leadership / Lee G. Bolman, Terrence E. Deal.-3rd ed.
     p. cm.
   "A joint publication in The Jossey-Bass business & management series and The Jossey-Bass higher & adult education series."
   Includes bibliographical references and index.
   ISBN 0-7879-6426-3 (alk. paper) - ISBN 0-7879-6427-1 (alk. paper)
   1. Management. 2. Organizational behavior. 3. Leadership. I. Deal, Terrence E. II. Title. III. Jossey-Bass business & management series. IV. Jossey-Bass higher and adult education series.
HD31.B6135 2003
658.4'063-dc21   2003006453

Printed in the United States of America
THIRD EDITION

HB Printing   10 9 8 7 6 5 4 3 2
PB Printing   10 9 8 7 6 5 4 3

A joint publication in

THE JOSSEY-BASS BUSINESS
& MANAGEMENT SERIES

and

THE JOSSEY-BASS HIGHER &
ADULT EDUCATION SERIES

CONTENTS

PREFACE

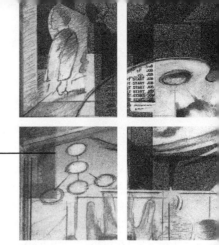

This is the fourth release of a work that began in 1984 as *Modern Approaches to Understanding and Managing Organizations*. It reappeared twice in the 1990s as *Reframing Organizations* and has been translated into multiple languages. We're grateful to readers around the world who have told us the book gave them ideas that make a difference—in their everyday life at work and elsewhere in their lives.

It is time for an update, and we're gratified to be back by popular demand. Organizations and leadership challenges have been changing rapidly in recent years, and scholars have been running hard to keep up. This edition tries to capture the new-millennial frontiers of both knowledge and art.

The four-frame model, with its view of organizations as factories, families, jungles, and temples, remains the book's conceptual heart. But so much else has changed. We have updated our case examples extensively to keep up with the latest developments in managerial practice. We have added a new feature, a series we call "greatest hits in organization studies." These sidebars represent pithy summaries of key ideas from the most influential works in the scholarly literature (as indicated by a new citation analysis, described in the Appendix). As a counterpoint to the scholarly works, we have also added occasional summaries of recent management best-sellers.

Life in organizations has also produced many new examples. The introductory chapters and our section on the structural frame (Part Two) both benefit from extensive updating of case material. In our discussion of human resource management, we have added new material on diversity and included other developments at the HR frontier. We have added new case material and research findings to our discussion of organizational politics and symbols. We have also deepened our discussion of organizational culture.

There is new material throughout the book, but we worked zealously to minimize bloat by tracking down and expunging every redundant sentence, marginal concept, or extraneous example. At the same time, we've tried to keep it fun. Organizational life is an endless source of examples as entertaining as they are instructive, and we've sprinkled them throughout the text. We apologize to anyone who finds that an old favorite fell to the cutting-room floor, but we think most readers will find the book an even clearer and more efficient read.

As always, our primary audience is managers and future leaders. We have tried to answer the question, What do we know about organizations and leadership that is genuinely important and useful to practitioners? We have worked to present a large, complex body of theory, research, and practice as clearly and simply as possible. We tried to avoid watering it down or presenting simplistic views of how to solve managerial problems. We try to avoid solutions in favor of more powerful and provocative ways of thinking about organizational opportunities and pitfalls.

We continue to focus on both management *and* leadership. Leading and managing are different, but both are important. If an organization is overmanaged but underled, it eventually loses any sense of spirit or purpose. A poorly managed organization with a strong, charismatic leader may soar briefly only to crash shortly thereafter. Malpractice can be as damaging and unethical for managers and leaders as for physicians. Myopic managers or overzealous leaders usually harm more than just themselves. The challenges of modern organizations require the objective perspective of managers as well as the brilliant flashes of vision wise leadership provides. We need more people in managerial roles who can find simplicity and order amid organizational confusion and chaos. We need versatile and flexible leaders who are artists as well as analysts, who can reframe experience to discover new issues and possibilities. We need managers who love their work, their organizations, and the people whose lives they affect. We need leaders and managers who appreciate management as a moral and ethical undertaking. We need leaders who combine hard-headed realism with passionate commitment to larger values and purposes. We hope to encourage and nurture such qualities and possibilities.

As in the past, we have tried to produce a clear and readable synthesis and integration of the field's major theoretical traditions. We concentrate mainly on organization theory's implications for practice. We draw on examples from every sector and around the globe.

Historically, organization studies have been divided into several intellectual camps, often isolated from one another. Works that seek to give a comprehensive overview of organization theory and research often drown in social science jargon and abstraction and have little to say to practitioners. We try to find a balance between misleading oversimplification and mind-boggling complexity.

The bulk of work in organization theory has focused almost exclusively on either the private *or* the public sector, but not both. We think this is a mistake. Managers need to understand similarities and differences among all types of organizations. The public and private sectors increasingly interpenetrate one another. Public administrators who regulate airlines, nuclear power plants, or pharmaceutical companies face the problem of "indirect management" every day. They struggle to influence the behavior of organizations over which they have very limited authority. Private firms need to manage relationships with multiple levels of government. The situation is even more complicated for managers in multinational companies coping with the subtleties of governments with very different systems and traditions. Across sectors and cultures, managers often harbor narrow, stereotypic conceptions of one another that impede effectiveness on both sides. We need common ground and a shared understanding that can help strengthen public and private organizations in the United States and throughout the world. The dialogue between public and private, domestic and multinational organizations has become increasingly important. Because of their generic application, the frames offer an ecumenical language for the exchange. Our work with a variety of organizations around the world has continually reinforced our confidence that the frames are relevant everywhere. Political issues, for example, are universally important, even though the specifics vary greatly from one country or culture to another.

The idea of *reframing* continues to be a central theme. Throughout the book, we show how the same situation can be viewed in at least four ways. In Part Six, we include a series of chapters on reframing critical organizational issues such as leadership, change, and ethics. Two chapters are specifically devoted to reframing real-life situations.

We also continue to emphasize artistry. Overemphasizing the rational and technical side of an organization often contributes to decline or demise. Our counterbalance emphasizes the importance of art in both management and leadership. Artistry is neither exact nor precise; the artist interprets experience, expressing it in forms that can be felt, understood, and appreciated. Art fosters emotion, subtlety, and ambiguity. An artist represents the world to give us a deeper understanding of what is and what might be. In modern organizations, quality, commitment, and creativity are highly valued but often hard to find. They can be developed and encouraged by leaders or managers who embrace the expressive side of their work.

OUTLINE OF THE BOOK

The first part of the book, "Making Sense of Organizations," tackles a perplexing question about management: Why is it that smart people so often do dumb things? Chapter One, "The Power of Reframing," explains why: Managers often misread situations. They have not learned how to use multiple lenses to get a better sense of what they're up against and what they might do. Chapter Two, "Simple Ideas, Complex Organizations," uses several famous cases (destruction of a Korean Airlines jet plane by the Soviet Air Force, the collapse of Enron, and a friendly-fire tragedy in the skies over Iraq in 1994)to show how managers' everyday theories can lead to catastrophe. We explain basic factors that make organizational life complicated, ambiguous, and unpredictable; discuss common fallacies in managerial thinking; and spell out criteria for more effective approaches to diagnosis and action.

Part Two, "The Structural Frame," has been updated with new case material, including structural confusion that hindered rescue efforts during the September 11, 2001, terrorist incident in New York City. Chapter Three, "Getting Organized," describes basic issues managers must consider in designing structure to fit an organization's goals, tasks, and context. It shows why organizations—from Harvard University to McDonald's—need different structures in order to be effective in their unique environments. Chapter Four, "Structure and Restructuring," explains major structural pathologies and pitfalls. It presents guidelines for aligning structures to situations, along with several cases illustrating successful structural change. Chapter Five, "Organizing Groups and Teams," shows that structure is a key to high-performing teams of all kinds.

Part Three, "The Human Resource Frame," includes new material on the changing employment relationship; it updates best practices in human resource management.

Chapter Six, "People and Organizations," focuses on the relationship between organizations and human nature. It shows how a manager's practices and assumptions about people can lead either to alienation and hostility or to commitment and high motivation. It contrasts two strategies for achieving effectiveness: "lean and mean," or investing in people. Chapter Seven, "Improving Human Resource Management," is an overview of practices that build a more motivated and committed workforce—including participative management, job enrichment, self-managing workgroups, management of diversity, and organization development. Chapter Eight, "Interpersonal and Group Dynamics," presents an example of interpersonal conflict to illustrate how managers create effective or ineffective relationships. It also discusses how group members can increase their effectiveness by attending to group process, including informal norms and roles, interpersonal conflict, leadership, and decision making.

Part Four, "The Political Frame," views organizations as arenas. Individuals and groups compete to achieve their parochial interests in a world of conflicting perspectives, scarce resources, and struggles for power. Chapter Nine, "Power, Conflict, and Coalition," analyzes the tragic loss of the space shuttle *Challenger,* illustrating the influence of political dynamics in decision making. It shows how scarcity and diversity lead to conflict, bargaining, and games of power; the chapter also distinguishes constructive and destructive political dynamics. Chapter Ten, "The Manager as Politician," illustrates basic skills of the constructive politician: diagnosing political realities, setting agendas, building networks, negotiating, and making choices that are both effective and ethical. Chapter Eleven, "Organizations as Political Arenas and Political Agents," highlights organizations as both arenas for political contests and political actors influencing broader social, political, and economic trends. The story of Ross Johnson and a $25 billion leveraged buyout explores the intersection of politics both inside and outside organizations.

Part Five explores the symbolic frame. Chapter Twelve, "Organizational Culture and Symbols," spells out basic symbolic elements in organizations: culture, myths, heroes, metaphors, stories, humor, play, rituals, and ceremonies. It defines organizational culture and shows its central role in shaping performance. The power of symbol and culture is illustrated in organizations as diverse as Harley-Davidson, Volvo France, the U.S. Congress, and Nordstrom department stores. Chapter Thirteen, "Organization as Theater," reveals how organizational structures, activities, and events serve as secular dramas, expressing our fears and joys, arousing our affect, and kindling our spirit. It also shows how organizational structures and processes, such as planning, evaluation, and decision making, are often more important for what they *express* than for what they *accomplish.* Chapter Fourteen, "Organizational Culture in Action," uses the case of a computer development team to show what leaders and group members can do collectively to build a culture that bonds people in pursuit of a shared mission. Initiation rituals, specialized language, group stories, humor and play, and ceremonies all combine to transform diverse individuals into a cohesive team with purpose, spirit, and soul.

Part Six, "Improving Leadership Practice," focuses on the implications of the frames for central issues in managerial practice, including leadership, change, and ethics. Chapter Fifteen, "Integrating Frames for Effective Practice," shows how managers can blend the frames to improve their effectiveness. It looks at organizations as multiple realities and gives guidelines for aligning frames with situations. Chapter Sixteen, "Reframing in Action," presents four scenarios, or scripts, derived from the frames. It applies the scenarios to the harrowing experience of a young manager whose first day in a new job turns out to be far more challenging than she expected. The discussion illustrates how a leader can expand her options and enhance her effectiveness by considering alternative approaches. Chapter Seventeen, "Reframing Leadership," discusses limitations in traditional views of leadership and proposes a more comprehensive view of how leadership works in organizations. It summarizes and critiques current knowledge on the characteristics of leaders. It shows how frames generate distinctive images of effective leaders as architects, servants, advocates, and prophets. New in this edition is a section on gender and leadership. Chapter Eighteen, "Reframing Change," describes four fundamental issues that arise in any change effort: individual needs, structural alignment, conflict, and loss. It uses cases of successful and unsuccessful change to document key strategies, such as training, realigning, creating arenas, and using symbol and ceremony.

Chapter Nineteen, "Reframing Ethics and Spirit," discusses four ethics that emerge from the cognitive lenses: excellence, caring, justice, and faith. It argues that leaders can build more ethical organizations through gifts of authorship, love, power, and significance. Chapter Twenty, "Bringing It All Together," is an integrative treatment of the reframing process. It takes a troubled school administrator through a weekend of reflection on critical difficulties he faces. The chapter shows how reframing can help managers move from feeling confused and stuck to a renewed sense of clarity and confidence. The

Epilogue (Chapter Twenty-One) describes strategies and characteristics needed in future leaders. It explains why they will need an artistic combination of conceptual flexibility and commitment to core values. Efforts to prepare future leaders have to focus as much on spiritual development as on the intellectual.

ACKNOWLEDGMENTS

We noted in our first edition, "Book writing often feels like a lonely process, even when an odd couple is doing the writing." This odd couple keeps getting older (sexagenarians both, now)—and, some would say, even odder. Yet the process seems less lonely because of our close friendship and our contact with many other colleagues and friends. The best thing about teaching is that you learn so much from your students. Students at Harvard, Vanderbilt, the University of Missouri–Kansas City, and the University of Southern California have given us invaluable criticism, challenge, and support over the years. We wish we could thank personally all of the leaders and managers from whom we have learned so much in seminars, workshops, and consultations. Their experience and wisdom are the foundation and touchstone for our work.

As in the past, we owe much to our colleagues. Thanks again to all who helped us in the prior editions; your contribution still lingers in this work. But we particularly want to mention those who have made more recent contributions.

We have learned much from collaboration with a number of teaching fellows and graduate assistants at the University of Missouri–Kansas City; in particular, we are very grateful for the help of Mary Yung and Hooilin Chan. They did an outstanding job helping us develop the citation analysis that appears in Appendix A.

We also wish we could thank all the colleagues and readers in the United States and around the world who have offered valuable comments and suggestions, but the list is long and our memories keep getting shorter. Elena Granell de Aldaz of the Institute for Advanced Study of Management in Caracas collaborated with us on developing a Spanish-language adaptation of *Reframing Organizations* as well as on a more recent project that studied frame orientations among managers in Venezuela. We are proud to consider her a valued colleague and wonderful friend. Bob Marx, of the University of Massachusetts, deserves special mention as a charter member of the frames family. Bob's interest in the frames, creativity in developing teaching designs, and eye for video material have aided our thinking and teaching immensely. Lt. Cdr. Gary Deal, USN; Maj. Kevin Reed, USAF; Dr. Peter Minich, a transplant surgeon; and Jan and Ron Haynes of FzioMed all provided valuable case material. Our friends at the Ritz-Carlton Club in Phoenix, Ann Hamilton, Yunen Silverio, Perla Silverio, and Jean Wright gave us some important insights into the delightful inner workings of a great hotel chain. Peter Frost, at the University of British Columbia, and Peter Vaill, at St. Thomas University, have both been a continuing source of ideas, support, and inspiration. A number of individuals, including many friends and colleagues at the Organizational Behavior Teaching Conference, have given us helpful ideas and suggestions. We apologize for any omissions, but we want to thank Joe Aniello, Jim Begun, Lars Bjork, Irwin Blumer, Grady Bogue, Gordon D. Brown, Jean Brown, Mark Denke, Eric Dent, Susan C. Eaton, Max Elden, Ellen Ensher, Kent Fairfield, Maureen Farrell, Kenneth E. Galea'i, Daniel Gutmore, Margaret Heffernan, Tom Hickock, Richard M. Jacobs, Jeanne King, Patricia Klinck, Harald Koht, Bob Kramer, Mark Kriger, Mark Maier, Magid Mazen, John Mirocha, Christopher Morphew, Ken Murrell, Sandra Parkes, Sally Power, Jeffrey A. Routsong, Peter Sevastos, Jody Spiro, Niki Steckler, Susan S. Stratton, Michael Thies, J. Douglas Toma, and Suzanne Waalfort. We only wish we had succeeded in implementing all the wonderful ideas we received from these and other colleagues.

Bill Eddy, dean emeritus of the Bloch School at the University of Missouri–Kansas City, gets special thanks for nurturing an environment that helps scholarship flourish. His successors, Al Page and Homer Erekson, have kept that tradition alive. Other Bloch School colleagues who have helped more than they know are Dave Bodde, Nancy Day, Dick Heimovics, Bob Herman, Rick Lytle, Deborah Noble, Stephen Pruitt, David Renz, Eleanor Schwartz, Beth Smith, and Marilyn Taylor. Lee's colleagues in the Department of Organization, Leadership, and Management at the Bloch School have done their part by generating many experiential opportunities to learn more about leadership. In addition to colleagues already mentioned, he thanks Raj Arora, Gene Brown, Rita Cain, Rich Hamilton, and Patti Greene. At the Rossier School, University of Southern California, Dean Karen Gallagher presides over a stimulating, well-grounded place to be. Colleagues Carl Cohn, Stu Gothald, and Gib Hentschke offer both intellectual stimulation and moral support.

Others to whom our debt is particularly clear are Chris Argyris, Pat Arnold, Sam Bacharach, Cliff Baden, Estella Bensimon, Al Bertani, Pat Bower, Barbara Bunker, Tom

Burks, Ellen Castro, Sharon Conley, Linton Deck, Tom Johnson (always a source of creative ideas), Ralph Kilmann, Grady McGonagill, John Meyer, Harrison Owen, Kent Peterson, Michael Sales, Mary Jane Saxton, Dick Scott, Joan Vydra, Roy Williams, and Karl Weick. Thanks again to Dave Brown, Phil Mirvis, Barry Oshry, Tim Hall, Bill Kahn, and Todd Jick of the Brookline Circle, now in its third decade of searching for joy and meaning in lives devoted to the study of organizations.

Outside the United States, we are grateful to Rolf Kaelin, Cüno Pumpin, and Peter Weisman in Switzerland; Ilpo Linko in Finland; Tom Case in Brazil; Einar Plyhn and Haakon Gran in Norway; Peter Normark and Dag Bjorkegren in Sweden; and H.R.H. Prince Philipp von und zu Lichtenstein.

Closer to home, we owe more than we can say to Bruce Kay and Homa Aminmadani, without whom our sanity and health would be significantly diminished. Homa's Persian elegance and extraordinary determination continue to wrest about as much efficiency from Terry as possible, given the material she's had to work with for more years than she likes to admit. She is becoming a legend around the world for her attention to detail, her negotiating skills, and her extraordinary caring and compassion—all this despite working for someone who is, she is sure, a "legend in his own mind." Bruce's genial and unflappable approach to work, coupled with high levels of organization and follow-through, have all had a wonderfully positive impact since he took on the challenge of bringing a modicum of order and sanity to Lee's professional functioning. We also continue to be grateful for the long-term support and friendship of Linda Corey, who still serves as our resident representative at Harvard.

Lee's six children—Edward, Shelley, Lori, Scott, Christopher, and Bradley—all continue to enrich his life and contribute to his growth. He still wishes he could give them as much as they have given him. Chris Bolman also served as a valuable consultant on contemporary music. Janie Deal has delighted her father in becoming a fascinating and independent entrepreneur with her (and her husband's) catering business, the Wild Rices. Her hopes that advancing years would temper her father's outrageousness have not yet been fully answered; she is still waiting for maturity to blossom. Special mention also to Terry's parents, Bob and Dorothy Deal. Entering their nineties, they are pleasantly surprised that their oft wayward son could write a book.

We dedicate the book to our wives, who have more than earned all the credit and appreciation that we can give them. Joan Gallos, Lee's spouse and closest colleague, combines intellectual challenge and critique with support and love. She has been an active collaborator in developing our ideas, and her teaching manual for the last two editions was a frame-breaking model for the genre. Her contributions have become so integrated into our own thinking that we are no longer able to thank her for all the ways that the book has gained from her wisdom and insights.

Sandy Deal's psychological training enables her to approach the field of organizations with a distinctive and illuminating slant. Her concentration on individual and family therapy has helped us make some even stronger connections to the field of clinical psychology. (We are skeptical, though, that she ever really said, "I don't need to bring my work home, because he's always waiting there for me.") Sandy is a delightful partner whose love and support over the long run have made all the difference. She is a rare combination of courage and caring, intimacy and independence, responsibility and playfulness.

To Joan and Sandy, thanks again. As the years accumulate, we love you even more.

May 2003   Lee G. Bolman
                                               Kansas City, Missouri
                                               Terrence E. Deal
                                               San Luis Obispo, California

THE AUTHORS

Lee G. Bolman holds the Marion Bloch Missouri Chair in Leadership at the Bloch School of Business and Public Administration, University of Missouri–Kansas City. He received a B.A. (1962) in history and a Ph.D. (1968) in administrative sciences, both from Yale University. Bolman's interests lie at the intersection of leadership and organizations, and he has published numerous articles, chapters, and cases. He is coauthor of *Escape from Cluelessness: A Guide for the Organizationally Challenged* (2000). Bolman has been a consultant to corporations, public agencies, universities, and public schools in the United States, Asia, Europe, and Latin America. For twenty years, he taught at the Harvard Graduate School of Education, where he also chaired the Institute for Educational Administration and the School Leadership Academy. He has been director and board chair of the Organizational Behavior Teaching Society and director of the National Training Laboratories.

Bolman lives in Kansas City, Missouri, with his wife, Joan Gallos; the two youngest of his six children, Chris and Brad; and their Dalmatian, Vincent Van Gogh of KCMO.

Terrence E. Deal is a clinical professor of education at the University of Southern California's Rossier School of Education. Before joining USC, he served on the faculties of the Stanford University Graduate School of Education, the Harvard Graduate School of Education, and Vanderbilt University's Peabody College of Education. He received his B.A. (1961) in history from LaVerne College, his M.A. (1966) in educational administration from California State University at Los Angeles, and his Ph.D. (1972) in education and sociology from Stanford University. Deal has been a policeman, public school teacher, high school principal, district officer administrator, and university professor. His primary research interests are in organizational symbolism and change. He is the author of twenty-five books, including the best-seller *Corporate Cultures* (with A. A. Kennedy, 1982) and

Shaping School Culture (with K. Peterson, 1999). He has published numerous articles on organizations, change, and leadership. He is a consultant to business, health care, military, educational, and religious organizations domestically and in Europe, Scandinavia, the Middle East, Canada, South America, Japan, and Southeast Asia.

Deal lives in San Luis Obispo, California, with his wife, Sandy, and their cat, Max.

Bolman and Deal first met in 1976 when they were assigned to co-teach a course on organizations at Harvard University. Trained in different disciplines on opposite coasts, they disagreed on almost everything. It was the beginning of a challenging but very productive partnership. They have written a number of other books together, including *Leading with Soul: An Uncommon Journey of Spirit* (1995, 2001). Their books have been translated into multiple languages for readers in Asia, Europe, and Latin America.

For five years, Bolman and Deal also codirected the National Center for Educational Leadership, a research consortium of Harvard, Vanderbilt, and the University of Chicago.

The authors appreciate hearing from readers and welcome comments, questions, suggestions, or accounts of experiences that bear on the ideas in the book. Stories of success, failure, or puzzlement are all welcome. Readers can contact the authors at the following addresses:

Lee Bolman
Bloch School-UMKC
5100 Rockhill Road
Kansas City, MO 64113
bolmanl@umkc.edu

Terry Deal
6625 Via Piedra
San Luis Obispo, CA 93401
sucha@slocoast.net

Reframing Organizations

PART ONE

Making Sense of Organizations

CHAPTER 1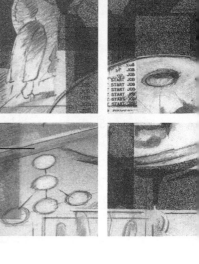

Introduction
The Power of Reframing

"The World's Leading Company," the lobby banner proclaimed in the gleaming corporate headquarters in Houston, Texas. With some justification. For six years running, Enron had been voted the most innovative of *Fortune*'s "Most Admired Companies" (McLean, 2001, p. 60). In September 2001, with reported earnings of over $1 billion a year and an annual growth rate of 68 percent, it ranked thirtieth on *Fortune*'s list of America's hundred fastest growing companies. Small wonder that CEO Kenneth W. Lay was one of America's most powerful business leaders, sometimes mentioned in the same breath with Jack Welch, GE's legendary CEO. Lay had the added advantage of a long-term friendship with President George W. Bush. He cemented this personal tie by giving more than half a million dollars to Bush's presidential campaign (the biggest individual donor). What could be better than a big, innovative, fast-growing, profitable, politically connected company?

The trouble was the books had been cooked, and external auditors were asleep at the switch. In December 2001, Enron collapsed in what was at the time history's largest corporate bankruptcy. Its stock plunged from eighty dollars to eighty *cents* a share in the space of a year. Tens of billions of dollars in shareholder wealth evaporated. Many jobs and most of the retirement funds of Enron's employees disappeared.[1]

What went wrong? After the collapse, critics offered plenty of plausible explanations. Yet Enron's leadership seemed baffled by the abrupt free fall. Former CEO Jeffrey K.

Skilling, regarded as the primary architect of Enron's high-flying, take-no-prisoners culture, was among those caught off-guard. Associates described him as "the ultimate control freak. The sort of hands-on corporate leader who kept his fingers on all the pieces of the puzzle" (Schwartz, 2002, p. C-1). Skilling resigned for unexplained "personal reasons" only three months before Enron imploded; many wondered if he had jumped ship because he foresaw the iceberg dead ahead. But when asked about Enron's crash, he claimed, "I had no idea the company was in anything but excellent shape" (p. C-1).

Skilling and his boss, Lay, were both viewed as brilliant men, yet both found refuge in cluelessness. They insisted that they either didn't know about, or didn't understand, the financial maneuvers and management misjudgments that led to Enron's fall. The chief executive of Enron's auditor, Andersen Worldwide, made the same claim, even though Andersen partners in Chicago had debated whether to drop Enron as a client because the company's accounting was so aggressively pushing acceptable boundaries. Carl Bass, a senior partner sent in to monitor the Enron audit, strongly objected to some of the company's high-risk accounting practices. Andersen moved him off the case. Andersen's top executive, Joseph F. Berardino, claimed he didn't know about any of this, even though he had visited Enron's headquarters a few weeks before Bass was reassigned (Byrne, 2002b).

Berardino, Lay, and Skilling weren't the first or last corporate leaders seemingly clueless about a looming disaster. A decade earlier, following General Motors's market-share dive in the 1980s, GM's CEO, Roger Smith, was asked what had gone wrong. The only response he could muster was, "I don't know. It's a mysterious thing" (Loomis, 1993, p. 41). Smith had once been hailed as a bold visionary leader; down the road he admitted ruefully, "I'm not as smart as people said a few years ago, and not as dumb as they say now" (Smith, 1987, p. 26).

The stories of Skilling, Lay, Berardino, and Smith are only a few examples of a ubiquitous leadership challenge: How do you know if you are seeing the real picture? It is a test that managers and leaders often fail. Cluelessness is an everyday fact of life, even for very smart people. The problem is not insufficient intellectual wattage but a lack of understanding of what they are up against and what remedies might work. If it was difficult to decipher clues and read signs in the past, it's even tougher now. The world is more turbulent and complex than it was fifty years ago; the stakes are higher, and challenges often outpace a leader's cognitive capabilities.

In the discussion that follows, we explore the origins and symptoms of cluelessness in organizations. Then we turn to "reframing"—the conceptual core of the book. Reframing requires an ability to understand and use multiple perspectives, to think about the same thing in more than one way. We introduce four frames: structural, human resource, political, and symbolic. Each is distinctive, each coherent and powerful in its own right. Together, they help capture a comprehensive picture of what's wrong and what might be done.

VIRTUES AND DRAWBACKS OF ORGANIZED ACTIVITY

The first humanlike primates appeared on earth about twelve million years ago. During most of human evolution, our ancestors were hunters and gatherers. Only the last ten or fifteen thousand years have seen the emergence of institutions more complex than small, simple, nomadic communities. Large organizations emerged to dominate the social landscape even more recently.

There was little need for professional managers when individuals managed their own affairs. Today, things are very different. The challenge of finding the right way to frame our world has become overwhelming in the twenty-first century's turbulent and roiling times. Forms of management and organization effective a few years ago are obsolete today. Sérieyx (1993) calls it the organizational big bang: "The information revolution, the globalization of economies, the proliferation of events that undermine all our certainties, the collapse of the grand ideologies, the arrival of the CNN society which transforms us into an immense, planetary village—all these shocks have overturned the rules of the game and suddenly turned yesterday's organizations into antiques" (pp. 14–15).

The proliferation of complex organizations has made most human activities collective endeavors. We grow up in and start families. We work in and rely on organizations for goods and services. We learn in schools and universities. We play sports in teams. We join clubs and associations. Many of us will grow old and die in hospitals or nursing homes. We build these human enterprises because of what they can do for us. They produce consumer goods, offer entertainment, provide social services and health care, and deliver the mail.

All too often, however, we experience the darker side. Organizations can frustrate and exploit people. Too often, products are flawed, families are dysfunctional, students fail to learn, patients stay sick, and policies make things worse instead of better. Many organizations infuse work with so little meaning that jobs have hardly any value beyond a paycheck. It's hard to find a company these days that doesn't aim officially to delight its customers, but a national survey found that customer satisfaction across industries mostly went downhill between 1995 and 2001 (American Customer Satisfaction Index, 2002). NASA, the same organization that put a man on the moon, launched America's ill-fated space shuttles *Challenger* and *Columbia*. Around the world, schools are blamed for social ills, universities are said to close more minds than they open, and government agencies are criticized for red tape and rigidity. The sarcastic phrase "good enough for government work" reflects widespread cynicism about the performance of public agencies. The private sector has its own problems. Automakers recall faulty cars, baby food producers apologize for adulterated fruit juice, and software companies deliver bugs and "vaporware." Industrial accidents dump chemicals, oil, toxic gas, and radioactive materials into the air and water. Too often, corporate greed and insensitivity create havoc for lives and communities. The bottom line: we are hard pressed to manage organizations so that benefits regularly exceed costs. The big question: Why should this be?

THE CURSE OF CLUELESSNESS

Year after year, the best and brightest managers maneuver or meander their way to the apex of great enterprises. Then they do really dumb things. How do bright people turn out so dim? One theory is that they're too smart for their own good. Feinberg and Tarrant (1995) label it the "self-destructive intelligence syndrome." They argue smart people act stupid because of personality flaws—things like pride, arrogance, and unconscious needs to fail. Lundin and Lundin (1998) came to a similar conclusion: "[Bosses'] dumb behavior is motivated by self-love and ego, which block the capacity for empathy."

It's true that psychic flaws have been apparent in such brilliantly self-destructive individuals as Adolph Hitler, Richard Nixon, and Bill Clinton. But on the whole, intellectually challenged people have as many psychological problems as the best and brightest. The real source of cluelessness is not personality or IQ. It's in *how we think and make sense of the world around us*. Regardless of intellectual wattage, we're out to lunch if we use the wrong ideas for the situation at hand. When you see a distorted picture, you react the wrong way. But you'll probably stick with erroneous ideas if they're all you have. The problem is they lead you into trouble and mask their flaws at the same time. You may be confident that everything is humming along. If not, at least it's not your fault.

Vaughan (1995), in trying to explain the *Challenger* space shuttle disaster, underscored how hard it is for people to surrender their ingrained mental models: "They puzzle over contradictory evidence, but usually succeed in pushing it aside—until they come across a piece of evidence too fascinating to ignore, too clear to misperceive, too painful to deny, which makes vivid still other signals they do not want to see, forcing them to alter and surrender the world-view they have so meticulously constructed" (p. 235).

Charan and Useem (2002) found that this tendency to see no evil is a common problem in organizational disasters. Cisco Systems, for example, had one of the most sophisticated forecasting systems in the business. The system worked superbly during ten years of phenomenal growth in the 1990s but misfired once demand started going downhill. Cisco's leadership had trouble believing that the bottom was really falling out.

> Customers began going bankrupt. Suppliers warned of a coming drop in demand. Even Wall Street wondered if the Internet equipment market was coming apart. "I have never been more optimistic about the future of our industry as a whole or of Cisco," CEO John Chambers declared in December 2000, still projecting 50 percent growth. For the perpetually sunny Chambers, [the critical piece of evidence] did not come until April 2001, when cratering sales forced Cisco to write down $2.5 billion in excess inventory and lay off 8,500 employees. Chambers may have been operating in real time, but he wasn't operating in the real world. (Charan and Useem, 2002, p. 54)

Floyd Norris wrote about Enron's former CEO: "There were no problems at Enron while Jeffrey K. Skilling was running the company. Or at least, none that he noticed: [in his testimony to Congress] Mr. Skilling may not have persuaded many listeners. But he did make it clear to those who are investigating Enron at the Justice Department and the S.E.C. that they will have to work to prove he was aware of anything at all during the period he was running one of America's largest companies" (Norris, 2002, p. C-1). Too often, psychic prisons prevent managers and leaders from seeing old problems in a new light or finding more promising ways to work on perennial challenges. When they don't know what to do, they do more of what they know. This helps explain a number of unsettling reports from the managerial front lines:

- In 2000, the United States was again the world's strongest economy, yet corporate America set a new record for failure: 176 public companies with $95 billion in assets went bankrupt. Aided by a business downturn, it got worse the following year, as 257 companies with $258 billion in assets went under (Charan and Useem, 2002). Charan and

Useem traced all that failure back to a single source: "Most companies founder for one reason: managerial error" (p. 52).

• The annual value of corporate mergers grew a hundredfold between 1980 and 2000 (Renner, 2000), even though a recent study found that "83 percent of mergers were unsuccessful in producing any business benefit as regards shareholder value" (KPMG, 2000). Mergers typically benefit shareholders of the acquired firm but harm almost everyone else—customers, employees, and the acquiring firm (Tichy, forthcoming). Despite this dismal record, the vast majority of the managers who engineered mergers believed they were successful (KPMG, 2000).

• Hogan, Curphy, and Hogan (1994) estimate that one-half to three-quarters of all American managers are incompetent. The authors didn't study managers in other countries, but, given America's comparative economic success, the results are probably no better elsewhere.

• A study by CSC Index (cited in Gertz and Baptista, 1995) found that fewer than one-third of reengineering initiatives met or exceeded their goals. The same could be said for almost any other popular business improvement scheme, including total quality management and strategic planning.

Small wonder that so many corporate veterans nod assent to Scott Adams's admittedly unscientific "Dilbert principle": "the most ineffective workers are systematically moved the place where they can do the least damage—management" (1996, p. 14).

STRATEGIES FOR IMPROVING ORGANIZATIONS: THE TRACK RECORD

We have certainly tried to improve organizations. Legions of managers go to work every day with that hope in mind. Authors and consultants spin out a steady flow of new answers and promising solutions. Policy makers develop laws and regulations to guide organizations on a more correct path.

The most common strategy aims at improving management. Modern mythology promises organizations will work splendidly if well managed. Managers are supposed to have the big picture and look out for their organization's overall health and productivity.

Unfortunately, they have not always been equal to the task, even when armed with computers, information systems, flowcharts, quality programs, and a panoply of other tools and techniques. They go forth with this rational arsenal to try to tame our wild and primitive workplace. Yet in the end, irrational forces most often prevail.

When managers cannot solve problems, they hire consultants. Today, the number and variety of advice givers is overwhelming. Most have a specialty: reengineering, quality, mergers and acquisitions, strategy, human resource management, information technology, executive search, outplacement, training, organization development, and many more. For every managerial question or issue, there is a consultant willing to offer assistance—at a premium price.

For all their sage advice and remarkable fees, consultants have yet to make a significant dent in pressing problems plaguing businesses, public agencies, military services, hospitals, or schools. Sometimes the consultants are more hindrance than help. More than a few managers wish that consultants, like physicians, were bound by the oath "Above all else, do no harm." Meanwhile, consultants grouse about clients' failure to implement their insights. McKinsey & Co., "the high priest of high-level consulting" (Byrne, 2002a, p. 66) worked so closely with Enron that managing partner Rajat Gupta sent his chief lawyer down to Houston after Enron's collapse to see if the consulting company might be in legal trouble. The lawyer reported that McKinsey was safe, and Gupta insisted bravely, "We stand by all the work we did. Beyond that, we can only empathize with the trouble they are going through. It's a sad thing to see" (Byrne, 2002a, p. 68). Clients can be confident that, no matter how bad the results, they are responsible if anything goes wrong. But at least they'll get empathy.

When managers and consultants fail, government frequently jumps in with legislation, policies, and regulations. Constituents badger elected officials to "do something" about a variety of ills: pollution, dangerous products, hazardous working conditions, and chaotic schools, to name a few. Governing bodies respond by making "policy." But policies regularly go awry while meandering from the legislative floor to the targeted problems. A sizable body of research records a continuing saga of perverse ways in which policy implementation distorts policy makers' intentions (Bardach, 1977; Elmore, 1978; Freudenberg and Gramling, 1994; Peters, 1999; Pressman and Wildavsky, 1973).

Difficulties surrounding each strategy for improving organizations are well documented. Exemplary intentions produce more costs than benefits. Problems outlast solutions. It is as if tens of thousands of hard-working, highly motivated pioneers keep hacking away at a swamp that continues to produce new growth faster than the old can be cleared.

There are reasons for optimism. Organizations have changed about as much in the past decade or two as in the previous century. To survive, they had to. Revolutionary changes in technology, the rise of the global economy, and shortened product life cycles have spawned a flurry of activity to design more fluid and more flexible organizational forms. These efforts have engendered a bewildering variety of labels: networks (Chaize, 1992), virtual organizations, adhocracies (Mintzberg, 1979), atomized organizations (Deal and Kennedy, 1982), spider plants (Morgan, 1993), PALs (Kanter, 1989), and many others. These new forms can be seen in network organizations such as the French packaging giant Carnaud et Metal Box. CEO Jean-Marie Descarpentries said his approach to management was simple: "You catalyze toward the future, you trust people, and they discover things you never would have thought of" (Aubrey and Tilliette, 1990, p. 142).

New organization models also flourish in companies such as Pret à Manger (the U.K.'s socially conscious sandwich shops), Saturn (the automobile producer with a soul), and Novo-Nordisk (the Danish pharmaceutical company that includes environmental and social metrics in its bottom line). All three are passionate about core values and create familylike bonds among employees and customers. The information technology revolution has bred an array of innovative forms visible in such firms as eBay, the phenomenally successful Internet auction company, and software innovator SAS Institute. Despite such successes, there are still too many failures. How can leaders and managers improve the odds for themselves as well as their organizations?

THEORY BASE

Managers, consultants, and policy makers draw, formally or otherwise, on a variety of theories in an effort to change or improve organizations. Yet only in the past few decades have social scientists devoted much time or attention to developing ideas about how organizations work (or why they often fail). In the social sciences, several major schools of thought have evolved. Each has its own concepts and assumptions and espouses a view of how to bring social collectives under control.

Each tradition claims a scientific foundation. But theories easily become theologies, preaching a single, parochial scripture. Competing gospels present limited versions of reality but expanded prophetic visions of what the future holds, along with a definite set of strategies for reaching the Promised Land. Modern managers trying to get on top of things encounter a cacophony of voices and visions.

Consider an executive browsing in the management section of her local bookstore on a brisk winter day early in 2003. She is worried about her company's flagging performance and about the chance that her job might soon disappear. She spots the black-on-white spine of *The Six Sigma Way: How GE, Motorola, and Other Top Companies Are Honing Their Performance* (Pande, Neuman, and Cavanagh, 2000). She's not exactly sure what six sigma is, but she knows a lot of her peers are talking about it. Scanning the book, she is drawn to phrases such as "a flexible system for improved business leadership and performance," and "a new formula for 21st-century business success." Jumping to chapter two, she encounters, "In Figure 2.2 you see a model of a company as seen from a process-flow perspective. On the far left are the inputs to the process (or system); in the middle is the organization or process itself (depicted as a process map or flowchart). Finally, on the far-right, are the all-important customer, end products and (let's hope) profits."

"This stuff may be terrific," the executive tells herself, "but it seems a little dry."

Then she spots *Primal Leadership: Realizing the Power of Emotional Intelligence* (Goleman, McKee, and Boyatzis, 2002). The authors talk about how leaders can cultivate good feelings by developing the "four domains of emotional intelligence": self-awareness, self-management, social awareness, and relationship management.

"Nice," she mumbles, "but a little squishy. Let's look for something a little more down to earth."

She finds *What Would Machiavelli Do? The Ends Justify the Meanness* (Bing, 2000). She ponders the book's basic premise: those who get ahead in business aren't necessarily smarter, just meaner. She reads, "A simple, detailed plan for those with the courage to leave kindness and decency behind, to seize the future by the throat and make it cough up money, power, and superior office space."

"He can't be serious, can he?" she wonders. "Anyway, it's too cynical. Isn't there something more uplifting?"

She spots *From Worst to First: Behind the Scenes of Continental's Remarkable Comeback* (Bethune and Huler, 1999). She glances at some of the chapter titles: "The Last Suppers, or Whose Problem Is It?" "Fly to Win, or You Can Make Pizza So Cheap No One Wants to Eat It." "Crop Duster's Son." She reads that Gordon Bethune's first official act when he took charge of Continental was to unlock the executive suite doors to show employees he wasn't trying to shut them out. He also gathered a group of employees in the company's parking lot to burn the old restrictive policy manuals.

"Bonfires in my company?" she muses. "I don't think so."

FRAMES AND REFRAMING

Had the executive visited another store in another year, she might have encountered other works but a similar range of opinions. Our purpose in this book is to sort through multiple voices competing for managers' attention. In doing so, we consolidate major schools of organizational thought into four perspectives.[2] There are many ways to label such outlooks—mental models, maps, mind-sets, schema, and cognitive lenses, to name a few. We have chosen the label *frames*. In describing frames, we deliberately mix metaphors, referring to them as windows, maps, tools, lenses, orientations, and perspectives because all of those images capture part of the ecumenical idea we want to convey.

As a mental map, a frame is a set of ideas or assumptions you carry in your head. It helps you understand and negotiate a particular "territory." The territory isn't necessarily defined by geography. It could be a sport, an art form, an academic subject, or anything else you care about. Suppose you like to cook and particularly enjoy Chinese food. You might develop an extensive stock of knowledge and concepts about Chinese cuisine. Eventually your understanding of subtle regional differences in spicing and ingredients might enable you to pinpoint which part of China a dish came from. Someone else trying to identify the same dish might not be sure whether it came from Beijing or Bombay. As the example indicates, the better your map, the easier it is to negotiate a terrain. But every map is bounded. A map of New York won't be of much help trying to navigate San Francisco. Modern automobiles often come with computerized navigation systems that tell you where you are and guide you turn-by-turn to your destination. It would be a big help if organizations could provide the same thing to managers. Unfortunately, to avoid getting lost, managers still need to develop and carry accurate maps in their heads.

Our purpose in this book is to present lenses, or frames, that help you understand and find your way around. Frames are windows on the world of leadership and management.

A good frame makes it easier to know what you are up against and what you can do about it. Goran Carstedt, the talented executive who led the turnaround of Volvo's French division in the 1980s, put it this way: "The world simply can't be made sense of, facts can't be organized, unless you have a mental model to begin with. That theory does not have to be the right one, because you can alter it along the way as information comes in. But you can't begin to learn without some concept that gives you expectations or hypotheses" (Hampden-Turner, 1992, p. 167).

Artistic managers such as Carstedt learn fluidly because they are able to frame and reframe experience, sorting through the tangled underbrush to find solutions to problems. A critic once commented to Cézanne, "That doesn't look anything like a sunset." Pondering his painting, Cézanne responded, "Then you don't see sunsets the way I do." Like Cézanne, leaders have to find new ways to see things. They must also articulate and communicate their vision so others can learn to shift perspectives when needed.

Like maps, frames are both windows on a territory and tools for navigation. Every tool has distinctive strengths and limitations. The right tool makes a job easier, but the wrong one just gets in the way. One or two tools may suffice for simple jobs, but not for more complex undertakings. Managers who master the hammer and expect all problems to behave like nails find organizational life confusing and frustrating. The wise manager, like a skilled carpenter or a professional chef, wants at hand a diverse collection of high-quality implements. Experienced managers also understand the difference between possessing a tool and knowing how to use it. Only experience and practice bring the skill and wisdom to size up a situation and use tools well.

Our goal is usable knowledge. We have sought ideas powerful enough to capture the subtlety and complexity of life in organizations yet simple enough to be useful. Our distillation has drawn much from the social sciences—particularly from sociology, psychology, political science, and anthropology. Thousands of managers and scores of organizations have also been our mentors. They helped us sift through social science research to identify ideas that work in practice. We have sorted insights drawn from both research and practice into four major frames, used by academics and practitioners alike to make sense of organizations. The four frames that we first described in the early 1980s—structural, human resource, political, and symbolic (Bolman and Deal, 1984)—have since been explored and adapted by other organizational scholars (including Bergquist, 1992; Birnbaum, 1988, 1992; and Dunford, 1992). The worried executive earlier in the chapter, seeking revelation in a bookstore, rediscovered the same four perspectives.

The first book she stumbled on, *The Six Sigma Way*, extends a long tradition that treats an organization as a factory. Drawing from sociology and management science, the *structural frame* emphasizes goals, specialized roles, and formal relationships. Structures—commonly depicted by organization charts—are designed to fit an organization's environment and technology. Organizations allocate responsibilities to participants ("division of labor"). They then create rules, policies, procedures, and hierarchies to coordinate diverse activities into a unified strategy. Problems arise when structure is poorly aligned with current circumstances. At that point, some form of reorganization or redesign is needed to remedy the mismatch.

A simple but fateful example: Riebling (2002) documents the long history of conflict and head butting between America's two intelligence agencies, the Federal Bureau of Investigation and the Central Intelligence Agency. Both are charged to combat espionage and terrorism, but the FBI's writ runs within the United States, while the CIA's mandate is everywhere else. Structurally, the FBI is housed in the Department of Justice and reports to the Attorney General, while the CIA reports through the Director of Central Intelligence to the president. At a number of major junctures in American history (including the assassination of President John F. Kennedy, the Iran-Contra scandal, and the September 11 terrorist attack), each agency held pieces of a larger puzzle, but coordination snafus made it hard for anyone to identify the individual pieces, much less to put them together.

Our executive next encountered *Primal Leadership*, with its focus on an organization's human side. The *human resource frame*, based particularly on ideas from psychology, sees an organization as much like an extended family, made up of individuals with needs, feelings, prejudices, skills, and limitations. People have a great capacity to learn and often an even greater capacity to defend old attitudes and beliefs. From a human resource perspective, the key challenge is to tailor organizations to individuals—to find a way for people to get the job done while feeling good about what they are doing. The conflict between the FBI and the CIA, for example, was fueled in part by a long-running feud between the agencies' two patron saints, J. Edgar Hoover and "Wild Bill" Donovan. When he first became FBI director in the 1920s, Hoover reported to Donovan, who tried to get him fired. When World War II broke out, Hoover wanted the FBI to become the nation's worldwide intelligence agency. He fumed when President Franklin D. Roosevelt instead created a new agency and made Donovan its director.

What Would Machiavelli Do? is a contemporary application of the *political frame*, rooted in the work of political scientists. It sees organizations as arenas, contests, or jungles.

Parochial interests compete for power and scarce resources. Conflict is rampant because of enduring differences in needs, perspectives, and lifestyles among competing individuals and groups. Bargaining, negotiation, coercion, and compromise are a normal part of everyday life. Coalitions form around specific interests and change as issues come and go. Problems arise when power is concentrated in the wrong places or is so broadly dispersed that nothing gets done. Solutions arise from political skill and acumen—as Machiavelli suggested centuries ago in *The Prince* ([1514] 1961). Conflict between the FBI and the CIA was exacerbated by competition for support and funding from Congress and the White House.

Finally, our executive encountered *From Worst to First*, with its emphasis on cultural change as the key to organizational transformation. The *symbolic frame,* drawing on social and cultural anthropology, treats organizations as tribes, theaters, or carnivals. It abandons assumptions of rationality more prominent in other frames. It sees organizations as cultures, propelled more by rituals, ceremonies, stories, heroes, and myths than by rules, policies, and managerial authority. Organization is also theater: actors play their roles in the organizational drama while audiences form impressions from what is seen onstage. Problems arise when actors blow their parts, when symbols lose their meaning, or when ceremonies and rituals lose their potency. We rebuild the expressive or spiritual side of organizations through the use of symbol, myth, and magic. The FBI, which built its image with the dramatic capture or killing of notorious gang leaders, bank robbers and foreign agents, liked to pounce quickly and publicly on suspects. The CIA preferred to work in the shadows, believing that patience and secrecy were a better route to its long-term goal of collecting intelligence and rooting out foreign spies.

The overview of the four-frame model in Table 1.1 shows that each of the frames has its own image of reality. You may be drawn to one or two frames and repelled by others. Some frames may seem clear and straightforward, while others seem puzzling. But learning to apply all four deepens your appreciation and understanding of organizations. Galileo discovered this when he devised the first telescope. Each lens he added contributed to a more accurate image of the heavens. Successful managers take advantage of the same truth. They reframe until they understand the situation at hand. They do this by using more than one frame, or perspective, to develop both a diagnosis of what they are up against and strategies for moving forward.

This claim has stimulated a growing body of research. Dunford and Palmer (1995) found that management courses teaching multiple frames had significant positive effects

TABLE 1.1. Overview of the Four-Frame Model.

	Frame			
	Structural	**Human Resource**	**Political**	**Symbolic**
Metaphor for organization	Factory or machine	Family	Jungle	Carnival, temple, theatre
Central concepts	Rules, roles, goals, policies, technology, environment	Needs, skills, relationships	Power, conflict, competition, organizational politics	Culture, meaning, metaphor, ritual, ceremony, stories, heroes
Image of leadership	Social architecture	Empowerment	Advocacy	Inspiration
Basic leadership challenge	Attune structure to task, technology, environment	Align organizational and human needs	Develop agenda and power base	Create faith, beauty, meaning

over both the short run and the long—in fact, 98 percent of their respondents rated reframing as helpful or very helpful, and about 90 percent felt it gave them a competitive advantage. Another series of studies has shown that the ability to use multiple frames is associated with greater effectiveness for managers and leaders (Bensimon, 1989, 1990; Birnbaum, 1992; Bolman and Deal, 1991, 1992a, 1992b; Heimovics, Herman, and Jurkiewicz Coughlin, 1993, 1995; Wimpelberg, 1987).

Multiframe thinking requires elastic movement beyond narrow and mechanical approaches for understanding organizations. Table 1.2 presents two distinctive ways of approaching management and leadership. One is a rational-technical approach emphasizing certainty and control. The other is a more expressive, artistic conception encouraging flexibility, creativity, and interpretation. The first sees managers as technicians; the second sees them as leaders and artists.

We cannot count the number of times managers have told us that they handled some problem the "only way" it could be done. Such statements betray a failure of both imagi-

TABLE 1.2. Expanding Managerial Thinking.

How Managers Think	How Managers Might Think
They often have a limited view of organizations (for example, attributing almost all problems to individuals' flaws and errors).	They need a holistic framework that encourages inquiry into a range of significant issues: people, power, structure, and symbols.
Regardless of a problem's source, managers often choose rational and structural solutions: facts, logic, restructuring.	They need a palette that offers an array of options: bargaining as well as training, celebration as well as reorganization.
Managers often value certainty, rationality, and control while fearing ambiguity, paradox, and "going with the flow."	They need to develop creativity, risk taking, and playfulness in responses to life's dilemmas and paradoxes, focusing as much on finding the right question as the right answer, on finding meaning and faith amid clutter and confusion.
Leaders often rely on the "one right answer" and the "one best way"; they are stunned at the turmoil and resistance they generate.	Leaders need passionate, unwavering commitment to principle, combined with flexibility in understanding and responding to events.

nation and courage. It may be comforting to think that failure was unavoidable and we did all we could. But it can be enormously liberating to realize there is *always* more than one way to respond to any problem or dilemma. Those who master the ability to reframe report a liberating sense of choice and power. Managers are imprisoned only to the extent that their palette of ideas is impoverished.

This lack of imagination—Langer (1989) calls it "mindlessness"—is a major cause of the shortfall between the reach and the grasp of so many organizations—the empty chasm between dreams and reality, between noble aspirations and disappointing results. The gap is painfully acute in a world in which organizations dominate so much of our lives.

Akira Kurosawa's film *Rashomon* recounts the same event through the eyes of several witnesses. Each tells a very different story. Organizations are filled with people who have their own interpretations of what is and should be happening. Each version contains a glimmer of truth, but each is a product of the prejudices and blind spots of its maker.

No single story is comprehensive enough to make an organization truly understandable or manageable. Effective managers need multiple tools, the skill to use each of them, and the wisdom to match frames to situations.[3]

Artistry is neither exact nor precise. Artists interpret experience and express it in forms that can be felt, understood, and appreciated by others. Art embraces emotion, subtlety, ambiguity. An artist reframes the world so others can see new possibilities. Modern organizations often rely too much on engineering and too little on art in searching for attributes such as quality, commitment, and creativity. Art is not a replacement for engineering but an enhancement. Artistic leaders and managers help us see beyond today's reality to new forms that release untapped individual energies and improve collective performance. The leader as artist relies on images as well as memos, poetry as well as policy, reflection as well as command, and reframing as well as refitting.

CONCLUSION

As organizations have become pervasive and dominant, they have also become formidably difficult to understand and manage. The result is that managers are often nearly as clueless as the Dilberts of the world think they are. The consequences of myopic management and leadership show up every day, sometimes in small and subtle ways, sometimes in catastrophes like the collapse of Enron or WorldCom. Our basic premise is that a primary cause of managerial failure is faulty thinking rooted in inadequate ideas. Managers and those who try to help them too often rely on narrow models that capture only part of the realities of organizational life.

Learning multiple perspectives, or frames, is a defense against cluelessness. Frames serve multiple functions. They are maps that aid navigation, and tools for solving problems and getting things done. This book is organized around four frames that are rooted in both managerial practice and social science research. The *structural frame* focuses on the architecture of organization—the design of units and subunits, rules and roles, goals and policies—that shape and channel decisions and activities. The *human resource frame* emphasizes an understanding of people, with their strengths and foibles, reason and emotion, desires and fears. The *political frame* sees organizations as competitive arenas characterized by scarce resources, competing interests, and struggles for power and advantage.

Finally, the *symbolic frame* focuses on issues of meaning and faith. It puts ritual, ceremony, story, play, and culture at the heart of organizational life.

Each of the frames is both powerful and coherent. Collectively, they make it possible to reframe, viewing the same thing from multiple perspectives. When the world seems hopelessly confusing and nothing is working, reframing is a powerful tool for gaining clarity, generating new options, and finding strategies that work.

NOTES

1. Enron's reign as history's greatest corporate catastrophe was brief. An even bigger behemoth, WorldCom, with assets of more than $100 billion, thundered into Chapter 11 seven months later in July 2002. Stock worth more than forty-five dollars a share two years earlier fell to nine cents.
2. Among the possible ways of talking about frames are schemata or schema theory (Fiedler, 1982; Fiske and Dyer, 1985; Lord and Foti, 1986), representations (Frensch and Sternberg, 1991; Lesgold and Lajoie, 1991; Voss, Wolfe, Lawrence, and Engle, 1991), cognitive maps (Weick and Bougon, 1986), paradigms (Gregory, 1983; Kuhn, 1970), social categorizations (Cronshaw, 1987), implicit theories (Brief and Downey, 1983), mental models (Senge, 1990), and root metaphors. We follow Goffman (1974) in using the term *frame*.
3. A number of management scholars (including Allison, 1971; Bergquist, 1992; Birnbaum, 1988; Elmore, 1978; Morgan, 1986; Perrow, 1986; Quinn, 1988; Quinn, Faerman, Thompson, and McGrath, 1996; and Scott, 1981) have made similar arguments for a multiframe approach to organizations.

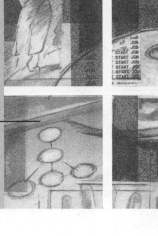

CHAPTER **2**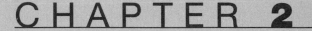

Simple Ideas, Complex Organizations

Early in the morning of August 31, 1983, Kim Eui Donz, a Korean Airlines flight engineer, took his place in the cockpit of KAL Flight 007. His responsibility was clear-cut: to program the inertial navigation system (INS) to direct the flight on its forty-one-hundred-mile course from Anchorage to Seoul. Routinely, Donz entered the plane's position, unaware that his computer entry was 10 degrees off, pinpointing the plane's location as W139 instead of W149. A warning light blinked when he programmed the incorrect position, but he wrote it off to a technical malfunction. Unfortunately, this miscalculation caused the INS to conclude the plane was taking off some three hundred miles *east* of Anchorage.

The mistake should have been caught. Elaborate cross-checking is built into flight procedures of airline pilots. But pilots are human—and we all sometimes shortcut standard operating rules. Another error occurred when the aircraft commander Captain Chun, in the interest of time, hastily revised his flight plan. As a result, the crew had to rush through its routine preflight checks.

The Anchorage control tower cleared Flight 007 to proceed directly to the normal Bethel checkpoint, and Captain Chun switched on the INS without verifying its settings. After takeoff, air traffic control provided a more direct route to save time and fuel. But the new route bypassed Bethel, the last chance before the plane flew over water without further checkpoints until reaching Asia. The crew and passengers were now en route to a mistaken destination. The oversight might still have been detected if Captain Chun had stayed on the flight deck. But after turning off the seat belt sign, he visited the first-class cabin to mix with dignitaries and chat with deadheading KAL pilots.

By coincidence, the "finger error" of 10 degrees put the plane on a course similar to a route flown regularly by American reconnaissance flights near Soviet airspace. Routinely, each reconnaissance mission probed the perimeter of the Soviet border and then veered off. To Soviet radar, the approaching KAL flight looked like a familiar blip, until it did the unexpected. Instead of turning away, the plane crossed into Soviet airspace.

Now the Soviet Air Defense Force became an active player in the unfolding drama. When radar operators could not identify the intruding aircraft, four interceptors were deployed. On the ground, Soviet commanders were thrown into panic and confusion. An unidentified intruder was as potentially dangerous as it was puzzling. If this was a reconnaissance plane, why wasn't it turning away? Still unable to identify Flight 007, they scrambled more fighters. The flight was now well inside Soviet territory, on a course headed directly between two major Soviet air bases.

At 3:12 A.M., Lieutenant Colonel Gennadi Osipovich flew his SU-15 fighter alongside KAL 007. He was surprised to see flashing lights—unprecedented for a U.S. reconnaissance plane. He was even more surprised to identify the plane as a Boeing civilian aircraft. Osipovich told ground control about the lights, and two senior Russian officers speculated that the intruder might be a passenger plane. But Osipovich never mentioned that he had identified a Boeing 747. "They did not ask me," he said later (Gordon, 1996, p. A6). In his mind, the aircraft had to be on a spy mission, and he expected both a hero's welcome and a substantial cash bonus for destroying the enemy target. But time was short; KAL 007 would soon leave Soviet airspace. Ordered to force KAL 007 to land, Osipovich concluded radio was useless, because the foreign pilots would not speak Russian. He flashed his lights and fired more than five hundred cannon rounds as a signal—but the shells contained no tracers and were invisible. There was no response. At 3:26 A.M., less than half a minute before KAL 007 was to exit Soviet airspace, Osipovich fired two missiles. He reported to ground control, "The target is destroyed." Two hundred sixty-nine people fell to their deaths (Gordon, 1996; Hersch, 1986; Witkin, 1993).

The ensuing international incident produced outraged charges, countercharges, and the usual spate of conspiracy theories. Was the plane on an American spy mission? Had the Russians intentionally shot down a civilian aircraft? Had the passengers survived and then been hidden away in Soviet prisons?

More likely, KAL Flight 007 is a dramatic version of an old story: human error leading to tragedy. The flight engineer's initial mistake was compounded by actions of other crew members, including Captain Chun himself. If we look deeper, though, we find that the human-error explanation is deceptive and simplistic. In organizational life, there are almost always organizational causes upstream of human foibles. Korean Airlines had systems to prevent human errors. The systems failed. There were additional procedures to detect and correct such errors; these backup measures also failed. Similar glitches appear in many other well-publicized disasters: nuclear accidents at Chernobyl in the Ukraine and at Three Mile Island in the United States, and the 1995 collapse of a department store in Seoul, for example. Each illustrates a similar chain of error, miscommunication, and misguided actions.

The KAL tragedy happened years ago, but a more recent disaster, discussed in Chapter One, shows that traumatic events are not limited to airline travel or foreign intrigue. In the late 1990s and early 2000, America's Enron Corporation was flying high. It was poised to replace General Electric in size and influence. In a rapidly expanding energy market, it seemed that little could derail the company's ambitious plans.

Two competing strategies vied for the company's future. One, championed by Jeffrey Skilling, sought to position Enron in an exploding financial environment. Rather than own plants and pipelines, why not make deals on the open market? And why limit the portfolio to energy, when broadband and even weather investments offered potentially more lucrative rewards? The other strategy was the brainchild of Skilling's internal competitor, Rebecca Mark. Her vision of the company's future focused on big investments in plants and infrastructure, particularly in underdeveloped overseas markets. Mark wanted to own things. Skilling didn't want to own anything, just buy and sell. Above the fray, Enron's chairman, Ken Lay, concentrated on schmoozing analysts and Washington dignitaries and sponsoring charity events.

Enron had systems and controls to monitor financial transactions, but none seemed to catch the debts and losses accumulating behind the scenes. Arthur Andersen, the company's external auditor, was either oblivious to or complicitous in Enron's precarious financial position. Once the damage could no longer be hidden, the stock price fell precipitously. This exposed even more glaring shortfalls and obligations. Top executives held corporate rallies to build confidence and faith among the rank and file. At the same time, they were selling stock and jumping ship. In the end, the fall of Enron evaporated employee savings, shortchanged the company's creditors, damaged the credibility of corporate America, and helped derail a long-standing bull market. Once again, human error and system failure took their toll.

The KAL and Enron stories made headlines, but errors, failures, and chaos are an everyday of life in organizations. Consider a less dramatic public sector case:

> Helen Demarco arrived in her office to discover a local newspaper clipping. The headline read, "Osborne Announces Plan." Paul Osborne had arrived two months earlier as Amtran's new chief executive. His mandate was to "revitalize, cut costs, and improve efficiency." After twenty years of service, Demarco had achieved a senior management position at Amtran. She had never talked directly with Osborne, but her boss reported to him. Along with her other long-term colleagues, Demarco waited with curiosity and apprehension to learn what the new chief had in mind. She was startled as she read the newspaper account. Osborne's plan made technical assumptions directly related to her area of expertise. She knew that he was a manager, not a technical expert. She saw immediately the new plan's fatal technical flaws. *If he tries to implement this, it'll be the worst management mistake since the Edsel,* she thought to herself.
>
> Two days later, Demarco and several colleagues received a memo instructing them to form a committee and begin work on the revitalization plan. When the group met, everyone agreed the plan was crazy.
>
> "What do we do?" someone asked.
>
> "Why don't we just tell him it won't work?" said one hopeful soul.
>
> "He's already gone public! You want to tell him his baby is ugly?"
>
> "Not me. Besides, he already thinks a lot of us are deadwood. If we tell him it's no good, he'll just think we're defensive."
>
> "Well, we can't just go ahead with it. It's bound to fail!"
>
> "That's true," said Demarco thoughtfully. "But what if we tell him we're conducting a study of how to implement the plan?"
>
> Her suggestion was approved overwhelmingly. The group informed Osborne a study was under way. They even got a substantial budget to support their "research." No one mentioned the study's real purpose: finding a way to kill the plan without alienating Osborne.
>
> Over time, the group developed a strategy. They assembled a lengthy, technical report, filled with graphs, tables, and impenetrable jargon. The report offered Osborne two options.

Option A, his original plan, was presented as technically feasible but phenomenally expensive—well beyond anything Amtran could afford. Option B, billed as a "modest downscaling" of the original plan, was projected as much more cost-effective.

When Osborne pressed the group on the huge cost difference between the two proposals, he received a barrage of technical jargon and quotations. No one mentioned that behind the smoke screen, even Option B offered few benefits at a very high cost. Osborne argued and pressed for more information. But given the apparent reality, he finally agreed to proceed with Option B. Since the plan required several years to implement, he moved to another position before it became operational. Even so, the "Osborne plan" was widely heralded as an extraordinary innovation, supporting once again Paul Osborne's reputation as a manager who could revitalize ailing organizations.

Helen Demarco came away from the experience with deep feelings of frustration and failure. The Osborne plan, in her view, was a wasteful mistake, and she had knowingly participated in a charade. "But," she rationalized to herself, "I really didn't have much choice. Osborne was determined to go ahead. It would have been career suicide to try to stop him."

In fact, Demarco did have other options. There are always alternatives in any managerial quandary. Tragedies occur because managers cannot foresee the issues, are unaware of their choices, or lack the artistry and skill to chart a different course. Helen Demarco, Paul Osborne, the crew of KAL Flight 007, and Enron's management team all thought they were performing effectively. They were tripped up in part by human fallibility. But they were also blinded by a limited understanding of the circumstances. The first step in managerial wisdom and artistry is to understand the situation at hand.

That first step is often a big one, because understanding an organization is not easy. In the remainder of this chapter, we explain why. In the next section, we describe some of the properties of organizations that make them so difficult to understand and manage. Then, we discuss how properties of human nature can get in the way of understanding and magnify organizational difficulties.

PROPERTIES OF ORGANIZATIONS

Human organizations can be exciting and challenging places. That is how things are usually depicted in management texts and corporate annual reports. But they are just as likely deceptive, confusing, and demoralizing. It is a mistake to assume that an organization is either a snake pit or a rose garden (Schwartz, 1986). Managers need to be mindful of several natural characteristics of life at work that create opportunities for the wise as well as traps for the unwary.

First, *organizations are complex.* They are populated by people, whose behavior is notoriously hard to understand and predict. Interactions among diverse individuals and groups make organizations even more complicated. The transactions in the flight crew of KAL Flight 007 suggest some of the intricacies that arise even in relatively simple systems like a three-person cockpit. Larger organizations have a bewildering array of people, departments, technologies, goals, and environments. The complexity is compounded with transactions across multiple organizations. The KAL disaster resulted from a chain of events within and among several separate systems. Enron's demise was hastened by a falling stock market, demanding creditors, credulous outside auditors, and declining public confidence. Almost anything can affect anything else in collective activity. Permutations produce complex, causal knots very hard to disentangle. Paul Osborne probably never understood the real story of what happened to his plan. Even after exhaustive investigation, our understanding of what really happened to KAL Flight 007 is still woven from conjecture and supposition. We may never know the full story behind Enron's collapse.

Second, *organizations are surprising.* What you expect is often dramatically different from what happens. Paul Osborne saw his plan as a bold leap forward; Helen and her group thought it was an expensive albatross. If she was right, then he made matters *worse* by trying to improve them. He might have produced better results by leaving things alone. Until shortly before the bottom fell out, Enron's leadership team was supremely confident that they were building a pioneering new model of corporate success. Their efforts to pump up confidence when things were falling apart seemed contrived and duplicitous when the company finally collapsed.

The solution to yesterday's problems often creates future impediments to getting anything done. It may even create new possibilities for disaster. Think of the procedural hurdles and bureaucratic obstacles often created after a disaster such as Flight 007, the meltdown of Enron, or the loss of the space shuttle *Challenger.* A friend of ours was the president of a chain of retail stores. In the firm's early years, he had a problem with two sisters who worked in the same store. To prevent this situation from recurring, he established a nepotism policy. It prohibited two members of the same family from working for the company. Years later, two of his employees met at work, fell in love, and began to live together. The president was stunned when they asked if they could get married without being fired. What goes around often comes around, to the detriment of an organization's well-being. Taking action in a collective enterprise is like shooting a wobbly cue ball into a large and complex array of self-directed billiard balls. So many balls careen in so many directions that it is impossible to know how things will eventually sort out.

Third, *organizations are deceptive.* They defy expectations and then camouflage surprises. The Soviet Air Defense Force tried to hide its surprise and confusion for fear of revealing critical strategic weaknesses. Enron raised financial camouflage to an art form with a series of sophisticated partnerships (carrying *Star Wars* names like Chewco, Jedi, and Kenobe). These initiatives generated artificial revenue balanced by hidden off-the-books debt (Babineck, 2002). Helen Demarco and her colleagues did their best to ensure that Paul Osborne never learned that their research was a holding action and their technical report was mostly artful camouflage.

It is tempting but too easy to blame deception on individual character flaws or personality disorders. Helen Demarco disliked deception and regretted doing it, yet she believed she had no other choice. Sophisticated managers know that what happened to Paul Osborne happens routinely. Even though the new quality initiative might be flawed or the new product doomed, subordinates often clam up. Warning voices at Enron were silenced until the dissenters "blew the whistle" in Congressional hearings and the press. Subordinates legitimately fear that the boss will not listen or might punish them for being resistant or insubordinate. A friend who occupies a senior position in a large government agency put it simply: "Communications in organizations are rarely candid, open, or timely."

Fourth, *organizations are ambiguous.* The sum of complexity, unpredictability, and deception is rampant ambiguity. Figuring out what is really happening in businesses, hospitals, schools, or public agencies is difficult. Even if we think we know what is happening, it is hard to know what it means or what to do about it. Helen Demarco was never sure how Paul Osborne really felt, how receptive he would be to other points of view, or how much he was willing to compromise. She and her peers heightened ambiguity by trying to keep him in the dark. As the KAL and Enron cases show, when you incorporate additional organizations—or cultures—into the human equation, the level of ambiguity quickly becomes overwhelming.

Ambiguity originates from a number of sources. Sometimes information is incomplete or vague. The same information may be interpreted in a variety of ways. At other times, ambiguity is deliberately created to hide problems or avoid conflict. Much of the time, events and processes are so complex, scattered, and uncoordinated no one can fully understand—let alone control—what is happening. Exhibit 2.1, adapted from McCaskey (1982), lists some of the most important sources of organizational ambiguity.

ORGANIZATIONAL LEARNING

An environment filled with complexity, surprise, deception, and ambiguity makes it hard to extract lessons for future action. Yet an increasingly turbulent, rapidly shifting environment requires contemporary organizations to learn better and faster just to survive. Michael Dell, founder and CEO of Dell Computer Corporation, explained it this way: "In our business, the product cycle is six months, and if you miss the product cycle,

EXHIBIT 2.1. Sources of Ambiguity.

We are not sure what the problem is. Definitions are vague or competing, and any given problem is intertwined with other messy problems.

We are not sure what is really happening. Information is incomplete, ambiguous, and unreliable. People disagree on how to interpret information that is available.

We are not sure what we want. We all have multiple goals that are unclear or conflicting. Different people want different things. This leads to political and emotional conflict.

We do not have the resources we need. Shortages of time, attention, or money make difficult situations even more chaotic.

We are not sure who is supposed to do what. Roles are unclear, there is disagreement about who is responsible for what, and things keep shifting as players come and go.

We are not sure how to get what we want. Even if we agree on what we want, we are not sure (or we disagree) about how to make it happen.

We are not sure how to determine if we have succeeded. We are not sure what criteria to use to evaluate success. Or if we do know the criteria, we are not sure how to measure the outcome.

Source: Adapted from McCaskey (1982).

you've missed the opportunity. In this business, there are two kinds of people, really: the quick and the dead" (Farkas and De Backer, 1996).

With stakes so high, organizational learning has emerged as a topic of increasing urgency. Decades ago, scholars debated whether the idea of collective learning even made sense; could organizations learn, or was learning inherently individual? That debate died out as scholars and practitioners discovered instances where individuals learned and organizations didn't, or vice versa. Complex firms such as Microsoft, Toyota, and British Airways have "learned" capabilities that go far beyond individual knowledge. Yet individuals often master lessons their system cannot. From the late 1980s onward, for example, even senior officials in China recognized the nation was heading in two contradictory directions at once, promoting capitalism economically while defending communist political rule. A longtime Communist party member mused, "What does the Party stand for now? Nothing. Stability, maybe. But really, no ideas at all" (Rosenthal, 2002, p. A3). Behind the scenes, individual party members began an increasingly urgent search for a way to bridge the gap. Publicly, though, the party tried to keep the lid on dissent and pretend that bringing capitalists into the party was just one more sign of socialist progress (Kahn, 2002). Almost everyone knew they were on the road to perdition, but the system had great difficulty acknowledging and acting on that reality.

A variety of perspectives on organizational learning have emerged, exemplified in the work of Peter Senge (1990) and Barry Oshry (1995). Senge sees a core learning dilemma in organizations: "We learn best from our experience, but we never directly experience the consequences of many of our decisions" (1990, p. 23). It is relatively easy for people to learn when cause and effect are close enough that the connection is easy to see. Complex systems often sever that linear linkage: cause may be far removed from effect, solutions remote from problems, and feedback delayed or misleading (Cyert and March, 1963; Senge, 1990). At home, you flip a switch and the light goes on. In an organization, you flip the switch and nothing happens until long after you leave the room—or a toilet may flush in a building ten miles away. You are still in the dark, and the user of the toilet is unpleasantly surprised. To understand what is going on, you need to master the system's complex circular causality.

Senge emphasizes the value of "system maps" that clarify how a system works. Consider "Chainsaw Al" Dunlap, CEO of Scott Paper in the early 1990s. Dunlap was proud of his nickname and his turnaround at Scott. He raised profits and market value substantially by slashing head count and cutting frills such as research and development. But he rarely talked about Scott's steady loss of market share (Byrne, 1996). As the case illustrates, actions that produce short-term improvements often create more serious long-term problems. A corresponding systems model might look like Figure 2.1.

The strategy might be to cut training to improve short-term profitability, or drink martinis to relieve stress, or offer big rebates to entice customers to buy now, or borrow from a loan shark to cover gambling debts. In each case, a strategy that seems to work in the short run produces long-term costs that become apparent only too late.

Oshry (1995) makes the same basic point—system blindness is widespread—but emphasizes causes rooted in asymmetric relationships: between tops and bottoms, vendors and customers. When we are at the apex of an organization, for example, we lose track of what it is like in the middle or at the bottom. We cannot see that system dynamics are producing a "dance of blind reflex" (p. 54). In this rhythmic decoupling, various partners live in different worlds. Top managers feel overwhelmed by complexity, responsibility, and overload. They are chronically disappointed in middle management's lack of

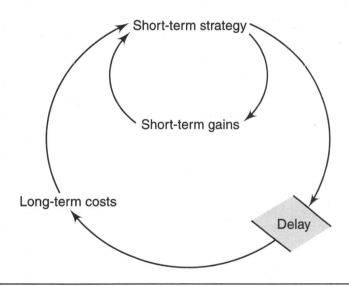

FIGURE 2.1. Systems Model with Delay.

initiative and creativity. Middle managers, meanwhile, feel torn by conflicting signals and pressures. Top managers tell them to take risks and then punish mistakes. Subordinates and bosses tug those in the middle in opposite directions, causing them to feel confused and weak. At the bottom of the mix, workers feel vulnerable, unappreciated, and oppressed: "They give us lousy jobs with lousy pay, they order us around all the time but never tell us what's really going on, and then they wonder why we don't love our work." If you do not see the dance, says Oshry, you continue to play your part blindly, unaware of any other option.

Oshry and Senge both argue that failure to read system dynamics traps us in a cycle of blaming and self-defense. The enemy is out there somewhere, and problems are always caused by someone else. This same theme appears in the work of Chris Argyris and Donald Schön (1978, 1996). They focus less on system dynamics and more on individual and group defenses. Senge argues that we fail to learn from experience because we don't see the consequences of our actions. Argyris and Schön believe that "the actions we take to promote productive organizational learning actually inhibit deeper learning" (1996, p. 281). Actions are counterproductive because we try to solve problems while avoiding undiscussable issues and tip-toeing around organizational taboos. We ignore important but "sensitive" issues and tell ourselves only a fool would do otherwise. Such strategies often seem to work in the short run but eventually create a double bind: we can't solve problems without facing issues that we have tried to bury, but that would reveal our cover-up. Facing that double bind, Helen Demarco and her colleagues chose to camouflage their strategy. The consequence, according to Argyris and Schön, is escalating games of deception. This is exactly what happened at both Enron and WorldCom, but increasingly desperate maneuvers only made the day of reckoning more catastrophic when it finally arrived.

COPING WITH AMBIGUITY AND COMPLEXITY

How do organizations cope with a complex and ambiguous environment? Basically, they try to make it simpler. One way is to develop systems and technology to collect and process information. Another is to break complexity into smaller pieces and assign chunks to specialized individuals or units. Still another approach is to hire or develop sophisticated professionals with skills in handling specific segments of environmental complexity. These and other methods are all helpful but not always sufficient. Despite organizations' best efforts, bad things still happen.

On April 14, 1994, three years after Iraq's surrender ended the Gulf War, two U.S. F-15C fighter jets took off from a base in Turkey to fly into the no-fly zone in Northern Iraq. Their mission was to "clear the area of any hostile aircraft" (Snook, 2000, p. 4). There had been no violations of the no-fly zone in more than two years. But Iraqi antiaircraft fire was a continuing risk. There were media reports that Saddam Hussein might be planning to move a large force north. At 10:22 A.M., the fighter pilots reported to AWACS (Airborne Warning and Control System) controllers that they had made radar contact with two slow, low-flying aircraft. The fighter pilots attempted to identify the aircraft with an electronic friend-or-foe system but were unsuccessful. They flew down to attempt a visual identification. The lead pilot, Tiger 01, passed above and to the left of the targets and spotted two "Hinds"—a label for Soviet-made helicopters used by the Iraqis. He reported his sighting, and an AWACS controller responded, "Copy, 2 Hinds" (Snook, 2000, p. 6). The fighter pilots circled back to begin a firing run. They informed AWACS that they were "engaged," and, at 10:30 A.M., each pilot brought down one of the two helicopters.

Both pilots felt "pumped" after their success—exactly as Gennadi Osipovich felt after bringing down KAL 007. Destroying enemy aircraft is the Holy Grail of fighter pilots. Only later did the pilots learn that they had destroyed two American UH-60 Black Hawk helicopters, killing all twenty-six UN relief workers aboard.

Tiger 01 was sure he saw Hinds, even though Hinds are tan and Black Hawks forest green, and despite the six American flags painted on each UH-60. How could two highly trained and experienced U.S. pilots see what wasn't there? Snook's painstaking analysis offers a compelling explanation.

To begin with, the camouflage paint on the Black Hawks was, by design, difficult to see against the terrain, particularly for fighters flying very fast at an angular distance of more than a thousand feet. To attempt a visual identification, the pilots had to fly at a danger-ously low altitude in a valley with mountains on either side. Terrain awareness was criti-cal, and they were eager to get back above the mountains as quickly as possible. An extensive postmortem showed that the helicopters would have been difficult to identify. The pilots did the normal human thing in the face of ambiguous perceptual data: they filled in gaps in what they saw based on what they knew, what they expected, and what they wanted.

The Black Hawk and the Hind have certain similarities in size and appearance: both have a tapered, downward-sloping tail and winglike appendages (ordnance sponsons on the Hinds, fuel tanks on the Black Hawk) that look somewhat similar from above. The pilots had received limited training on identifying helicopters, because fighter pilots train primarily for high-speed combat at altitudes where helicopters never fly. In the training they did receive, they saw only photos taken from *below.* (The photos came from the Army, whose troops would usually be on the ground looking up.) The lead pilot said later that "Black Hawks did not even cross my mind. The only helicopter that crossed my mind was the Hind" (Snook, 2000, p. 81).

What You Expect to See Is What You See

It is easy to understand why the pilots were only thinking about enemy aircraft. They were flying heavily armed over unfriendly territory. Their preflight briefings had covered a number of possible threats but included no mention of friendly helicopters. Once the mission commenced, Tiger 01 was in continual contact with AWACS controllers, and he expected that they would alert him to any friendly aircraft in the vicinity. (In fact, one of the AWACS controllers was monitoring the helicopters. But the AWACS team was in its first day on the job and its members were still learning how to work together.) "By the time Tiger 01 saw the helicopters, he already *believed* that they were enemy. All that remained was for him to selectively match up incoming scraps of visual data with a rea-sonable cognitive scheme of an enemy silhouette. As he flipped through the photos in his onboard 'goody book,' the ordnance sponsons of the Hind were too easy a match with the top view of UH-60 external fuel tanks. His book contained no photos of Black Hawks" (Snook, 2000, p. 80).

Situations can be even more complicated when history casts its shadow. In May 1987, the frigate *USS Stark* established radar contact on an aircraft flying out of Iraq. The target appeared friendly because, at the time, Iraq and the United States were in a coalition opposing Iran. Unexpectedly, the fighter attacked the *Stark,* inflicting substantial damage and casualties. Fourteen months later, a similar situation presented itself to the com-mander of the *USS Vincennes,* operating in the Straits of Hormuz. Radar contact pinpointed an aircraft originating from Iran, a hostile source. The *Vincennes* fired two missiles and destroyed the aircraft—an Iran Air Airbus with 290 souls aboard. All perished. The experience of the *Stark* no doubt influenced the decision of the *Vincennes* captain. What happened before affects the current decisions.

Some events are so clear and unambiguous that it is easy for people to agree on what is happening. Determining if a train is on schedule, if a plane landed safely, or if a clock is keeping accurate time is straightforward. But most of the important issues confronting managers are not so clear-cut. Solid facts and simple problems in everyday life at work are hard to find. Will a reorganization work? Was a meeting successful? Why did a consensual decision backfire? Our ability to make sense in complicated and ambiguous situations depends very much on the frames, or mental models, we bring to the task. As the friendly-fire episode illustrates, those frames are determined by history and circumstance, which can lead even well-trained experts into making poor choices. Since our interpretations hinge on our expectations, beliefs, and values, our internal world is as important as what is outside—sometimes more so, because we manage to see what we expect and want. The fuzziness of everyday life makes it easy for people to make the world conform to their favored internal maps.

Managers regularly face an unending barrage of puzzles or "messes." To act without creating more trouble, they must first establish an accurate picture of what is happening. Then they must proceed to a deeper level, asking, "What is *really* going on here?" This important step in reading a situation is often overlooked. As a result, managers may form superficial analyses and leap on solutions nearest at hand or most in vogue. Market share declining? Try strategic planning. Customer complaints? Put in a quality program. Profits down? Time to reengineer or downsize.

A better alternative is to think, to probe more deeply into what is *really* going on. As a former chief of naval operations remarked, "The first responsibility of a leader is to figure out what is going on. . . . That is never easy to do because situations are rarely black or white, they are a pale shade of gray . . . they are seldom neatly packaged." Sometimes a more careful assessment defines a real problem. Other times, we find ourselves caught on the horns of a dilemma, like a university professor who said, "I'm in a situation where my options are to take an administrative job that I don't want or to work for someone I don't respect." A problem can be solved, but a dilemma requires a choice based on values and ethics—or enough patience to let things take their own course.

The ideas, or theories, we carry with us determine whether a given situation is confusing or clear, meaningful or cryptic, a paralyzing disaster or a genuine learning experience. Personal theories are essential because of a basic fact about human perception: in any situation, there is simply too much happening for us to attend to it all. To help us understand what is going on and what to do next, well-grounded personal theories offer two advantages: (1) they tell us what is important and what can be safely ignored, and (2) they group scattered bits of information into manageable patterns or concepts.

The Dilemma of Changing Versus Conserving

To a nonpilot, a fighter jet's cockpit is a confusing array of controls, switches, and gauges. Yet an experienced pilot can discern the aircraft's status in a glance. Like other professionals, a pilot learns patterns that cluster seemingly fragmented bits of information into a few manageable chunks. It takes many hours to learn the key concepts, but once they've been learned, they help the pilot size things up with ease, speed, and accuracy. In the same way, an experienced manager can read a situation very rapidly, decide what needs to be done, and make it happen. This intuition and skill are based on extensive prior learning of effective patterns of thought and action.

It takes time and effort to learn these lessons. Helen Demarco's prior experience gave her a set of lenses for making sense of Paul Osborne's behavior and deciding how to respond. Because she read the situation through a limited framework, she could not see other options. The good and bad news is that our theories shield us from confusion, uncertainty, and anxiety. Tiger 01 knew exactly what to do because he knew what he saw. The captain of the *Vincennes* did not want a reprise of what happened to the *Stark*. We get anxious and stuck if we have tried every lens we know and nothing works. Letting go of a preferred mind-set sacrifices our investment in learning the ropes. We are caught in a dilemma: holding on to old patterns is ineffective, but developing new mental models entails substantial time and effort. It is also risky; it might lead to analysis paralysis and further erosion of our confidence and effectiveness.

This dilemma still exists even if we see no flaws in our current mind-set, because our theories are self-sealing—they block us from seeing our errors. An extensive body of research documents the many ways in which individuals spin reality to protect existing beliefs (see, for example, Garland, 1990; Kühberger, 1995; Staw and Hoang, 1995; Tetlock, 2000). This helps to explain why Enron's Ken Lay and Andersen's Joe Berardino were sure they had done the right thing, even though their companies collapsed during their watch. Heath and Gonzalez (1995) found that decision makers rely on others not so much to gain new information as to strengthen preconceived thinking. Tetlock (2000) showed that managers' judgments of performance were influenced by cognitive preferences and political ideologies. Extensive research on the "framing effect" (Kahneman and Tversky, 1979) shows how powerful subtle cues can be. Relatively modest changes in how a problem or decision is framed can have a dramatic impact on how people respond (Shu and Adams, 1995; Gegerenzer, Hoffrage, and Kleinbölting, 1991). Decision makers, for example, tend to respond more favorably to an option that has a "70 percent chance of success" than one that has a "30 percent chance of failure," even though they are statistically identical.

Some of us recognize that mental maps influence how we interpret the world around us. Less widely understood is that what we expect often determines what we get. Rosenthal and Jacobson (1968) studied schoolteachers who were told that certain students in their classes were "spurters"—students who were "about to bloom." The so-called spurters had been randomly selected, but they still achieved above-average gains on achievement tests. They really *did* spurt. Somehow the teachers' expectations were communicated to and assimilated by the students. Modern medical science is still trying to understand the power of the placebo effect—the ability of sugar pills to make people better. Results are attributed to an unexplained change in the patient's belief system. Patients believe they will get better; therefore they do. The similar, so-called Pygmalion effect has been replicated in countless reorganizations, new product launches, and new approaches to performance appraisal.

COMMON FALLACIES IN ORGANIZATIONAL DIAGNOSIS

Albert Einstein once said that a thing should be made as simple as possible, but no simpler. When we ask students and managers to diagnose cases like KAL Flight 007, Helen Demarco, or Enron, they often make things simpler than they are. They do this by relying on one of three oversimplified, one-size-fits-all concepts.

The first and most common is to *blame people*. This approach explains everything in terms of individual error. Problems result from bad attitudes, abrasive personalities, neurotic tendencies, stupidity, or incompetence. It's an easy way to explain anything that goes

Greatest Hits from Organization Studies No. 5: James G. March and Herbert A. Simon, *Organizations* (New York: Wiley, 1958).*

March and Simon's pioneering 1958 book *Organizations* sought to define a new field that barely existed, by offering a structure and language for studying organizations. It was one of the works that helped to earn Simon the 1978 Nobel Prize for economics.

No brief summary can do justice to the range of topics and issues that March and Simon considered. In essence, they offered a cognitive, social-psychological view of organizational behavior with an emphasis on thinking, information processing, and decision making. The book begins with extensive attention to a model of behavior that sees humans as continually seeking to satisfy motives expressed in the form of aspiration levels. The aspirations that are operative at any given time are a function of both the individuals' history and the environment in which they find themselves. If aspirations are unsatisfied, individuals engage in search; they look for better, more satisfying options. An important implication of the March and Simon model is that organizations influence individuals primarily by managing the available information and options, the "decision premises" that individuals consider.

March and Simon followed Simon's earlier work (1947) in critiquing the traditional economic view of "rational man," who maximizes utility by considering all available options and choosing the best. Instead, they argue, both individuals and organizations have limited information and limited ability to process what they have. They never know all the options. Instead, they become aware of alternatives and gradually alter aspirations in the course of searching the environment. Instead of maximizing, individuals and organizations "satisfice": looking not for the best option but for the first that is good enough to meet their current aspirations.

Organizational decision making is additionally complicated because the environment is very complex, resources (time, attention, money, and so on) are scarce, and there is ongoing conflict among individuals and groups. Organizational design occurs through a piecemeal bargaining process that holds no guarantee of optimal rationality. Of necessity, organizations seek to simplify the environment so as to reduce the load on limited capacities for decision making and information processing. A major way to simplify is to create "programs"—standardized ways of performing repetitive tasks. Once a program is in place, there is an incentive to keep using it so long as the results are at least marginally satisfactory. Otherwise, the organization is forced to expend time and energy to innovate. But programming tends to drive out innovation, because individuals find it easier and less taxing to devote their limited time and energy to programmed tasks (which are automatic, well practiced, and more certain of success). Thus, a would-be author may find it much easier to make tea, rearrange her desk, and sort the mail than to figure out how to write the opening paragraph of her novel.

March and Simon's book falls primarily within the structural and human resource frames. But their discussions of scarce resources, power, conflict, and bargaining recognize the reality of organizational politics. They postulate, for example, that organizational decision making is more analytic when groups have common goals, but more political otherwise. Although they do not use the term explicitly, March and Simon recognize framing as an essential component of individual and organizational choice. Decision making, they say, is always based on a simplified model of the world. Organizations develop unique vocabulary and classification schemes, which determine what people are likely to see and talk about. Things that don't fit the organization's frame are likely to be either ignored or reframed into terms the organization can understand.

* We used citation analysis (how often a work is referenced in the scholarly literature) to develop a list of "scholars' greatest hits"—the works that organizational scholars rely on most. Appendix A shows our results and discusses how we developed our analysis. At appropriate points in the book (where the ideas are most relevant, as here), we present a brief summary of key ideas from works that were at the top of our list.

wrong. Once Enron went bankrupt, the hunt was on for someone to blame, and the top executives became the target of both prosecutors and talk-show comedians. One CEO said, "We want the bad guys exposed and the bad guys punished" (Toffler and Reingold, 2003, p. 229). As children, we learned it was important to assign blame for every broken toy, stained carpet, or wounded sibling. Pinpointing the culprit is comforting. Assigning blame resolves ambiguity, explains mystery, and makes clear what must be done next: punish the guilty. No doubt the Enron story had its share of culpable individuals. But the larger story is about the organizational and social context that set the stage for individual malfeasance. Targeting individuals while ignoring larger system failures oversimplifies the problem and does little to prevent a recurrence.

When it is hard to identify a guilty individual, then a second popular alternative is to *blame the bureaucracy.* Things went haywire because the organization is stifled by rules and red tape—or because it's out of control for lack of clear goals and roles. One or the other explanation almost always applies. If things are out of control, then the system needs clearer rules and procedures, and tighter job descriptions. The problem between

Helen Demarco and Paul Osborne could have been averted if roles had been clear and everyone had behaved rationally. Tighter financial controls could have prevented Enron's free fall. The problem is that piling on rules and regulations typically leads to bureaucratic rigidity. Rules inhibit freedom and flexibility, stifle initiative, and generate oceans of red tape. Could Enron have achieved its status as America's most innovative company if it had played only by conventional rules? When things become too tight, the solution is to "free up" the system so red tape and rigid rules don't stifle creativity and bog things down. But many organizations vacillate endlessly between being too loose and too tight.

A third fallacy attributes problems to a *thirst for power*. From this viewpoint, Paul Osborne and Helen Demarco were both playing political games and looking out for themselves. In the case of Enron, Skilling and Mark were more interested in expanding their own turf than in the company's best interests. This view sees organizations as jungles filled with predators and prey. Victory goes to the more adroit, or the more treacherous. Political games and turf wars cause most organizational problems. The best you can do is to play the game better than your opponent—and watch your backside.

The problem is not that these three fallacies are entirely wrong but that they oversimplify a more complicated reality. Each is based on a partial truth. Blaming people points to the perennial importance of individual culpability. Some problems *are* caused by personal characteristics: rigid bosses, slothful subordinates, bumbling bureaucrats, greedy union members, or insensitive elites. Much of the time, though, faulting people blocks us from seeing system weaknesses and offers few workable options. If, for example, the problem is someone's abrasive or pathological personality, what do we do? Even psychiatrists find it hard to alter character disorders, and firing everyone with a less-than-ideal persona is rarely a viable option.

The blame-the-bureaucracy perspective starts from a reasonable assumption: organizations are created to achieve specific goals. They are most effective when goals and policies are clear (but not excessively restrictive), jobs are well defined (but not too limiting), control systems are in place (but not oppressive), and employees behave reasonably and prudently. Disagreements between Helen Demarco and Paul Osborne ideally could have been resolved through rational discourse and careful consideration of the facts. If people always behaved that way, organizations would presumably work a lot better than most do. In practice, this perspective is better at explaining how organizations should work than why they often don't. Managers who cling to rationality become discouraged and frustrated when confronted by intractable irrational forces. Year after year, we witness the introduction of new control systems, hear of new ways to reorganize, and are dazzled by emerging management consultants and the latest management methods. Yet old problems persist, seemingly immune to every rational cure we devise.

The thirst-for-power view highlights some enduring features of organizations. Helen Demarco and Paul Osborne, like Jeffrey Skilling and Rebecca Mark, had differing interests and sources of power. Demarco was a career employee with a stake in protecting her status. She could afford to take a long-term view. An unrealistic crash program that failed could hurt her career. Osborne's situation was different; he came with a mandate for change—the sooner the better. A program drawn out over many years would not enhance his reputation as a leader who got results. He needed a dramatic and visible initiative that promised big improvements quickly. The dog-eat-dog, thirst-for-power perspective offers a plausible analysis of almost anything that goes wrong in organizations or society. Demarco and her colleagues, for example, played their cards adeptly and, apparently, achieved a significant victory. But neither Demarco nor Osborne really wanted political games to dominate decision making. In that sense, both lost. At Enron, Skilling won the internal political battle, but he and Mark both built businesses that contributed to the company's downfall. Both also bailed out before the company folded.

Blaming people, the bureaucracy, or human nature leads to a false sense of clarity and optimism. Surprises, complexities, and ambiguities of organizational life require more powerful and comprehensive approaches to give managers the flexibility to look at organizations from more than one angle. In Western cultures, particularly, there is a tendency to embrace one theory or ideology and to try to make the world conform. If it works, we persist in our view. If discrepancies arise, we try to rationalize them away. If people challenge our view, we ignore them or put them in their place. Only poor results over a long period of time call our theories into question. Even then, we often simply entrench ourselves in a new worldview, triggering the cycle again.

In Japan, there are four major religions, each with unique beliefs and assumptions: Buddhism, Confucianism, Shintoism, and Taoism. Though the religions differ greatly in history, traditions, and basic tenets, many Japanese feel no need to choose only one. They use them all, taking advantage of the strengths of each for suitable purposes or occasions. The four frames can play a similar role for managers in modern organizations. Rather than portraying the field of organizational theory as fragmented, we present it as pluralistic. Seen this way, the field offers a rich and varied assortment of lenses for viewing organizations. Each theoretical tradition is helpful. Each has blind spots. Each tells its own story about organizations. The ability to shift from one to another helps redefine situations so that they become understandable and manageable. The ability to reframe is one of the most powerful capacities of great artists. It can be equally powerful for managers. Undergraduates at Vanderbilt University captured this in a class-initiated rap (for best results, rap fans should imagine the rapper Common doing these lines in a neo-soul, hip-hop style):

Reframe, reframe, put a new spin on the mess you're in.
Reframe, reframe, try to play a different game.
Reframe, reframe, when you're in a tangle, shoot another angle;
look at things a different way.

CONCLUSION

Because organizations are complex, surprising, deceptive, and ambiguous, they are formidably difficult to understand and manage. Our preconceived theories and images determine what we see, what we do, and what we accomplish. Narrow, oversimplified perspectives become fallacies that often cloud rather than illuminate managerial action. The world of most managers and administrators is a world of messes: complexity, ambiguity, value dilemmas, political pressures, and multiple constituencies. For managers whose images blind them to important parts of this messy reality, it is a world of frustration and failure. For those with better theories and the capacity to use them with skill and grace, it is a world of excitement and possibility. A mess can be defined as both a troublesome situation and a group of people who eat together. The core challenge of leadership is to move an organization from the former to something more like the latter.

In succeeding chapters, we examine four perspectives, or frames, that have helped managers and leaders find clarity and meaning amid the confusion of organizational life. We cannot guarantee your success as a manager or a change agent. We believe, though, that you can improve your odds with an artful appreciation of the four lenses and how to use them to understand and influence what's really going on.

PART TWO

The Structural Frame

A frame, as explained in Chapter Two, is a coherent set of ideas that enable you to see and understand more clearly what goes on day to day. In Parts Two to Five, we embark on a tour of the frames—four very different ways of making sense of life at work or anywhere else. Each frame is presented in three chapters: one that introduces the basic concepts, and two that focus on key applications and extensions. We begin with one of the oldest and most widely used ways of thinking about organizations, the structural frame.

If someone asked you to describe your organization—your workplace, your school, or even your family—what image would come to mind? A likely possibility is a traditional organization chart, a series of boxes and lines depicting job responsibilities and levels. The chart might be shaped roughly like a pyramid, with a small number of authority figures at the top and a much larger number of grunts at the bottom. Such a chart is only one of many images that reflect how the structural frame views organizations. The frame is rooted in traditional rational images but goes much deeper to develop versatile and powerful ways to understand social architecture and its consequences.

We begin Chapter Three with two cases, contrasting the structural features of a highly disciplined aircraft carrier with the structural lapses that hampered rescue efforts in New York City's September 11 terrorist attacks. We then highlight the basic assumptions of the structural view with emphasis on two key dimensions: dividing work and coordinating it thereafter. We emphasize how structural design depends on an organization's circumstances, including its goals, technology, and environment. In addition, we show why tightly controlled, top-down forms may work well in simple, stable situations but fail badly in more fluid and ambiguous ones.

In Chapter Four, we turn to issues of structural change and redesign. We describe basic structural tensions, explore alternatives to consider when new circumstances require structural revisions, and discuss challenges of the restructuring process. We close the chapter with examples of successful structural change.

Finally, in Chapter Five, we apply structural concepts to groups and teams. When teams work badly, members often blame one another for problems that reflect structural rather than individual failings. We begin by examining structural configurations in five-person teams. Then we contrast the games of baseball, American football, and basketball to show how optimal structure depends on what a team is trying to do and under what conditions. We close with an examination of the structural characteristics of high-performance teams.

CHAPTER 3

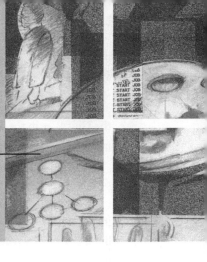

Getting Organized

"It may look like chaos, but we always know what is going on," says Lt. Cdr. Gary Deal, a naval officer who once served aboard the aircraft carrier *USS Kennedy*. When equipped for deployment, the *Kennedy* is home to more than five thousand men and women. About half of these people are assigned to the ship, the other half to the air wing. The ship is organized into nineteen departments, including operations, engineering, supply, navigation, and air (which controls all functions of the flight deck). The air wing is organized into nine squadrons. Each squadron ensures that its flight crews and aircraft are ready to conduct an assigned mission at any time. The flight deck is responsible for the safe and efficient launch and recovery of the aircraft. Fifty functional roles are involved in the process. Individuals' functions are immediately obvious from their uniforms: blue for "grunts," red for weapons and fire-control personnel, brown for those who direct the taxiing and towing of aircraft, and purple for fuelers (they are affectionately referred to as "grapes"). Supervisory personnel, including catapult officers known as "shooters," wear yellow, while safety personnel wear white. On the bridge, officers dress in standard khaki uniforms; the Officer of the Deck wears a gold-emblazoned baseball cap. The captain has overall command of the ship, while the commander of the air group (CAG) is responsible for the air wing.

In combat, the *USS Kennedy*'s primary goal is clear: bombs on target. To reach that goal, all functions have to work together. Anything anyone does affects everyone else, especially in close quarters under battle conditions. Individuals know their own job even if they are unaware of the big picture. A carrier succeeds only if roles are clear and everyone responds uniformly to the chain of command. The performance of the carrier fleet in the Gulf War in the early 1990s and a decade later in Afghanistan and the 2003 campaign in Iraq is ample evidence that warships like the *Kennedy* can do their job.

A naval carrier can plan for most of the contingencies combat might bring. Tragically, the same thing was not true for New York City's fire and police departments in the face of the September 11 terrorist strikes on the World Trade Center. That day saw countless inspiring examples of individual heroism and personal sacrifice. At the risk of their own lives, emergency personnel rescued thousands of people. Many died in the effort. But extraordinary individual efforts were hindered or thwarted by breakdowns in communication, command, and control. Police helicopters hovering near the north tower radioed that it was near collapse more than twenty minutes before it fell. The warning was relayed to police officers, and most escaped. But it reached very few firefighters. There was no link between fire and police radios, and the commanders in the two departments could not communicate because their command posts were three blocks apart. It might not have helped even if they had talked, because the fire department's radios had been notoriously unreliable in high-rise buildings for years. The failures of communication and coordination magnified the death toll—including 121 firefighters who died when the north tower collapsed. The absence of a clear and appropriate structure seriously impaired the effectiveness of highly motivated, skilled professionals who gave their all in the face of an unprecedented catastrophe (Dwyer, Flynn, and Fessenden, 2002).

Comparing the situation aboard the *USS Kennedy* with rescue efforts at the World Trade Center points to a core premise of the structural perspective: clear, well-understood roles and relationships and adequate coordination are key to how well an organization performs. We begin our examination of the structural frame by discussing its core assumptions, origins, and basic forms. The possibilities for designing an organization's structure are almost limitless, but any design must address two core issues. In this chapter, we explain those issues, describe the major options, and discuss structural imperatives to consider when arranging a particular work setting.

STRUCTURAL ASSUMPTIONS

The assumptions of the structural frame are reflected in current approaches to social architecture and organizational design. These assumptions reflect a belief in rationality and a faith that the right formal arrangements minimize problems and maximize performance. A human resource perspective emphasizes the importance of changing people (through training, rotation, promotion, or dismissal), but the structural perspective champions a pattern of well-thought-out roles and relationships. Properly designed, these formal arrangements can accommodate both collective goals and individual differences.

Six assumptions undergird the structural frame:

1. Organizations exist to achieve established goals and objectives.

2. Organizations increase efficiency and enhance performance through specialization and a clear division of labor.

3. Appropriate forms of coordination and control ensure that diverse efforts of individuals and units mesh.

4. Organizations work best when rationality prevails over personal preferences and extraneous pressures.

5. Structures must be designed to fit an organization's circumstances (including its goals, technology, workforce, and environment).

6. Problems and performance gaps arise from structural deficiencies and can be remedied through analysis and restructuring.

ORIGINS OF THE STRUCTURAL PERSPECTIVE

The structural view has two main intellectual roots. The first is the work of industrial analysts bent on designing organizations for maximum efficiency. The most prominent of them, Frederick W. Taylor (1911), was the father of time-and-motion studies; he founded an approach that he labeled "scientific management." Taylor broke tasks into minute parts and retrained workers to get the most from each motion and every second spent at work. Other theorists contributing to the scientific management approach were Henri Fayol ([1919] 1949), Lyndall Urwick (1937), and Luther Gulick (Gulick and Urwick, 1937). Their work led to principles focused on specialization, span of control, authority, and delegation of responsibility.

The second branch of structural ideas stems from the work of the German economist and sociologist Max Weber. Weber wrote around the beginning of the twentieth century. At the time, formal organization was a relatively new phenomenon. Patriarchy, rather than rationality, was still the primary organizing principle. Patriarchal organizations were dominated by a father figure, an individual with almost unlimited power. He could reward, punish, promote, or fire on personal whim. Sensing an evolution of new models in late-nineteenth-century Europe, Weber described "monocratic bureaucracy" as an ideal form that maximized norms of rationality. His model outlined several major features: (1) a fixed division of labor, (2) a hierarchy of offices, (3) a set of rules governing performance, (4) separation of personal from official property and rights, (5) technical qualifications (not family ties or friendship) for selecting personnel, and (6) employment as primary occupation and long-term career.

After World War II, Weber's work was rediscovered and spawned a substantial body of theory and research. Blau and Scott (1962), Perrow (1986), Thompson (1967), and Hall (1963), among others, extended the bureaucratic model. Their work examined relationships among the elements of structure; looked closely at why organizations choose one structure over another; and analyzed the effects of structure on morale, productivity, and effectiveness.

STRUCTURAL FORMS AND FUNCTIONS

How does structure influence what happens in the workplace? Essentially, it is a blueprint for formal expectations and exchanges among internal players (executives, managers, employees) and external constituencies (such as customers and clients). Like an animal's skeleton or a building's framework, structural form both enhances and constrains what an organization can accomplish. The alternative design possibilities are infinite, limited only by human preferences and capacities.

We often assume that people prefer structures with more choices and latitude (Leavitt, 1978). But this is not always the case. A study by Moeller (1968), for example, explored the effects of structure on teacher morale in two school systems. One was structured loosely and encouraged wide participation in decision making. The other was tightly controlled, with a centralized hierarchy and a clear chain of command. Moeller found the opposite of what he expected: faculty morale was higher in the district with tighter structure. Adler and Borys (1996) argue that the type of structure is as important as the amount. There are good rules and bad ones. Formal structure enhances morale if it helps us get our work done. It has a negative impact if it gets in our way, buries us in red tape, or makes it easier for management to control us. According to Adler and Borys, stereotypical images of machine bureaucracy confuse "two very different kinds of machine—machines designed to de-skill work and those designed to leverage users' skills" (p. 69). Even this may be too simple, as shown by the experience of People's Express, an airline launched in the early 1980s. Donald Burr, the airline's CEO, saw advantages in rotating employees from job to job. He assumed that it would reduce boredom and give people a better appreciation for the overall operation. Instead, rotating employees through unfamiliar jobs eventually resulted in excessive burnout and inefficiency. The intention was noble; the outcome reinforced the importance of specialization and routine.

Stereotypes aside, the structural perspective is not inherently machinelike or inflexible. Structures in stable environments are hierarchical and rules-oriented. But recent years have witnessed remarkable inventiveness in designing structures emphasizing flexibility, participation, and quality. Saturn is a prime example. The company transferred General Motors employees from Michigan, where they were told what to do, to Tennessee, where they gained a say in how work would be done. This high level of autonomy and participation enabled them to produce one of the finest cars in the world. Nordstrom department stores have achieved a reputation for extraordinary customer service, loyalty, and satisfaction. Much of the company's success can be attributed to the wide discretion given to its sales force. When new employees arrive, they are handed a rule book. It contains only one rule: "Rule # 1—Use your good judgment in all situations. There will be no additional rules." The structural dance between rigidity and flexibility is ongoing. The trick is achieving a balance between autonomy and inconsistency. The former, for example, can enhance customer service; the latter can kill it.

Dramatic changes in technology and the business environment have rendered old structures obsolete at an unprecedented rate, spawning a new interest in organizational design (Nadler, Gerstein, and Shaw, 1992). Pressures of globalization, competition, technology, customer expectations, and workforce dynamics have prompted organizations worldwide to rethink and redesign structural patterns. A swarm of items compete for managers' attention—money, markets, people, and technological competencies, to name a few. But a significant amount of time and attention must be devoted to social architecture, designing an infrastructure that allows people to do their best: "How a firm organizes its efforts can be a source of tremendous competitive advantage, particularly in times

Greatest Hits from Organization Studies No. 4: Michael C. Jensen and William H. Meckling, "Theory of the Firm: Managerial Behavior, Agency Costs, and Ownership Structure," *Journal of Financial Economics,* **1976, 3, 305–360.**

This classic article, fourth on our list (see Table A.1 in the Appendix) of works most often cited by scholars, focuses on two central questions: (1) What are the implications of the "agency problem,"—that is, the conflicts of interest between principals and their agents? (2) Given those conflicts, why do corporations even exist?

An agency relationship is created whenever one party engages another to undertake some task. But Jensen and Meckling's primary focus is the relationship between a corporation's owners (shareholders) and their agents, the corporation's managers. The authors assume principals and agents both seek to maximize utility, but their interests often diverge. If you are a sole proprietor, a dollar of the firm's money is a dollar of yours as well. If you own only 1 percent, that same dollar represents only a penny of your money. The lower your ownership stake, the greater your incentive to spend the firm's money on things that benefit you more than the business. A notorious example is Tyco's chief executive, Dennis Kozlowski, who reportedly spent more than $30 million of company money to buy, furnish, and decorate his palatial apartment in New York City (Sorkin, 2002). Shareholders, of course, hate this kind of thing and would like to minimize unproductive management perks. But it is difficult for them to stay abreast of everything management does, and they can't do it without incurring "monitoring costs," time and money spent on things like supervision and auditing. One implication these authors draw is that the primary value of stock analysts is the monitoring function they perform. Analysts' ability to pick stocks is notoriously poor. But their oversight puts more heat on managers to serve shareholder interests. The article also shows that, despite the agency conflicts, the corporate form still makes economic sense for the parties involved.

The authors elaborate that the agency problem is a pervasive structural feature of cooperative activity. The relationship between a team and individual members, or between a boss and a subordinate, is like that between principal and agent. If members of a team share rewards equally, for example, there is an incentive for "free riders" to let someone else do most of the work. In each case, the principal has to find a way to ensure that the agent doesn't diverge too far from the principal's interests and instructions.

where premiums are placed on flexibility, adaptation, and the management of change" (Nadler, Gerstein, and Shaw, 1992, p. 3).

BASIC STRUCTURAL TENSIONS

Two design issues are at the heart of organizational structure: how to allocate work (*differentiation*) and how to coordinate roles and units once responsibilities have been parceled out (*integration*). Division of labor—or allocating jobs—is the cornerstone. Every living system finds a way to create specialized roles. Consider an ant colony: "Small workers . . . spend most of their time in the nest feeding the larval broods; intermediate-sized workers constitute most of the population, going out on raids as well as doing other jobs. The largest workers . . . have a huge head and large powerful jaws. These individuals are . . . soldiers; they carry no food but constantly run along the flanks of the raiding and emigration columns" (Topoff, 1972, p. 72).

Like ants, humans long ago discovered the virtues of specialization. A job (or position) channels behavior by prescribing what someone is to do—or not do—to accomplish a task. Prescriptions take the form of job descriptions, procedures, routines, or rules (Mintzberg, 1979). Formal constraints can be burdensome, leading to apathy, absenteeism, and resistance (Argyris, 1957, 1964), but they help ensure predictability, uniformity, and reliability. If manufacturing standards, airline maintenance, hotel housekeeping, or prison sentences were left solely to individual discretion, problems of quality and equity would abound.

Once an organization specifies positions or roles, managers face a second set of key decisions: how to group people into working units, the task of integration. There are several basic options (Mintzberg, 1979):

- Functional groups based on *knowledge or skill*, as in the case of a university's academic departments or the classic industrial units of research, engineering, manufacturing, marketing, and finance
- Units created on the basis of *time*, as by shift (day, swing, or graveyard shift)
- Groups organized by *product*: detergent versus bar soap, wide-body versus narrow-body aircraft

- Groups established around *customers or clients,* as in hospital wards created around patient type (pediatrics, intensive care, or maternity), computer sales departments organized by customer (corporate, government, education, individual), or schools targeting students in particular age groups

- Groupings around *place or geography,* such as regional offices in corporations or government agencies, or neighborhood schools in different parts of a city

- Grouping by *process:* a complete flow of work, as with "the order fulfillment process. This process flows from initiation by a customer order, through the functions, to delivery to the customer" (Galbraith, 1993, p. 34); organization by process attained new prominence from the reengineering movement of the 1990s (Hammer and Champy, 1993)

Creating roles and units yields the benefit of specialization but creates problems of coordination and control. Units tend to focus on their priorities and strike out on their own, as happened to New York's police and fire departments on September 11. The result is *suboptimization,* an emphasis on achieving unit goals rather than focusing on the overall mission. Efforts become fragmented, and performance suffers. This problem plagued Gov. Tom Ridge, who was named by Pres. George W. Bush as the director of homeland security in the aftermath of the terrorist attacks. Ridge's attempts to informally integrate various agencies dealing with security struggled to pull autonomous units together. As a result, President Bush proposed and obtained a cabinet-level Department of Homeland Security. The goal was to cluster security agencies under one authority.

Successful organizations employ a variety of methods to coordinate individual and group efforts and to link local initiatives with corporationwide goals. They do this in two primary ways: *vertically,* through the formal chain of command; and *laterally,* through meetings, committees, coordinating roles, or network structures. We next look at each of these strategies in detail.

VERTICAL COORDINATION

With vertical coordination, higher levels coordinate and control the work of subordinates through authority, rules and policies, and planning and control systems.

Authority

The most basic and ubiquitous way of integrating the efforts of individuals, units, or divisions is to designate "a boss,"—someone with formal authority. Authorities—executives, managers, and supervisors—are officially charged with keeping activities aligned with goals. They control by making decisions, resolving conflicts, solving problems, evaluating performances and output, and distributing rewards and sanctions. A chain of command is a hierarchy of managerial and supervisory strata, each with legitimate power to shape and direct the behavior of those at lower levels. It works best when authority is both endorsed by subordinates and authorized by superiors (Dornbusch and Scott, 1975). On the *USS Kennedy,* for example, the chain of command is clear and universally accepted.

Rules and Policies

Rules, policies, standards, and standard operating procedures limit discretion and help ensure predictability and uniformity. Rules govern conditions of work and specify standard processes for carrying out tasks, handling personnel issues, and relating to the external environment. This helps to ensure that similar situations are handled uniformly. It reduces "particularism" (Perrow, 1986)—responding to specific issues on the basis of personal or political forces unrelated to organizational goals. Two citizens' complaints about a tax bill are supposed to be treated the same way, even if one is a prominent politician and the other a shoe clerk. Once a situation is defined as one where a rule applies, the course of action is clear, straightforward, and almost automatic.

A standard is a benchmark to ensure that goods and services maintain a specified level of quality. Measurement against the standard makes it possible to identify and fix problems. During the 1970s and 1980s, American manufacturing standards lagged, while Japanese manufacturers were scrupulous in ensuring that high standards were widely known and universally accepted. In one case, an American company ordered ball bearings from a Japanese plant. The Americans insisted on what was for them an unusually high standard—only twenty defective parts per thousand. When the order arrived, it included a separate bag of twenty defective bearings, and a note: "We were not sure why you wanted these, but here they are." Globalization's pressures for world-class quality spawned growing interest in "six sigma," a statistical standard of near perfection.

Standard operating procedures (SOPs) reduce performance variance in tasks requiring high levels of predictability and allowing little margin for error. Commercial airline pilots typically fly in a different crew every month. Because interdependence is high and mistakes are critical, SOPs govern all significant aspects of their work. All pilots are trained extensively in the procedures; so long as they follow the rules, actions of crew members mesh. If not, disaster may follow. A significant percentage of aviation accidents occur after someone violates SOPs. More than one airplane has crashed on takeoff because the crew overlooked a required checklist item.

SOPs can fail, however, under conditions of anomaly—freak, unforeseen situations. In the September 11 terrorist attacks, pilots followed standard procedures for dealing with hijackers: cooperate with their demands, and try to get the plane quickly on the ground. These SOPs were based on prior histories of hijackers who wanted to make a statement, not commit suicide. This traditional approach was abandoned by passengers on United Airlines Flight 93, who learned via cell phones that the hijackers were using aircraft as bombs rather than a bully pulpit. Passengers lost their lives fighting to regain control of the plane. But theirs was the only one of four hijacked jets that crashed in a rural field instead of demolishing a high-profile urban target.

Planning and Control Systems

Reliance on planning and control systems, forecasting and measuring, has mushroomed since the dawn of the computer era. Retailers, for example, need to know what's selling and what isn't. Point-of-sale terminals now yield instant information once requiring weeks to obtain. Performance data flow freely up and down the hierarchy, greatly enhancing management's ability to control performance and outcomes.

Mintzberg (1979) distinguishes two major approaches to control and planning: performance control and action planning. *Performance control* imposes outcome objectives (for example, "increase sales by 10 percent this year") without specifying how the results are to be achieved. Performance control measures and motivates, particularly when targets are reasonably clear and measurable. It is less successful when goals are ambiguous, hard to measure, or of dubious relevance. A notorious example was the use of enemy body counts by the U.S. Army to measure combat effectiveness in Vietnam; field commanders became obsessed with "getting the numbers up," regardless of whether the information was accurate or reflected actual military progress.

Action planning specifies methods and time frames for decisions and actions, as in "increase this month's sales by using a companywide sales pitch" (Mintzberg, 1979, pp. 153–154). Action planning works best when it is easier to assess *how* a job is done than to measure whether its objectives were achieved. This is often true of service jobs. McDonald's has very clear specifications for how counter employees are to greet customers (for example, with a smile and a cheerful welcome). The objective is customer satisfaction, but it is easier to monitor employees' behavior than customers' reactions.

LATERAL COORDINATION

Though efficient, vertical coordination is not always effective. People's behavior is often remarkably untouched by commands, rules, and systems. Lateral techniques—formal and informal meetings, task forces, coordinating roles, matrix structures, and network organizations—arise to fill the void. Lateral forms of coordination are typically less formalized and more flexible than authority-bound systems and rules. They can be simpler and quicker as well.

Meetings

Informal communication and formal meetings form the cornerstone of lateral coordination. All organizations have regular meetings. Boards confer to make policy. Executive committees gather to make strategic decisions. In some government agencies, review committees (sometimes known as "murder boards") convene to examine proposals from lower levels. Formal meetings provide a lion's share of lateral coordination in relatively simple, stable organizations—for example, a railroad with a predictable market, a manufacturer with a stable product, or a life insurance company selling policies that have changed little over time.

Task Forces

As organizations become more complex, technologies grow in sophistication, and environments become more turbulent, the demand for lateral communication mushrooms. Additional face-to-face coordination devices are needed. Task forces assemble when new problems or opportunities require collaboration of a number of specialties or functions. High-technology firms rely heavily on project teams or task forces to coordinate development of new products or services.

Coordinating Roles

To augment efforts of formal groups, coordinating roles or units spring up, using persuasion and negotiation to help others integrate their efforts. A product manager in a consumer goods company, responsible for the performance of a laundry detergent or low-fat snack, spends much of her time pulling together people and units critical to the product's success: research, manufacturing, marketing, and sales. Cooper Industries grew dramatically in the 1980s and 1990s by aggressively cultivating crosscutting manufacturing expertise. It created a coordinating unit, a kind of SWAT team of manufacturing experts, to spread production know-how across Cooper's business units (Farkas and De Backer, 1996).

Matrix Structures

Beginning in the 1960s, many organizations in complex environments developed matrix structures, spelling out crosscutting coordination responsibility. By the mid-1990s, Asea Brown Boveri (ABB), the electrical engineering giant, had grown to encompass some thirteen hundred separate companies and more than two hundred thousand employees worldwide. ABB maintained a very small corporate headquarters (fewer than two hundred people) in Zürich, where CEO Percy Barnevik rarely spent more than a day or two a week (often Saturday and Sunday). The energetic Barnevik spent much of his time in an airborne office traveling around ABB's far-flung empire ("The ABB of Management," 1996).

To cobble together this complex collection, ABB developed a matrix structure crisscrossing approximately one hundred countries with about sixty-five business sectors (Rappaport, 1992). Each subsidiary reported to both a country manager (Sweden, Germany, and so on) and a sector manager (power transformers, transportation, and the like). The design carried the inevitable risk of tension and conflict between sector and country managers. ABB tried to create structural cohesion at the top with a small executive coordinating committee (thirteen individuals from eight countries), an elite cadre of some five hundred global managers, and a policy of doing business in English, even though it was a second language for the majority of ABB's employees.

The structure worked through the 1990s, and ABB became one of Europe's most admired companies. But the inherent tensions eventually took a toll. Barnevik turned over the reins to a successor in 1996, and after the market crash in 2000 ABB began to generate more bad news than good (Reed and Sains, 2002). Nonetheless, variations on ABB's structure—a matrix with business or product lines on one axis and countries or regions on the other—are common in global corporations.

Networks

Networks have always been around, but the proliferation of microcomputers beginning in the 1980s spawned an explosive growth of computer networks—everything from small local grids to the global Internet. These powerful new lateral communication devices often supplanted vertical strategies and spurred the development of network structures within and between organizations (Steward, 1994). Powell, Koput, and Smith-Doerr (1996) describe the mushrooming of "interorganizational networks" in such rapidly developing fields as biotechnology, where knowledge is so complex and widely dispersed that no organization can go it alone. They give an example of work on Alzheimer's disease. The knowledge was developed by thirty-four scientists from three corporations, a university, a government laboratory, and a private research institute.

Ghoshal and Bartlett (1990) argue that many large global corporations have evolved into interorganizational networks. Horizontal linkages supplement and sometimes supplant vertical coordination. Such a firm is multicentric: initiatives and strategy emerge from many places, taking shape through a variety of partnerships and joint ventures.

Strengths and Weaknesses of Lateral Strategies

Every lateral coordination strategy has strengths and weaknesses. A formal or informal meeting is an opportunity for dialogue and decision, but it risks squandering an excessive amount of time and energy. A task force fosters creativity and integration around specific problems but often diverts attention from ongoing operating issues. The effectiveness of coordinators who span boundaries of a number of units is heavily dependent on their skills and credibility. Matrix structures create means of lateral linkage and integration but are notorious for creating conflict and confusion. For example, Digital Equipment's CEO Robert Palmer blamed the firm's matrix design for delaying by several years the company's badly needed shift from minicomputers to PCs; competitors moved ahead while Digital debated (Dwyer, Engardio, Schiller, and Reed, 1994). The faltering Digital ultimately was acquired by Compaq, which itself was swallowed up a few years later by Hewlett-Packard.

The self-organizing network's bias toward decentralization, teaming, and cross-functional and cross-geographical work makes it well attuned to complexity and change (Steward, 1994). But networks are inherently difficult to control, and evolution produces vipers as well as orchids—there is no guarantee that we will like the results.

MCDONALD'S AND HARVARD: A STRUCTURAL ODD COUPLE

The optimal blend of vertical and lateral strategies depends on the unique coordination challenges in any given situation. Vertical coordination is generally superior if an environment is stable, tasks are well understood and predictable, and uniformity is at a premium. Lateral communications work best when a complex task is performed in a turbulent, fast-changing environment. Every organization must find a design that works for its circumstances. Otherwise it will falter or fail. Consider the contrasting structures of two highly successful organizations: McDonald's and Harvard University.

McDonald's first Indian restaurant, and its first in the world with no beef on the menu, opened Sunday in New Delhi with a traditional Hindu ceremony and a rush of enthusiastic customers. O. P. Sahani, a seventy-five-year-old retired civil servant, came all the way from Vrindavan, ninety miles south, to show his support for McDonald's efforts to do business with India. "They have not brought raw materials from overseas," Sahani said, proudly wearing a red-and-yellow McDonald's cap. Other customers didn't seem all that interested that mutton for Maharaja Macs came from Indian sheep, the potatoes for fries from Indian farms, and Coke from an Indian bottler. The menu also featured rice-based Vegetable Burgers patties flavored with peas, carrots, red pepper, beans, coriander, and other spices. Sahani, a vegetarian who was the first customer, praised the Vegetable Burgers but had one word of advice for owners:

"It was nice, but you require some improvement in the chips," he said, describing the fries as "too soft." (Associated Press, 1996)

McDonald's, the company that made the Big Mac a household word, has been enormously successful. For forty years after its founding in the 1950s, the company was an unstoppable growth engine that came to dominate the worldwide fast-food business. McDonald's has a relatively small staff at its world headquarters near Chicago; the vast majority of its employees are salted across the world in thousands of local outlets. But despite its size and geographic reach, McDonald's is a highly centralized, tightly controlled organization. Most major decisions are made at the top.

Managers and employees of McDonald's restaurants have limited discretion about how to do their jobs. Their work is controlled by technology; machines time the french fries and measure the soft drinks. The parent company has powerful systems to ensure that food and service conform to standard specifications. A Big Mac tastes virtually the same whether purchased in New York or Los Angeles, Hong Kong or Moscow. Guaranteed standard quality inevitably limits the discretion of people who own and work in an individual outlet. Cooks are not expected to develop creative new versions of the Big Mac or Quarter Pounder (although the Egg McMuffin and other innovations were created by local franchises). Creative departures from standard product lines are neither encouraged nor tolerated except when a new item is tested for adoption across local outlets.

All that structure might sound oppressive, but one of McDonald's major miscues in the 1990s resulted from trying to loosen up. Responding to pressure from some frustrated franchisees, McDonald's in 1993 stopped sending out inspectors to grade all its restaurants on standard criteria for service, food, and ambience. When left to police themselves, some restaurants slipped badly. Customers noticed, and McDonald's image sagged. Ten years later, a new CEO brought back inspectors and grading in an effort to correct lagging standards (David, 2003).

Harvard University is also highly successful. Like McDonald's, it has a very small administrative group at the top, but in most other respects the two organizations diverge. Even though Harvard is more geographically concentrated than McDonald's, it is significantly more decentralized. Virtually all of Harvard's activities occur within a few square miles of Boston and Cambridge, Massachusetts. Most employees are housed in the university's several schools: Harvard College (the undergraduate school), the graduate faculty of arts and sciences, and various professional schools. Each school has its own dean and its own endowment and, in accordance with Harvard's philosophy of "every tub on its own bottom," largely controls its own destiny.

Harvard is one of few universities in which each school chooses its own academic calendar. In a typical year, classes might begin on August 28 in the medical school, September 3 in the law school, and September 17 in the faculty of arts and sciences. Each school has fiscal autonomy and responsibility. Individual professors also have enormous autonomy and discretion. In many schools, they have almost total control over courses they teach; research they do; and which university activities they pursue, if any. Faculty meetings are typically sparsely attended. If a dean or a department head wants a faculty member to chair a committee or offer a new course, the request is more often a humble entreaty than an authoritative command.

The contrast between McDonald's and Harvard is particularly strong at the level of service delivery. No one expects individual personality to influence the quality of McDonald's hamburgers. But everyone expects each course at Harvard to be the unique creation of an individual professor. Two schools might offer courses with the same title, covering entirely different content with widely divergent teaching styles.

STRUCTURAL IMPERATIVES

Why do McDonald's and Harvard have such radically different structures? Is one more effective than the other? Or has each organization evolved a design that fits its circumstances? Every organization needs to respond to a generic set of structural parameters (outlined in Table 3.1). An organization's size, age, core process, environment, strategy and goals, information technology, and workforce characteristics combine to dictate its preferred social architecture. Each factor must be taken into account in designing a workable structure.

Size and Age

An organization's size and age affect structural shape and character. Unless growth (or downsizing) is matched with corresponding adjustment in roles and relationships, problems inevitably arise. A small, entrepreneurial organization typically has very simple,

TABLE 3.1. Structural Imperatives.

Dimension	Structural Implications
Size and age	Complexity and formalization increase with size and age.
Core process	Core processes or technologies must align with structure.
Environment	Stable environment rewards simpler structure; uncertain, turbulent environment requires more complex, adaptable structure.
Strategy and goals	Variation in clarity and consistency of goals requires appropriate structural adaptations.
Information technology	Information technology permits flatter, more flexible, and more decentralized structure.
Nature of the workforce	More educated and professional workers need and want greater autonomy and discretion.

informal structural arrangements. Over time, as the organization grows, pressures for efficiency and discipline spawn greater formalization and complexity (Greiner, 1972; Quinn and Cameron, 1983). If carried too far, this ultimately leads to the suffocating bureaucratic rigidity often seen in large, mature organizations.

In the beginning, McDonald's was not the complex, standardized, tightly controlled company it is today. It began as a single hamburger stand in San Bernardino, California, owned and managed by the McDonald brothers. They virtually invented the concept of fast food and were phenomenally successful. The two tried to expand by selling franchise rights, with little success. They were making more than enough money, disliked travel, and had no heirs. If they were richer, said one brother, "we'd be leaving it to a church or something, and we didn't go to church" (Love, 1986, p. 23).

The concept took off when Ray Kroc arrived on the scene. He had achieved modest success selling milk shake machines to restaurants. When he began to get calls from people wanting the McDonalds' milk shake mixer, he decided to visit the brothers. Seeing the original stand, Kroc realized the potential: "Unlike the homebound McDonalds, Kroc had traveled extensively, and he could envision hundreds of large and small markets where a McDonald's could be located. He understood the existing food services businesses, and understood how a McDonald's unit could be a formidable competitor" (pp. 39–40).

Kroc persuaded the McDonald brothers to let him take over the franchising effort. The rest is history.

Core Process

Structure has to be built around an organization's procedure for transforming raw materials into finished products. Every organization has a central process, or core technology, with at least three elements: raw materials, activities transforming raw materials into desired ends, and underlying beliefs about cause-and-effect linking inputs and actions to outcomes (Dornbusch and Scott, 1975).

Core technologies vary in clarity, predictability, and effectiveness. Assembling a Big Mac is relatively routine and programmed. The task is clear, most potential problems are known in advance, and the probability of a good outcome is high. Its relatively simple technology allows McDonald's to function successfully by relying mostly on vertical coordination.

In contrast, Harvard's two core processes—research and teaching—are far more complex and less predictable. Teaching objectives are complicated and amorphous. Unlike hamburger buns, students are active agents. Their needs and skills vary widely; moods fluctuate in response to weather, time of day, and the season. Their preoccupation with extracurricular activities is a fact of life. Which teaching strategies yield desired outcomes is more a matter of faith than of fact. Even if students could be molded predictably, it would be hard to know which molds are best. Mystery surrounds the knowledge and skills they will eventually need. Feedback is slow or absent; professors rarely learn about the long-term benefits, if any, students derive from a course. This complex technology, heavily dependent on the skills and knowledge of highly trained professionals, is a key source of Harvard's highly decentralized, loosely coordinated structure.

Because structure must align with an organization's core process, significant technical change implies structural change (Barley, 1990), but existing structures often hinder adaptation. In recent decades, differential ability to integrate new technologies has become fateful for a firm's effectiveness and survival (Henderson and Clark, 1990). This means that new entrants often have an advantage over established firms in exploiting new technologies, since the latter are tempted to force new technology to fit into their current structure. When high-strength, low-alloy steel was introduced into the manufacture of automobiles in the 1970s, for example, one firm's engineers persisted in using traditional manufacturing methods. It didn't work, and the company fell behind younger firms less wedded to the old ways (Henderson and Clark, 1990).

Environment

Although organizations buffer internal activities from external fluctuations and interference, circumstances outside are still a potent force. The environment provides raw materials and receives finished products and services. Stable, mature businesses—such as railroads, furniture manufacturers or elementary schools—deal with relatively homogeneous, stable, and predictable outside influences. As a result, they rely on simpler organizational forms.

Organizations with rapidly changing technologies or markets—such as high-technology electronics firms—cope with a much higher degree of uncertainty. New state-of-the-art products may be obsolete in six months or less. Uncertainty and turbulence press for more sophisticated architectural forms. New specialties and roles are required to deal with emerging problems. More specialized and diversified structures require more elaborate approaches to vertical and lateral coordination. An uncertain environment also demands a high level of flexibility and adaptability. Traditional managers, steeped in the tradition of the top-down pyramid, struggle to adapt to strange new forms where chains of command are flat rather than multilayered, and coordination arises mainly from a dense network of horizontal relationships (Chaize, 1992; Sérieyx, 1993).

All organizations are dependent on the environment, but some are more vulnerable than others. Public schools, for example, have low power with respect to external constituencies and struggle to get resources they need. Small size, powerful competitors, well-organized external constituencies, limited flexibility, and scarcity of resources tend to increase dependence. An organization such as Harvard University is insulated by size, elite status, and a large endowment. Harvard can afford to offer low teaching loads, generous salaries, and substantial autonomy to its faculty. A small college with serious financial pressures is likely to have tighter controls, higher workloads, and limited discretion in using its funds.

Strategy and Goals

Strategic decisions are oriented to the future and are concerned with long-term direction (Chandler, 1962). Most organizations, particularly in the business world, devote considerable effort to developing strategy, which is "the determination of long-range goals and objectives of an enterprise, and the adoption of courses of action and allocation of resources necessary for carrying out these goals" (p. 13).

Goals of varying specificity are embedded in strategy. In business firms, goals such as profitability, growth, and market share are relatively specific and easy to measure. This is one reason McDonald's can structure its resources so tightly. Goals in educational or human services organizations are typically much more diffuse: "producing educated men and women" or "improving individual well-being." This is another reason Harvard adopts a more decentralized, loosely integrated system of roles and relationships.

Goals vary in number and complexity. Historically, McDonald's goals were fewer, less complex, and less controversial than Harvard's, which aligned well with McDonald's centralized, top-down structure. Uncertainty and conflict over goals are typically much higher in public agencies, universities, and schools. In the early twenty-first century, even McDonald's is beginning to find that changing circumstances require a more complex set of goals. Globalization makes for a much more turbulent and complex environment, and shifting consumer preferences have begun to outrun McDonald's ability to adapt, leading to a series of earnings disappointments in 2001 and 2002 (Stires, 2002).

To complicate matters further, stated goals are not the only ones (or even the most important ones) an organization pursues. Westerlund and Sjostrand (1979) suggest various others:

- Honorific: fictitious goals crediting the organization with desirable qualities
- Taboo: goals an organization pursues but does not talk about
- Stereotypical: goals any reputable organization should have
- Existing: goals quietly pursued even though inconsistent with the organization's stated values and self-image

Understanding linkages among goals, structure, and strategy requires a look beyond formal statements of purpose. Schools, for example, are often criticized if structure does not coincide with the goal of scholastic achievement. But schools have other, less visible goals. One is character development. Another is the taboo goal of certification and selection, as schools channel students into tracks and sort them into careers. Still a third goal is custody and control, keeping kids off the streets and out from underfoot. Finally, schools often herald honorific goals such as excellence. Strategy and goals shape structure, but the process is often complex and subtle.

Information Technology

Computers and new technologies continue to revolutionize the amount of available information and the speed at which it travels. Once available exclusively to top-level or middle managers, information is now easily accessible and widely shared. This makes it possible to move decisions closer to the action. E-mail has made communication immediate and far reaching. With the press of a key, anyone can reach another person—or carpet the entire network. In the war in Iraq in 2003, the U.S. and British forces had an obvious advantage in military hardware. They also had a powerful structural advantage because their superior information technology let them develop a much more flexible and decentralized decision-making structure. Commanders in the field could change their plans immediately in response to new developments. Iraqi forces, meanwhile, had a much slower, more vertical structure. Iraqi commanders relied on decisions from the top. A major reason that Iraqi resistance was lighter than expected was that commanders had no idea what to do when they were cut off from their chain of command (Broder and Schmitt, 2003).

The implications of improved technology for the design of organizations are enormous. Information is a central structural determinant. Galbraith (1973) defines uncertainty as the difference between the information an organization has and needs. As uncertainty increases, more information—possibly hard to get—is required to make decisions. Organizations then have two options: reduce the need for information or increase the capacity to process it (Galbraith, 1973). Organizations reduce the need for information by creating slack resources or by establishing self-contained units that work independently.

Before the proliferation of personal computers, information technology (IT) was centralized and controlled by specialists. Mainframes could do things previously impossible.

But coordinating user needs with IT offerings was often very frustrating and time-consuming for both sides. The spread of personal computers created a slack resource (more computing power than users needed), often reducing the need to coordinate vertically. Linking desktop machines opened new possibilities for structuring organizations as networks or "complex adaptive systems" (Waldrop, 1992, p. 145). Such systems are assemblies of loosely connected units, or agents, each with its own agenda. Control is dispersed and emerges from a bottom-up series of interactions. Agents pursue their own interests and needs, rather than respond to edicts from headquarters (Chaize, 1992; Holland, 1995; Waldrop, 1992). These characteristics can be found in systems as diverse as prairies, cities, economies, and the Internet.

The development of Microsoft's widely used (but not always widely loved) Windows NT operating system is an example of a network in action. The product was one of the most complex pieces of software ever written. It had to work as a unified whole, yet more than two hundred developers in dozens of small units were organized "right on the edge of chaos" (Zachary, 1994, p. 107). Each unit had its own goals and working style. Many developers never talked to one another, and some didn't like one another. Reporting relationships were "a crazy quilt, not a hierarchy. Formal reporting lines were often ignored" (p. 108). What held it together? Basically, a requirement set down by the boss, David Cutler. After the first year, he decreed, programmers had to "eat their own dog food" (p. 1) by developing NT on computers operating under NT itself. A daily "build" stitched the operating system together electronically (Cusumano and Selby, 1995). Initially, developers were stunned at the poor quality of the dog food; the system crashed all the time. But each crash let developers know immediately if their latest code had defects or crashed into someone else's. There were powerful incentives to find problems and fix them. One spur was Cutler's authoritative harangue: "If you break the build, your ass is grass, and I'm the lawnmower" (Zachary, 1994, pp. 129–130). Even more important was an emerging appreciation for interdependence and contributions to the whole. If your code broke the build, your pride suffered, and you jeopardized everyone else's ability to get on with the work.

Innovations and investments in information technology make flatter structures inevitable: "Only five years ago it was treated as sensational news when I pointed out that the information-based organization needs far fewer levels of management than the traditional command-and-control model. By now a great many—maybe most—American companies have cut management levels by one-third or more. But the restructuring of corporations—middle-sized ones as well as large ones, and, eventually, even smaller ones—has barely begun" (Drucker, 1989, p. 20).

These changes create tensions and complexities that can lead to disaster. In July 2001, two aircraft, a Russian passenger jet and a DHL cargo plane, were unknowingly headed on a collision course at thirty-six thousand feet. Both planes were equipped with a computerized crash avoidance system, TCAS. The TCAS in the DHL plane gave an order to descend, while the Russian jet's system ordered the pilot to pull up. But a Swiss air controller, belatedly spotting the potential collision, ordered the Russian plane to descend. Faced with directly conflicting inputs, the Russian captain did as he had been trained and followed the controller's order. In this case, lateral control would have worked better than vertical control—the computer, not the human, gave the better advice. The planes collided and all on board perished—including forty-five Russian students headed for a beach vacation in Spain (Landler, 2002; Rising, 2002).

People: Nature of the Workforce

Human resource requirements have changed dramatically in recent decades. Many lower-level jobs now require a high level of skill. A better-educated workforce expects and often demands more discretion in daily work routines. Increasing specialization of knowledge has professionalized many functions. Professionals typically know more than their supervisors about technical aspects of their work. Socialized to expect autonomy, they prefer reporting to professional colleagues. Lawyers who report to engineers, or engineers who report to lawyers, often question the boss's competence to evaluate their work. Trying to tell a Harvard professor what to teach is an exercise in futility. On the other hand, giving too much discretion to a youthful, low-skilled McDonald's worker could easily be a disaster for both the employee and the customers.

Like changes in technology, changes in the workforce put pressure on traditional hierarchical forms. Dramatically different structural forms are emerging as a result. Deal and Kennedy (1982) predicted the emergence of the atomized or network organization, made up of small, autonomous, often geographically dispersed work groups tied together by information systems and organizational symbols. Drucker makes a similar observation in noting that businesses will increasingly "move work to where the people are, rather than people to where the work is" (1989, p. 20).

Citibank International

In sum, numerous forces affecting structural design combine to create a complicated mix of challenges and tensions. It is not simply a matter of deciding, for example, whether we should be hierarchical and centralized like McDonald's or flat and decentralized like Harvard. Many organizations find that they have to do both and somehow accommodate the structural tensions involved.

Beginning in the 1980s, New York-based Citibank bet a large chunk of its future on consumer banking outside the United States, particularly in Asia and the Pacific Rim (Hansell, 1996). Serving consumers in places as diverse as Australia, Hong Kong, India, Indonesia, Malaysia, the Philippines, and Singapore required coping with a confusing mélange of cultures, governments, competitors, and business climates. At the same time, a key element of the bank's strategy was to develop a consistent, global brand name and image: "Citibank is working to make its outposts as consistent as McDonald's restaurants, with the offerings, advertising images and branch décor identical from country to country" (p. 12). The idea was that Citibank customers should be able to go anywhere in the world and find an automatic teller machine that spoke their language and provided the same services they found at home. But that strategy inevitably carried great risks: "No company can operate effectively on a global scale by centralizing all key decisions and then farming them out for implementation. It doesn't work. The conditions in each market are too varied, the nuances of competition too complex, and the changes in climate too subtle and too rapid for long-distance management. No matter how good they are, no matter how well supported analytically, the decision-makers at the center are too far removed from individual markets and the needs of local customers" (Ohmae, 1990, p. 87).

The challenge was to globalize and localize at the same time: centralizing such functions as product development and computer services while finding and developing managers around the globe who had the resources and flexibility to respond to local conditions.

CONCLUSION

The structural frame looks beyond individuals to examine the social architecture of work. Though sometimes equated with red tape, mindless memos, and rigid bureaucrats, the structural approach is broader and more subtle. It encompasses the freewheeling, loosely structured entrepreneurial task force as well as the more tightly controlled railway company or postal department. If structure is overlooked, an organization often misdirects energy and resources. It may, for example, waste time and money on massive training programs in a vain effort to solve problems that have much more to do with social architecture than people's skills or attitudes. It may fire managers and bring in new ones, who then fall victim to the same structural flaws that doomed their predecessors.

At the heart of organizational design are the twin issues of differentiation and integration. Organizations divide work by creating a variety of specialized roles, functions, and units. They must then tie the many elements together by means of both vertical and horizontal techniques for integration. There is no one best way to organize. The right structure depends on prevailing circumstances and considers an organization's goals, strategies, technology, and environment.

Organizations operating in simpler and more stable environments are likely to employ less complex and more centralized structures. They rely on authority, rules, and policies as the primary vehicles for coordinating the work. But the top levels in highly centralized systems get overwhelmed in more fluid, complicated environments. They cannot process all the information pouring in on them, and urgent decisions back up at their office door. Organizations operating in rapidly changing, turbulent, and uncertain environments need much more complex and flexible structures. Understanding the complexity and variety of design possibilities can help create structures that work for, rather than against, both the people and the purposes of organizations.

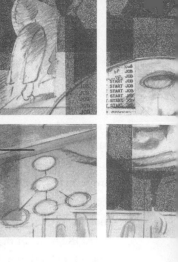

CHAPTER 4

Structure and Restructuring

In Chapter Three, we contrasted the structures of McDonald's and Harvard University. The comparison may soon be due for an update. Larry Summers took the helm as president of Harvard in 2001. An economist and former U.S. treasury secretary, Summers concluded that the venerable university needed an overhaul. From the president's office, he issued a series of authoritative new directives. He first attacked the undergraduate grading system, in which half of the students received A's and 90 percent graduated with honors. Next he stiffened standards for awarding tenure, encouraged more foreign study, and asked faculty (especially senior professors) to spend more time with students. He stepped across curricular boundaries to call for an emphasis on educational reform and more interdisciplinary courses. He proposed a center for medicine and science to encourage more applied research. Finally, he announced a bold move to build an additional campus across the Charles River to house new growth and development. Summers's initiatives aimed to tighten Harvard's famously decentralized structure and to imbue the president's office with more authority. How will his plans pan out? Prior experience with restructuring is not entirely reassuring. Major initiatives to redesign structure and processes have often proved neither durable nor beneficial.

In 1984, strategy guru Michael Porter suggested a sweeping reorganization of the billion-dollar publishing giant McGraw-Hill—which had been divided into book, magazine, and financial services divisions—into twenty-one "market focus" segments. "But Porter's scheme backfired," writes Beam (1989, p. 40). "The elaborate mix mastering of McGraw-Hill assets cost hundreds of staffers their jobs, but has fallen far short of management's expectations. Revenues in 1988 grew only 3.8 percent to $1.8 billion, trailing the rate of inflation. McGraw-Hill is no longer a leader in trade magazine publishing, an industry it once dominated." The divisions that performed best were those reorganized least. A McGraw-Hill executive commented ruefully, "Market focus was the atom [bomb] that blew the company apart. It was like our first whiff of coke, this seductive idea that the solution to our problems could be found inside the company, by reorganizing the pieces. Now, when things are going badly, we reorganize" (Beam, 1989).

Reorganizing, or restructuring, is a powerful but high-risk approach to improvement. An organization's structure at any moment represents its resolution of an enduring set of basic tensions or dilemmas. We start this chapter by discussing those dilemmas. Then, drawing on the work of Henry Mintzberg and Sally Helgesen, we describe some of the major configurations that organizations employ as they try to align structure with mission and environment. We conclude with several case examples illustrating both opportunities and challenges managers encounter when attempting to create a more workable structural design.

STRUCTURAL DILEMMAS

Finding a satisfactory system of roles and relationships is an ongoing, universal struggle. Managers rarely face well-defined problems with clear-cut solutions. Instead, they confront enduring structural dilemmas, tough trade-offs without easy answers.

Differentiation Versus Integration

The tension between allocating work and coordinating diverse efforts creates a classic dilemma, as we saw in Chapter Three. The more complex a role structure (lots of people doing many different things), the harder it is to maintain a focused, tightly coupled enterprise. Think about the challenge facing Larry Summers as he tries to bring a higher level of coordination to a university that historically has been highly decentralized. As complexity grows, organizations require more sophisticated—and more costly—coordination strategies. Rules, policies, and commands have to be augmented by lateral strategies.

Gap Versus Overlap

If key responsibilities are not clearly assigned, important tasks fall through the cracks. Conversely, roles and activities can overlap, creating conflict, wasted effort, and unintended redundancy. A patient in a prestigious teaching hospital, for example, calls her husband and pleads with him to rescue her before she goes crazy. At night, she can't sleep because hospital staff keep waking her up, often to do something someone else has already done. Conversely, when she wants something, her call button rarely produces any response.

The new cabinet-level Department of Homeland Security, created in the wake of the September 11 terrorist attacks, was intended to reduce both gaps and overlaps among the many agencies responsible for responding to threats. Activities incorporated into the new department included immigration, border protection, emergency management, and intelligence analysis. Yet the two most prominent antiterrorism agencies, the FBI and the CIA—with their long history of mutual gaps, overlaps, and bureaucratic squabbling—remained separate from the new agency and from one another (Firestone, 2002). Time will tell how well the new structure achieves its intended goals.

Underuse Versus Overload

If employees have too little work, they become bored and get in other people's way. In one physician's office, for example, clerical staff were able to complete most of their tasks during the morning. After lunch, they filled their time talking to family and friends. As a result, the office's telephone lines were constantly busy, making it difficult for patients to schedule appointments. Meanwhile, nurses were swamped with clients and routine paperwork. Too busy for informal talk with patients, they were often brusque and curt. Patients complained about impersonal care. A better structural balance was accomplished by reassigning many of the nurses' clerical duties to office staff.

Lack of Clarity Versus Lack of Creativity

If employees are unclear about what they are supposed to be doing, they often shape their role around personal preferences instead of organizational goals, frequently leading to problems. A creative new approach to each Big Mac, for example, is not what most McDonald's customers are seeking. But when responsibilities are overdefined, people conform to prescribed roles in "bureaupathic" ways. They rigidly follow job descriptions regardless of how much the service or product suffers. "You lost my bag!" an angry passenger shouted, confronting an airline manager. The manager's response was to inquire, "How was the flight?" "I asked about my bag," the passenger said. "That's not my job," the manager replied; "see someone in baggage claim." The passenger was not a happy customer.

Excessive Autonomy Versus Excessive Interdependence

If the efforts of individuals or groups are too autonomous, people often feel isolated and unsupported. Schoolteachers feel lonely and without support as a result of working in self-contained classrooms, rarely seeing other adults. Yet efforts to create closer teamwork have repeatedly run aground because of teachers' difficulties in working together. In contrast, if units and roles are too tightly linked, people are distracted from work and waste time on unnecessary coordination. One reason IBM lost its early lead in the personal computer business was that new initiatives required so many approvals—from levels and divisions alike—that new products were overdesigned and late to market. Hewlett-Packard's ability to innovate in the late 1990s was hindered by the same problem.

Too Loose Versus Too Tight

A critical structural challenge is how to hold an organization together without holding it back. If structure is too loose, people go their own way or get lost, with little sense of what others are doing. Structures that are too tight stifle flexibility and cause people to spend much of their time trying to beat the system.

We can see some of the perils of too loose a structure in the accounting firm Andersen Worldwide, indicted in 2002 for its role in the Enron scandal. Andersen's Houston office shredded documents and altered memos to cover up its role in Enron's questionable accounting procedures. At its Chicago headquarters, Andersen had an internal audit team, the Professional Standards Group (PSG), which was charged with reviewing the work of regional offices. But unlike other big accounting firms, Andersen let frontline partners closest to the clients overrule PSG. This loose control allowed local discretion, which was a selling point to customers, but it came back to haunt the firm. The lax controls created a situation where "the rainmakers were given the power to overrule the accounting nerds" (McNamee and Borrus, 2002, p. 33).

The opposite problem is common in managed health care. Medical decisions are reviewed by insurance companies, giving clerks far removed from patients the authority to approve or deny treatment. Many physicians lament spending more time on the phone with insurance representatives than seeing patients. As a result of these tight controls, insurance providers sometimes deny treatments that physicians might see as urgent. In one case, a hospital-based psychologist diagnosed an adolescent as a likely perpetrator of sexual assault. The insurer questioned the diagnosis and denied hospitalization. The next day, the teen-ager raped a five-year-old girl.

Goalless Versus Goalbound

In some situations, few people know what the goals are; in others, people cling to goals long after they have become irrelevant or outmoded. In the sixties, for example, polio was virtually eradicated by new vaccines. This eliminated the goal of the March of Dimes organization, which for years championed finding a cure for the crippling disease. The organization chose to shift its purpose to focus on preventing birth defects.

Irresponsible Versus Unresponsive

If people abdicate their responsibilities, performance suffers. However, adhering too rigidly to policies or procedures can be equally harmful. In public agencies, "street-level bureaucrats" (Lipsky, 1980) who deal with the public are often asked, "Could you do me this favor?" or "Couldn't you bend the rules a little bit in this case?" Turning down every request, no matter how reasonable, alienates the public and perpetuates images of bureaucratic rigidity and red tape. But agency workers who are too accommodating create problems of inconsistency and favoritism.

STRUCTURAL CONFIGURATIONS

Responding to structural dilemmas with an appropriate structural configuration is a recurrent management challenge. Achieving the right balance is tied closely to an organization's circumstances: its environment, workforce, technology, and past structural commitments. Structural design rarely starts from scratch. Managers search for options among existing blueprints from their experience or the popular literature. Henry Mintzberg and Sally Helgesen offer two conceptions of structural options.

Mintzberg's Fives

As the two-dimensional lines and boxes of a traditional organization chart have become increasingly obsolete, students of organizational design have developed a variety of new structural images. One influential example is Mintzberg's five-sector "logo," depicted in Figure 4.1. At the base of Mintzberg's image is the *operating core*, consisting of people who perform the basic work. The core is made up of workers who produce or provide products or services to customers or clients: teachers in schools, assembly-line workers in factories, physicians and nurses in hospitals, and flight crews in airlines.

Directly above the operating core is the *administrative component:* managers who supervise, control, and provide resources for the operators. School principals, factory foremen, and echelons of middle management fulfill this role. At the top of Mintzberg's figure, senior managers in the strategic apex focus on the outside environment, determine the mission, and shape the grand design. In school systems, the strategic apex includes superintendents and school boards. In corporations, the apex houses senior executives and the board of directors.

Two more components sit alongside the administrative component. The *technostructure* houses specialists and analysts who standardize, measure, and inspect outputs and processes. Accounting and quality control departments in industry, audit departments in government agencies, and flight standards departments in airlines perform such technical functions. The *support staff* performs tasks that support or facilitate the work of others. In schools, for example, the support staff includes nurses, secretaries, custodians, food service workers, and bus drivers.

From this basic blueprint, Mintzberg (1979) derived five structural configurations: simple structure, machine bureaucracy, professional bureaucracy, divisionalized form, and adhocracy. Each creates its unique set of management challenges.

SIMPLE STRUCTURE. A simple structure has only two levels: the strategic apex and an operating level (see Figure 4.2). Coordination is accomplished primarily through direct supervision, as in a small mom-and-pop operation. Either mom or pop constantly monitors what is going on and exercises total authority over daily operations. A startup

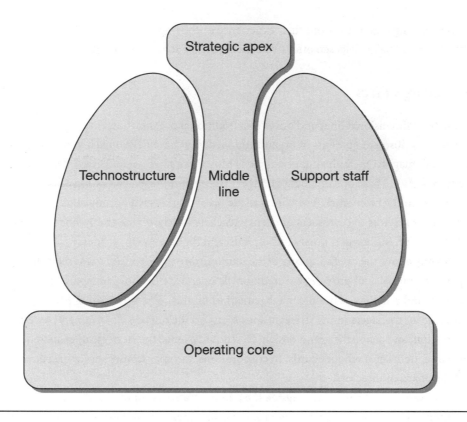

FIGURE 4.1. Mintzberg's Model.
Source: Mintzberg (1979), p. 20. Copyright ©1979. Reprinted by permission of Prentice Hall, Upper Saddle River, N.J.

company typically begins with a simple structure. William Hewlett and David Packard began their business in a garage, as did Apple Computer's Steve Jobs and Steve Wozniak; General Electric had its humble beginnings in Thomas Edison's laboratory. The virtues of simple structure are its flexibility and adaptability; one person directs the entire operation. But virtues can become vices. Authorities block as well as initiate change, and they punish capriciously as well as reward handsomely. A boss too close to day-to-day operations is easily distracted by immediate problems, neglecting long-range strategic issues.

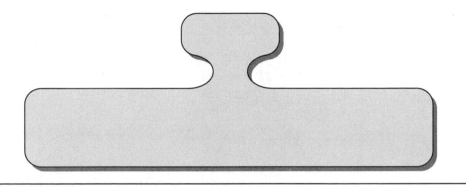

FIGURE 4.2. Simple Structure.
Source: Mintzberg (1979), p. 307. Copyright ©1979. Reprinted by permission of Prentice Hall, Upper Saddle River, N.J.

MACHINE BUREAUCRACY. McDonald's is a classic machine bureaucracy. Important decisions are made at the strategic apex; day-to-day operations are controlled by managers and standardized procedures. Unlike simple hierarchies, machine bureaucracies have large support staffs and a sizeable technostructure, with many layers between apex and operating levels (see Figure 4.3).

For routine tasks, such as making hamburgers and manufacturing automotive parts, machine bureaucracy is both efficient and effective. A key challenge is how to motivate and satisfy workers in the operating core. People tire quickly of repetitive work and standardized procedures. Yet offering too much creativity and personal challenge in, say, a McDonald's outlet could undermine consistency and uniformity—two keys to the company's success.

Like other machine bureaucracies, McDonald's deals constantly with tension between local managers and headquarters. Middle managers are heavily influenced by local concerns and tastes. Top executives, aided by analysts, rely more on generic and abstract information and pursue corporationwide concerns. As a result, a solution from the top may not always match the needs of individual units. Faced with declining sales and market share, McDonald's introduced a new food preparation system in 1998 under the marketing banner "Made for you." CEO Jack Greenberg was convinced the new cook-to-order

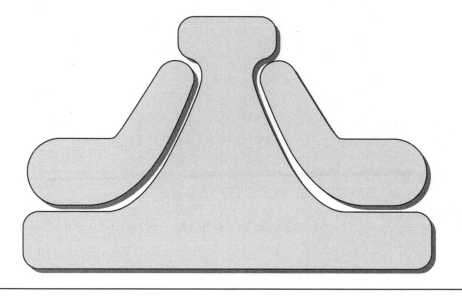

FIGURE 4.3. Machine Bureaucracy.
Source: Mintzberg (1979), p. 325. Copyright ©1979. Reprinted by permission of Prentice Hall, Upper Saddle River, N.J.

system would produce the fresher, tastier burgers the company needed to get back on the fast track, but franchisees soon complained that the system led to long lines and frustrated customers. Unfazed by the criticism, Greenberg invited a couple of skeptical financial analysts to flip burgers at a McDonald's outlet in New Jersey so they could see firsthand that the concerns were unfounded. The experiment backfired. The analysts concluded that the system was too slow and decided to pass on the stock (Stires, 2002). Greenberg was replaced at the end of 2002.

Beginning with the precepts of scientific management in the early twentieth century, there have been recurring efforts to improve public schools by getting them to work more like a machine bureaucracy in which teachers are the production workers. The initiatives have included "teacher-proof" curriculum, incentive pay schemes, and promoting test scores as the primary indicator of school effectiveness. But educators cling to a view of themselves as professionals who need sufficient autonomy to use their experience and judgment in finding the best way to teach. They want to work in an organization that mirrors the third of Mintzberg's types, the professional bureaucracy.

PROFESSIONAL BUREAUCRACY. Harvard University affords a glimpse into the inner workings of a professional bureaucracy (see Figure 4.4). Its operating core is large relative to its other structural parts, particularly the technostructure. Few managerial levels exist between the strategic apex and the professors, creating a flat and decentralized profile. Control relies heavily on professional training and indoctrination. Professionals are insulated from formal interference, freeing them to use their expertise. Though producing many benefits, this arrangement leads to problems of coordination and quality control. Tenured professors, for example, are largely immune to formal sanctions. As a result, universities have to find other ways to deal with incompetence and irresponsibility.

A professional bureaucracy responds slowly to external change. Waves of reform typically produce little impact because professionals often view any change in their surroundings as an annoying distraction from their chosen work. The result is a paradox: individual professionals may be at the forefront of their specialty, while the institution as a whole changes at a glacial pace. Professional bureaucracies regularly stumble when they try to exercise greater control over the operating core; requiring Harvard professors to follow standard teaching methods might do more harm than good. In his efforts to achieve greater presidential control over Harvard's fractious faculty, new president Larry Summers quickly ran into predictable challenges. In one famous case, he suggested that superstar African American studies professor Cornel West redirect his scholarly output. Summer's advice was given in private, but West's feeling of being insulted made the front page of the *New York Times*. Summers's profuse public apologies failed to deter the offended professor from decamping to Princeton.

DIVISIONALIZED FORM. In a divisionalized structure (see Figure 4.5), the bulk of the work is done in quasi-autonomous units, as with campuses in a multicampus university, specialties in a large multispecialty hospital, or divisions in a Fortune 500 company (Mintzberg, 1979). One of the oldest businesses in the United States, Berwind, houses divisions in sectors as diverse as manufacturing, financial services, real estate, and land management. Each division serves a distinct market and supports its own functional units. Division presidents are accountable to the corporate office in Philadelphia for

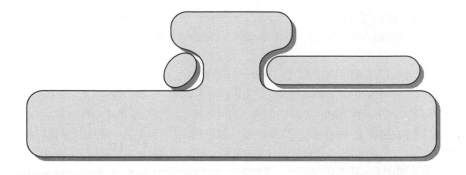

FIGURE 4.4. Professional Bureaucracy.
Source: Mintzberg (1979), p. 355. Copyright ©1979. Reprinted by permission of Prentice Hall, Upper Saddle River, N.J.

specific results: profits, sales growth, and return on investment. As long as they deliver, divisions have relatively free rein. Philadelphia manages the strategic portfolio and allocates resources on the basis of its assessment of market opportunities.

Divisionalized structure offers economies of scale, ample resources, and responsiveness without undue economic risks, but it creates other tensions. One is a cat-and-mouse game between headquarters and divisions. Headquarters wants tighter oversight, while divisional managers try to evade corporate control:

> Our top management likes to make all the major decisions. They think they do, but I've seen one case where a division beat them. I received . . . a request from the division for a chimney. I couldn't see what anyone would do with a chimney, so I flew out for a visit. They've built and equipped a whole plant on plant expense orders. The chimney is the only indivisible item that exceeded the $50,000 limit we put on plant expense orders. Apparently they learned that a new plant wouldn't be formally received, so they built the damn thing. I don't know exactly what I'm going to say. (Bower, 1970, p. 189)

Another risk in the divisionalized form is that headquarters may lose touch with operations. (As one manager put it, "Headquarters is where the rubber meets the air.") Divisionalized enterprises become unwieldy unless goals are measurable and reliable vertical information systems are in place (Mintzberg, 1979).

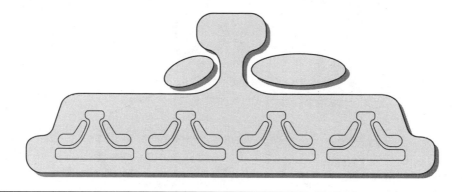

FIGURE 4.5. Divisionalized Form.
Source: Mintzberg (1979), p. 393. Copyright ©1979. Reprinted by permission of Prentice Hall, Upper Saddle River, N.J.

ADHOCRACY. Adhocracy is a loose, flexible, self-renewing organic form tied together mostly through lateral means (see Figure 4.6). Usually found in a diverse, freewheeling environment, adhocracy functions as an "organizational tent," exploiting benefits that structural designers traditionally regarded as liabilities: "Ambiguous authority structures, unclear objectives, and contradictory assignments of responsibility can legitimize controversies and challenge traditions. Incoherence and indecision can foster exploration, self-evaluation, and learning" (Hedberg, Nystrom, and Starbuck, 1976, p. 45).

Ad hoc structures are most often found in conditions of turbulence and rapid change. Examples are advertising agencies, think-tank consulting firms, and the recording industry. In the 1970s and 1980s, Digital Equipment was a well-known pioneer of adhocracy: "In many ways [DEC] is a big company in small company clothes. It doesn't believe much in hierarchy, rule books, dress codes, company cars, executive dining rooms, lofty titles, country club memberships, or most trappings of corpocracy. It doesn't even have assigned parking spots. Only the top half-dozen executives have sizable offices. Everyone else at the company headquarters in Maynard, Mass., makes do with dinky doorless cubicles" (Machan, 1987, p. 154).

Digital's structural arrangements helped make it the world leader in minicomputers. But the design became a problem when the market shifted away from Digital's minicomputer stronghold toward personal computers, where aggressive new competitors like

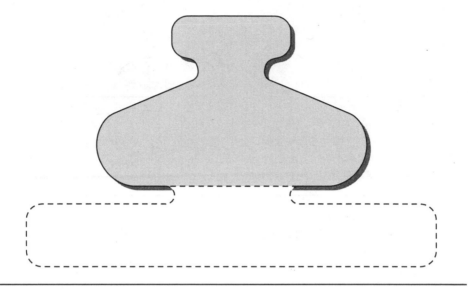

FIGURE 4.6. Adhocracy.
Source: Mintzberg (1979), p. 443. Copyright ©1979. Reprinted by permission of Prentice Hall, Upper Saddle River, N.J.

Compaq and Dell were dominant. "They flew so high and crashed so hard," said one observer, because "at DEC, the internal mattered so much. They spent their lives playing with each other" (Johnson, 1996, p. F-11). The strength of Digital's adhocracy, a flowering of local creativity, became a liability when the company needed a timely and coordinated shift throughout the organization.

Helgesen's Web of Inclusion

Mintzberg's five-sector imagery adds a new dimension to the conventional line-staff organization chart but retains much of the traditional image of structure as a top-down pyramid. Helgesen argues that the idea of hierarchy is primarily a male-driven image, quite different from versions created by female executives: "The women I studied had built profoundly integrated and organic organizations in which the focus was on nurturing good relationships; in which the niceties of hierarchical rank and distinction played little part; and in which lines of communication were multiplicitous, open, and diffuse. I noted that women tended to put themselves at the center of their organizations rather than at the top, thus emphasizing both accessibility and equality, and that they labored constantly to include people in their decision-making" (Helgesen, 1995, p. 10).

Helgesen coined the expression "web of inclusion" to describe an architectural form more circular than hierarchical. The web builds from the center out. Its architect works much like a spider, spinning new threads of connection and reinforcing existing strands. The web's center and periphery are interconnected; action in one place ripples across the entire configuration, forming "an interconnected cosmic web in which the threads of all forces and events form an inseparable net of endlessly, mutually conditioned relations" (Fritjof Capra, quoted in Helgesen, 1995, p. 16). As a consequence, weaknesses in either the center or the periphery of the web undermine the strength of the organic network.

Helgesen's concept started to take form while she was an assistant at the *Village Voice*, an alternative newspaper in New York City's Greenwich Village. Dan Wolf, the editor, ran a very lean operation: no fact checkers, department heads, or consultants, and only a few assistants. Missing entirely were formal staff meetings, memos, and a rational chain of command. The only visible source of information was a centrally located corkboard to which staff affixed a variety of notices and scribbled responses. Yet for all the supposed ambiguity and chaos, communication at the *Voice* was excellent. Wolf was at the center of the communication hub, readily accessible in his centrally located office. Anyone could walk through his door, no appointment needed. An agenda was unnecessary—just talk about whatever was on your mind. Most operational details were delegated to the paper's four editors. Wolf invited people to lunch regularly, to eat, talk, and get to know one another. Everyone, irrespective of role or level, was included in an ongoing dialogue, characterized as "fractious togetherness." The architecture of the *Voice* was an organically connected web rather than a clearly defined pyramid. It had a recognizable, well-understood structure, observable in its employees' daily behavior.

The web form encounters increasing challenges as an organization gets bigger. When Meg Whitman become CEO of Internet phenomenon eBay in 1998, she joined an organization with fewer than fifty employees configured in an informal web centered around founder Pierre Omidyar. One of her first steps was to set up appointments with her new staff. She was surprised to learn that scheduled meetings were a foreign concept in a company where no one kept a calendar or made appointments. Omidyar had built a company with a strong culture and powerful sense of community but no explicit strategy, no regular meetings, no marketing department, and almost no other identifiable structural elements. Despite the company's phenomenal growth and profitability, Whitman concluded that it was in danger of imploding without more structure and discipline. Omidyar agreed. He had worked hard to recruit Whitman because he believed she brought the big-company management experience that eBay needed to keep growing (Hill and Farkas, 2000).

GENERIC ISSUES IN RESTRUCTURING

As Digital's rise and fall illustrates, sooner or later every structure has to be remodeled as a result of internal or external changes. When the time for restructuring comes, managers need to take account of tensions specific to each structural configuration. Consultants and managers often apply general principles without recognizing key differences across architectural forms. Restructuring an adhocracy, for example, is radically different from restructuring a machine bureaucracy. Reweaving a web is a far cry from tinkering with a professional bureaucracy. Subjecting radically differing organizations to the same organizing logic is a recipe for disaster.

Mintzberg's imagery suggests general principles to guide restructuring across a range of circumstances. Each major component of his model exerts its own pressures. Restructuring triggers a multidirectional tug-of-war that eventually determines the shape of the structure. Unless various pushes and pulls are acknowledged and managed effectively, the result may be a catastrophe.

The strategic apex tends to exert centralizing pressures. Through commands, rules, or less obtrusive means, top managers continually try to develop a unified mission or strategy. Deep down, they long for a simple structure they can control. By contrast, middle managers resist control from the top and tend to pull the organization toward balkanization. Navy captains, school principals, department heads, and bureau chiefs become committed to their own domain and seek to protect and enhance their unit's parochial interests. Tensions between centripetal forces from the top and centrifugal forces from middle management are especially prominent in divisionalized structures but are critical issues in any restructuring effort.

The technostructure exerts pressures to standardize; analysts want to measure and monitor the organization's progress against well-defined criteria. Depending on the circumstances, they counterbalance (or complement) top administrators who want to centralize and middle managers who seek greater autonomy. Technocrats feel most at home in a machine bureaucracy.

The support staff pulls in the direction of greater collaboration. Its members usually feel happiest when authority is given to small work units. There they can influence, directly and personally, the shape and flow of everyday decisions. They prefer adhocracy. Meanwhile, the operating core seeks to control its own destiny and minimize influence from the other components. Its members often look outside—to a union or to their professional colleagues—for support.

Attempts to restructure must acknowledge the natural tensions among various components. Depending on the configuration—simple structure, machine bureaucracy, professional bureaucracy, divisionalized form, or adhocracy—each component has more or less influence on the final outcome. In a simple structure, the boss has the edge. In machine bureaucracies, the technostructure and strategic apex possess the most clout. In professional bureaucracies, chronic conflict between administrators and professionals is the dominant tension, while members of the technostructure play an important role in the wings. In the adhocracy, a variety of actors can play a pivotal role in shaping the emerging structural patterns.

Beyond internal negotiations lurks a more crucial issue. A structure's workability ultimately depends on its fit with the organization's environment and technology. Natural selection weeds out the field, determining survivors and victims. It is always a poker game among the major players to negotiate a structure that meets the needs of each component and still works in the organization's environment.

WHY RESTRUCTURE?

Restructuring is a challenging process that consumes time and resources with no guarantee of success. Organizations typically embark on that path when they feel compelled to respond to major problems or opportunities. Various pressures can lead to that conclusion:

- *The environment shifts.* At American Telephone & Telegraph, a mandated shift from regulated monopoly to a market with multiple competitors required a massive reorganization of the Bell System.
- *Technology changes.* The aircraft industry's shift from piston to jet engines profoundly affected the relationship between engine and airframe. Some established firms faltered because they underestimated the complexities; Boeing rose to lead the industry because it understood them (Henderson and Clark, 1990).
- *Organizations grow.* Digital Equipment thrived with a very informal and flexible structure during the company's early years, but the same structure produced major problems when it grew into a multibillion-dollar corporation.
- *Leadership changes.* Reorganization is often the first initiative of new leaders. It is a way to try to put their stamp on the organization, even if no one else sees a need to restructure.

Miller and Friesen (1984) studied a sample of successful as well as troubled firms undergoing structural change and found that those in trouble typically fell into one of three configurations:

1. *The impulsive firm:* a fast-growing organization controlled by one individual or a few top people in which structures and controls have become too primitive and the firm is increasingly out of control. Profits may fall precipitously, and survival may be at stake. Many once-successful entrepreneurial organizations stumble at this stage; they have failed to evolve beyond their simple structure.

2. *The stagnant bureaucracy:* an older, tradition-dominated organization with an obsolete product line. A predictable and placid environment has lulled everyone to sleep, and top management is slavishly committed to old ways. Information systems are too primitive to detect the need for change, and lower-level managers feel ignored and alienated. Many old-line corporations and public bureaucracies fit this group of faltering machine bureaucracies.

3. *The headless giant:* a loosely coupled, divisional organization that has turned into a feudal barony. The administrative core is weak, and most of the initiative and power resides in autonomous divisions. With no real strategy or leadership at the top, the firm

is adrift. Collaboration is minimal because departments compete for resources. Decision making is reactive and crisis-oriented. WorldCom is a recent example of how bad things can get. CEO Bernie Ebbers built the company rapidly from a tiny start-up in Mississippi to a global telecommunications giant through some sixty-five acquisitions. His shopping spree culminated in the 1998 purchase of long-distance giant MCI for $37 billion in WorldCom's high-flying stock. But "for all its talent in buying competitors, the company was not up to the task of merging them. Dozens of conflicting computer systems remained, local network systems were repetitive and failed to work together properly, and billing systems were not coordinated. 'Don't think of WorldCom the way you would of other corporations,' said one person who has worked with the company at a high level for many years. 'It's not a company, it's just a bunch of disparate pieces. It's simply dysfunctional.'" (Eichenwald, 2002c, p. C-6)

Miller and Friesen (1984) found that even in troubled organizations, structural change is episodic: long periods of little change are followed by brief episodes of major restructuring. Organizations are reluctant to make major changes because a stable structure reduces confusion and uncertainty, maintains internal consistency, and protects the existing equilibrium. The price of stability is a structure that grows increasingly misaligned with the environment. Eventually, the gap gets so big that a major overhaul is inevitable. Restructuring, in this view, is like spring cleaning: we accumulate debris over months or years until we are finally forced to face up to the mess.

MAKING RESTRUCTURING WORK: THREE CASE EXAMPLES

In this section, we look at three case examples of restructuring. We focus particularly on examples of reengineering, which rose to prominence in the 1990s as an umbrella concept for a set of emerging trends in structural thinking: "When a process is reengineered, jobs evolve from narrow and task oriented to multidimensional. People who once did as they were instructed now make choices and decisions on their own instead. Assembly-line work disappears. Functional departments lose their reason for being. Managers stop acting like supervisors and behave more like coaches. Workers focus more on customers' needs and less on their bosses'. Attitudes and values change in response to new incentives. Practically every aspect of the organization is transformed, often beyond recognition" (Hammer and Champy, 1993, p. 65).

The process of reengineering and the results it produces vary significantly. Some initiatives have been catastrophic, a notorious example being the American long-haul bus company, Greyhound Lines. As the company came out of bankruptcy in the early 1990s, a new management team announced a major reorganization, with sizable cuts in staffing and routes and development of a new, computerized reservation system. The new initiative played well on Wall Street, where the company's stock soared, but it fared very poorly on Main Street as both customer service and the new reservations system collapsed. Rushed, underfunded, and insensitive to both employees and customers, it was a textbook example of how not to restructure. Eventually, Greyhound's stock crashed, and management was forced out. One observer noted wryly, "They reengineered that business to hell" (Tomsho, 1994, p. A1).

But there have also been examples of notable restructuring success. Here we discuss three of them, drawn from different eras and industries. The first, from Citibank, dates to the 1970s, well before the term *reengineering* was applied to structural change yet anticipating many of its principles.

Citibank's Back Room

The "back room" at Citibank—the department that processed checks and other financial instruments—was in trouble when John Reed took charge in 1970 (Seeger, Lorsch, and Gibson, 1975). Productivity was disappointing, errors were frequent, and expenses were rising almost 20 percent every year. Reed soon determined that the area needed dramatic structural change. Traditionally, it was viewed as a service for the bank's customer-contact offices, though it was structured as a machine bureaucracy. Reed decided to think of it not as a support function but as a factory: an independent, high-volume production facility. To implement this concept, he imported high-level executives from the automobile industry. One was Robert White, who came from Ford to become the primary architect of new structure and systems for the back room. White arrived with a strong faith in top-down management: "We use a pass/fail system as a management incentive. A manager passes or fails in terms of the objectives he himself has set within the top-down framework. He is rewarded, or not rewarded, accordingly. No excuses or rationalization of events beyond one's control are accepted" (Seeger, Lorsch, and Gibson, 1975, p. 3).

White began by developing a "phase one action plan" that called for cutting costs, putting in new computer systems, and developing a financial control system capable of both forecasting and measuring performance. In effect, the strategy retained the machine bureaucracy but tightened it. After phase one was implemented, White concluded that "we hadn't gone back to the basics enough. We found that we did not really understand the present processes completely" (p. 8). What followed was an intensive, detailed study of how the back room's processes worked. White and his associates developed a detailed flowchart that covered the walls of a room. They realized that the current structure was, in effect, one very large, functional pipeline. Everything flowed into "preprocessing" at the front end of the pipe, then to "encoding," and on through a series of functional areas until it eventually came out at the other end. Reed and White decided to break the pipe into several smaller lines, each carrying a different "product" and each supervised by a single manager with responsibility for an end-to-end process. The key insight was to change the structure from machine bureaucracy to a divisionalized form.

White also instituted extensive performance measures and tight accountability procedures:

> We currently measure 69 different quality indicators, and we are meeting the standards 87 percent of the time. When a given indicator is met or beaten consistently, we tighten the standard; we expect to continue this process indefinitely. We have defined 129 different standards for time lines, and we expect that number to continue to grow. Today, we are meeting 85 percent of those standards. Moreover, we also continually tighten these standards as soon as they can be consistently met. I think it is fair to say that our service performance has improved greatly since we began to hold costs flat—if for no other reason than that we really know what we are doing. (p. 8)

Not surprisingly, this demanding, top-down approach produced fear and loathing among many old-timers in the back room and nearly led to rebellion. As Mintzberg's model predicts, the technical core strongly resisted this intrusion. Reed and White decided to implement the new structure virtually overnight, and the short-term result was chaos and a major breakdown in the system. It took two weeks to get the system functioning normally and five months to recover from the problems generated by the transition. But once past that crisis, the new system led to a dramatic improvement in operating results: production was up, and costs and errors were down. The back room had unexpectedly become a major source of competitive advantage.

The basic concepts behind restructuring the back room are not new. The change from a large, functional bureaucracy to a divisionalized form first occurred in the 1920s at General Motors and Du Pont. By the 1970s, it was the dominant form for large organizations. What was unusual was to apply the concept of a divisionalized organization to the back room of a bank. Reed and White did not, in fact, begin with that in mind. It emerged from their intense mapping of the existing processes and recognition that dramatic change was possible.

Kodak's Black-and-White Division

The Citibank restructuring was strongly driven from the top down and focused primarily on internal efficiencies. This has been true of many, but by no means all, reengineering efforts. A more recent example from Eastman Kodak began with a push from the top but put much greater emphasis on customers and on empowering employees at multiple levels. Kodak traces its origins to the late 1880s, when George Eastman began to manufacture wooden boxes capable of capturing one hundred personal images on film. He also conceived of an innovative, "no fuss, no muss" way to process the pictures: just send the whole box back to Kodak. Kodak processed the pictures, reloaded the camera, and shipped it back to the customer.

A century later, Kodak was a giant in trouble. Its name and film were known around the world, but the company had been rocked by intense competition, high costs, declining customer satisfaction, threats of a hostile takeover, and low employee morale. At a top management meeting in 1989, Kodak's normally gentle, soft-spoken CEO, Colby Chandler, wielded a machete to hack a wooden lectern to pieces. The message was clear and dramatic: Kodak needed fundamental change, and its functional, "stovepipe" structure had to give way to an organization based on process—a seamless flow from raw materials to finished products (Hammer and Champy, 1993).

Kodak chose to reorganize into six flows, one of which was black-and-white film. Implementation was to begin immediately, and any laggard operations would be shut down. In the black-and-white division, a group of executives focused on creating three streams: graphics, health sciences, and solvent coatings. All other areas (financial services, human resources, and engineering support) would be "dedicated" to supporting the flows.

One of the first tasks was to create performance measures and standards for the flows (productivity, inventory, waste, quality, conformance to specifications). With the operating flow as the center of attention, managers and supervisors became coaches and cheerleaders. Frequent informal meetings were an opportunity to air concerns and identify problems. Employees were encouraged to develop local visions and determine priorities and improvement plans for everything from reducing inventory and cutting waste to establishing relationships with suppliers and speeding delivery time: "In the old days, there wasn't much real interaction between the people on the shop floor and the product engineers. When you needed a repair or a modification, you called MEMO [the Manufacturing, Engineering, and Maintenance Operation]. No one ever encouraged you to figure out ways to solve problems yourself" (Frangos, 1993, p. 108).

The overall flow focused on satisfying external customers; each step in the process emphasized satisfying internal customers and building cooperation among employees. Cross-functional teams began to achieve breakthroughs in quality and cost reduction; "We demonstrated that the internal customers can focus their energy on a common problem," Frangos commented (1993, p. 110).

Two years after the restructuring was launched in the black-and-white division, performance standards were being surpassed, the division was one of the company's shining stars in terms of profitability, and it was widely heralded as one of the company's best places to work. The division's new title, "Team Zebra," summarized the structural transformation. The zebra was selected as a symbol because "every zebra is unique. No two zebras' stripes are the same—kind of like fingerprints. They also run in herds. Being animals that are preyed upon, they understand that to the extent they can stay together, they can defend themselves from lions and other predators. In fact, predators probably have a hard time distinguishing the individuals from the mass of black and white stripes. We also need to band together as part of a team—when we're operating in synch, we baffle the competition" (p. 126).

Beth Israel Hospital

Boston's Beth Israel Hospital is an example from health care of a restructuring effort that sought to move toward greater autonomy and teamwork. When Joyce Clifford became Beth Israel's director of nursing, she found a top-down structure common in hospitals:

> The nursing aides, who had the least preparation, had the most contact with the patients. But they had no authority of any kind. They had to go to their supervisor to ask if a patient could have an aspirin. The supervisor would then ask the head nurse, who would then ask a doctor. The doctor would ask how long the patient had been in pain. Of course the head nurse had absolutely no idea, so she'd have to track down the aide to ask her, and then relay that information back to the doctor. It was ridiculous, a ludicrous and dissatisfying situation, and one in which it was impossible for the nurse to feel any satisfaction at all. The system was hierarchical, fragmented, impersonal, and [overmanaged]. (Helgesen, 1995, p. 134)

Within units, the responsibilities of nurses were highly specialized: some were assigned to handling medications, others to monitoring vital signs, and still others to taking blood pressure readings. Add to the list specialized housekeeping roles—bedpan, bed making, and food services—and an individual patient's day was filled with interruptions from a multitude of virtual strangers. No one really knew what was going on with the patient.

With the support and cooperation of Mitchell Rabkin, Beth Israel's progressive CEO, Clifford instituted a major structural change, from a pyramid with nurses at the bottom to an inclusionary web with nurses at the center. The concept was called primary nursing. Each primary nurse assumes responsibility for the care of a specific patient. The nurse takes information when the patient is admitted, develops a comprehensive plan, assembles a team to provide round-the-clock care, and lets the family know what to expect. A nurse manager sets goals for the unit, deals with budget and administrative matters, and makes sure that primary nurses have ample resources to provide quality care.

The primary nurse's role ensures a central point for information about the patient's progress. As the primary nurse assumed more responsibility, connections with physicians and other hospital workers had to be revised. Instead of simply carrying out the orders of physicians, the primary nurse became a professional partner, attending rounds and participating as an equal in treatment decisions. Housekeepers reported to primary nurses rather than to housekeeping supervisors. The same housekeeper was assigned to make a patient's bed, attend to the patient's hygiene, and deliver trays. Laundry workers brought in clean items on demand rather than making a once-a-day delivery. Beth Israel's inclusivity web was further strengthened by sophisticated technology that gave all points of the network easy access to patient information and administrative data.

Primary nurses themselves performed a variety of tasks for a single patient. Rather than being seen as menial undesirable work, for example, bed making became an opportunity to evaluate a patient's condition and assess how well a treatment plan is working:

> At the center of all patient care at Beth Israel, Joyce Clifford linked the various intersecting points of the inclusive web: "A big part of my job is to keep nurses informed on a regular basis of what's going on out there—what the board is doing, what decisions are confronting the hospital as a whole, what the issues are in health care in this country. I also let them know that I'm trying to represent what the nurses here are doing—to our vice-presidents, to our board, and people in the outside world, . . . to the nursing profession and the health care field as a whole." (p. 158)

No one knows whether more reorganization efforts succeed than fail, but the percentage of failures is high. The Kodak, Citibank, and Beth Israel efforts succeeded by following several basic principles of successful structural change:

- The change architects developed a new conception of the organization's goals and strategies.

- They carefully studied the existing structure and process so that they understood how things worked. Many efforts at structural change fail because they start from an incomplete picture of current processes.

- They designed the new structure in light of changes in goals, technology, and environment.

- Finally, they experimented, retaining things that worked and discarding things that did not.

CONCLUSION

At a given moment, an organization's structure represents its effort to align internal processes with the external environment, while simultaneously resolving an enduring set of organizational dilemmas: Are we too loose, or too tight? Are employees underworked, or overwhelmed? Are we too rigid, or do we lack standards? Do people spend too much or too little time coordinating with one another? Structure also represents a resolution of contending claims from various groups within an organization.

Mintzberg differentiates five major components in organizational structure: strategic apex, middle management, operating core, technostructure, and support staff. Distinct configurations of these components lead to specific organizational forms: simple structure, machine bureaucracy, professional bureaucracy, divisionalized form, and adhocracy. Helgesen adds a less hierarchical model, the web of inclusion.

A given resolution of structural tensions may be right for a particular time and circumstance, but changes in the organization and its environment eventually require some form of structural adaptation. Restructuring is a powerful but high-risk tool for organizational change. In the short term, it almost invariably produces confusion, resistance, and even a decline in effectiveness. Success or failure in the long run depends on how well the new model aligns the organization with its environment, task, and technology, and on the effectiveness of the processes for putting the new structure in place. Effective restructuring requires both a microscopic view of typical structural problems as well as an overall, topographical sense of structural options.

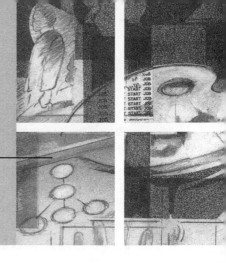

CHAPTER 5

Organizing Groups and Teams

In Seattle, a seventeen-year-old girl is mortally injured in an automobile accident. She is pronounced brain-dead, and her parents give permission to harvest her organs. Her kidney tissue type is entered into a national database. In Nashville, a potential recipient is identified: a forty-two-year-old mother of three no longer able to continue dialysis treatments. Without a new kidney, she will die.

Dr. Peter Minich, the Nashville surgeon who will perform the transplant, contacts his counterpart in Seattle to check the condition of the kidney. Weighing several factors, he decides to accept the organ. A Seattle surgical team procures the kidney, checks for a tissue match, and transports the iced kidney to the airport for its flight to Nashville. Simultaneously, the Nashville transplant team hospitalizes the recipient, gives her a complete physical, and dialyzes her. They also notify the hospital and give an estimate of how long the operation will take. The lab is alerted to perform the final cross-match once the kidney arrives, a procedure that takes three hours.

On arrival, the kidney is taken to the lab. Ninety minutes before the results of the cross-match are complete, nurses begin to prepare the operating room. They clean it, sterilize equipment, and bring in the necessary instruments—clamps, scissors, and retractors. The lab calls in a positive result, so the transplant can go forward. Members of the transplant team scrub in and go about their respective duties. The surgeon cleans up the kidney. The first assistant trims the fat and helps the surgeon pack the organ in fresh ice slush. A scrub nurse and a circulating nurse prepare the instrument table. The anesthesiologist and nurse assistant prepare the patient for surgery. During the transplant procedure, the circulating nurse brings instruments and sutures. The scrub nurse watches the surgery and anticipates which instruments the surgeon will need. The surgeon focuses on the procedure. The first assistant retracts tissue. The anesthesiologist monitors the patient's vital signs and supervises the nurse assistant.

Success depends as much on the performance of the team as on the technical skills of the surgeon. Roles are clearly defined, but people also have flexibility to cross role boundaries to do what needs to be done. The surgeon is in charge, yet there is also substantial lateral coordination. A good scrub nurse, for example, anticipates which instruments to hand off, with the discretion to "give me what I want, not what I'm asking for." According to Dr. Minich, "the more often team members work together the greater the chance for a successful outcome. Building a cohesive team is critical. The surgeon has to be a team leader as well as a good technician." Minich has had a perfect success record as a result.

The impact of structure on a team's performance is not restricted to the operating suite. During the Second World War, an unusual U.S. Army commando team compiled a distinctive record. It accomplished every mission it was assigned, including extremely high-risk, behind-the-lines operations. Deaths and injuries were among the lowest of any U.S. military unit. A research team was charged with finding out what made the unit so successful. Were the enlisted men and officers especially talented? Was their training longer or more intensive than normal? Or was the group just plain lucky?

Researchers pinpointed the reason for the group's success: the ability to reconfigure its structure to fit the situation. Planning for missions, the group functioned democratically. Anyone, irrespective of specialty or rank, could volunteer ideas and make suggestions. Decisions were reached by consensus, and the engagement strategy was approved by the group as a whole. The unit's planning structure resembled that of a research and development team, or a creative design group. Amorphous roles, lateral coordination, and a flat hierarchy encouraged participation, creativity, and productive conflict. Battle plans reflected the group's best ideas.

Executing the plan was another story. The group's structure transformed from a loose, creative confederation to a well-defined, tightly controlled chain of command. Each individual had a specific assignment. Tasks had to be done with split-second precision. The commanding officer had sole responsibility for making operational decisions or revising the plan. Everyone else obeyed orders without question, though they were allowed to offer suggestions if time permitted. In battle, the group relied on the traditional military structure: clear-cut responsibilities, and decisions made at the top and executed by the rank and file.

The group's ability to tailor its structure captured the best of two worlds. Participation encouraged creativity, ownership, and understanding of the battle plan. Authority, accountability, and clarity enabled the group to function with speed and efficiency during the operation.

Much of the work in large organizations is now done in groups or teams. When these units work well, they elevate the performance of ordinary individuals to extraordinary heights. When teams malfunction, as too often happens, they erode the potential contributions of the most talented members. What determines how well groups perform? As illustrated by the surgical team and the commando team, the performance of a small group depends heavily on structure. A key ingredient of a top-performing team is an effective pattern of roles and relationships focused on attaining common goals.

In this chapter, we explore the structural features of small groups and how to restructure to improve group performance. We begin by describing various design options and the relationship between design and tasks. Next, using sports as an example, we discuss patterns of differentiation, coordination, and interdependence in teams. Finally, we describe the characteristics of high-performing teams.

TASKS AND LINKAGES IN SMALL GROUPS

In organizing, groups have a number of structural options. The one that is chosen or that evolves must maximize individuals' contributions while minimizing pathologies that often plague small groups. A key to group structure is the work to be done. Tasks vary in clarity, predictability, and stability. The task-structure relationship is the same for small groups as for larger organizations.

As suggested in Chapter Four, complex tasks present challenges different from simpler ones. Planning a commando mission or transplanting a kidney is not the same as painting a house. Simple tasks align with basic structures—clearly defined roles, elementary forms of interdependence, and coordination by plan or command. More complicated projects generally require more complex forms: flexible roles, reciprocal interdependence, and coordination through lateral relationships and mutual feedback. If a situation becomes exceptionally ambiguous and fast-paced, particularly when time is a factor, more centralized authority often works best. Otherwise, a group may be unable to make decisions quickly enough. Without a workable structure, performance and morale suffer, and problems multiply.

Ferreting out the appropriate group structure requires careful consideration of multiple situational variables, some ambiguous or hard to assess:

- What are we trying to accomplish?
- What needs to be done?
- Who should do what?
- How should we make decisions?
- Who is in charge?
- How do we coordinate efforts?
- What do individual members care about most: time, quality, participation?
- What are the special skills and talents of each group member?
- What is the relationship between this group and others?
- How will we determine success?

To illustrate design options, we next look at several basic structural configurations identified in studies of five-member teams. The first is a one-boss arrangement; one person has authority over others (see Figure 5.1). Information and decisions flow from the top. Group members offer information to and communicate primarily with the official leader rather than with one another. Although this arrangement is efficient and fast, it works best with a relatively simple and straightforward task. More complicated situations overload the boss, producing delays or bad decisions, unless the person in charge has an unusual level of skill, expertise, and energy. Subordinates quickly become frustrated when directives they receive are poorly timed or ill-suited to their work.

A second option creates another management level below the boss (see Figure 5.2). Two individuals are given authority over specific areas of the group's work. Information and decisions flow through them. This arrangement works when a task is divisible; it reduces the span of control, allowing the person in charge to concentrate on mission,

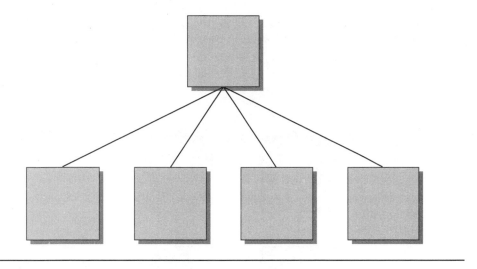

FIGURE 5.1. One Boss.

strategy, or relationships with higher-ups. But adding a new management layer limits access from the lower levels to the boss and may eventually erode morale and perform-ance. With added layers, communication becomes slower and more cumbersome.

Another possibility is to create, in effect, a simple hierarchy, with a middle manager who reports to the boss and in turn supervises and communicates with others (see Figure 5.3). This arrangement is used extensively at the White House. It frees the president to focus on mission and external relations while leaving operational details to the chief of staff. Though this further limits access to the top, it can be more efficient than a dual-manager arrange-ment. At the same time, friction between operational and top-level managers is common-place and can lead to attempts by number two to usurp number one's position.

A fourth possibility is a circle network, where information and decisions flow sequen-tially from one group member to another (see Figure 5.4). Each can add to or modify whatever comes around. This configuration is more egalitarian and simplifies communi-cation. Each person has to deal directly with only two others; transactions are therefore easier to manage. But one weak link in the chain can undermine the entire enterprise, and the circle can bog down with complex tasks that require more reciprocity.

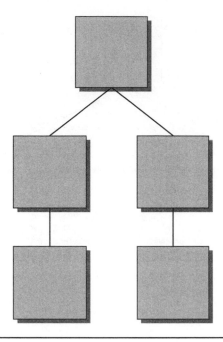

FIGURE 5.2. Dual Authority.

A final possibility is to create what small group researchers call the all-channel, or star, network (see Figure 5.5). This design is similar to Helgesen's web of inclusion. It creates multiple connections so that each person can talk to anyone else. Information flows freely; decisions require touching multiple bases. Morale in an all-channel network is usually very high. The arrangement works well if a task is amorphous or complicated, but it is slow and inefficient for a simpler task. It works best when team members bring well-developed communication skills, enjoy participation, tolerate ambiguity, embrace diversity, have good communication skills, and manage conflict.

In small groups, such as school boards, families, task forces, and leadership teams, many day-to-day problems are caused by poorly understood or inappropriate structural forms. Creating effective teamwork requires a design of roles and relationships well suited to the situation.

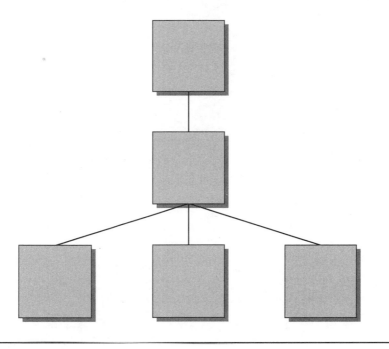

FIGURE 5.3. Simple Hierarchy.

TEAMWORK AND INTERDEPENDENCE

The research described in the previous section shows that even in the relatively simple case of five-person teams, structure is critical to team functioning. In the real world of organizations, things get more complicated. Teams come in many sizes, and tasks vary greatly in structural demands. Team sports offer a helpful analogy to clarify the impact of task differences on teamwork. Every game calls for its own unique patterns of differentiation and coordination. How closely team members depend on one another (the level of interdependence) varies widely from sport to sport. Because of this, unique team structures are required for different sports (Keidel, 1984). Teams, just like organizations, must be aligned with the task at hand. Social architecture is remarkably different for baseball, football, and basketball teams.

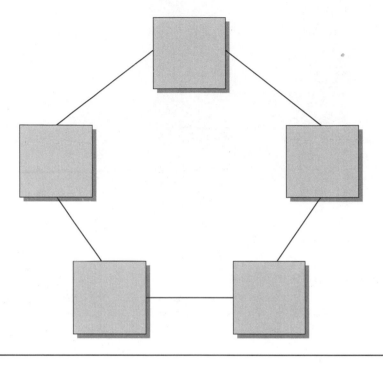

FIGURE 5.4. Circle.

Baseball

As Pete Rose once noted, "Baseball is a team game, but nine men who meet their individual goals make a nice team" (Keidel, 1984, p. 8). A baseball team is a loosely integrated confederation. Individual efforts are mostly independent, seldom involving more than two or three players at a time. Particularly on defense, players are separated from one another by significant distance. Because of the differentiated, loosely linked nature of a baseball team, very little coordination is required among the various positions. The pitcher and catcher must each know what the other is going to do, and at times, infielders must anticipate how a teammate will act, particularly in a double play or squeeze situation. Most managerial decisions are tactical, normally involving individual substitutions or actions. Managers come and go without seriously disrupting the team's playing ability.

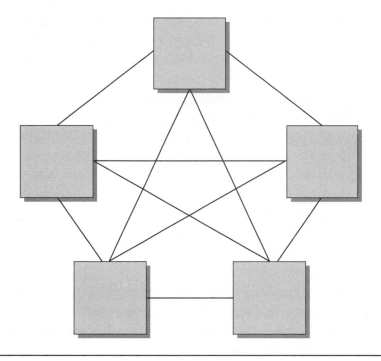

FIGURE 5.5. All-Channel Network.

Players can be transferred from one team to another with relative ease. A newcomer can carry out responsibilities without significant adjustment.

John Updike summed it up well: "Of all the team sports, baseball, with its graceful intermittence of action, its immense and tranquil field sparsely salted with poised men in white, its dispassionate mathematics, seemed to be best suited to accommodate, and be ornamented by, a loner. It is an essentially lonely game" (Keidel, 1984, pp. 14–15).

Football

American football is a different story. Unlike baseball, players perform in close proximity to one another. Linemen and offensive backs hear, see, or touch one another. Each play involves every player on the field. Efforts are sequentially linked in a plan or play. The actions of linemen pave the way for the movement of backs; a defensive team's field position becomes the starting point for the offense, and vice versa. In the transition from offense to defense, specialty platoons play a pivotal role (Keidel, 1984). Unlike baseball, the efforts of individual players are tightly coordinated. George Allen, coach of the Washington Redskins, put it this way: "A football game is a lot like a machine. It's made up of parts. If one part doesn't work, one player pulling against you and not doing his job, the whole machine fails" (Keidel, 1984, p. 9).

Because of the interdependence among parts, a football team must be well integrated, mainly through planning and hierarchical control. The primary units are the offensive, defensive, and specialty platoons, each with its own coordinator. Under the direction of the head coach, the team uses scouting reports and other surveillance to develop a strategy or game plan in advance. During the game, strategic decisions are typically made by the head coach. Tactical decisions are made by assistants or by designated players on either offense or defense (Keidel, 1984).

A football team's systemic characteristics make it hard to swap players from one team to another. Irv Cross, of the Philadelphia Eagles, once remarked, "An Eagles player could never make an easy transition to the Dallas Cowboys; the system and philosophies are just too different" (Keidel, 1984, p. 15). A coach is not easily replaced. Tom Landry, Vince Lombardi, and Don Shula led their Cowboys, Packers, and Dolphins teams to many victories over the years. Their success was rooted significantly in their ability to create a well-coordinated team from available talent. Unlike baseball, football requires sound strategy and tightly meshed execution (Keidel, 1984).

Basketball

Basketball players perform in even closer proximity than football players. In quick, rapidly moving transitions, offense becomes defense—with the same players. The efforts of basketball players are highly reciprocal; each player depends on the effort of all the others. Each player may be involved with any of the other four. Anyone can handle the ball or attempt to score.

Basketball is much like improvisational jazz: teams require a high level of spontaneous, mutual adjustment. Everyone is on the move, often in an emergent way rather than a predetermined direction. A successful basketball season depends heavily on a flowing relationship among team members who "read" and anticipate one another's moves. Players who are together a long time develop a sense of what each will do in various circumstances. A team of newcomers experiences difficulty in adjusting to individual predispositions or quirks. Keidel (1984) notes that coaches serve as integrators whose periodic interventions reinforce team cohesion, helping players coordinate laterally. Unlike baseball teams, basketball teams cannot function as a collection of individual stars. Unlike football, basketball has no platoons. It is wholly a group effort.

A study of Duke University's successful women's basketball team in 2000 documented the importance of group interdependence and cohesion. The team won because players could anticipate the actions of others. The individual *I* deferred to the collective *we*. Passing to a teammate was valued as highly as making the shot yourself. Basketball is "fast, physically close, and crowded, 20 arms and legs in motion, up, down, across, in the air. The better the team, the more precise the passing into lanes that appear blocked with bodies" (Lubans, 2001, p. 1).

Determinants of Successful Teamwork

In sports and elsewhere, successful teamwork depends on the game—on what a team is trying to do. Keidel (1984) suggests several important questions in determining an appropriate structural design:

- What is the nature and degree of task-related interaction among individuals?
- What is the geographic distribution of unit members?
- Given a group's objectives and constraints, where does autonomy reside?
- How is coordination achieved?
- Which word best describes the required structure: conglomerate, mechanistic, or organic?
- What sports expression metaphorically captures the task of management: filling out the line-up card, preparing the game plan, or influencing the game's flow?

Beyond sports, team structures vary, even within the same organization. For example, a senior research manager in a pharmaceutical firm observed a structural progression in discovering and developing a new drug: "The process moves through three distinct stages.

It's like going from baseball to football to basketball" (Keidel, 1984, p. 11). In basic research, individual scientists work independently to develop a body of knowledge. As in baseball, individual efforts are the norm. Once identified, a promising drug passes from developmental chemists to pharmacy researchers to toxicologists. If the drug receives preliminary federal approval, it moves to clinical researchers for experimental tests. These sequential relationships are reminiscent of play sequences in football. In the final stage ("new drug application") physicians, statisticians, pharmacists, pharmacologists, toxicologists, and chemists work closely and reciprocally to win final approval from the Food and Drug Administration. Their efforts resemble the closely linked and flowing patterns of a basketball team (Keidel, 1984).

Jan Haynes of FzioMed, a California developer of new approaches to preventing scar tissue in surgical procedures, echoes the pharmaceutical executive's observations. But she adds, "In sports a game lasts only a short period of time. In our business, each game goes on for months." Ron Haynes, the firm's CEO, points out how difficult it is to change his leadership style as the rules of the game change: "I have to know when I need to shift from [baseball manager Tommy] Lasorda to [football coach Vince] Lombardi to [basketball coach Pat] Riley. Otherwise, our operation won't get the job done right." Doing the right job requires a structure well suited to what an organization is trying to accomplish.

TEAM STRUCTURE AND TOP PERFORMANCE

The importance of a clear and appropriate structure to team performance is well documented. Katzenbach and Smith (1993), for example, interviewed hundreds of people on more than fifty teams in developing their book *The Wisdom of Teams.* Their sample encompassed thirty enterprises in settings as diverse as Motorola, Hewlett-Packard, Operation Desert Storm, and the Girl Scouts. They drew a clear distinction between undifferentiated "groups" and sharply focused "teams": "A team is a small number of people with complementary skills, who are committed to a common purpose, set of performance goals and approach for which they hold themselves mutually accountable" (p. 112).

Katzenbach and Smith's research highlights six distinguishing characteristics of high-performing teams:

1. *High-performing teams shape purpose in response to a demand or an opportunity placed in their path, usually by higher management.* Top managers clarify the team's charter, rationale, and challenge while permitting flexibility for the team to work out specific goals and plans of operation. By giving a team clear authority and then staying out of the way, management releases collective energy and creativity.

2. *High-performing teams translate common purpose into specific, measurable performance goals.* Purpose yields an overall mission, but successful teams take the additional step of recasting purpose into specific and measurable performance goals: "If a team fails to establish specific performance goals or if those goals do not relate directly to the team's overall purpose, team members become confused, pull apart, and revert to mediocre performance. By contrast, when purpose and goals are built on one another and are combined with team commitment, they become a powerful engine of performance" (p. 113). Specific goals define collective "work products," facilitate clear communication and constructive conflict, keep the team focused on getting results, and offer a yardstick for gauging small wins along the way.

3. *High-performing teams are of manageable size.* Katzenbach and Smith (1993) fix the optimal size for an effective team somewhere between two and twenty-five people: "Ten people are far more likely than fifty to work through their individual, functional, and hierarchical differences toward a common plan and to hold themselves jointly accountable for the results" (p. 114).

4. *High-performing teams develop the right mix of expertise.* The structural frame stresses the critical link between specialization and expertise. Effective teams seek out the full range of necessary technical fluency; "product development teams that include only marketers or engineers are less likely to succeed than those with the complementary skills of both" (p. 115). In addition, exemplary teams find and reward expertise in problem solving, decision making, and interpersonal skills to keep the group focused, on task, and free of debilitating personal squabbles.

5. *High-performing teams develop a common commitment to working relationships.* "Team members must agree on who will do particular jobs, how schedules will be set and adhered to, what skills need to be developed, how continuing membership in the team is to be earned, and how the group will make and modify decisions" (p. 115). Effective teams take the time to explore who is best suited for a particular task as well as how

individual roles come together. Achieving structural clarity varies from team to team, but it takes more than an organization chart to identify roles and pinpoint one's place in the official hierarchy. Most teams require a more detailed understanding of who is going to do what and how people relate to each other in carrying out diverse tasks. One possibility is to use responsibility charting (Galbraith, 1977). Responsibility charting presents a framework and a language for hammering out how people work together. For a given task, responsibility is assigned to the individual or group with overall accountability. The next step is to outline how that role relates to others on the team. Does someone need to approve the actions of the responsible person? Are there people who need to be consulted? Are there others who must be kept informed? Whatever form it takes, an effective team "establishes a social contract among members that relates to their purpose and guides and obligates how they will work together" (Katzenbach and Smith, 1993, p. 116).

6. *Members of high-performing teams hold themselves collectively accountable.* Pinpointing individual responsibility is crucial to a well-coordinated effort, but effective teams find ways to hold the collective accountable: "Teams enjoying a common purpose and approach inevitably hold themselves responsible, both as individuals and as a team, for the team's performance" (p. 116).

A focused, cohesive structure is a foundation for high-performing teams. Even highly skilled people zealously pursuing a shared mission will falter and fail if group structure constantly generates confusion and frustration.

SATURN: THE STORY BEHIND THE STORY

After it was launched by its parent, General Motors, Saturn quickly achieved levels of quality, consumer satisfaction, and customer loyalty that surpassed those of much of the American automotive industry. What was the secret of the company's success? Credit has been given both to its sophisticated technology and its enlightened approach to managing people. On the technology side, Saturn made extensive use of computers and deployed robots for many repetitive or dangerous jobs. Its human resource practices emphasized training, conflict management, and extensive employee participation. Yet it is easy to overlook Saturn's distinctive team structure as an important element of its achievements.

Companywide, Saturn employees were granted authority to make decisions, within a few flexible guidelines. Restrictive rules and ironclad, top-down work procedures were left behind as the company moved away from what employees call the "old world" of General Motors. Early in the company's history, a new manager imported from General Motors was walking the line and noticed an assembly worker standing beside a pile of parts. He asked the employee why the parts were not being used. The worker replied that they did not meet quality standards. The manager told him to use the parts anyway. The worker refused. "Very quickly the UAW [United Automobile Workers] president and a top manager came to the scene. They flat out told [the new manager] that things aren't done that way here at Saturn and that he'd better learn his job. To which the manager replied, 'What is my job?' The union president retorted, 'That's for you to discover'" (Deal and Jenkins, 1994, p. 244).

Saturn's engineers and assembly-line workers worked together to solve problems and design manufacturing processes. Relationships between UAW and Saturn management were cordial and cooperative, governed by an official agreement just one page in length.

Most of the actual assembly of the Saturn automobile was done by teams. More than 150 production teams of eight to fifteen cross-trained, highly interdependent workers assembled the car on a half-mile-long assembly line. The traditional system of sequential, repetitive efforts by isolated individuals became a thing of the past. Saturn created "a work environment where people provide leadership for themselves and others. It is cooperation and self and team management that make Saturn tick. Problems are solved by people working together—they are not kicked upstairs for others to solve" (p. 230).

Across the subassembly groups—body systems, power train, and general assembly, operating in three shifts, twenty-four hours a day—Saturn teams exemplified the successful profile from *Wisdom of Teams*. The design of the car, corporate values, and quality standards came down from the executive suite, but each team translated broad objectives into measurable performance goals. Teams were empowered to deal with budget, safety procedures, ergonomics, vacations, time off, and other matters. In effect, each team managed its own business within general guidelines. An employee in body systems described how it worked on her team: "The working conditions are like running your own business. We decide when the shifts are, who starts where, break and eating times, and vacation schedules" (Deal and Jenkins, 1994, p. 242).

Saturn teams were of manageable size, usually staffed with the right mix of expertise to handle all aspects of the team's tasks. When necessary, additional expertise could be borrowed from other teams through a process called augmentation.

Saturn teams designed their own working relationships. Prior to the beginning of a shift, team members conferred in a team center for five or ten minutes. They determined the day's rotation. A team of ten would have ten jobs to do and typically rotated through them, except that rotation was more frequent for jobs involving heavy lifting or stress. Every week the plant shut down to let teams review quality standards, budget, safety, and the ergonomics of assembly. A WUC (work unit counselor) was designated as official team leader. WUCs normally rose through the ranks to assume the role. The level of responsibility teams assumed was illustrated by an interior design team that chose to eliminate sixteen team jobs. In looking for ways to trim costs, the team identified an inefficient practice: walking too far to pick up parts for the assembly. Moving the parts closer to the line eliminated the extra distance, but it also made the extra positions unnecessary. The team—including those who eventually moved to other positions at Saturn—made decisions about which positions to eliminate.

Group accountability became an accepted way of life for Saturn teams. Workers watched the numbers every day. At least $10,000 in salary was put at risk each year. If the company met its performance objectives, everyone gained. If it did not, the loss was also shared. Everyone at Saturn admitted that things were not perfect. But there was general agreement that teams were learning from mistakes and constantly refining the structure of teamwork.

CONCLUSION

Every group evolves a structure as its members work together, but the design may help or hinder effectiveness. Conscious attention to structure and roles can make an enormous difference in group performance. As in any organization, team structure emphasizing hierarchy and top-down control tends to work well for simple, well-understood and stable tasks. As tasks become more complex or the environment gets more turbulent, structure must also grow more complex, and lateral forms of communication and coordination become more important. Team sports suggest images of task variations. The simple structure of a baseball team mirrors the leisurely pace and emphasis on individual performance that are part of the game. The need for a game plan in football, or on-the-spot improvisation and coordination in basketball, requires a more complex structure.

Many teams never learn the lesson of the commando team: vary the structure in response to changes in task and circumstance. A task force that meets to study a problem and develop a report, for example, goes through several phases, each calling for different patterns of roles, linkages, and interdependence. Loose, nonhierarchical forms may work extremely well in the early phases of goal setting and brainstorming, particularly if the group has enough time to work through the challenges of getting under way. Later phases of report writing and editing may require a more centralized and specialized structure. Leaders, as Ron Haynes of FzioMed pointed out, must know when the rules of the game change, and redesign the structure accordingly.

When a group encounters the inevitable vicissitudes of group life—such things as overload, conflict, confusion, communication gaps, or bungled handoffs—the members often pin the blame on each other. Few groups are blessed with flawless members, but it is much easier and more profitable to restructure the team than to reconstruct each member's personality.

PART THREE

The Human Resource Frame

"Our most important resource is our people."

"Organizations exploit people, chew them up, and spit them out."

Both of these views of the relationship between people and organizations are often expressed, but which is true? How you answer affects everything you do at work.

The human resource frame centers on how characteristics of organizations and people shape what they do for one another. We begin in Chapter Six by laying out the basic human resource assumptions, focusing on the fit between human needs and organizational rationality. Organizations generally hope for a cadre of talented, highly motivated employees who will give their best. Often, though, these same organizations rely on outdated assumptions and counterproductive management practices that cause workers to give less and demand more.

After examining how organizations get it wrong in Chapter Six, Chapter Seven turns to how smart managers and progressive organizations find better ways to manage human resources. We describe "high-involvement" or "high-commitment" practices that help build and retain a talented and motivated workforce.

In Chapter Eight, we examine human issues in interpersonal relations and small groups. We describe effective and ineffective strategies for managing relationships and look at how interpersonal dynamics can make or break a group or team.

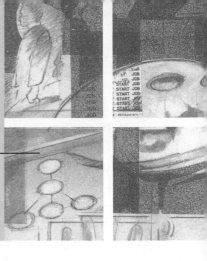

CHAPTER 6

People and Organizations

Home from the Korean War, David Swanson took a management position with American consumer products giant Procter & Gamble. His joy in landing a good civilian job was short-lived. He was discouraged to find that P&G managed its production plants much as the U.S. Army managed combat units, with a strong emphasis on rank, command, and top-down control. The results were debilitating: militant unions, deep-seated mistrust, and perennial labor-management antagonism. During a strike at one P&G plant, managers flown in as replacement workers never got beyond the airport. It was surrounded by union members in pickup trucks with shotguns. Swanson felt there must be a better way.

Swanson had studied at MIT with Douglas McGregor, one of few Americans in the 1950s who believed that workers actually cared about doing good work. McGregor felt that workers would be much more productive if management was smart enough to align jobs with workers' needs. After working his way up the management ranks, Swanson was assigned to manage a new P&G plant in Augusta, Georgia. He enlisted McGregor to help him design it. They built the plant as an "open system" featuring then-radical innovations: communication of both good and bad news, self-managing teams, and a peer-controlled pay system. The experiment became a huge success. "By the mid-1960s, and by almost any productivity measure Swanson and his colleagues could muster, Augusta was 30 percent more productive than any other P&G plant" (Waterman, 1994, p. 41).

McGregor was building on a tradition with roots in the early work of pioneers such as Mary Parker Follett (1918) and Elton Mayo (1933). They questioned a deeply held, invisible assumption that guided managerial efforts for centuries: workers had no rights beyond a paycheck; their duty was to work hard and follow orders. Pioneers who helped lay the human resource frame's foundation criticized this view on two grounds: it was unfair, and it was bad psychology. They argued that people's skills, attitudes, energy, and commitment are vital resources that can make or break an enterprise.

Everyone knows that organizations can be alienating, dehumanizing, and frustrating. Such conditions waste talent, distort lives, and motivate people to pull out or fight back, devoting much of their time and effort to beating the system. The human resource frame offers another possibility: an organization can also be energizing, productive, and mutually rewarding. This potential exists despite the widespread image of organizations as oppressive places dominated by callous and selfish bosses who care only about accumulating money and power. In Franz Kafka's novel *The Trial,* for example, the protagonist faces a mysterious, impersonal, and hostile system destroying people at will, seemingly for no reason. Countless books and films follow Kafka's lead (while very few depict happy workers or caring bosses).

There is more than a grain of contemporary truth in these fictional accounts. Consider McWane, one of the world's largest manufacturers of cast-iron pipes, whose management philosophy could come from a Dickens novel. McWane "has by far the worst safety record in an industry that, for three of the last four years, has had the highest injury rate in the nation" (Barstow and Bergman, 2003c, p. A-1). In 1995, McWane bought Tyler Pipe, a foundry in central Texas. Over the next two years, McWane cut nearly two-thirds of employees, eliminating quality control and safety inspectors, while pushing to maintain production at prior levels. Profits soared, but so did turnover and injuries (including at least three deaths). The employee handbook told workers they were expected to work "as quickly and efficiently as possible without compromising safety rules or safe practices in any way" (Barstow and Bergman, 2003a, p. A-14). But federal safety inspectors concluded that the safety program was a "charade"; the company routinely violated safety standards in its push to avoid production downtime. Since many rookie employees got hurt and left, injuries and turnover fed one another. A nurse resigned in disgust after four months on the job. She concluded that the company targeted injured workers for dismissal. In 2002, McWane admitted in federal court and in a settlement with federal regulators that it had willfully ignored or violated safety rules (Barstow and Bergman, 2003a).

Sacrificing people for profits continually reinvigorates age-old images of insensitive and heartless organizations. Every economic downturn produces waves of layoffs and downsizing that reinforce workers' vulnerability in the face of forces over which they have little control. One of America's most popular cartoon strips in recent years has been "Dilbert," whose white-collar, cubicle-class hero wanders mindlessly through an office landscape of incompetent bosses, bureaucratic inertia, and corporate doublespeak.

HUMAN RESOURCE ASSUMPTIONS

Is the workplace really this bleak across the board? Are individuals simply pawns, sacrificed to collective purposes and casually cast aside when no longer needed? Is there hope that work can ever fully engage people's talent and energy? Such questions have intensified with globalization and the growth in size and power of modern institutions. How can people find freedom and dignity in a world dominated by economic fluctuations and an emphasis on short-term results? Answers are not easy. They require a sensitive understanding of people and their symbiotic relationship with organizations. The human resource frame is built on core assumptions that highlight this linkage:

- Organizations exist to serve human needs rather than the reverse.
- People and organizations need each other. Organizations need ideas, energy, and talent; people need careers, salaries, and opportunities.
- When the fit between individual and system is poor, one or both suffer. Individuals are exploited or exploit the organization—or both become victims.
- A good fit benefits both. Individuals find meaningful and satisfying work, and organizations get the talent and energy they need to succeed.

People want to know, "How well will this place fulfill my needs?" Organizations universally ask, "How do we find and retain people with the skills and attitudes needed to do the work?" In this chapter, we first examine the human side of organizations: how people's needs are satisfied or frustrated at work. Then we look at the changing employment contract and its impact on both people and organizations.

HUMAN NEEDS

The concept of need is controversial. Some theorists argue that the idea is too vague and refers to something difficult to observe. Others say that whatever needs people might have are so variable and so strongly influenced by the environment that the concept offers little help in explaining how they behave (Salancik and Pfeffer, 1977). Economists such as Jensen and Meckling (1994) argue that the individual's willingness to trade off one thing for another (time for money, or sleep for entertainment) disproves the idea of needs. Despite this academic skepticism, needs are a central element in everyday psychology. Parents worry about the needs of their children, politicians pride themselves on responding to the needs of constituents, and managers try to understand the needs of workers. Common sense tells us needs are important, but it is less clear what they are.

A horticultural analogy may help clarify matters. A gardener knows that every plant has specific requirements. The right combination of temperature, moisture, soil conditions, and sunlight allows a plant to grow and flourish. Within design limits, plants do their best to get what they need. They orient leaves sunward to get more light or sink roots deeper in search of water. A plant's capabilities generally increase with maturity. Highly vulnerable seedlings become more self-sufficient as they grow (better able to fend off insects and competition from other plants). These capabilities decline as the plant nears the end of its life cycle.

Human needs are similar. Conditions or elements in the environment allow people to survive and evolve. Needs for oxygen, water, and food are clear; the idea of universal psychic needs is more controversial. A genetic, or "nature," perspective argues that certain psychological needs are basic to being human (Maslow, 1954; McClelland, 1985; White 1960). A "nurture" view argues that people are so shaped by environment, socialization, and culture that it is fruitless to talk about generic psychic needs.

In extreme forms, both nature and nurture arguments mislead us. No degree in psychology is needed to know people are capable of enormous amounts of learning and adaptation and are influenced by their surroundings. Nor do we need advanced training in biology to recognize that many individual differences are present at birth. Genes determine so many physical characteristics that it is surprising to find some proponents of the nurture view wedded to their argument that behavioral differences are *always* caused by environmental factors.

An emerging consensus sees human behavior as resulting from the interplay between heredity and environment. Genes initially determine potential and predispositions. Research has shown, for example, that certain genetic patterns are associated with such behavioral tendencies as criminality. But learning profoundly modifies and sometimes reverses the original instructions.

The nature-nurture seesaw suggests a more powerful way of thinking about human needs. A need can be defined as a genetic predisposition to prefer some experiences over others. Needs energize and guide behavior and vary in strength at different times. We enjoy the company of others, yet sometimes want to be alone. Since the genetic instructions cannot anticipate all situations an individual encounters, both the form and the expression of each person's needs are significantly modified by experiences after birth.

WHAT NEEDS DO PEOPLE HAVE?

The existential psychologist Abraham Maslow (1954) developed one of our most influential theories about needs. He started with the notion that people are motivated by a variety of wants, some more fundamental than others. The desire for food dominates the lives of the chronically hungry, but other motives drive people with enough to eat. Maslow grouped human needs into five basic categories, arrayed in a hierarchy (with self-actualization at the top):

1. Physiological (needs for oxygen, water, food, physical health, and comfort)
2. Safety (to be safe from danger, attack, and threat)
3. Belongingness and love (needs for positive and loving relationships with other people)
4. Esteem (needs to feel valued and to value oneself)
5. Self-actualization (needs to develop to one's fullest, to actualize one's potential)

In Maslow's view, basic needs for physiological well-being and safety are "prepotent"; they have to be satisfied first. Once lower needs are satisfied, individuals are motivated by higher needs of belongingness, esteem, and self-actualization. The order is not iron-clad. Parents may sacrifice themselves for their children, and martyrs sometimes give their lives for a cause. Maslow believed that such reversals occur when lower needs are so well satisfied early in life that they recede into the background later on.

Attempts to validate Maslow's theory have proved inconclusive (Alderfer, 1972; Lawler and Shuttle, 1973; Schneider and Alderfer, 1973). The skimpy evidence has made many academics skeptical, but Maslow's view is still widely accepted and enormously influential among managers. Take, for example, the advice that the *Manager's Guide* at Federal Express offers employees: "Modern behavioral scientists such as Abraham Maslow . . . have shown that virtually every person has a hierarchy of emotional needs, from basic safety, shelter, and sustenance to the desire for respect, satisfaction, and a sense of accomplishment. Slowly these values have appeared as the centerpiece of progressive company policies, always with remarkable results" (Waterman, 1994, p. 92). Academic skepticism didn't prevent FedEx from building a highly successful management philosophy on that belief.

THEORY X AND THEORY Y

David Swanson's professor, Douglas McGregor (1960), built on Maslow's theory by adding another central idea: that managers' assumptions about people tend to become self-fulfilling prophecies. McGregor argued that most managers harbor "Theory X" assumptions, believing that subordinates are passive and lazy, have little ambition, prefer to be led, and resist change. Most conventional management practices, in his view, have been built on either hard or soft versions of Theory X. The hard version emphasizes coercion, tight controls, threats, and punishments. Over time, it generates low productivity, antagonism, militant unions, and subtle sabotage—exactly the conditions that Swanson found at Procter & Gamble in the 1950s. Soft versions of Theory X try to avoid conflict and satisfy everyone's needs. The usual result is superficial harmony with undercurrents of apathy and indifference. McGregor's key point was that a hard or soft Theory X approach is self-fulfilling: if you treat people as if they're lazy and need to be directed, they conform to your expectations.

Old-line managers often pointed to years of experience proving that Theory X was the only way to get anything done because workers "are never satisfied" and "just don't seem to give a damn." McGregor advocated another view, which he called Theory Y. Maslow's hierarchy of needs was the foundation:

> We recognize readily enough that a man suffering from a severe dietary deficiency is sick.
> The deprivation of physiological needs has behavioral consequences. The same is true—

although less well recognized—of deprivation of higher-level needs. The man whose needs for safety, association, independence, or status are thwarted is sick as surely as the man who has rickets. And his sickness will have behavioral consequences. We will be mistaken if we attribute his resultant passivity, hostility, and refusal to accept responsibility to his inherent human nature. These forms of behavior are symptoms of illness—of deprivation of his social and egoistic needs. (McGregor, 1960, pp. 35–36)

Theory Y's key proposition is that "the essential task of management is to arrange organizational conditions so that people can achieve their own goals best by directing their efforts toward organizational rewards" (McGregor, 1960, p. 61). If individuals find no satisfaction in their work, management has little choice but to rely on Theory X and external control. Conversely, the more managers align organizational requirements with employee self-interest, the more they can rely on Theory Y's principle of self-direction.

PERSONALITY AND ORGANIZATION

Like his contemporary McGregor, Chris Argyris (1957, 1964) also saw a basic conflict between human personality and how organizations were typically structured and managed. Argyris argued that people have basic "self-actualization trends"—akin to the efforts of a plant to reach its biological potential. From infancy into adulthood, people advance from dependence to independence, from a narrow to a broader range of skills and interests. They move from a short time perspective (interests quickly developed and forgotten, with little ability to anticipate the future) to a much longer-term horizon. The child's impulsivity and limited self-knowledge are replaced by a more mature level of self-awareness and self-control.

Like McGregor, Argyris felt organizations often treated workers like children rather than adults—a view eloquently expressed in Charlie Chaplin's 1936 film *Modern Times*. In one scene, Chaplin's character works furiously on an assembly line, trying to tighten bolts on every piece that goes past. His time perspective can be measured in seconds. Skill requirements are minimal; he has almost no control over the pace of his work. An efficiency expert selects Chaplin as the guinea pig for a new machine designed to feed him lunch while he continues to tighten bolts. It goes haywire and begins to assault Chaplin with food. The film's message is clear: industrial organizations exploit workers and treat them like infants.

Argyris saw person-structure conflict built into traditional principles of organizational design and management. The structural concept of task specialization defines jobs as narrowly as possible to improve efficiency. But the rational logic often backfires. Consider the experience of autoworker Ben Hamper. His introduction to life on the automobile assembly line came while he was still a child. His first impressions mirror a story many other American workers could tell:

> I was seven years old the first time I ever set foot inside an automobile factory. The occasion was Family Night at the old Fisher Body plant in Flint where my father worked the second shift. If nothing else, this annual peepshow lent a whole world of credence to our father's daily grumble. The assembly line did indeed stink. The noise was very close to intolerable. The heat was one complete bastard.
>
> After a hundred wrong turns and dead ends, we found my old man down on the trim line. His job was to install windshields using this goofy apparatus with large suction cups that resembled an octopus being crucified. A car would nuzzle up to the old man's work area and he would be waiting for it, a cigarette dangling from his lip, his arms wrapped around the windshield contraption as if it might suddenly rebel and bolt off for the ocean. Car, windshield. Car, windshield. Car, windshield. No wonder my father preferred playin' hopscotch with barmaids. (Hamper, 1992, pp. 1–2)

Following in his father's and grandfather's footsteps, Ben Hamper became an autoworker. He soon discovered a familiar pattern. Though his career began twenty years after Argyris and McGregor questioned the fallacies of traditional management techniques, little had changed. Hamper held down a variety of jobs, each as mindless and repetitious as the next: "The one thing that was impossible to escape was the monotony. Every minute, every hour, every truck, and every movement was a plodding replica of the one that had gone before" (p. 41).

The specialization Ben Hamper saw in the auto plant calls for a clear chain of command to coordinate discrete jobs. Bosses direct and control people at lower levels, thus encouraging the passivity and dependence Argyris saw as conflicting with needs of healthy human beings. The conflict worsens as one moves down the hierarchy—more mechanized jobs, more directives, and tighter controls. As people mature, conflict intensifies. Argyris argued that employees inevitably look for ways to respond to these frustrations. He identified six possibilities:

1. *They withdraw—through chronic absenteeism or simply by quitting.* Ben Hamper chronicled many examples of absenteeism and quitting, including his friend Roy, who lasted only a couple of months:

> My pal Roy was beginning to unravel in a real rush. His enthusiasm about all the money we were makin' had dissipated and he was having major difficulty coping with the drudgery of factory labor. He wallowed in the slow-motion injustice of the time clock. His job, like mine, wasn't difficult. It was just plain monotonous. . . .
>
> The day before he quit, he approached me with a box-cutter knife sticking out of his glove and requested that I give him a slice across the back of the hand. He felt sure this ploy would land him a few days off. Since slicing Roy didn't seem like a solid career move, I refused. Roy went down the line to the other workers where he received a couple of charitable offers to cut his throat, but no dice on the hand. He wound up sulking back to his job. After that night, I never saw Roy again. (pp. 40, 43)

2. *They stay on the job but withdraw psychologically, becoming indifferent, passive, and apathetic.* Like many other workers, Ben Hamper didn't want to quit, so he looked for ways to cope with the tedium. His favorite was to "double up" by making a deal with another worker to take turns covering each other's job. This made it possible to get full pay for half a day's work:

> What a setup. Dale and I would both report to work before the 4:30 horn. We'd spend a half hour preparing all the stock we'd need for the evening. At 5:00, I would take over the two jobs while Dale went to sleep in a makeshift cardboard bed behind our bench. He'd stuff some plugs into his ears, crawl into his bed, and often be sound asleep before I had even finished my first truck. I'd work the jobs from 5:00 until 9:24, the official lunch period. When the line stopped, I'd give Dale's cardboard coffin a good kick. It was time for the handoff. I would give my ID badge to Dale so that he could punch me out at quitting time. (p. 61)

If doubling up didn't work, workers invented other diversions, like Rivet Hockey (sailing rivets into a coworker's foot or leg) and Dumpster Ball (kicking cardboard boxes high enough to clear a dumpster). And if games weren't enough, there was always alcohol: "Drinking right on the line wasn't something everyone cared for. But plenty did, and the most popular time to go snagging for gusto was the lunch break. As soon as that lunch horn blew, half of the plant put it in gear, sprinting out the door in packs of three or four, each pointed squarely for one of those chilly coolers up at one of the nearby beer emporiums." (p. 56)

3. *They resist by restricting output, deception, featherbedding, or sabotage.* Hamper (1992) reports what happened when the company removed a popular foreman because he was "too close to his work force" (p. 205):

> With a tight grip on the whip, the new bossman started riding the crew. No music. No Rivet Hockey. No horseplay. No drinking. No card playing. No working up the line. No leaving the department. No doubling-up. No this, no that. No questions asked.
>
> No way. After three nights of this imported bullyism, the boys had had their fill. Frames began sliding down the line minus parts. Rivets became cross-eyed. Guns mysteriously broke down. The repairmen began shipping the majority of the defects, unable to keep up with the repair load.

Sabotage was drastic, but it got the point across and brought the new foreman into line. The boss's strong-arm tactics engendered an equally strong reaction from workers. To survive, the foreman had to fall into step. Otherwise, he would be replaced, and the cycle would start anew.

4. *They try to climb the hierarchy to better jobs.* Moving up works for some, but there are rarely enough "better" jobs to go around. Many workers are reluctant to take promotions anyway. Hamper (1992) reports what happened to a coworker who tried to crack down after he was promoted to foreman: "For the next eight days, we made Calvin Moza's short-lived career switch sheer hell. Every time he'd walk the aisle, someone would pepper his steps with raining rivets. He couldn't make a move without the hammers banging and loud chants of 'suckass' and 'brown snout' ringin' in his ears. He got everything he deserved. There was simply no room for pity when dealing with a hypocrite who was about as pure as freshly driven snot" (p. 208). Hamper himself was lucky: he started to moonlight as a writer during one of the periodic layoffs punctuating his automaking career. Styling himself "The Rivethead," he wrote a column about factory life from the

inside. His writing eventually led to a best-selling book. Most of his buddies weren't nearly as fortunate.

5. *They form alliances (such as labor unions) to redress the power imbalance.* Union movements grow out of workers' desire for a more equal footing with management. Argyris cautioned, however, that leaders would run unions much like factories, because they knew no other way to manage. In the long run, employees' sense of powerlessness would change little. Ben Hamper, like most autoworkers, was a union member, yet the union is largely invisible in his accounts of life on the assembly line. He rarely sought union help and even less often got any. He appreciated wages and benefits earned at the bargaining table, but nothing in the labor agreement protected workers from boredom, frustration, or feeling powerless.

6. *They teach their children to believe that work is unrewarding and hopes for advancement are slim.* Hamper's account of life on the line is a vivid illustration for Argyris's contention that organizations treat adults like children. The company made halfhearted efforts to do otherwise: they assigned an employee to wander through the plant dressed in costume as "Howie Makem, the Quality Cat." (Howie was mostly greeted with groans, insults, and an occasional flying rivet.) Message boards were plastered with inspirational phrases such as "Riveting is fun." A usually invisible plant manager would give an annual speech promising to talk more with workers. All this hypocrisy took its toll: "Working the Rivet Line was like being paid to flunk high school the rest of your life. An adolescent time warp in which the duties of the day were just an underlying annoyance. No one really grew up here. No pretensions to being anything other than stunted brats clinging to rusty monkeybars. The popular diversions—Rivet Hockey, Dumpster Ball, intoxication, writing, rock 'n' roll—were just reinventions of youth. We were fumbling along in the middle of a long-running cartoon" (Hamper, 1992, p. 185). Researchers in the 1960s began to note that children of farmers grew up believing hard work paid off, while the offspring of urban blue-collar workers did not. As a result, many U.S. companies began to move facilities away from old industrial states like Michigan (where Ben Hamper worked) to more rural states like North Carolina and Tennessee, in search of employees who still embodied the "work ethic." Argyris predicted, however, that industry would eventually demotivate even the most committed workforce unless management practices changed.

Argyris and McGregor formed their views on the basis of observations of American organizations in the 1950s and 1960s.[1] Since then, investigators everywhere have documented similar conflicts between people and organizations. Orgogozo (1991), for example, contended that typical French management practices caused workers to feel humiliation, boredom, anger, and exhaustion "because they have no hope of being recognized and valued for what they do" (p. 101). She depicted relations between superiors and subordinates in France as tense and distant because "bosses do everything possible to protect themselves from the resentment that they generate" (p. 73).

Early on, human resource frame ideas were often overlooked or ignored by scholars and practicing managers. The frame's influence has grown with the realization that misuse of human resources depresses profits as well as people. Legions of consultants, managers, and researchers have pursued answers to the vexing human problems of organization. In the process, they have developed a range of strategies for improving the fit between individuals and organizations. These are discussed in depth in Chapter Seven.

HUMAN CAPACITY AND THE NEW EMPLOYMENT CONTRACT

The symbiotic relationship between individuals and organizations has evolved in response to changes in the needs and capabilities of both. In recent years, both sides of the person-organization relationship has become problematic as a result of dramatic trends pushing organizations in two contrasting directions. On the one hand, global competition, rapid technical change, and shorter product life cycles have produced a turbulent, intensely competitive environment placing an enormous premium on being free, fast, and facile: "*Free* means having components (work units and people) that are autonomous and able to respond to problems and opportunities in market segments. *Fast* means having the capability to assess and respond quickly to these situations. *Facile* means being able to change thinking practices and established routines in the light of new information or developments" (Mirvis and Hall, 1996, p. 74).

Handy (1993) sees organizations adopting a "shamrock" form, with three clusters of people:

1. A core group of managers and professionals with skills and capacities critical to the enterprise

2. The basic workforce, "increasingly working part-time or in shifts to provide the necessary flexibility" (p. 366)

3. A "contractual fringe" of people who do work that can be done more cheaply by outsiders

Beginning in the 1990s, more and more organizations have turned to downsizing, outsourcing, and reliance on part-time and temporary employees to cope with business fluctuations. In 1996, for example, Volkswagen opened a new manufacturing plant in Brazil with 80 percent of the workforce employed by subcontractors. Volkswagen's CEO described it as a "dream factory" that would revolutionize auto manufacturing (Schemo, 1996, p. C1). Analysts disagreed whether the new factory was lean or merely mean. Even in Japan, traditional notions of a lifetime career began to erode in the face of "a bloated work force, particularly in the white collar sector, which proved to be an economic drag prolonging [Japan's] economic troubles" (WuDunn, 1996, p. 8). Around the world, employees looking for career advice encountered a set of new mantras:

Job security is dead.

There is no guarantee of employment, only of employability.

Everyone is self-employed (Hakim, 1994).

If you're searching for excellence, become excellent at searching for new jobs (Paul Hirsch, cited in Kanter, 1989).

Focus on learning and credibility rather than promotions (Kanter, 1989).

Meanwhile, some of the same global forces are also pushing in another direction, toward a growing dependence on well-trained human capital. Organizations have become much more complex as a consequence of globalization and shifts to an information-intensive economy. More decentralized structures, like the networks discussed in Chapter Three and the webs of inclusion described in Chapter Four, are proliferating in response to greater complexity and turbulence. These new configurations depend on a higher level of skill, intelligence, and commitment across a broader spectrum of employees. A network of decentralized decision nodes is a blueprint for disaster if decision makers lack capacity or desire to make sensible choices. Skill requirements have been changing so fast that individuals are hard pressed to keep up. The result is a troubling gap: organizations struggle to find people who bring the skills and qualities needed, while individuals with yesterday's skills face dismal job prospects. "The evidence is that skill problems in the U.S. work force are widespread and growing. Moreover, there is little evidence that U.S. employers, for the most part, are doing what is required to address this problem" (Pfeffer, 1994, p. 17).

The shift from a production-intensive to an information-intensive economy is not helping to close the gap. There used to be far more jobs that involved making *things*. In the first three decades after World War II, high-paying work in developed nations was heavily concentrated in blue-collar work (Drucker, 1993). These jobs generally required little formal training and few specialized skills, but they afforded pay and benefits to sustain a reasonably comfortable and stable lifestyle. No more. Blue-collar workers accounted for more than one-third of the U.S. workforce in the late 1970s; by the mid-1990s, the percentage was less than one-fifth and still declining (Drucker, 1993; Handy, 1989). Surviving production jobs often require much higher skill levels than in the past. When U.S. automobile manufacturers began to replace retiring older workers in the mid-1990s, they emphasized quick minds more than strong bodies and put applicants "through a grueling selection process that emphasized mental acuity and communication skills" (Meredith, 1996, p. 1).

This skill gap is even greater in many developing nations. China's population of 1.3 billion people consists mostly of farmers and workers with old-economy skills. Beginning in the 1980s, China began a gradual shift to a market economy, reducing regulations, welcoming foreign investment, and selling off fading state-owned enterprises. The strategy worked economically. But even as China became one of the world's fastest-growing economies, with compound growth at approximately 7 percent in the five years from 1998 to 2002, unemployment grew even faster as state-owned enterprises succumbed to nimbler foreign competitors.

Trying to increase flexibility and employee skills simultaneously creates an increasingly vexing human resource dilemma. Should an organization seek flexibility and adaptability (through a downsized, outsourced, part-time workforce), or commitment and loyalty (through a long-term commitment to people)? Should it seek high skills (by hiring the best and training them well), or low costs (by hiring the cheapest and investing no more than necessary)?

LEAN AND MEAN: MORE BENEFITS THAN COSTS?

The advantages of a smaller, more flexible workforce seem compelling: lower costs, higher efficiency, and greater ability to respond to business cycle fluctuations. Many economists and business analysts argued that U.S. competitive success in the 1980s was directly related to corporate willingness to shed unnecessary staff (Lynch, 1996). For some companies, it worked well: "The formula of cutting staff and investing heavily in computerized equipment has paid off particularly in manufacturing, which enjoys a much greater productivity growth rate—more than 3 percent a year on average in the 1990s—than business as a whole. General Electric is a winner. So is the Chrysler Corporation. Chrysler made 1.72 million cars in the United States [in 1995], the same as in 1988, but with 9,000 fewer workers. The departure of those workers meant that the remaining 93,700 produced more cars per hour" (Uchitelle, 1996, p. 1).

Downsizing works best when a combination of new technology and smarter management produces significant productivity gains, making it possible for fewer people to do more. Yet even when downsizing works, it risks trading short-term gains for long-term decay. As mentioned in Chapter Two, "Chainsaw Al" Dunlap became a hero of the downsizing movement. As chief executive of Scott Paper, he more than doubled profits and market value. His strategy? Cut people—half the managers, half of research and development, and a fifth of blue-collar workers. For good measure, he told managers not to get involved in community activities, eliminated all corporate contributions to charity, and moved company headquarters from Philadelphia (where it had been for more than a century) to Boca Raton, Florida (where Dunlap had a new home). Financial outcomes were impressive, but employee morale sank, and Scott lost market share in every major product line. Dunlap did not stay around long enough to find out if he had sacrificed Scott's future for short-term gains. After less than two years on the job, he sold the company to its biggest competitor and walked away with almost $100 million for his efforts. On the same day that officials in Boca Raton received Dunlap's request for a $156,000 incentive grant for job creation, Scott's new owners announced that the Boca Raton headquarters would close (Byrne, 1996).

Companies have eliminated millions of jobs in recent decades, many in middle management (Pennar, 1996; Uchitelle and Kleinfeld, 1996), yet firms have found benefits elusive or nonexistent. A survey by the American Management Association found that less than half of downsized companies went on to report higher profits subsequently (Gertz and Baptista, 1995) and that cost cutting almost never led to profitable growth. Conversely, another survey found that stability rather than major change characterized 90 percent of firms that outperformed the average in their industry over a ten-year period ("Fire and Forget," 1996). Markels and Murray (1996) reported that downsizing too often turned into "dumbsizing": "Many firms continue to make flawed decisions—hasty, across-the-board cuts—that come back to haunt them, on the bottom line, in public relationships, in strained relationships with customers and suppliers, and in demoralized employees." In shedding staff, firms too often found that they had also sacrificed knowledge, skill, and loyalty (Reichheld, 1993, 1996).

Downsizing and outsourcing also have a corrosive effect on employee motivation and commitment. A 1996 poll found that 75 percent of U.S. workers felt that companies had become less loyal to their employees, and 64 percent felt that employees were less loyal to their companies (Kleinfeld, 1996). Workers reported the mood in the workplace was angrier and colleagues were more competitive. The resultant cynicism was palpable in many places. When Chemical Bank and Chase Manhattan went through a difficult merger in the mid-1990s, management tried to allay anxiety by publishing a periodic newsletter. Many employees found it "saccharine and platitudinous" (Kleinfeld, 1996, p. 8), and some skeptics began distributing their own more candid updates. One mock memo, ostensibly from the chief executive, offered the following answers to "frequently asked questions" (p. 8):

Q: Why am I being laid off, why is my career in ruins, why can't I sleep at night?
A: Your largely insignificant life is being sacrificed to bring into existence the best banking and financial services company in the world, bar none, without equal, post no bills, void where prohibited.
Q: When will I know if I'm being laid off?
A: You, you, you. Is that all you care about, you? Please understand that we need to think about "us," which probably doesn't include you. It's about time you started thinking about the greater whole, buddy. It should be an honor to be laid off.

All this foment has implications for both people and systems. For individuals, an age of downsizing and insecurity has personal and social costs: low wages, minimal benefits, job insecurity, stress, and burnout. Pfeffer (1994, 1998) and Lawler (1996) argue that a skilled and motivated workforce is a powerful source of strategic advantage precisely because few employers invest time and resources to develop a cadre of committed, talented employees. The most successful company in the U.S. airline industry in recent decades, Southwest Airlines, paid employees a competitive wage but had an enormous cost advantage over competitors because its highly committed workforce was far more productive. Competitors tried to imitate Southwest's approach but found that "the real difference is in the effort Southwest gets out of its people. That is very, very hard to duplicate" (Labich, 1994, p. 52).

INVESTING IN PEOPLE

The picture is not totally bleak, however. Many successful organizations have embraced creative and powerful ways to align individual and organizational needs. All these reflect the human resource frame's core assumptions by viewing the workforce as an investment rather than a cost. Pfeffer (1998) and Waterman (1994) argue that a pervasive characteristic of high-performing companies is doing a better job of understanding and responding to the needs of both employees and customers. As a result, they attract better people who are motivated to do a superior job. The downward spiral now takes a more positive upward spin.

Ewing Kauffman grew a pharmaceutical business begun in a Kansas City basement into a multibillion-dollar company (Morgan, 1995). His approach was heavily influenced by his personal experiences as a young pharmaceutical salesman:

> I worked on straight commission, receiving no salary, no expenses, no car, and no benefits in any way, shape, or form—just straight commission. By the end of the second year, my commission amounted to more than the president's salary. He didn't think that was right, so he cut my commission. By then I was Midwest sales manager and had other salesmen working for me under an arrangement whereby my commission was three percent of everything they sold. In spite of the cut in my commission, that year I still managed to make more than the president thought a sales manager should make. So this time he cut the territory, which was the same as taking away some of my income. I quit and started Marion Laboratories.

I based the company on a vision of what it would be. When we hired employees, they were referred to as "associates," and they shared in the success of the company. Once again, the two principles that have guided my entire career, which were based on my experience working for that very first pharmaceutical company, are these: "Those who produce should share in the profits," and "Treat others as you would be treated." (Kauffman, 1996, p. 40)

Few managers in 1950 shared Kauffman's faith, and there are still many skeptics. An urgent debate is under way about the future of the relationship between people and organizations. Some visions are apocalyptic: the "end of the job," a massive underclass of underemployed and unemployed, increasing polarization and social unrest (Rifkin, 1995). A more optimistic scenario depicts a continuing increase in the number of organizations worldwide that recognize the importance of human assets and find their own version of Kauffman's principles for success.

Ben Hamper's employer, General Motors, began to recognize the challenge in the late 1960s at a time when the company's profits were declining though sales were increasing. Just as Argyris and McGregor predicted, human resource issues were becoming increasingly expensive and difficult to manage. In 1972, GM's new plant at Lordstown, Ohio, became a notorious site of conflict between the individual and the system. Lordstown was GM's newest and most automated plant when it opened, with a design that emphasized sophisticated technology, rather than new approaches to engaging employees. A year later, new managers, brought in because the plant had failed to achieve production targets, added fuel to employee foment by cutting jobs rather than fixing the people problems. They downsized the workforce and increased the workload of those who remained. Wages and benefits for survivors were excellent. But the grievance rate soon soared, from five hundred complaints a year to more than five hundred a month. Employee sabotage slowed or stopped the assembly line multiple times, and the local union finally voted to strike over working conditions. One of the major issues was "doubling up." Cars moved down the line at a rate of one hundred per hour, meaning each worker normally had about thirty-six seconds to perform one job. Doubling up cut that to eighteen seconds. That was a fast pace, but, like Ben Hamper, many employees preferred working faster with an occasional break to facing another car every half-minute all day long. Management tried to eliminate the practice for fear it would produce inferior work. Asked about the strike, employees said wages were not the issue: "The job pays good, but it's driving me crazy." "It's just like the army. No, it's worse than the army, 'cause you're welded to the line. You just about need a pass to piss."

After the costly strike at Lordstown, GM began to get the message. In 1973, GM and the UAW signed a contract establishing a joint union-management National Committee to Improve the Quality of Working Life. Subsequently, GM joined a growing list of corporations worldwide that invested heavily in improving human resource management (Deal and Jenkins, 1994; Kanter, 1983; Lawler, 1986; Maccoby, 1981). The results at GM and elsewhere have sometimes been dramatic. We discuss some of the successes—and failures—in Chapter Seven, where we explore the state of the art in managing human assets.

The battle between the two competing philosophies just discussed—lean and mean versus invest in people—is still very much alive. In pipe manufacturing, two of the dominant players are cross-town rivals in Birmingham, Alabama. In managing people, they have followed very different roads. One of the companies is McWane, discussed at the beginning of the chapter. McWane has become notorious for its abysmal record on safety and environmental protection—nine deaths, four hundred safety violations, and 450 environmental violations between 1995 and 2002 (Barstow & Bergman, 2003b). The other is American Cast Iron Pipe (Acipco), ranked sixth in the *Fortune* 2002 survey of the best places to work in America (Levering and Moskowitz, 2003). Barstow and Bergman write that "several statistical measures show how different Acipco is from McWane. At some McWane plants, turnover rates approach 100 percent a year. Acipco—with a work force of about 3,000, three-fifths the size of McWane—has annual turnover of less than half a percent; 10,000 people recently applied for 100 openings. McWane has also been cited for 40 times more federal safety violations since 1995, OSHA records show" (2003c, p. A15).

Which of these two competing visions works better? Financially, it is difficult to judge, since both companies are privately held. We know only that both companies have succeeded in the same industry since early in the twentieth century. But in January 2003, at the same time that *Fortune* was lauding Acipco for its progressive human resource practices, the *New York Times* and a television documentary pilloried McWane for its callous disregard of both people and the law. Stay tuned for further updates; this story continues to evolve.

CONCLUSION

The human resource frame highlights the relationship between people and organizations. Organizations need people (for their energy, effort, and talent), and people need organizations (for the many intrinsic and extrinsic rewards they offer), but their respective needs are not always well aligned. When the fit between people and organizations is poor, one or both suffer: individuals may feel neglected or oppressed, and organizations sputter because individuals withdraw their efforts or even work against organizational purposes. Conversely, a good fit benefits both: individuals find meaningful and satisfying work, and organizations get the talent and energy they need to succeed.

Global competition, turbulence, and rapid change have heightened an enduring organizational dilemma: Is it better to be lean and mean, or to invest in people? A variety of strategies to reduce the workforce—downsizing, outsourcing, use of temporary and part-time workers—have been widely applied to reduce costs and increase flexibility. They risk a loss of talent and loyalty that leads to organizations that are mediocre, even if flexible. Emerging evidence suggests that downsizing has often produced disappointing results. Many highly successful organizations have gone in another direction: investing in people on the premise that a highly motivated and skilled workforce is a powerful competitive advantage.

NOTE

1. Argyris, Maslow, McGregor, and their contemporaries built on a tradition with roots going back well into the nineteenth century. In *Capital*, Karl Marx (1887) posited his own version of a fundamental conflict between individual and organization: "The capitalist gets rich, not like the miser, in proportion to his personal labour and restricted consumption, but at the same rate as he squeezes out the labour-power of others, and enforces on the laborer abstinence from all life's enjoyments." Marx did not foresee the twentieth-century realization that conflict and exploitation are fundamental issues in *organization*, regardless of economic system. That these problems were at least as severe in communist societies is illustrated by a joke popular among Soviet workers in the 1980s: "We pretend to work, and they pretend to pay us." In China in the early twenty-first century, many workers now eagerly seek to escape the state sector and go to work for capitalist firms such as Sony and Motorola because the jobs are better.

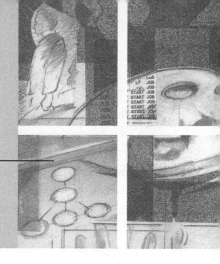

CHAPTER 7

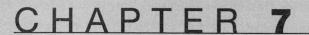

Improving Human Resource Management

Separated by centuries, Bill Gates (born in Seattle in 1955) and Robert Owen (born in Wales in 1771) obviously never met but still had much in common. Both were wildly successful entrepreneurs before the age of thirty. Both exploited the day's hot technology: software for Gates, spinning mills for Owen. Both were highly controversial. Gates, founder of Microsoft, the software giant, was widely envied as well as feared for his wealth and take-no-prisoners approach to competition. Owen was bitterly loathed and attacked for being the only capitalist of his time to conclude that it was not good for business to have eight-year-olds working a thirteen-hour factory shift. At his New Lanark, Scotland, knitting mill, bought in 1799, Owen took a new approach:

> Owen provided clean, decent housing for his workers and their families in a community free of controllable disease, crime, and gin shops. He took young children out of his factory and put them in a school he founded. There he invented preschool, day care, and the brand of progressive education that stresses learning as a pleasurable experience (along with the first adult night school). The entire business world was shocked when he prohibited corporal punishment in his factory and dumbfounded when he retrained his supervisors in humane disciplinary practices. While giving his workers an extremely high standard of living compared to other workers of the era, Owen was making a fortune at New Lanark. This conundrum drew twenty thousand visitors between 1815 and 1820. (O'Toole, 1995, pp. 201, 206)

Owen anticipated the growing importance of human capital. He tried to convince fellow capitalists that investing in people could produce an even greater return than investing in machinery. Eager to spread his heretical philosophy, Owen left New Lanark and entered the political arena. He thereafter encountered continual frustration that ended, ultimately, in failure. Though he attracted a number of admirers (including Thomas Jefferson, Ralph Waldo Emerson, and Karl Marx), the business world rejected his ideas *in toto*. He was portrayed as a wild radical whose ideas hurt the very people he wanted to help (O'Toole, 1995).

Owen was 150 years ahead of his time. Only in the late twentieth century did business leaders come to understand that investing in people was a key to successful financial performance. In recent years, periodic waves of restructuring and downsizing have raised age-old questions about the relationship between the individual and the organization. A number of persuasive reports suggest Owen was right: one sure route to long-term success *is* investing in employees and responding to their needs (Applebaum, Bailey, Berg, and Kalleberg, 2000; Collins and Porras, 1994; Deal and Jenkins, 1994; Farkas and De Backer, 1996; Kotter and Heskett, 1992; Lawler, 1996; Levering and Moskowitz, 1993; Pfeffer, 1994; 1998; Waterman, 1994). Yet many organizations still don't believe it, and numerous others have trouble putting it into practice:

> Something very strange is occurring in organizational management. Over the past decade or so, numerous rigorous studies conducted both within specific industries and in samples of organizations that cross industries have demonstrated the enormous economic returns obtained through the implementation of what are variously called high involvement, high performance, or high commitment management practices. Furthermore, much of this research serves to validate earlier writing on participative management and employee involvement. But even as these research results pile up, trends in actual management practice are, in many instances, moving in a direction exactly *opposite* to what this growing body of evidence prescribes. (Pfeffer, 1998, p. xv)

Such resistance has a long history. Owen encountered it in the nineteenth century, as did Elton Mayo in the early twentieth. Mayo demonstrated that an occasional rest break made textile plant workers more productive. As soon as Mayo left, foremen killed the breaks, and productivity plunged (Trahair, 2001). Why do managers persist in pursuing less effective strategies when better ones work so well?

For one thing, managers operating with Theory X assumptions fear losing control or indulging workers. For another, investing in people is a long-term process. It needs time and persistence to yield results. Faced with relentless pressure to get immediate results, managers too often conclude that slashing costs, or changing strategy, or reorganizing has a better chance of producing a quick hit. Pfeffer (1998) believes another barrier is the increased dominance of a "financial" perspective portraying the organization simply as a portfolio of financial assets. In this view, people issues are subjective, soft, and secondary in comparison to hard financial numbers.

Despite such barriers, many organizations get it right. They're not perfect, but they're better than most. That's usually good enough so both an organization and its workforce come out ahead. The company prospers because of having a more talented, motivated, loyal, and free-spirited team than its competitors. Its employees are more productive and innovative; they provide better customer service. They are less likely to make costly errors or to jump ship the first time someone offers them a better deal. Work is more fun and more rewarding. That's a potent edge—in sports, business, or anywhere else. Each organization with sensitive people management has its own unique approach, but most variations rest on a set of generic strategies, summarized in Table 7.1 and examined in depth in the remainder of the chapter.

BUILD AND IMPLEMENT AN HR PHILOSOPHY

An effective human resource philosophy provides overall guidance and direction. Principles come alive through activities and practices, making the commitment a reality.

Develop a Public Statement of the HR Philosophy

Many, if not most, organizations either lack an explicit human resource philosophy or ignore the one they espouse. Yet success often hinges on a thoughtful, explicit strategy for managing people. In the 1990s, Federal Express explained the company's philosophy in its *Manager's Guide:* "Take care of our people; they in turn will deliver the impeccable service demanded by our customers who will reward us with the profitability necessary to secure

TABLE 7.1. Basic Human Resource Strategies.

Human Resource Principle	Specific Practices
Build and implement an HRM strategy	Develop a shared philosophy for managing people Build systems and practices to implement the philosophy
Hire the right people	Know what you want Be selective
Keep them	Reward well Protect jobs Promote from within Share the wealth
Invest in them	Invest in learning Create development opportunities
Empower them	Provide information and support Encourage autonomy and participation Redesign work Foster self-managing teams Promote egalitarianism
Promote diversity	Be explicit and consistent about the organization's diversity philosophy Hold managers accountable

our future. People-Service-Profit, these three words are the very foundation of Federal Express."

Build Systems and Practices to Implement the Philosophy

FedEx's philosophy might have been little more than words if the company were not so diligent about reinforcing it. Managers were rated annually by subordinates on a leadership index containing questions about how well they helped subordinates, listened to their ideas, and showed them respect. Managers with subpar scores had to repeat the process in six months—a distinction to be avoided at all costs. Collectively, if the index fell below the corporate standard, the top three hundred managers lost their bonuses (Waterman, 1994).

HIRE THE RIGHT PEOPLE: KNOW WHAT YOU WANT AND BE SELECTIVE

Strong companies are clear about the kinds of people they want. They hire only those who fit the mold. Southwest Airlines became the most successful firm in its industry by hiring people with positive attitudes and interpersonal skills, particularly a good sense of humor (Farkas and De Backer, 1996; Labich, 1994; Levering and Moskowitz, 1993). The word is out, and enthusiastic applicants clamor for jobs at Southwest. The airline can be selective, with well over a hundred applicants for every job opening. A group of pilots applying for a job were asked to change into Bermuda shorts before hiring interviews. One pilot refused. He did not get a job at Southwest.

Serving a much smaller, more upscale clientele than Southwest, the Ritz Carlton hotel group uses a careful selection process to hire only those who can commit themselves to its basic philosophy: "We are ladies and gentlemen serving ladies and gentlemen." A focus on customer service enabled Enterprise Rent-a-Car to become the fastest-growing company in its industry. Enterprise wooed its midmarket clientele by deliberately hiring "from the half of the class that makes the top half possible"—college graduates more successful on the playing field and at fraternity parties than in the classroom. Enterprise was looking more for people skills than raw intelligence (Pfeffer, 1998, p. 71). In contrast, Microsoft's formidably bright CEO, Bill Gates, insisted on "intelligence or smartness over anything else, even, in many cases, experience" (Stross, 1996, p. 162). A study of highly successful midsized companies in Germany (Simon, 1996) found that a carefully selected, highly motivated workforce was a key strength. Companies in Simon's sample had very little employee turnover—except among new hires: "Many new employees leave, or are terminated, shortly after joining the work force, both sides having learned that a worker does not fit into the firm's culture and cannot stand its pace" (p. 199).

KEEP EMPLOYEES

To get people they want, companies such as SAS Institute, Costco, and Southwest Airlines start by offering attractive pay and benefits. To keep them, they protect jobs, promote from within, and give people a piece of the action.

Reward Well

"In a cavernous, no-frills retail warehouse setting, where bulk sales determine stockholder profits, knowledgeable, dependable service usually isn't part of the low-cost package. Don't tell that to Costco Wholesale Corp., where employee longevity and high morale are as commonplace as overloaded shopping carts. 'We like to turn over our inventory faster than our people,' said Jim Sinegal, president and CEO of Costco, a membership warehouse store headquartered in Washington State with more than 300 stores across the country" (Montgomery, 2000).

Costco has a weird success formula: pay employees more and charge customers less than its biggest competitor, Sam's Club (a subsidiary of retail giant Wal-Mart). It sounds like a foolproof recipe for failure, but in recent years Costco has been the industry's most profitable firm. How? In CEO Sinegal's view, the answer was easy: "If you pay the best wages, you get the highest productivity. By our industry standards, we think we've got the best people and the best productivity when we do that." Compared with its competitors, Costco achieved higher sales volumes, faster inventory turn, and lower shrinkage ("Average Sales Per Store . . ., 2002"). It all added up to industry-leading profits and customer satisfaction (American Customer Satisfaction Index, 2000).

Costco is a specific example of a more general principle: pay should reflect value added. Overcompensating people who contribute little of value is a losing proposition. But skilled, motivated, and involved employees justify high pay for their exemplary contributions (Lawler, 1996).

To get and keep good people, selective companies also offer attractive benefits. Osterman (1995) found, for example, that firms with "high-commitment" human resource practices were more likely to offer work and family benefits such as day care and flexible hours. Software powerhouse SAS is an example:

> In the software industry, where turnover rates hover around 20%, SAS maintains a level below 4%, which results in about $50 million a year in HR-related savings, according to a recent Harvard Business School study. In addition, the company believes that its stable workforce enables it to produce new versions of its data-mining and statistical-analysis software more cheaply and efficiently. "The well-being of our company is linked to the well-being of our employees," says SAS CEO Jim Goodnight. "Employees determine whether we flourish or

fail. If we make the effort and invest resources in our employees' professional welfare, every-one wins—the employee, the customer, and the company." Some of those benefits include low-cost day-care facilities for 700 kids; a cafeteria outfitted with high chairs, so employees can eat lunch with their children; free access to a 36,000-square-foot gym, a putting green, onsite massages; and an office with a door for every white-collar employee. (Stein, 2000)

One of the most popular benefits at FedEx (a perennial honoree on the *Fortune* list of America's one hundred best places to work) is "jump-seating"—a free ride in the cockpit of a FedEx plane anywhere the company flies. One service agent in San Francisco averaged more than one hundred thousand miles a year during her first eleven years at FedEx (Levering, 2001).

Protect Jobs

Job security seems an anachronism today, a relic of old slow-moving, paternalistic times. In a turbulent, highly competitive environment, how is long-term commitment to employees possible? It's not easy and not always doable. Companies (and even countries) historically offering long-term security have abandoned their commitment in the face of severe economic reversals; AT&T, Delta Airlines, and IBM are notable corporate examples. At the national level, the largest downsizing process in history has been occurring in China. Economic reforms have forced state-owned enterprises (SOEs) to sink or swim in a competitive market. Many have been foundering and forced to abandon the guarantee of lifetime employment (Smith, 2002). In three years, from 1998 to 2001, a government report counted more than 25 million layoffs from SOEs, many of them unskilled older workers. About a third of these remained unemployed in 2002 ("China Says 'No' . . .," 2002; Lingle, 2002; Smith, 2002).

Still, many firms continue to honor job security as a cornerstone of their human resource philosophy. Publix is an employee-owned, Fortune 500 supermarket chain in the southeastern United States. The company has never had a layoff since its 1930 founding. Not coincidentally, Publix, in 2002, had the highest rating of customer satisfaction in its industry, for the eighth consecutive year. Similarly, Lincoln Electric, the world's largest manufacturer of arc welding equipment, has, since 1914, honored a policy that no employee with more than three years of service would be laid off. This commitment was tested in the 1980s, when the company experienced a 40 percent year-to-year drop in demand for its products. To avoid layoffs, production workers were converted to salespeople. They canvassed businesses rarely reached by the company's regular distribution channels. "Not only did these people sell arc welding equipment in new places to new users but since much of the profit of this equipment comes from the sale of replacement parts, Lincoln subsequently enjoyed greater market penetration and greater sales as a consequence" (Pfeffer, 1994, p. 47). Japan's Mazda, facing similar circumstances, had a parallel experience: "At the end of the year, when awards were presented to the best salespeople, the company discovered that the top ten were all former factory workers. They could explain the product effectively, and when business picked up, the fact that factory workers had experience talking to customers yielded useful ideas about product characteristics" (Pfeffer, 1994, p. 47).

Promote from Within

Costco has an explicit target of promoting at least 80 percent of its managers from inside. Some 90 percent of managers at FedEx started in a nonmanagement job. Promoting from within offers several advantages (Pfeffer, 1998):

- It encourages both management and employees to invest time and resources in upgrading skills.
- It is a powerful performance incentive.
- It fosters trust and loyalty.
- It capitalizes on knowledge and skills of veteran employees.
- It reduces serious errors by newcomers unfamiliar with history and proven ways.
- It increases the likelihood that employees will think longer-term and avoid impetuous, short-sighted decisions. Collins and Porras (1994) found that highly successful corporations almost never hired a chief executive from the outside; less effective companies did so regularly.

Share the Wealth

Many employees feel little responsibility for an organization's performance. They expect any gains in efficiency and profitability to benefit executives and shareholders. People-oriented organizations have devised a variety of ways to link employee rewards more directly to corporate productivity. These include gain sharing, profit sharing, and employee stock ownership plans (ESOPs). Scanlon plans, first introduced in the 1930s, give workers an incentive to reduce costs and improve efficiency by offering them a share of any gains. Profit-sharing plans give employees a bonus commensurate with the firm's overall profitability or the performance of their local unit.

Generally, both gain-sharing and profit-sharing plans have been shown to have a positive impact on performance and profitability. Kanter (1989) suggests gain-sharing plans have spread slowly because they require significant changes: cross-unit teams, suggestion systems, and in particular more open communication of financial information to employees. Similar barriers have slowed the progress of ESOPs: "Evidence shows that, to be effective, ownership has to be combined with ground-floor efforts to involve employees in decisions through schemes such as work teams and quality-improvement groups. Many companies have been doing this, of course, including plenty without ESOPs. But employee-owners often begin to expect rights that other groups of shareholders have: a voice in broad corporate decisions, board seats, and voting rights. And that's where the trouble can start, since few executives seem comfortable with this level of power-sharing" (Bernstein, 1996, p. 101).

The ups and downs of employee ownership are illustrated at United Airlines. After employees took a pay cut of 15 percent in exchange for 55 percent of the company and three of its twelve board seats in 1994, the company's stock more than doubled in the next two years. United gained in profits, productivity, and market share in the years immediately following the employee buyout (Chandler, 1996). But the airline never fully overcame a long history of combative employee relations. Although United grew impressively in the boom years of the 1990s, everything unraveled after the September 11 terror attacks. As the airline began to burn cash, management's push for cost savings ran up against the unions' commitment to protecting jobs. After failing to obtain a government bailout, United was forced to declare bankruptcy in December 2002.

Bonus and profit-sharing plans spread rapidly in the boom years of the 1990s. Top managers were more likely than other employees to benefit, but many successful firms spread benefits more widely. Plans based awards on overall corporate performance, or subunit performance, or a mixture. Some targeted specific priorities, such as innovation and developing new businesses. But skeptics noted a significant downside risk to profit-sharing plans: they work well so long as there are rewards but breed disappointment and anger if the company experiences a financial downturn. United Airlines employees were enthusiastic when the stock soared to almost $100 a share but crushed when bankruptcy made their shares virtually worthless.

INVEST IN EMPLOYEES

As products, markets, and organizations become more complex, the value of people's knowledge and skills increases. Undertrained workers hurt organizations in many ways: shoddy quality, poor service, higher costs, and costly mistakes. Pfeffer (1994), for example, reports that a high proportion of petrochemical industry accidents involve contract employees. Yet many organizations are reluctant to invest in developing their human capital. Training costs are immediate and easy to measure; benefits are more elusive and long-term. Training temporary or contract workers carries added disincentives. Still, many companies report a sizable return on their training investment. An internal study at Motorola, for instance, found a gain of twenty-nine dollars for every dollar invested in sales training (Waterman, 1994).

The human resource–oriented organization also recognizes that learning must occur on the job as well as in the classroom. Carnaud et Metal Box in France, the world's third largest packaging company, puts great emphasis on creating a learning organization: "Learning in an organization takes place when three elements are in place: good mentors who teach others, a management system that lets people try new things as much as possible, and a very good exchange with the environment" (Aubrey and Tilliette, 1990, pp. 144–145). Carnaud's chief executive, Jean-Marie Descarpentries, felt the biggest flaw in managers was their failure to be as aggressive and systematic about learning as they needed to be.

At Ritz Carlton, employees must be recertified annually and participate in a daily "lineup," where they review the company's service credo, with an emphasis on the "basic of the day." Ask any Ritz Carlton employee about today's basic—it might be "uncompromising standards of cleanliness," "never lose a client," "smile—we're on stage," or any of twenty principles. They'll know. If not, they'll be embarrassed and look quickly for a copy of the credo to refresh their memory.

EMPOWER EMPLOYEES

Progressive organizations empower employees as well as invest in their development. Empowerment includes making information available, but it doesn't stop there. It also involves encouraging autonomy and participation, redesigning work, fostering teams, promoting egalitarianism, and giving work meaning.

Provide Information and Support

A key factor in Enron's dizzying collapse was that no one understood its financial picture. Wall Street analysts, the board of directors, perhaps even the chief executive and auditors were operating in the dark. Eight months before the crash, *Fortune* reporter Bethany McLean asked new CEO Jeffrey Skilling, "How, exactly, does Enron make money?" She was attacked as incompetent and unethical, and Enron executives tried unsuccessfully to get *Fortune* to kill her story. Her March 2001 article in *Fortune* pointed out that the financial reports were almost impenetrable and the stock price could implode if the company missed its earnings forecasts.

Over the last twenty years, a very different philosophy, "open-book management," has begun to take root in many progressive companies. This movement is inspired by the near-death experience of an obscure plant in Missouri, Springfield Remanufacturing (now SRC Holdings). SRC was created in 1983 when a group of managers and employees purchased it from International Harvester for about $100,000 in cash and almost $9 million in debt. It was one of history's most highly leveraged buyouts (Pfeffer, 1998; Stack and Burlingham, 1994). Less awesome levels of debt had strangled many other companies, and CEO Jack Stack figured the only way the business could make it was with everyone's best efforts. He developed the open-book philosophy as a way to survive. The system is built around three basic principles (Case, 1995):

1. All employees at every level should see and learn to understand financial and performance measures. All the important numbers should be readily available, and all employees should get Financial Literacy 101 so they can understand what the numbers mean.

2. All employees are encouraged to think like owners—doing whatever they can to improve the numbers.

3. Everyone gets a piece of the action—a stake in the company's financial success.

Since SRC's initial success, companies in a variety of industries have had similar success stories. In 1984, Bob Frey and a partner bought Cin-Made, a small, low-tech container manufacturer with a history of weak results and poor employee relations. In the early months after taking over, Frey employed traditional, get-tough methods of improving performance. He stood over people with a stopwatch, cut their pay, and insulted their intelligence. This triggered massive mistrust, soaring grievances, and a bitter strike. Frey finally figured there had to be a better way. He started to hold monthly "state of the business" meetings where he shared financial results and explained what they meant. He put in a profit-sharing program. Employees were deeply skeptical at first, but a shared sense that "we're all in this together" gradually took root. Eventually, employees became deeply involved in decision making. Productivity more than doubled, and profit sharing expanded to more than a third of workers' annual pay.

Open-book management works for several reasons. First, it sends a clear signal that management actually trusts people. Second, it is a powerful incentive for employees to contribute. They can see the big picture—how their work affects the bottom line and how the bottom line affects them. Finally, it furnishes information they need to do a better job. If efficiency is dropping, scrap is increasing, or a certain product has stopped selling, employees know right away. They are then in a better position to do something about it.

Encourage Autonomy and Participation

Information is necessary but not sufficient for fully engaging employees. The work itself needs to offer opportunities for autonomy, influence, and intrinsic rewards.

The classical approach assumed that managers made decisions and employees did what they were told. This made employees dependent on their boss, with little control over what they did or how. They were treated like children, and as McGregor and Argyris predicted, they tended to behave that way. As more companies faced up to the costs in motivation, morale, and productivity, they began to develop programs that were often given the generic label *participation*. The idea is to give workers more opportunity to influence decisions about their work and working conditions. The results have often been remarkable.

A classic illustration comes from a group of manual workers—all women—who painted dolls in a toy factory (Whyte, 1955). In a reengineered process, each woman took a toy from a tray, painted it, and put it on a passing hook. The women received an hourly rate, a group bonus, and a learning bonus. Although management expected little difficulty with the new system, production was disappointing and morale worse. Workers complained that the room was too hot and the hooks moved too fast.

Reluctantly, the foreman followed a consultant's advice and met face to face with the employees. After hearing the women's complaints, the foreman agreed to bring in fans. Though he and the industrial engineer who designed the new manufacturing process expected no benefit, it made a significant improvement in morale. Discussions continued, and after several meetings, the employees came up with a radical suggestion: let them control the belt's speed. The engineer argued vehemently against this; he had already carefully calculated the optimal speed. The foreman was also skeptical but, against the engineer's protests, agreed to give the women's suggestion a try. The employees developed a complicated production schedule: start slow at the beginning of the day, increase the speed once they had warmed up, slow it down before lunch, and so on.

Results of this inadvertent experiment in participation were stunning. Morale skyrocketed. Production increased far beyond the engineer's most optimistic calculations. The women's bonuses escalated so much that they were earning more than many workers with significantly higher levels of skill and experience. For that reason, the experiment ended unhappily. The women's production and high pay became a problem because higher-skilled workers in the rest of the plant protested. To restore harmony, management reverted to the engineer's earlier recommendation: a fixed speed for the belt. Production plunged, morale plummeted, and most of the women quit.

Worldwide, satisfying examples of successful participative management experiments have multiplied. A Venezuelan example is illustrative. Historically, the nation's health care was provided by a two-tier system: small, high-quality, private health care for the affluent and a large, public system for everyone else. The public system, operated by the national ministry of health, was in a state of perpetual crisis. It suffered from overcentralization, chronic deficits, poor hygiene, decaying facilities, and theft of everything from cotton balls to X-ray machines (Palumbo, 1991).

A small group of health care providers founded Ascardio to provide cardiac care in one part of rural Venezuela (Palumbo, 1991; Malavé, 1995). Participative management helped Ascardio become an extraordinary success with remarkably high standards of patient care: "The Ascardio style requires, beyond mastery of a technical specialty, the willingness to get involved in an environment of team decision making instead of working in isolation. This is particularly evident in the General Assembly, which brings together doctors, technical personnel, workers, board members, and community representatives (none of whom are physicians). In its monthly meetings, the Assembly discusses everything from the poor performance of a doctor to the repercussions of giving salary increases decreed by the President of Venezuela" (Malavé, 1995, p. 16).

Research on participation shows it to be one of the most promising ways to increase both morale and productivity (Appelbaum, Bailey, Berg, and Kalleberg, 2000; Blumberg, 1968; Katzell and Yankelovich, 1975; Levine and Tyson, 1990). A systematic recent study (Appelbaum, Bailey, Berg, and Kalleberg, 2000) of practices in three industries—steel, apparel, and medical instruments—found that participation was consistently associated with higher performance. Workers in "high performance" plants had more confidence in management, liked their jobs better, and were paid better. The authors suggested participation improves productivity through two mechanisms: increasing the effectiveness of individual workers and enhancing organizational learning (Appelbaum, Bailey, Berg, and Kalleberg, 2000).

But even when it works, participation often creates the need for systemic changes resisted by other parts of the organization. Moreover, participative management too often exists more in rhetoric than in reality (Argyris, 1998; Argyris and Schön, 1974, 1996). Efforts at fostering participation have failed for two main reasons: (1) difficulty in designing workable participative systems and (2) managers' ambivalence—they espouse participation but fear subordinates will abuse it. Without realizing what they are doing, managers mandate participation in a controlling, top-down fashion, sending mixed messages of the form, "You make the decision, so long as it's what I want. Do what you think is right, but make sure I agree." Such contradictions virtually guarantee failure.

Redesign Work

In the name of efficiency and scientific management, many organizations spent much of the twentieth century trying to drive out the human element by designing jobs to be simple, repetitive, and low-skill. When this approach also dampened motivation and enthusiasm, management's habitual response was to blame workers for being uncooperative. It took several decades before opinion began to shift toward the view that problems might have more to do with the jobs than the workers. One key moment occurred when a young English social scientist took a trip to a coal mine:

> In 1949 trade unionist and former coal miner Ken Bamforth made a trip back to the colliery where he used to work in South Yorkshire. At the time, he was a postgraduate fellow being trained for industrial fieldwork at the Tavistock Institute for Social Research in London and had been encouraged to return to his former industry to report any new perceptions of work organization. At a newly opened coal seam, Bamforth noticed an interesting development indeed. Technical improvements in roof control had made it possible to mine "shortwall," and the men in the pits, with the support of their union, proposed to reorganize the labor process. Instead of each miner being responsible for a separate task, as had become characteristic of mechanized "longwall" mining, workers organized relatively autonomous groups that rotated tasks and shifts among themselves with a minimum of supervision. To take advantage of new technical opportunities, they reinvigorated a tradition of small group autonomy and responsibility dominant in the days before mechanization. (Sirianni, 1995)

Bamforth's observations helped to spur the "socio-technical systems" approach (Rice, 1953; Trist and Bamforth, 1951). Trist and Bamforth (1951) noted that the long-wall method isolated individual workers and disrupted old informal groupings that fostered powerful social support in the difficult and dangerous environment of a coal mine. They argued for the creation of "composite" work groups. Each individual was cross-trained in multiple jobs so each group could work relatively autonomously. Their approach made relatively little headway in England in the 1950s but got a major boost when two of Tavistock's researchers (Eric Trist and Fred Emery) were invited to Norway by Einar Thorsrud of the Norwegian Industrial Democracy Project, a joint labor-management effort to give workers more impact on their work.

At about the same time, in a pioneering American study, Frederick Herzberg (1966) asked employees to talk about their best and worst work experiences. "Good feelings" stories featured achievement, recognition, responsibility, advancement, and learning; Herzberg called these *motivators*. "Bad feelings" stories centered around company policy and administration, supervision, and working conditions; Herzberg labeled them *hygiene factors.* Motivators dealt mostly with the work itself; hygiene factors clustered around the work context. Attempts to motivate workers with better pay and fringe benefits, improved working conditions, communications programs, or human relations training missed the point, said Herzberg. He called such efforts "KITA motivators"—the belief that a kick in the tail is the best way to get people to work harder. Herzberg saw job enrichment as central to motivation but distinguished it from simply adding more dull tasks to a tedious job. Enrichment meant giving workers more freedom and authority, more feedback, and greater challenges. It made them more accountable and let them use more skills.

Hackman and his colleagues (Hackman and Oldham, 1980) extended Herzberg's ideas by identifying three critical factors in job redesign: "Individuals need (1) to see their work as meaningful and worthwhile, more likely when jobs produce a visible and useful 'whole,' (2) to use discretion and judgment so they can feel personally accountable for results, and (3) to receive feedback about their efforts so they can improve" (Hackman, Oldham, Janson, and Purdy, 1987, p. 320).

Experiments with job redesign have grown significantly over the last several decades. Many efforts have been successful, and some resoundingly so (Kopelman, 1985; Lawler, 1986; Yorks and Whitsett, 1989; Pfeffer, 1994; Parker and Wall, 1998). Typically, job enrichment has a stronger impact on quality than on productivity. The reason: there is more satisfaction in doing good work than in simply doing more work (Lawler, 1986). Most workers prefer redesigned jobs, though some still favor old ways. Hackman emphasized that employees with "high growth needs" would welcome job enrichment, while others with "low growth needs" would not.

Recent years have witnessed a gradual reduction in dull, routine, and unchallenging jobs. Routine work is either redesigned or turned over to machines and computers. But significant obstacles block the progress of job enrichment, and monotonous jobs will not soon disappear. One barrier is the lingering assumption that jobs should be organized around technical imperatives, and that repetition makes people more efficient. Another barrier is the enduring belief that workers produce more in a Theory X environment. A third barrier is economic; many jobs cannot be altered significantly without major investments in redesigning physical plant and machinery.

A fourth barrier was illustrated in the doll manufacturing experiment. When it works, job enrichment leads to pressures for basic systemwide changes. Workers on enriched jobs often develop a higher opinion of themselves. They may demand more from the organization—sometimes increased benefits, sometimes new career opportunities and training for new tasks (Lawler, 1986).

Foster Self-Managing Teams

From the beginning, the sociotechnical systems perspective emphasized a close connection between work design and teamwork. Another influential early advocate of teaming was Rensis Likert, who argued in 1961 that an organization chart should depict not a hierarchy of individual jobs but a set of interconnected teams. Each team would be highly effective in its own right and linked to other teams via individuals who served as "linking pins." It took decades for such ideas to take hold, but an increasing number of firms now embrace the idea. One is Whole Foods Markets, a very successful, fast-growing grocery chain based in Texas. Whole Foods even cites the team concept in its annual report: "Everyone who works at Whole Foods Market is a Team Member. This reflects our philosophy that we are all partners in the shared mission of giving our customers the very best in products and services. The stores are organized in self-managing work teams that are responsible and accountable for their own performance" (cited in Pfeffer, 1998, p. 76).

Each Whole Foods store is a profit center, organized into about ten self-managed teams. Team leaders in each store make up another team, as do the store leaders in each region and the company's six regional vice presidents. New hires have to be approved by two-thirds of team members. An elaborate system of peer review puts strong emphasis on people's learning from one another (Pfeffer, 1998).

More and more firms around the world (including Cummins Engine, Procter & Gamble, and Saturn in the United States; SAP, the enterprise software firm in Germany; and Matsushita and Toyota in Japan) are experimenting with autonomous teams. Some experiments have been conducted in existing facilities, others in facilities designed from the outset to accommodate work teams.

As at Whole Foods, the central idea is giving a group responsibility for a meaningful whole—a product, subassembly, or complete service—with ample autonomy and resources and collective accountability for results. Teams meet regularly to discuss and decide work assignments, scheduling, and current production. Supervision typically rests with a team leader, either appointed or left to emerge from the group. Levels of discretion vary. At one extreme, a team may have authority to hire, fire, determine pay rates, specify work methods, and manage inventory. Decisions are made with the assistance of a computerized system generating up-to-date information on the team's results. In other cases, the team's scope of decision making is narrower, focusing on issues of production, quality, and work methods.

The team concept rarely works unless accompanied by ample training. Workers need to learn group skills and a broader range of technical skills so that each person understands and can perform someone else's job. "Pay for skills" often gives teams an incentive to keep expanding the range of competencies:

> At Topeka's General Foods pet food plant . . . new employees are paid a starting rate, and then advance one pay grade for each job they learn. All jobs earn equal amounts of additional pay, and they can be learned in any sequence. All in all, pay for skills is a clever approach. It stresses individual responsibility but does not have the drawbacks of other pay-for-performance systems that pit team member against team member in contention for the highest ratings. Because there is no limit to the number who can reach the highest pay levels, there is little formal inducement to maintain a monopoly of skills or withhold training from newcomers in order to preserve a superior position. (Kanter, 1989, pp. 248–249)

Promote Egalitarianism

Participative management is often viewed as a matter of style and climate rather than as a way to share authority. Managers—whether participative or not—still make key decisions. Broader, more egalitarian sharing of power is resisted worldwide. Managers have particularly resisted organizational democracy, the idea of building worker participation into formal structure and thus protecting it from managerial discretion. Most U.S. firms report one or another form of employee involvement, but many are approaches (such as a suggestion box or quality circle) that "do not fundamentally change the level of decision-making authority extended to the lowest levels of the organization" (Ledford, 1993, p. 148). Pfeffer (1998) and Ledford (1993) both observe that techniques for workforce involvement are less visible in American companies than evidence of their effectiveness would warrant.

A more formal effort to democratize the workplace has been attempted in some parts of Europe. In the 1950s, the communist government in Yugoslavia instituted a formal system of worker self-management. Elected workers' councils had the right to veto management decisions and even to fire the managers. The system ultimately gave way to political turmoil and national disintegration, but in the years after it was first established, the Yugoslav economy grew at an unprecedented rate (Bolman and Deal, 1984). Sweden and Norway legally mandated worker participation in decision making in the 1970s. In 1977, Norway passed a law against alienating and dehumanizing jobs and requiring quality-of-work-life councils in Norwegian firms (Elden, 1983, 1986). Major Scandinavian corporations pioneered efforts to democratize and improve the quality of work life. In Kalmar, Sweden, Volvo built one of the world's first plants designed to accommodate self-managing work groups.

The Brazilian manufacturer Semco offers a dramatic illustration of organizational democracy in action (Killian, Perez and Siehl, 1998; Semler, 1993). Ricardo Semler took over the company from his father in the 1980s and gradually evolved an unorthodox philosophy of management:

> The key to management is to get rid of all the managers.
>
> The key to getting work done on time is to stop wearing a watch.
>
> The best way to invest corporate profits is to give them to the employees.
>
> The purpose of work is not to make money. The purpose of work is to make the employees, whether working stiffs or top executives, feel good about life. (Ricardo Semler, cited in Killian, Perez, and Siehl, 1998, p. 2)

At Semco, workers hire new employees, evaluate bosses, and vote on major decisions. In one instance, employees outvoted Semler, preventing him from acquiring a company he wanted to buy. On another, they voted to buy an abandoned factory Semler didn't want. The workers proceeded to make the new plant a remarkable success. Semco's experiments produced dramatic gains in productivity, and the company was repeatedly rated the best place to work in Brazil. Semler no longer sees a need for his company to grow, but it grows anyway because innovative employee groups keep inventing new businesses.

Organizational democracy has been viewed in two ways: as an enormously powerful timely idea or as an unrealistic, overrated fad. The truth is somewhere in between. Like almost any significant organizational change, transition toward greater democracy is often difficult and messy. But long-term results show either a gain in productivity or maintenance of the status quo.

Despite generally positive evidence, many managers and union leaders continue to oppose the idea. Managers resist democracy for fear of losing existing prerogatives they enjoy and believe essential to success. Union leaders sometimes see democracy as a management ploy to get workers to accept gimmicks in place of gains in wages and benefits. Some union leaders also worry that organizational democracy might undermine the union if it leads to too much worker-management collaboration. In contrast, a number of pioneering union leaders, including Irving Bluestone of the United Auto Workers, have pushed for greater union-management collaboration.

Organizations that stop short of formal democracy can still become more egalitarian by reducing both real and symbolic status differences (Pfeffer, 1994, 1998). It is easy to discern an individual's place in the company pecking order from such cues as office size and access to perks like limousines and corporate jets. Companies that invest in people, by contrast, often reinforce participation and job redesign by replacing symbols of hierarchy with symbols of cooperation and equality. At the American automaker Saturn, conference tables are round rather than square. There is no head of the table, and leadership rotates according to the topic at hand. Semco has no organization chart, secretaries, or personal assistants, and even top executives type their letters and make their own photocopies.

Reducing symbolic differences is helpful, but reducing real ones is at least as important. A key issue is the pay differential from one end of the organization to the other. In the 1980s, Peter Drucker suggested that no leader should earn more than twenty times the pay of the lowest-paid worker, reasoning that outsized gaps undermine trust and devalue workers. Corporate America paid little heed. During the 1990s, the rich got richer and the poor mostly stood still—CEOs' pay increased by 571 percent, while hourly workers' take-home went up only 37 percent, barely beating inflation (Anderson, Cavanagh, Hartman, and Leondar-Wright, 2002; Mishel, Bernstein, and Schmitt, 2001). In 2001, with an average annual compensation of $15.5 million, CEOs of large American companies earned more than 400 times as much as the average factory worker (Byrne, Lavelle, Byrnes, and Vickers, 2002). In the year before going bankrupt, Enron was a pioneer in the golden paycheck movement, handing out a total of $283 million to its five top executives (Ackman, 2002).

In contrast, a number of progressive companies, such as Costco, Whole Foods, and Southwest Airlines, have traditionally underpaid their CEO by comparison to their competitors. Whole Foods Markets has had a policy limiting executives' pay to ten times the average salary of employees. In 2001, *Forbes* magazine ranked Costco's James Sinegal the second-best CEO in America in delivering performance for pay. But companies like Costco are the exception to a trend that has been spreading from the United States to the rest of the world. Until recently, European companies paid senior executives about half as much as American firms, but globalization is creating pressure to reduce those differences. When Daimler-Benz took over Chrysler in 1998, an immediate problem was that Chrysler's top executives were paid far more than Daimler's. Something had to give, and raising the salary of the Germans was more popular with the executives (Ewing, Baker, Echikson, and Capell, 1999).

PROMOTE DIVERSITY

A good workplace is serious about treating everyone well—workers as well as executives; women as well as men; Asians, African Americans, and Hispanics as well as whites; gay as well as straight. Sometimes they do it because they think it's right. Often, they do it because they were forced to by bad publicity, a lawsuit, or government pressure. In 1994, Denny's Restaurants suffered a public relations disaster and paid $54 million to settle discrimination lawsuits. The bill was even higher for Shoney's, at $134 million. Both restaurant chains got religion as a result (Colvin, 1999). So did Coca-Cola, which settled a class action suit by African American employees for $192 million in November 2000 (Kahn, 2001), and Texaco, after the company's stock market value dropped by half a billion dollars in the wake of a controversy over racism at the top (Colvin, 1999). Denny's transformation was so thorough that the company made it to the top spot on the *Fortune* 2001 list of the fifty best companies for minorities. Coke cracked the same list, in the number forty-nine spot (Esposito and others, 2002).

Companies promote diversity primarily because it makes good business sense. In recent years, affirmative action has been a political football much more in Washington than in the executive suite. If you devalue certain groups as employees, the word tends to get out and alienate a lot of potential customers. In the United States, more than half the workforce is female and about a fourth is Asian, African American, or Hispanic. California and New Mexico have become the first two states in which everyone is a minority because non-Hispanic whites are no longer a majority. These two states will be joined soon by Texas and New York, and eventually the United States as a whole. It is tough to build a workforce if your business practices write off much of the available talent. This is one reason so many public agencies in the United States have long been committed to diversity. One of the most successful is the U.S. Army, as exemplified in Colin Powell's ability to rise through the ranks to head the Joint Chiefs of Staff and, subsequently, to become the nation's secretary of state.

Promoting diversity mostly comes down to focus and persistence. Organizations have to take it seriously and build it into day-to-day management. They tailor recruiting practices to diversify the candidate pool. They develop a variety of internal diversity initiatives, such as mentoring programs to help people learn the ropes and get ahead. They tie executive bonuses to success in diversifying the workforce. They work hard at eliminating the glass ceiling. They diversify their board of directors. They buy from minority vendors. It takes more than lip service, and it won't happen overnight. Many organizations still don't get it. But many that would have had trouble spelling *diversity* a decade or so ago have made impressive strides since.

PUTTING IT ALL TOGETHER: TQM AND NUMMI

If human resource management strategies described in this chapter are implemented in a halfhearted, piecemeal fashion, they lead to predictable failure. Success requires a comprehensive strategy and long-term commitment many organizations espouse but few deliver. One example of a comprehensive strategy that combines structural and human resource elements is total quality management (TQM), which swept across corporate America in the 1980s. Quality gurus such as W. Edwards Deming (1986), Joseph Juran (1989), Philip Crosby (1989), and Kaoru Ishikawa (1985) differed on specifics, but they all emphasized workforce involvement, participation, and teaming as essential components of a serious quality effort. Hackman and Wageman (1995) analyzed the theory and practice of the quality movement and concluded that it represented a coherent and distinctive philosophy, consistent on the whole with existing research on effective human resource management.

Hackman and Wageman (1995) summarized four core assumptions in TQM:

1. High quality is actually cheaper than low quality.
2. People want to do good work.
3. Quality problems are cross-functional.
4. Top management is ultimately responsible for quality.

In practice, many organizations diluted the philosophy by implementing only certain parts, usually the easiest and least disruptive to the status quo. It is no surprise a majority of quality programs failed to achieve their objectives (Gertz and Baptista, 1995; Port, 1992), even though companies such as Ford, Motorola, and Xerox have obtained extraordinary results (Engardio and DeGeorge, 1994; Greising, 1994; Waterman, 1994).

The power of an integrated approach to TQM is illustrated in the case of New United Motors Manufacturing, Inc. (NUMMI), the General Motors–Toyota joint venture. In 1985, NUMMI reopened an old GM plant in Fremont, California, and began to build cars. It drew the workforce from five thousand employees laid off by GM the previous year. These workers had a reputation at GM for militancy, poor attendance, alcohol and drug abuse, and even fistfights on the assembly line (Holusha, 1989; Lawrence and Weckler, 1990; Lee, 1988). Two years later, absenteeism had declined from 20 percent under GM to 2 percent under NUMMI, and the plant was producing cars of higher quality at a lower labor cost than any other GM plant. NUMMI's Chevrolets ranked second among all cars sold in the United States in initial owner satisfaction; no other GM car was even in the top fifteen.

What accounted for this manufacturing miracle? The answer, in a word, was Toyota, GM's partner in the joint venture. GM provided the plant, the workers, and an American nameplate, but both car and production processes were designed in Japan. Toyota managed the plant, and production was split fifty-fifty between Chevrolets and Toyotas. NUMMI's success was built on a comprehensive human resource philosophy. There was symbolic egalitarianism: workers and executives wore the same uniforms, parked in the same lots, and ate in the same cafeteria. Grouped in small, self-managing teams, employees participated in designing their own jobs and rotated through different jobs. NUMMI's motto was "There are no managers, no supervisors, only team members."

Lee (1988) used images of dance and poetry to capture NUMMI's production process:

Every motion should be flowing and natural, like a ballet. If a worker has to bend awkwardly to do his job, then the symmetry of his motion is disturbed, and he will tire. One should never have to fight the car to build it, the NUMMI trainer explains. If you must hold nine bolts in one hand and fumble with an air wrench in the other, that is clumsy and wasteful. One understands that the sin of awkwardness, of assembly in fits of effort, is as much an esthetic fault as it is a flaw in the quest for efficiency. The entire system is pure oriental poetry that emphasizes the beauty of the process of life, the grace of 10,000 stalks of rice bending in unison in the winds.

Both union and management stressed collaboration. If a worker took a complaint to the union, the union representative was likely to be accompanied by a member of the company's human relations staff. The three would try to work the problem out on the spot. If workers fell behind, they could pull a cord to stop the line, and help would arrive quickly. NUMMI's president, Kan Higashi, saw the cord as a sign of trust between management and labor: "We had heavy arguments about installing the cord here. We wondered if workers would pull it just to get a rest. That has not happened." When car sales slumped in 1988, NUMMI laid off no one. Workers were sent at full pay to training sessions on problem solving and interpersonal relations. One worker commented, "With GM, if the line slowed down, some of us would have been on the street" (Holusha, 1989).

Even union leaders liked NUMMI. Bruce Lee, a UAW official, said that the team system liberated workers by giving them more control over their jobs and that it is "increasing the plant's productivity and competitiveness while making jobs easier" (Holusha, 1989). UAW president Owen Bieber said when he toured the plant, "I was most struck that there is hardly any management here at all" (Lee, 1988, pp. 232–233).

NUMMI was not a trouble-free paradise. A dissident union group complained that the brisk pace of work amounted to "management by stress" and the plant's policy on absenteeism was inhumane. A worker absent on more than three occasions within a three-month period was charged with an "offense"; four offenses in a year meant dismissal. But even dissidents conceded things were better than in the past. Most workers were happy simply for the chance to make automobiles. As one worker said, "We got a second chance here, and we are trying to take advantage of it. Many people don't get a second chance" (Holusha, 1989).

GM was sufficiently impressed to try to transfer NUMMI techniques to other plants. Sometimes it worked; innovations such as self-managing teams doing their own quality audits led to a 21 percent reduction in costs and a substantial increase in quality at GM's Lansing plant (Hampton and Norman, 1987). But transplants often failed to root because bits of the NUMMI philosophy were implemented piecemeal, with predictably marginal results. "Team decision making" became a fad at GM but often backfired because managers dictated to the teams (Lee, 1988). Higashi told a *Wall Street Journal* reporter at one point that he was "afraid that the GM upper management does not understand the basic concept" (Schlesinger, 1987, p. 30).

As the NUMMI case illustrates, successful human resource applications are neither as idyllic as an idealist might hope nor as soft as an old-line manager often fears. The NUMMI experiment combined creative human resource management with demanding work standards to produce an automobile highly competitive in terms of both cost and quality. Such combinations have become more and more common in recent decades.

GETTING THERE: TRAINING AND ORGANIZATION DEVELOPMENT

Why do so many organizations fail to implement the noble human resource practices they espouse? One problem is managerial reluctance and ambivalence. Progressive practices cost money, and many managers are skeptical about getting a return on investment. They also change the relationships between superiors and subordinates, which many people in roles of authority find disquieting. Another major barrier is that the implementation process requires skill and understanding often in short supply. Over the last several decades a number of approaches have been developed to help convert intention to reality.

Group Intervention

One provocative and influential example was "sensitivity training" in "T-groups." What came to be known as the T-group (T for training) was a serendipitous discovery by social psychologists in the late 1940s. During a conference on race relations, participants met in groups. Researchers were stationed in each group to take notes. In the evening, researchers reported their observations to program staff. When participants heard about the sessions, they asked to be included. They were fascinated to hear things about themselves and their behavior they had never learned before. Researchers soon recognized that they had discovered something important and began a more systematic program of "human relations laboratories." Trainers and participants joined in small groups, working together and learning from their work at the same time.

As word spread, T-groups replaced lectures as a way to develop human relations skills. But evidence of limited systemic impact stimulated T-group trainers to experiment with new approaches. "Conflict laboratories" were designed for situations involving friction among groups and organizational units. "Team-building" programs were created to help groups work better. "Future search" (Weisbord and Janoff, 1995), "open space" (Owen, 1993, 1995), and other large-group designs (Bunker and Alban, 1996) brought together large numbers of people from a variety of constituencies to work cooperatively on a set of key issues or challenges.

A recent example of a large-group intervention is the "work-out" conferences initiated by Jack Welch, CEO of General Electric. Frustrated by the slow pace of change in his organization, Welch convened a series of town hall meetings, typically with one hundred to two hundred employees, to identify and resolve issues "that participants thought were dumb, a waste of time, or needed to be changed" (Bunker and Alban, 1996, p. 170). The conferences were generally viewed as highly successful and spread throughout the company (Bunker and Alban, 1996).

Survey Feedback

As laboratory training was getting its start in the late 1940s, a group of researchers at the University of Michigan began to develop surveys to measure human resource patterns. They focused on motivation, communication, leadership styles, and organizational climate. Likert helped found the Survey Research Center at Michigan. His 1961 book, *New Patterns of Management,* became a classic in the human resource tradition. Likert used survey data to show that "employee-centered" supervisors, who focused more on people and relationships, typically managed higher-producing units than "job-centered" supervisors, who ignored human issues, made decisions themselves, and dictated to subordinates.

Survey research paved the way for survey feedback as an approach to organizational improvement. The process begins with questionnaires aimed at human resource issues. The results are tabulated and then shown to managers. The results might show, for example, that information within a unit flows well but that decisions are made in the wrong place using the wrong information. Members of the work unit, perhaps with the help of a consultant, would discuss the results and explore how to improve their effectiveness.

Evolution of OD

T-groups and survey research gave birth to the field of organization development (OD), a set of change strategies, such as group intervention and survey research, that emphasize data collection, open communication, and experiential learning, usually with the assistance of consultants or change agents. Since its early beginnings, OD has continued to evolve as a discipline (Mirvis, 1988, 1990). In 1965, few managers had heard of OD; by the 1990s, there were few who had not. Most major organizations (particularly in the United States) have experimented with OD: General Motors, the U.S. Postal Service, IBM, the Internal Revenue Service, Texas Instruments, Exxon, and the U.S. Navy have all employed their own brand.

CONCLUSION

If the individual finds satisfaction and meaning in work, the organization profits from effective use of individual talent and energy. If not, individuals withdraw, resist, or rebel. In the end, everyone loses. Progressive organizations implement a variety of "high-involvement" strategies for improving human resource management. Some approaches strengthen the bond between individual and organization by paying well, offering job security, promoting from within, training the workforce, and sharing the fruits of organizational success. Others empower workers and give work more significance through participation, job enrichment, teaming, democracy, egalitarianism, and valuing diversity. No single strategy is likely to be effective by itself. Success typically requires a comprehensive strategy undergirded by a long-term human resource management philosophy.

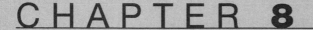
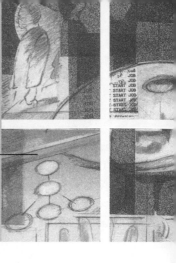

CHAPTER **8**

Interpersonal and Group Dynamics

Anne Barreta was excited but scared when she became the first woman and the first Hispanic American ever promoted to district marketing manager at the Hillcrest Corporation. She knew she could do the job, but also that she would be watched carefully. Her boss, Steve Carter, the regional marketing manager, was very supportive. Others were less enthusiastic—like the coworker who smiled as he patted her on the shoulder and said, "Congratulations! I just wish *I* was an affirmative action candidate."

Anne was responsible for one of two districts in the same city. Her counterpart in the other district, Harry Reynolds, was twenty-five years older and had been with Hillcrest twenty years longer. Some said that the term *good old boy* could have been invented to describe Harry. Usually genial, his temper flared quickly when someone got in his way. Anne tried to maintain a positive and professional relationship but often found Harry to be condescending and arrogant.

Things came to a head one afternoon as Anne, Harry, and their immediate subordinates were discussing marketing plans. Anne and Harry were disagreeing politely. Mark, one of Anne's subordinates, tried to support her views, but Harry kept cutting him off. Anne saw Mark's frustration building, but she was still surprised when he angrily told Harry, "If you'd listen to anyone besides yourself, and think a little before you open your mouth, we'd make a lot more progress." With barely controlled fury, Harry declared that "this meeting is adjourned" and stormed out.

A day later, Harry phoned to demand that Anne fire Mark. Anne tried to reason with him, but Harry was adamant. Worried about the fallout, Anne talked to Steve, their mutual boss. He agreed that firing Mark was too drastic but suggested a reprimand. Anne agreed and informed Harry. He again became angry and shouted, "If you want to get along in this company, you'd better fire that guy!" Anne calmly replied that Mark reported to her. Harry's final words were, "You'll regret this!"

Three months later, Steve called Anne to a private meeting. "I just learned," he said, "that someone's been spreading a rumor that I promoted you because you and I are having an affair."

Anne was stunned by a jumble of feelings—confusion, rage, surprise, shame. She groped for words, but none came.

"It's crazy, I know," Steve continued. "But the company hired a private detective to check it out. Of course, they didn't find anything. So they're dropping it. But some of the damage is already done. I can't prove it, but I'm pretty sure who's behind it."

"Harry?" Anne asked.

"Who else?"

The human resource frame focuses on the relationship between the individual and the organization, but people at work relate mostly to others. Managers spend most of their time in conversations and meetings, in groups and committees, over coffee or over lunch, on the phone, or on the Net (Kotter, 1982; Mintzberg, 1973). Relationships, then, figure prominently in both individual job satisfaction and organizational effectiveness.

Psychological theory and folk wisdom agree that social needs and interpersonal styles are substantially influenced by experiences early in life. Those patterns do not change quickly or easily in response to organizational requirements. Thompson (1967) and others have argued that the socializing institutions of a bureaucratic society shape people to make them better suited to the workplace. Schools, for example, train students to be punctual, complete assignments, and follow rules. But schools are not always fully successful. The human input of an organization is shaped initially by a decentralized cottage industry known as the family, and the family seldom produces raw materials exactly to specification.

To be human is to be an imperfect cog in the bureaucratic machinery. People conduct relationships to fit their individual styles and preferences, often disregarding what the organization wants. They may work, but never *only* on assigned tasks. They also attend to personal and social needs that often diverge from formal rules and requirements. A project falters because no one likes the manager's style. A committee gets little done because of tension that everyone sees but no one mentions. A school principal spends an inordinate amount of time dealing with a handful of abrasive or ineffectual teachers responsible for most discipline problems and parental complaints. Protracted warfare arises because of friction between two department heads. We saw in Chapter One, for example, that the relationship between the CIA and the FBI was crippled for decades by the personal animosity between William J. Donovan and J. Edgar Hoover.

This chapter begins by looking at basic sources of effective or ineffective interpersonal relations at work. We examine why individuals are often blind to their self-defeating actions in relationships. We describe theories of interpersonal competence and emotional intelligence and explain how they might contribute to greater effectiveness in workplace relationships. We also explore ways of understanding the importance of individual differences in style. Finally, we discuss key issues in how groups and teams work (or don't work): roles, norms, conflict, and leadership.

INTERPERSONAL DYNAMICS

In organizations, as elsewhere in life, many of the greatest joys and most intense sorrows occur in relationships with other people. Three recurrent questions regularly haunt managers:

1. What is really happening in this relationship?
2. Why do other people behave as they do?
3. What can I do about it?

All were questions for Anne Barreta. What was happening between her and Harry Reynolds? Did he really start the vicious rumor? If so, why? How should she deal with someone as difficult and devious as he seemed? Could she talk to him? What options did she have?

Some observers assume the obvious: Harry resents a young, minority woman who has become his peer. He becomes even more bitter when she rejects his demand to fire Mark. Harry seeks revenge through a sneak attack. The case resembles many others in which men dominate or victimize women (Collinson and Collinson, 1989). What should Anne, or any woman in similar circumstances, do? Confront the larger issues? That might help in the long run, but a woman who initiates confrontation is often branded a trouble-maker (Collinson and Collinson, 1989). Should Anne try to get Harry before he gets her? If she does, she might kindle a war no one wins.

Human resource theorists acknowledge political dynamics but suggest that constructive responses are possible. Argyris (1962) emphasizes the importance of "interpersonal competence" as a basic managerial skill. He shows that managers' effectiveness is often impaired because they are overcontrolling, excessively competitive, uncomfortable with feelings, closed to others' ideas, and blind to their own impact.

Argyris and Schön's Theories for Action

Argyris and Schön (1974, 1996) carry the issue of interpersonal effectiveness a step further. They argue that individual behavior is controlled by personal theories for action—assumptions that inform and guide behavior. Argyris and Schön distinguish two kinds of theory. *Espoused theories* are accounts individuals provide whenever they try to describe, explain, or predict their behavior. *Theories-in-use* guide what people actually do. A theory-in-use is an implicit program or set of rules that specifies how to behave.

Argyris and Schön found significant discrepancies between espoused theories and theories-in-use. Managers' self-descriptions are often unconnected to their actions. They typically see themselves as rational, open, concerned for others, and democratic. They don't realize that their actions are competitive, controlling, and defensive. Such blindness is pervasive because most managers employ a self-protective model of interpersonal behavior, particularly in dealing with issues that are embarrassing or threatening. Argyris and Schön refer to this theory-in-use as Model I (see Table 8.1).

MODEL I ASSUMPTIONS. Lurking in Model I is the core assumption that an organization is a dangerous place where you have to look out for yourself or someone else will do

TABLE 8.1. Model I Theory-in-Use.

Core Values (Governing Variables)	Action Strategies	Consequences for Behavioral World	Consequences for Learning
Define and achieve your goals	Design and manage the environment unilaterally	You will be seen as defensive, inconsistent, fearful, selfish	Self-sealing (so you won't know about the negative consequences of your actions)
Maximize winning, minimize losing	Own and control whatever is relevant to your interests	You create defensiveness in interpersonal relationships	Single-loop learning (you don't question your core values and assumptions)
Minimize generating or expressing negative feelings	Unilaterally protect yourself (from criticism, discomfort, vulnerability, etc.)	You reinforce defensive norms (mistrust, risk-avoidance, conformity, rivalry, etc.)	You test your assumptions and beliefs privately, not publicly
Be rational	Unilaterally protect others from being upset or hurt (censor bad news, hold private meetings, etc.)	Key issues become undiscussable	Unconscious collusion to protect yourself and others from learning

Source: Adapted from Argyris and Schön (1996), p. 93.

you in. This assumption leads individuals to follow a predictable set of steps in their attempt to influence others. We can see the progression in the exchanges between Harry and Anne:

1. *Assume that the problem is caused by the other person(s).* Harry seems to think that his problems are caused by Mark and Anne; Mark is insulting, and Anne protects him. Anne, for her part, blames Harry for being biased, unreasonable, and devious. This is the basic assumption at the core of Model I: "I'm OK, (s)he's not." So long as problems are someone else's fault, it is that person, not you, who needs to change.

2. *Develop a private, unilateral diagnosis and solution.* Harry develops his own diagnosis and solution: Anne should fire Mark. When she declines, he apparently develops another, more private strategy: undermine Anne without her knowledge.

3. *Since the other person is the cause of the problem, get that person to change.* Use one or more of three basic strategies: (1) facts, logic, and rational persuasion (argue the merits of your point of view); (2) indirect influence (ease in, ask leading questions, manipulate the other person); or (3) direct critique (tell the other person directly what he or she is doing wrong and how he or she should change). Harry starts with logic, moves quickly to direct critique, and, if Steve's diagnosis is correct, finally resorts to subterfuge and sabotage.

4. *If the other person resists or becomes defensive, it confirms that the other person caused the problem.* Anne's refusal to fire Mark presumably confirms Harry's perception of her as an ineffective troublemaker.

5. *Respond to resistance through some combination of intensifying pressure and protecting or rejecting the other person.* When Anne resists, Harry intensifies the pressure. Anne tries to soothe him without firing Mark. Harry apparently concludes that she is impossible to deal with and that the best solution is to sabotage her.

6. *If your efforts are unsuccessful or less successful than hoped, it is the other person's fault. You need feel no personal responsibility.* Harry does not succeed in getting rid of Mark or Anne. He stains Anne's reputation but damages his own in the process. Everyone is hurt. But Harry probably never realizes the error of his ways. The incident may confirm to Harry's colleagues that he is too temperamental and defensive and not fully trustworthy. Such perceptions will probably block Harry's promotion to a more senior position. But Harry may persist in believing that he is right and Anne is wrong, because no one wants to confront someone as defensive and cranky as Harry.

MODEL II ASSUMPTIONS. The result of Model I assumptions is wasted energy, strained relationships, and deterioration in decision-making processes—all predictable consequences of Model I. What else can be done about a situation like Anne's? Argyris and Schön (1996) propose Model II as an alternative:

1. *Emphasize common goals and mutual influence.* Even in a situation as difficult as the Anne Barreta case, shared goals are possible. Anne and Harry both want to be effective. Neither benefits from mutual destruction. At times, each needs help and might learn and profit from the other. To emphasize common goals, Anne might ask Harry, "What kind of relationship do we want? Do we want an ongoing battle? Wouldn't we both be better off if we worked together?"

2. *Communicate openly, and publicly test assumptions and beliefs.* Model II suggests that Anne talk directly to Harry and test her assumptions. She *believes* Harry deliberately started the rumor, but she is not *certain*. She suspects Harry will lie if she confronts him, another untested assumption. Anne might say, for example, "Harry, someone started a rumor about me and Steve. What do you know about that story and how it got started?" Though many managers see directness as startling and dangerous, Model II argues that Anne has little to lose and much to gain. Even if she does not get the truth, she lets Harry know she is aware of his game and is not afraid to confront him.

3. *Combine advocacy with inquiry.* Advocacy includes statements that communicate what an individual thinks, knows, wants, or feels. Inquiry seeks to learn what others think, know, want, or feel. Figure 8.1 presents a simple model of the relationship between advocacy and inquiry.

Model II emphasizes integration of advocacy and inquiry. It asks managers to express openly what they think and feel, and actively seek understanding of others' thoughts and feelings. Harry's demand that Anne fire Mark combines *high* advocacy with *low* inquiry. He tells her what he wants while showing no interest in her point of view. Such behavior

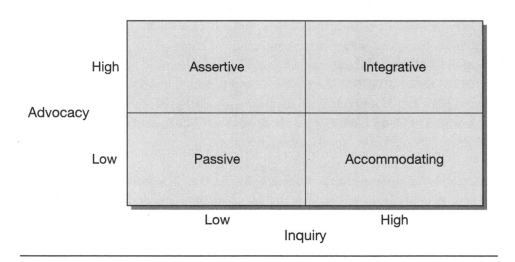

FIGURE 8.1. Advocacy and Inquiry.

tends to be perceived as assertive at best, dominating or arrogant at worst. Anne's response is low in both advocacy and inquiry. In her discomfort, she tries to get out of the meeting without making any concessions. Harry might see her as apathetic, unresponsive, or weak.

Model II counsels Anne to combine advocacy and inquiry in an open dialogue. She can tell Harry what she thinks and feels while testing her assumptions and trying to learn from him. This is difficult to learn and practice. Openness carries risks, and it is hard to be effective when you are ambivalent, uncomfortable, or frightened. It gets easier as you become more confident that you can cope with other people's responses. Anne's ability to confront Harry depends a lot on her confidence in herself and her interpersonal skills. Beliefs can be self-fulfilling. If you tell yourself that it's too dangerous to be open and that you do not know how to deal with difficult people, you will probably be right, but a more optimistic prediction can also be self-fulfilling.

THE PERILS OF SELF-PROTECTION. When managers feel vulnerable, they revert to self-protection. They skirt issues or attack others and escalate games of camouflage and deception (Argyris and Schön, 1978). Feeling inadequate, they try to camouflage their inadequacy. To avoid detection, they pile subterfuge on top of camouflage. This generates even more uncertainty and ambiguity and makes it difficult or impossible to detect errors. As a result, an organization often persists in following a course everyone privately thinks is a path to disaster. No one wants to be the one to speak the truth. Who wants to be the messenger bearing bad news?

The result is often catastrophe because critical information never reaches decision makers who need to act on it. In a number of well-documented aviation accidents, the copilot believed the captain was making a serious mistake yet chose not to say so directly. Instead, he used vague questions to nudge the captain gently. In each case, the captain missed the message. Perhaps the copilots feared upsetting their commander. Or perhaps they were not sure the captain was wrong. In any event, the errors were fatal. More direct communication could not have made things any worse and might have saved airplane, passengers, and crew.

Some of the same issues emerged in the well-publicized collapse of Enron:

> In April, 2000, Enron was still flying high, at least publicly. Jeffrey K. Skilling, the president
> and chief operating officer at the time, faced a video camera and spoke enthusiastically about

the corporate culture that would, he insisted, enable Enron to go from the world's largest energy-trading company to the world's leading company, period. "People have an obligation to dissent in this company," Mr. Skilling said, detailing Enron's core values of respect, communication, excellence, and integrity. "I mean, I sit up here on the 50th floor, so I have no idea what's going on down there. If you've got a problem with it, speak up. And if you don't speak up, that's not good." (Dewan, 2002, pp. C1, C7)

It sounded good, but Skilling was described by subordinates as a Darth Vader who created an environment of fear and cutthroat competition while turning a deaf ear to anyone who offered input he didn't want to hear. "After Enron's collapse in late 2001, one of the interviewers, Professor Robert F. Bruner of the University of Virginia, said that Skilling was 'very smooth, very, very smooth.' But, he added, it later became clear that Skilling was not doing what he said he was doing" (Dewan, 2002, p. C7).

Salovey and Mayer's Emotional Intelligence

The capacity that Argyris (1962) labeled *interpersonal competence* harked back to Thorndike's 1920 definition of *social intelligence* as "the ability to understand and manage men and women, boys and girls—to act wisely in human relations" (p. 228). Salovey and Mayer (1990) updated Thorndike in coining the term *emotional intelligence* as a label for a set of skills that include awareness of self and others and the ability to handle emotions and relationships. Salovey and Mayer found that individuals who scored relatively high in the ability to perceive accurately, understand, and appraise others' emotions could respond more flexibly to changes in their social environments and were better able to build supportive social networks (Cherniss, 2000; Salovey, Bedell, Detweiler, and Mayer, 1999). In the early 1990s, Daniel Goleman popularized Salovey and Mayer's work in his best-selling book *Emotional Intelligence.*

Interpersonal skills and emotional intelligence are vital because, as mentioned earlier, personal relationships are a central element of daily life in organizations. Many change efforts fail not because managers' intentions are incorrect or insincere but because they are unable to handle the social challenges of implementation. Popular remedies such as quality improvement, process reengineering, and self-managing teams often bog down in

Management Best-Sellers: Daniel Goleman, *Emotional Intelligence* (New York: Bantam, 1995).

Daniel Goleman didn't invent the idea of emotional intelligence, but he made it famous. His best-selling *Emotional Intelligence* focused more on children and education than on work, but it still attracted great interest from the business community. It was followed by articles in the *Harvard Business Review,* as well as two additional books (*Working with Emotional Intelligence* in 2000 and, with Annie McKee and Richard E. Boyatzis, *Primal Leadership* in 2002) focusing on the implications of emotional intelligence for leadership and work. Goleman's basic argument was that emotional intelligence (EI), rather than intellectual abilities (or intelligence quotient, IQ), accounts for most of the variance in effectiveness among managers, particularly at the senior level.

In *Primal Leadership,* Goleman, McKee, and Boyatzis (2002) define four dimensions of emotional intelligence. Two are internal (self-awareness and self-management), and two are external (social awareness and relationship management). Self-awareness includes awareness of one's feelings and one's impact on others. Self-management was broadly defined to include a number of positive psychological characteristics, among them emotional self-control, authenticity, adaptability, drive for achievement, initiative, and optimism. Social awareness included empathy (attunement to the thoughts and feelings of others), organizational awareness (sensitivity to the importance of relationships and networks), and commitment to service. The fourth characteristic, relationship management, includes inspiration, influence, developing others, catalyzing change, managing conflict, and teamwork.

Critics have made two main complaints about Goleman's work: (1) there's nothing new, just an updating of old ideas and common sense, and (2) Goleman is much better at explaining why EI is important than at suggesting practical ideas for enhancing it. There is some validity to both criticisms. Goleman borrowed the EI label from Salovey and Mayer, and the idea of multiple forms of intelligence was developed earlier by Howard Gardner (1993) at Harvard and Robert J. Sternberg (1985) at Yale. The dimensions of EI in *Primal Leadership* (inspiration, teamwork, and so forth) look as if they were culled from the leadership literature of the last decade or so. But even if Goleman is offering old wine in new bottles, those bottles have found a large and receptive audience because of the labels—the way he has framed the issue. He has offered a way to think about the relative importance of intellectual and social skills in organizational success and has made a persuasive case that managers with high IQ but low EI are a danger to themselves and everyone they work with.

interpersonal misunderstanding and miscommunication. Not long ago, a manufacturing organization proudly announced its "Put Quality First" program. A young manager was assigned to chair a quality team in the plant where she worked. She and her team began eagerly. But her plant manager tended to drop in on team meetings and dismiss almost every suggestion for change as impractical or unworkable. The team's enthusiasm quickly faded. The plant manager thought he was demonstrating accessibility and "management by walking around." The manager felt too cowed to tell him he was intrusive and dictatorial.

MANAGEMENT STYLES

Argyris and Schön's work on theories for action and Salovey and Mayer's work on emotional intelligence emphasize common elements of effectiveness that apply regardless of the individual. The assumption is that certain understandings and skills are helpful to anyone. Another body of research focuses on differences among individuals in personality and style. In a classic experiment (Lewin, Lippitt, and White, 1939), researchers compared autocratic, democratic, and laissez-faire leadership in a study of boys' clubs. They found that leadership style had a powerful impact on both productivity and morale. Under autocratic leadership, the boys were productive but joyless and experienced a high level of dependence and frustration. Laissez-faire leadership led to aimlessness and confusion. The boys strongly preferred democratic leadership, which produced a more positive group climate.

A number of subsequent researchers have examined leadership in the work setting (much of that work is reviewed in Stogdill, 1974; and Bass, 1981, 1990). Fleishman and Harris (1962) conducted an influential series of studies focusing on two dimensions or styles: *consideration* (how much a manager shows concern for and sensitivity to people), and *initiating structure* (to what degree a manager actively structures subordinate activity). Subsequent research on these dimensions has produced a complex pattern of findings. Higher consideration for employees is generally associated with lower turnover, fewer grievances, and less absenteeism. Overall, more effective supervisors tend to be high on both consideration and structure. Similar results were produced by Likert (1961), who presented evidence that "employee-centered" managers were more effective in the long run than "task-centered" managers.

Countless theories, books, workshops, and tests have been devoted to helping managers identify their own and others' personal or interpersonal styles. Are leaders introverts or extroverts? Are they friendly helpers, tough battlers, or objective thinkers? Do managers care more about control, inclusion, or affection? Do they behave more like parents or like children? Are they superstars concerned for both people and production, "country club" managers who care only about people, or hard-driving taskmasters who ignore human needs and feelings (Blake and Mouton, 1969)?

In the 1980s, the forty-year-old Myers-Briggs Type Indicator (Myers, 1980) became (and has since remained) an enormously popular tool for examining management styles. Built on principles from Jungian psychology, the inventory assesses four dimensions: introversion versus extroversion, sensing versus intuition, thinking versus feeling, and perceiving versus judging. On the basis of scores on those dimensions, it categorizes an individual into one of sixteen types. A central assumption underlying the Myers-Briggs approach is that each style has its strengths and weaknesses and no one style is universally better than any other. A second key assumption is that interpersonal relationships are much less confusing and frustrating if individuals understand and appreciate both their own style and those of co-workers.

One, and maybe both, of the authors of this book, for example, are ENFPs (extraverted, intuitive, feeling, perceiving). The good news is that ENFPs tend to be warmly enthusiastic, high-spirited, ingenious, and imaginative. But they dislike rules and bureaucracy and tend to start more projects than they finish. Their desks are usually messy, and they tend to be disorganized, impatient with details, and uninterested in planning. One of us was once paired with an ISTJ (introverted, sensing, thinking, judging), who was serious, quiet, thorough, practical, and dependable. The task was to manage an educational program, but the relationship got off to a rocky start. The ISTJ arrived at meetings with a detailed agenda and a trusty notepad. Her ENFP counterpart arrived with enthusiasm and a few vague ideas. As decisions were reached, the ISTJ carefully wrote down both her assignments and his on her to-do list. Her counterpart made brief, semi-legible notes on random scraps of paper. She would follow through on each of her tasks in a timely manner. He usually misplaced the scraps of paper, was often late, and did only the assignments that he remembered and thought were important. She became distraught at his lack of organization and began to wonder if he was trying to undermine her. He got annoyed at her bureaucratic rigidity. The relationship might have collapsed had not the two discussed their respective Myers-Briggs styles and recognized that they needed one other; each brought something different but essential to the relationship.

The Myers-Briggs is not so popular with academic psychologists, many of whom have come to prefer the "Big 5" model of personality on the ground that it has stronger research support (Goldberg, 1992; John, 1990). As its name implies, the model interprets personality in terms of five major dimensions. The names of the five vary from one author to another, but a typical list would include extraversion (enjoying other people and seeking their company), agreeableness (getting along with others), conscientiousness (a tendency to be orderly, planful and hard-working), neuroticism (difficulty in controlling negative feelings), and openness to experience (preference for creativity and new experience). For popular use, though, the Big 5 has disadvantages. Compared to the Myers-Briggs, its dimensions convey stronger value judgments; it is hard to argue that being disagreeable and neurotic is every bit as good as being at the opposite ends of those two dimensions. Moreover, some of the labels (such as neuroticism) make more sense to psychologists than to laypeople.

Despite the risk of turning managers into amateur psychologists, it often helps to have shared language and concepts to make sense of the elusive, complex world of individual styles. When managers are blind to their own style, they usually need help from others to learn about it. Their friends and colleagues may be more helpful if they have some way to talk about the issues. Tests like the Myers-Briggs provide this shared language.

GROUPS AND TEAMS IN ORGANIZATIONS

Anne Barreta's case shows how demanding even a two-person relationship can be. Managers face even more difficult challenges because they spend much of their time in groups. Groups, as we saw in Chapter Five, can take many forms: standing committees, task forces, project teams, boards of trustees, faculty committees, advisory groups, and cliques, to name a few. Whatever the labels, groups continually challenge and frustrate participants. Cynics offer witty but jaundiced perspectives on committees as "a cul-de-sac down which ideas are lured and then quietly strangled" or "a group of the unwilling, chosen by the unfit, to do the unnecessary." Painful experience has led many managers to conclude that groups are almost invariably inefficient, confused, and frustrating. But even people who hate groups can often recall at least one peak experience.

Groups, in fact, have both assets and liabilities (Collins and Guetzkow, 1964; Hackman, 1989; McGrath, 1984). Groups have more knowledge, diversity of perspective, time, and energy than individuals working alone. Groups often improve communication and increase acceptance of decisions. On the downside, groups may overrespond to social pressure or individual domination, bog down in inefficiency, or let personal agendas smother collective purposes (Maier, 1967).

Groups can be wonderful or terrible, productive or stagnant, imprisoning or freeing, conformist or creative. Whether paradise or inferno, groups are indispensable in modern organizations. They solve problems, make decisions, coordinate work, promote information sharing, build participation and commitment, and negotiate disputes (Handy, 1993). As modern organizations rely less on hierarchical coordination, groups have become even more important in such forms as self-managing teams, quality circles, and, increasingly, virtual groups whose members are linked by information technology.

Groups operate on two levels: an overt, conscious level focused on *task* and a more implicit level of *process*, emphasizing group maintenance and interpersonal dynamics (Bales, 1970; Bion, 1961; Leavitt, 1978; Maier, 1967; Schein, 1969). Many people see only confusion in group process. The informed eye sees much more. Groups, like modern art, are complex and subtle. A few basic dimensions can offer a map for bringing clarity and order out of apparent chaos and confusion. Our map emphasizes four central issues in group process: informal roles, informal norms, interpersonal conflict, and leadership and decision making.

Informal Roles

In a small group, as in a large organization, the fit between the individual and the larger system is a central human resource concern. The structural frame emphasizes the importance of formal roles, traditionally defined by a title and a job description. In groups and teams, roles are often much more informal and implicit, with both task and personal dimensions. A group's role system is critical. The right set of *task roles* helps get the work done and makes optimal use of each member's resources. But without a corresponding set of informal roles, individuals will feel frustrated and dissatisfied, which may lead them to become unproductive or disruptive.

Every work group needs a structure of task roles so members understand who is going to do what. The roles are often fluid, evolving over time as the group moves through the phases of its task. Groups do better when the task roles align with individual differences. Group members bring different interests (some love research but hate writing), skills (some may communicate better in writing, while others are better on their feet), and varying degrees of enthusiasm (some may be highly committed to the project, while others drag their feet). It is risky, for example, to assign the writing of a final report to a poor writer or to put your most insecure member on stage in front of a demanding group of senior executives.

Anyone entering a group hopes to find a comfortable and satisfying personal role. Imagine a three-person task force. One member, Karen, is happiest when she feels influential and visible. Bob prefers to be quiet and inconspicuous. Teresa finds it hard to participate unless she feels liked and valued. In the early going in any new group, members send implicit signals about roles they prefer, usually without realizing they are doing it. In the first meeting, Karen jumps in, takes the initiative, and pushes hard for her ideas. Teresa smiles, compliments other people, asks questions, and says she hopes everyone will get along. Bob watches, speaking only when asked a direct question.

If the three individuals' preferred roles dovetail, things may go well. Karen is happy to have Bob as a listener, and Bob is pleased that Karen lets him be inconspicuous. Teresa is content if she feels that Karen and Bob like her. But suppose that Tony, who likes to be in charge, joins the group. Karen and Tony may collide—both want the same role. The prognosis looks bleaker. Now suppose that one more member, Susan, signs on. Susan's mission in life is to help other people get along. If Susan can help Karen feel visible, Teresa feel loved, and Tony feel powerful while Bob is left alone, everyone will be happy—and the group should be productive.

Some groups are blessed with a rich set of resources and highly compatible individuals, but most groups are less fortunate. They have a limited quantity of talent, skill, and motivation. They have areas of both compatibility and potential conflict. The challenge is to capitalize on their assets while minimizing the negative impact of their liabilities. But many groups never recognize issues that need attention or avoid talking about them if they do see them. Avoidance often backfires. Neglected issues come back to haunt team performance, often at the worst possible moment, when a deadline looms and everyone feels the heat.

It usually works better to deal with issues early on. A major consulting firm produced a dramatic improvement in effectiveness and morale by conducting a team-building process whenever an "engagement team" formed to work on a new project. Members discussed the roles they preferred, how the group would operate, and the resources each individual brought along. Initially, many skeptics viewed the team building as a waste of time with doubtful benefits. But the extra time for group process at the beginning more than paid for itself in effectiveness down the road.

The absence of such advance team building can be catastrophic. In the friendly-fire incident discussed in Chapter Two, where American fighter jets accidentally shot down two U.S. helicopters over Iraq, the postaccident investigation focused on what the pilots did (misidentified friendly helicopters and then shot them down) and on what the airborne AWACS controllers didn't do (failed to give fighter pilots any information or warning about the presence of friendly helicopters in their vicinity, even though the controllers had this information). Snook (2000) attributes the inaction to a weak team, which, as luck would have it, was making its maiden flight. All the individuals were technically trained and knew their own jobs, but they had not yet jelled as a working team. Before going operational in the Iraqi theater, the team was supposed to experience two full-mission simulations to test their functioning under real-time conditions. But because of a last-minute assignment, they only got one. The one they got was based on out-of-date information, and three of the four key team leaders were not there. Some of the *individuals* on the team, then, got half the prescribed "spin-up" training. The *team as a whole* got none.

Informal Group Norms

Every group develops informal rules to live by—norms that govern how the group functions and how the members conduct themselves. We once observed two families in adjacent sites in the same campground. At first glance, both were alike: two adults, two small children, and California license plates. Further observation made it clear that the families had very different unwritten rules. Family A practiced a strong form of "do your own thing." Everyone did what he or she wanted, and no one paid much attention to anyone else. Their two-year-old wandered around the campground until he fell down a fifteen-foot embankment. He lay there wailing while a professor of leadership pondered the risks and rewards of intervening in someone else's family. Finally, the professor rescued and returned the child to his parents, who seemed oblivious to their son's mishap.

Family B, in contrast, was a model of interdependence and efficiency, operating like a well-oiled machine. Everything was done collectively; each member had a role. A drill sergeant would have admired the speed and precision with which they packed up for departure. Even their three-year-old approached her tasks with purpose and enthusiasm.

Every group, including a family, evolves a set of informal norms for "how we do things around here." Eventually, such rules are taken for granted. They come to be accepted as an unalterable social reality. The parents in Family A envied Family B. They were plainly puzzled as they asked, "How did they ever get those kids to help out like that? *Our* kids would never do that!"

With norms, as with roles, early intervention helps. Do we want to be task-oriented, no-nonsense, and get on with the job? Or would we prefer to be more relaxed, playful, and responsive to one another? Do we insist on full attendance at every meeting, or should we be more flexible? Must people be unerringly punctual, or would that cramp our style? If individuals fail to complete assignments, do we hang them from the nearest tree or gently encourage them to do better? Do we prize boisterous debate, or courtesy and restraint? Groups develop norms to answer such questions.

Interpersonal Conflict in Groups

Personal conflicts spawn many of the worst horror stories about group life. Interpersonal strife can block progress and waste time. It can make things unpleasant at best, painful at worst. Some groups are blessed with little conflict, but most encounter predictable differences in goals, perceptions, preferences, and beliefs. The larger and more diverse the group, the greater the likelihood of conflict.

How can a group cope with interpersonal conflict? The Model I manager typically relies on two strategies: "pour oil on troubled waters" and "might makes right." As a result, things get worse instead of better. The oil-on-troubled-waters strategy views conflict as something to avoid at all costs: minimize it, deny its existence, smooth it over, bury it, or circumvent it. Suppose, for example, that Tony says that the group needs a leader and Karen replies that a leader would selfishly dominate the group. Teresa, dreading conflict, might rush to say, "I think we're all basically saying the same thing" or "We can talk about leadership later; right now, why don't we find out a little more about each other?"

Smoothing tactics may work if the issue is temporary or peripheral. In such a case, conflict may disappear of its own accord—much to everyone's relief. But conflict early in a group's life has a remarkable tendency to resurface again and again. If smoothing tactics fail and conflict continues, another option is might-makes-right. If Tony senses conflict between Karen and himself, he may employ Model I thinking: since we disagree, and my view is right, she is the problem. Since she is the problem, the only way to get anything done is for her to change. Tony may try any of several strategies to change Karen. He may try to persuade her of the validity of his position. He may opt to get others in the group to side with him and put pressure on Karen. He may subtly, or not so subtly, criticize or attack her. If Karen thinks she is right and Tony is the problem, the two are headed for collision. The result may be painful for everyone.

If Model I is a costly approach to conflict, what else might a group do? Here are some guidelines that often prove helpful.

DEVELOP SKILLS. More and more organizations are recognizing that group effectiveness depends heavily on members' ability to understand what is happening and contribute effectively. Such skills as listening, communicating, managing conflict, and building consensus are critical building blocks in a high-performing group.

AGREE ON THE BASICS. Too often, a group plunges ahead without taking the time to agree on goals and procedures. Down the road, people continually stumble over unresolved issues. Shared understanding and commitment around the basics are a powerful glue to hold things together in the face of the inevitable stress and strain of group life.

SEARCH FOR INTERESTS IN COMMON. How does a group reach agreement if it begins divided? It helps to keep asking, "What do we have in common? If we disagree on the issue at hand, can we put it in a larger framework where we can agree?" If Tony and Karen clash on the need for a leader, can they find other areas of agreement? Perhaps both want to do the task well. Recognizing commonalities makes it easier to discuss differences. It also helps to remember that sometimes common interest is rooted in complementary differences (Lax and Sebenius, 1986). Karen's desire to be visible is compatible with Bob's preference to be in the background. Conversely, similarity (as when Karen and Tony both want to lead) is often the source of conflict.

EXPERIMENT. If Tony is sure the group needs a leader (namely, him) and Karen is equally convinced it does not, the group could bog down in endless debate. Susan, the group's social specialist, might propose an experiment: since Karen sees it one way and Tony sees it another, how could we gather more information to help the group decide? Could we try one meeting with a leader and one without to see what happens?

Experiments can be a powerful response to conflict. They are a way to move beyond stalemate without forcing either party to lose face or admit defeat. Parties may agree on a test even if they cannot agree on anything else. Equally important, they may learn something that moves the conversation to a new, more productive point.

DOUBT YOUR INFALLIBILITY. This was the advice that Benjamin Franklin offered his fellow delegates to the U.S. constitutional convention in 1787: "Having lived long, I have experienced many instances of being obliged by better information, or fuller consideration, to change opinions even on important subjects, which I once thought right, but found to be otherwise. It is therefore that the older I grow, the more apt I am to doubt my own judgment, and to pay more respect to the judgment of others" (Rossiter, 1966).

Groups possess diverse resources, ideas, and perspectives. A group that sees diversity as an asset and a source of learning has a good chance for a productive discussion of differences. In the heat of the moment, though, a five-person group can easily turn into five teachers in search of a learner, or a lynch mob in search of a victim. At such times, it helps if at least one person asks, "Are we all sure we're infallible? Are we really hearing one another?"

TREAT DIFFERENCES AS A GROUP RESPONSIBILITY. If Tony and Karen are on a collision course, it is tempting for others to stand aside. But everyone is aboard the same social vehicle; all will suffer if it careens off the road. The debate between Karen and Tony reflects personal feelings and preferences but deals with an issue of importance to the entire group. Leadership is an issue for everyone, not just Karen and Tony.

Leadership and Decision Making in Groups

A final problem that every group must resolve is the question of navigation: "How will we steer the ship, particularly in stormy weather?" Groups often get lost. Meetings are punctuated with statements like "I'm not sure where we're going" or "We've been talking for an hour without getting anywhere" or "Does anyone know what we're talking about?"

One task of leadership is to help groups develop a shared sense of direction and commitment. Otherwise, a group becomes rudderless or moves in directions that no one supports. Though leadership is essential, it need not come from only one person. A single leader focuses responsibility and clarifies accountability. But the same individual may not be equally effective in all situations. Groups often do better with a shared and fluid approach, regularly asking, "Who can best lead in *this* situation?" Katzenbach and Smith (1993) found that a key characteristic of high-performance teams was mutual accountability, fostered when leaders shared in the work and team members shared in the leadership.

Leadership, whether shared or individual, plays a critical role in group effectiveness and individual satisfaction. Maier (1967) found that leaders who overcontrol or understructure tend to produce frustration and ineffectiveness. Good leaders are sensitive to both task and process. They enlist others actively in managing both. Effective leaders help group members communicate and work together, while less effective leaders try to dominate and get their own ideas accepted.

CONCLUSION

Employees are hired to do a job but always bring social and personal needs with them to the workplace. Moreover, they spend much of their time interacting with others, one on one and in groups. Both individual satisfaction and organizational effectiveness depend heavily on the quality of interpersonal relationships.

An individual's social skills or competencies are a critical element in the effectiveness of relationships at work. Argyris and Schön argue that interpersonal dynamics in organizations are counterproductive as often as not. People employ theories-in-use (behavioral programs) that emphasize self-protection and the control of others. Argyris and Schön developed an alternative model of effectiveness built on values of mutuality and learning. Salovey and Mayer, as well as Goleman, underscore the importance of emotional intelligence—social skills that include awareness of self and others and the ability to handle emotions and relationships.

Small groups are often condemned for wasting time while producing little, but groups *can* be both satisfying and efficient. In any event, organizations cannot function without them. Managers need to understand that groups always operate at two levels: task and process. Both levels need to be managed if groups are to be effective. Among the significant process issues that groups have to manage are informal roles, group norms, interpersonal conflict, and leadership.

PART FOUR

The Political Frame

Pondering the word *politics,* what images come to mind? Are any of them positive or productive? The answer is probably no.

Although they came from very different persuasions, the last two American presidents, Bill Clinton and George W. Bush, were repeatedly accused of being "political." Opponents complained that they responded to self-interest and political pressures rather than championed the common good. Politics and politicians are universally despised and viewed as an unavoidable evil. In organizations, phrases like "they're playing politics" or "it was all political" are invariably terms of disapproval.

A jaundiced view of politics constitutes a serious threat to individual and organizational effectiveness. Viewed from the political frame, politics is simply the realistic process of making decisions and allocating resources in a context of scarcity and divergent interests. This view puts politics at the heart of decision making.

We introduce the elements of the political frame in Chapter Nine. We begin by examining dynamics lurking in the background of the tragic loss of the space shuttle *Challenger.* We lay out the frame's key assumptions and discuss basic issues of power, conflict, and ethics.

Chapter Ten, "The Manager as Politician," looks at the constructive side of politics. It is organized around the basic skills of the effective organizational politician: setting agendas, mapping the political terrain, networking, building coalitions, and negotiating. We also discuss four principles of moral judgment—mutuality, generality, openness, and caring—to offer guidance in dealing with ethically slippery political issues.

Chapter Eleven moves from the individual level to the organizational level. It looks at organizations as both arenas for political contests and active political players or actors. As arenas, organizations have an important duty to shape the rules of the game. As players or actors, organizations are powerful tools for achieving the broad agendas of whoever is in control. We close with a discussion of the relative power of organizations and society. Will giant corporations take over the world? Or will other institutions channel and constrain their actions in productive directions?

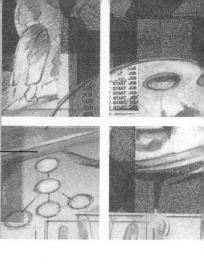

CHAPTER 9

Power, Conflict, and Coalition

Early on the morning of February 1, 2003, the U.S. space shuttle *Columbia* was returning to earth from a smooth and successful mission. Then something terrible went wrong. For perhaps half a minute, the crew was flooded with emergency signals—the noise of alarms and the glare of indicator lights signaling massive system failure. The craft tumbled out of control before it was finally blown apart. Cabin and crew were destroyed (Schwartz and Wald, 2003; Wald, 2003).

Second-guessing of the shuttle's sponsor, the National Aeronautics and Space Administration (NASA), and its attention to safety began almost immediately. Inquiries were fueled by memories of another space shuttle disaster seventeen years earlier.

January 28, 1986. At sunrise, it was clear but very cold in Cape Canaveral, Florida. The weather was more like New Hampshire, where Christa McAuliffe was a high school teacher. Curtains of ice greeted ground crews as they inspected the space shuttle *Challenger.* The temperature had plunged overnight to a record low of 24 degrees Fahrenheit (-4 degrees Celsius). The ice team removed as much as they could. Temperatures gradually warmed, but it was still brisk at 8:30 A.M. *Challenger*'s crew of seven astronauts noted the ice as they climbed into the capsule. As McAuliffe, the first teacher to venture into space, entered the ship, a technician offered her an apple. She beamed, and asked him to save it until she returned. At 11:38 A.M., *Challenger* lifted off. A minute later, there was a massive explosion in the booster rockets. Millions watched television screens in horror as the shuttle and its crew were destroyed.

On the eve of the launch, an emergency teleconference had been called between NASA and the Morton Thiokol Corporation, the contractor for the shuttle's solid–fuel rocket motor. During the teleconference, Thiokol engineers pleaded with superiors and NASA to delay the launch. They feared cold temperatures would cause a failure in synthetic rubber O-rings sealing the rocket motor's joints. If the rings failed, the motor could blow up. The problem was simple and familiar: rubber loses elasticity at cold temperatures. Freeze a rubber ball and it won't bounce; freeze an O-ring, and it might not seal. Engineers recommended strongly that NASA wait for warmer weather. They tried to produce a persuasive engineering rationale, but their report was hastily thrown together, and the data seemed equivocal (Vaughan, 1995). Meanwhile, Thiokol and NASA both faced strong pressure to get the shuttle in the air:

> Thiokol had gained the lucrative sole source contract for the solid rocket boosters thirteen years earlier, during a bitterly disputed award process. It was characterized by some veteran observers as a low point in squalid political intrigue. At the time of the award, a relatively small Thiokol Chemical Company in Brigham City, Utah, had political clout. Both the newly appointed chairman of the Senate Aeronautics and Space Science Committee, Democratic Senator Frank Moss, and the new NASA administrator, Dr. James Fletcher, were insiders in the tightly knit Utah political hierarchy. By summer 1985, however, Thiokol's monopoly position was under attack, and the corporation's executives were afraid to risk their billion-dollar contract by halting shuttle flight operations long enough to correct flaws in the booster joint design. (McConnell, 1987, p. 7)

Meanwhile, NASA managers were experiencing their own pressures. As part of the effort to build congressional support for the space program, NASA promised that the shuttle would eventually pay for itself in cargo fees, a boxcar in space. Projections of profitability were based on a very ambitious plan: twelve flights in 1984, fourteen in 1985, and seventeen in 1986. NASA had fallen well behind schedule—only five launches in 1984 and eight in 1985. The promise of "routine access to space" and self-supporting flights looked more and more dubious. With every flight costing taxpayers about $100 million, NASA needed a lot of cash from Congress, but prospects were dimming. NASA's credibility was eroding as the U.S. budget deficit soared.

That was the tense context in which Thiokol's engineers recommended canceling launch the next day. The response from NASA officials was swift and pointed. One NASA manager said he was "appalled" at the recommendation, and another said, "My God, Thiokol, when do you want me to launch? Next April?" (McConnell, 1987, p. 196). Thiokol asked for time to caucus. Senior managers huddled and decided, against the advice of engineers, to recommend the launch. NASA accepted the recommendation and launched Flight 51-L the next morning. The O-rings failed almost immediately, and the flight was destroyed (Bell and Esch, 1987; Jensen, 1995; McConnell, 1987; Marx, Stubbart, Traub, and Cavanaugh, 1987; Vaughan, 1990, 1995).

It is disturbing to see political agendas corrupting decision making, particularly for a life-threatening technical issue. It is tempting to explain *Challenger* by blaming individual selfishness and short-sightedness. But such explanations are little help in understanding or avoiding such a tragedy. As we saw in Chapter Two's friendly-fire case (where U.S. fighter jets mistakenly shot down two of their own helicopters), individual errors are downstream of powerful forces channeling decision makers over a precipice no one sees until too late. With *Challenger*, as in the friendly-fire case, key decision makers were experienced, highly trained, and intelligent. If we tried to get better people, where would we find them? Even if found, how could we ensure that they too would not become ensnared by the political forces at work?

In traditional structural views, organizations are guided by goals and policies set at the top. In the *Challenger* case, though, we find a welter of dispersed and conflicting goals. Some were set by the White House and Congress; others were established by NASA administrators. Many gradually emerged like weeds from a political swamp.

The human resource frame emphasizes malfunctions arising from person-organization misalignment or from flawed interpersonal and group dynamics. Though Model I pathologies (see Chapter Eight) were rampant in the NASA-Thiokol teleconference, the human resource frame glosses over political forces setting the stage for conflict and power plays.

Challenger was an extraordinary tragedy, but it illustrates political dynamics that are normal and universal in organizational life. The political frame does not blame politics on such individual characteristics as selfishness, myopia, or incompetence. Instead, it asserts that interdependence, divergent interests, scarcity, and power relations inevitably spawn political activity. It matters not who the individual players are. It is naïve and romantic to hope organizational politics can ever be eliminated in organizations. Managers can, however, learn to understand and manage political dynamics.

The goal of this chapter is explain why political processes are universal, why they won't go away, and how they can be better understood and managed. First, we describe the basic assumptions of the political frame and explain how they were at work in the *Challenger* case and others. Next, we highlight organizations as coalitions, rather than hierarchies. Coalitions are tools for exercising power, so we then turn to a discussion of power. We contrast it with authority and discuss tensions between authorities (who try to keep things under control) and partisans (who try to influence the system to get what they want). We also delineate multiple sources of power. Since conflict is normal among members of a coalition, we highlight its role in organizations. Finally, we discuss an issue at the heart of concern about organizational politics: Do political dynamics inevitably undermine principles and ethics?

POLITICAL ASSUMPTIONS

The political frame views organizations as living, screaming political arenas that host a complex web of individual and group interests. Five propositions summarize the perspective:

1. Organizations are *coalitions* of diverse individuals and interest groups.
2. There are *enduring differences* among coalition members in values, beliefs, information, interests, and perceptions of reality.
3. Most important decisions involve allocating *scarce resources*—who gets what.
4. Scarce resources and enduring differences make *conflict* central to organizational dynamics and underline *power* as the most important asset.
5. Goals and decisions emerge from *bargaining, negotiation,* and *jockeying for position* among competing stakeholders.

All five propositions of the political frame came to the fore in the *Challenger* incident:

1. *Organizations are coalitions.* NASA did not run the space shuttle program in isolation. The agency was part of a complex coalition including contractors, Congress, the White House, the military, the media—even the American public. Consider, for example, why Christa McAuliffe was aboard. Her expertise as a social science teacher was not critical to the mission. But the American public was bored with white male pilots in space. Human interest was good for both NASA and Congress; it built public support for the space program. McAuliffe's participation was a magnet for the media because it made for a great human interest story. Three years earlier, Sally Ride generated excitement as the first female astronaut. Now the idea of putting an ordinary citizen in space—especially a teacher—caught the public's imagination. Symbolically, Christa McAuliffe represented all Americans. Everyone flew with her.

2. *There are enduring differences among coalition members.* NASA's hunger for funding competed with the public's interest in lower taxes. Astronauts' concerns about safety were at odds with pressures on NASA and its contractors to maintain an ambitious flight schedule.

3. *Important decisions involve allocating scarce resources.* On the eve of the *Challenger* launch, key parties struggled to balance conflicting pressures. Everyone from Pres. Ronald Reagan to the average citizen was waiting for the first teacher to fly in space. Higher safety carried a high price—not just money, but further erosion of support from key constituents for both Morton Thiokol and NASA. *Survivor,* a pioneer of "reality" television, guaranteed political infighting because the rules allowed for only one winner.

4. *Scarce resources and enduring differences make conflict central and power the most important asset.* The teleconference on the eve of the launch began as a debate between the contractor and NASA. As a sole customer, NASA was in the driver's seat. When managers at Morton Thiokol sensed NASA's level of disappointment and frustration, they asked for time to caucus. The scene shifted to a tense standoff between engineers and managers. Engineers were unable leverage their expertise, their primary source of power, into a sufficiently persuasive case. Managers used their authority to recommend the launch despite the opposition.

5. *Goals and decisions emerge from bargaining, negotiation, and jockeying for position among competing stakeholders.* Political bargaining with the help of powerful allies got Morton Thiokol into the rocket motor business. Thiokol's engineers had been attempting to increase management's attention to the booster joint problem for many months. But acknowledging a problem, in addition to costing substantial time and money, risked

eroding Morton Thiokol's credibility. A large and profitable contract was hanging in the balance.

The assumptions of the political frame outline sources of power dynamics. A coalition forms because of interdependence among its members; they need one another, even though their interests may only partly overlap. The assumption of enduring difference implies that political activity is more visible and dominant under conditions of diversity than of homogeneity. Agreement and harmony are easier to achieve when everyone shares similar values, beliefs, and culture.

The concept of scarce resources suggests that politics will be more salient and intense in difficult times. Schools and colleges, for example, have lived through alternating times of feast and famine in response to peaks and valleys in economic and demographic trends. When money and students are plentiful (as they were in the 1960s and again in the 1990s), administrators spend time determining which buildings to erect and programs to initiate. Conversely, when resources dry up, conflict mushrooms and administrators often succumb to political forces they neither understand nor control.

Another key political issue is power—its distribution and exercise. Power in organizations is basically the capacity to get things done. Pfeffer (1992, p. 30) defines power as "the potential ability to influence behavior, to change the course of events, to overcome resistance, and to get people to do things they would not otherwise do." Russ (1994, p. 38) puts it more strongly as the ability to "make one's will prevail and to attain one's goal." Social scientists have often emphasized tight linkage between power and dependency: if A has something B wants, A has leverage. In much of organizational life, individuals and groups are interdependent; they need things from one another, and power relationships are multidirectional. From the view of the political frame, power is a "daily mechanism of our social existence" (Crozier and Friedberg, 1977, p. 32).

The final proposition of the political frame emphasizes that goals are set not by fiat at the top but through an ongoing process of negotiation and interaction among key players. To illustrate, consider another example: a commitment China made in December 2001 to promote its accession to the World Trade Organization. The Chinese government promised to get serious about protecting intellectual property, ensuring that products carrying labels such as Coca-Cola, Microsoft, Sony, and Rolex were authentic. The central government passed laws, threw the book at the occasional unlucky offender, blustered in the media, and put pressure on local governments. Yet six months later, name-brand knockoffs and pirated software were still on sale all over China, even a few blocks from Tiananmen Square.

Why did the antipiracy efforts have so little impact? The central government was far from monolithic and was only one of many players in a complex power game. Newly affluent Chinese consumers wanted foreign brands. Lots of large and small Chinese businesses knew, for example, that a homemade carbonated fluid fetched a better price if it carried an American name. The problem was so widespread that, in some cases, Coca-Cola's Chinese affiliate found itself not only raiding factories but chasing pirates who were slapping Coke labels on bottles in delivery trucks en route to retail outlets.

Stopping piracy ran into a range of obstacles. Pirates were often local businesses with plenty of *guanxi* (connections) who generously shared the loot with local government and police officials. Moreover, the concept of intellectual property rights was new to many Chinese. They found it hard to see the merit of punishing a hard-working Chinese entrepreneur to protect a big, foreign corporation. Multiple power centers, fierce bargaining, and continuing internal and external divisions seriously limited senior officials' ability to translate intention into action.

The antipiracy effort got a jump start from an emerging ally that began to shift the balance of power. Chinese companies increasingly began to develop their own brands, patents, and copyrights. They became just as eager as their foreign counterparts to keep poachers off their turf. *People's Daily* reported in April 2002 that Chinese software producers were losing almost $5 billion a year to pirates ("China Issues White Paper . . .," 2002). These producers, who were as passionate as Microsoft about protecting copyrights, added important local muscle to the government's antipiracy efforts.

ORGANIZATIONS AS COALITIONS

Viewing an organization as a coalition rather than a pyramid questions many orthodox views. Academics and managers alike have assumed that organizations have, or ought to have, clear and consistent goals set at the apex of authority. In a business, the owners or top managers set goals such as growth and profitability. Goals in a government agency are presumably set by the legislature and elected executives. The political frame questions such views, emphasizing that organizations are coalitions. Individuals and groups have their insular objectives and resources, and they bargain with other players to influence goals and decisions. Cyert and March articulate the difference between structural and political views of goals:

> To what extent is it arbitrary, in conventional accounting, that we call wage payments "costs" and dividend payments "profit" rather than the other way around? Why is it that in our quasi-genetic moments we are inclined to say that in the beginning there was a manager, and he recruited workers and capital? . . . The emphasis on the asymmetry has seriously confused the understanding of organizational goals. The confusion arises because ultimately it makes only slightly more sense to say that the goal of a business enterprise is to maximize profit than to say that its goal is to maximize the salary of Sam Smith, assistant to the janitor. (1963, p. 30)

Cyert and March are saying something like this: Jones, the assistant janitor; Ford, the foreman; and Cohen-Peters, the company president, are members of a grand coalition, Cohen-Peters Enterprises. All make demands on resources, and each bargains to get as much as possible. Cohen-Peters has more authority than Jones or Ford but no divine or inalienable right to determine goals. Her influence depends on how much power she mobilizes in comparison with that of Jones, Ford, and other members of the coalition.

If political pressures on goals are visible in the private sector, they are blatant in the public arena. As we saw in the *Challenger* incident, public agencies operate amid a welter of constituencies, each making demands and trying to get its way. The result is a confusing multiplicity of goals, many in conflict. In the early 1990s, for example, the French national airline, Air France, found itself in a tightening vise. Survival in an era of deregulation depended on cutting its bloated costs, but powerful unions fought tooth and nail to protect workers' pay and jobs. Was Air France's goal to serve the passengers, protect the workers, or relieve the suffering of French taxpayers? All of the above, because passengers, workers, managers, government officials, taxpayers, and more were all participants in the Air France coalition. Can outsiders be part of the coalition? Yes, if they are able to influence the carrier's goals and decisions, regardless of whether they get Air France paychecks.

Greatest Hits from Organization Studies No. 2: Richard M. Cyert and James G. March, *A Behavioral Theory of the Firm* (Upper Saddle River, N.J.: Prentice Hall, 1963).

Coming in at number two on the scholars' lists of greatest hits is a forty-year-old work by two professors who were colleagues at Carnegie-Mellon university: an economist, Richard Cyert, and a political scientist, James G. March. Cyert and March defined their basic purpose as developing a predictive theory of organizational decision making rooted in realistic understanding of how decisions were actually made. They rejected as unrealistic the traditional economic view of a firm as a unitary entity (a corporate "person") with a singular goal of maximizing profits. Cyert and March chose instead to view organizations as coalitions made up of individuals and subcoalitions. This view implied a central idea of the political frame: goals emerge out of a bargaining process among coalition members. Cyert and March also insisted that "side payments" are critical, since preferences are partly incompatible and not every decision can satisfy everyone. A coalition can survive only if it offers enough side payments to keep essential coalition members on board. This is not easy because of limited resources—(money, time, information, and decision-making capacity).

In analyzing decision making, Cyert and March developed four "relational concepts," implicit rules that firms use to make decisions more manageable:

1. *Quasi-resolution of conflict.* Instead of resolving conflict, organizations break problems into pieces and farm pieces out to different units. Units make decisions that are locally rational (for example, marketers do what they think is best for marketing). Decisions are never fully consistent but need only be good enough to keep the coalition functioning.
2. *Uncertainty avoidance.* Organizations employ a range of simplifying mechanisms—SOPs, organizational and industry traditions, contracts—that enable them to act as if information is clearer than it is.
3. *Problemistic search.* Organizations look for solutions in the neighborhood of the presenting problem and grab the first acceptable solution.
4. *Organizational learning.* Over time, organizations evolve by adapting goals and aspiration levels, altering what they attend to and what they ignore, and changing search rules.

POWER AND DECISION MAKING

A coalition forms because members have interests in common and believe they can do more together than apart. To accomplish their aims, they need power. Power can be viewed from multiple perspectives. Structural theorists typically emphasize authority, the legitimate prerogative to make binding decisions. Managers make rational decisions (optimal and consistent with purpose), monitor actions to ensure decisions are implemented, and evaluate how well subordinates carry out directives. In contrast, human resource theorists place little emphasis on power, though they often promote the idea of empowerment (Bennis and Nanus, 1985; Block, 1987). More than the structuralists do, they emphasize limits of authority. As an asymmetric source of influence, authority often stands in the way of integrating organizational and individual needs. If A can influence B but not vice versa, there is a good chance that the relationship will be more satisfying for A. Human resource theorists tend to focus on influence that enhances mutuality and collaboration. The implicit hope is that participation, openness, and collaboration make power a nonissue.

The political frame views authority as only one among many forms of power. It recognizes the importance of human (and group) needs but emphasizes that scarce resources and incompatible preferences cause needs to collide. Consider a case of policy conflict. A group of graduate students in an academic department wants the university to become more democratic and responsive, while faculty members insist on tightening controls and standards. The human resource theorist is likely to ask: What are the needs and perspectives of each group? How can the two engage in a productive dialogue to learn from one another, explore differences, and find a mutually satisfactory solution? A structural analysis would focus on finding the right decision, one based on sound analysis or producing better outcomes. Political theorists are more likely to view divergent interests as an enduring fact of life and are less optimistic about distinguishing better from worse solutions. The question becomes, How does each group articulate preferences and mobilize power to get what it wants? Power, in this view, is not necessarily bad: "We have to stop describing power always in negative terms: [as in] it excludes, it represses. In fact, power produces; it produces reality" (Foucault, 1975, p. 12).

Authorities and Partisans

Our example of conflict in an academic department illustrates the relationship between two political roles that are often central to the politics of both organizations and society. Professors are *authorities*; their role entitles them to make decisions binding on the students. Students are *partisans*; they want to exert bottom-up influence. Gamson (1968) describes the relationship in this way: "Authorities are the recipients or targets of influence, and the agents or initiators of social control. Potential partisans have the opposite roles—as agents or initiators of influence, and targets or recipients of social control" (p. 76).

In a family, parents function as authorities and children as partisans. Parents make binding decisions about bedtime, television viewing, or which child uses a particular toy. Parents initiate social control, and children are the recipients of parental decisions. Children in turn try to influence the decision makers. They argue for a later bedtime or point out the injustice of giving one child something another wants. They try to split authorities by lobbying one parent after the other has refused. They may form a coalition (with siblings, grandparents, and so on) in an attempt to strengthen their bargaining position.

Social control is essential to anyone in a formal position because authority depends on it. Officeholders can exert control only so long as partisans respect or fear them enough that their authority remains intact. If partisan opposition becomes too powerful to control, authority may collapse. The process can be very swift, as events in Eastern Europe in 1989 illustrated. Established regimes lost much of their legitimacy years earlier but held on through coercion and control of access to decision making. Senior government officials had reason to hold on: their power and privilege were tied to maintaining the "leading role" of the Communist party. As massive demonstrations erupted, authorities faced an unnerving choice: activate the police and army in the hope of preserving power, or watch their power evaporate. Authorities in China and Romania chose the first course. It led to bloodshed in both cases, but only the Chinese were able to quash the opposition. In Eastern Europe, authorities' attempts to quell dissent were futile, and their power evaporated as swiftly as water in a desert.

The period of evaporation is heady but dangerous. The question is whether new authority can reconstitute itself quickly enough to avoid chaos. Authorities and partisans both have reason to fear a specter such as Lebanon in the 1980s or Bosnia and Liberia in the 1990s—perpetual turmoil with no authority able to bring partisan strife under control. In the spring of 2002, a senior member of the Chinese communist party admitted that it was hard to say what the party stood for except for one thing: stability (Rosenthal, 2002). China's twentieth century was chronically chaotic, with a continuing series of wars, revolutions, crop failures, and social turmoil. The party's greatest strength was widespread fear that the social and economic progress of recent years might crash into still another period of conflict and turbulence. Government leaders were wary of any change, because they knew their hold on the reins could be put at risk. If partisans are convinced that the existing authorities are too evil or too incompetent to continue, they will run the risk of trying to wrest power away—unless they regard the authorities as too formidable. Conversely, if partisans trust authority, they will leave it alone and even support it in the event of an attack (Gamson, 1968; Baldridge, 1971).

Sources of Power

Even though partisans lack authority, they may have other power sources. A number of social scientists (Baldridge, 1971; French and Raven, 1959; Kanter, 1977; Pfeffer, 1981, 1992; Russ, 1994) have tried to identify the various wellsprings of power. Their alternatives include:

1. *Position power (authority).* Positions confer certain levels of formal authority; professors assign grades, and judges decide disputes. Positions also place incumbents in more or less powerful locations in communications and power networks. It helps to be in the right unit as well as the right job; though a lofty title in a backwater department may not mean much, junior members of a powerful unit may have substantial clout (Pfeffer, 1992).

2. *Information and expertise.* Power flows to those with the information and know-how to solve important problems. It flows to marketing experts in consumer products industries, to the faculty in elite universities, and to superstar conductors of symphony orchestras.

3. *Control of rewards.* The ability to deliver jobs, money, political support, or other rewards brings power. France and Italy were among many countries rocked in the 1990s by scandals involving political bosses who kept themselves in power through control of patronage, public services, and other payoffs.

4. *Coercive power.* Coercive power rests on the ability to constrain, block, interfere, or punish. A union's ability to walk out, students' ability to sit in, and an army's ability to clamp down exemplify coercive power. Even information can be used coercively. In the early 1970s, Students for a Democratic Society (SDS) created havoc at Stanford University by stealing and publishing a listing of faculty salaries. Publicizing a list that had been a well-guarded secret revealed enormous disparities in how much faculty members, even in the same department, were making. This strategy bolstered the sit-ins and other coercive measures the SDS employed in its bid for power.

5. *Alliances and networks.* Getting things done in an organization involves working through a complex network of individuals and groups. Friends and allies make things a lot easier. Kotter (1982) found that a key difference between more and less successful senior managers was attentiveness to building and cultivating links with friends and allies. Managers who spent too little time building networks had much more difficulty getting things done.

6. *Access and control of agendas.* A by-product of networks and alliances is access to decision arenas. Organizations and political systems typically give some groups more access than others. When decisions are made, the interests of those with "a seat at the table" are well represented, while the concerns of absentees are often distorted or ignored (Lukes, 1974; Brown, 1986).

7. *Framing: control of meaning and symbols.* "Establishing the framework within which issues will be viewed and decided is often tantamount to determining the result" (Pfeffer, 1992, p. 203). Elites and opinion leaders often have substantial ability to define and even impose the meanings and myths that define identity, beliefs, and values. Viewed positively, this fosters meaning and hope. Viewed cynically, the elites can convince others to accept and support things not in their best interests (Brown, 1986). This can be a very subtle and unobtrusive form of power: when the powerless accept the myths promulgated by the powerful, overt conflict and power struggles may disappear (Brown, 1986; Frost, 1985; Gaventa, 1980). In China in the early twenty-first century, senior government leaders repeatedly invoked the mantra that the alternative to Communist rule was chaos. Whether this assertion was myth or reality, many Chinese were reluctant to test it.

8. *Personal power.* Individuals with charisma, energy and stamina, political skills, verbal facility, or the capacity to articulate a vision are imbued with power independent of other sources.

Multiple sources of power constrain authorities' capacity to make binding decisions. If they rely solely on position power, they generate resistance and are outflanked, out-maneuvered, or overrun by those more versatile in exercising power. Kotter (1985) argues that managerial jobs come with a built-in "power gap" because position power is rarely enough to get the job done. Expertise, rewards, coercion, allies, access, framing, and personal power help close the gap.

A decision maker's power also depends on constituents' leverage and satisfaction. An organization that sets new profit records every year is rarely besieged by complaints and demands for change. As many company presidents have learned, however, the first bad quarter triggers a stream of calls and letters from board members, stockholders, and financial analysts. In the boom of the late 1990s, "everyone" was getting rich in the stock market, and charismatic CEOs such as Jack Welch of General Electric and Jean-Marie Messier of France's Vivendi became popular heroes. But when the economy, the market, and the image of business crashed in the first years of the new century, so did their heroic images. In 2002, Welch found himself deeply embarrassed by public revelation of the generous postretirement payouts his old company was bestowing on him. In the same year, Messier was booted out by a coalition of American board members dissatisfied with the stock price and French board members concerned about Messier's arrogant "American" leadership style.

One college president remarked ruefully that his primary job seemed to be to provide "sex for the students, parking for the faculty, and football for the alumni." The remark was half facetious, but it reflects an important reality: a president's power lies particularly in zones of indifference—areas few people care much about. The zone of indifference can expand or contract markedly, depending on how an organization is doing in the eyes of its major constituents.

Distribution of Power: Overbounded and Underbounded Systems

One key way in which organizations and societies differ is in how power is distributed. Alderfer (1979) and Brown (1983) distinguish between overbounded and underbounded systems. In an overbounded system, power is highly concentrated and everything is tightly regulated. In an underbounded system, power is diffuse and the system is very loosely controlled. An overbounded system regulates politics tightly; an underbounded system is an open invitation to conflict and power games.

If power is concentrated at the top of a highly regulated system, political activity is often forced underground. Before the emergence of Mikhail Gorbachev and *glasnost* ("openness") in the 1980s, it was common for Westerners to view the Soviets as a vast, undifferentiated mass of like-minded people, brainwashed by decades of government propaganda. The truth was otherwise, but even so-called experts on Soviet affairs missed its significance (Alterman, 1989). Ethnic, political, philosophical, and religious differences simmered quietly beneath the surface so long as the Kremlin maintained a tightly regulated society. *Glasnost* took the lid off, leading to an outpouring of debate and dissent that rapidly caused the collapse of the old order in the Soviet Union and throughout Eastern Europe. Almost overnight, much of Eastern Europe went from overbounded to underbounded. The war in Iraq in 2003 produced the same result. The collapse of an overbounded system created a power vacuum that attracted a host of contenders.

CONFLICT IN ORGANIZATIONS

A basic proposition of the political frame is that the combination of scarce resources and divergent interests produces conflict as surely as night follows day. Unlike other frames, the political frame does not view conflict as something that can or should be stamped out. The structural frame in particular views conflict as a problem that undermines effectiveness. Hierarchical conflict raises the possibility of lower levels ignoring or subverting management directives. Conflict among major partisan groups can undermine leadership's ability to function. Such dangers are precisely why the structural perspective champions a well-defined chain of command. A basic function of authority is to resolve conflict. If two individuals or departments cannot reach agreement, a higher level can adjudicate the dispute and make a final decision consistent with plans and goals.

From a political perspective, conflict is not necessarily a problem or a sign that something is amiss. Organizational resources are notoriously in short supply; there is rarely enough to give everyone everything they want. There are too many lower-level jobs and too few at the top. If one group controls the policy process, others may be frozen out. Individuals compete for jobs, titles, and prestige. Departments compete for resources and power. Interest groups vie for policy concessions. Conflict is natural and inevitable.

The focus of the political frame is not on resolution of conflict (as is often the case in both the structural and human resource frames) but on strategy and tactics. If conflict will not go away, the question becomes how to make the best of it. Conflict has benefits as well as costs: "a tranquil, harmonious organization may very well be an apathetic, uncreative, stagnant, inflexible, and unresponsive organization. Conflict challenges the status quo [and] stimulates interest and curiosity. It is the root of personal and social change, creativity, and innovation. Conflict encourages new ideas and approaches to problems, stimulating innovation" (Heffron, 1989, p. 185). An organization can experience too much or too little conflict (Brown, 1983; Heffron, 1989; Jehn, 1995). Intervention may be needed to increase or decrease conflict, depending on the situation. Even more important than the amount of conflict is how it is managed. Poor conflict management leads to the kind of infighting and destructive power struggle we saw in the *Challenger* case. But well-handled conflict can stimulate the creativity and innovation that make an organization a livelier, more adaptive, and more effective place (Kotter, 1985).

Conflict is particularly likely to occur at boundaries, or interfaces, between groups and units. Horizontal conflict occurs in interfaces between departments or divisions; vertical conflict occurs between levels. Cultural conflict occurs between groups with differing values, traditions, beliefs, and lifestyles. Cultural conflict in the larger society is often imported into the workplace. Tension forms around gender, racial, and other differences. But organizations also create their own cultural conflict. The culture of management is different from that of blue-collar workers. Workers who move up the ladder sometimes struggle with cultural adjustments required by their new role.

The challenge for both managers and organizations is to recognize and manage interface conflict. Like other forms of conflict, it can be productive or debilitating. One of the most important tasks of unit managers or union representatives is to be a persuasive and influential advocate for their group on a political field having many players representing competing interests. They need negotiation skills to develop alliances and cement deals that enable their group to move forward.

MORAL MAZES: THE POLITICS OF GETTING AHEAD

Is a world of power, conflict, self-interest, and political games inevitably a jungle in which the only rule is that the strong devour the weak? Is it almost invariably a nasty, brutish environment in which values and ethics are irrelevant? The corporate ethics scandals of

2001–02 reinforced a recurrent suspicion that the morals of the marketplace amount to no morals at all. Consider this example:

> Not long after the big purge at Covenant Corporation, when 600 people were fired, the CEO spent $1 million for a Family Day to bring everyone together. The massive party was attended by over 14,000 people and featured clowns, sports idols, and booths complete with beanbag and ring tosses, foot and bus races, computer games, dice rolls, and, perhaps appropriately, mazes. In his letter to his Fellow Employees following the event, the CEO said, "I think Family Day made a very strong statement about the 'family' of employees at Corporate Headquarters. And that is that we can accomplish whatever we set out to do if we work together; if we share the effort, we will share the rewards." (Jackall, 1988, p. 37)

Jackall adds that "wise and ambitious managers resist the lulling platitudes of unity, though they invoke them with fervor, and look for the inevitable clash of interests beneath the bouncy, cheerful surface of corporate life" (p. 37). Beneath the surface is a world of circles and alliances, dominance and submission, conflict and self-interest, and (in Jackall's phrase) "moral mazes." Moving up the ladder inevitably involves competition for the scarce resource of status. The preferred myth is that free and fair competition ensures better performers will win, at least in the long run.

But assessing performance in a managerial job is fraught with ambiguity. There are multiple criteria, some of which can be assessed only through subjective judgment (particularly by the boss and other superiors). It is often hard to separate individual performance from the group's, or from a host of external factors. It may also make a big difference who is doing the judging. When bright, creative energy traders at Enron developed clever techniques with names like "Get Shorty" and "Fat Boy" to exploit the crisis in California's electricity market in 2001, did they deserve commendation for their contribution to the bottom line? Or jail time in the Golden State? Did Thiokol engineers who fought to stop the launch of *Challenger* deserve a high grade for persistence and integrity, or a low grade because they failed to make a convincing case? When some of those same engineers went public with their criticism, were they demonstrating courage, or disloyalty? Whistleblowers are regularly lauded by the press yet punished or banished by their employers. This is exemplified by *Time* magazine's 2002 Person of the Year award, which was given to three women who blew the whistle on their employers: Enron, WorldCom, and the FBI.

Managers frequently learn that getting ahead is a matter of personal "credibility," which comes from doing what is socially and politically correct. Definitions of political correctness reflect tacit forms of power deeply embedded in organizational patterns and structure (Frost, 1986). Because getting ahead and making it to the top dominate the attention of many managers (Dalton, 1959; Jackall, 1988; Ritti and Funkhouser, 1982), both organizations and individuals need to develop constructive and positive ways to master the political game. The question is not whether organizations will have politics but rather what kind of politics they will have. Jackall's view is bleak:

> Bureaucracy breaks apart the ownership of property from its control, social independence from occupation, substance from appearances, action from responsibility, obligation from guilt, language from meaning, and notions of truth from reality. Most important, and at the bottom of all these fractures, it breaks apart the traditional connection between the meaning of work and salvation. In the bureaucratic world, one's success, one's sign of election, no longer depends on an inscrutable God, but on the capriciousness of one's superiors and the market; and one achieves economic salvation to the extent that one pleases and submits to new gods, that is, one's bosses and the exigencies of an impersonal market. (Jackall, 1988, pp. 191–192)

This is not a pretty picture, but it is often accurate. Productive politics is possible but not easy. In the next chapter, we explore some of the ways that a manager can become a constructive politician.

CONCLUSION

The traditional view sees organizations as created and controlled by legitimate authorities who set goals, design structure, hire and manage employees, and ensure pursuance of the right objectives. The political view frames a very different world. Authorities have position power, but they must vie with many other contenders for other forms of clout. Contenders bring their own beliefs, values, and interests. They seek access to various forms of power and compete for their share of scarce resources in a limited organizational pie.

From a political perspective, goals, structure, and policies emerge from an ongoing process of bargaining and negotiation among major interest groups. Sometimes legitimate authorities are the dominant members of the coalition; this is likely to be the case in a small, entrepreneurial organization where the chief executive is also the owner. But large corporations are often controlled by senior management rather than by stockholders or the board of directors. Government agencies may be controlled more by the permanent civil servants than by the political leaders at the top. The dominant group in a school district may be the teachers' union rather than the school board or the superintendent. In all such cases, rationalists feel that the wrong people are setting the agenda. But the political view suggests that the exercise of power is a natural part of an ongoing contest. Those who get and use power best will be winners.

There is no guarantee that those who gain power use it wisely or justly. But it is not inevitable that power and politics are demeaning and destructive. Constructive politics is a possibility—indeed, a necessary possibility if we are to create institutions and societies that are both just and efficient.

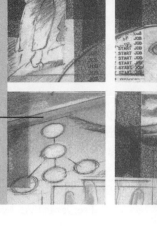

CHAPTER 10

The Manager as Politician

Bill Gates was standing in the right place in the early 1980s when IBM's fledgling personal computer business came looking for an operating system. Gates didn't have one, but his partner, Paul Allen, knew someone who did. Gates paid $75,000 for QDOS (Quick and Dirty Operating System) in the deal—or steal—of the twentieth century. Gates changed the name to DOS and resold it to IBM, but he shrewdly retained the right to license it to anyone else. DOS quickly became the primary operating system for most of the world's personal computers. Gates himself was on the road to becoming one of the world's richest men (Manes and Andrews, 1994; Zachary, 1994).

Windows, a graphic interface riding atop DOS, fueled another great leap forward for Gates's Microsoft empire. But by the late 1980s, Gates had a problem. He and everyone else knew that DOS was obsolete, woefully deficient for existing personal computers and even more inadequate for those to come. Millions of PC users were stuck in a high-tech version of *Waiting for Godot*.

The solution was supposed to be OS/2, an operating system developed jointly by Microsoft and IBM. It was a tense partnership. IBMers saw "Microsofties" as undisciplined adolescents. Microsoft folks moaned that "Big Blue" was a hopelessly bureaucratic producer of "poor code, poor design, poor process and other overhead" (Manes and Andrews, 1994, p. 425). Increasingly pessimistic about the viability of OS/2, Gates decided to hedge his bets by developing a new operating system to be called Windows NT. Gates recruited the brilliant but crotchety Dave Cutler from Digital Equipment to head the effort. Cutler had led the development of the VMS operating system that helped DEC dominate the minicomputer industry for many years. Zachary (1993) described Cutler as a rough-cut combination of Captain Bligh and Captain Ahab. Gates agreed that Cutler was known "more for his code than his charm" (Zachary, 1993, p. A1).

Things started well, but Cutler insisted on keeping his team small and wanted no responsibility beyond the "kernel" of the operating system. He figured someone else could worry about such things as the user interface. Gates began to see a potential disaster looming, but issuing orders to the temperamental Cutler was as promising as telling Picasso to paint differently. Gates then brought in the calm, understated Paul Maritz. Born in South Africa, Maritz had studied mathematics and economics in Cape Town before deciding that software was his destiny. After five years with Intel, Maritz joined Microsoft in 1986 and became the leader of its OS/2 effort. When he was assigned informal oversight of Windows NT, no one told Cutler, who adamantly refused to work for Maritz. Twelve years Cutler's junior, Maritz got a frosty welcome:

> As he began meeting regularly with Cutler on NT matters, Maritz often found himself the victim of slights. Once Maritz innocently suggested to Cutler that "We should—" Cutler interrupted, "We! Who's we? You mean you and the mouse in your pocket?" Maritz brushed off such retorts, even finding humor in Cutler's apparently inexhaustible supply of epithets. He refused to allow Cutler to draw him into a brawl. Instead, he hoped Cutler would "volunteer" for greater responsibility as the shortcomings of the status quo became more apparent. (Zachary, 1994, p. 76)

Maritz enticed Cutler with tempting challenges. In early 1990, he asked Cutler if it would be possible to put together a demonstration of NT in November for COMDEX, the industry's biggest convention. Cutler took the bait. Maritz knew that the effort would expose NT's weaknesses (Zachary, 1994). When Gates subsequently seethed that NT was too late, too big, and too slow, Maritz scrambled to "filter that stuff from Dave" (p. 208). Maritz's patience eventually paid off when he was promoted to head all operating systems development: "The promotion gave Maritz formal and actual authority over Cutler and the entire NT project. Still, he avoided confrontations, preferring to wait until Cutler came to see the benefits of Maritz's views. Increasingly Cutler and his inner circle viewed Maritz as a powerhouse and not an empty suit. 'He's critical to the project,' said [one of Cutler's most loyal lieutenants]. 'He got into it a little bit at a time. Slowly he blended his way in until it was obvious who was running the show. Him.'" (p. 204)

The *Challenger* case (see Chapter Nine) teaches a chilling lesson about how political pressures distort momentous decisions. Similarly, the implosion of firms such as Enron and WorldCom shows how the unfettered pursuit of self-interest by powerful executives can bring even a giant corporation to its knees. Many believe that the antidote is to free management from politics. But this is unrealistic so long as the political frame's basic conditions apply. Enduring differences lead to multiple interpretations of what is important, and even what is true. Scarce resources require tough decisions about who gets what. Interdependence means that people cannot ignore one another; they need each other's assistance, support, and resources. Under such conditions, efforts to eliminate politics drive differences under the rug or into the closet. There they fester into counterproductive, unmanageable forms. In our search for more positive images of the manager as constructive politician, Paul Maritz offers an example.

Kotter (1985) contends that too many managers are either naïve or cynical. Naïve managers view the world through rose-colored glasses, insisting that most people are good, kind, and trustworthy. Cynical managers believe the opposite: everyone is selfish, things are always political, and "get them before they get you" is the best survival tactic. Neither stance is effective: "Organizational excellence . . . demands a sophisticated type of social skill: a leadership skill that can mobilize people and accomplish important objectives despite dozens of obstacles; a skill that can pull people together for meaningful purposes despite the thousands of forces that push us apart; a skill that can keep our corporations and public institutions from descending into a mediocrity characterized by bureaucratic infighting, parochial politics, and vicious power struggles" (p. 11).

Organizations need "benevolent politicians" who steer a course between naïveté and cynicism: "Beyond the yellow brick road of naïveté and the mugger's lane of cynicism, there is a narrow path, poorly lighted, hard to find, and even harder to stay on once found. People who have the skill and the perseverance to take that path serve us in countless ways. We need more of these people. Many more" (Kotter, 1985, p. xi).

In a world of chronic scarcity, diversity, and conflict, the astute manager has to develop a direction, build a base of support, and learn how to manage relations with both allies and opponents. In this chapter, we start by laying out four basic skills for the manager as politician. Then we tackle ethical issues, the soft underbelly of organizational politics. Is it possible to be political and still do the right thing? We discuss four instrumental values to guide ethical choice: mutuality (is everyone playing by the same rules?); generality (would it be good if everyone did it?); openness (are we open to public scrutiny?), and caring (are we looking out for anyone beyond ourselves?).

POLITICAL SKILLS

The manager as politician exercises four key skills: agenda setting (Kanter, 1983; Kotter, 1988; Pfeffer, 1992; Smith, 1988), mapping the political terrain (Pfeffer, 1992; Pichault, 1993), networking and forming coalitions (Kanter, 1983; Kotter, 1982, 1985, 1988; Pfeffer, 1992; Smith, 1988), and bargaining and negotiating (Bellow and Moulton, 1978; Fisher and Ury, 1981; Lax and Sebenius, 1986).

Agenda Setting

Structurally, an agenda outlines a goal and a scheduled series of activities. Politically, agendas are statements of interests and scenarios. In reflecting on his experience as a university president, Warren Bennis (1989) arrived at a deceptively simple observation: "It struck me that I was most effective when I knew what I wanted" (p. 20). Kanter's study of internal entrepreneurs in American corporations (1983), Kotter's analysis of effective corporate leaders (1988), and Smith's examination of effective U.S. presidents (1988) all reached a similar conclusion: the first step in effective political leadership is setting an agenda.

The effective leader creates an "agenda for change" with two major elements: a *vision* balancing the long-term interests of key parties and a *strategy for achieving the vision,* recognizing competing internal and external forces (Kotter, 1988). The agenda must impart direction while addressing the concerns of major stakeholders. Kanter (1983) and Pfeffer (1992) underscore the close relationship between gathering information and developing a vision. Pfeffer's list of key political attributes includes "sensitivity,"—knowing how others think and what they care about so that your agenda responds to their concerns: "Many people think of politicians as arm-twisters, and that is, in part, true. But in order to be a successful arm-twister, one needs to know which arm to twist, and how" (Pfeffer, 1992, p. 172).

Kanter (1983) adds: "While gathering information, entrepreneurs can also be 'planting seeds'—leaving the kernel of an idea behind and letting it germinate and blossom so that it begins to float around the system from many sources other than the innovator" (p. 218). This was exactly Paul Maritz's approach. Ignoring Dave Cutler's barbs and insults, he focused on getting information, building relationships, and formulating an agenda. He quickly concluded that the NT project was in disarray and that Cutler had to take on more responsibility. But Maritz's strategy was exquisitely attuned to his quarry: "Maritz protected Cutler from undue criticism and resisted the urge to reform him. [He] kept the peace by exacting from Cutler no ritual expressions of obedience" (Zachary, 1994, pp. 281–282).

A vision without a strategy remains an illusion. A strategy has to recognize major forces working for and against the agenda. Smith (1988, p. 333) makes this point about the American presidency:

> In the grand scheme of American government, the paramount task and power of the president is to articulate the national purpose: to fix the nation's agenda. Of all the big games at the summit of American politics, the agenda game must be won first. The effectiveness of the presidency and the capacity of any president to lead depend on focusing the nation's political attention and its energies on two or three top priorities. From the standpoint of history, the flow of events seems to have immutable logic, but political reality is inherently chaotic: it contains no automatic agenda. Order must be imposed.

Agendas never come neatly packaged. The bigger the job, the more difficult it is to wade through clamoring issues to find order amid chaos. Contrary to Woody Allen's dictum, success requires more than just showing up. High office, even if the incumbent enjoys great personal popularity, is no guarantee. Ronald Reagan was remarkably successful in his first year as president following a classic strategy for winning the agenda game: "First impressions are critical. In the agenda game, a swift beginning is crucial for a new president to establish himself as leader—to show the nation that he will make a difference in people's lives. The first one hundred days are the vital test; in those weeks, the political community and the public measure a new president—to see whether he is active, dominant, sure, purposeful" (Smith, 1988, p. 334).

Reagan began with a vision but without a strategy. He was not gifted as a manager or a strategist, despite extraordinary ability to portray complex issues in broad, symbolic brushstrokes. Reagan's staff painstakingly studied the first hundred days of four predecessors. They concluded that it was essential to move with speed and focus. Pushing competing issues aside, they focused on two: cutting taxes and reducing the federal budget. They also discovered a secret weapon in David Stockman, the only person in the Reagan White House who really understood the federal budget process. Stockman later admitted that he was astounded by the "low level of fiscal literacy" of Reagan and his key advisers (Smith, 1988, p. 354). According to Smith, "Stockman got a jump on everyone else for two reasons: he had an agenda and a legislative blueprint already prepared, and he understood the real levers of power. Two terms as a Michigan congressman plus a network of key Republican and Democratic connections had taught Stockman how to play the power game" (p. 351). Reagan and his advisers had the vision; Stockman brought strategic direction.

Mapping the Political Terrain

It seems foolhardy to plunge into a minefield without knowing where explosives are buried, yet managers unwittingly do it all the time. They launch a new initiative with little or no effort to scout the political turf. Pichault (1993) suggests four steps for developing a political map:

1. Determine channels of informal communication.
2. Identify principal agents of political influence.
3. Analyze possibilities for both internal and external mobilization.
4. Anticipate strategies that others are likely to employ.

Pichault offers an example of planned change in a large government agency in Belgium. The agency wanted to replace antiquated, manual records with a fully automated, paperless computer network. But proponents of the new system had virtually no understanding of how the status quo actually functioned. Nor did they anticipate the interests and power of key middle managers and front-line bureaucrats. It seemed obvious to the techies that better access to data would dramatically improve efficiency. In reality, front-line bureaucrats made almost no use of the data. They applied standard procedures in 90 percent of the cases they encountered and asked their bosses what to do about the rest. Their queries were partly to get the "right" answer, but even more important they wanted to cover themselves politically. Even if the new technology were installed, front-line bureaucrats were likely to ignore or work around it. After a consultant clarified the political map, a new battle erupted between unrepentant techies, insisting their solution was correct, pitted against senior managers arguing for a less ambitious, more grounded approach. The two sides ultimately compromised.

A simple way to develop a political map for any situation is to create a two-dimensional diagram mapping players (who is in the game), power (how much clout each player is likely to exercise), and interests (what each player wants). Figures 10.1 and 10.2 present two hypothetical versions of the Belgian bureaucracy's political map. Figure 10.1 shows the map as seen by proponents of the new technology (the techies). Their view of the terrain shows little serious opposition to the new system, and they hold all the high cards; their map suggests a quick and easy win. Figure 10.2, the real map (as it might be seen by an objective analyst), paints a very different picture. Resistance is more intense and opponents more powerful. This view of the political terrain forecasts a stormy process imbued with protracted conflict. Though less comforting, the second map has an important message: success requires substantial effort to realign the existing field of political forces. The third and fourth key skills of the manager as politician, discussed in the next two sections, include strategies for doing that.

Networking and Building Coalitions

The *Challenger* disaster occurred despite recognition of the O-ring problem by engineers at both Morton Thiokol and NASA. For a long time, they tried to get their superiors' attention, mostly through memos. Six months before the accident, Roger Boisjoly, an engineer at Morton Thiokol, wrote: "The result [of an O-ring failure] would be a catastrophe of the highest order—loss of human life" (Bell and Esch, 1987, p. 45). Two months later, another Thiokol engineer wrote a memo that opened, "HELP! The seal task force is constantly being delayed by every possible means" (p. 45). The memo detailed resistance from other departments in Thiokol. A memo to the boss is sometimes effective, but it is just as often a sign of political innocence. Kotter (1985) suggests four basic steps for exercising political influence:

1. Identify relevant relationships (figure out who needs to be led).
2. Assess who might resist, why, and how strongly (figure out where the leadership challenges will be).

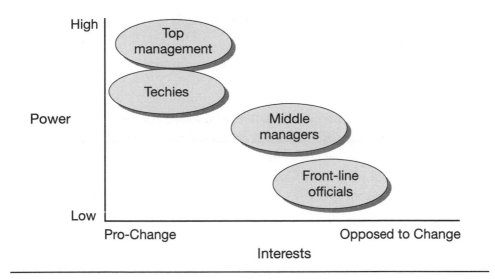

FIGURE 10.1. The Map the Techies See.

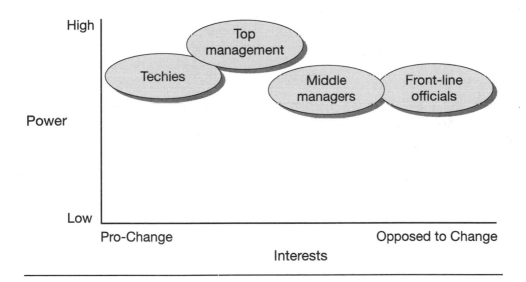

FIGURE 10.2. The Real Political Map.

3. Develop, wherever possible, relationships with potential opponents to facilitate communication, education, or negotiation.

4. If step three fails, carefully select and implement either more subtle or more forceful methods.

These steps underscore the importance of developing a sufficient power base. Moving up the ladder confers authority but also incurs increasing dependence, because success depends on the cooperation of many others (Kotter, 1985, 1988). People rarely give their best efforts and fullest cooperation simply because they were ordered to do so. They accept directions when they perceive the people in authority as credible, competent, and sensible.

The first task in building networks and coalitions is to figure out whose help you need. The second is to develop relationships so people will be there when you need them. Middle managers seeking to promote change typically begin by getting their boss on board (Kanter, 1983). They then move to "preselling" or "making cheerleaders": "Peers, managers of related functions, stakeholders in the issue, potential collaborators, and sometimes even customers would be approached individually, in one-on-one meetings that gave people a chance to influence the project and [gave] the innovator the maximum opportunity to sell it. Seeing them alone and on their territory was important: the rule was to act as if each person were *the* most important one for the project's success" (p. 223).

Once you cultivate cheerleaders, you can move to "horse trading": promising rewards in exchange for resources and support. This builds a resource base that helps in getting the necessary approvals and mandates from higher management (Kanter, 1983). Kanter found that the usual route to success in "securing blessings" is to identify critical senior managers and to develop a polished, formal presentation to sway their support. The best presentations respond to both substantive and political concerns. Senior managers typically care about two questions: Is it a good idea? How will my constituents react? Once innovators obtain higher management's blessing, they can formalize the coalition with their boss and make specific plans for pursuing the project (Kanter, 1983).

The basic point is simple: as a manager, you need friends and allies to get things done. To get their support, you need to cultivate relationships. Hard-core rationalists and incurable romantics sometimes react with horror to such a scenario. Why should you have to play political games to get something accepted if it's the right thing to do? One of the great works in French drama, Molière's *The Misanthrope,* tells the story of a protagonist whose rigid rejection of all things political is destructive for him and everyone around him. The point that Molière made four centuries ago still has merit: it is hard to dislike politics without also disliking people. Like it or not, political dynamics are inevitable under conditions most managers face every day: ambiguity, diversity, and scarcity.

Ignoring or misreading those dynamics is costly. Smith (1988) reports a case in point. Thomas Wyman, board chairman of the CBS television network, went to Washington in 1983 to lobby U.S. Attorney General Edwin Meese. A White House emergency forced Meese to miss the meeting, and Wyman was sent to the office of Craig Fuller, one of Meese's top advisers:

"I know something about this issue," Fuller suggested, "Perhaps you'd like to discuss it with me."

Wyman waved him off, unaware of Fuller's actual role, and evidently regarding him as a mere staff man.

"No, I'd rather wait and talk to Meese," Wyman said.

For nearly an hour, Wyman sat leafing through magazines in Fuller's office, making no effort to talk to Fuller, who kept working at his desk just a few feet away.

Finally, Meese burst into Fuller's office, full of apologies that he simply wouldn't have time for substantive talk. "Did you talk to Fuller?" he asked.

Wyman shook his head.

"You should have talked to Fuller," Meese said. "He's very important on this issue. He knows it better than any of the rest of us. He's writing a memo for the president on the pros and cons. You could have given him your side of the argument." (Smith, 1988, pp. xviii-xix)

Wyman missed an important opportunity because he failed to test his assumptions about who actually had power.

Bargaining and Negotiation

We often associate bargaining with commercial, legal, and labor relations settings. From a political perspective, though, bargaining is central to all decision making. The horse trading Kanter describes as part of coalition building is just one of many examples. Negotiation is needed whenever two or more parties with some interests in common and others in conflict need to reach agreement. Labor and management may agree that a firm should make money and offer good jobs to its employees but disagree on how to balance pay and profitability. Engineers and top managers at Morton Thiokol had a common interest in the success of the shuttle program. They differed sharply on how to balance technical and political trade-offs.

A fundamental dilemma in negotiations is choosing between "creating value" and "claiming value":

> Value creators tend to believe that, above all, successful negotiators must be inventive and cooperative enough to devise an agreement that yields considerable gain to each party, relative to no-agreement possibilities. Some speak about the need for replacing the win-lose image of negotiation with win-win negotiation. In addition to information sharing and honest communication, the drive to create value can require ingenuity and may benefit from a variety of techniques and attitudes. The parties can treat the negotiation as solving a joint problem; they can organize brainstorming sessions to invent creative solutions to their problems:

> Value claimers, on the other hand, tend to see this drive for joint gain as naive and weak-minded. For them, negotiation is hard, tough bargaining. The object of negotiation is to convince the other guy that he wants what you have to offer much more than you want what he has; moreover, you have all the time in the world, while he is up against pressing deadlines. To "win" at negotiating—and thus make the other fellow "lose"—one must start high, concede slowly, exaggerate the value of concessions, minimize the benefits of the other's concessions, conceal information, argue forcibly on behalf of principles that imply favorable settlements, make commitments to accept only highly favorable agreements, and be willing to out wait the other fellow. (Lax and Sebenius, 1986, pp. 30–32)

One of the best-known win-win approaches to negotiation was developed by Fisher and Ury (1981) in *Getting to Yes*. They argue that people too often engage in "positional bargaining": they stake out positions and then reluctantly make concessions to reach agreement. Fisher and Ury contend that positional bargaining is inefficient and misses opportunities to create an agreement beneficial to both parties. They propose an alternative: "principled bargaining," built around four strategies.

The first strategy is to *separate the people from the problem*. The stress and tension of negotiations can easily escalate into anger and personal attack. The result is that a negotiator sometimes wants to defeat or hurt the other person at almost any cost. Because every negotiation involves both substance and relationship, the wise negotiator will "deal with the people as human beings and with the problem on its merits." Maritz demonstrated this principle in dealing with the prickly Cutler. Even though Cutler continually baited and insulted him, Maritz refused to be distracted and persistently focused on getting the job done.

The second rule of thumb is to *focus on interests, not positions*. If you get locked into a particular position, you might overlook other ways to achieve the goal. An example is the 1978 Camp David treaty, resolving issues between Israel and Egypt. The sides were at an impasse over where to draw the boundary between the two countries. Israel wanted to keep part of the Sinai, while Egypt wanted all of it back. Resolution became possible only when they looked at each other's underlying interests. Israel was concerned about security: no Egyptian tanks on the border. Egypt was concerned about sovereignty: the Sinai had been part of Egypt from the time of the Pharaohs. The parties agreed on a plan that gave all of the Sinai back to Egypt while demilitarizing large parts of it (Fisher and Ury, 1981). That solution led to a durable peace agreement.

Fisher and Ury's third recommendation is to *invent options for mutual gain*, looking for new possibilities that bring advantages to both sides. Parties often lock on to the first alternative that comes to mind and stop searching. Efforts to generate more options increase the chance of a better decision. Maritz recognized this in his dealings with Cutler. Instead of trying to bully Cutler, he asked innocently, "Could you do a demo at November COMDEX?" It was a new option that created gains for both parties.

Fisher and Ury's fourth strategy is to *insist on objective criteria*—standards of fairness for both substance and procedure. When a school board and a teachers' union are at loggerheads over the size of a pay increase, they can look for independent standards, such as the rate of inflation or the terms of settlement used in other districts. A classic example of fair procedure finds two sisters deadlocked over how to divide a pie between them. They agree that one will cut the pie into two pieces and the other will choose the piece that she wants.

Fisher and Ury devote most of their attention to creating value—finding better solutions for both parties. They downplay the question of claiming value. Yet there are many examples in which shrewd value-claimers have done very well. In 1980, Bill Gates offered to license an operating system to IBM about forty-eight hours before he had actually obtained the rights. Meanwhile, Microsoft neglected to mention to QDOS's owner, Tim Paterson of Seattle Computer, that they were buying his operating system to resell it to IBM. Microsoft gave IBM a great price: only $30,000 more than the $50,000 they'd paid for it. But they were smart enough to retain the rights to license it to anyone else. At the time, IBM was an elephant and Microsoft was a flea. Almost no one except Gates saw the possibility that people would want an IBM computer made by anyone but IBM. But the new PC was so successful, IBM couldn't make enough of them. Within a year, Microsoft had licensed MS-DOS to fifty companies, and the number kept growing (Mendelson and Korin, n.d.). Onlookers who wondered why Microsoft was so aggressive and unyielding in battling the Justice Department's antitrust suit twenty years later might not have known that Gates had been a dogged value claimer for a long time.

A classic treatment of value claiming is Schelling's 1960 essay *The Strategy of Conflict*, which focuses on the problem of how to make a credible threat. Suppose, for example, that I want to buy your house and am willing to pay $250,000. How can I convince you that I'm willing to pay only $200,000? Contrary to a common assumption, I'm not always better off if I'm stronger and have more resources. If you believe that I'm very wealthy, you might take my threat less seriously than if I can get you to believe that $200,000 is the farthest I can go. Common sense also suggests that I should be better off if I have considerable freedom of action. Yet I may get a better price if I can convince you my hands are tied—for example, I'm negotiating for a very stubborn buyer who won't go above $200,000, even if the house is worth more. Such examples suggest that the ideal situation for a bargainer is to have substantial resources and freedom while convincing the other side of the opposite. Value claiming gives us a picture of the bargaining process:

1. Bargaining is a mixed-motive game. Both parties want an agreement but have differing interests and preferences. (IBM and Microsoft both wanted an operating system deal. But the IBM negotiators probably thought they were stealing candy from babies by buying it royalty-free for a measly $80,000. Meanwhile, Gates was already dreaming about millions of computers running his code.)

2. Bargaining is a process of interdependent decisions. What each party does affects the other. Each player wants to be able to predict what the other will do while limiting the other's ability to reciprocate. (IBM was racing to bring its PC to market; a key challenge was making sure they had an operating system to go with it.)

3. The more player A can control player B's level of uncertainty, the more powerful A is. (Microsoft was an intermediary between Seattle Computer and IBM but kept each in the dark about the other.)

4. Bargaining involves judicious use of *threats* rather than sanctions. Players may threaten to use force, go on strike, or break off negotiations. In most cases, they much prefer not to bear the costs of carrying out the threat.

5. Making a threat credible is crucial. It is effective only if your opponent believes it. A noncredible threat weakens your bargaining position and confuses the process.

6. Calculation of the appropriate level of threat is also critical. If I underthreaten, I may weaken my own position. If I overthreaten, you may not believe me, may break off the negotiations, or may escalate your own threats.

Creating value and claiming value are both intrinsic to the bargaining process. How does a manager decide how to balance the two? At least two questions are important: "How much opportunity is there for a win-win solution?" and "Will I have to work with these people again?" If an agreement can make everyone better off, it makes sense to emphasize creating value. If you expect to work with the same people in the future, it is risky to use value-claiming tactics that leave anger and mistrust in their wake. Managers who get a reputation for being manipulative and self-interested have a hard time building networks and coalitions they need for future success.

Axelrod (1980) found that a strategy of conditional openness works best when negotiators need to work together over time. This strategy starts with open and collaborative behavior and maintains the approach if the other responds in kind. If the other party becomes adversarial, however, the negotiator responds in kind and remains adversarial until the opponent makes a collaborative move. It is, in effect, a friendly and forgiving version of tit for tat—do unto others as they do unto you. Axelrod's research revealed that this conditional openness strategy worked better than even the most fiendishly diabolical adversarial strategy.

A final consideration in balancing collaborative and adversarial tactics is ethics. Bargainers often deliberately misrepresent their positions—even though lying is almost universally condemned as unethical (Bok, 1978). This leads to a profoundly difficult question for the manager as politician: What actions are ethical and just?

MORALITY AND POLITICS

Block (1987), Burns (1978), and Lax and Sebenius (1986) explore ethical issues in bargaining and organizational politics. Block's view assumes that individuals empower themselves through understanding: "The process of organizational politics as we know it works against people taking responsibility. We empower ourselves by discovering a positive way of being political. The line between positive and negative politics is a tightrope we have to walk" (Block, 1987, p. xiii).

Block argues that bureaucratic cycles often leave individuals feeling vulnerable, powerless, and helpless. If we confer too much power to the organization or others, we fear that the power will be used against us. Consequently, we develop manipulative strategies to protect ourselves. To escape the dilemma, managers need to support organizational structures, policies, and procedures that promote empowerment. They must also empower themselves.

Block urges managers to begin by building an "image of greatness,"—a vision of what their department can contribute that is meaningful and worthwhile. Then they need to build support for their vision by negotiating agreement and trust. Block suggests dealing differently with friends than with opponents. Adversaries, he says, are simultaneously the most difficult and most interesting people to deal with. It is usually ineffective to pressure them; a better strategy is to "let go of them." He offers four steps for letting go: (1) tell them your vision, (2) state your best understanding of their position, (3) identify your contribution to the problem, and (4) tell them what you plan to do without making demands.

Such a strategy might work for conflict originating in a misunderstanding of one's self-interest. But in a situation of scarce resources and durable differences, bringing politics into the open may backfire. It can make conflict more obvious and overt but offer little hope of resolution. Block argues that "war games in organizations lose their power when brought into the light of day" (1987, p. 148), but the political frame questions that assumption.

Burns's conception of positive politics (1978) draws on examples as diverse and complex as Franklin Roosevelt and Adolph Hitler, Gandhi and Mao, Woodrow Wilson and Joan of Arc. He sees conflict and power as central to leadership. Searching for firm moral footing in a world of cultural and ethical diversity, Burns turned to the motivation theory of Maslow (1954) and the ethical theory of Kohlberg (1973). From Maslow he borrowed the idea of the hierarchy of motives. Moral leaders, he argued, appeal to a higher level on the needs hierarchy.

From Kohlberg he adopted the idea of stages of moral reasoning. At the lowest, "preconventional" level, moral judgment is based primarily on perceived consequences: an action is right if you are rewarded and wrong if you are punished. In the intermediate or "conventional" level, the emphasis is on conforming to authority and established rules. At the highest, "postconventional" level, ethical judgment rests on general principles: the greatest good for the greatest number, or universal and comprehensive moral principles.

Maslow and Kohlberg offered a foundation on which Burns (1978) constructed a positive view of politics:

> If leaders are to be effective in helping to mobilize and elevate their constituencies, leaders must be whole persons, persons with full functioning capacities for thinking and feeling. The problem for them as educators, as leaders, is not to promote narrow, egocentric self-actualization, but to extend awareness of human needs and the means of gratifying them, to improve the larger social situation for which educators or leaders have responsibility and over which they have power. What does all this mean for the teaching of leadership as opposed to manipulation? "Teachers"—in whatever guise—treat students neither coercively nor instrumentally but as joint seekers of truth and of mutual actualization. They help students define moral values not by imposing their own moralities on them but by positing situations that pose moral choices and then encouraging conflict and debate. They seek to help students rise to higher stages of moral reasoning and hence to higher levels of principled judgment. (pp. 448–449)

In Burns's view, positive politics evolve when individuals choose actions appealing to higher motives and higher stages of moral judgment. Lax and Sebenius (1986), regarding ethical issues as inescapable, present a set of questions to help managers decide what is ethical:

1. Are you following rules that are mutually understood and accepted? (In poker, for example, everyone understands that bluffing is part of the game.)

2. Are you comfortable discussing and defending your action? (Would you want your colleagues and friends to be aware of it? Your spouse, children, or parents? Would you be comfortable if it were on the front page of your local newspaper?)

3. Would you want someone to do it to you? To a member of your family?

4. Would you want everyone to act that way? Would the resulting society be desirable? (If you were designing an organization, would you want people to act that way? Would you teach your children to do it?)

5. Are there alternatives that rest on firmer ethical ground?

Although these questions do not yield a comprehensive ethical framework, they embody four important principles of moral judgment. These are instrumental values—guidelines not about the right thing to do but about the right way of doing things. They do not guarantee right action, but they substantially reduce ethical risks. As evidence, we note that these values are regularly ignored wherever we find an organizational scandal.

1. *Mutuality.* Are all parties to a relationship operating under the same understanding about the rules of the game? Enron's Ken Lay was talking up the company's stock to analysts and employees even as he and others were selling shares. In the period when WorldCom illegitimately improved its profits by booking some of its operating expenses as capital investments, it made major competitors look bad and generated considerable puzzlement. Top executives at both AT&T and Sprint felt the heat from analysts and shareholders and wondered, *What are we doing wrong? Why can't we get the results they're getting?*

2. *Generality.* Does a specific action follow a principle of moral conduct applicable to all comparable situations? When WorldCom violated a basic accounting principle to inflate their results, they were secretly breaking the rules, which does not amount to following a broadly applicable rule of conduct.

3. *Openness.* Are we willing to make our thinking and decisions public and confrontable? It was Justice Oliver Wendell Holmes who observed many years ago that "sunlight is the best disinfectant." Keeping others in the dark was a consistent theme in the

corporate ethics scandals of 2001–02. Enron's books were almost impenetrable, and the company was hostile to anyone who asked questions, such as *Fortune* reporter Bethany McLean. Enron's techniques for manipulating the California energy crisis had to be secret to work. One device involved creating the appearance of congestion in the California power grid, and then getting paid by the state for "moving energy to relieve congestion without actually moving any energy or relieving any congestion" (Oppel, 2002, p. 1).

4. *Caring.* Does this action show care for the legitimate interests of others? Enron's effort to protect its share price by locking in employees so they couldn't sell Enron shares in retirement accounts as the market plunged is only one of many examples of putting the interests of senior executives ahead of everyone else's.

The scandals of the early 2000s were not unprecedented; such a wave is a predictable feature of the trough that follows every business boom. The 1990s, for example, gave us Ivan Boesky and the savings and loan crisis. There was another wave of corporate scandals back in the 1970s, and in the 1930s the president of the New York Stock Exchange literally went to jail in his three-piece suit (Labaton, 2002). There will always be temptation whenever gargantuan egos and large sums of money are at stake. Top managers too rarely think or talk about the moral dimension of management and leadership. Porter (1989) notes the dearth of such conversation: "In a seminar with seventeen executives from nine corporations, we learned how the privatization of moral discourse in our society has created a deep sense of moral loneliness and moral illiteracy; how the absence of a common language prevents people from talking about and reading the moral issues they face. We learned how the isolation of individuals—the taboo against talking about spiritual matters in the public sphere—robs people of courage, of the strength of heart to do what deep down they believe to be right" (p. 2).

If we choose to banish moral discourse and leave managers to face ethical issues alone, we invite dreary and brutish political dynamics. In a pluralistic secular world, an organization cannot impose a narrow ethical framework on employees. But, as we argue in Chapter Nineteen, it can and should take a moral stance. It can make its values clear, hold employees accountable, and validate the need for dialogue about ethical choices. Positive politics, absent an ethical framework and a moral dialogue, is no more likely to occur than farming without sunlight or water.

CONCLUSION

The question is not whether organizations are political but rather what kind of politics they will have. Political dynamics can be sordid and destructive. But politics can also be the vehicle for achieving noble purpose. Organizational change and effectiveness depend on managers' political skills. Constructive politicians recognize and understand political realities. They know how to fashion an agenda, map the political terrain, create a network of support, and negotiate with both allies and adversaries. In the process, they encounter a practical and ethical dilemma: when to adopt an open, collaborative strategy or when to choose a tougher, more adversarial approach. They have to consider the potential for collaboration, the importance of long-term relationships, and most important their own values and ethical principles.

CHAPTER 11

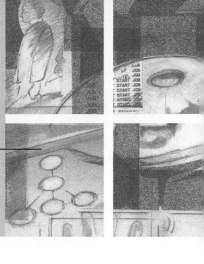

Organizations as Political Arenas and Political Agents

It's not easy to make *Time* magazine's cover as a poster boy for corporate greed and insensitivity, but Ross Johnson managed. In *Barbarians at the Gate,* Bryan Burrough and John Helyar (1990) explain how. Johnson began his career in the 1960s plodding through a series of middle-management jobs for General Electric in Canada. At age thirty-two, he was earning a modest $14,000 a year and teaching at night to bring in extra cash. Frustrated, he left GE to seek his fortune elsewhere. His charm, humor, and charisma moved him along. Several jobs later, the mid-1970s found him in New York heading international operations for Standard Brands, a consumer products firm. Johnson's lavish spending (on limousines and sumptuous entertainment) soon put him on a collision course with his boss. Henry Weigl, a tightfisted autocrat, was proud of twenty consecutive years of profit growth on his watch as president of Standard Brands. Fed up with Johnson's extravagance, Weigl tried to push him out. Johnson's political acumen averted a personal disaster: "Johnson prepared for war. A headhunter who gathered employee intelligence for Weigl became a double agent, also reporting to Johnson. A gathering of conspirators descended upon Johnson's home over several weekends. Together they assembled a report that would show how Weigl's tightfisted ways were slowly strangling Standard Brands" (Burrough and Helyar, 1990, p. 19).

Knowing that Weigl was heading for a confrontation, Johnson networked with friends on the board of directors. He got unexpected help from a tragedy: two weeks before the board meeting, a popular executive died. Many blamed his death on overexposure to Weigl's caustic management style. At the board meeting, Weigl reviewed a long list of Johnson's expense account abuses. Johnson admitted minor excesses and said he would resign. The board caucused, kicked Weigl upstairs, and put Johnson in charge of the company. Johnson accepted on one condition: Weigl had to move out of the headquarters building.

Johnson fired many of the senior executives, promoted his friends to high office, and embarked on a spectacular period of lavish spending: corporate jets, country club memberships, corporate apartments, and generous contracts to star athletes. After four years of mediocre business results, an unexpected call came from Bob Schaeberle, chairman of the food giant Nabisco. Schaeberle wanted to talk merger. Within two weeks, the transaction was done: a $1.9 billion stock swap—a big deal in 1981.

Everyone knew who would be in charge: Nabisco was by far the stronger player. But people underestimated Ross Johnson. Schaeberle became chairman and chief executive of the merged company, Johnson president and chief operating officer:

> On paper, Schaeberle remained the top executive of Nabisco Brands, but Johnson found it easy to get his way. Their offices were adjacent, and Johnson wasted no time ingratiating himself with his boss. He consistently deferred to Schaeberle, obsequiously addressing him in meetings as "Mr. Chairman." Johnson donated $250,000 to Pace University to endow a Robert M. Schaeberle Chair in accounting. Surprised by the announcement at a Pace dinner, an honored but stunned Schaeberle asked, "Who's going to pay for this?" The company was, of course.
>
> Slowly but surely, Johnson closed his grip around Schaeberle's reign.
>
> One by one, veteran Nabisco executives began to vanish, replaced by Johnson men. . . . Within three years, twenty-one of the company's top twenty-four officers were Standard Brands men. The Nabisco officers had been killed so softly that Schaeberle never realized what happened. At meetings, he would say, "It's nice to see all these young people around the table." (Burrough and Helyar, 1990, pp. 33–35)

Johnson also impressed Schaeberle by selling some of Nabisco's weaker units for top dollar. He used his charm, telling potential buyers they could run the business much better than Nabisco. He won a cookie war: under attack in Kansas City by Frito-Lay and Procter & Gamble, Johnson upped the ante, virtually giving Nabisco's cookies away. After a few years, Schaeberle made Johnson chief executive. In return a grateful Johnson named the company's new research unit after Schaeberle.

Once in charge, Johnson seemed more interested in hobnobbing with celebrities than in running the company. But then, in 1985, he got a phone call from Tylee Wilson, chief executive of R. J. Reynolds. The huge Winston-Salem–based tobacco company wanted to talk merger. Wilson wanted a partner to help Reynolds reduce its heavy dependence on the profitable but controversial cigarette business. Johnson held out for more than Wilson wanted to pay, but the deal was soon done: Reynolds coughed up $4.9 billion for Nabisco.

More than one of Wilson's friends warned him about Johnson. Wilson discounted the risk: it was his deal, and he would be in charge. But Wilson, lacking Johnson's awesome skills at ingratiation, had alienated part of his board. Things came to a head when board members learned Wilson had authorized a huge effort to develop a smokeless cigarette without their approval. That tempest left Wilson vulnerable, and Johnson relied again on the Standard Brands strategy: he told several friends on the board that he would be leaving because there was only room for one CEO. A few weeks later, Wilson was startled to learn that a majority of his board wanted him gone. He took a multimillion-dollar settlement and left.

Johnson was now atop a business netting over a billion dollars a year—more money than even he could spend. He tried: a new headquarters building in Atlanta; a fleet of corporate jets known as the RJR Air Force; lavish directors' fees, and perks to senior executives and star athletes (top of the line: golfer Jack Nicklaus at $1 million a year). Johnson was having the time of his life—until RJR Nabisco's stock lost a third of its value in the market crash of October 1987. Convinced the stock was unfairly tainted by its tobacco business, Johnson wanted to get the price back up. He settled on a craze of the time: a management-led leveraged buyout (LBO) of his company.

The basic idea of an LBO is to find an undervalued company, buy up shares with someone else's money, fix it up or break it up, and sell it at a profit. It's a high-stakes, high-risk venture. Leverage from borrowed money can mean prodigious profits—or crushing losses. The interest burden can be staggering. Once you announce an LBO, your company is in play; It's open season for anyone to try to top your bid. *Anyone* in this case meant Henry Kravis: "Practically unknown five years before, Kravis and his secretive firm, KKR, had ridden Wall Street's leveraged buyout wave to prominence in the mid-eighties. Ranked as an industrial company, the businesses KKR controlled, from Duracell batteries to Safeway supermarkets, placed it among the top ten U.S. corporations. Now, with $45 billion in buying power, Kravis was the unquestioned king of Wall Street acquisitors. His war chest [was] greater than the gross national products of Pakistan or Greece, his clout rivaling that of any in financial history" (Burrough and Helyar, 1990, p. 130).

If anyone could compete with RJR Nabisco's management bid, it was Kravis. Before announcing the LBO, Johnson had declined several overtures from Kravis to meet and talk. Johnson didn't want to tip his hand, but he expected Kravis to stay out anyway. He figured the deal was too big: $17 billion—three times bigger than any LBO in history. And Kravis mostly did friendly deals. Johnson did not realize that he had annoyed a very dangerous adversary. "I can't believe this," Kravis fumed after he first got word of the deal. "We gave them the idea. He wouldn't even meet with us" (Burrough and Helyar, 1990, p. 191).

What followed was one of business history's biggest six-week poker games. Huge coalitions formed. Johnson engaged the merger department at Shearson Lehman Hutton to lead his charge. Shearson, the brokerage unit of American Express, brought the money and the LBO expertise Johnson needed. Johnson brought top management and the board. But being on the same team is no guarantee of having identical interests. Johnson insisted on the fattest management package in LBO history. Shearson reluctantly went along because Johnson was their ticket into the deal. Eventually, when details of the lucrative agreement hit the *New York Times,* it drove a huge wedge between Johnson and his board, who'd never seen it.

Millions of dollars in fees gushed into the hands of bankers, lawyers, and brokers. Just about every big player on Wall Street got a piece of the action. It had everything but sex: confusion, conflict, reams of computer printouts, sleepless nights, threats and bluffs, brilliant stratagems, childish mistakes. Ego, image, and personal antipathy regularly threw the process off track. It finally culminated in a frantic, last-minute bidding war. When the dust cleared, Henry Kravis and the KKR group won by a nose. RJR Nabisco was theirs for a cool $25 billion. It was a Pyrrhic victory. RJR Nabisco never performed as well as hoped, and KKR spent several years getting out from under the unprofitable deal.

The RJR Nabisco story illustrates two sides of organizational politics: organizations are both arenas and agents. As arenas, they house the ongoing interplay of diverse interests and agendas. As agents, they are powerful tools for achieving purposes of those who master the game. Ross Johnson was a consummate practitioner of internal politics, with no qualms about treating a corporation as a personal plaything. He won every battle—until he found himself playing as a novice against the grandmasters of the LBO game.

From a political view, there is no such thing as permanent improvement; "happily ever after" exists only in fairy tales. In the real world, today's winners may quickly become tomorrow's losers or vice versa. Change and stability are paradoxical: organizations constantly change and yet never change. There is continual jockeying for position, and yesterday's elite may be tomorrow's also-ran. Yet, as in any competitive match, players come and go, but the game continues.

This chapter explores organizations first as political arenas and then as political agents. Viewing organizations as political arenas is a way to reframe many organizational processes. Organization design, for example, can be viewed not as a rational expression of an organization's goals but as a political embodiment of contending claims. In our discussion of organizations as arenas, we examine the political dimensions of organizational change, contrasting top-down and bottom-up efforts. As political agents, organizations operate in complex ecosystems—interdependent networks of organizations engaged in similar activities and occupying similar niches. We illustrate several forms ecosystems can take—business, public policy, business/government, and society. Finally, we look at the dark side of organizational power. We explore the concern that large, multinational organizations represent a growing risk to the world because they are too powerful for anyone to control.

ORGANIZATIONS AS ARENAS

As arenas, organizations house contests. An arena helps determine the rules of the game, the players, and what is up for grabs. From this perspective, every organizational process is political. Consider the process of shaping and structuring an organization. Most theories, built on structural premises, assume that the best design is one that contributes to efficient attainment of the organization's goals and strategy. Pfeffer (1978) offers an explicitly political conception as an alternative: "Since organizations are coalitions, and the different participants have varying interests and preferences, the critical question becomes not how organizations should be designed to maximize effectiveness, but rather, whose preferences and interests are to be served by the organization. . . . What is effective for students may be ineffective for administrators. What is effectiveness as defined by consumers may be ineffectiveness as defined by stockholders. The assessment of organizations is dependent upon one's preferences and one's perspective" (p. 223).

Even though groups have conflicting preferences, they have a shared interest in avoiding continuously destructive conflict. So they agree on ways to divide power and resources, and those settlements are reflected in organizational design. Structures are "the resolution, at a given time, of the contending claims for control, subject to the constraint that the structures permit the organization to survive" (Pfeffer, 1978, p. 224).

An example is Johnson's controversial decision to move RJR's headquarters from Winston-Salem, where it had been for a century, to Atlanta. Reynolds was the commercial heart of Winston-Salem. It engendered fierce pride and loyalty among much of the citizenry, many of whom were substantial stockholders. But Johnson and his key lieutenants saw the small city in the heart of tobacco country as boring and provincial. The move to Atlanta had scant business justification, was unpopular with the RJR board, and made Johnson the most hated man in Winston-Salem. But he headed the dominant coalition. He got what he wanted.

Gamson's distinction (1968) between authorities and partisans (see our Chapter Nine) implies two major sources of political initiative: bottom-up, relying on mobilization of groups to assert their agendas; and top-down, relying on authorities' capacity to influence subordinates. We discuss examples of both to illustrate some of the basic processes of political action.

Bottom-Up Political Action

The rise of trade unions and the emergence of the civil rights movement in the United States exemplify the process of bottom-up change. In both cases, the impetus for change was a significant disruption in previous patterns. Trade unions developed in the context of the industrial revolution, rapid urbanization, and the decline of family farms. The civil rights movement arose after massive occupational and geographic shifts for black citizens. In each case, changing conditions unfroze old patterns and intensified dissatisfaction for a disenfranchised group. Both movements reflected a classic pattern of revolutions: a period of rising expectations followed by widespread disappointment.

The initial stimulus in both cases was grassroots mobilizing and organizing—the formation of trade unions or of civil rights groups. Elites bitterly contested the legitimacy of such grassroots activity and launched coercive blocking tactics. At various times, to battle unionization employers used everything from lawsuits to violence. The civil rights movement, particularly in its early stages, experienced violent repression by whites. In the face of intense opposition, newly organized groups engaged the policy process and fought to have their rights embodied in law. Either movement might have failed had it been weaker or its opposition stronger. Both suffered profound setbacks but mobilized enough power to survive and grow. Compared to many bottom-up change efforts, they were relatively successful. Most such efforts fail; even the most successful yield only modest reforms. Union busting is still practiced in the United States and elsewhere, and union power has diminished considerably in recent decades in the face of global competition, the shift to a service economy, and the decline in blue-collar work. The difficulties of bottom-up political action lead many people to believe that you have to begin at the top to get anything done. Yet research on top-down efforts catalogues many failures, as we discuss in the next section.

Political Barriers to Control from the Top

Deal and Nutt (1980) conducted a revealing secondary analysis of local school districts that received federal funding to develop experimental programs for comprehensive changes in education. A typical scenario for these projects included these steps:

1. The central administration learned of the opportunity to obtain government funding.

2. A small group of administrators met to develop a proposal for improving some aspect of the educational program. (The process was usually rushed. Few people were involved because there was so little time to meet the proposal deadline.)

3. When funding was approved, the administration announced with pride and enthusiasm that the district's success in a national competition would bring it substantial money to support an exciting new project to improve instruction.

4. Teachers were stunned to learn the administration had committed to new teaching approaches without faculty input. Administrators were startled and perplexed when teachers greeted the news with resistance, criticism, and anger.

5. Caught in the middle between teachers and the funding agency, administrators interpreted teacher resistance as a sign of defensiveness and unwillingness to change.

6. The new program became a political football, producing more disharmony, mistrust, and conflict than tangible improvement in education.

The programs studied by Deal and Nutt represented examples of top-down change efforts under comparatively favorable circumstances. The districts were not in crisis. The change efforts were well funded and blessed by the federal government. Yet across the board, the new initiatives set off heated political battles. In many cases, administrators found themselves outgunned. Only one superintendent survived over the program's five-year funding cycle.

In most instances, administrators never anticipated a major political battle. They were confident their proposed programs would be progressive, effective, and good for everyone. They overlooked the risks in proposing change that someone else was expected to carry out. As a result, they got conflict instead of the expected huzzahs.

A similar pattern appears repeatedly in attempts to achieve top-down change. Countless efforts mounted by chief executives, frustrated managers, hopeful study teams, and high-status management consultants end in failure. The usual mistake is assuming that the right idea (as perceived by the idea's champions) and legitimate authority ensure success. This assumption neglects the agendas and power of the "lowerarchy"—partisans and groups in midlevel and lower-level positions, who devise creative and maddening ways to resist, divert, undermine, ignore, or overthrow change efforts.

ORGANIZATIONS AS POLITICAL AGENTS

Organizations are arenas for internal politics. They are also political agents in larger arenas or "ecosystems" (Moore, 1993). Since organizations depend on their environment for the resources they need to survive, they are inevitably enmeshed in relationships with external constituents whose expectations or demands must be met. These constituents often speak with conflicting voices, making management's job highly difficult (Hoskisson, Hitt, Johnson, and Grossman, 2002). The situation of the organization as political actor is parallel in many ways to the manager as politician. The organization has to develop an agenda, map its environment, manage relationships with both allies and enemies, and negotiate effectively.

Many of an organization's key constituents are other organizations. Just as frogs, flies, and lily pads coevolve in a swamp, organizations develop in tandem in a shared environment. Moore (1993) illustrates with two ecosystems in the personal computer business, one pioneered by Apple Computer and the other by IBM. Apple's ecosystem dominated the PC industry before IBM's entry. But IBM's ecosystem rapidly surpassed Apple's worldwide. IBM had enormous business clout, and the open architecture of its PC induced new players to flock into its arena. Some of these players competed head-on (for example, Compaq and Dell in hardware, Microsoft and Lotus in software). Others were related much like bees and flowers, each performing an indispensable cross-pollinating service. One symbiotic pairing was particularly fateful. As Microsoft gained control of the operating system and Intel of the microprocessor in the IBM ecosystem, the two increasingly became mutually indispensable. More sophisticated software needed faster microprocessors, and vice versa, so the two had every reason to cheer each other on. Two companies that began as servants to IBM eventually took over what became the "Wintel" ecosystem. Industry terminology changed to reflect the shift in power—what were once called "IBM-clones" and proudly advertised as "100-percent IBM compatible!" became simply "Windows PCs."

The same factors that generate internal politics also create political dynamics within and between ecosystems. Organizations have parochial interests and compete for scarce resources. The RJR Nabisco bidding war created a fluid, temporary ecosystem illustrating many of the complexities. Dozens of individuals, groups, and organizations were involved. RJR Nabisco itself, the big prize in the contest, was largely a bystander, with its board on the sidelines for most of the game. Johnson and his Shearson allies pursued their private interests more than the corporation's. Financial stakes were enormous, yet the game was often driven by issues of power, reputation, and personal animosity. Everyone wanted the prize, but you could win by losing and lose by winning.

Organizational ecosystems come in many forms and sizes. Some are small and local (consider the ecosystem of laundries in Dallas, or Milan). Others are very large and complex (the global automobile industry). We examine several significant types of ecosystem to illustrate the dynamics involved.

Business Ecosystems

General Motors, founded by Billy Durant in 1906 and rebuilt by Alfred Sloan in the 1920s, became the world's largest industrial corporation. It pioneered in the auto industry's ecosystem and became the dominant player for more than half a century. Its resources and power were and still are immense. In 2001, GM earned $601 million on sales of about $177 billion. But GM's niche crumbled in the 1970s and 1980s with the arrival of powerful foreign competitors. Environmental shifts revealed all too clearly that GM had become a lumbering, slow-to-adapt beast. Despite all its power, the company struggled to convince consumers to keep buying its cars. In 1992, GM reported a loss of $23.5 billion, at the time "the largest ocean of red ink that has ever engulfed a *Fortune 500* company" (Loomis, 1993, p. 41). GM's size and financial strength were an enormous cushion; a lesser beast might not have survived its marketing and management problems. But history shows that even great companies falter.

In contrast, General Electric thrived during the 1980s. Its success stemmed from adroit adaptation to a changing environment. In the first two decades after World War II, engineers who ran GE's functional structure created an efficient system for producing whatever *they* thought consumers needed. Almost a stereotype of old-fashioned hierarchy, it would have been a disaster in the late-twentieth-century world of frenetic global competition. But it was hugely successful in an era when much of the world's industrial capacity (outside the United States) had been devastated, and pent-up consumer demand gobbled up anything GE could manufacture.

By the time Jack Welch became CEO in 1981, GE had evolved considerably from its postwar engineering mentality. Welch concluded that only dramatic change could save the company from a downhill slide. He set to work to build a culture that emphasized quality, entrepreneurship, and candor. He made a key decision to compete only in markets where GE could be a dominant player. He insisted that every GE business be number one or two in its industry. If not, said Welch, "we'll fix it, sell it, or close it" (Morris, 1995, p. 90). He radically revised GE's business mix, selling off about a third of the businesses he inherited and moving resources into more promising opportunities. In four years, GE reduced its payroll from more than 400,000 to about 330,000. Welch's "destaffing" initiatives earned him the nickname "Neutron Jack," after the bomb that wipes out people but leaves buildings intact (Bartlett and Elderkin, 1991). Welch was not infallible; some of his investments soured, and GE was troubled by periodic ethics scandals (Paré, 1994). But earnings growth made GE a very profitable company. Market value increased from $21.6 billion in 1982 to $73.9 billion in 1992 and then to more than $300 billion in 2002. In 1982, IBM had more than twice the market value of GE; ten years later, their positions were reversed (Loomis, 1993, p. 37).

Public Policy Ecosystems

In the public sector, a policy arena forms around virtually every government activity. Air carriers, airplane manufacturers, travelers, legislators, and regulators are all active participants in the commercial aviation ecosystem. In the United States, the Federal Aviation Administration has been a troubled key player for several decades. Charged with divergent goals of defending safety, promoting the economic health of the industry, and keeping its own costs down, it has perennially come under heavy fire from virtually every direction. Feeble oversight permitted marginal carriers to shortcut safety but continue flying. A ten-year, $10 billion air traffic modernization plan first announced in 1981 yielded little success, ringing up billions of dollars in bills by the end of the 1990s. Things improved under Jane Garvey, who was appointed to direct the agency for a five-year term from 1997 to 2002. She was widely praised for introducing pay for performance, improving management systems, expediting the long-delayed overhaul of air traffic control, and improving the FAA's relationship with air traffic controllers. But the agency was still faulted for weak accounting systems and bureaucratic lethargy (Cahlink, 2002). After the terrorist attacks of September 11, 2001, the agency came under heavy fire for its delay in toughening requirements for companies and personnel that screened airline passengers and baggage.

Education is another illustration of a complex policy ecosystem. In recent years, one side of an intense debate has argued strongly that American public schools could be improved by giving parents and students more choice about which schools children would attend. Choice plans, such as educational vouchers, gave families grants to send their children to private schools. Proponents argued that parents would choose the school that fit their children's needs and competition would have an invigorating effect on schools. But school boards and school administrators almost universally resisted the idea. Coalitions formed on both sides of the issue and lobbied at both the state and national levels. The debate is ongoing.

Business-Government Ecosystems

Government and business inevitably evolve in tandem, spawning a multitude of intersecting ecosystems. Perrow (1986) discusses one example: pharmaceutical companies, physicians, and government. A major threat to the companies' profit margin is generic drugs, which sell at a price much lower than that of their brand-name equivalents. In the United States, the industry trade association, an interorganizational coalition, successfully lobbied many state legislatures to prohibit the sale of generic drugs, ostensibly to protect consumers. The industry also persuaded the American Medical Association (AMA) to permit drugs to be advertised by brand name in its journals. Consumers normally buy whatever the doctor prescribes, and drug companies wanted doctors to think brand labels rather than chemical names. As a result of the policy shift, the AMA's advertising income tripled in seven years, and the manufacturers strengthened the position of their respective brands (Perrow, 1986).

More recently, the ecosystem shifted again with the rapid rise of a newly powerful player: managed health care providers. HMOs used their increasing political leverage to push physicians to prescribe less expensive generic drugs. In an effort to save consumers' money, several states required pharmacists to offer the generic equivalent when a brand name is prescribed.

Drug companies are by no means unique in their attention to politics: "Firms search feverishly for sources of competitive advantage. One such source . . . is government policy, which determines the rules of commerce; the structure of markets (through barriers to entry and changes in cost structures due to regulations, subsidies, and taxation); the offerings of goods and services that are permissible; and the sizes of markets based on government subsidies and purchases. Consequently, gaining and maintaining access to those who make public policy may well be a firm's most important political goal" (Schuler, Rehbein and Cramer, 2002, p. 659).

Schuler and colleagues found that politically active firms use a range of strategies for influencing government. FedEx illustrates the possibilities. In Chapter Seven, we noted the company's sophisticated approach to managing people. FedEx has been equally agile in managing its political environment. The *New York Times* described it as "one of the most formidable and successful corporate lobbies in the capital" (Lewis, 1996, p. 17). Its CEO, Fred Smith, "spends considerable time in Washington, where he is regarded as Federal Express's chief advocate. It was Mr. Smith who hit a lobbying home run in 1977 when he persuaded Congress to allow the fledgling company to use full-sized jetliners to carry its cargo, rather than the small planes to which it had been restricted. That was the watershed event that allowed the company to grow to its present dominating position with almost $10.3 billion in business" (p. 30).

FedEx's political action committee ranked among the nation's top ten, making generous donations to hundreds of candidates for Congress. Its board is adorned with popular former congressional leaders from both major political parties. Its corporate jets regularly ferry officeholders to events around the country. All this generosity paid off. In October 1996, when FedEx wanted two words inserted into a 1923 law regulating railway express companies, the Senate stayed in session a couple of extra days to get it done, even with elections only a month away. A first-term senator commented, "I was stunned by the breadth and depth of their clout up here" (Lewis, 1996, p. 17).

A similar coevolution of business and politics occurs around the world:

> No one would dispute that business and politics are closely intertwined in Japan. As one leading financial journalist puts it, "If you don't use politicians, you can't expand business these days in Japan—that's basic." Businessmen provide politicians with funds, politicians provide businessmen with information. If you wish to develop a department store, a hotel or a ski resort, you need licenses and permissions and the cooperation of leading local political figures. And it is always useful to hear that a certain area is slated for development, preferably several years before development starts, when land prices are still low (Downer, 1994, p. 299)

Society as Ecosystem

On a still larger scale, we find society: the massive ecosystem in which business, government, and the public are embedded and coevolve. A critical question in this arena is the power relationship between organizations and society. All organizations have power. Large organizations have a lot: "Of the 100 largest economies in the world, 51 are corporations, and only 49 are countries. Wal-Mart is bigger than Israel, Poland or Greece. Mitsubishi is bigger than Indonesia. General Motors is bigger than Denmark. If governments can't set the rules, who will? The corporations? But they're the players. Who's the referee?" (Longworth, 1996, p. 4)

A number of organizational scholars (including Korten, 1995; Perrow, 1986; and Stern and Barley, 1996) emphasize that whoever controls a multibillion-dollar tool wields enormous power. Korten's view is particularly dark:

> An active propaganda machinery controlled by the world's largest corporations constantly reassures us that consumerism is the path to happiness, government restraint of market excess is the cause of our distress, and economic globalization is both a historical inevitability and a boon to the human species. In fact, these are all myths propagated to justify profligate greed and mask the extent to which the global transformation of human institutions is a consequence of the sophisticated, well-funded, and intentional interventions of a small elite whose money enables them to live in a world of illusion apart from the rest of humanity. These forces have transformed once beneficial corporations and financial institutions into instruments of a market tyranny that is extending its reach across the planet like a cancer, colonizing ever more of the planet's living spaces, destroying livelihoods, displacing people, rendering democratic institutions impotent, and feeding on life in an insatiable quest for money. (Korten, 1995, p. 12)

Do sophisticated consumer marketing firms create and control consumer tastes, or do they simply react to needs created by larger social forces? Critics like Korten are convinced that the advantage lies with the corporations, but Pfeffer and Salancik (1978) see it the other way around, as do many proponents of "the marketing concept":

> The marketing concept of management is based on the premise that over the longer term all businesses are born and survive or die because people (the market) either want them or don't want them. In short, the market creates, shapes, and defines the demand for all classes of products and services. Almost needless to say, many managers tend to think that they can design goods and services and then create demand. The marketing concept denies this proposition. Instead, the marketing concept emphasizes that the creative aspect of marketing is discovering, defining, and fulfilling what people want or need or what solves their life-style problems. (Marshall, 1984, p. 1)

Greatest Hits from Organization Studies No. 1: Jeffrey Pfeffer and Gerald Salancik, *The External Control of Organizations* (New York: Harper & Row, 1978).

Pfeffer and Salancik's 1978 book has fallen out of print and is little known outside academic circles, but scholars love it; it occupies the top rung in our ranking of most-cited works. As its title suggests, the book's principal theme is that organizations are much more creatures than creators of their environment. In the authors' words: "The perspective [in this book] denies the validity of the conceptualization of organizations as self-directed, autonomous actors pursuing their own ends and instead argues that organizations are other-directed, involved in a constant struggle for autonomy and discretion, confronted with constraint and external control" (p. 257). The authors follow Cyert and March (1963) in viewing organizations as coalitions that are both "markets in which influence and control are transacted" (p. 259) and players that need to negotiate their relationships with a range of external constituents.

Pfeffer and Salancik emphasize that organizations depend on their environment for inputs that they need to survive. Much of the job of management is to understand and respond to demands of key external constituents whose support is vital to organizational survival. This job is made more difficult by two challenges:

1. Organizations' understanding of their environment is often distorted or imperfect (because organizations only act on the information they're geared to collect and know how to interpret)
2. Organizations confront multiple constituents whose demands are often inconsistent.

Organizations comply where they have to, but they also look for ways to increase their autonomy by making their environment more predictable and favorable. They may merge to gain greater market power, form coalitions (alliances, joint ventures) to gain greater influence, or enlist government help (by seeking subsidies or protective tariffs, for example). But there is a dilemma: every entanglement, even as it produces greater influence over a part of the environment, also produces some erosion of the organization's autonomy.

Pfeffer and Salancik describe three roles for managers, two political and one symbolic. There is a *responsive role* in which managers adjust the organization's activities to comply with pressures from the environment. There is the *discretionary role* where managers seek to alter the organization's relationship with its environment. And there is a *symbolic role* arising from the widely accepted myth that managers make a difference. This means, for example, that replacing managers is one way to create the appearance of change without actually changing anything (an idea that we discuss further in the next two chapters).

Proponents of this view note even the most successful marketers have had their share of Edsels—products released with great fanfare and a huge marketing budget that fluttered briefly and then sank like a stone.

Are large multinational corporations so powerful that they have become a law unto themselves, or are they strongly shaped by the need to respond to the governments, people, and cultures in the countries where they operate? An ecological view suggests that the answer is some of both. Ecosystems and competitors within them rise and fall. Power relations are never static, and even the most powerful have no guarantee of immortality. Of the top twenty-five U.S. companies at the beginning of the twentieth century, all but one had dropped off the list or vanished altogether as the century came to a close. The lone survivor? General Electric.

Over much of the twentieth century, as corporations grew and became more powerful, control shifted from owners and shareholders to management. So long as the companies performed well, stakeholders retained enough confidence in management not to raise serious questions. The myth of accountability—that managers are accountable to both the shareholders and the market—was accepted at face value. But periodically, confidence has shattered in the face of a downturn in the business cycle or corruption in the executive suite. This happened after the market crash of 1929, and again in the 1970s and 1980s, when *Business Week* noted, "By any measure, the current crop of corporate managers has reigned over an era of unprecedented American economic decline. For at least a decade, America's standard of living has been eroding, its share of the world market shrinking, and its products retreating in the face of foreign competition. So it's no accident that the dominance of management is being challenged today" (Nussbaum and Dobrzynski, 1987, pp. 102–103).

The 1990s brought a reprieve for embattled managers. Just as worries about the decline and fall of the U.S. economy reached a crescendo, productivity and profits soared. Shareholder returns and CEO salaries reached unprecedented heights. America once again fell in love with heroic CEOs like GE's Jack Welch. It was a wild and wonderful party while it lasted, but it also bred the climate of "infectious greed" (in Alan Greenspan's phrase) that led to a large and painful hangover afterwards. A seemingly endless list of executive misdeeds and accounting scandals undermined a shaky stock market and wiped out much of the public's confidence in corporate leaders. Once again a chorus of critics attacked the concentration of power and wealth in the hands of a selfish, corrupt elite.

The view that bigger is better came under fresh attack: "Giant companies dominate the landscape. But talented people don't want to work in them, customers hate doing business with them, and Wall Street doesn't want to invest in them" (Hammonds, 2002, p. 78).

The battle over corporate power will continue on a global scale. Large multinational companies have enormous power but must also cope with the demands of other powerful players: governments, labor unions, investors, and consumers. Useem (1996) argues that much of the turbulence in corporate America—shake-ups, breakups, downsizings, and the like—is the result of pressure from institutional investors. Big pension and mutual funds with millions or billions to invest often use "voice" (that is, influence and pressure) because they cannot easily exit; it is easy to sell a few hundred shares of General Electric but much harder to sell a few hundred thousand. Unquestionably, senior executives feel the heat from the investment community. At both Enron and WorldCom, external pressures to deliver better numbers every quarter led to financial reports that increasingly depicted a fantasy world of manufactured profits.

Barber (1995) sees a tension between "Jihad" and "McWorld" dominating the world scene for the foreseeable future. He uses *jihad* as shorthand for tribalism—identifying tightly with members of one's own ethnic and religious group. *McWorld* stands for global capitalism—represented by the brands that are increasingly dominant around the globe. Barber sees the tension between these two forces as potentially devastating:

> Jihad and McWorld operate with equal strength in opposite directions, the one driven by parochial hatreds, the other by universalizing markets, the one re-creating ancient subnational and ethnic borders from within, the other making national borders porous from without. Yet Jihad and McWorld have this in common: they both make war on the sovereign nation-state and thus undermine the nation-state's democratic institutions. Their common thread is indifference to civil liberty. Jihad forges communities of blood rooted in exclusion and hatred, communities that slight democracy in favor of tyrannical paternalism or consensual tribalism. McWorld forges global markets rooted in consumption and profit, leaving to an untrustworthy, if not altogether fictitious, invisible hand issues of public interests and common good that once might have been nurtured by democratic citizenries and their watchful governments. Unless we can offer an alternative to the struggle between Jihad and McWorld, [then] the epoch on whose threshold we stand—postcommunist, postindustrial, postnational, yet

sectarian, fearful, and bigoted—is likely also to be terminally postdemocratic. (Barber, 1995, pp. 68)

In a cacophonous global village, this is the biggest political contest of all.

CONCLUSION

Organizations are both arenas for internal politics and political agents with their own agendas, resources, and strategies. As arenas, they house contests and offer a setting for the ongoing interplay of divergent interests and agendas. The nature of an arena and the rules it creates help determine the game to be played, who's on the field, and the interests to be pursued. From this perspective, every significant organizational process is inherently political.

As agents, organizations are tools, often very powerful tools, for achieving the purposes of whoever controls them. But they are also inevitably dependent on their environment for needed support and resources. They exist, compete, and co-evolve in business or political ecosystems with clusters of organizations, each pursuing its own interests and seeking a viable niche. As in nature, relationships within and between ecosystems are sometimes fiercely competitive, sometimes collaborative and interdependent.

A particularly urgent and controversial question is the relative power of organizations and society. Giant multinational corporations have achieved scale and resources unprecedented in human history. Some critics foresee them increasingly dominating and distorting politics and society. More optimistic observers argue that organizations are inherently dependent on a changing and turbulent environment. In the long run, they retain their clout only by adapting to larger social forces.

PART FIVE

The Symbolic Frame

What images or associations come to mind when you think about each of these?

- American flag

- Nazi

- General Motors

- Princess Diana

- Declaration of Independence

- Al-Qaeda

- McDonald's

- Pearl Harbor

- Paris

It is likely that you had emotional, even visceral, reactions to many of these items. Each refers to a specific person, group, place, or event, but each has also acquired symbolic resonance.

Symbols carry powerful intellectual and emotional messages; they speak to both the mind and the heart.

The symbolic frame focuses on how humans make sense of the messy, ambiguous world in which they live. Meaning, belief, and faith are its central concerns. Meaning is not given to us; we have to create it. There are, for example, many who revere the American flag and many others who burn it. The flag is symbolically powerful for both groups, but each finds very different meanings in it. Symbols are the basic building blocks of the meaning systems, or cultures, that we inhabit. We live in cultures in the same way that fish live in water. Just as fish are said to discover water last, our own cultural ways are often invisible to us.

Chapter Twelve uses a variety of examples to demonstrate what culture is and why it is so important. It then explores the many forms symbols take in social life, including myth, vision, story, heroes and heroines, ritual, and ceremony.

Chapter Thirteen takes a dramaturgical perspective. In it, we view organizations as akin to theater companies that seek to please by staging the dramas their audiences expect. We show that many activities and processes in organizations—such as evaluation and strategic planning—rarely achieve supposed goals yet are remarkably persistent because they project vital messages that audiences want to hear.

In Chapter Fourteen, we apply symbolic concepts to team dynamics. We use a famous case of a highly successful computer development team to show that the essence of its success was cultural and spiritual. The team used initiation rituals, humor, play, specialized language, ceremony, and other symbolic forms to weld a diverse and fractious group of individuals into a spirited, successful team.

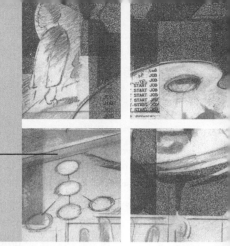

CHAPTER **12**

Organizational Culture and Symbols

In 2002, Harley-Davidson celebrated its one hundredth birthday. The festivities lasted for fourteen months and included events in Mexico City, Sydney, Tokyo, Barcelona, and Munich. In a spectacular culminating extravaganza, a million bikers roared into the company's headquarters in Milwaukee to showcase their bikes and revel in Harley-Davidson's unique culture. To the HOGs (Harley Owner's Groups), owning a Harley is a way of life:

> Despite their diversity, Harley riders have something in common: a fanatical dedication to their Harleys. It's a feeling that many cannot articulate, and for them there's a Harley T-shirt inscribed: "Harley-Davidson—If I Have To Explain You Wouldn't Understand" [. . .] One thing is certain: This incredible brand loyalty is emotional. It is based on a pattern of associations that includes the American flag and another American symbol, the eagle (which is also a Harley symbol), as well as camaraderie, individualism, the feeling of riding free, and the pride of owning a product that has become a legend. On the road, one Harley rider always helps another in distress—even though one may be a tattooed biker and the other a buttoned-down bank president. (Reid, 1989, p. 5)

Harley-Davidson is only one example of how symbols permeate every fiber of organizations. After September 11, 2001, the American people turned to symbols to cope with the aftermath of the country's most devastating terrorist attack. Flags flew everywhere. Makeshift monuments were erected to honor victims and the heroic acts of police and firefighters who gave their lives. Members of Congress gathered on the Capitol steps to sing "God Bless America" on national television. Across the country, people gathered in both formal and informal healing ceremonies. Especially in times of tragedies and triumphs, we embrace the spiritual magic symbols represent.

In our highly complex world, persistent questions haunt us. In the wake of the Twin Towers tragedy, the most frequently voiced question was "Why?" It was a question raised by those who lost someone as well as by the firefighters, police, and others who survived. There is no satisfactory answer, only faith and hope that such a mind-numbing tragedy could somehow be rendered understandable.

The symbolic frame seeks to interpret and illuminate basic issues of meaning and belief that make symbols so powerful. It depicts a world far different from traditional canons of rationality, certainty, and linearity.

The frame forms a conceptual umbrella for ideas from a variety of disciplines, including organization theory and sociology (Selznick, 1957; Blumer, 1969; Clark, 1975; Corwin, 1976; March and Olsen, 1976; Meyer and Rowan, 1978; Weick, 1976; Davis and others, 1976; Hofstede, 1984) and political science (Dittmer, 1977; Edelman, 1971). Freud and Jung relied heavily on symbolic concepts in attempting to understand the human psyche. Anthropologists have traditionally focused on symbols and their place in the culture and lives of humans (Ortner, 1973). Joseph Campbell's book *The Power of Myth* became a widely watched television special.

SYMBOLIC ASSUMPTIONS

The symbolic frame distills ideas from these diverse sources into several core assumptions:

- What is most important is not what happens but what it means.

- Activity and meaning are loosely coupled; events have multiple meanings because people interpret experience differently.

- In the face of widespread uncertainty and ambiguity, people create symbols to resolve confusion, increase predictability, find direction, and anchor hope and faith.

- Many events and processes are more important for what is expressed than what is produced. They form a cultural tapestry of secular myths, heroes and heroines, rituals, ceremonies, and stories that help people find purpose and passion in their personal and work lives.

- Culture is the glue that holds an organization together and unites people around shared values and beliefs.

The symbolic frame sees life as more *serendipitous* than linear. Organizations function like complex, constantly changing, organic pinball machines. Decisions, actors, plans, and issues continuously carom through an elastic, ever-changing labyrinth of cushions, barriers, and traps. Managers who turn to Peter Drucker's *Effective Executive* for guidance might do better to study Lewis Carroll's *Through the Looking Glass*. But all the apparent chaos has a deeper sense of emblematic order. In recent years, the importance of symbols in corporate life has become more widely appreciated.

This chapter begins our examination of the symbolic frame. Symbols embody and express an organization's *culture*: the interwoven pattern of beliefs, values, practices, and artifacts that defines for members who they are and how they are to do things. Accordingly, we first look at organizations as unique cultures or tribes. We then reinforce the importance of symbols by describing their effects in two companies, Volvo France and Continental Airlines. Next, we move on to discuss the various forms symbols assume: myths, visions and values; heroes and heroines; stories and fairy tales; ritual; ceremony; and metaphor, humor, and play. All these are basic elements of organizational culture.

ORGANIZATIONS AS CULTURES

Culture: What is it? What is its role in an organization? Both questions are hotly contested. Some people argue that organizations *have* cultures; others insist that organizations *are* cultures. Schein (1992, p. 12) offers a more formal definition of culture: "a pattern of shared basic assumptions that a group learned as it solved its problems of external adaptation and integration, that has worked well enough to be considered valid and therefore to be taught to new members as the correct way to perceive, think, and feel in relation to those problems." Deal and Kennedy (1982, p. 4) define culture more succinctly as "the way we do things around here." Culture is both a product and a process.

As a product, it embodies accumulated wisdom from those who came before us. As a process, it is constantly renewed and re-created as newcomers learn the old ways and eventually become teachers themselves.

There is controversy about the relationship between culture and leadership. Do leaders shape culture, or are they shaped by it? Is symbolic leadership more often empowering, or manipulative? Do organizations with strong cultures outperform those relying on policies and rules? Does success breed a cohesive culture, or is it the other way around?

Over time, every organization develops distinctive beliefs, values, and patterns. Many of them are unconscious or taken for granted, reflected in myths, fairy tales, stories, rituals, ceremonies, and other symbolic forms. Managers who understand the power of symbols are much better equipped to understand and influence their organizations. From a symbolic perspective, meaning is the basic human need. Managers who understand symbolic forms and activities and encourage their use help shape an effective organization—so long as the organizational culture is aligned with the challenges of the marketplace.

Nordstrom department stores exemplify the power of culture at work. Customers rave about its no-hassle, no-questions-asked commitment to high-quality service: "not service the way it used to be, but service that never was" (Spector and McCarthy, 1995, p. 1). Founder John Nordstrom was a Swedish immigrant who settled in Seattle after an odyssey across America and a brief stint in Alaska looking for gold. He and Carl Wallin, a shoemaker, opened a shoe store. Nordstrom's sons Elmer, Everett, and Lloyd joined the business. Collectively, they anchored the firm in an enduring philosophical principle: the customer is always right. The following generation of Nordstroms expanded the business while maintaining a tight connection with its historical roots.

The company relies on experienced, acculturated "Nordies" to induct new employees into customer service the Nordstrom way. Newcomers always begin in sales, learning traditions from the ground up: "When we are at our best, our frontline people are lieutenants because they control the business. Our competition has foot soldiers on the front line and lieutenants in the back" (Spector and McCarthy, 1995, p. 106).

Nordstrom's unique commitment to customer service is heralded in true tales of heroes and heroines going out of their way:

• One customer fell in love with a particular pair of pleated burgundy slacks that were on sale at Nordstrom's downtown Seattle store. Unfortunately, the store was out of her size. The sales associate got some cash from her department managers, marched across the street, bought the slacks at full price from a competitor, brought them back, and sold them to the customer at Nordstrom's reduced price (Spector and McCarthy, 1995, p. 26).

• When a customer inadvertently left her airline ticket on a Nordstrom counter, the sales associate tried to solve the problem with a call to the airline. When that didn't work, she hopped into a cab, headed for the airport, and made a personal delivery to the customer (p. 125).

• A Nordie cheerfully issued a refund on a set of automobile tires, even though Nordstrom had never sold tires. In 1975, Nordstrom had bought three stores from Northern Commercial in Alaska. The customer had bought the tires from Northern Commercial— so Nordstrom took them back (p. 27).

Nordstrom's commitment to customer service is regularly reinforced in storewide rituals. Newcomers to Nordstrom encounter the company's values in the initial employee orientation. They are given a five-inch-by-eight-inch card labeled the "Nordstrom Employee Handbook," which reads:

> Welcome to Nordstrom
> We're glad to have you with our company. Our number one goal is to provide outstanding customer service.
> Set both your personal and professional goals high. We have great confidence in your ability to achieve them.
> Nordstrom Rules:
> Rule #1: Use your good judgment in all situations.
> There will be no additional rules. (pp. 15–16)

At staff meetings, Nordstrom sales associates compare and discuss sales techniques and role-play customer encounters. Periodic ceremonies reinforce the company's cherished values. From the company's early years, the Nordstrom family sponsored summer picnics and Christmas dance parties. More recently, numerous events create occasions to celebrate customer service: "We do crazy stuff. Monthly store pow-wows serve as a kind of revival meeting, where customer letters of appreciation are read and positive achievements are recognized, while co-workers whoop and cheer for one another. Letters of complaint about Nordstrom customer service are also read over the intercom (omitting the names of offending salespeople)" (pp. 120, 129).

At one spirited sales meeting, the regional manager asked all present to call out their sales targets for the year, which he posted on a large chart. Then the regional manager uncovered his own target for each individual. Anyone whose target was below the regional manager's was roundly booed. Anyone whose individual goals were higher than the regional manager's was rewarded with enthusiastic cheers (Spector and McCarthy, 1995).

The delicate balance of competition, cooperation, and customer service has served Nordstrom well. In a sermon titled "The Gospel According to Nordstrom," one California minister "praised the retailer for carrying out the call of the gospel in ways more consistent and caring than we sometimes do in the church" (p. 21).

ORGANIZATIONAL SYMBOLS

An organization's culture is revealed and communicated most clearly through its symbols. McDonald's franchises are united as much by golden arches, core values, and the legend of Ray Kroc as by sophisticated control systems. Harvard professors, remarkably free of structural limits, are tightly constrained by historically anchored rituals of teaching, enduring values of scholarship, and the myths and mystique of Harvard.

In recent years, the importance of symbols in corporate life has become more widely appreciated. Such books as Kotter and Heskett's *Corporate Culture and Performance* (1992) and Collins and Porras's *Built to Last* (1994) offer impressive longitudinal evidence linking symbols to the financial bottom line. A case in point is Goren Carstedt's arrival to head Volvo France in the 1980s. It was a big challenge. Volvo had hoped to double sales to twenty thousand cars a year in France. Instead, sales were declining while other imported cars were increasing market share. Even more troubling was the net of excuses offered to rationalize the dismal performance: "The products were said to be too old, too heavy, too stodgy, too expensive, and all had stiff rear axles, which were not *pointé* (hip) in France. Too much performance had been sacrificed to safety. Deliveries were slow, and promised new models were late. Carstedt was told time and time again that 'this is France.' It was a Latin nation, passionate and hot-blooded, whereas Volvo was a cerebral car, something melancholy Scandinavians thought about on long winter evenings" (Hampden-Turner, 1992, pp. 156–157).

Rejecting excuses, Carstedt was determined to put a more positive spin on an otherwise dreary situation. His actions illustrate the possibilities for someone who understands the power of symbols and culture. He began by listening: he convened nine regional meetings with Volvo's 150 French dealers. Seated around tables, he asked for their ideas: "I want to know what you think should be done and what Volvo can do to help you sell more cars. Tell me what we are doing wrong, what you want from us, and I'll see that it is done if I possibly can" (Hampden-Turner, 1992, p. 158). His approach was a dramatic departure from anything the dealers had seen before. His straightforward, open style soon earned him the nickname *le vol du nord* (the north wind).

Carstedt's next steps relied heavily on values, ritual, ceremony, and humor to show he was listening and willing to make real changes. He drew a cartoon that turned the traditional chain of command upside down. As Carstedt describes it, "The customer was king. The dealers were his courtiers, and it was our job—mine, Volvo France's and HQ's— to make sure the dealers had what they needed" (Hampden-Turner, 1992, p. 159).

He invited dealers and their spouses to a conference center near Paris. The meeting opened with a humorous film, *Où est Volvo?* ("Where's Volvo?"). French citizens were shown answering questions about Volvo and its dealers. Shrugs and gestures of indifference told the story: *"Je ne sais pas"* ("I don't know"). Next, Volvo's new models were shown via telecast from a beautifully appointed showroom somewhere in France. When asked to reveal the location, Carstedt raised the curtain behind him. There it was, a showroom assembled on the spot to show the dealers what a little ingenuity could do.

Next, Carstedt took dealers on an excursion in Sweden. He wanted them to experience the culture behind the car: "Eighty percent of our marketing efforts are internal to help dealers assume the Volvo identity and take pride in the quality of the vehicles and see their own service is an inseparable part of this" (Hampden-Turner, 1992, p. 161). The group flew by chartered plane to Gothenburg, where they toured the factory and met with top managers. Later, said Carstedt, "we gave out prizes to our best dealers in front of our president and senior managers" (p. 162). The following day, the group traveled by train through the countryside. They met Volvo workers, toured old Stockholm, and were feted at a Viking party, complete with Swedish musicians and folksingers in traditional costume, where "they drank Schnapps, wore helmets, ate with their fingers, and threw the debris over their shoulders" (p. 162).

Carstedt closed with a speech—in French:

For two years now, I've been trying to explain to you that there is something special about Volvo: our philosophy and values are important to our success. And to understand Volvo, it helps to understand something about Sweden. So we've invited you on a trip to see our lakes, forests, trees and houses for yourselves. Now we're here, in the heart of Sweden, in the room where Nobel dinners are served before the prizes are given, and you have the Nobel menus before you to remind you that this is the place that gives hospitality to the greatest achievements and the finest quality of which you are all a part. (Hampden-Turner, 1992, p. 162)

Back in France, Carstedt declared war on memos of excuse and defense. To convey the difference between where they had been and where they needed to go, he created two visual images. The first was a square made of four fingers, each pointing out what was wrong with someone else. The second depicted four hands in a supportive grasp. A graphic advertisement emphasized safety by showing a little girl strapped snugly in the rear seat of a Volvo. The caption read, "You need to protect the future, especially when the future is behind you." Volvo was cited that year for the best automotive advertising in France. The work paid off. In the next four years, Volvo's sales and market share doubled.

Greatest Hits of Organization Studies No. 7: Geert Hofstede, *Culture's Consequences: International Differences in Work-Related Values* (Newbury Park, Calif.: Sage, 1984).

Geert Hofstede pioneered research on the impact of national culture on the workplace. Defining culture as "the collective programming of the mind that distinguishes the members of one human group from another" (p. 21), he focused particularly on work-related values.

The heart of Hofstede's book is a survey of a large U.S. multinational company's employees. Some 117,000 surveys were collected from workers and managers in forty countries and twenty languages. The data were collected in two waves, one in 1968 and another in 1972. Hofstede then searched for variables that reliably differentiated managers of various nations. He ultimately settled on four dimensions of national culture:

1. *Power distance*: a measure of power inequality between bosses and subordinates. High power-distance countries (such as the Philippines, Mexico, and

---

Venezuela) display more autocratic relationships between bosses and subordinates. Low power-distance countries (including Denmark, Israel, and Austria) tend to have more democratic and decentralized patterns.

2. *Uncertainty avoidance*: the level of comfort or discomfort with uncertainty and ambiguity. Countries high on uncertainty avoidance (Greece, Portugal, Belgium, and Japan) tend to make heavy use of structure, rules, and specialists to maintain control. Countries low on the index (Hong Kong, Denmark, Sweden, and Singapore) put less emphasis on structure and are more tolerant of risk taking.

3. *Individualism*: the importance of the individual versus the collective (group, organization, or society). Countries highest on individualism (the United States, Australia, Great Britain, and Canada) put emphasis on autonomous, self-reliant individuals who try to meet their own needs. Countries lowest on individuality (Peru, Pakistan, Colombia, and Venezuela) emphasized mutual loyalty between individual and collective.

4. *Masculinity-femininity:* In countries highest in masculinity (Japan, Austria, Venezuela, Italy), men tend to feel strong pressures for career success; there are relatively few women in high-level positions, and job stress is high. The opposite is true in countries low in masculinity (such as Denmark, Norway, the Netherlands, and Sweden).

Hofstede argues that management practices and theories about effective management are inevitably culture-bound. Most management theory has been developed in the United States, which is culturally similar to nations where people speak English or other northern European languages with Germanic roots but distinct from most countries in Asia (as well as those speaking a language derived from Latin). To Hofstede, managers and scholars have too often assumed that what works in their culture will work anywhere, an assumption that often has disastrous results.

Hofstede also explores the relationship between national and organizational culture, noting that a common culture is a powerful form of organizational glue. He argues this is usually easier for multinational companies when a dominant home country culture is accepted companywide. This can only work if managers, particularly those from outside the home culture, become bicultural. A failing of many American managers who work abroad, in Hofstede's view, is that they tend to live in American enclaves and remain both monolingual and monocultural.

Hofstede's research was limited in many ways. His sample came from only one American company, and many nations were absent (China, Russia, most of Africa and eastern Europe). His data were far from perfect and are now more than three decades old. But no other work has been as influential in demonstrating the pervasive impact of national culture on organizations.

Gordon Bethune, CEO of Continental Airlines, demonstrated a comparable flair for drama in his amazing turnaround of what was once heralded as the worst air carrier in the United States. In 1994, the airline was dead last in on-time performance, worst in mishandling luggage, highest in customer complaints, and among the bottom performers in overbooking. It was losing money so fast that Bethune's early meetings to develop plans for reform were each labeled "the last supper."

Bethune quickly launched a series of symbolic actions to get the company headed in a new direction:

• He opened the doors to the executive suite, which were previously locked and accessible only with an ID. Security cameras were removed.

• He convened open houses with food and drink for all employees in the executive offices. He personally led tours of his office, opening a closet door to prove that Frank Lorenzo, the previous CEO, was really gone.

• He sat in a different chair at each management meeting.

• He gathered up the old employee manuals full of rules and regulations and, joined by a group of employees, took them to the parking lot and set them afire.

• He ordered the paint department to redo Continental's fleet with a completely new paint scheme. When the operations managers complained the time frame was too short, Bethune told them, "I have a Beretta at home with a fifteen-round magazine, and if you don't get those airplanes painted by July 1 I'm going to come in here and empty the clip. You're wonderful people and I love you, but you're going to get those airplanes painted or I'm going to shoot every last one of you."

• He invited a hundred of the airline's best customers and their spouses to his home for dinner and apologized to them for what they had put up with prior to 1974.

• He used metaphors to illustrate principles of cultural cohesion. An example was the watch, which, Bethune noted with a flourish, requires every part to function.

• He backed up intangible values with tangible rewards. Reliability, for example, became a core value. This meant being on time all the time. When Continental's flights hit 71 percent, each employee received a check for $65; when the company topped all other U.S. airlines in on-time performance, each employee received $100. But the true value of the money was illustrated in stories of how it was spent, by employees buying something for themselves or giving their kids a treat.

As a result of these and other actions, Continental, received the J. D. Power Award for customer satisfaction in 1996 and 1997. In 1997, the company received the distinction of being named 1996 Airline of the Year. Equally important, the company became profitable in 1995 and remained so for the next five years. In 2002, the company achieved enviable placements on several of *Fortune* magazine's A lists: number two on "most admired global airlines," number thirty on "most admired global corporations," and number forty-two on "100 best companies to work for in America."

Carstedt's strategy at Volvo and Bethune's at Continental are only two examples of using symbols to find meaning in chaos, clarity in confusion, and predictability in mystery. In the sections that follow, we use additional examples to illustrate other symbols and symbolic activities. Different symbolic forms play distinctive cultural roles in organizations. *Myth, vision, and values* give an organization a deep sense of purpose and resolve. *Heroes and heroines,* through their words and deeds, serve as living logos to demonstrate what is cherished and sanctified. Narrative forms such as *fairy tales* and *stories* offer explanations, reconcile contradictions, and resolve dilemmas (Cohen, 1969). Symbolic events—such as *rituals* and *ceremonies*—give direction over uncharted and seemingly unchartable terrain (Ortner, 1973). *Metaphor, humor, and play* loosen things up and take participants to a deeper level.

Myths, Vision, and Values

Myths, operating at the deepest reaches of consciousness, are the story behind the story (Campbell, 1988). They explain. They express. They maintain solidarity and cohesion. They legitimize. They communicate unconscious wishes and conflicts. They mediate contradictions. They are a narrative to anchor the present in the past (Cohen, 1969). All organizations rely on myths or sagas of varying strength and intensity (Clark, 1975). Myths support claims of distinctiveness, transforming a place of work into a revered institution and an all-encompassing way of life.

Myths often originate in the founding or launching of an enterprise. The original plan for Southwest Airlines, for example, was sketched on a cocktail napkin in a San Antonio, Texas, bar. It envisioned connecting three cities: Dallas, Houston, and San Antonio. As legend has it, Rollin King, one of the original founders, said to his counterpart Herb Kelleher, who later became Southwest's CEO, "Herb, let's start an airline." Kelleher replied,

"Rollin, you're crazy. Let's do it!" (Freiberg and Freiberg, 1998, p. 15). As the new airline moved ahead, it met staunch resistance from established carriers. Four years of intense legal wrangling kept the upstart grounded. In 1971, the Texas Supreme Court ruled in Southwest's favor, and its planes were ready to fly. The possibility that a local sheriff might enforce a lingering injunction from a lower court to halt the flights prompted a terse directive from Kelleher: "You roll right over the son of a bitch and leave our tire tracks on his uniform if you have to" (Freiberg and Freiberg, 1998, p. 21). The persistence and zaniness of Southwest's mythologized beginnings have helped shaped its unique culture: "The spirit and steadfastness that enabled the airline to survive in its early years is what makes Southwest such a remarkable company today" (Freiberg and Freiberg, 1998, p. 14).

Myths anchor an organization's *values*. Values define what an organization stands for, those qualities worthy of esteem or commitment for their own sake. Unlike goals, values are intangible and define a fundamental character that distinguishes an enterprise from others. Values create a sense of identity, from boardroom to factory floor, and make people feel special. When an organization attempts to articulate values in mission statements or other formal documents, they often lose their meaning.

Southwest Airlines has never codified its values formally. But its Symbol of Freedom billboards and banners express the company's defining purpose: extending the freedom to fly to everyone, not just the elite, and doing it with an abiding sense of fun. In contrast, the Edina (Minnesota) School District, following the suicide of a female superintendent, involved staff, parents, and students in formally articulating shared values: "We care. We share. We dare." The values of the U.S. Marine Corps are condensed into a simple phrase: "Semper Fi." It is more than a motto; it stands for the deeply held sentiments that are instilled into each recruit and perpetuated by every veteran Marine: "The values and assumptions that shape its members . . . is all the Marines have. They are the smallest of the U.S. military services, and in many ways the most interesting. Theirs is the richest culture: formalistic, insular, elitist, with a deep anchor in their own history and mythology" (Ricks, 1997, p. 15).

Vision turns an organization's core ideology, or sense of purpose, into an image of what the future might become. It is a shared fantasy illuminating new possibilities within the realm of existing myths and values. Martin Luther King's "I have a dream" speech, for example, foresaw a new future for race relations in the United States rooted in the ideals of America's founding fathers.

Vision is vital in contemporary organizations. In their book *Built to Last,* Collins and Porras profile many of America's visionary companies. According to the authors, "The essence of a visionary company comes in the translation of its core ideology and its own unique drive for progress into the very fabric of the organization" (Collins and Porras, p. 201). Johnson and Johnson's commitment to the elimination of "pain and disease" and to "the doctors, nurses, hospitals, mothers, and all others who use our products" motivated the company to make the costly decision to pull Tylenol from store shelves when several bottles tainted by product tampering were discovered. 3M's principle of "thou shalt not kill a new product idea" originated when someone dug in his heels and refused to stop working on an idea that became Scotch Tape. The same principle years later paved the way for Post-its, a product resurrected from a failed adhesive. An abstract vision offers concrete imagery linking historical legend and core philosophical precepts to future events. A shared vision imbues an organization with spirit, resolve, and élan.

Subtle distinctions among intangible ideas such as myths, values, and visions are difficult to draw. In reality, these ideas often conjoin. Take eBay, a highly visible success amid a sea of dot com disasters. In eBay, a seamless interplay of myth, values, and vision contributes to top performance, even in an unfavorable economic environment. Much of eBay's success is attributed to its founder, Pierre Omidyar. He envisioned creation of a perfect marketplace where buyers would have equal access to products and prices, and sellers would have an open market for their goods. Prices would be set by the laws of supply and demand. But Omidyar's vision went beyond economic exchange to incorporate another benefit of the marketplace: community. In true marketplace stalls and cafes, people swap gossip, trade suggestions for solving a variety of issues, and pass the time of day. Omidyar wanted eBay to be both a virtual business site and a caring community. That vision led to eBay's core values: commerce and community. Embedded in these are corollary values: "Treat other people on line as you would like to be treated, and when disputes arise, give other people the benefit of the doubt."

eBay is also awash in myths and legends. Omidyar's vision is said to have taken root over dinner with his fiancée. She complained to him that their move from Boston to the Silicon Valley had severed her ties with fellow collectors of Pez dispensers. He came to her rescue by writing code that laid the foundation for a new company. Did it happen this way? Not quite. This story was hatched by Mary Lou Song, in an effort to get eBay some media exposure. Her conclusion: "Nobody wants to hear about a thirty-year-old genius who wanted to create a perfect market. They want to hear that he did it for his fiancée." The myth continues because myths are truer than true.

Heroes and Heroines

In the wake of scandals involving CEOs at Enron and elsewhere, *Business Week* (Byrnes, Byrne, Edwards, and Lee, 2002) profiled six "good" CEOs. They were not flashy media celebrities like Lee Iacocca or Jack Welch. Nor were they symbols of corporate greed like Ken Lay, Bernie Ebbers, or Dennis Kozlowski. They were solid leaders who built companies that had stood the test of time and delivered exemplary results.

Just as important, these six leaders modeled the corporate values they hoped to instill in others. One of the featured executives, Colgate Palmolive's Ruben Mark, refused to comment on *Business Week*'s story because he felt talking to the press added little value to his company's operation. Another, Costco's James Sinegal, took pride in his disdain for corporate perks. He answered his own phone and personally escorted guests to his spartan office—no bathroom, no walls, twenty-year-old furniture. Sinegal commented on his penuriousness: "We're low-cost operators, and it would be a little phoney if we tried to pretend that we're not and had all the trappings" (Byrnes, Byrne, Edwards, and Lee, 2002, p. 82).

All six of these executives, at some level, seemed to understand their role as cultural heroes. They were living logos, human icons, whose words and deeds exemplified and reinforced important core values. The impact of such well-placed cultural heroes and heroines is underscored by Bernie Marcus, cofounder of Home Depot: "People watch the titular heads of companies, how they live their lives, and they know [if] they are being sold a bill of goods. If you are a selfish son-of-a-bitch, well that usually comes across fairly well. And it comes across no matter how many memos you send out [stating otherwise]" (Roush, 1999, p. 139).

Home Depot also realized that cultural heroes and heroines were not concentrated at the top. They were salted everywhere, ordinary people doing extraordinary things. Home Depot made a practice of regularly anointing and celebrating its heroes and heroines, among them:

- A mentally retarded worker at a California store who cleaned bathrooms and swept floors ("He doesn't shy back from anything")

- An employee who developed a coloring book for children
- A manager who stripped nude in a high-level meeting to protest a severe cost-cutting measure in his lumber operation
- An employee who, on her own, went to a competitor after hours to purchase merchandise with a personal credit card so that it would be available to a Home Depot customer the next day

The top-to-bottom cultural recognition of heroes and heroines helped Home Depot be recognized from 1995 to 1999 as one of *Fortune* magazine's most admired companies.

Some heroic exploits happen out of view. For many years, Southwest Airlines has annually recognized the contribution of its behind-the-scene employees in a Heroes of the Heart award ceremony. The award is given to the backstage group that has contributed the most to Southwest's unique culture and successful performance. During the year following the awards event, a Southwest aircraft flies with the name of the group printed on its fuselage as a symbol of the employees' contribution. A song written for the occasion expresses the value Southwest places on its heroes and heroines—even those whose important work is often hidden:

> Heroes come in every shape and size;
> Adding something very special to others in their lives
> No one gives you medals and the world won't know your name
> But in Southwest's eyes you're heroes just the same.

In recent memory, the Twin Towers tragedy reminded all Americans of the vital role heroism plays in fueling the human spirit. New York City police officers and firefighters in particular touched people's hearts. These courageous men and women risked their lives to save others. Many perished as a result:

- A police officer had just turned in his retirement papers at headquarters but raced to the scene to see what he could do to help. He was killed.
- A firefighter was playing golf in New Jersey. Hearing of the disaster in progress, he packed up his clubs and reported for duty. He was also killed.

Sacrifices such as these reaffirmed Americans' spirit and resolve in the face of one of the nation's most costly human tragedies.

Every day, less dramatic acts of heroism occur as people go out of their way to help customers or serve their communities. Home Depot, for example, abounds in stories of employees who volunteer personal time to help needy customers fix their homes or finish household projects. The products come from Home Depot, but the labor comes from the hearts of employees motivated by the values of the company. *Newsweek* periodically has an "everyday heroes" feature showcasing the uncommon exploits of common people.

Exploits of heroes and heroines are lodged in our psyches. We call on their examples in times of uncertainty and stress. American POWs, interred in North Vietnam prisons, drew upon stories of Capt. Lance Sijan, Adm. James Stockdale, and Col. Bud Day, who had courageously endured injury and torture in captivity, refusing to capitulate to their Viet Cong captors. "[Their examples] when passed along the clandestine prison communications network . . . helped support the resolve that eventually defeated the enemy's efforts" (McConnell, 1986, p.30). During the Bosnian conflict, the ordeal of Scott O'Grady, a U.S. Air Force fighter pilot, was widely publicized. To survive after being shot down over enemy territory, O'Grady drew on the example of Sijan: "His strong will to survive and be free was an inspiration to every pilot I knew" (O'Grady, 1997, p. 67). Although these examples are drawn from the harrowing challenges of war, they demonstrate how human models can influence our everyday decisions and actions. We all carry the lessons of teachers, parents, and others with us. Their examples serve as guides to the everyday choices we make in our personal lives and at work.

Stories and Fairy Tales

The chancellor of Vanderbilt University, Joe B. Wyatt (now chancellor emeritus), once stood in front of several hundred professors and staff members at the university's convocation. Its purpose was to kick off another school year. Wyatt wended his way through facts about the university's status and awarded chairs to professors who had retired. He closed his presentation with a story:

> I'd like to share with you a story about a young second grade teacher in Austin, Texas. Her name is Roberta Wright. Among her young students was a little girl who was stealing materi-

als from the classroom each day. Ms. Wright called the mother and scheduled a parent conference. She told the mother about the daily thefts and let her know that the stealing could not continue. The mother sat silent for a few seconds and then said, "Oh, Ms. Wright, you don't understand, do you? She comes home each afternoon and plays that she's still in school. She pretends she's you."

Chancellor Wyatt paused for a few moments, his eyes moving from person to person in the assembled crowd. He then concluded: "And ladies and gentleman, that does not stop in second grade." He was reminding everyone of the sacred side of teaching, one of the university's core values. The story conveyed his message in a powerful way.

Like fairy tales, stories are more than entertainment or moral instruction for small children. They offer comfort, reassurance, direction, and hope to people of all ages. They externalize inner conflicts and tensions (Bettelheim, 1977). Stories are sometimes dismissed as the last resort of people with nothing of substance—(like a professor accused of telling "war stories," offering entertainment rather than truth or wisdom). Yet stories also convey information, morals, values, and myths vividly and convincingly (Mitroff and Kilmann, 1975). They perpetuate values and keep the historical exploits of heroes and heroines alive. B. Lopez has captured poetically the role of stories in the human experience:

Remember only this one thing,
The stories people tell have a way of taking care of them.
If stories come to you, care for them.
And learn to give them away where they are needed.
Sometimes a person needs a story more than food to stay alive.
That is why we put these stories in each other's memories.
This is how people care for themselves.
　　　(Lopez, 1998)

Stories are commonly told and retold around the campfire and during family reunions. But stories play a wider role in the human experience. David Armstrong, CEO of Armstrong International, says in his book *Managing by Storying Around* (1992) that storytelling has played a powerful role in history through the teachings of Jesus, Buddha, and Mohammed, among others. Potentially it plays an equally influential role in contemporary organizations: "Rules, either in policy manuals or on signs, can be intimidating. But the morals in stories are invariably inviting, fun and inspiring. Through story telling our people can know very clearly what the company believes in and what needs to be done" (Armstrong, p. 6). To Armstrong, storytelling is a simple, timeless, memorable, and demographic-proof way to do a number of things (pp. 7–8):

- Pass along corporate traditions
- Train employees
- Empower people
- Recognize accomplishments
- Spread the word
- Have fun
- Recruit and hire the right people
- Make sales
- Develop better managers

Effective organizations are full of good stories. They often focus on the exploits and legends of corporate heroes. For example, Marriott Hotels founder J. W. Marriott, Sr., died years ago, but his presence is still felt. Stories of his unwavering commitment to customer service are told and retold. His aphorism "Take good care of your employees and they'll take good care of your customers" is still vital to Marriott's philosophy. According to legend, Marriott visited every new hotel general manager and took the manager for a walk around the property. He would point out every broken branch, sidewalk pebble, and obscure cobweb. By tour's end, the new manager left with a long to-do list. More important, the manager took away an indelible lesson in what really mattered at Marriott.

Another story involves the late Thomas Frist, Sr., one of the founders of Hospital Corporation of America (HCA). Frist would sit through meetings of the company's board of directors as financial details and strategy were discussed and debated. Near the end of the meeting, he typically rose to read letters from patients who had received treatment in HCA's hospitals. In doing so, he reminded senior management of the company's primary purpose.

Not all stories center on the founder or chief executive. Ritz-Carlton is famous for the unique, upscale treatment it offers guests around the world. "My pleasure" is employees' universal response to requests, no matter how demanding or trivial. One hurried guest jumped into a taxi to the airport but left his briefcase on the sidewalk. The doorman retrieved the briefcase, abandoned his post, sped to the airport, and delivered the briefcase to the panicked guest. Instead of being fired, the doorman became a permanent part of the legends and lore—a living example of the company's commitment to going the extra mile (Deal and Jenkins, 1994).

Stories are a key medium for communicating corporate myths. They establish and perpetuate tradition. They are recalled and embellished in formal meetings and informal coffee breaks. They convey the value and identity of the organization to insiders and outsiders, thereby building confidence and support. One school administrator responded to criticisms of a new reading program by recounting stories of several children whose ability to read had increased dramatically. The stories spread through the community, and test scores became almost irrelevant because the stories built so much confidence and support. Stories can communicate the success of a good program, or obscure the failure of a bad one. If reading scores go down, a few dramatic success stories might prevent a close look at the program's actual effectiveness.

Ritual

Around the world, at home and at work, ritual gives structure and meaning to daily life. "We find these magical moments every day—drinking our morning coffee, reading the daily paper, eating lunch with a friend, drinking a glass of wine while admiring the sunset, or saying, 'Good night, sleep tight . . .' at bedtime. The holy in the daily; the sacred in the single act of living" (Fulghum, 1995, p. 3).

For sunrise and sundown, for moon and rain, for stars.
A time for the first breath—"ah"—and the last breath—"oh"
But in the meantime, there is the infinite moment—
A time to do the dishes.
And a time to walk the dog. (p. 254)

Humans create both personal and communal rituals. Those that work and carry meaning become the dance of life. "Rituals anchor us to a center," Fulghum writes, "while freeing us to move on and confront the everlasting unpredictability of life. The paradox of ritual patterns and sacred habits is that they simultaneously serve as a solid footing and spring-board, providing a stable dynamic in our lives" (p. 261). The power of ritual is palpable if one experiences the emptiness of losing it. When the Roman Catholic Church changed its liturgy from Latin to the vernacular, many Catholics felt a profound loss of conviction and faith in the Mass. Conversely, in 2001 and 2002, when the Catholic Church in the United States suffered a seemingly endless series of scandals involving sexual misbehavior by priests, many shaken laypersons turned to the rituals of the mass for comfort and reassurance.

Historically, cultures have relied on ritual and ceremony to create order, clarity, and predictability—particularly around issues or dilemmas too complex, mysterious, or random to be controlled otherwise. Rain dances, harvest celebrations, and annual meetings invoke supernatural assistance in the critical but unpredictable processes of raising crops and building market share. Conventions are a yearly opportunities to renew old ties and revive deep collective commitments. "Convention centers are the basilicas of secular religion" (Fulghum, 1995, p. 96).

Rituals of initiation induct newcomers into communal membership. "Greenhorns" encounter powerful symbolic issues from the moment they join a group or organization:

> The first problem faced by the new member of any group is gaining entry into the men's hut—of gaining access to the basic organizational secrets. A key episode here is the rite of passage. This is more or less an affirmation to the individual of the fact that he has been accepted into the men's hut. And, as in the tribe, simply attaining puberty is not sufficient. There must be an accompanying trial and appropriate ritual to mark the event. The so-called primitives had the good sense to make these trials meaningful and direct. Upon attaining puberty you killed a lion and were circumcised. After a little dancing and whatnot, you were admitted as a junior member and learned some secrets. The hut is a symbol of, and a medium for maintaining, the *status quo* and the good of the order. (Ritti and Funkhouser, 1982, p. 3)

Modern amenities (central heating, flush toilets, Novocain) insulate us from the discomfort and uncertainties of earlier eras. It is tempting to believe that we are equally far beyond the primitive drives, sexism, and superstition that gave rise to age-old institutions such as the men's hut. But consider the experience of a new member of the U.S. Senate:

> Paul Tsongas attended his first meeting of the Senate Energy Committee in January 1979.
> At the time, Tsongas had just finished a well-publicized race against Senator Edward Brooke,
> his name having thus appeared almost daily in the Washington newspapers for weeks. Tak-
> ing his seat quietly at the far end of the table as befits a freshman, he listened intently as
> Chairman Henry Jackson welcomed everyone back for the new Congress and greeted the
> new members, including Senator "Ton'gas." Repeatedly stumbling over the name, Jackson
> drew ripples of laughter from the audience of lobbyists, staff, and press while Tsongas
> squirmed in the mandatory silence of freshmen (Weatherford, 1985, pp. 32–33)

Henry "Scoop" Jackson was no juvenile prankster; he was a savvy, powerful, and widely
respected veteran of the Senate. He was simply welcoming Tsongas to the men's hut in a
ritual that employed a verbal surrogate for ritual circumcision. Nor are women spared
Senate initiation rituals:

> One of the early female victims was a representative who was a serious feminist. Soon after
> arriving in Congress, she broke propriety by audaciously proposing an amendment to a mili-
> tary bill of Edward Hebert, Chief of the Defense Clan. When the amendment received only
> a single vote, she supposedly snapped at the aged committee chairman: "I know the only
> reason my amendment failed is that I've got a vagina." To which Herbert retorted, "If you'd
> been using your vagina instead of your mouth, maybe you'd have gotten a few more votes."
> (Weatherford, 1985, p. 35)

That last exchange seems particularly harsh and offensive, but its diverse meanings and
various interpretations take us right to the heart of the symbolic frame. A kinder and gen-
tler anecdote would lose some of the power of this demonstration of how much can happen in a multilayered transaction. Let's look at some possible interpretations.

One interpretation highlights the age-old battle between the sexes. The female representative raises the specter of sexual discrimination; Hebert responds with a highly offensive sexist remark.

The exchange can also be seen as a classic negotiation about the newcomer's agenda
for reforming the organization. Newcomers are expected to bring new ideas and perspectives; it is their *destiny* to be agents of evolution and reform. Old-timers act as a force
for stability and the wisdom of the past; they are supposed to pass along old values and

practices. If newcomers fully succumb to the press of historical tradition, an organization risks stultification and decay. Conversely, if old-timers fail to induct new arrivals properly, an organization risks chaos and disarray.

If we frame the transaction as an initiation ritual, we focus on the clash between a new arrival and an established veteran. Here, the exchange is very similar to what Senator Tsongas experienced. Decoded this way, the exchange is a universal feature of initiation rituals, independent of time, place, or gender: the old-timer is reminding the rookies about how things work and who's in charge. Rarely does any family, group, organization, or society with cohesion and a sense of itself offer free admission to newcomers. The price is usually higher for those who are different or who question or threaten existing values, norms, and patterns. People who differ in gender, race, ethnicity, or religion cannot become full-fledged members of a group or organization until they are initiated into the inner sanctum. The initiation may be bitterly painful and raise poignant questions for the newcomer: "What price am I willing to pay to join this group? Where is the line between legitimate adjustment to a new culture and sacrificing my own values or identity? Why should I have to tolerate values or practices that I see as wrong or unjust?" Yet only a weak culture accepts newcomers with no initiation. The stronger a culture, the stronger the message to newcomers that "you are different and not yet one of us." The initiation reinforces the existing culture at the same time that it tests the newcomer's ability to become a member. It became clear that Hillary Rodham Clinton, a Democrat from New York, had survived her initiation and achieved full membership in the United States Senate when she and Sen. Don Nickles, a Republican from Oklahoma, partnered on an unemployment bill in early 2003. This was particularly impressive because Nickles had been a leader of the effort to impeach her husband, Pres. Bill Clinton.

Initiation, then, is one important role of ritual. Rituals play an equally powerful role in bonding a group together and imbuing the enterprise with the traditions and values that enable people to carry out the organization's mission. In strong cultures, this often means making sacrifices—sometimes risking life or limb. All Americans saw the resolve in the eyes of firefighters who climbed the stairs of the Trade Towers to rescue people trapped above. Even knowing they might not survive, the firefighters moved ahead. Their steely courage and close comradeship are buttressed by a multitude of rituals such as living and cooking together.

Rituals also prepare combat pilots to slip into a fighter cockpit not knowing whether they will return:

> For me, there can be no fighter pilots without fighter pilot rituals. The end result of these ritu-
> als is a culture that allows individuals to risk their lives and revel in it. If the normal American
> finds it difficult to understand the circumstances that compel an individual to willingly hurtle
> their body through space encased in several tons of steel while determined people are
> actively trying to kill them, it is because the normal American has not been indoctrinated
> into the fighter pilot culture. (Broughton, 1988, p. 131)

Maj. Kevin Reed, an F-16 pilot, recently outlined the Air Force's comprehensive liturgy (Reed, 2001). Some rituals recognize accomplishments. When Capt. Sijan received his Medal of Honor, the president of the United States attended:

> In the large room, men in impressive uniforms and costly vested suits and women [in uni-
> forms] and cheerful spring pastels stood motionless and silent in their contemplation of the
> words. The stark text of the citation contained a wealth of evocative imagery, some of it sav-
> age, some tender to the point of heartbreak. President Ford left the rostrum: a group of senior
> officers drew up beside him to hand forward the glass-covered walnut case containing the
> medal. There was a certain liturgical quality to this passing of a sanctified object among
> a circle of anointed leaders. (McConnell, 1986, pp. 245–246)

Other rituals soften grief. The most solemn of the Air Force rituals is the death notifica-
tion. Once a fatality has been confirmed, a team of three officers is dispatched to the home of the nearest relative. An officer of superior rank passes the news: "The Chief of Staff of the Air Force conveys his deep sympathies." A flight surgeon is there for physical support. A chaplain offers spiritual sustenance. The notification ritual is the first step in the consolation ceremony (Reed, 2001, p. 10).

On the flip side are the numerous fun rituals, but even they have a serious side:

> On a Friday night at a base officers club, four Marine A-6 Intruder pilots joined a packed
> crowd of Air Force officers. One of the Marine aviators put his cap on the bar while fishing for
> some money to pay for his drink. The bartender rang a foot-tall bell and yelled "Hat on the
> bar!" This infraction automatically means the guilty party buys a round of drinks. Surveying
> the size of the crowd, the Marine calculated that his supposed breach of decorum could cost
> him several hundred dollars. He refused to pay. An Air Force colonel approached him and
> asked him if he really intended to flout the tradition. When the Marine responded in the

affirmative, the colonel called the base security and ordered the A-6s on the ramp impounded. The Marine left and called his superior to report the colonel's action. Shortly thereafter, he returned and asked sheepishly, "What's everyone having?"

Rituals also govern key relationships. In a fighter squadron, one of the most important relationships is that between a pilot and a crew chief. A preflight ritual transfers ownership between someone who cares for an aircraft on the ground and the one who will fly it:

> The ground ceremony is a ritual we have formalized to signify the handing off of the aircraft to the pilot where the pilot is assured his aircraft is ready and safe for flight. The marching reinforces our teamwork while the drill and ceremony keeps our customs alive, enabling us to demonstrate our pride in our profession:
>
> 1. The first salute is a courtesy greeting that signifies respect between the aircraft mechanic and his pilot.
>
> 2. The handshake takes the greeting to a new level and is the personal bond between the mechanic and his pilot.
>
> 3. The second salute after the pilot has operationally checked the aircraft signifies the aircraft's airworthiness and that the aircraft is now in the hands of the pilot.
>
> 4. The thumbs-up is the personal gesture wishing a good flight to the pilot. [R. Mola, cited in Reed, 2001, p. 5]

Interwoven, the many rituals of combat flying bond the participants together and bind them to the service's traditions and values. The same is true for cohesive cultures in every sector.

Ceremony

The distinction between ritual and ceremony is subtle. Ceremonies are grander, more elaborate, less frequent occasions. Rituals are simpler, day-to-day routines, though still meaningful. A manager might marry only once but insist on a newspaper, croissant, and coffee at the same hour each morning. Ritual and ceremony are both illustrated in an account from Japan:

It has been the same every night since the death in 1964 of Yasujiro Tsutsumi, the legendary patriarch of the huge Seibu real-estate and transportation group. Two employees stand an overnight vigil at his tomb. There are always plenty of volunteers from a business that owns about one-sixth of the real estate in Japan, along with a large collection of hotels, resorts and railways. On New Year's, the weather is often bitter, but at dawn the vigil expands to include five or six hundred top executives—directors, vice presidents, presidents—arrayed by company and rank, the most senior in front. A limousine delivers Yasujiro's third son, Yoshiaki Tsutsumi, the head of the family business and Japan's richest man. A great brass bell booms out six times as Yoshiaki approaches his father's tomb. He claps his hands twice, bows deeply, and says, "Happy New Year, Father, Happy New Year." Then he turns to deliver a brief-but-stern sermon to the assembled congregation. The basic themes change little from year to year: last year was tough, this year will be even tougher, and you'll be washing dishes in one of the hotels if your performance is bad. Finally, he toasts his father with warm sake and departs. (Downer, 1994)

Ceremonies punctuate our lives at special moments. Baptisms, bar mitzvahs, graduations, weddings, and anniversaries offer meaning and spiritual connection at important transitions. Ceremonies serve four major roles: they socialize, stabilize, reassure, and convey messages to external constituencies. Consider the example of Mary Kay Cosmetics. Several thousand people gather at the company's annual seminar to hear (now posthumous) personal messages from Mary Kay, to applaud the achievements of star salespeople, to hear success stories from people who replaced soap operas with sales calls, and to celebrate. The ceremony brings new members into the fold and helps maintain uniformity in the Mary Kay family long after the seminar ends. It creates a distinctive pageant and makes the Mary Kay culture accessible to outsiders, particularly to consumers. Failure recedes and obstacles disappear as the "you can do it" spirit of the company manifests itself in the symbol of the bumblebee—a creature that, according to aerodynamics experts, should not be able to fly. Apparently unaware of its limitations, it flies anyway.

In the U.S. Congress, ceremony is almost always the order of the day:

Ceremony operates best in a symbolically rich setting that calls for special seating arrangements, particular forms of dress, and various ritual accoutrements such as crosses, thrones, flags, and masks. The full panoply of these objects marches around the congressional chamber in the process of legislation, but it is in the particular use of ritual language that the real nature of congressional ceremony emerges. Because of the sanctity of words, special speech forms are often used . . . to separate normal human interaction from interaction with particularly powerful beings such as gods or potentates. Taboos on the use of personal names and certain pronouns reach an inordinate level in the American Congress, where neither the word *I* nor *you* is proper. Nor can the legislators address one another directly by name, as in "Edward Kennedy," "Ted," or even the more formal "Senator Kennedy." A simple phrase such as "I would like to ask you . . ." becomes "Mr. President, the Senator from Texas would like to ask the Senator from California. . . ." (Weatherford, 1985, pp. 189–190)

Ceremony is also evident in other matters of national importance. In the United States, political conventions select candidates, even though there is rarely much suspense about the outcome, which is carefully scripted for television. Then follow several months in which competing candidates trade clichés and exchange epithets. The same pageantry unfolds each election year. Rhetoric and spontaneous demonstrations are staged in advance. Campaigning is notoriously repetitious and superficial, and voting often seems disconnected from the main drama. The process of electing a president is still a momentous ceremony. It entails a sense of social involvement. It is an outlet for expression of discontent and enthusiasm. It stages live drama for citizens to witness and debate. It gives millions of people a sense of participation in an exciting adventure. It lets candidates reassure the public that there are answers to our most important questions and solutions to our biggest problems. It draws attention to common social ties and to the importance of accepting whichever candidate eventually wins (Edelman, 1977).

Ritual and ceremony are equally significant in business. Rituals communicate meaning from one individual to another and from an organization to its environment. Some organizational events, like retirement dinners and welcoming speeches for new employees, are clearly ceremonial. But many others happen at moments of triumph or times of transition. The ceremony marking the rollout of the first Saturn automobile was a momentous occasion:

I will never forget that day as long as I live. . . . I was totally caught up in the pride and confidence that literally oozed from [everyone]. The applause and whistles and laughter and tears at Inspiration Point and down the aisles leading to the audit area were deafening. But I don't think anyone was prepared for the decibel level when that car slowly wheeled into audit (the final quality checkpoint), with Roger [Smith] and Owen [Bieber] smiling and waving, followed by every team member in the plant who had previously lined the aisles. When Roger stepped out of that car, raised both of his fists jubilantly into the air and shouted "We did it!" the house came down. . . . There wasn't a dry eye in the house [O'Toole, 1996, p. 43]

The bittersweet moments of transition also command ceremony. When Phil Condit took over the reins of Boeing, he invited senior managers to his home for dinner. Afterward, the group gathered around a giant fire pit to tell stories about Boeing. Condit asked them to tell negative stories and toss them into the flames. It was a ceremonial way to banish the dark side of the company's past (Deal and Key, 1998).

Expressive events provide order and meaning and bind an organization or a society together. When properly conducted and attuned to valued myths, rituals fire the imagination and deepen faith; otherwise, they become cold, empty forms that people resent and avoid. Rituals and ceremonies can release creativity and transform meanings. They can also cement the status quo and block adaptation and learning. Like other symbols, they cut both ways.

Metaphor, Humor, and Play

Metaphors, humor, and play illustrate the important "as if" quality of symbols. They are indirect ways to grapple with issues that are too complex, mysterious, or threatening to approach head-on. Metaphors make the strange familiar and the familiar strange. They help us capture subtle themes that normal language can overlook. Consider the metaphors from managers asked to produce one for their agency as it is and one as they hope it might become:

As It Is	As It Might Become
A maze	A well-oiled wheel
Wet noodle	Oak tree
Aggregation of tribes with competing agenda	Symphony orchestra
Three-ring circus	Championship team

A puzzle no one can put together	A smooth-running machine
Twilight zone	Utopia
Herd of horses	Tribe
Herd of cattle on the rampage	Fleet of ships heading for the same port
Oldsmobile 98	Honda Civic

Metaphors compress complicated issues into understandable images, influencing our attitudes, evaluations, and actions. A university head who views the institution as a factory establishes different policies than one who conceives of it as a craft guild or a shopping center. Consultants who see themselves as physicians are likely to differ from those who see themselves as salespeople or rain dancers.

Fine (1996) suggests that metaphors are also central to the process of defining and justifying one's work identity. He found that restaurant cooks use four metaphors to describe who they are and what they do: as professionals (like lawyers or doctors), artists (like painters or architects), businesspersons (like executives or entrepreneurs), and workers (like manual laborers). Each image gives rise to its own "occupational rhetoric," and cooks draw on all of them according to the times and situations.

Humor serves important as-if functions. Hansot (1979) argues that it is less important to ask why people use humor in organizations than to ask why they are so serious. She contends that humor plays a number of important functions: it integrates, expresses skepticism, contributes to flexibility and adaptiveness, and signals status. Though a classic device for distancing, humor can also socialize, include, and convey membership. It can establish solidarity and facilitate face saving. Above all, it is a way to illuminate and break frames, indicating that any single definition of a situation is arbitrary.

In most work settings, play and humor are sharply distinguished from work. Play is what people do when they are not working. Images of play in the conversation of managers typically connote aggression, competition, and struggle ("We've got to beat them at their own game"; "We dropped the ball on that one"; "The ball is in his court now") rather than relaxation and fun. But if play is viewed as a state of mind (Bateson, 1972; Goffman, 1974), any activity can be playful. Play permits relaxing the rules to explore alternatives. It encourages experimentation, flexibility, and adaptiveness. March (1976) suggests five guidelines for play in organizations:

1. Treat goals as hypotheses.

2. Treat intuition as real.

3. Treat hypocrisy as transition.

4. Treat memory as an enemy.

5. Treat experience as a theory.

CONCLUSION

In contrast to traditional views emphasizing rationality and objectivity, the symbolic frame highlights the tribal aspect of contemporary organizations. It centers on complexity and ambiguity in organizational phenomena and on the many uses of symbols to mediate the meaning of organizational events and activities. Myths, values, and vision bring cohesiveness, clarity, and direction in the presence of confusion and mystery. Heroes and heroines are role models for people to admire and emulate. Stories carry values and serve as powerful modes of communication. Rituals and ceremonies are ways to take action in the face of success or calamity. Metaphors, humor, and play offer escape from the tyranny of facts and logic; they stimulate creative alternatives to old choices. In *The Feast of Fools,* Cox (1969, p. 13) summarizes the importance of symbolism in modern life: "Our links to yesterday and tomorrow depend also on the aesthetic, emotional, and symbolic aspects of human life—on saga, play, and celebration. Without festival and fantasy, man would not really be a historical being at all."

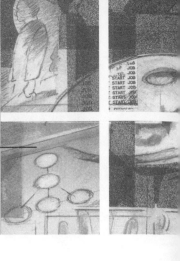

CHAPTER 13

Organization as Theater

Theater as an activity, as a staging of reality, depends on the ability of the audience to frame what they experience. It depends precisely on the audience recognizing, being aware, that they are an audience; they are witnesses to, not participants in, a performance. It depends further on a distinction between actors and the parts they play—characters may die on stage, but actors will live to take a bow. Finally, theater depends on a recognition that performances play with reality in such a way as to turn the taken-for-granted into a plausible appearance.

Mangham and Overington, 1987, p. 49

The symbolic frame encourages us to view organizations as theater and organizational activities as dramaturgical performances played to both internal and external audiences. The success story of the U.S. Navy's Polaris missile system is a fascinating example. The Polaris project was heralded in its time as an exemplar of effective, efficient government activity. One of its distinctive attributes was reliance on modern management techniques such as PERT charts and the Program Planning and Budgeting System. The techniques were embodied in several structural forms: specialist roles, technical divisions, management meetings, and the Special Projects Office. In the wake of the Polaris success—it was produced on time and under budget—analysts concluded that the project's management approach was a major factor. The admiral in charge received a plaque recognizing his role in bringing modern management techniques to the U.S. Navy. A team of visiting British experts recommended PERT to their admiralty.

A later study by Sapolsky (1972) revealed a more symbolic explanation for the stellar accomplishment. The management innovations were highly visible but only marginally connected to ongoing efforts. Specialists' work was loosely linked to other aspects of the project. The technical division produced plans and charts that were mostly ignored. Management meetings served as public arenas in which to chide poor performers, and as revival meetings to reinforce the project's religious fervor. The Special Projects Office served as an official briefing area. Visiting dignitaries were regaled with impressive diagrams and charts unrelated to the project's actual progress. Upon its visit, the team from the British Navy apparently surmised all this and still recommended a similar approach to their own admiralty (Sapolsky, 1972).

Instead of serving their intended rational purposes, modern management techniques contributed to a myth that built external legitimacy and support and kept critics at bay. The Polaris myth afforded a breathing space for the work to go forward and kept spirits and self-confidence high. Polaris demonstrates the virtues of theater in engaging the attention and appreciation of both internal and external audiences: "An alchemist's combination of whirling computers, bright-colored charts, and fast-talking public relations officers gave the Special Projects Office a truly effective management system. It mattered not whether the parts of the system functioned, or even existed. It mattered only that certain people, for a certain period of time, believed that they did" (Sapolsky, 1972, p. 129).

The symbolic frame views structures and processes as secular theater—drama that expresses our fears, joys, and expectations. Drama arouses emotions and kindles our spirit. It reduces uncertainty and soothes bewilderment. It provides a shared basis for understanding the present and a vision of a more promising future. Institutional theorists have described the role of drama in organizations, and we begin this chapter by discussing their views. We then look at organizational structure as theater and do the same with a number of common organizational processes: meetings, planning, evaluation, collective bargaining, and the exercise of power.

INSTITUTIONAL THEORY

Institutional theorists extend the example of Polaris to the everyday workings of contemporary organizations: "In technical organizations, the development of a rational plan is a prelude to the reconstruction and reintegration of a pattern of production activities. In institutionalized organizations, the creation of a rational plan constitutes a dramaturgical alternative to actual changes. Plans are regarded as ends in themselves—as evidence that we are a humane and scientific people who have brought yet another problem under rational control" (Meyer and Rowan, 1983a, p. 126).

DiMaggio and Powell (1983), for example, conclude that organizations in specific fields worry more about how innovations appear than what they add to performance: "New practices become infused with value beyond the technical requirements of the task at hand. . . . As an innovation spreads, a threshold is reached beyond which adoption provides legitimacy rather than improves performance" (p. 142). Staw and Epstein (2000) present empirical evidence that adoption of modern management techniques accentuates a company's legitimacy and heightens CEO compensation, even if the techniques are not fully implemented. Economic performance does not improve, but perceptions of innovativeness and management quality rise.

Institutional theory's theatrical view of organizations is a recent addition to the management literature. Organizations were long viewed as closed systems that protected the technical core from external pressures. Functional demands shaped social architecture. The environment served as a source of raw materials and a market for finished products. The name of the game was efficiency, internal control of the means of production, and economic performance. External fluctuations and production uncertainties were buffered by rational devices such as forecasting, stockpiling, leveling the peaks and valleys of supply and demand, and growth (so as to get more leverage over the environment).

Greatest Hits from Organization Studies No. 3: Paul J. DiMaggio and Walter Powell, "The Iron Cage Revisited: Institutional Isomorphism and Collective Rationality in Organizational Fields," *American Sociological Review,* **Apr. 1983,** *48,* **147–160.**

Third on our list of scholars' greatest hits is an article by Paul J. DiMaggio and Walter Powell. The authors' argument parallels our view of organization as theater. *Isomorphism,* as DiMaggio and Powell use the word, refers to processes that cause organizations to become more like other organizations, particularly when they belong to the same "organizational field." The authors define an organizational field as a set of organizations that "constitute a recognized area of institutional life: key suppliers, resource and product consumers, regulatory agencies, and other organizations that produce similar services or products" (p. 148). This is similar to the concept of an organizational ecosystem, discussed in Chapter Eleven. As an example, think about public schools. They are very like each other but unlike most other kinds of organization. They have similar buildings, classrooms, curricula, staffing patterns, gyms, parent-teacher organizations, and so on. The structural frame would explain these similarities in terms of the need to align structure with goals, task, and technology. DiMaggio and Powell counter that isomorphism occurs for reasons that may have little to do with efficiency or effectiveness.

They describe three kinds of isomorphism: coercive, mimetic, and normative. *Coercive isomorphism* occurs when organizations become more similar in response to outside pressures or requirements. For example, MBA programs in graduate schools of business all tend to have very similar admission requirements and curricula because so many of them are accredited by the same body using the same standards. *Mimetic isomorphism* occurs when one organization simply copies another, as when a university of modest reputation adopts a set of freshman requirements borrowed from those at Harvard or Yale. DiMaggio and Powell suggest that such copying is particularly likely in the presence of fuzzy goals and uncertain technology. When uncertainty makes it hard to prove that one approach is any better than another, imitation saves time and may buy legitimacy.

Normative isomorphism, DiMaggio and Powell's third type, occurs because professionals (lawyers, doctors, engineers, teachers) bring shared ideas, values, and norms from their training to the workplace. DiMaggio and Powell argue that professionally trained individuals are becoming much more numerous and, as a result, influential. Growing numbers of managers with MBAs from accredited business schools carry shared values, beliefs, and practices wherever they go. Latest ideas from the business schools may or may not produce better results, but they still spread rapidly because the newly minted professionals believe in them.

DiMaggio and Powell contend that the primary benefit of isomorphism is to improve an organization's image rather than its products and services: "Each of the institutional isomorphic processes can be expected to proceed in the absence of evidence that they increase internal organizational efficiency. To the extent that organizational effectiveness is enhanced, the reason will often be that organizations are rewarded for being similar to other organizations in their fields. This similarity can make it easier for organizations to transact with other organizations, to attract career-minded staff, to be acknowledged as legitimate and reputable, and to fit into administrative categories that define eligibility for public and private grants and contracts" (p. 153).

Institutional theorists present a less rational dramaturgical image. Organizations, particularly those with vague goals and weak technologies, cannot seal themselves off from external events and pressures. Their environment is never passive or neutral. They are constantly buffeted by larger social, political, and economic trends. The name of the game is maintaining legitimacy and support in the eyes of multiple constituencies. Organizations must therefore reflect contemporary beliefs and expectations. Widely held myths shape social architecture. Correct appearance, rather than efficient production, is the prevailing measure of effectiveness.

Highly technical organizations concentrate attention on production processes. Organizations with higher levels of ambiguity and uncertainty turn their backs on technical processes and stage dramatic performances for internal and external audiences (Meyer and Rowan, 1983a). Decision making is more ritual than rational (March and Olsen, 1976). Evaluations serve purposes other than assessing performance (Dornbusch and Scott, 1975). Events affect leadership more than leaders influence events (Edelman, 1977). Structure, decoupled from actual work, serves as a theatrical, ceremonial portrayal of prevailing social myths (Meyer and Rowan, 1983b).

Activities without tangible results? The very thought casts doubt on a substantial proportion of organized endeavor. Might such heresy lead to wholesale cynicism, undercutting confidence in organizations—undermining faith and morale for anyone struggling to make a real difference? The symbolic frame offers a more hopeful interpretation. Institutionalized structures, activities, and events become expressive components of organizational theater. They create ongoing drama that entertains, creates meaning, and portrays the organization to itself. Geertz observed this same phenomenon in Balinese pageants, where "the carefully crafted and scripted, assiduously enacted ritualism of court culture was . . . 'not merely the drapery of political order but its substance'" (Mangham and Overington, 1987, p. 39).

As the work of Sapolsky, DiMaggio and Powell, and Staw and Epstein demonstrates, good drama signals to the outside world that all is well: well-crafted decisions and plans, new innovations in response to emerging problems, sophisticated evaluation and control systems to ensure accountability. All this theatrical face-work creates an image of a well-managed, legitimate organization worthy of confidence and support. Getting the drama right is particularly critical in sectors where outputs are ambiguous and success is hard to measure. But good theater also plays a role in highly technical organizations. Fluctuations in stock prices of American businesses are a case in point. When organizations announce a currently popular improvement strategy, their stock price often improves on the news. We saw an example in Chapter Four, when new management at Greyhound Lines announced staffing cuts and a reengineering initiative; the stock price went up, though the change efforts ultimately proved disastrous. If external constituencies question the worth of existing practices, organizations promise improvement and stage a familiar drama called *Change.* If consumers complain about quality, businesses create a "total quality program" and promise tighter quality standards. Crises stimulate a call for new leaders, who in turn promise major reform.

ORGANIZATIONAL STRUCTURE AS THEATER

Recall that the structural frame depicts a workplace as a network of interdependent roles and units coordinated through a variety of horizontal and vertical linkages. Structural patterns align with purpose and are determined by goals, technologies, and environment (Lawrence and Lorsch, 1967; Perrow, 1979; Woodward, 1970). In contrast, a symbolic view approaches structure as stage design: an arrangement of space, lighting, props, and costumes that make the drama vivid and credible to its audience.

One dramaturgical role of structure is to reflect and convey prevailing social values and myths. In many schools, churches, personnel departments, and mental health firms, goals are multiple and elusive, technology is underdeveloped, linkages between means and ends are poorly understood, and effectiveness is difficult to determine. Building legitimacy requires an appearance conforming to society's expectations. Settings and costumes should be appropriate: a church should have a building, religious artifacts, and a properly attired member of the clergy. A clinic should have examination rooms, uniformed nurses, and licensed physicians with diplomas prominently featured on the wall.

Meyer and Rowan (1978) depict the structure of public schools as largely symbolic. A school has difficulty sustaining public support unless it offers fashionable answers to three questions: Does it offer appropriate topics (for example, third-grade mathematics, world history)? Are topics taught to age-graded students by certified teachers? Does it look like a school (with classrooms, a gymnasium, a library, and a flag near the front door)?

An institution of higher education is judged by age, the size and beauty of the campus, the size of its library collection, its faculty-student ratio, and the number of professors who received doctorates from prestigious institutions. Kamens (1977) suggests that the major function of a college or university is to redefine novice students as graduates who possess special qualities or skills. The value of the transformation must be negotiated with important constituencies. This is done through constant references to the quality and rigor of educational programs and is validated by the structural characteristics or appearance of the institution.

The correct structural configuration, in Kamens's view, depends on whether an institution is elite or not and whether it allocates graduates to a specific social or corporate group. Ivy League schools such as Harvard, Yale, and Princeton are well known for producing graduates who occupy elite roles in society. Each type of institution espouses its own myth and dramatizes its own aspects of structure. The main considerations are casting the right actors, writing a suitable script, and setting the appropriate stage. Elite schools, for example, dramatize selectivity, develop an attractive residential campus, advertise a favorable ratio of faculty to students, and develop a core curriculum that restrains specialization in favor of a unified core of knowledge.

If an institution or its environment changes, theatrical adaptation is needed. New audiences require revisions in actors, scripts, or settings. Since legitimacy and worth are anchored primarily in alignment of structural characteristics to prevailing myths, organizations alter appearances to mirror changes in social expectations. Until the 1930s, America's elite Ivy League colleges were essentially finishing schools for the aristocracy. Admission depended on wealth and breeding more than talent. When the Great Depression cast the rich as predators and villains, the old way became indefensible. The colleges revised admission policy to admit the academically talented regardless of economic background (Delbanco, 1996).

Formal structures are built largely from "blocks" of contemporary myth. Legitimate organizations project a "modern" appearance, constructed of contemporary issues and dilemmas. For example, if total quality management, or reengineering, becomes the badge of honor for progressive companies, programs and consultants spread like fire in a parched forest. As laws mandate education for children with special needs, schools hire specialists who perform highly visible functions that classroom teachers rarely see or understand. In response to criticisms of antiquated management methods, universities adopt sophisticated control systems producing elaborate printouts, often with little effect on operations. Legislatures pass laws on occupational safety, and factories create safety units to post signs no one observes. New structures reflect legal and social expectations and represent a bid for legitimacy and support from the attending audience. An organization, for example, without an affirmative action program is suspiciously out of step with prevailing concerns for diversity and equity. Nonconformity invites questions, criticism, and inspection. It is much easier to appoint an affirmative action officer than to change hiring practices deeply embedded in both individual and institutional beliefs and practices. Since the presence of the affirmative action officer is more visible than revisions in hiring priorities, the addition of a new role may successfully signal to external constituencies that there has been improvement, even if only as a formality. Beginning in the mid-1990s, affirmative action was increasingly challenged in the United States. If its popularity wanes or the Supreme Court overturns its Bakke decision, revisions in the institutional facade may be in order.

Government agencies encapsulate existing ambivalence or conflicts to assure us that things are under control (Edelman, 1977). In the United States, conflict between shippers and railroads led to the founding of the Interstate Commerce Commission. Conflict between labor and management produced the National Labor Relations Board. Conflict between consumers and producers resulted in the Food and Drug Administration. Concern over pollution gave rise to the Environmental Protection Agency. The events of September 11, 2001, led to creation of the Homeland Security Department. In practice, these agencies serve mostly political and symbolic functions: "Congress passes on to these agencies a type of symbolic control; they represent our belief in the virtues of planning and the value of an integrated program of action. But the agencies are given no formal authority over the organizations whose services they are to control and few funds to use as incentives to stimulate the cooperation of these existing organizations" (Scott, 1983, p. 126).

Politically, regulatory agencies are often "captured" by the very entities they are supposed to regulate. Major drug companies are far more effective than the public in lobbying and influencing decisions about drug safety. The Federal Aviation Administration has repeatedly come under fire for its perceived "coziness" with airline companies. In 2002 the Securities and Exchange Commission was criticized for failing to prevent fraudulent practices at well known companies such as Enron and Tyco.

In practice, agencies legitimize elite values, reassure the public that they are zealously protecting its interests, and struggle for funding from the legislature. They reduce tension and uncertainty and increase the public's sense of confidence and security. Only in a crisis is their actual performance called into question (Edelman, 1977), and then the drama of reform ensures that perpetrators are caught and punished and the situation is under control so the crises will never happen again.

ORGANIZATIONAL PROCESS AS THEATER

Administrative processes coordinate work through formal meetings, evaluation systems, accounting systems, management information systems, and labor negotiations. Technical processes produce goods and services. Factory workers assemble parts into products. Professors give lectures to impart knowledge and wisdom. Physicians diagnose illnesses and prescribe medical treatment. Social workers write case reports to identify and remedy social ills.

People spend much of their time engaged in such work processes. To justify their labor, they need to believe their work produces intended outcomes. But even the best intentions do not always lead to desired results. Meetings may not make decisions or solve problems, though they often lead to more meetings. Planning often produces documents few ever see or use. Even without tangible results, activities play a vital role in theatrical performance. They serve as scripts and stage markings that create an opportunities for self-expression, forums for airing grievances, and arenas for negotiating new understandings. Next, we look more closely at these functions in the context of meetings, planning, performance appraisals, collective bargaining, and the exercise of power.

Meetings

March and Olsen (1976) were ahead of the times in their depiction of meetings as "garbage cans." Organizations are notorious as settings for managers looking for ways to expend time and energy, problems in search of solutions, and people with solutions looking for problems. Meetings attract all three: people, problems, and solutions. Outcomes depend on a complicated and often serendipitous interplay among the inputs that happen to arrive: Who came to the meeting? What problems, concerns, or needs did they bring? What solutions or suggestions were available? Garbage can dynamics are particularly likely for meetings dealing with emotionally powerful, symbolically visible, technically fuzzy issues. A conversation on mission is likely to attract a larger, more diverse set of people, problems, and solutions than one on cost accounting. Reorganization (Olsen, 1976b), choosing a new chief administrator (Olsen, 1976a), and conflicts over desegregation (Weiner, 1976) are well-documented occasions for dramatic performances. Meetings may not always produce rational discourse, sound plans, or radical improvements. But they serve as symbolic arenas to help prevent individual and organizational disintegration. They are expressive occasions. Some players become clearer about their role in the collective drama and get a chance to practice and polish their lines. Others revel in the chance to find some excitement at work. Audiences take comfort that issues are getting attention and that better times may lie ahead.

Planning

An organization without a plan is seen as reactive, shortsighted, and rudderless. Planning, then, is a ceremony any reputable organization must conduct periodically to maintain legitimacy. A plan is a badge of honor that organizations wear conspicuously and with pride. A strategic plan carries even higher status. Mintzberg's insightful book *The Rise and Fall of Strategic Planning* (1994) presents an impressive array of survey and anecdotal evidence questioning how well strategic planning really achieves its rational objectives. He shows that the presumed linear progression from analysis to objectives to action to results is more fanciful than factual. Many executives, at some level of awareness, clearly recognize the shortcomings yet continue to champion strategic planning: "Recently I asked three corporate executives what decisions they had made in the last year that they would not have made were it not for their corporate plans. All had difficulty identifying one such decision. Since each of their plans [was] marked 'secret' or 'confidential,' I asked them how their competitors might benefit from the possession of their plans. Each answered with embarrassment that their competitors would not benefit. Yet these executives were strong advocates of corporate planning" (Russell Ackoff, quoted in Mintzberg, 1994, p. 98).

An activity that rarely achieves its intended results may persist because it plays a vital role in the ongoing organizational drama. Quinn notes: "A good deal of the corporate planning I have observed is like a ritual rain dance; it has no effect on the weather that follows, but those who engage in it think it does. Moreover, it seems to me that much of the advice and instruction related to corporate planning is directed at improving the dancing, not the weather" (quoted in Mintzberg, 1994, p. 139).

Cohen and March (1974) list four symbolic roles for plans in universities, but these roles apply to other organizations as well:

1. *Plans are symbols.* Academic organizations have few real pieces of objective evidence to evaluate performance. They have nothing comparable to profit or sales figures. How are we doing? No one really knows. Planning is a signal that all is well or improvement is just around the corner. A failing institution can announce that it has a plan to revitalize itself. An institution without a nuclear reactor, an economics department, or a Division I football team can announce a plan to get one; its stock may then soar. A school or university undergoing an accreditation review engages in a "self-study" and lays out an ambitious strategic plan, which can then gather dust until it is time to repeat the process.

2. *Plans become games.* Especially where goals and technology are unclear, planning becomes a test of will. If a department wants a new program badly, it must justify the expenditure by substantial planning efforts. If an administrator wishes to avoid saying yes but has no real basis for saying no, she can test commitment by asking for a plan. Benefits come more from the process than the result.

3. *Plans become excuses for interaction.* Developing a plan forces discussion and may increase interest in and commitment to new priorities. Occasionally, interaction yields positive results. But rarely does it yield an accurate forecast. Discussions of the future modify views of what should be done differently today. Conclusions about what will happen next year are notoriously susceptible to alteration as people, politics, policies, or preferences change.

4. *Plans become advertisements.* What is frequently called a plan is more like an investment brochure. It is an attempt to persuade private and public donors of an institution's attractiveness. Plans are typically adorned with glossy photographs of beautiful people in pristine settings, official pronouncements of excellence, and a noticeable absence of specific information.

Cohen and March (1974) asked college presidents their views of the linkage between plans and decisions. Responses fell into four main categories:

"Yes, we have a plan. It is used in capital project and physical location decisions."

"Yes, we have a plan. Here it is. It was made during the administration of our last president. We are working on a new one."

"No, we do not have a plan. We should. We're working on one."

"I think there's a plan around here someplace. Miss Jones, do we have a copy of our comprehensive, ten-year plan?" (p. 113)

There is little to suggest that the results would be much different today.

A study of a large-scale planning project in a suburban school district (Edelfson, Johnson, and Stromquist, 1977) offers another example of planning's symbolic importance. Project Redesign, a five-year planning effort supported by federal funds, involved a significant proportion of the district's professionals and citizens in creating ways to meet the next decade's key challenges. Ultimately the process produced no major decisions or significant changes. But it did produce many benefits. It gave participants the chance to participate and interact, which they liked. It was a forum for engaging a variety of problems, solutions, and conflicts that might have been more troublesome had they surfaced in some other arena. It enabled the district to present itself as a model district. Finally, it renewed the district's faith in the virtues of participation, the merits of grassroots democracy, the value of good ideas, and the efficacy of modern planning techniques.

Evaluation

Assessing the performance or productivity of individuals, departments, or programs is a major undertaking. Evaluation consumes substantial time, effort, and money. It typically yields a lengthy report presented with considerable ceremony. A university convenes a visiting committee or accrediting team to evaluate schools or departments. Government mandates assessment of program efficacy. A social service agency commissions a study or audit whenever an important problem or issue arises. Yet rarely are insights or recommendations implemented. Results typically disappear into the recesses of people's minds or the far reaches of administrators' file cabinets.

From another perspective, evaluation ensures a responsible, serious, and well-managed image. Its widespread use persists largely for symbolic reasons. Evaluation produces magic numbers to help us believe that things are working. It shows that an organization takes goals seriously, cares about its performance, and wants to improve. The evaluation process gives participants an opportunity to share opinions and have them recognized publicly. Evaluation results help people relabel old practices, escape the normal routine, and build new beliefs (Rallis, 1980). Even if rarely used for decision making, evaluation also serves as a weapon in political battles or as a justification for a decision already made (Weiss, 1980).

In public organizations, Floden and Weiner (1978) argue, "Evaluation is a ritual whose function is to calm the anxieties of the citizenry and to perpetuate an image of government rationality, efficiency, and accountability. The very act of requiring and commissioning evaluations may create the impression that government is seriously committed to the pursuit of publicly espoused goals, such as increasing student achievement or reducing malnutrition. Evaluations lend credence to this image even when programs are created to appease interest groups" (p. 17).

The evaluation process often takes the form of high drama. Prestigious evaluators are hired, and the process receives considerable publicity. Participants wear costumes that are more formal than usual. New roles are enacted: evaluators ask penetrating questions, and respondents give answers that portray the world as it is supposed to be. The results are often presented dramatically, especially when they are favorable. Negative results, by contrast, are often couched in vacuous language with high-sounding recommendations that no one is likely to take very seriously. Attempts to solve the problems disappear after the ceremony is over.

Occasionally, an evaluator blows the whistle by producing a highly critical report. The drama then becomes a tragedy that is often injurious to both parties. In the United States, a widely publicized report on public education (Coleman, 1966) advanced the thesis that schools don't make a difference. The report and the subsequent debate undermined public confidence in the schools and at the same time raised questions about the cohesion and maturity of the social sciences in their evaluation role.

Collective Bargaining

In collective bargaining, labor and management meet and confer to reshape divisive standoffs into workable agreements. The process typically pits two reasonable sets of interests against each other: unions want better working conditions and benefits for members; management tries to keep costs down and maximize profits for shareholders.

Negotiating teams come together on a public stage and follow a well-known script: "Negotiators have to act like opponents, representatives and experts, showing that they are aligned with teammates and constituents, willing to push hard to achieve constituent goals, and constantly in control. On the public stage, anger and opposition dominate; rituals of opposition, representation and control produce a drama of conflict. At the same time, there are mechanisms for private understanding between opposing lead bargainers, such as signaling and sidebar discussions" (Friedman, 1994, pp. 86–87).

On the surface, the negotiation process appears to be a political contest where power determines the distribution of scarce resources (see Chapter Eleven). On a deeper plane, negotiation is a carefully crafted ritual that delivers the performance audiences demand. Departures from the script carry high risk: "A young executive took the helm of a firm with the intention of eliminating bickering and conflict between management and labor. He commissioned a study of the company's wage structure and went to the bargaining table to present his offer. He informed the union representatives what he had done, and offered them more than they had expected to get. The astonished union leaders berated the executive for undermining the process of collective bargaining and asked for another five cents an hour beyond his offer" (Blum, 1961, pp. 63–64).

Similar problems have been documented by Friedman in his studies of mutual gains bargaining (which emphasizes cooperation and a win-win outcome rather than conflict). A disillusioned participant in an abortive mutual gains process lamented: "It hurt us. We got real chummy. Everyone talked. Then in the final hours, it was the same old shit. Maybe we should have been pounding on the table" (Friedman, 1994, p. 216).

In theater, actors who deviate from the script disrupt everyone else's ability to deliver their lines. The bargaining drama is designed to convince each side the outcomes were the result of a heroic battle. If well performed, the drama conveys the message that two opponents fought hard and persistently for what they believed was right (Blum, 1961; Friedman, 1994). It obscures the widespread reality that actors almost always know in advance how the play will end.

Power

Power is usually viewed as a tangible attribute that individuals or systems possess— as something that can be seized, exercised, or redistributed. But power is inherently ambiguous. It is not always easy to determine what power is, who has it, or how to get it. Sometimes it is even harder to know when power is being used. You are powerful if others think you are.

Power is often attributed to certain behaviors. People who talk a lot, belong to committees, and seem close to the action are typically perceived as powerful. Yet there may be little real relationship between observed behavior and the ability to get what one wants. The relationship may even be negative; the frustrated may talk a lot, and the disgruntled may resort to political intrigue or posturing without discernible impact (Enderud, 1976).

Power is also often attributed to particular individuals or groups to account for observed outcomes. If the unemployment rate improves, political incumbents take credit. If a firm's profits jump, we give credit to the chief executive. If a program is started when things are getting better anyway, it inherits success. Myths of leadership attribute causality to individuals in high places. Whether things are going well or badly, we like to hold someone responsible. Cohen and March (1974) have this to say about college presidents:

> Presidents negotiate with their audiences on the interpretations of their power. As a result, during recent years of campus troubles, many college presidents sought to emphasize the limitations of presidential control. During the more glorious days of conspicuous success, they solicited a recognition of their responsibility for events. This is likely to lead to popular impressions of strong presidents during good times and weak presidents during bad times. Persons who are primarily exposed to the symbolic presidency (for example, outsiders) will tend to exaggerate the power of the presidency. Those people who have tried to accomplish something in the institution with presidential support (for example, educational reforms) will tend to underestimate presidential power or presidential will (pp. 198–199).

As Edelman (1977) puts it: "Leaders lead, followers follow, and organizations prosper. While this logic is pervasive, it can be misleading. Marching one step ahead of a crowd moving in a chosen direction may define realistically the connection between leadership and followership. Successful leadership is having followers who believe in the leader. By believing, people are encouraged to link positive events with leadership behaviors. George Gallup once remarked, 'People tend to judge a man by his goals, by what he is trying to do, and not necessarily by what he accomplishes or how well he succeeds'" (p. 73).

Leaders are typically judged by their style and their coping skills. Dramatic performances emphasizing traits popularly associated with leadership—such as forcefulness, responsibility, courage, and decency—contribute to a leader's image. Though reassuring, the assumption that leaders make a real difference is often misleading. Cohen and March (1974) compare the college president to the driver of a skidding automobile: "The marginal judgments he makes, his skill, and his luck will probably make some difference to the life prospects of his riders. As a result, his responsibilities are heavy. But whether he is convicted of manslaughter or receives a medal for heroism is largely outside his control" (p. 203).

As with other processes, a leader's power is less a matter of action than of appearance. When a leader does make a difference, it is by enriching and updating the drama—constructing new myths that alter beliefs and generate faith. When George W. Bush stood on a platform at New York City's Ground Zero shortly after September 11, 2001, he pulled a firefighter to his side. When the crowd yelled, "We can't hear you," he shouted back, "Well, I can hear you. The world can hear you, and those who did this will be hearing from us soon." The right words on the right occasion greatly buttressed Americans' confidence that an untested president had the strength and determination to avenge the terrorist attacks.

CONCLUSION

From a symbolic perspective, organizations are judged primarily by appearance. The right image provides a ceremonial stage, projecting to audiences the dramatic performance they expect. The drama reassures, fosters belief in the organization's purposes, and cultivates faith. Structures that do little to coordinate activity and processes that rarely achieve their ostensible goals still serve important symbolic functions. They provide internal glue. They help participants cope, find meaning, and play their role without reading the wrong lines, upstaging the lead actors, or confusing tragedy with comedy. Externally, they provide a basis for confidence and hope.

The symbolic frame introduces and elaborates concepts rarely applied to organizations in the past. These concepts sharply redefine organizational dynamics and have significant implications for managing and changing organizations. Historically, theories of management and organization have focused on instrumental issues. We see problems, try to develop and implement solutions, and then ask, "What did we accomplish?" Often, the answer is "nothing" or "not much." We find ourselves repeating the old saw that the more things change, the more they remain the same. Such a message is disheartening and disillusioning. It produces a sense of helplessness and a belief that things will never get much better.

The symbolic frame sounds a more hopeful note. For a variety of reasons, we have decided to reframe our organization. We may be restless, frustrated, or searching to renew our faith. We therefore mount a new play called *Change*. At the end of the pageant, we can ask three questions:

1. What was expressed?
2. What was attracted?
3. What was legitimized?

The answers are often enormously uplifting. The drama allows us to resolve contradiction and envision solutions to our problems. Old conflicts, new blood, borrowed expertise, and vital issues are attracted onto the stage, where they combine and begin to produce new myths and beliefs. Change becomes exciting, uplifting, and vital. The message is heartening and spiritually invigorating. There is always hope; the world is always different. Each day is potentially more exciting and full of meaning than the next. If not, change the symbols, revise the drama, develop new myths—or dance.

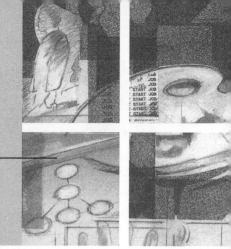

CHAPTER 14

Organizational Culture in Action

Prescriptions and theories for developing better teamwork abound in management literature. But they often miss the deeper secret of how groups and teams reach the state of grace and peak performance. Former Visa CEO Dee Hock captured the heart of the issue: "In the field of group endeavor, you will see incredible events in which the group performs far beyond the sum of its individual talents. It happens in the symphony, in the ballet, in the theater, in sports, and equally in business. It is easy to recognize and impossible to define. It is a mystique. It cannot be achieved without immense effort, training, and cooperation, but effort, training, and cooperation alone rarely create it" (Quoted in Schlesinger, Eccles, and Gabarro, 1983, p. 173).

Who would have predicted that the Minnesota Twins or the Anaheim Angels would have reached major league baseball play-offs in 2002? During the preseason, both teams were written off. Neither was seen as having the individual talent to prevail in postseason play.

Who would have imagined that David Packard and William Hewlett or the founders of Compaq would create highly successful companies that later would merge into one?

Did anyone other than the pilots believe that Britain's Royal Air Force could have defended the island country against Hitler's Luftwaffe? As Winston Churchill later commented, "Never have so many owed so much to so few."

Are such peak performances simply a great mystery—beautiful when they happen but no more predictable or controllable than the next earthquake in California? In this chapter, we analyze a well-documented case of a team that *did* achieve a state of transcendence. The story takes us directly into the symbolic roots of flow, spirit, and magic. Tracy

Kidder, in *The Soul of a New Machine* (1981), writes a dazzling account of a small group of engineers at Data General who created a new computer in record time in the 1970s. Despite scant resources and limited support, the Eagle Group outperformed all other Data General divisions to produce a new, state-of-the-art machine. The machine they produced is now antiquated, but lessons learned from how they did it are as current as ever.

THE EAGLE GROUP'S SOURCES OF SUCCESS

Why did the Eagle Group succeed? So many groups of engineers—or educators, physicians, executives, or graduate students—start out with high hopes but falter and fail. Were the individuals on the Eagle project extraordinarily talented? Not really. Each was highly skilled, but there were equally talented engineers working on other Data General projects. Were team members always treated with dignity and respect? Quite the contrary. As one engineer noted, "No one ever pats anyone on the back" (Kidder, 1981, p. 179). Instead, the group experienced what they called mushroom management: "Put 'em in the dark, feed 'em shit, and watch 'em grow" (p. 109). For over a year, group members jeopardized their health, their families, and their careers: "I'm flat out by definition. I'm a mess. It's terrible. It's a lot of fun" (p. 119).

Were financial rewards a motivating factor? Group members said explicitly that they did not work for money. Nor were they motivated by fame. Heroic efforts were rewarded neither by formal appreciation nor by official applause. The group quietly dissolved shortly after completing the new computer, and most members of the team moved unrecognized to other parts of Data General, or to other companies. Their experience fits that of later successes at Cisco Systems, where Paulson (2001) concludes, "All personnel are driven by the desire to be a part of a winning organization" (p. 187).

Perhaps the group's structure accounted for its success. Were its members pursuing well-defined and laudable goals? The group leader, Tom West, offered the precept that "not everything worth doing is worth doing well." Pushed to translate his maxim, he elaborated, "If you can do a quick-and-dirty job and it works, do it" (Kidder, 1981, p. 119). Did the group have an especially clear and well-coordinated set of roles and relationships? According to Kidder, it kept no meaningful charts, graphs, or organization tables. One of the group's engineers put it bluntly: "The whole management structure—anyone in Harvard Business School would have barfed" (p. 116).

Can the political frame unravel the secret of the group's phenomenal performance? Perhaps its members were motivated more by power than by money: "There's a big high in here somewhere for me that I don't fully understand. Some of it's a raw power trip. The reason I work is because I win" (p. 179). They were encouraged to circumvent the formal structure to advance the group's interests: "If you can't get what you need from some manager at your level in another department, go to his boss—that's the way to get things done" (pp. 109–191). Group members were also unusually direct and confrontational: "Feeling sorely provoked, [David] Peck one day said to this engineer, 'You're an asshole.' Ordered by his boss to apologize, Peck went to the man he had insulted, looking sheepish, and said, 'I'm sorry you're an asshole'" (p. 224).

The group was highly competitive with others in the company: "There's a thing you learn at Data General, if you work here for any period of time . . . that nothing ever happens unless you push it" (p. 111). They also competed with one another. Their collectively anointed "tube wars" are a typical example. Carl Alsing, the head of a subgroup known as the Microkids, came back from lunch one day to find that all of his files had been turned into empty shells: the names were there, but the contents had vanished. It took him an hour to find the real files hidden elsewhere. Alsing counterattacked by creating an encrypted file and tantalizing the team, "There's erotic writing in there and if you can find it, you can read it'" (p. 107).

Here we begin to encounter the secrets of the group's success. The tube wars—and other exchanges among group members—were more than power struggles. They were a form of play that released tensions, created bonds, and contributed to an unusual group spirit. A shared and cohesive culture, rather than a clear, well-defined structure, was the real invisible force that gave the team its drive.

LEADING PRINCIPLES

From the Eagle Group's experience we can distill several important tenets of the symbolic frame that apply to any group or team:

- How someone becomes a group member is important.
- Diversity supports a team's competitive advantage.
- Example, not command, holds a team together.

- A specialized language fosters cohesion and commitment.

- Stories carry history and values and reinforce group identity.

- Humor and play reduce tension and encourage creativity.

- Ritual and ceremony lift spirits and reinforce values.

- Informal cultural players make contributions disproportionate to their formal role.

- Soul is the secret of success.

Becoming a Member

Joining a team involves more than a rational decision. It is a mutual choice marked by some special form of ritual. In the Eagle Group, the process of becoming a member was called "signing up." When interviewing recruits, Alsing conveyed the message that they were volunteering to climb Mount Everest without a rope and probably lacked the "right stuff" to keep up with the other climbers in the party. When the new recruits protested that they wanted to climb Mount Everest anyway, Alsing told them they would have to wait to find out if they were good enough. After it was all done and the selections had been made, Alsing summed it up this way: "It was kind of like recruiting for a suicide mission. You're gonna die, but you're gonna die in glory" (Kidder, 1981, p. 66).

Through the signing-up ritual, an engineer became part of a special effort and agreed to forsake family, friends, and health to accomplish the impossible. It was a sacred declaration: "I want to do this job and I'll give it my heart and soul" (p. 63).

Diversity Is a Competitive Advantage

Though nearly all the group's members were engineers, each had unique skills and style. West, the group's leader, was by reputation a highly talented technical debugger. He was also aloof and unapproachable, the "Prince of Darkness." Steve Wallach, the group's computer architect, was a highly creative maverick. According to Kidder (1981, p. 75), before accepting West's invitation to join the group, he went to Edson de Castro, the president of Data General, to find out precisely what he'd be working on:

> "Okay," Wallach said, "what the fuck do you want?"
> "I want a thirty-two-bit Eclipse," de Castro told him.

"If we can do this, you won't cancel it on us?" Wallach asked. "You'll leave us alone?"

"That's what I want, a thirty-two," de Castro assured him, "a thirty-two-bit Eclipse and no mode bit."

Wallach signed up. His love of literature, stories, and verse provided a literary substructure for the technical architecture of the new machine. Alsing, the group's microcode expert, was as warm and approachable as West was cold and remote. He headed the Microkids, the group of young engineers who programmed the new machine. Ed Rasala, Alsing's counterpart, headed the Hardy Boys, the group's hardware design team. In contrast to Alsing's creative fecundity, Rasala was a solid, hyperactive, risk-taking, and detail-oriented mechanic: "I may not be the smartest designer in the world, a CPU giant, but I'm dumb enough to stick with it to the end" (p. 142).

Diversity among the group's top engineers was institutionalized in specialized functions. One engineer, for example, was viewed as a creative genius who liked inventing an esoteric idea and then trying to get it to work. Another was a craftsman who enjoyed fixing things, working tirelessly until the last bug had been tracked down and eliminated. West buffered the team from upper management interference and served as a group "devil." Wallach created the original design. Alsing and the Microkids created "a synaptic language that would fuse the physical machine with the programs that would tell it what to do" (p. 60). Rasala and the Hardy Boys built the physical circuitry. Understandably, there was tension among these diverse individuals and groups. Harnessing the resulting energy galvanized all the parts into a working team.

Example, Not Command

Wallach's design generated modest coordination for Eagle's autonomous individuals and groups. The group had some rules but paid little attention to them. De Castro, the CEO, was viewed as a distant god. He was never there physically, but his presence was always felt. West, the group's official leader, rarely interfered with the actual work, nor was he particularly visible in the laboratory. One Sunday morning in January, however, when the team was supposed to be resting, a Hardy Boy happened to come by the lab and found West sitting in front of one of the prototypes. The next Sunday, West wasn't in the lab, and after that they rarely saw him there. For a long time he did not even hint that he might again put his own hands inside the machine.

West contributed primarily by causing problems for the engineers to solve and making mundane events and issues appear to be special. He created an almost endless series of "brushfires" so he could inspire his staff to put them out. He had a genius for finding drama and romance in everyday routine. Other members of the group's formal leadership followed de Castro and West in creating ambiguity, encouraging inventiveness, and leading by example. Heroes of the moment gave inspiration and direction. Subtle and implicit signals rather than concrete and explicit guidelines or decisions held the group together and directed it toward a common goal.

Specialized Language

Every group develops words, phrases, and metaphors unique to its circumstances. A specialized language both reflects and shapes a group's culture. Shared language allows team members to communicate easily, with minimal misunderstanding. To the members of the Eagle Group, for example, a *kludge* was a poor, inelegant solution—such as a machine with loose wires held together with adhesive tape. A *canard* was anything false. *Fundamentals* were the source of thinking that enlightened. The word *realistically* typically prefaced flights of fantasy. "Give me a *core dump*" meant tell me your thoughts. A *stack overflow* meant that an engineer's memory compartments were too full, and a *one-stack-deep mind* indicated shallow thinking. "Eagle" was a label for the project, while "Hardy Boys" and "Microkids" gave identity to the subgroups. Two prototype computers were named Woodstock and Trixie.

A shared language binds a group together and is a visible sign of membership. It also sets a group apart and reinforces unique values and beliefs. Asked about the Eagle Group's headquarters, West observed, "It's basically a cattle yard. What goes on here is not part of the real world." Asked for an explanation, West remarked, "Mm-hmm. The language is different" (Kidder, 1981, p. 50).

Stories Carry History, Values, and Group Identity

In high-performing organizations and groups, stories keep traditions alive and provide examples to guide everyday behavior. The group's lore extended and reinforced the subtle yet powerful influence of Eagle's leaders—some of them distant and remote. West's reputation as a "troublemaker" and an "excitement junkie" was conveyed through stories about computer wars of the mid-1970s. Alsing said of West that he was always prepared and never raised his voice. Still, he conveyed intensity and conviction that he knew the way out of whatever storm was currently battering the group. West also had the skills of a good politician. He knew how to develop agendas, build alliances, and negotiate with potential supporters or opponents. When he had a particular objective in mind, he would first go upstairs to sign up senior executives. Then he went to people one at a time, telling them the bosses liked the idea and asking them to come on board: "They say, 'Ah, it sounds like you're just gonna put a bag on the side of the Eclipse,' and Tom'll give 'em his little grin and say, 'It's more than that, we're really gonna build this fucker and it's gonna be fast as greased lightning.' He tells them, 'We're gonna do it by April'" (p. 44).

Stories of persistence, irreverence, and creativity encouraged others to go beyond themselves, adding new exploits and tales to Eagle's lore. For example, as the group neared completion, a debugging problem threatened the entire project. Jim Veres, one of the engineers, worked day and night to find the error. Ken Holberger, one of the Hardy Boys, drove to work early one morning, pondering problems of the project and wondering if it would ever be finished. He was awakened from his reverie by an unexpected scene as he entered the lab. "A great heap of paper lies on the floor, a continuous sheet of computer paper streaming out of the carriage at [the] system console. Stretched out, the sheet would run across the room and back again several times. You could fit a fairly detailed description of American history . . . on it. Veres sits in the midst of this chaos, the picture of the scholar. He's examined it all. He turns to Holberger. 'I found it,' he says" (Kidder, 1981, p. 207).

Humor and Play

Groups often focus single-mindedly on the task at hand, shunning anything not directly work-related. Seriousness replaces godliness as a cardinal virtue. Effective teams balance seriousness with play and humor. Surgical teams, cockpit crews, and many other groups have learned that joking and playful banter are an essential source of invention and team spirit. Humor releases tension and helps resolve issues that arise from day-to-day routines as well as from sudden emergencies.

Play among the members of the Eagle project was an essential part of the group process. When Alsing wanted the Microkids to learn how to manipulate the computer known as Trixie, he made up a game. As the Microkids came on board, he told each of them to figure how to write a program in Trixie's assembly language. The program had to fetch and print contents of a file stored inside the computer. The Microkids went to work, learned their way around the machine, and felt great satisfaction—until Alsing's perverse sense of humor tripped them up. When they finally found the elusive file, they were greeted with the message "Access Denied." Through such play, the Microkids learned to use the computer, coalesced into a team, and learned to negotiate their new technical environment. They also learned their playful leader cared about creativity.

Humor was a continuous thread as the team struggled with its formidable task. Humor often stretched the boundaries of good taste, but that too was part of the group's identity:

> [Alsing] drew his chair up to his terminal and typed a few letters—a short code that put him in touch with Trixie, the machine reserved for the use of his microcoding team. "We've anthropomorphized Trixie to a ridiculous extent," he said.
>
> He typed, WHO.
>
> On the dark-blue screen of the cathode-ray tube, with alacrity, an answer appeared: CARL.
>
> WHERE, typed Alsing.
>
> IN THE ROAD, WHERE ELSE! Trixie replied.
>
> HOW.
>
> ERROR, read the message on the screen.
>
> "Oh, yeah, I forgot," said Alsing, and he typed, PLEASE HOW.
>
> THAT'S FOR US TO KNOW AND YOU TO FIND OUT.
>
> Alsing seemed satisfied with that, and he typed, WHEN.
>
> RIGHT FUCKING NOW, wrote the machine.
>
> WHY, wrote Alsing.
>
> BECAUSE WE LIKE TO CARL. (pp. 90–91)

Throughout the year and a half it took to build their new machine, engineers of the Eagle project relied on play and humor as a source of relaxation, stimulation, enlightenment, and spiritual renewal.

Ritual and Ceremony

Ritual and ceremony are expressive occasions. As parentheses in an ordinary workday, they enclose and define special forms of behavior. What occurs on the surface is not nearly so important as the deeper meaning communicated beneath visible behavior. Despite the stereotype of narrowly task-focused engineers with little time for anything nonrational, the Eagle Group was very aware of the importance of symbolic activity. Leadership encouraged ritual and ceremony from the beginning.

As one example, Rasala, head of the Hardy Boys, established a rule requiring that changes in the boards of the prototype be updated each morning. This activity allowed efforts to be coordinated formally. More important, the daily update was an occasion for informal communication, bantering, and gaining a sense of the whole. The engineers disliked the daily procedure, so Rasala changed it to once a week—on Saturday. He made it a point always to be there himself.

Eagle's leaders met regularly, but their meetings focused more on symbolic issues than on substance. "'We could be in a lot of trouble here,' West might say, referring to some current problem. And Wallach or Rasala or Alsing would reply, 'You mean *you* could be in a lot of trouble, right, Tom?' It was Friday, they were going home soon, and relaxing, they could half forget that they would be coming back to work tomorrow" (Kidder, 1981, p. 132). Friday afternoon is a traditional time to wind down and relax. Honoring such a tradition was all the more important for a group whose members often worked all week and then all weekend. West made himself available to anyone who wanted to chat. Near the end of the day, before hurrying home, West would lean back in his chair with his office door open and entertain any visitor.

In addition to recurring rituals, the Eagle Group convened periodic ceremonies to raise their spirits and reinforce their sense of shared mission. Toward the end of the project, Alsing instigated a ceremony to trigger a burst of renewed energy for the final push. The festivities called attention to the values of creativity, hard work, and teamwork. A favorite pretext for parties was presentation of the Honorary Microcoder Awards that Alsing and the Microcoder Team instituted. Not to be outdone, the Hardy Boys cooked up the PAL Awards (named for the programmable array logic chips used in the machines). The first was presented after work at a local establishment called the Cain Ridge Saloon. The citation read as follows (p. 250):

Honorary PAL Award

In recognition of unsolicited contributions

to the advancement of Eclipse hardware

above and beyond the normal call of duty,

we hereby convey unto you our thanks and congratulations

on achieving this "high" honor.

The same values and spirit were reinforced again and again in a continued cycle of celebratory events: "Chuck Holland [Alsing's main submanager] handed out his own special awards to each member of the Microteam, the Under Extraordinary Pressure Awards. They looked like diplomas. There was one for Neal Firth, 'who gave us a computer before the hardware guys did,' and one to Betty Shanahan, 'for putting up with a bunch of creepy guys.' Having dispensed the Honorary Microcoder Awards to almost every possible candidate, the Microteam instituted the All-Nighter Award. The first of these went to Jim Guyer, the citation ingeniously inserted under the clear plastic coating of an insulated coffee cup" (Kidder, 1981, p. 250).

The Contribution of Informal Cultural Players

Alsing was the main organizer and instigator of parties. He was also the Eagle Group's conscience and nearly everyone's confidant.

> For a time, when he was still in college, Alsing had wanted to become a psychologist. He adopted that sort of role now. Although he kept track of his team's technical progress, he acted most visibly as the social director of the Microteam, and often of the entire Eclipse Group. Fairly early in the project, Chuck Holland had complained, "Alsing's hard to be a manager for, because he goes around you a lot and tells your people to do something else." But Holland also conceded, "The good thing about him is that you can go and talk to him. He's more of a regular guy than most managers." (Kidder, 1981, p. 105)

Every group or organization has a "priest" or "priestess" who ministers to spiritual needs. Informally, these people hear confessions, give blessings, maintain traditions, encourage ceremonies, and intercede in matters of gravest importance. Alsing did all these things and, like the tribal priest, was a counterpart and interpreter of the intentions of the chief:

West warned him several times, "If you get too close to the people who work for you, Alsing, you're gonna get burned." But West didn't interfere, and he soon stopped issuing warnings.

One evening, while alone with West in West's office, Alsing said: "Tom, the kids think you're an ogre. You don't even say hello to them."

West smiled and replied. "You're doing fine, Alsing." (Kidder, 1981, pp. 109–110)

The duties of Rosemarie Seale, the group's secretary, also went well beyond formal boundaries. If Alsing was the priest, she was the mother superior. She did all the usual secretarial chores—answering the phones, preparing documents, and preparing budgets. But she found particular joy in solving the minor crises that arose almost daily and serving as a kind of den mother for the members of the Eagle team. When new members came on, it was Rosemarie Seale who worried about finding them a desk and some pencils. When paychecks went astray, she would track them down and get them to their intended recipient. She liked the job, she said, because she felt that she was doing something important.

In any group, a network of informal players deals with human issues outside formal channels. On the Eagle project, their efforts were encouraged, appreciated, and rewarded outside the formal chain of command; they helped keep the project on track.

Soul Is the Secret of Success

The symbolic side of the Eagle Group was the real secret of its success. Its soul, or culture, created a new machine: "Ninety-eight percent of the thrill comes from knowing that the thing you designed works, and works almost the way you expected it would. If that happens, part of *you* is in that machine" (Kidder, 1981, p. 273). All the members of the Eagle Group put something of themselves into the new computer. Individual efforts went well beyond the job and were supported by a way of life that encouraged each person to commit to doing something of significance. This commitment was elicited through the ritual of signing up and then maintained and accentuated by shared diversity, exceptional leaders, common language, stories, rituals, ceremonies, play, and humor. In the best sense of the word, the Eagle Group was a team, and the efforts of the individual members were knitted together by a cohesive culture. Symbolic elements were at the heart of the group's success.

The experience of the Eagle Group is not unusual. After extensive research on high-performing groups, Vaill (1982) concluded that spirit was at the core of every such group he studied. Members of such groups consistently "felt the spirit," a feeling essential to the meaning and value of their work.

More and more teams and organizations now realize that culture, soul, and spirit are the wellspring of high performance. The U.S. Air Force, in the aftermath of the Vietnam War, embarked on a vigorous effort to reaffirm traditions and rebuild its culture. "Cohesion is a principle of war" was added to the list of core values. Project Warrior brought heroes—living and dead—forward as visible examples of the right stuff. Rituals were revitalized and reinforced. For example, the Air Force instituted a "reblue-ing" ceremony to encourage recommitment to its traditions and values.

Countless other organizations have taken similar steps. Facing intense foreign competition and a severe profit squeeze, Ford set out in the 1980s to build a culture committed to the principle that "quality is job one." Mitsubishi, with more than twenty-five thousand products ranging from "noodles to space satellites" (Lifson and Takagi, 1981, p. 11), used an elaborate entrance ceremony for newly hired employees as part of its effort to reinforce a corporate culture that stressed professionalism, cooperation, and entrepreneurship. Jan Carlzon revitalized the culture of the Scandinavian Air System around the precepts that every encounter between a customer and an SAS employee was a "moment of truth" and that SAS "flies people, not planes" (Carlzon, 1987, p. 27). The commitment at Outback Steakhouse to "No rules, just right" has distinguished the company among its competitors. Instilling in employees the theme of creating a cheerful, comfortable, enjoyable and fun atmosphere has made the restaurant chain a huge success in an industry littered with failures (Taylor, Ramaya, and Puia, 1999).

CONCLUSION

Symbolic perspectives question traditional views that building a team mainly means finding the right people and designing an appropriate structure. The essence of high performance is spirit. If we were to banish play, ritual, ceremony, and myth, we would destroy teamwork, not enhance it. There are many signs that contemporary organizations are at a critical juncture because of a crisis of meaning and faith. Managers wonder how to build team spirit when turnover is high, resources are tight, and people worry about losing their jobs. Such questions are important, but by themselves they limit managerial imagination and divert attention from deeper issues of faith and purpose. Managers are inescapably accountable for budget and bottom line; they have to respond to individual needs, legal requirements, and economic pressures. But they can serve a deeper and more durable function if they recognize that team building at its heart is a spiritual undertaking. It is both a search for the spirit within and creation of a community of believers united by shared faith and shared culture. Peak performance emerges as a team discovers its soul.

Improving Leadership Practice

Up to now, we have emphasized the unique features of each frame. In practice, of course, our messy, turbulent world rarely presents us with well-defined, single-frame problems. In this part of the book, we focus on multiframe approaches to the challenges of leadership.

In Chapter Fifteen, we look at salient characteristics of everyday managerial life, contrasting a stereotype of crisp, orderly rationality with a more frantic, reactive reality. We show how routine activities and processes such as strategic planning, decision making, and conflict take on different meanings depending on how they are viewed. We provide an example to illustrate the misunderstanding and cacophony that arise when parties are seeing different realities. Finally, we look at studies of effective organizations and senior managers to examine how research aligns with the frames.

In Chapter Sixteen, we examine a case example of a middle manager who encounters an unexpected crisis on her first day in a new job. We show how, in a situation where the stakes and the risks are very high, each frame generates both effective and ineffective scenarios for responding.

We turn in Chapter Seventeen to a discussion of leadership in theory and practice. We begin with two examples of prominent leaders in crisis, one more successful than the other. We examine the idea of leadership and review research on the characteristics of effective leaders. After discussing some popular leadership models, we show how each frame provides a distinct image of leaders and leadership.

Chapter Eighteen moves to a perennial challenge of leadership: creating change. We examine what each frame has to say about barriers to change and how make change efforts successful. We then combine the frames with a model of stages of change developed by John Kotter to show how the two in combination provide a powerful map.

Ethics and spirit are the focus in Chapter Nineteen. We begin with an in-depth discussion of what went wrong at Enron (extending our treatment of a case that has threaded throughout the book). We conclude that while Enron had plenty of smart, aggressive people, it lacked wisdom and soul. We then examine ethics, showing how each frame offers a different criterion for ethical behavior.

Chapter Twenty presents an integrative case in which we zoom in on a new principal in his perilous early weeks at a troubled urban high school. We show how the frames generate a more comprehensive diagnosis of the issues and a more promising set of strategies for moving ahead.

Finally, in the Epilogue, we summarize the basic messages of the book and lay out implications for the development of future leaders.

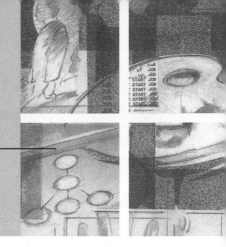

CHAPTER 15

Integrating Frames
for Effective Practice

No one could have forecast what New York City Mayor Rudolph Giuliani faced on September 11, 2001. During a breakfast meeting at the Peninsula Hotel, an aide informed him that a plane had hit one of the World Trade Center's twin towers. He went directly to the scene and observed firsthand the devastating strike on the second tower. It was now clear that this was planned terrorism. Giuliani immediately took command of the situation and set up a central post to open communications with emergency personnel on the scene as well as with the governor and the White House. This was consistent with the mayor's reputation as a no-nonsense, take-charge, in-control manager. Then the unimaginable happened—both towers collapsed, vaporizing thousands of people and creating a mountain of twisted steel, concrete, and debris. It was an unprecedented human tragedy and a deep symbolic wound for the city.

In the aftermath, the American public observed what many assumed was a transformed Giuliani—a sensitive, emotional, and deeply caring leader whose ubiquitous presence was a source of inspiration to New Yorkers, as well as to Americans everywhere. But His Honor disputes his supposed personal transformation: "The events of September 11 affected me more deeply than anything I have ever experienced; but the idea that I somehow became a different person on that day—that there was a pre–September 11 Rudy and a wholly other post-September Rudy—is not true. I was prepared to handle September 11 precisely because I was the same person who had been doing his best to take on challenges my whole career. . . . You can't be paralyzed by any situation. It's about balance" (Giuliani and Kurson, pp. x, xiii).

When the situation changed, Giuliani found himself drawing upon different aspects of his cognitive and behavioral repertoire—lessons learned from prior experience. Both the mayor and his constituents faced dramatically altered circumstances, which in turn required reframing and creating a new balance among frames. The symbolic frame, for example, had always been important in Giuliani's leadership but became even more predominant after September 11. Meanwhile, the political dynamics on which Giuliani had historically thrived receded in their relative significance.

Balancing the frames, and recalibrating in response to new circumstances, is essential to both management and leadership. This chapter considers the frames in combination. How do you choose a frame? How do you integrate multiple frames in the same situation? We begin by revisiting the turbulent world of managers. We then explore what happens when people employ different frames. We offer questions and guidelines to stimulate thinking about which frames are likely to apply in specific situations. Finally, we examine literature on effective managers and organizations to see which frames dominate current theory.

LIFE AS MANAGERS KNOW IT

Prevailing mythology depicts managers as rational men and women who plan, organize, coordinate, and control the activities of subordinates. Periodicals, books, and business schools portray a certain image of modern managers: unruffled, well organized, with clean desks, power suits, and sophisticated information systems. Such "supermanagers" develop and implement farsighted strategies, producing predictable and effective results. It is a reassuring picture of clarity and order. Unfortunately, it's wrong.

Another picture emerges if you watch managers at work (Carlson, 1951; Kotter, 1982; Mintzberg, 1973; Luthans, 1988). It's a hectic life, shifting rapidly from one situation to another, each with its own blend of challenges. In months of observing senior managers, Kotter (1982) rarely saw them *making* a decision. Decisions *emerged* from a fluid, swirling vortex of conversations, meetings, and memos. Information systems ensure an overload of detail about what happened last month or last year. Yet they fail to answer a far more important question: What will happen tomorrow? In deciding what to do next, managers operate mostly on the basis of intuition. Like Giuliani, they draw on hunches and judgment derived from prior experience. Too busy to spend time thinking or reading, they get most of their information orally, in meetings or over the phone. They are hassled priests, modern muddlers, and corporate wheeler-dealers.

How does one reconcile the actual work of managers with the heroic imagery? "Whenever I report this frenetic pattern to groups of executives," says Harold Leavitt, "regardless of hierarchical level or nationality, they always respond with a mix of discomfiture and recognition. Reluctantly, and somewhat sheepishly, they will admit that the description fits, but they don't like to be told about it. If they were really good managers, they seem to feel, they would be in control, their desks would be clean, and their shops would run as smoothly as a Mercedes engine" (1996, p. 294). Led to believe that they should be rational and on top of things, managers become confused and bewildered. They are supposed to plan and organize, yet they find themselves muddling and playing catch-up. They want to solve problems and make decisions. But problems are ill defined and options murky. Control is an illusion, and rationality an afterthought.

ACROSS FRAMES: ORGANIZATIONS AS MULTIPLE REALITIES

Organizational life is full of events that can be interpreted in a number of ways. Table 15.1 examines familiar processes through four lenses. As the table shows, any event can be framed in several ways and serve multiple purposes. Planning, for example, produces specific objectives. But it also creates arenas for airing conflict and becomes a sacred occasion to renegotiate symbolic meanings.

Multiple realities produce confusion and conflict as the individuals view the same event through their own lenses. A hospital administrator once called a meeting to make an important decision. The chief technician viewed it as a chance to express feelings and build relationships. The director of nursing hoped to gain power vis-à-vis physicians. The medical director saw it as an occasion for reaffirming the hospital's distinctive approach to medical care. The meeting became a cacophonous jumble, like a group of musicians each playing from a different score.

TABLE 15.1. Four Interpretations of Organizational Process.

Process	Structural Frame	Human Resource Frame	Political Frame	Symbolic Frame
Strategic planning	Creating strategies to set objectives and coordinate resources	Gatherings to promote participation	Arena to air conflict and realign power	Ritual to signal responsibility, produce symbols, negotiate meanings
Decision making	Rational sequence to produce right decision	Open process to produce commitment	Opportunity to gain or exercise power	Ritual to confirm values and create opportunities for bonding
Reorganizing	Realign roles and responsibilities to fit tasks and environment	Maintain a balance between human needs and formal roles	Redistribute power and form new coalitions	Maintain an image of accountability and responsiveness; negotiate new social order
Evaluating	Way to distribute rewards or penalties and control performance	Process for helping individuals grow and improve	Opportunity to exercise power	Occasion to play roles in shared drama

Approaching conflict	Maintain organizational goals by having authorities resolve conflict	Develop relationships by having individuals confront conflict	Develop power by bargaining, forcing, or manipulating others to win	Develop shared values and use conflict to negotiate meaning
Goal setting	Keep organization headed in the right direction	Keep people involved and communication open	Provide opportunity for individuals and groups to make interests known	Develop symbols and shared values
Communication	Transmit facts and information	Exchange information, needs, and feelings	Influence or manipulate others	Tell stories
Meetings	Formal occasions for making decisions	Informal occasions for involvement, sharing feelings	Competitive occasions to win points	Sacred occasions to celebrate and transform the culture
Motivation	Economic incentives	Growth and self-actualization	Coercion, manipulation, and seduction	Symbols and celebrations

The confusion that results when everyone sees the world through a unique lens is illustrated in this classic case:

Doctor Fights Order to Quit Maine Island

Dr. Gregory O'Keefe found himself the focus of a fierce battle between 1,200 year-round residents of Vinalhaven, Maine (an island fishing community), and the National Health Service Corps (NHSC), which pays his salary and is insisting he take a promotion to an administrator's desk in Rockville, Md.

O'Keefe doesn't want to go, and his patients don't want him to either. The islanders are so upset that, much to the surprise of NHSC officials, they have enlisted the aid of Sen. William Cohen (R-Maine) and U.S. Health and Human Services Secretary Margaret Heckler to keep him here.

It's certainly not the prestige or glamour of the job that is holding O'Keefe, who drives the town's only ambulance and, as often as twice a week, takes critically ill patients to mainland hospitals via an emergency ferry run or a Coast Guard cutter, private plane, or even a lobster boat.

Apparently unyielding in their insistence that O'Keefe accept the promotion or resign, NHSC officials seemed startled last week by the spate of protests from angry islanders, which prompted nationwide media attention and inquiries from the Maine Congressional delegation. NHSC says it probably would not replace O'Keefe on the island, which, in the agency's view, is now able to support a private medical practice.

Cohen described himself as "frustrated by the lack of responsiveness of lower-level bureaucrats." But to the NHSC, O'Keefe is a foot soldier in a military organization of more than 1,600 physicians assigned to isolated, medically needy communities. And he's had the audacity to question the orders of a superior officer.

"It's like a soldier who wanted to stay at Ft. Myers and jumped on TV and called the Defense Secretary a rat for wanting him to move," Shirley Barth, press officer for the federal Public Health Service, said in a telephone interview Thursday. (Goodman, 1983, p. 1)

The NHSC officials had trouble seeing beyond the structural frame; they had a task to do and a strategy for achieving it. O'Keefe's opposition was illegitimate. O'Keefe saw the situation in human resource terms. He felt the work he was doing was meaningful and satisfying, and the islanders needed him. For Senator Cohen, it was a political issue; could minor bureaucrats be allowed to harm his constituents through mindless abuse of power? For the hardy residents of Vinalhaven, O'Keefe was a heroic figure of mythic proportions: "If he gets one night's sleep out of twenty, he's lucky, but he's always up there smiling and working." The islanders were full of stories about O'Keefe's humility, skill, humaneness, dedication, wit, confidence, and caring.

With everyone peering through distinct frames, confusion and conflict were predictable. The inability of NHSC officials to understand and acknowledge the existence of other perceptions illustrates costs of clinging to a single view of a situation. Whenever someone's actions seem to make no sense, it is worth asking if you and they are seeing contrasting realities. It helps to understand their perspective, even if it seems inappropriate. Their frame—not yours—determines how they act.

MATCHING FRAMES TO SITUATIONS

For a given time and situation, one perspective may be more helpful than others. At a strategic crossroads, a rational process focused on gathering and analyzing information may be exactly what is needed. At other times, developing commitment or building a power base may be more critical. In times of great stress, such as what AT&T experienced after divesting its regional operating companies, decision processes may become a form of ritual that brings comfort and support. Choosing a frame, or understanding others' perspectives, involves a combination of analysis, intuition, and artistry. Table 15.2 poses questions to facilitate analysis and stimulate intuition. It also suggests conditions under which each frame is likely to be most effective.

Are commitment and motivation essential to success? The human resource and symbolic frames need to be considered whenever issues of individual commitment, energy, and skill are the key to effective implementation. A new curriculum in a school district will fail without teacher support. Support might be strengthened by human resource approaches, such as participation and self-managing teams, or through symbolic approaches linking the innovation to values and symbols teachers cherish.

Is the technical quality important? When a good decision needs to be technically correct, the structural frame's emphasis on rationality and logical procedure is essential. But

TABLE 15.2. Choosing a Frame.

Question	If yes:	If no:
Are individual commitment and motivation essential to success?	Human resource; symbolic	Structural; political
Is the technical quality of the decision important?	Structural	Human resource; political; symbolic
Is there a high level of ambiguity and uncertainty?	Political; symbolic	Structural; human resource
Are conflict and scarce resources significant?	Political; symbolic	Structural; human resource
Are you working from the bottom up?	Political; symbolic	Structural; human resource

if a decision must be acceptable to major constituents, then human resource, political, or symbolic issues loom more significant. In the R. J. Reynolds leveraged buyout story (Chapter Eleven), none of the bidders wanted to win the battle but lose the war by paying more than RJR's real value. Massive effort went into data collection and analysis to determine how much the company was worth. Could the technical quality of a decision ever be *unimportant?* Yes, particularly for decisions allocating scarce resources. A college found itself embroiled in a three-month battle over the choice of a commencement speaker. The faculty pushed for a great scholar, the students for a movie star. The president was more than willing to invite anyone acceptable to both groups; she could find no technical criterion to prove that one choice was better than the other.

Are ambiguity and uncertainty high? If goals are clear, technology is well understood, and behavior is reasonably predictable, the structural and human resource frames are likely to apply. As ambiguity increases, the political and symbolic frames become more relevant. The political frame expects people to be rational in pursuing self-interest, but contests among individuals and parochial groups often become confused and chaotic, requiring political intervention. The symbolic frame sees symbols as a way of finding order, meaning, and "truth" in situations too complex, uncertain, or mysterious for rational or political analysis. In the R. J. Reynolds case, the most critical ambiguity was what other bidders were doing and what it meant. Everyone scouted the competition intensely and tried to interpret even the weakest signals. At a key point in the endgame, Henry Kravis hinted that he might drop out. To make the hint credible, he went off for a long weekend in Colorado just before final bids were due. The opposition picked up the signals and started telling one another, "Henry's not bidding." It was, according to one member of the Shearson team, "our fatal error."

Are conflict and scarce resources significant? Human resource logic fits best in situations favoring collaboration—as in profitable, growing firms or highly unified schools. But when conflict is high and resources are scarce, dynamics of conflict, power, and self-interest regularly come to the fore. In a situation like the Reynolds bidding war, sophisticated political strategies are vital to success. In other cases, skilled leaders may find that an overarching symbol helps would-be adversaries transcend their differences and work together. In the early 1980s, for example, Yale University was paralyzed by a clerical and technical workers' strike. No one, including Yale's president, A. Bartlett Giamatti, knew how to settle the dispute. Then Phil Donahue invited the Yale community to appear on his television show. Union members energetically presented their side, and Giamatti represented the administration. The audience was active and vocal but polarized. Near the end of the program, Giamatti told a story about his father, an Italian immigrant, who was admitted to the neighborhood university, which happened to be Yale. His father couldn't pay the tuition, but Yale had a core value of "admission by ability, support by need." The story and the invocation of a shared value helped bridge the chasm dividing the parties. Because symbols play a part in every culture and every social class, the symbolic frame may be appropriate across a range of situations.

The structural frame fits situations in the middle. Structure imposes limits on available options, which in turn implies conditions of moderate scarcity. Extreme scarcity fosters conflict that exceeds the capacity of existing authority systems.

Are you working from the bottom up? Restructuring is an option primarily for those in a position of authority. Human resource approaches to improvement—such as training, job enrichment, and participation—need support from the top to be successful. The political frame, in contrast, fits well for making change from the bottom up. Because partisans—bottom-up change agents—rarely have much formal clout, they must find other bases of power. Bottom-up change efforts also use symbolic acts to draw attention to their cause and embarrass their opponents. The September 11 terrorists could have chosen from an almost unlimited array of possible targets in the United States, but the World Trade Towers and the Pentagon were deliberately selected for their symbolic visibility.

The questions in Table 15.2 are no substitute for judgment and intuition in deciding how to frame or respond to a situation. But they can guide and augment the process. Consider once again the Helen Demarco case (Chapter Two). Her boss, Paul Osborne, had a plan for major change. Demarco thought the plan was a mistake but did not feel she could directly oppose her boss. What should she do? The issue of commitment and motivation was important, both in terms of her lack of commitment to Osborne's plan and her concern about finding a solution he could accept. The table suggests that the human resource frame was worth considering, though Demarco never did. The technical quality of the plan was critical in her judgment, but she was convinced that Osborne was immune to technical arguments.

Ambiguity played a significant role in the case. Even if technical issues were reasonably clear, the key issue of how to influence Osborne was shrouded in ambiguity. Implicitly, Demarco acknowledged the importance of the symbolic frame in using a form of theater (the research that wasn't research, a technical report that was window dressing) as her key strategy. Above all, Table 15.2 suggests that Demarco's situation aligns with the political frame: resources were scarce, conflict was high, and she was trying to influence from the bottom up. The logic ran toward politics and symbols. She went with the flow.

The questions in Table 15.2 cannot be followed mechanically to arrive at a correct response for every situation. In some cases, the analysis might lead you to a familiar frame. If the old frame shows signs of inadequacy, though, it may still be appropriate to reframe. You may discover an exciting and creative new lens for deciphering the situation. Then you face another problem: how to communicate your discovery to others who still see another reality.

EFFECTIVE MANAGERS AND ORGANIZATIONS

Does the ability to use multiple frames actually help managers decipher events and determine how to respond? If so, how are the frames combined and integrated in everyday situations? We will examine several strands of research. First, we look at three influential reports on organizational excellence: *In Search of Excellence* (Peters and Waterman, 1982), *Built to Last* (Collins and Porras, 1994), and *From Good to Great* (Collins, 2001). Then we review three studies of managerial work, *The General Managers* (Kotter, 1982), *Managing Public Policy* (Lynn, 1987), and *Real Managers* (Luthans, Yodgetts, and Rosenkrantz, 1988). Finally, we look at recent studies of managers' frame orientations.

Organizational Excellence

Peters and Waterman's spectacularly best-selling *In Search of Excellence* (1982) explored the question, "What do high-performing corporations have in common?" They studied more than sixty large companies in six major industries: high technology (Digital Equipment and IBM, for example), consumer products (Kodak, Procter & Gamble), manufacturing (3M, Caterpillar), service (McDonald's, Delta Airlines), project management (Boeing, Bechtel), and natural resources (Exxon, Du Pont). The companies were chosen on the basis of both objective performance indicators (such as long-term growth and profitability) and the judgment of knowledgeable observers.

Collins and Porras (1994) attempted a similar study of what they termed "visionary" companies but tried to address two methodological limitations in Peters and Waterman's study. Collins and Porras included a comparison group (missing in Peters and Waterman) by matching each of their excellent companies with another firm in the same industry founded at about the same time. Their pairings included Citibank with Chase Manhattan, General Electric with Westinghouse, Sony with Kenwood, Hewlett-Packard with Texas Instruments, and Merck with Pfizer. Collins and Porras emphasized long-term results by restricting their study to companies at least fifty years old with evidence of consistent success over many decades.

Collins (2001) used a comparative approach similar to that of Collins and Porras but focused on another criterion for success: instead of organizations that had excelled for many years, he identified a group of companies that had made a dramatic breakthrough from middling to superlative and compared them with similar companies that had remained ordinary.

All three studies identified seven or eight critical characteristics of excellent companies, similar in some respects and distinct in others, as Table 15.3 shows. All three studies suggest that excellent companies manage to embrace paradox. They are loose yet tight, highly disciplined yet entrepreneurial. Peters and Waterman's "bias for action" and Collins and Porras's "try a lot, keep what works" both point to risk and experiment as a way to learn and avoid bogging down in analysis paralysis. All three studies emphasize a clear core identity that helps firms stay on track, stick to the knitting, and be clear about what they will *not* do.

Two of the studies emphasized one thing they did not find: charismatic, larger-than-life leadership. Collins and Porras (1994) and Collins (2001) both found leaders who were usu-

TABLE 15.3. Characteristics of Excellent/Visionary Companies.

Frame	Peters and Waterman (1982)	Collins and Porras (1994)	Collins (2001)
Structural	Autonomy and entrepreneurship; bias for action; simple form, lean staff	Clock building, not time telling; try a lot, keep what works	Confront the brutal facts; "hedgehog concept" (best in world, economic engine); technology accelerators; "flywheel," not "doom loop"
Human resource	Close to the customer; productivity through people	Home-grown management	"Level 5 leadership"; first who, then what
Political			
Symbolic	Hands on, value-driven; simultaneous loose and tight properties; stick to the knitting	Big, hairy, audacious goals; cultlike cultures; good enough never is; preserve the core, stimulate progress; more than profits	Never lose faith; hedgehog concept (deeply passionate); culture of discipline

ally homegrown and focused on building their organization rather than their personal reputation. Collins's "level 5" leaders were driven but self-effacing, extremely disciplined and hardworking but consistent in attributing success to their colleagues rather than themselves.

As Table 15.3 shows, all three studies produced three-frame models. None of the characteristics of excellence are political. Does the effective organization eliminate politics? Or did the authors miss something? By definition, their samples focused on companies with a strong record of growth and profitability. Infighting and backbiting tend to be less salient and visible on a winning team than on a losing one. With relatively abundant resources, political dynamics are less prominent because slack resources can be used to buy off conflicting interests. Recall, too, that a strong culture tends to increase homogeneity and reduce pluralism. A unifying culture reduces conflict and political strife—or makes them easier to manage.

Even in successful companies, it is likely that power and conflict are more important than these reports suggest. Ask a few managers, "What makes your organization successful?" They rarely talk about coalitions, conflict, or jockeying for position. Even if it exists, politics is typically kept in the closet—secrets known to insiders but not on public display. If we change our focus from effective organizations to effective managers, we find a different picture.

The Effective Senior Manager

Kotter (1982) conducted an intensive study of fifteen corporate general managers (GMs). His sample included "individuals who hold positions with some multifunctional responsibility for a business" (p. 2); each managed an organization with at least several hundred employees. Lynn (1987) analyzed five subcabinet-level executives in the U.S. government, political appointees with responsibility for a major federal agency. Luthans, Yodgetts, and Rosenkrantz (1988) studied a larger but less elite sample of managers than Kotter and Lynn. With a sample of about 450 managers at a variety of levels, they examined managers' day-to-day activities, and how those activities related to success and effectiveness. Table 15.4 shows the characteristics that these studies emphasize as being the keys to the effectiveness of senior managers.

Kotter and Lynn both described jobs of enormous complexity and uncertainty, coupled with substantial dependence on networks of people whose support and energy were

TABLE 15.4. Challenges in Managers' Jobs.

Frame	Kotter (1982)	Lynn (1987)	Luthans, Yodgetts, and Rosenkrantz (1988)
Structural	Keep on top of large, complex set of activities; set goals and policies under conditions of uncertainty	Attain intellectual grasp of policy issues	Communication* (paperwork, exchange routine information); traditional management (planning, goal-setting, controlling)
Human resource	Motivate, coordinate, and control large, diverse group of subordinates	Use their personalities to best advantage	Human resource management* (motivating, managing conflict, staffing, etc.)
Political	Achieve "delicate balance" in allocating scarce resources; get support from bosses; get support from corporate staff and other constituents	Exploit all opportunities to achieve strategic gains	Networking** (politics, interacting with outsiders)
Symbolic	Develop credible strategic premises; identify and focus on core activities that give meaning to employees		

Notes: * Managers judged "effective" by their subordinates
** Managers who were "successful" (achieved rapid promotions to higher positions faster than peers)

essential for the executives to do their job. Both focused on three basic challenges: setting an agenda, building a network, and using the network to get things done. Lynn's work is consistent with Kotter's observation: "As a result of these demands, the typical GM faced significant obstacles in both figuring out what to do and in getting things done" (Kotter, 1982, p. 122).

Kotter and Lynn both emphasized the political dimension in senior managers' jobs. Lynn described the need for a significant dose of political skill and sophistication: "building legislative support, negotiating, and identifying changing positions and interests"

(1987, p. 248). Kotter's model includes elements of all four frames; Lynn's includes all but the symbolic.

A somewhat different picture emerges from the study by Luthans, Yodgetts, and Rosenkrantz. In their sample, middle- and lower-level managers spent almost two-thirds of their time on structural activities (routine communications and traditional management functions like planning and controlling), about one-fifth on "human resource management" (people-related activities like motivating, disciplining, training, staffing), and about a fifth on "networking"(political activities like socializing, politicking, and relating to external constituents). The results suggest that, compared to the senior executives Kotter and Lynn studied, middle managers spend less time grappling with complexity and more time on routine.

Luthans, Yodgetts, and Rosenkrantz distinguished between "effective" and "successful" managers and found each group used time differently. The criteria for effectiveness were (1) quantity and quality of unit performance and (2) subordinates' satisfaction with their boss. Success was defined in terms of promotions per year—how fast people got ahead.

The most "effective" managers spent much of their time on communications and human resource management and relatively little time on networking. But networking was the only activity that was strongly related to getting ahead. "Successful" managers spent almost half their time on networking, and only about 10 percent on human resource management. At first glance, this might seem to confirm the cynical suspicion that getting ahead in a career is more about politics than performance. More likely, the results confirm that performance is in the eye of the beholder. Subordinates rate their boss primarily on criteria internal to the unit—effective communications and treating people well. Bosses, on the other hand, focus on how well a manager handles relations to external constituents, including, of course, the bosses themselves. The researchers found that the 10 percent or so of their sample high on both success and effectiveness had a balanced approach emphasizing both internal and external issues. They were, in effect, multiframe managers.

Comparing all six studies reveals similarities and differences. All give roughly equal emphasis to structural and human resource considerations. But political issues are invisible in the organizational excellence studies, whereas they are prominent in all the studies of individual managers. Politics was as important for Kotter's corporate executives as for Lynn's political appointees and was the key to getting ahead for middle managers. Conversely, symbols and culture were more prominent in the studies of organizational excellence. For various reasons, each study tended to neglect one frame or another. In assessing any framework for improving organizations, ask if anything is left out. The frame overlooked could be the one that derails the effort.

The Manager's Frame Preferences

In recent years, a new line of research on managers' cognitive styles has yielded additional data on how frame preference influences leadership effectiveness. Bolman and Deal (1991, 1992a, 1992b) and Bolman and Granell (1999) studied populations of managers and administrators in both business and education. They found that the ability to use multiple frames was a consistent correlate of effectiveness. Effectiveness as a *manager* was particularly associated with the structural frame, whereas the symbolic and political frames tended to be the primary determinants of effectiveness as a *leader*.

Bensimon (1989, 1990) studied college presidents and found that multiframe presidents were viewed as more effective than presidents wedded to a single frame. In her sample, more than a third of the presidents used only one frame, and only a quarter relied on more than two. Single-frame presidents tended to be less experienced, relying mainly on structural or human resource perspectives. Presidents who relied solely on the structural frame were particularly likely to be seen as ineffective leaders. Heimovics, Herman, and Jurkiewicz Coughlin (1993) found the same thing for chief executives in the nonprofit sector, and Wimpelberg (1987) found comparable results in a study of eighteen school principals. His study paired nine effective and less effective schools. Principals of ineffective schools relied almost entirely on the structural frame, whereas principals in effective schools used multiple frames. When asked about hiring teachers, principals in less effective schools talked about standard procedures (how vacancies are posted, how the central office sends a candidate for an interview), while more effective principals emphasized "playing the system" to get the teachers they needed.

Bensimon found that presidents thought they used more frames than their colleagues observed. They were particularly likely to overrate themselves on the human resource and symbolic frames, a finding also reported by Bolman and Deal (1991). Only half of the presidents who saw themselves as a symbolic leader were perceived that way by others.

Despite the low image of organizational politics in the minds of many managers, political savvy appears to be a primary determinant of success in certain jobs. Heimovics, Herman, and Jurkiewicz Coughlin (1993, 1995) found this for chief executives of nonprofit organizations, and Doktor (1993) found the same thing for directors of family service organizations in Kentucky.

CONCLUSION

The image of firm control and crisp rationality often attributed to managers has little relevance to the messy world of complexity, conflict, and uncertainty that they inhabit. They need multiple frames to survive. They need to understand that any event or process can serve multiple purposes and that participants are often operating in different frames. They need a diagnostic map that helps them assess which frames are likely to be salient and helpful in a given situation. Among the key variables are motivation, technical constraints, uncertainty, scarcity, conflict, and whether an individual is operating from the top down or from the bottom up.

Several lines of recent research find that effective leaders and effective organizations rely on multiple frames. Studies of effective corporations, of individuals in senior management roles, and of public administrators all point to the need for multiple perspectives in developing a holistic picture of complex systems.

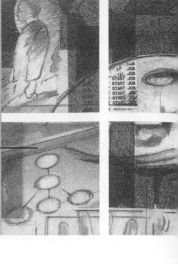

CHAPTER 16

Reframing in Action
Opportunities and Perils

Put yourself in the shoes of Cindy Marshall, headed to the office for your first day in a new job. Your company has transferred you to Kansas City to manage a customer service unit. It's a big promotion, with a substantial increase in pay and responsibility. You know you face a major challenge. You are inheriting a department with a reputation for slow, substandard service. Senior management credits much of the blame to your predecessor, Bill Howard, who is seen as too authoritarian and rigid. Howard is moving to another job, but the company asked him to stay on for a week to help you get oriented. One potential sticking point is that he hired most of your new staff. Many may still feel loyal to him.

When you arrive, you get a frosty hello from Susan Bond, the department secretary. As you walk into your new office, you see Howard behind the desk in a conversation with three other staff members. You say hello, and he responds by saying, "Didn't the secretary tell you that we're in a meeting right now? If you'll wait outside, I'll be able to see you in about an hour."

As Cindy Marshall, what would you do?

You're in the glare of the spotlight, and the audience eagerly awaits your response. If you feel threatened or attacked—as most of us would—you'll be emotionally pulled toward either fight or flight. Fighting back and escalating the conflict is risky and could damage both parties. Backing away or fleeing could suggest that you are too emotional or not tough enough.

This is a classic example of a manager's nightmare: a totally unexpected situation that threatens to career out of control. Howard's greeting is well-designed to throw you off stride and put you in a bind. It carries echoes of historic patterns of male arrogance and condescension in relating to women (similar to those we saw in the Anne Barreta case in Chapter Eight). Deliberately or not, Howard's response seems crafted to disconcert a younger, female colleague. This increases the odds that, as Marshall, you will feel trapped and powerless, or you will do something rash and regrettable. Either way, he wins and you lose.

The frames suggest another set of possibilities. They offer the advantage of multiple lenses to size up the situation. What's really going on here? What options do you have? What script does the situation demand? How might you reinterpret the scene to create a more effective scenario? Reframing is a powerful tool in a tough situation for generating possibilities other than fight or flight.

As Marshall, an immediate question is whether to respond to Howard on the spot or to buy time. If you're at a loss for what to say or if you fear you will make things worse instead of better, take time to "go to the balcony"—try to get above the confusion of the moment long enough to get a better perspective and develop a workable strategy. Even better, though, find an effective response on the spot.

Each of the frames generates its own possibilities that can be translated into alternative scenarios. They can also be misapplied or misused. Success depends on the skill and artistry of the person using a given scenario. In this chapter, we describe scenarios for both effective and ineffective responses Marshall could make using the four lenses to show that *each* can generate effective or ineffective responses. We conclude with a summary of the power and risks of reframing and highlight the importance of reframing for outsiders and newcomers.

STRUCTURAL FRAME

You may wonder what structure has to do with a direct, personal confrontation, but the structural scenario in Exhibit 16.1 can be used to generate a variety of responses. Here's one example:

Howard: Didn't the secretary tell you that we're in a meeting right now? If you'll wait outside, I'll be able to see you in about an hour.

EXHIBIT 16.1. A Structural Scenario.

A structural scenario casts managers and leaders in the fundamental roles of clarifying goals, attending to the relationship between structure and environment, and developing a clearly defined structure appropriate to what needs to be done. Without a workable structure, people become unsure about what they are supposed to be doing. The result is confusion, frustration, and conflict. In an effective organization, individuals are relatively clear about their responsibilities and their contribution. Policies, linkages, and lines of authority are straightforward and widely accepted. With the right structure—one that people understand and accept—the organization can achieve its goals, and individuals can see their role in the big picture.

The main job of a leader is to focus on task, facts, and logic, rather than personality and emotions. Most people problems stem from structural flaws, not personal limitation or liability. The structural leader is not rigidly authoritarian and does not attempt to solve every problem by issuing orders (though that is sometimes appropriate). Instead, the leader tries to design and implement a process or structure appropriate to the circumstances.

Marshall: My appointment as manager of this office began at nine this morning. This is now my office, and you're sitting behind my desk. Either you relinquish the desk immediately, or I will call headquarters and report you for insubordination.

Howard: I was asked to stay on the job for one more week to try to help you learn the ropes. Frankly, I doubt that you're ready for this job, but you don't seem to want any help.

Marshall: I repeat, I am now in charge of this office. Let me also remind you that headquarters assigned you to stay this week to assist me. I expect you to carry out that assignment. If you don't, I will submit a letter for your file detailing your lack of cooperation. Now, *(firmly)* I want my desk.

Howard: Well, we were working on important office business, but since the princess here is more interested in giving orders than in getting work done, let's move our meeting down to your office, Joe. Enjoy the desk!

In this exchange, Cindy places heavy emphasis on her formal authority and the chain of command. By invoking her superiors and her legitimate authority, she takes charge and gets Howard to back down, but at a price. She risks long-term tension with her new subordinates, who surely feel awkward during this combative encounter. They may see their new boss as autocratic and defensive. She also risks reinforcing an old stereotype of women managers as "critical, bossy, and overcontrolling" (Kanter, 1977, p. 189).

There are other structural options. Here's another example of how Marshall might respond:

> **Howard:** Didn't the secretary tell you that we're in a meeting right now? If you'll wait outside, I'll be able to see you in about an hour.
>
> **Marshall:** She didn't mention it, and I don't want to interrupt important work, but we also need to set some priorities and work out an agenda for the day anyway. Bill, have you developed a plan for how you and I can get to work on the transition?
>
> **Howard:** We can meet later on, after I get through some pressing business.
>
> **Marshall:** The pressing business is just the kind of thing I need to learn about as the new manager here. What issues are you discussing?
>
> **Howard:** How to keep the office functioning when the new manager is not ready for the job.
>
> **Marshall:** Well, I have a lot to learn, but I feel I'm ready. With your help, I think we can have a smooth and productive transition. How about if you continue your meeting and I just sit in as an observer? Then, Bill, you and I could meet to work out a plan for how we'll handle the transition. After that, I'd like to schedule a meeting with each manager to get an individual progress report. I'd like to hear from each of you about your major customer service objectives and how you would assess your progress against objectives. Now, what were you talking about before I got here?

This time, Marshall is still clear and firm in establishing her authority, but she does it without appearing harsh or dictatorial. She underscores the importance of setting priorities. She asks if Howard has a plan for making the transition productive. She emphasizes shared goals and defines a temporary role for herself as an observer. She focuses steadfastly on the task and not on Howard's provocations. In keeping the exchange on a rational level and outlining a transition plan, she avoids escalating or submerging the conflict. She also communicates to her new staff that she has done her homework, is organized, and knows what she wants. When she says she would like to hear their personal objectives and progress, she communicates an expectation that they should follow her example.

HUMAN RESOURCE FRAME

The human resource frame values listening and responsiveness, but sometimes people go a little too far:

Howard: Didn't the secretary tell you that we're in a meeting right now? If you'll wait outside, I'll be able to see you in about an hour.

Marshall: Oh, gosh, no, she didn't. I just feel terrible about interrupting your meeting. I hope I didn't offend anyone because to me, it's really important to establish good working relationships right from the outset. While I'm

EXHIBIT 16.2. A Human Resource Scenario.

The human resource leader believes that people are the center of any organization. If people feel the organization is responsive to their needs and supportive of their personal goals, you can count on commitment and loyalty. Administrators who are authoritarian or insensitive, who don't communicate effectively, or who don't care about their people can never be effective leaders. The human resource leader works on behalf of both the organization and its people, seeking to serve the best interests of both.

The job of the leader is support and empowerment. Support takes a variety of forms: showing concern for people, listening to their aspirations and goals, and communicating personal warmth and openness. The leader empowers through participation and openness and by ensuring that people have the autonomy and resources they need to do their job.

waiting, is there anything I can do to help? Would anyone like a cup of coffee?

Howard: No. We'll let you know when we're finished.

Marshall: Oh. Well, have a good meeting, and I'll see you in an hour.

In the effort to be friendly and accommodating, Marshall acts more like a waitress than a manager. She defuses the conflict, but her staff is likely see their new boss as weak. She could instead capitalize on an interest in people:

Howard: Didn't the secretary tell you that we're in a meeting right now? If you'll wait outside, I'll be able to see you in about an hour.

Marshall: I'm sorry if I'm interrupting, but I'm eager to get started, and I'll need all your help. *(She walks around, introduces herself, and shakes hand with each member of her new staff. Howard scowls silently.)* Bill, could we take a few minutes to talk about how we can work together on the transition, now that I'm coming in to manage the department?

Howard: You're not the manager yet. I was asked to stay on for a week to get you started—though, frankly, I doubt that you're ready for this job.

Marshall: I understand your concern, Bill. I know how committed you are to the success of the department. If I were you, I might be worried about whether I was turning my baby over to someone who wouldn't be able to take care of it. But I wouldn't be here if I didn't feel ready. I want to benefit as much as I can from your experience. Is it urgent to get on with what you were talking about, or could we take some time first to talk about how we can start working together?

Howard: We have some things we need to finish.

Marshall: Well, as a manager, I always prefer to trust the judgment of the people who are closest to the action. I'll just sit in while you finish up, and then we can talk about how we move forward from there.

Here, Marshall is unfazed and relentlessly cheerful; she avoids a battle and acknowledges Howard's perspective. When he says she is not ready for the job, she resists the temptation to debate or return his salvo. Instead, she acknowledges his concern but calmly communicates her confidence and her focus on moving ahead. She demonstrates an important skill of a human resource leader: the ability to combine advocacy with inquiry. She listens carefully to Howard but gently stands her ground. She asks for his help while expressing confidence that she can do the job. When he says they have things to finish, she responds with the agility of a martial artist, using Howard's energy to her own advantage. She expresses part of her philosophy—she prefers to trust her staff's judgment—and positions herself as an observer, thus gaining an opportunity to learn more about her staff and the issues they are addressing. By reframing the situation, she is off to a better start with Howard and is able to signal to others the kind of people-oriented leader she intends to be.

POLITICAL FRAME

Some managers translate the political approach into management by intimidation and manipulation. It sometimes works, but the risks are high. Here's an example:

Howard: Didn't the secretary tell you that we're in a meeting right now? If you'll wait outside, I'll be able to see you in about an hour.

Marshall: In your next job, maybe you should train your secretary better. Anyway, I can't waste time sitting around in hallways. Everyone in this room knows why I'm here. You've got a choice, Bill. You can cooperate with me, or you can lose any credibility you still have in this company.

Howard: If I didn't have more experience than you do, I wouldn't be so quick to throw my weight around. But if you think you know it all already, I guess you won't need any help from me.

Marshall: What I know is that this department has gone downhill under your leadership, and it's my job to turn it around. You can go home right now, if you want—you know where the door is. But if you're smart, you'll stay and help. The vice president wants my report on the transition. You'll be a lot better off if I can tell him you've been cooperative.

Moviegoers cheer when bullies get their comeuppance. It can be satisfying to give the verbal equivalent of a kick in the groin to someone who deserves it. In this exchange, Mar-

EXHIBIT 16.3. A Political Scenario.

The political leader believes that managers have to recognize political reality and know how to deal with conflict. Inside and outside any organization, a variety of interest groups, each with its own agenda, compete for scarce resources. There is never enough to give all parties what they want, so there will always be struggles.

The job of the leader is to recognize major constituencies, develop ties to their leadership, and manage conflict as productively as possible. Above all, leaders need to build a power base and use power carefully. They can't give every group everything it wants, but they can create arenas where groups can negotiate differences and come up with a reasonable compromise. They also need to work at articulating what everyone has in common. It is wasteful for people to expend energy fighting each other when there are plenty of enemies outside to battle. Any group that doesn't get its act together internally tends to get trounced by outsiders.

---

shall establishes that she is tough, even dangerous. But such coercive tactics can be expensive in the long run. She is likely to win this battle because her hand is stronger. But she may lose the war. She increases Howard's antagonism, and her attack may offend him and frighten her new staff. Even if they dislike Howard, they might see Marshall as arrogant and callous. She may have done political damage that will be difficult to reverse.

Sophisticated political leaders prefer to avoid naked demonstrations of power, looking instead for ways to appeal to the self-interests of potential adversaries:

Howard: Didn't the secretary tell you that we're in a meeting right now? If you'll wait outside, I'll be able to see you in about an hour.

Marshall: *(pleasantly)* Bill, if it's OK with you, I'd prefer to skip the games and go to work. I expect this department to be a winner, and I hope that's what we all want. I also would like to manage the transition in a way that's good for your career, Bill, and for the careers of others in the room.

Howard: If I need advice from you on my career, I'll ask.

Marshall: OK, but the vice president has asked me to let him know about the cooperation I get here. I'd like to be able to say that everyone has been helping me as much as possible. Is that what you'd like, too?

Howard:	I've known the vice president a lot longer than you have. I can talk to him myself.
Marshall:	I know, Bill, he's told me that. In fact, I just came from his office. If you'd like, we could both go see him right now.
Howard:	Uh, no, not right now.
Marshall:	Well, then, let's get on with it. Do you want to finish what you were discussing, or is this a good time for us to develop some agreement on how we're going to work together?

In this politically based response, Marshall is both direct and diplomatic. She uses a light touch in dismissing Howard's opening salvo ("I'd prefer to skip the games."). She speaks directly to both Howard's interest in his career and her subordinates' interest in theirs. She deftly deflates his posturing by asking if he wants to go with her to talk to the vice president. Clearly, she is confident of her political position and knows that his bluster has little to back it up.

Note that in both political scenarios, Marshall draws on her power resources. In the first, she uses them to humiliate Howard. In the second, her approach is more subtle. She conserves her political capital and takes charge while leaving him with as much pride as possible. It is closer to a win-win than a win-lose outcome.

SYMBOLIC FRAME

At first glance, Cindy Marshall's encounter with Bill Howard might seem a poor candidate for a symbolic approach. An ineffective effort could produce embarrassing results, making the would-be symbolic leader look foolish:

Howard:	Didn't the secretary tell you that we're in a meeting right now? If you'll wait outside, I'll be able to see you in about an hour.
Marshall:	It's great to see that you're all hard at work. It's proof that we all share a commitment to excellence in customer service. In fact, I've already made up buttons for all the staff. Here—I have one for each of you. They read, "The customer is always first." They look great, and they communicate the

EXHIBIT 16.4. A Symbolic Scenario.

The symbolic leader believes that the most important part of a leader's job is inspiration—giving people something they can believe in. People become excited about and committed to a place with a unique identity, a special place where they feel that what they do is really important. Effective symbolic leaders are passionate about making the organization the best of its kind and communicating that passion to others. They use dramatic, visible symbols to get people excited and to give them a sense of the organization's mission. They are visible and energetic. They create slogans, tell stories, hold rallies, give awards, appear where they are least expected, and manage by wandering around.

Symbolic leaders are sensitive to an organization's history and culture. They seek to use the best in an organization's traditions and values as a base for building a culture that has cohesiveness and meaning. They articulate a vision that communicates the organization's unique capabilities and mission.

---

                spirit that we all want in the department. Go on with your meeting. I can use the hour to talk to some of the staff about their visions for the department. *(She walks out of the office.)*

Howard: *(to remaining staff)* Did you believe that? I told you they hired a real space cadet to replace me. Maybe you didn't believe me, but you just saw it with your own eyes.

Marshall's symbolic direction might be on the right track, but symbols work only when they are attuned to people and place. As a newcomer to the department culture, she needs to pay close attention to her audience. Meaningless symbols antagonize, and empty symbolic events backfire.

Conversely, a more skillful symbolic leader understands that a situation of challenge and stress can serve as a powerful opportunity to articulate values and build a sense of mission. Marshall demonstrates how, in a well-formed symbolic approach to Howard's gruffness:

Howard: Didn't the secretary tell you that we're in a meeting right now? If you'll wait outside, I'll be able to see you in about an hour.

Marshall: *(smiling)* Maybe this is just the traditional initiation ritual in this department, Bill, but let me ask a question. If one of our customers came through the door right now, would you ask her to wait outside for an hour?

Howard: If she just came barging in like you did, sure.

Marshall: Are you working on something that's more important than responding to our customers?

Howard: They're not *your* customers. You've only been here five minutes.

Marshall: True, but I've been with this company long enough to know the importance of putting customers first.

Howard: Look, you don't know the first thing about how this department functions. Before you go off on some customer crusade, you ought to learn a little about how we do things.

Marshall: There's a lot I can learn from all of you, and I'm eager to get started. For example, I'm very interested in your ideas on how we can make this a department where as soon as a person walks in, he or she gets the sense that this is a place where people care, are responsive, and genuinely want to be helpful. I'd like that to be true for anyone who comes in—a staff member, a customer, or just someone who got lost and came into the wrong office. That's not the message I got from my initiation a couple of minutes ago, but I'm sure we can think of lots of ways to change that. How does that fit with your image of what the department should be like?

Notice how Marshall reframes the conversation. Instead of engaging in a personal confrontation with Howard, she focuses on the department's core values. She brought her "customer first" commitment with her, but she avoids positioning that value as something imposed from outside. Instead, she grounds it in an experience everyone in the room has just shared: the way she was greeted when she entered. Like many successful symbolic leaders, she is attuned to the cues about values and culture that are expressed in everyday life. She communicates her philosophy, but she also asks questions to draw out Howard and her new staff members. If she can use the organization's history to an advantage in rekindling a commitment to customer service, she is off to a good start.

BENEFITS AND RISKS OF REFRAMING

The multiple replays of the Howard-Marshall incident illustrate both the power and the risks of reframing. The frames are powerful because of their ability to spur imagination and generate new insights and options. But each frame has limits as well as strengths, and each can be applied well or poorly.

The Cindy Marshall case shows how frames can be used as scripts, or scenarios, to guide action in high-stakes circumstances. By changing our script, we can change how we appear, what we do, and how our audience sees us. We can create the possibility of transformation in everyday life. Few of us have the dramatic skill and versatility of a professional actor, but we *can* alter what we do by choosing an alternative script or scenario. We have been learning how to do this since birth. Both men and women typically employ different scenarios for same-sex and opposite-sex encounters, for example. Students who are guarded and formal when talking to a professor become energized and intimate when talking to friends. Managers who are polite and deferential with the boss may be gruff and autocratic with subordinates and then come home at night to romp playfully with their kids. The tenderhearted neighbor becomes a ruthless competitor when his company's market share is threatened. Consciously or not, we all read situations to figure out what scene we're in and the role we've been assigned so that we can respond in character. But it's important to ask ourselves whether the drama is the one we want and to recognize that we have latitude about which character to play and how to interpret the script.

The essence of reframing is examining the same situation from multiple vantage points. The effective leader changes lenses when things don't make sense or aren't working. Reframing offers the promise of powerful new options, but it cannot guarantee that every new strategy will be successful. Each frame offers distinctive advantages, but each has its blind spots and shortcomings.

The *structural frame* risks ignoring everything that falls outside the rational scope of tasks, procedures, policies, and organization charts. Structural thinking can overestimate the power of authority and underestimate the authority of power. Paradoxically, overreliance on structural assumptions and a narrow emphasis on rationality can lead to an irrational neglect of human, political, and cultural variables crucial to effective action.

Adherents of the *human resource frame* sometimes cling to a romanticized view of human nature in which everyone hungers for growth and collaboration. Human resource enthusiasts can be overly optimistic about integrating individual and organizational needs while neglecting structure and the stubborn realities of conflict and scarcity.

The *political frame* captures dynamics that other frames miss but has its own limits. A fixation on politics easily becomes a cynical self-fulfilling prophecy, reinforcing conflict and mistrust while sacrificing opportunities for rational discourse, collaboration, and hope. *Political* is too often interpreted as amoral, scheming, and oblivious to the common good.

The *symbolic frame* offers powerful insight into fundamental issues of meaning and belief, and possibilities for bonding people into a cohesive group with a shared mission. But its concepts are also elusive; effectiveness depends on the artistry of the user. Symbols are sometimes mere fluff or camouflage, the tools of a scoundrel who seeks to manipulate the unsuspecting, or an awkward attempt that embarrasses more than energizes people at work.

REFRAMING FOR NEWCOMERS AND OUTSIDERS

Marshall's initial encounter with Howard exemplifies challenges and tests that she and other managers confront as they move forward in their careers. The different scenarios offer a glimmer of what managers might encounter, depending on how they size up a situation. Managers feel powerless and trapped when they rely on only one or two frames. This is particularly true for newcomers, as well as for women and members of other groups who experience "the dogged frustration of people living daily in a system not made for them and with no plans soon to adjust for them or their differences" (Gallos and Ramsey, 1996, p. 216). Outsiders are less likely to get a second or third chance when they fail. Judicious reframing enables them to transform a managerial trap into a leadership opportunity.

Though progressive organizations have made heroic strides in building a more just opportunity structure (Levering and Moskowitz, 1993; Morrison, 1992), the path to success is still fraught with obstacles blocking women and minorities. But the more often individuals break through the glass ceiling or out of the corporate ghetto, the quicker those barriers will disappear. Career barriers can feel as foreboding and impenetrable as the Berlin Wall until it suddenly fell. Learning to reframe can speed the day when gender and racial barriers disappear.

One or two frames may be enough to build a successful career in middle management, but they do not equip you to rise to the top. The ability to reframe and use multiple lenses helps you advance while feeling less strain and confusion along the way.

CONCLUSION

Managers can use frames as scenarios, or scripts, to generate alternative approaches to challenging circumstances. In planning for a high-stakes meeting or a tense encounter, they can imagine and try out novel ways to play their roles. Until reframing becomes automatic, it takes more than the few seconds that Cindy Marshall had to generate an effective response in every frame. In practicing any new skill—playing tennis, flying an airplane, or handling a tough leadership challenge—the process is often slow and painstaking at first. But as skill improves, it gets easier, faster, and more fluid.

CHAPTER **17**

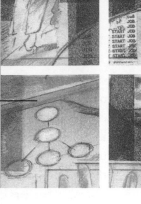

Reframing Leadership

Imagine yourself in the august role of Elizabeth II, queen "by the Grace of God, of the United Kingdom of Great Britain and Northern Ireland and Her other Realms and Territories." It is August 31, 1997, and your traditional summer holiday in Scotland is interrupted by tragic news that your former daughter-in-law, Princess Diana, and her new boyfriend have been killed in a Paris automobile accident. Your relationship with Diana was distant and frosty for years, going back even before she and your son, Prince Charles, were divorced in 1996. But Diana is immensely popular in England and around the world. She is also the mother of your grandson, Prince William, who is expected to inherit your throne. What do you do?

Or try another challenge. As in Chapter Fifteen, rejoin New York City Mayor Rudolph Giuliani the morning of September 11, 2001. It is a beautiful late summer day in New York City, and the polls are opening for the primary election to choose your successor. Being mayor used to be fun, but now you're a lame duck, widely viewed as yesterday's news. Shortly before 9:00 A.M., you learn that an airplane has crashed into one of the twin towers of the World Trade Center. What do you do?

Unforeseen tragedy is only one of many leadership tests, but when it strikes, a leader's choices are both difficult and fateful. Queen Elizabeth and Rudy Giuliani chose distinct paths, with contrasting results.

Her Britannic Majesty decided to stay in Scotland. She and her husband, Prince Phillip, issued a terse statement that they were "deeply shocked and distressed by this terrible news." As millions mourned in one of Britain's most intense outpourings of grief, the queen came under withering criticism. As London's *Daily Mirror* put it, "Your people are suffering. Speak to us, Ma'am." Public support for the monarchy dropped 40 percent in a week (Barton, 2001). Belatedly, the queen scheduled a televised address to the nation. Fortunately for the monarchy, Prince Charles recognized better than his mother the depth of public sentiment. He flew to Paris to accompany Diana's body back to England and insisted that she receive royal honors at her funeral (Varin, 2002).

Rudy Giuliani could have shrunk from the awesome burdens created by the terrorist attacks. He woke up that morning a virtual has-been, a wounded, end-of-term mayor whose ratings in New York and elsewhere had been in steady decline. New Yorkers were tired of his arrogance and bullying. A messy, very public divorce battle with his estranged wife was beginning to turn him into an object of ridicule—(she and their children were living at Gracie Mansion, the mayor's official residence, while His Honor bunked in a friend's spare bedroom). Yet, as we saw in Chapter Fifteen, Giuliani seemed transformed on New York's bloodiest day. He sped immediately to the scene, arriving in time to see smoke, chaos, and bodies falling from the sky. He brought his hand to his mouth as he battled back tears, and then he went to work. He closed bridges and tunnels, ordered the evacuation of the disaster area, and postponed the primary elections. "By mid-day, he had all of the city's commissioners sitting at a makeshift conference table at a temporary command center reporting on how their agencies were responding. Not just the police and fire and emergency management agencies: Every agency was present. That process created an immediate sense of discipline for a government that otherwise might have spun in confusion" (Coles, 2002).

Giuliani appeared repeatedly on television to offer calm, reassuring accounts of complex and horrible news. He resisted pressure to speculate beyond what he knew about the death toll, saying simply that it would be "much more than any of us can bear." Wearing spattered boots and a New York Fire Department baseball cap, he gave tours to visiting dignitaries. Determined to prove New York's resilience, the mayor pushed relentlessly to get Broadway theaters and the New York Stock Exchange reopened as soon as possible, overriding naysayers who said it couldn't or shouldn't be done. "He attended funerals, comforted survivors, urged residents to dine out and tourists to come in, all the while exuding compassion and resolve. The man who had seemed so finished just a few weeks earlier was now greeted with cheers wherever he went: Rudy! Rudy!" (Barry, 2001, p. A-1).

As both examples show, in times of crisis we expect leadership from people in high places, and we are grievously disappointed if they fail to provide it. But it is misleading to imagine that leadership comes *only* from people in high positions. Such a view causes us to ask too much of too few. Rudy Giuliani insisted that the real heroes of September 11 were firefighters, police officers, and rescue workers who risked, and in many cases lost, their lives trying to help others. Under conditions of enormous danger and confusion, often cut off from communication with their commanding officers, they improvised and exercised on-the-spot leadership that significantly reduced the death toll. They demonstrate clearly that we need *more* leaders as well as *better* leadership.

This chapter begins by exploring the idea of leadership: what it is and is not, what it can and cannot do. We look at the difference between leadership and other forms of power, as well as the relationship between leadership and management. We emphasize that leadership is always situated in both a context and a relationship. We then turn to a brief review of research on the characteristics of effective leaders and to some of the leadership models that have been most popular with practitioners. We also examine the important issue of gender and leadership, noting that the traditional equation of leadership with maleness is beginning to fade. Finally, we look at leadership through the frames, showing that each frame generates its own distinctive image of what leadership is and how it works.

THE IDEA OF LEADERSHIP

Leadership is universally offered as a panacea for almost any social problem. Around the world, middle managers say their enterprise would thrive if only senior management showed "real leadership." A widely accepted canon holds that leadership is a very good thing that we need more of—at least, more of the right kind. "For many—perhaps for most—Americans, leadership is a word that has risen above normal workaday usage as a conveyer of meaning and has become a kind of incantation. We feel that if we repeat it often enough with sufficient ardor, we shall ease our sense of having lost our way, our sense of things unaccomplished, of duties unfulfilled" (Gardner, 1986, p. 1). Yet there is confusion and disagreement about what leadership means and how much difference it can make.

Sennett (1980, p. 197) writes, "Authority is not a thing; it is a search for solidity and security in the strength of others which will seem to be like a thing." The same is true of leadership. It is not a tangible thing. It exists only in relationships and in the imagination and perception of the engaged parties. Most images of leadership suggest that leaders get things done and get people to do things; leaders are powerful. Yet many examples of the exercise of power fall outside our image of leadership: armed robbers, extortionists, bullies, traffic cops. Implicitly, we expect leaders to persuade or inspire rather than to coerce or give orders. We also expect leaders to produce cooperative effort and to pursue goals that transcend narrow self-interest.

Leadership is also distinct from authority, though authorities may be leaders. Weber (1947) linked authority to legitimacy. People choose to obey authority so long as they believe the authority is legitimate. Authority and leadership are both built on voluntary obedience. If leaders lose legitimacy, they lose the capacity to lead. But many examples of obeying authority fall outside the domain of leadership. As Gardner (1989, p. 7) put it, "The meter maid has authority, but not necessarily leadership."

Heifetz (1994) argues that authority can be an impediment to leadership: "Authority constrains leadership because in times of distress, people expect too much. They form inappropriate dependencies that isolate their authorities behind a mask of knowing. [The leadership role] is played badly if authorities reinforce dependency and delude themselves into thinking that they have the answers when they do not. Feeling pressured to know, they will surely come up with an answer, even if poorly tested, misleading, and wrong" (p. 180).

Leadership is also different from management, though the two are easily confused. One may be a leader without being a manager, and many managers could not "lead a squad of seven-year-olds to the ice-cream counter" (Gardner, 1989, p. 2). Bennis and Nanus (1985) offer the distinction that "managers do things right, and leaders do the right thing" (p. 21). Kotter (1988) echoes many writers in seeing management as primarily about structural nuts and bolts: planning, organizing, and controlling. He views leadership as a change-oriented process of visioning, networking, and building relationships. But Gardner (1989) argues against contrasting leadership and management too sharply because leaders may "end up looking like a cross between Napoleon and the Pied Piper, and managers like unimaginative clods" (p. 3). He suggests several dimensions for distinguishing leadership from management. Leaders think long-term, look outside as well as inside, and influence constituents beyond their immediate formal jurisdiction. They emphasize vision and renewal and have the political skills to cope with the challenging requirements of multiple constituencies.

THE CONTEXT OF LEADERSHIP

In story and myth, leaders are often lonely heroes and itinerant warriors, wed only to their honor and their cause. Think of Joan of Arc, Sir Lancelot, the Lone Ranger, or Rambo. But traditional notions of solitary, heroic leaders can lead led us to focus too much on individuals and too little on the stage where they play their parts. Leaders make things happen, but things also make leaders happen. We need only look at the transformation in Giuliani's image after September 11 to see that situation influences what leaders must do and what they can do. Giuliani found himself on-stage in an unplanned theater of horror, and he delivered the performance of his life. Another stage would have required, and permitted, different leadership. No single formula is possible or advisable for the great range of situations potential leaders encounter.

Heroic images of leadership convey the notion of a one-way process: leaders lead and followers follow. This view blinds us to the reality of the relationship between leader and follower. Leaders are not independent actors; they both shape and are shaped by their constituents (Gardner, 1989; Simmel, 1950). Leaders often promote a new idea or initiative only *after* a large number of their constituents already favor it (Cleveland, 1985). Leadership, then, is not simply a matter of what a leader does but of what occurs in a relationship. Leaders' actions generate responses from others that in turn affect the leaders' capacity for taking further initiatives (Murphy, 1985). As Briand (1993, p. 39) puts it, "A 'leader' who makes a decision and then attempts to 'sell' it to the public is not a wise leader and will likely not prove an effective one. The point is not that those who are already leaders should do less, but that everyone else can and should do more. Everyone must accept responsibility for the people's well-being, and everyone has a role to play in sustaining it."

It is common to equate leadership with position, but this relegates all those in the lowerarchy to the passive role of follower. It also reinforces the widespread tendency of senior executives to take on more responsibility than they can adequately discharge (Oshry, 1995). Administrators are leaders only to the extent that others grant them cooperation and follow their lead. Conversely, one can be a leader without a position of formal authority. Good organizations encourage leadership from many quarters (Kanter, 1983; Barnes and Kriger, 1986).

Leadership is thus a subtle process of mutual influence fusing thought, feeling, and action to produce cooperative effort in the service of purposes and values embraced by *both* the leader and the led. Single-frame managers are unlikely to understand and attend to the intricacies of a holistic process.

WHAT DO WE KNOW ABOUT GOOD LEADERSHIP?

Perhaps the two most widely accepted propositions about leadership are that all good leaders must have the right stuff—such qualities as vision, strength, and commitment that are essential to leadership—and that good leadership is situational; what works in one setting will not work in another. A proposition from the "effective schools" literature illustrates the right-stuff perspective: a good school is headed by a strong and visionary instructional leader. An example of the situational view is an assumption like "It takes a different kind of person to lead when you're growing and adding staff than when you're cutting budgets and laying people off."

Despite the apparent tension between the one-best-way and contingency views of leadership, both capture part of the truth. Studies have found shared characteristics among unusually effective leaders across a variety of sectors and situations. Another body of research has identified situational variables that critically influence the kind of leadership that works best.

One Best Way

Recent decades have spawned a series of studies of good leadership in organizations (Bennis and Nanus, 1985; Clifford and Cavanagh, 1985; Collins, 2001; Collins and Porras, 1994; Conger, 1989; Farkas and De Backer, 1996; Kotter, 1982, 1988; Kouzes and Posner, 1987; Levinson and Rosenthal, 1984; Maccoby, 1981; Peters and Austin, 1985; Vaill, 1982). Most have been qualitative studies of leaders, primarily corporate executives. Methodology has varied from casual impressions to systematic interviews and observation.

No characteristic is universal in these reports, though vision and focus come closest. Effective leaders help articulate a vision, set standards for performance, and create focus and direction. A related characteristic explicit in some reports (Clifford and Cavanagh, 1985; Kouzes and Posner, 1987; Peters and Austin, 1985) and implicit in others is the ability to communicate a vision effectively, often through the use of symbols. Another characteristic mentioned in many studies is commitment or passion (Clifford and Cavanagh, 1985; Collins, 2001; Peters and Austin, 1985; Vaill, 1982). Good leaders care deeply about their work and the people who do it. They believe little in life is more important than doing good work well. A third frequently mentioned characteristic is the ability to inspire trust and build relationships (Bennis and Nanus, 1985; Kotter, 1988; Maccoby, 1981). Kouzes and Posner (1987) found that honesty came first on a list of traits that managers most admired in a leader.

Beyond vision, passion, and trust, consensus breaks down. The studies cited so far, along with extensive reviews of the literature (Bass, 1981, 1990; Gardner, 1987; Hollander, 1978; Yukl, 2001), generate a long list of attributes associated with effective leadership: risk taking, flexibility, self-confidence, interpersonal skills, managing by walking around, task competence, intelligence, decisiveness, understanding of followers, and courage, to name a few. The oldest reliable finding about effective leaders—they are smarter and work harder than other people—continues to find research support (O'Reilly and Chatman, 1994), but such characteristics are found in people who are better at almost anything, and there are many brilliant hard workers who are hopeless leaders.

Blake and Mouton's "managerial grid" (1969, 1985) is a classic and still popular example of a one-best-way approach. Diffused through scores of books, articles, and training programs, the grid postulates two fundamental dimensions of leader effectiveness: concern for task and concern for people. The model arrays approaches to leadership on a two-dimensional grid shown in Figure 17.1. Theoretically, the grid contains eighty-one cells, though Blake and Mouton emphasize only five.

- 1,1 The manager who has little concern for task or people and is simply going through the motions
- 1,9 The friendly manager who is concerned about people but has little concern for task
- 9,1 The hard-driving taskmaster

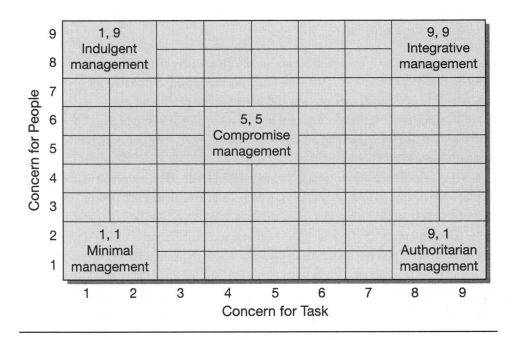

FIGURE 17.1.

Source: Adapted from Blake and Mouton (1985).

- 5,5 The compromising manager who tries to balance task and people
- 9,9 The ideal manager who integrates task and people and produces outstanding performance

Blake and Mouton have vigorously defended their conviction that a 9,9 style is a leadership approach for all situations and all seasons (Blake and Mouton, 1982), but this claim has been heavily criticized. The grid approach focuses almost exclusively on issues of task and human resources. It gives little attention to constituents other than direct subordinates and assumes that a leader who integrates concern for task with concern for people is effective in almost any situation. If structure is unwieldy, political conflict is debilitating, or the organization's culture is threadbare, the grid model may have little to say.

Contingency Theories

The dearth of attributes consistently associated with effective leadership reinforces the argument that leadership varies with the situation. Leadership is different for first-level supervisors than for chief executives. It is different in the public and private sectors. The job of a college president is very different in China from what it is in France. The kind of leadership needed for skilled and highly motivated followers may not work for followers who are alienated and untrained.

Several writers have offered situational theories of leadership (including Fiedler, 1967; Fiedler and Chemers, 1974; Hersey, 1984; Hersey and Blanchard, 1977; Reddin, 1970; and Vroom and Yetton, 1973), but all are limited in their conceptualization of leadership and in the strength of empirical support. Most fail to distinguish between leadership and management, typically treating leadership as synonymous with relationships between managers and their subordinates. In contrast, Burns (1978), Gardner (1986), and Kotter (1985) argue persuasively that leaders need skill in managing relationships with all significant stakeholders, including superiors, peers, and external constituents. Contingency theories are a major area for further research. Almost everyone believes that widely varying circumstances require different forms of leadership, but research is still sparse.

This has not kept approaches such as the Hersey and Blanchard (1977) situational leadership model from becoming widely popular in management development programs. The Hersey/Blanchard model uses two dimensions of leadership similar to those in the managerial grid: task and people. Hersey (1984, p. 31) defines task behavior as "the extent to which the leader engages in spelling out the duties and responsibilities of an individual or group." Relationship behavior is "the extent to which the leader engages in two-way or multi-way communication." It includes "listening, encouraging, facilitating, providing clarification, and giving socioemotional support" (p. 32). Hersey combines task and people into a two-by-two chart, which shows four possible "leadership styles": telling, selling, participating, and delegating (Figure 17.2).

When should a manager use each style? The model says it depends on subordinates' "maturity" (Hersey and Blanchard, 1977) or "readiness level" (Hersey, 1984). Hersey defines readiness in terms of subordinate attitudes (how *willing* they are to do a good job) and skills (how *able* they are to do the job well). The model distinguishes four levels of subordinate readiness and argues that the appropriate style depend on the situation.

High Relationship, Low Task: **Leadership Through Participation** Use when followers are "able" but "unwilling" or "insecure"	*High Relationship, High Task:* **Leadership Through Selling** Use when followers are "unable" but "willing" or "motivated"
Low Relationship, Low Task: **Leadership Through Delegation** Use when followers are "able" and "willing" or "motivated"	*Low Relationship, High Task:* **Leadership Through Telling** Use when followers are "unable" and "unwilling" or "insecure"

FIGURE 17.2. Situational Leadership Model.
Source: Adapted from Hersey (1984).

For subordinates at the lowest level (unable and unwilling to do a good job), the model counsels managers to "tell": such people need direction from their boss. At the next level up (willing but unable), subordinates want to do the job but lack skills. The model tells leaders to "sell" in such situations: explain their decision and give subordinates an opportunity for clarification. At the next level, when subordinates are able but unwilling, the leader should use "participating" to increase motivation: share ideas and discuss what to do. At the highest level, with subordinates who are both able and willing, the leader should simply delegate: the subordinates will do fine without leader input.

Though at first glance the model may seem plausible, research casts doubts on its validity (Hambleton and Gumpert, 1982; Graeff, 1983; Blank, Weitzel, and Green, 1990). If, for example, managers give unwilling and unable subordinates high direction and low support, what would cause their motivation to improve? The manager of a computer company design team told us ruefully, "I treated my group with a 'telling' management style and found that in fact they became both less able and less willing." Furthermore, like Blake and Mouton, Hersey and Blanchard focus mostly on the relationship between managers and immediate subordinates and say little about issues of structure, politics, or symbols.

The Leadership Models as Secular Faiths

Dealing with people is a perennially perplexing aspect of managing. Managers are always looking for ideas to make the job easier. Too often, the search for simplicity overlooks important realities. Even so, a manager may conclude that any model is better than nothing in the face of confusion and mystery. True believers may defend their commitment with fervor, as a case study illustrates.

> A major corporation was developing a new management training program for a group of two thousand technical managers. A task force with representatives from two divisions in the company came together to decide what to teach. The representatives from Division A had participated in managerial grid seminars. They knew in their hearts that the grid was the one best way and that it should be the foundation of the seminar. The managers in Division B had attended situational leadership seminars, and their faith in the situational model was equally unshakable.
>
> Initially, the two sides engaged in polite talk and rational argument. When that failed, the conversation gradually became more heated. Eventually, the group found itself hopelessly deadlocked. An outside consultant came in to mediate the dispute. He listened while the representatives from each division reviewed the conversation. The consultant then said to the group, "I'm impressed by the passion on both sides. I'm curious about one thing. If you all believe so deeply in these models and if it makes a difference which model someone learns, why can't I see any difference in the behavior of your two groups?" Stunned silence fell over the room. Finally one member said, "You know, I think he's right. We don't use the damn models, we just preach them." That ended the impasse.

GENDER AND LEADERSHIP

Until recently, research and writing on leadership focused mostly on men. The implicit, taken-for-granted assumption was that leadership is basically a male activity. In recent years, however, there has been a surge of interest in gender and leadership, stimulated by the dramatic shifts in women's roles and by the accomplishments of individual women.

One such woman is Karren Brady, who became managing director of the Birmingham (England) City Football Club in 1993. At twenty-three, she was the youngest person, and the only woman, heading a professional English soccer team. She ran into a few challenges. There was the strapping forward who told her on the team bus that he liked her blouse because he could see her breasts through it. She looked him in the eye and replied, "Where I'm going to send you, you won't be able to see them from there." A week later, he'd been downgraded to a club a hundred miles away. There was the time the directors of another team told her how fortunate she was that they were willing to let her into their owners' box. She fired back, "The day I have to feel grateful for half a lager and a pork pie in a dump of a little box with a psychedelic carpet is the day I give up" (Hoge, 2002, p. A14).

Brady got plenty of media attention, but it often focused on her looks and wardrobe. One newspaper ran a full-page photo of her in a short skirt under the headline, "Sex Shooter." Another described her entry into a meeting: "Every inch the modern woman, she totters into the room on high-heeled strappy sandals and a short and sexy black suit." Brady was continually perplexed: "I came here to run a business, to put right a dilapidated, rundown operation with a series of business solutions. But the media, with the combination of my age, the way I look, and obviously the fact that I was a female— the first in a male-dominated world—went into a frenzy. It was unbelievable. I'd be in press conferences, and journalists would actually ask me my vital statistics" (Hoge, 2002, p. A14).

Still, Brady understood that publicity, even tinged with notoriety, was good for business. She took a team that had never shown a profit from the edge of bankruptcy to become one of the England's strongest teams, both on the field and at the cash register. She even overcame the complications that might have arisen after she married one of her players. She bought and sold her husband twice, making over a million pounds in the process. She won businesswoman-of-the-year awards, and eventually even her fellow football executives recognized her talent; they named her to represent them in negotiations for the national television contract that yielded a big chunk of their revenue.

Women like Karren Brady have proven that they can lead in a man's world. But do men and women lead differently? Are they seen differently in leadership roles? Why do men have such a disproportionate hold on positions of institutional and organizational power? Research on gender and leadership has asked these and other questions, and we turn next to some of the emerging answers.

Do Men and Women Lead Differently?

Helgesen (1990), Rosener (1990), and others have argued that women bring a "female advantage" to leadership. They believe that modern organizations need the leadership characteristics that women are more likely to bring, such as concern for people, nurturance, and willingness to share information. But the research evidence for gender differences in leadership is equivocal. We might expect, for example, that women would be rated higher on the human resource frame (warm, supportive, participative) and lower on the political frame (powerful, shrewd, aggressive). We need only look at examples like Karren Brady, Hewlett-Packard CEO Carly Fiorina, and former British Prime Minister Margaret Thatcher to see that things are not that simple. In fact, studies give such stereotypes limited support. Bolman and Deal (1991, 1992a) found no differences in frame orientation among men and women. Eagly and Johnson (1990) found no gender differences in emphasis on people versus task, though they found that women tended to be somewhat more participative and less directive than men. For the most part, the available evidence suggests that men and women in comparable positions are more alike than different, at least in the eyes of their subordinates (Carless, 1998; Komives, 1991; Morrison, White, and Van Velsor, 1987). When differences are detected, they generally show women scoring somewhat higher than men on a variety of measures of leadership and managerial behavior (Bass, Avolio, and Atwater, 1996; Edwards, 1991; Hallinger, Bickman, and Davis, 1990; Weddle, 1991; and Wilson and Wilson, 1991), but the differences are not great and researchers have debated whether they have practical significance.

Why the Glass Ceiling?

If women lead at least as well as men, why does the so-called glass ceiling keep them from high positions? In the United States and many other nations, women are now in the pipeline leading to the top. In the United States they now represent a substantial percentage of students in professional schools—more than half of education and law students and close to half in business and medical schools, a dramatic increase in recent decades (except in education, where they have long been a majority). But women still represent less than 10 percent of senior executives in business (Ragins, Townsend, and Mattis, 1998). *Fortune*'s 2002 list of the "fifty most powerful women in business" had to be filled out with vice presidents because fewer than twenty CEOs were identified (Sellers, 2002). In American schools, women constitute the great majority of teachers and a growing percentage of middle managers, yet in 1998 they accounted for only 12 percent of school superintendents. That was about the same as in 1930, though it was up from only 2 percent in 1981 (Keller, 1999).

There is no consensus about what sustains the glass ceiling, but evidence points to several contributing factors:

1. *Stereotypes associate leadership with maleness.* Schein (1975, 1990) found that both men and women tend to believe that men do, but women do not, have the characteristics associated with successful managers.

2. *Women, more than men, must walk a tightrope of conflicting expectations.* Simply put, high-level jobs are "powerful, but women, in the minds of many people, should not be. According to this set of beliefs, a powerful woman is distasteful, unfeminine, and even ludicrous. A strong woman can make both men and women uncomfortable by challenging the conventional understanding—unless, that is, she finds a way to exercise power that is recognizably different from the norm" (Keller, 1999). The challenge for women is to be powerful and "feminine" at the same time, which "is an incredibly difficult role negotiation" (Brunner, cited in Keller, 1999).

3. *Women encounter discrimination.* In ancient fairy tales as well as modern films, powerful women usually turn out to be witches (or worse). Shakespeare's *The Taming of the Shrew* is only one of many stories carrying the message that a strong woman is dangerous until tamed by a stronger man. The historical association of powerful men with leadership and of powerful women with evil produces unspoken and often unconscious bias. Valian (1999) argues that widely held gender schemata (ways of thinking about what men and women are like) subtly associate competence with maleness. Even though these differences are small and nonconscious, she argues, they accumulate over the course of individual careers to give men a growing advantage.

4. *Women pay a higher price.* Shakeshaft (cited in Keller, 1999) argues that the rewards of senior positions may be lower for women because, compared with men, they

have higher needs for success in their family and personal lives but lower needs for esteem and status. Almost 70 percent of women in one study named personal and family responsibilities as the biggest barrier to their career success, far higher than any other factor (Morris, 2002). Executive jobs in any sector tend to impose a crushing workload on incumbents. That burden is even more overwhelming for women, who still do the majority of the housework and child rearing in most dual-career families. That helps to explain why fast-track women are less likely to marry and, if they do marry, are more likely to get divorced (Heffernan, 2002; Keller, 1999). It also explains why many women who do make it to the top turn out to be blessed with "trophy husbands" in the form of hard-to-find, stay-at-home dads (Morris, 2002).

Women have made progress. Attitudes have changed slowly, support mechanisms (such as day-care for working mothers) have gradually increased, and cultural views have shifted. Perhaps the single strongest force for continued advancement of women into leadership roles is the growing recognition by progressive organizations that they cannot afford to sacrifice access to the tremendous talent pool that women, as slightly over half the population, represent. The proportion of woman who were presidents of American universities doubled to almost 20 percent between 1986 and 2001 (Jacobson, 2002). Princeton, one of America's elite Ivies, accepted no women until 1969. Thirty years later, some of its mostly male alumni worried that their beloved *alma mater* might be on the skids when the first female president, Shirley Tilghman, appointed the first female provost as well. But grumbling at alumni gatherings could not change the fact that women were making gains even in America's most elite institutions.

REFRAMING LEADERSHIP

Reframing offers a way to get beyond narrow and oversimplified views of leadership. Each of the frames offers a distinctive image of the leadership process. Depending on leader and circumstance, each view can lead to compelling and constructive leadership images, but none is right for all times and seasons. In this section, we discuss four images of leadership summarized in Table 17.1. For each, we examine skills and processes and propose rules of thumb for successful leadership practice.

TABLE 17.1. Reframing Leadership.

	Leadership Is Effective When:		Leadership Is Ineffective When:	
Frame	Leader Is:	Leadership Process Is:	Leader Is:	Leadership Process Is:
Structural	Analyst, architect	Analysis, design	Petty tyrant	Management by detail and fiat
Human resource	Catalyst, servant	Support, empowerment	Weakling, pushover	Abdication
Political	Advocate, negotiator	Advocacy, coalition building	Con artist, thug	Manipulation, fraud
Symbolic	Prophet, poet	Inspiration, framing experience	Fanatic, fool	Mirage, smoke and mirrors

Architect or Tyrant? Structural Leadership

Structural leadership often evokes images of petty tyrants and rigid bureaucrats who never met a rule they didn't like. Little literature exists on structural leadership in comparison to other frames. Some structural theorists have argued that leadership is neither important nor basic (Hall, 1987). But the effects of structural leadership can be powerful and enduring, even if the style is subtler and less obviously heroic than other forms. Collins and Porras (1994) reported that the founders of many highly successful companies, such as Hewlett-Packard and Sony, had neither a clear vision for their organization nor even a particular product in mind. They were "clock builders": social architects who focused on designing and building an effective organization.

One of the great architects in business history was Alfred P. Sloan, Jr., who became president of General Motors in 1923 and remained a dominant force in the company until his retirement in 1956. The structure and strategy he established made GM the world's largest corporation. He has been described as "the George Washington of the GM culture" (Lee, 1988, p. 42), even though his "genius was not in inspirational leadership, but in organizational structures" (p. 43).

At the turn of the twentieth century, some thirty manufacturers produced automobiles in the United States. In 1899, they produced a grand total of about six hundred cars. Most of these small carmakers stumbled out of the starting gate, leaving two late entries, the Ford Motor Company (founded by Henry Ford in 1903) and GM (founded by William Durant in 1908) as front-runners in the race to dominate the American automobile industry. Henry Ford's single-minded determination to build an affordable car pushed Ford into a commanding lead when Sloan took over General Motors.

Under GM's founder, Billy Durant, the company's divisions operated as independent fiefdoms. Durant had built GM by buying everything in sight, thus forming a loose combination of previously independent firms. "GM did not have adequate knowledge or control of the individual operating divisions. It was management by crony, with the divisions operating on a horse-trading basis. The main thing to note here is that no one had the needed information or the needed control over the divisions. The divisions continued to spend lavishly, and their requests for additional funds were met" (Sloan, 1965, pp. 27–28).

Uncontrolled costs and a business slump in 1920 created a financial crisis. Chevrolet lost $5 million in 1921, and only Du Pont money and Buick's profitability kept GM afloat (Sloan, 1965). In Sloan's first year, 1923, matters got worse. GM's market share dropped from 20 percent to 17 percent, while Ford's increased to 55 percent. But change was afoot. Henry Ford had a disdain for organization and clung to his original vision of a single, low-priced, mass-market car. The Model T was cheap and reliable, but Ford stuck with the same design for almost twenty years. The "Tin Lizzie" was a marketing miracle when customers would buy anything with four wheels and a motor. Ford saw no great need for creature comforts in the Model T, but Sloan surmised that consumers would pay more for amenities (like windows to keep out rain and snow). His strategy worked, and Chevrolet soon began to gnaw off large chunks of Ford's market share. By 1928, Model T sales had dropped so precipitously that Henry Ford was forced to close his massive River Rouge plant for a year to retool. General Motors took the lead in the great auto race for the first time in twenty years. For the rest of the twentieth century, no company ever sold more cars than General Motors.

Sloan recognized that GM needed a better structural form. The dominant model of the time was a centralized, functional organization, but Sloan felt that such a structure would not work for GM. Instead, he created one of the world's first decentralized organizations. His basic principle was simple: centralize planning and resource allocation; decentralize operating decisions. Under Sloan's model, divisions focused on making and selling cars, while top management focused on long-range strategy and major funding decisions. The central staff made sure that top management had the information and control systems it needed to make strategic decisions.

The structure worked. By the late 1920s, GM had a more versatile organization with a broader product line than Ford. With Henry Ford still dominating his highly centralized company, Ford was poorly positioned to compete with GM's multiple divisions, each producing its own cars at different prices. GM's pioneering structural form eventually set the standard for others: "Although they developed many variations and although in very recent years they have been occasionally mixed into a matrix form, only two basic organizational structures have been used for the management of large industrial enterprises. One is the centralized, functional departmentalized type perfected by General Electric and Du Pont before World War I. The other is the multidivisional, decentralized structure initially developed at General Motors and also at Du Pont in the 1920s" (Chandler, 1977, p. 463).

In the 1980s, GM found itself with another structural leader, Roger Smith, at the helm. The results were less satisfying. Like Sloan, Smith ascended to the top job at a difficult time. In 1980, his first year as GM's chief executive, all American automakers lost money. It was GM's first loss since 1921. Recognizing that the company had serious competitive problems, Smith relied on structure and technology to make it "the world's first 21st century corporation" (Lee, 1988, p. 16). He restructured vehicle operations and spent billions of dollars in a quest for paperless offices and robotized assembly plants. The changes were dramatic, but the results were dismal:

> [Smith's] tenure has been a tragic era in General Motors history. No GM chairman has disrupted as many lives without commensurate rewards, has spent as much money without returns, or has alienated so many along the way. An endless string of public relations and internal relations insensitivities has confused his organization and complicated the attainment of its goals. Few employees believe that [Smith] is in the least concerned with their well-being, and even fewer below executive row anticipate any measure of respect, or reward, for their contributions. No GM chief executive's motives have ever been as universally questioned or his decisions as thoroughly mistrusted. (Lee, 1988, pp. 286–287)

Why did Smith stumble where Sloan had succeeded? They were equally uncharismatic. Sloan was a somber, quiet engineer who habitually looked as if he were sucking a lemon. Smith's leadership aura was not helped by his blotchy complexion and squeaky voice. Neither had great sensitivity to human resource or symbolic issues. Why, then, was Sloan's structural contribution so durable and Smith's so problematic? The answer comes down to how well each implemented the right structural form. Structural leaders succeed not because of inspiration but because they have the right design for the times and are able to get their structural changes implemented.

Effective structural leaders share several characteristics.

STRUCTURAL LEADERS DO THEIR HOMEWORK. Sloan was a brilliant engineer who had grown up in the auto industry. Before coming to GM, he was chief executive of an auto accessories company where he implemented a divisional structure. When GM bought his firm in 1916, Sloan became a vice president and board member. Working under Durant, he devoted much of his energy to studying GM's structural problems. He pioneered the development of more sophisticated internal information systems and better market research. He was an early convert to group decision making and created a committee structure to make major decisions.

Roger Smith had spent his entire career with General Motors, but most of his jobs were in finance. Much of his vision for General Motors involved changes in production technology, an area where he had little experience or expertise.

STRUCTURAL LEADERS RETHINK THE RELATIONSHIP OF STRUCTURE, STRATEGY, AND ENVIRONMENT. Sloan's new structure was intimately tied to a strategy for reaching the automotive market. He foresaw a growing market, improvements in automobiles, and more discriminating consumers. In the face of Henry Ford's stubborn attachment to the Model T, Sloan introduced the "price pyramid" (cars for every pocketbook) and the annual model change. Automotive technology in the 1920s was evolving almost as fast as electronics in the 1990s, and the annual model change soon became the industry norm.

For a variety of reasons, GM in the 1960s began to move away from Sloan's concepts. Fearing a government effort to break up the corporation, GM reduced the independence of the car divisions and centralized design and engineering. Increasingly, the divisions became marketing groups required to build and sell cars the corporation designed. In the early 1980s, "look-alike cars" became the standard across divisions. Many consumers became confused and angry when they found it hard to see the subtle differences between a Chevrolet and a Cadillac.

Smith's vision was truncated, focused more on reducing costs than on selling cars. As he saw it, GM's primary competitive problem was high costs driven by high wages. He hoped to solve that by replacing workers with machines. He gave little support to efforts already under way at GM to improve working conditions on the shop floor. Ironically, his two best investments—NUMMI and Saturn—succeeded precisely because of innovative approaches to managing people: "With only a fraction of the money invested in GM's heavily robotized plants, [the NUMMI plant at] Fremont is more efficient and produces better-quality cars than any plant in the GM system" (Hampton and Norman, 1987, p. 102).

STRUCTURAL LEADERS FOCUS ON IMPLEMENTATION. Structural leaders often miscalculate difficulties of putting their design in place. They underestimate resistance, skimp on training, fail to build a political base, and misread cultural cues. As a result, they are often thwarted by neglected human resource, political, and symbolic barriers. Sloan was no human resource specialist, but he intuitively saw the need to get understanding and acceptance of major decisions. He did that by continually asking for advice and by establishing committees and task forces to address major issues.

EFFECTIVE STRUCTURAL LEADERS EXPERIMENT, EVALUATE, AND ADAPT. Sloan tinkered constantly with GM's structure and strategy and encouraged others to do likewise. The Great Depression produced a drop of 72 percent in sales at GM between 1929 and 1932, but the company adapted very adroitly to hard times. It increased its market share and made money every year. Sloan briefly centralized operations to survive the depression but decentralized again once business began to recover. In the 1980s, Smith spent billions on his campaign to modernize the corporation and cut costs, yet GM lost market share every year and continued to be the industry's highest-cost producer: "Much of the advanced technology that GM acquired at such high cost hindered rather than improved productivity. Runaway robots started welding doors shut at the new Detroit-Hamtramck Cadillac plant. Luckily for Ford and Chrysler, poverty prevented them from indulging in the same orgy of spending on robots" ("On a Clear Day . . .," 1989, p. 77).

Catalyst or Wimp? Human Resource Leadership

The tiny trickle of writing about structural leadership is swamped by a torrent of human resource literature (among the best: Argyris, 1962; Bennis and Nanus, 1985; Blanchard and Johnson, 1982; Bradford and Cohen, 1984; Fiedler, 1967; Fiedler and Chemers, 1974; Hersey, 1984; Hollander, 1978; House, 1971; Levinson, 1968; Likert, 1961, 1967; Vroom and Yetton, 1973; and Waterman, 1994). Human resource theorists typically advocate openness, mutuality, listening, coaching, participation, and empowerment. They view the leader as a facilitator and catalyst who motivates and empowers subordinates. The leader's power comes from talent, sensitivity, and service rather than position or force. Greenleaf (1973) argues that followers "will freely respond only to individuals who are chosen as leaders because they are proven and trusted as servants" (p. 4). He adds, "The servant-leader makes sure that other people's highest priority needs are being served. The best test [of leadership] is: do those served grow as persons; do they, *while being served,* become healthier, wiser, freer, more autonomous, more likely themselves to become servants?" (p. 7).

Will managers who adhere to such images be respected leaders who make a difference? Or will they be seen as naïve and weak, carried along on the current of other people's energy? The Cindy Marshall case illustrates both sides. In one human resource encounter, Marshall seems more a flunky than a leader. In the other, she combines some of the virtues of both servant and catalyst. The leadership tightrope is real, and some managers hide behind participation and sensitivity as an excuse not to walk it.

There are also many human resource leaders whose skill and artistry produce extraordinary results. A good example is Martín Varsavsky, an Argentine native who wound up in New York as a teenager after a political murder forced his family to flee the military dictatorship in his homeland. Varsavsky became a serial entrepreneur and was eventually named entrepreneur of the year in 1999 by a major industry group in Europe. His successful start-ups included Urban Capital, a real-estate development firm in New York; Viatel, an international telephone service; Jazztel, a computer network provider in Spain and Portugal; and EinsteiNet, an online software supermarket based in Germany. His approach to managing people was central to his success: "Martín developed management practices that would be keys throughout his career: create horizontal organizations without any hierarchy, communicate clearly what you intend before doing it, delegate as much as possible, trust your colleagues, and leave operating decisions in the hands of others" (Ganitsky and Sancho, 2002).

Gifted human resource leaders such as Varsavsky typically apply a consistent set of leadership principles.

HUMAN RESOURCE LEADERS BELIEVE IN PEOPLE AND COMMUNICATE THEIR BELIEF. Human resource leaders are passionate about "productivity through people" (Peters and Waterman, 1982). They demonstrate this faith in their words and actions and often build it into a core philosophy or credo. Fred Smith, founder and CEO of Federal Express, sees "putting people first" as the cornerstone of his company's success: "We discovered a long time ago that customer satisfaction really begins with employee satisfaction. That belief is incorporated in our corporate philosophy statement: People—Service—Profit" (Waterman, 1994, p. 89).

William Hewlett, cofounder of the electronics giant Hewlett-Packard, put it this way:

> The dignity and worth of the individual is a very important part of the HP Way. With this in mind, many years ago we did away with time clocks, and more recently we introduced the flexible work hours program. This is meant to be an expression of trust and confidence in people, as well as providing them with an opportunity to adjust their work schedules to their personal lives. Many new HP people as well as visitors often note and comment to us about another HP way—that is, our informality and our being on a first-name basis. I could cite other examples, but the problem is that none by [itself] really catches the essence of what the HP Way is all about. You can't describe it in numbers and statistics. In the last analysis, it is a spirit, a point of view. There is a feeling that everyone is part of a team, and that team is HP. It is an idea that is based on the individual. (Peters and Waterman, 1982, p. 244)

HUMAN RESOURCE LEADERS ARE VISIBLE AND ACCESSIBLE. Peters and Waterman (1982) popularized the notion of "management by wandering around"—the idea that managers need to get out of their offices and spend time with workers and customers. Patricia Carrigan, the first woman to be a plant manager at General Motors, modeled this technique in the course of turning around two GM plants, each with a long history of union-management conflict (Kouzes and Posner, 1987). In both situations, she began by going to the plant floor to introduce herself to workers and ask how they thought the plant could be improved. One worker commented that before Carrigan came, "I didn't know who the plant manager was. I wouldn't have recognized him if I saw him." When she left her first assignment after three years, the local union gave her a plaque. It concluded, "Be it resolved that Pat M. Carrigan, through the exhibiting of these qualities as a people person, has played a vital role in the creation of a new way of life at the Lakewood plant. Therefore, be it resolved that the members of Local 34 will always warmly remember Pat M. Carrigan as one of us" (Kouzes and Posner, 1987, p. 36).

EFFECTIVE HUMAN RESOURCE LEADERS EMPOWER OTHERS. Human resource leaders often refer to their employees as "partners," "owners," or "associates." They make it clear that employees have a stake in the organization's success and a right to be involved in making decisions. In the 1980s, Jan Carlzon, CEO of Scandinavian Air Systems (SAS), built a turnaround effort intent on making the company "the best airline in the world for business travelers" (Carlzon, 1987, p. 46). To find out what the business traveler wanted, he turned to SAS's front-line service employees for their ideas and suggestions. Focus groups generated hundreds of ideas and emphasized the importance of front-line autonomy to decide on the spot what passengers needed. Carlzon concluded that SAS's image to its customers was built out of a series of "moments of truth": fifteen-second encounters between employees and customers. "If we are truly dedicated toward orienting our company to each customer's individual needs, we cannot rely on rule books and instruction from distant corporate offices. We have to place responsibility for ideas, decisions, and actions with the people who are SAS during those 15 seconds. If they have to go up the organizational chain of command for a decision on an individual problem, then those 15 golden seconds will elapse without a response and we will have lost an opportunity to earn a loyal customer" (p. 66).

Advocate or Hustler? Political Leadership

Sometimes, even in the private sector leaders find that they have to plunge into a political arena to move their company where it needs to go. Consider two chief executives from quite dissimilar eras: Lee Iacocca, who became chief executive of Chrysler when the company was near death in the late 1970s, and Carleton "Carly" Fiorina, who became CEO of Silicon Valley giant Hewlett-Packard in July 1999.

Iacocca's career had taken him to the vaunted presidency of Ford Motor Company. But then, on July 1, 1978, his boss, Henry Ford II, fired him, reportedly with the simple explanation, "Let's just say I don't like you" (O'Toole, 1984, p. 231). Iacocca's unemployment was brief. Chrysler Corporation, desperate for new leadership, believed that Iacocca was the answer.

Even though Iacocca had done his homework before accepting Chrysler's offer, things were even worse than he expected. Chrysler was losing money so fast that bankruptcy seemed almost inevitable. He concluded that the only way out was to persuade the U.S. government to guarantee massive loans. It was a tough sell; much of Congress, the media, and the American public were against the idea. Iacocca had to convince all of them that government intervention was in their best interest as well as Chrysler's.

Like Iacocca, Fiorina came in to head a troubled giant. HP's problems were not as bad as Chrysler's; it was still a profitable company with more than $40 billion in annual revenue. But customer service was deteriorating, bureaucracy was stifling innovation, and HP seemed to be falling behind the technology curve. *Business Week* described HP as part of "the clueless establishment" (Burrows and Elstrom, 1999, p. 76). Fiorina's arrival was big news for more than one reason. She was only the fifth CEO in HP's sixty-year history, and she was the first to come from outside since Bill (Hewlett) and Dave (Packard) founded the company in a Palo Alto garage in 1938. She was also the first woman to head a company of HP's size in any industry. She brought many strengths, including "a silver tongue and an iron will" (Burrows and Elstrom, 1999, p. 76). But she faced daunting challenges, especially after she set her sights on a merger with another, floundering, $40 billion company, Compaq. Her board supported her initiative, but Bill and Dave's heirs, who controlled more than 15 percent of HP's stock, didn't. Fiorina had to win a massive gunfight at HP corral or lose her job.

Ultimately, Iacocca got his guarantees and Fiorina got her merger. Both won their battles by artfully employing a set of principles for political leaders.

POLITICAL LEADERS CLARIFY WHAT THEY WANT AND WHAT THEY CAN GET. Political leaders are realists. They avoid letting what they want cloud their judgment about what is possible. Iacocca translated Chrysler's survival into the realistic goal of getting enough help to make it through a couple of difficult years without going under. He was always careful to ask not for money but for loan guarantees, insisting that the guarantees would cost the taxpayers nothing because Chrysler would pay back its loans. Fiorina, too, was realistic. Once she knew she was in a nasty, public squabble, she zeroed in on one goal: getting enough votes to put the merger through.

POLITICAL LEADERS ASSESS THE DISTRIBUTION OF POWER AND INTERESTS. Political leaders map the political terrain by thinking carefully about the key players, their interests, and their power, asking: Whose support do I need? How do I go about getting it? Who are my opponents? How much power do they have? What can I do to reduce or overcome their opposition? Is this battle winnable?

Iacocca needed the support of Chrysler's employees and unions, but he knew that they had little choice. The key players were Congress and the public. Congress would vote for the guarantees only if Iacocca's proposal had sufficient popular support.

Fiorina knew she needed support from HP's board, from analysts, and ultimately from a majority of voting shares. She first went after her board's support, but she ran into a stroke of bad luck. Walter Hewlett, son of HP cofounder Bill, missed the July 2001 board meeting at which McKinsey consultants made the case for the merger. A month later, Hewlett voted reluctantly to approve the merger. But he had serious misgivings. The substantial layoffs that were touted as one of the merger's "synergies" amounted to abandoning the HP Way in Hewlett's mind. His doubts grew when HP's stock dropped some 40 percent after the merger announcement. A few weeks later, he announced that he would vote his shares against the merger (Burrows, 2001). Fiorina now faced an uphill battle, with her job and her vision for HP both hanging on the outcome. Her only chance was to make a case persuasive enough to win over the analysts and shareholders who were still on the fence.

POLITICAL LEADERS BUILD LINKAGE TO KEY STAKEHOLDERS. Political leaders focus their attention on building relationships and networks. They recognize the value of personal contact and face-to-face conversations. Iacocca worked hard to build linkages with Congress, the media, and the public. He spent hours meeting with members of Congress and testifying before congressional committees. After he met with thirty-one Italian American members of Congress, all but one voted for the loan guarantees. Said Iacocca, "Some were Republicans, some were Democrats, but in this case they voted the straight Italian ticket. We were desperate, and we had to play every angle" (Iacocca and Novak, 1984, p. 221).

Fiorina's primary target was institutional shareholders, who held about 57 percent of the company's stock, and the analysts whose opinions mattered. Armed with a fifty-page document that laid out the strategic and financial rationale for the merger, Fiorina and Compaq CEO Michael Capellas hit the road, speaking to every analyst they could find. Fiorina focused on big picture, strategic issues, while Capellas backed her up on the nitty-gritty details of integrating the two firms. A particularly vital target was Institutional Shareholders Services, an advisory firm whose clients held more than a fifth of HP's stock. ISS's recommendation could easily make or break the deal. Though initially skeptical, ISS's lead analyst for the merger, Ram Kumar, said that the Fiorina/Capellas team's persuasiveness and command of detail won him over. "They had a strong grasp of the technical aspects of the merger," Kumar said. "It was an exhaustive, detailed plan" ("Hewlett-Packard Merger Pitch . . .," 2002).

POLITICAL LEADERS PERSUADE FIRST, NEGOTIATE SECOND, AND COERCE ONLY IF NECESSARY. Wise political leaders recognize that power is essential to their effectiveness; they also know to use it judiciously. William P. Kelly, an experienced public administrator, put it well: "Power is like the old Esso ad—a tiger in your tank. But you can't let the tiger out, you just let people hear him roar. You use power terribly sparingly because it has a short half-life. You let people know you have it and hope that you don't have to use it" (Ridout and Fenn, 1974, p. 10).

Sophisticated political leaders know that influence begins with an understanding of others' concerns and interests. What is important to them? How can I help them get what they want? Iacocca knew that he had to address the widespread belief that federal guarantees would throw millions of taxpayer dollars down a rat hole. He used advertising to respond directly to public concerns. Does Chrysler have a future? Yes, he said, we've been here fifty-four years, and we'll be here another fifty-four years. Would the loan guarantees be a dangerous precedent? No, the government already had $400 billion in other loan guarantees on the books, and in any event, Chrysler was going to pay its loans back. Iacocca also spoke directly to congressional concerns. Chrysler prepared computer print-outs showing how many jobs would be lost in every district if Chrysler went under.

Fiorina knew her biggest hurdle was the poor track record for big mergers, particularly in the computer industry. Her most potent opponent, Walter Hewlett, used Compaq's acquisition of fading giant Digital Equipment in 1998 as evidence that the deal would be a disaster, noting the 80 percent decline in Compaq's share value after the deal. Fiorina developed a threefold argument based on competitive scale, cost savings, and management strength. She took this story on the road in countless meetings with analysts and institutional shareholders. Her audiences generally found her very persuasive. HP buttressed the case with a blizzard of press releases, advertising, and direct mail.

As the battle intensified, Fiorina even resorted to the business equivalent of attack ads. HP put out a press release designed to gently but firmly discredit Walter Hewlett as a semiclueless dilettante: "Walter Hewlett, an heir of HP co-founder Bill Hewlett, is a musician and academic who oversees the Hewlett family trust and foundation. While he serves on HP's board of directors, Walter has never worked at the company or been involved in its management" (Fried, 2002).

Iacocca and Fiorina both won their battles. Chrysler pulled out of its tailspin, repaid its loans, ignited the minivan craze, and had many profitable years before it was acquired by German automaker Daimler Benz in 1998. HP fell short of analysts' expectations with a loss of $2 billion in its first postmerger quarterly financial report, but it is still too soon to know if the merger will go down in management history as an example of inspired leadership or simply as Fiorina's Folly.

Prophet or Zealot? Symbolic Leadership

The symbolic frame represents a fourth turn of the leadership kaleidoscope. This lens sees an organization as both theater and temple. As theater, an organization creates a stage on which actors play their roles and hope to communicate the right impression to the right audience. As temple, an organization is a community of faith, bonded by shared beliefs, traditions, myths, rituals, and ceremonies.

Symbolically, leaders lead through both their actions and their words as they *interpret and reinterpret experience*. What are the real lessons of history? What is really happening in the world? What will the future bring? What mission is worthy of our loyalty and investment? Data and analysis offer few adequate answers to such questions. Symbolic leaders interpret experience so as to impart meaning and purpose through phrases of beauty and passion. Franklin D. Roosevelt reassured a nation in the midst of its deepest economic depression that "the only thing we have to fear is fear itself." At almost the same time, Adolph Hitler assured Germans that their severe economic and social problems were the result of betrayal by Jews and communists. Germans, he said, were a superior people who could still fulfill their nation's destiny of world mastery. Though many saw the destructive paranoia in Hitler's message, millions of fearful citizens were swept up in Hitler's bold vision of German ascendancy.

Burns (1978) was mindful of leaders such as Franklin Roosevelt; Mohandas Gandhi; and Martin Luther King, Jr., when he drew a distinction between "transforming" and "transactional" leaders. According to Burns, transactional leaders "approach their followers with an eye to trading one thing for another: jobs for votes, subsidies for campaign contributions" (p. 4). Transforming leaders are rarer. As Burns describes them, they evoke their constituents' better nature and move them toward higher and more universal needs and purposes. They are visionary leaders whose leadership is inherently symbolic. Symbolic leaders follow a consistent set of practices and rules.

THEY LEAD BY EXAMPLE. Symbolic leaders demonstrate their commitment and courage by plunging into the fray. In taking risks and holding nothing back, they reassure and inspire others. New York Mayor Rudy Giuliani's leadership in the aftermath of the September 11 terrorist attacks is again a dramatic case in point. Risking his own life, he moved immediately to the scene. When the first tower collapsed, he was caught for fifteen minutes in the rubble.

THEY USE SYMBOLS TO CAPTURE ATTENTION. When Diana Lam became principal of the Mackey Middle School in Boston in 1985, she faced a substantial challenge. Mackey had the usual problems of an urban school: decaying physical plant, poor discipline, racial tension, disgruntled teachers, and limited resources (Kaufer and Leader, 1987a). In such a situation, a symbolic leader does something visible and dramatic to signal that change is coming. During the summer before assuming her duties, Lam wrote a personal letter to every teacher requesting an individual meeting. She met teachers wherever they wanted (in one case driving two hours). She asked teachers how they felt about the school and what changes they wanted. Then she recruited members of her family as a crew to repaint the school's front door and some of the most decrepit classrooms. "When school opened, students and staff members immediately saw that things were going to be different, if only symbolically. Perhaps even more important, staff members received a subtle challenge to make a contribution themselves" (Kaufer and Leader, 1987b, p. 3).

When Iacocca became president of Chrysler, one of his first steps was to announce that he was reducing his salary from $360,000 to $1 a year. "I did it for good, cold pragmatic reasons. I wanted our employees and our suppliers to be thinking: 'I can follow a guy who sets that kind of example,'" Iacocca explained in his autobiography (Iacocca and Novak, 1984, pp. 229–230).

SYMBOLIC LEADERS FRAME EXPERIENCE. In a world of uncertainty and ambiguity, a key function of symbolic leadership is to offer plausible interpretations of experience. Jan Carlzon mobilized front-line staff at SAS around the idea that each short encounter with a customer was a "moment of truth" (Carlzon, 1987). When Martin Luther King, Jr., spoke at the March on Washington in 1963 and gave his extraordinary "I Have a Dream" speech, his opening line was, "I am happy to join with you today in what will go down in history as the greatest demonstration for freedom in the history of our nation." He could have interpreted the event in a number of other ways: "We are here because progress has been slow, but we are not ready to quit yet"; "We are here because nothing else has worked"; "We are here because it's summer and it's a good day to be outside." Each version is about as accurate as the next, but accuracy is not the real issue. King's assertion was bold and inspiring; it told members of the audience that they were making history by their presence at a momentous event.

SYMBOLIC LEADERS COMMUNICATE A VISION. One powerful way in which a leader can interpret experience is by distilling and disseminating a vision—a persuasive and hopeful image of the future. A vision needs to address both the challenges of the present and the hopes and values of followers. Vision is particularly important in a time of crisis and uncertainty. When people are in pain, when they are confused and uncertain, or when they feel despair and hopelessness, they desperately seek meaning and hope.

Where does such vision come from? One view is that leaders create a vision and then persuade others to accept it (Bass, 1985; Bennis and Nanus, 1985). An alternative view is that leaders discover and articulate a vision that is already there, even if in an inchoate and unexpressed form (Cleveland, 1985). Kouzes and Posner (1987) put it well: "Corporate leaders know very well that what seeds the vision are those imperfectly formed images in the marketing department about what the customers really wanted and those inarticulate mumblings from the manufacturing folks about the poor product quality, not crystal ball gazing in upper levels of the corporate stratosphere. The best leaders are the best followers. They pay attention to those weak signals and quickly respond to changes in the corporate course" (p. 114).

Early in his career, Jan Carlzon had learned this lesson the hard way when he and a group of young executives designed a set of tour packages offering Swedish senior citizens what Carlzon knew they wanted: safe, risk-free travel to familiar places. The product bombed because the seniors really wanted variety and adventure. For Carlzon it was a memorable lesson: listen to your customers and to the front-line staff who know their real desire (Carlzon, 1987).

Leadership is a two-way street. No amount of charisma or rhetorical skill can sell a vision that reflects only the leader's values and needs; Carlzon's team had spent a fortune on beautiful color brochures to promote the doomed tour packages. Effective symbolic leadership is possible only for those who understand the deepest values and most pressing concerns of their constituents. But leaders still play a critical role. They can bring a unique, personal blend of poetry, passion, conviction, and courage to articulating a vision. They can play a key role in distilling and shaping the direction to be pursued. Most important, they can choose which stories to tell as a means of communicating the vision.

SYMBOLIC LEADERS TELL STORIES. Symbolic leaders often embed their vision in a story—a story about "us" and about "our" past, present, and future. *Us* could be the Sorbonne, Chrysler, the people of Thailand, or any other audience a leader hopes to reach. The past is usually a golden one, a time of noble purposes, of great deeds, of heroes and heroines. The present is a time of trouble, challenge, or crisis—a critical moment when we have to make fateful choices. The future is the dream: a vision of hope and greatness often linked directly to greatness in the past.

This is just the kind of story that helped Ronald Reagan, a master storyteller, become president of the United States. Reagan's golden past was the frontier, a place of rugged, sturdy, self-reliant men and women who built a great nation and took care of themselves and their neighbors without the intervention of a monstrous national government. It was an America of small towns and volunteer fire departments. America had fallen into crisis, said Reagan, because "the liberals" had created a federal government that was levying oppressive taxes and eroding freedom through regulation and bureaucracy. Reagan offered a vision: a return to American greatness by "getting government off the backs of the American people" and restoring traditional American values of freedom and self-reliance. It worked for Reagan and worked again twenty years later for a Reagan acolyte, George W. Bush.

The success of such stories is only partly related to their historical validity or empirical support. The central question is whether they are credible and persuasive to their audiences. A story, even a flawed story, will work if it taps persuasively into the experience, values, and aspirations of listeners.

Mohammed Said Sahaf, Iraq's information minister during the war in 2003, was mostly dismissed by Westerners as a source of lies and misinformation. He repeatedly predicted Iraqi victories that never materialized. Two days before Baghdad fell, he brazenly told reporters that there were no American forces in the city, despite the conspicuous presence of an American armored battalion at a presidential palace less than half a mile away. But Sahaf became a media star in much of the Arab world, where many viewers saw him as more interesting and credible than the boring briefers for the U.S. military. His military uniform, pistol on hip, and rakish beret conveyed spirit and élan. Arabs admired his creativity in generating pungent insults for the Americans ("bloodsucking worms," "sick dogs," "donkeys"). They particularly liked the story Sahaf told with flair and conviction: the infidel invaders were plunging ever deeper into a trap in which they would soon be destroyed by heroic Iraqi fighters. Sahaf's star turn ended abruptly with the collapse of the government he served, but for a time millions of Arabs who felt enraged and humiliated by the invasion of Iraq could take delight in a man who told the story as they wanted it to be (Lamb, 2003).

Good stories are truer than true: this reflects both the power and the danger of symbolic leadership. In the hands of a Gandhi or a King, the constructive power of stories is immense. Told by a Hitler, their destructive power is almost incalculable. In the wake of World War I and the Great Depression, Germany in the 1930s was hungry for hope. Other stories might have caught the imagination of the German people, but Hitler's passion and single-mindedness brought his story to center stage and carried Europe to a catastrophe of war and holocaust.

SYMBOLIC LEADERS RESPECT AND USE HISTORY. When leaders make the mistake of assuming that history started when they walked in the door, they usually misread their circumstances and alienate their constituents. Wise leaders attend to history, and link their initiatives to the values, stories, and heroes of the past. Even as she unleashed massive changes at HP, Carly Fiorina told Bill and Dave stories and insisted on her fidelity to the HP Way.

Sometimes the use of history is deliberately selective. When Hu Jintao became chief of the Chinese Communist Party in the fall of 2002, many wondered whether he would ever escape the long shadow of his predecessor, Jiang Zemin, who had bequeathed a party leadership stacked with his loyalists. Hu was unstinting in his praise of Jiang's legacy but began to differentiate himself symbolically (Eckholm, 2003). Hu enlisted a symbolic ally, Mao Zedong, the supreme hero of the Chinese Communist revolution. In December 2002, only a month after coming to power, Hu traveled to Xibaipo, a town where Mao had given a famous speech in 1949. In contrast to Jiang, who consistently talked up the economic successes of his reign, Hu emphasized the need to help the poor and dispossessed deal with the changes sweeping over China. He referred often to Mao and rarely to Jiang. He repeated Mao's call to the faithful to practice "plain living and arduous struggle" more than sixty times. As the editor of a party paper commented, "He showed that his legitimacy comes ultimately from Mao, not Jiang" (Eckholm, 2003, p. A6).

CONCLUSION

Though leadership is universally accepted as a cure for all organizational ills, it is also widely misunderstood. Many views of leadership fail to recognize its relational and contextual nature and its distinction from power and position. Inadequate ideas about leadership often produce oversimplified advice to managers. We need to reframe leadership to move beyond the impasse created by oversimplified models.

Each of the frames highlights significant possibilities for leadership, but each is incomplete in capturing a holistic picture. Early in the twentieth century, implicit models of managerial leadership were narrowly rational. In the 1960s and 1970s, human resource leadership became fashionable. In recent years, symbolic leadership has moved to center stage, and the literature abounds with advice on how to become a visionary leader capable of transforming cultural patterns. Organizations need vision, but it is not their only need and not always their most important one. Ideally, managers combine multiple frames into a comprehensive approach to leadership. Still, it is unrealistic to expect everyone to be a leader for all times and seasons. Wise leaders understand their own strengths, work to expand them, and build teams that can offer an organization leadership in all four modes: structural, political, human resource, and symbolic.

CHAPTER 18

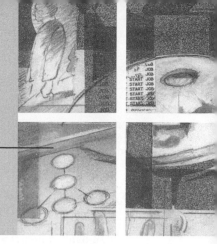

Reframing Change

Training, Realigning, Negotiating, Grieving, and Moving On

In 2002, the United States was almost the only nation not yet officially converted to the metric system. This seems strange, given that as far back as July 1958 the Federal Register contained provisions that "all calibrations in the U.S. customary system of weights and measurements carried out by the National Bureau of Standards will continue to be based on metric measurement and standards." It seems even more peculiar because in 1996 all federal agencies were ordered to adopt the metric system. For years, the United States has been urged to align its weights and measures with the rest of the world. Yet there has been little progress, even though America's adherence to a thousand-year-old English system (which the English have been slowly abandoning) has many costs. It handicaps international commerce, for example, and it led to measurement confusion in the design of the Hubble space telescope that cost taxpayers millions of dollars.

America's metric inertia illustrates a predictable dynamic of change that scuttles many bold new plans. Organizations spend millions of dollars on change strategies that either produce no change or make things worse. Mergers fail. Technology misses its potential. Strategies that are vital to success never make it into practice. This chapter opens by describing typical flaws in efforts to change organizations. It then moves from barriers to opportunities, developing a multiframe analysis of the change process to show how training, structural realignment, political bargaining, and symbolic rituals of letting go can achieve more positive outcomes. It goes on to describe an integrated model of the change process and concludes with a case study illustrating effective change.

A COMMON CHANGE SCENARIO

DDB Bank (a pseudonym) is one of the largest banks in Southeast Asia, with more than sixty branches and thirteen thousand employees, and a network of correspondent banks throughout the world. The bank has been uniformly profitable since its founding more than fifty years ago. Its loan portfolio is sound. Shareholders, capital markets, and government regulators universally give the bank high marks.

When he became general manager of DDB's main branch, Thomas Lo was one of a few managers dissatisfied with the bank's performance. In fourteen years with Citibank in various parts of the world, he had learned to think strategically and to feel at home in a dynamic, fast-moving organization. For years—generations, even—DDB's strategy had been very conservative. Its branches created a large deposit base. Particularly in rural areas, depositors stayed with DDB as long as they felt their money was safe and readily accessible. A low-cost deposit base enabled DDB to make loans at reasonable but profitable rates of interest—a key to the bank's solid profitability. It had stable, long-term relationships with both borrowers and depositors. In making decisions, managers could usually rely on explicit policies and procedures.

Staff and personnel policies also reflected DDB's reliance on stability and systems. Jobs and grades were defined in detail, with a clear career path from entry level position up to branch manager. Two main requirements governed upward movement: (1) complete the minimum time in grade, and (2) follow established rules and procedures to the letter. Meeting these criteria ensured a steady, predictable career.

The decision to hire Thomas Lo was controversial, and it split the management team. A faction led by Executive Vice President William Tun, head of all domestic branches, embraced the principle "If it's not broken, don't fix it." This group favored leaving well enough alone. An opposing group argued the bank had to anticipate changes on the horizon. This contingent was led by Philip Neo, executive vice president in charge of corporate banking.

The more progressive group emphasized the banking industry was becoming much more competitive as government regulation relaxed. This faction felt the traditional deposit base could no longer be taken for granted. To stay competitive, they maintained, DDB had to focus on superior customer service and innovative strategies to defend and extend its deposit base. Thomas Lo was recruited to make the main branch a role model for other DDB branches.

Lo hit the ground running. Within three months, a five-year plan was produced, and implementation got under way. Branch mangers received targets for loans, deposits, and profitability. This last item got highest priority. Information systems were revamped so that targets could be monitored continuously. The main branch was reorganized. New positions for a marketing manager and a planning manager were added. Though Lo advertised these positions internally so as to appear to be in line with existing policies, his real intention was to hire outsiders and inject new blood into the main branch.

Lo also pressed for other changes. He argued for a new performance appraisal system to identify strong performers and move them rapidly upward. He wanted a more flexible salary scale: less emphasis on time in grade and more room for merit increases. He encouraged the human resource department to develop new career paths for moving people between branches and for making lateral transfers between branches and the head office. Most of the staff had degrees in accounting or economics, but Lo wanted a new breed of movers and shakers—even if their studies were unrelated to banking.

Six months later, Lo concluded that his innovations were having almost no effect on day-to-day activities. The problem was not open resistance but covert foot dragging. Some managers claimed they were working to implement the changes but offered many excuses for falling behind schedule. Others nodded their heads in public agreement but privately carried on doing things the old way. Lo began seriously considering leaving DDB to join a smaller, more dynamic investment banking firm.

Lo's story is all too familiar: hopeful beginnings, a turbulent middle, and a discouraging ending. Alert readers might note that Lo's story has parallels to the Helen Demarco case in Chapter Two. Lo's subordinates may have felt much like Demarco: they were not resisting change but protecting the organization. Similarly, Paul Osborne and Thomas Lo had much in common: both brought in new, fresh ideas to revitalize stodginess, and both felt frustrated at the difficulty of moving change through their organization.

Such stories illustrate an ironclad law: change rationally conceived usually fails. Like Lo, change agents misread or overlook unanticipated consequences of their actions. They march blindly down their chosen path despite warning signs they are headed in the wrong direction. Over scores of change efforts, we continue to see managers whose strategies are limited because they are wedded to one or two frames. Some try to produce major change by redesigning formal structures, only to find people unable or unwilling to carry out new responsibilities. Others import new people or retrain old ones, only to find new blood and new ideas are rejected or assimilated, often disappearing without a trace.

As Machiavelli observed many years ago in *The Prince,* "It must be realized that there is nothing more difficult to plan, more uncertain of success, or more dangerous to manage than the establishment of a new order of [things]; for he who introduces [change] makes enemies of all those who derived advantage from the old order and finds but lukewarm defenders among those who stand to gain from the new one" ([1514] 1961, p.27).

Machiavelli's pessimistic observations about the process of change are as timely as ever, but the frames can help agents of change increase their odds of success. Organizational change is a multiframe undertaking. It never works to retrain people without revising roles, or to revamp roles without retraining. Managers who anticipate that new roles require new skills and vice versa have much greater likelihood of success. Change also alters power relationships and undermines existing agreements and pacts. Even more profoundly, it intrudes upon deeply rooted symbolic forms, traditional ways, and ritual behavior. Below the surface, the organization's social tapestry begins to unravel, threatening both time-honored traditions and prevailing cultural values and practices. In the remainder of the chapter, we look at the human resource, structural, political, and symbolic aspects of organizational change and integrate them with Kotter's model of the change process.

Each frame offers a distinctive view of major issues in change, as summarized in Table 18.1. The human resource frame focuses on needs and skills, the structural frame on alignment and clarity, the political frame on conflict and arenas, and the symbolic frame on loss of meaning and the importance of creating new symbols and ways. Each frame highlights a set of barriers and posits possibilities for making change stick.

CHANGE AND TRAINING

It sounds simplistic to point out that investment in change calls for collateral investment in training. Yet countless reform initiatives falter because managers neglect to spend time and money on developing necessary new knowledge and skills. In too many organizations, the human resource department is an afterthought no one really takes seriously.

Management Best-Sellers: Spencer Johnson, *Who Moved My Cheese?* *An A-Mazing Way to Deal with Change in Your Work and Your Life* (New York: Putnam, 1998).

Spencer Johnson's brief ninety-four-page parable about mice, men, and change topped *Business Week*'s best-seller list for three consecutive years (1999, 2000, and 2001), making it one of the most successful management books ever.

The essence of the book is a story about a maze and its four inhabitants: two mice named Sniff and Scurry and two "little people" named Hem and Haw. Life is good because they have found a place in the maze where they reliably discover a plentiful supply of high-quality cheese. But then the quality and quantity of cheese decline, and eventually the cheese disappears altogether.

The mice, being relatively simple creatures, figure "No cheese here? Let's go look somewhere else." Sniff is very good at sniffing out new supplies, and Scurry excels in scurrying after them once they're found. Before long, they're both back in cheese heaven.

But Hem and Haw, being human, are reluctant to abandon old ways. They figure someone has made a mistake because they're entitled to get cheese where they have always gotten it. They're confident that, if they wait, the cheese will return. It doesn't. As they get hungrier, Hem and Haw gripe and complain about the unfairness of it all. Eventually, Haw decides it's time to explore and look for something better. Hem, however, insists on staying where he is until the cheese comes back.

As he searches, Haw develops a new outlook. He posts signs on the walls to express his new thinking, with messages such as "Old beliefs do not lead you to new cheese." Haw's explorations eventually reunite him with Sniff, Scurry, and the new cache of cheese. Hem continues to starve.

Cheese, as the book points out, is a metaphor for whatever you might want in life. The maze represents the context in which you work and live; it could be your family, your workplace, or your life. The basic message is simple and clear: clinging to old beliefs and habits when the world around you has changed is self-defeating. Flexibility, experimentation, and the willingness to try on new beliefs are critical to success in a fast-changing world.

The book certainly has critics. But it has far more fans, for whom its simplicity is a virtue. The parable often enables its fans to see aspects of themselves and their own experience—times when, like Hem, they have hurt themselves by rigidly refusing to adapt to new circumstances.

TABLE 18.1. Reframing Organizational Change.

Frame	Barriers to Change	Essential Strategies
Human Resource	Anxiety, uncertainty; people feel incompetent and needy	Training to develop new skills; participation and involvement; psychological support
Structural	Loss of clarity and stability; confusion, chaos	Communicating, realigning, and renegotiating formal patterns and policies
Political	Disempowerment; conflict between winners and losers	Create arenas where issues can be renegotiated and new coalitions formed
Symbolic	Loss of meaning and purpose; clinging to the past	Create transition rituals; mourn the past, celebrate the future

In one large firm, for example, top management decided to purchase state-of-the-art technology. They were confident the investment would yield a 50 percent cut in cycle time from a customer order to delivery. Faster turnaround would yield a decisive competitive advantage. The strategy was crafted during hours of careful analysis. The new technology was launched with great fanfare. The CEO assured a delighted sales force it would now have a high-tech competitive edge. After the initial euphoria faded, though, the sales force realized its old methods were obsolete; years of experience were useless. Veterans suddenly felt like neophytes. When the CEO heard that the sales force was shaky about the new technology, he said, "Then find someone in human resources to throw something together. You know, what's-her-name, the new human resources vice president. That's why we hired her." A year later, the new technology had failed to deliver. The training never materialized. The company's investment ultimately yielded a costly, inefficient technology and a demoralized sales force. The window of opportunity was lost to the competition.

In contrast, a large hospital invested millions of dollars in a new integrated information system. The goal was to improve patient care by making updated information available to everyone involved in a treatment plan. Terminals linked patients' bedsides to nursing stations, attending physicians, pharmacy, and other services. To ensure that the new system would work, hospital administrators created a simulation lab. Individual representatives from all groups were brought into a room and seated at terminals. Hypothetical scenarios gave them a chance to practice and work out the kinks. Many, particularly physicians, needed to improve their computer skills. Coaches were there to help. Each group became its own self-help support system. Both skills and confidence improved in the training session. Relationships that formed across various functions were invaluable as the system was implemented.

From a human resource perspective, people have good reason to resist change. No one likes feeling anxious and incompetent. Changes in routine practice and procedure undermine existing knowledge and skills, and they undercut people's ability to perform with confidence and success. When asked to do something they don't understand, don't know how to do, or don't believe in, people feel puzzled, anxious, and insecure. Lacking skills and confidence to implement the new ways, they resist or even sabotage, awaiting the return of the good old days. Or, like Thomas Lo's subordinates, they may comply superficially while covertly dragging their feet. Even if they try to do what they are told, the results are predictably dismal. Sometimes, resistance is sensible; it produces better results than the new methods. Training, psychological support, and participation all increase the likelihood that people will understand and feel comfortable with the new methods.

Often overlooked in the training loop are those responsible for guiding the change. Kotter presents a vivid example of how training can prepare people to communicate the rationale for a new order of things. A company moving to a team-based structure developed by twenty top managers was concerned about how workers and trade unions would react. To make sure people would understand and accept the changes, the managers went through an intensive training regimen: "Our twenty 'communicators' practiced and practiced. They learned the responses, tried them out, and did more role plays until they felt comfortable with nearly anything that might come at them. Handling 200 issues well may sound like too much, but we did it. . . . I can't believe that what we did is not applicable nearly everywhere. I think too many people wing it" (Kotter and Cohen, 2002, p. 86).

CHANGE AND REALIGNMENT

Individual skills and confidence cannot guarantee success unless structure is also realigned to the new initiative. As an example, a school system created a policy requiring principals to assume a more active role in supervising classroom instruction. Principals were trained in how to observe and counsel teachers. Morale problems and complaints soon began to surface. No one had asked how changes in principals' duties might affect teachers. Nor had anyone thought to question existing agreements about authority. Was it legitimate, in teachers' eyes, for principals to spend time in classrooms observing them and suggesting ways to improve teaching? Most important, no one had asked who would handle administrative duties for which principals no longer had time. As a result, supplies were often delayed, parents felt neglected, and discipline deteriorated. By midyear, most principals were back to concentrating on their administrative duties and leaving teachers alone.

Structure confers clarity, predictability, and security. Formal roles prescribe duties and outline how work is to be performed. Policies and standard operating procedures synchronize diverse efforts into well-coordinated programs. Formal allocation of authority lets everyone know who is in charge, when, and over what. Change undermines existing arrangements, creating ambiguity, confusion, and distrust. People no longer know what is expected or what to expect from others. Everyone may think someone else in charge when, in fact, no one is.

Consider another example. In the wake of changes in health care, a hospital was experiencing substantial employee turnover and absenteeism, a shortage of nurses, poor communication, and low staff morale. There were rumors of an impending effort to organize a union. A consultant's report identified several structural problems:

> One set related to top management. Members of the executive committee seemed to be confused about their roles and authority. Many believed all important decisions were made (prior to the meetings) by Rettew, the hospital administrator. Many shared the perception that major decisions were made behind closed doors, and that Rettew often made "side deals" with different individuals, promising them special favors or rewards in return for support at the committee meetings. People at this level felt manipulated, confused, and dissatisfied.
>
> Major problems also existed in the nursing service. The director of nursing seemed to be patterning her managerial style after that of Rettew. . . . Nursing supervisors and head nurses felt that they had no authority, while staff nurses complained about a lack of direction and openness by the nursing administration. The structure of the organization was unclear. Nurses were unaware of what their jobs were, whom they should report to, and how decisions were made. (McLennan, 1989, p. 231)

As the school and hospital examples both illustrate, when things start to shift people become unsure about their duties, how to relate to others, and who has authority to

Greatest Hits from Organization Studies No. 6: Richard R. Nelson and Sidney G. Winter, *An Evolutionary Theory of Economic Change* (Cambridge, Mass.: Harvard University Press, 1982).

If you are an economist, how might you think about change in organizations? Nelson and Winter's book represents one side of a debate within economics that pits the dominant neoclassical view against a range of heretical perspectives. In essence, the neoclassical view sees both humans and organizations as rational decision makers who maximize their own interests (utility) in the face of available options and incentives. The problem of change is simple: rational maximizers will change if (1) their preferences change or (2) the environment changes the incentives they face.

An example of the neoclassical approach is greatest hit no. 4, Jensen and Meckling's paper on agency theory, discussed in Chapter Three. Nelson and Winter are dissenters. (So are the authors of two other works on our hit list: no. 2, Cyert and March, discussed in Chapter Eleven; and no. 5, March and Simon, discussed in Chapter Two.)

Nelson and Winter criticize maximization on the ground that "firms have but limited bases for judging what will work best; they may even have difficulty establishing the plausible range of alternatives to be considered"(p. 399). They develop an evolutionary theory intended to conform closely to change processes as observed in practice. Three concepts are central:

1. *Routine:* a regular and predictable pattern of behavior, a way of doing something that a firm uses repeatedly. This is what March and Simon (1958) refer to as "programmed activity."
2. *Search:* the process of assessing current options, acquiring new information, and potentially altering routines. "Routines play the role of genes in our evolutionary theory. Search routines stochastically generate mutations" (p. 400).
3. *Selection environment:* the set of considerations determining whether an organization adopts an innovation. They include costs and benefits, consumer and regulatory factors, and how an organization learns about innovation from others.

Nelson and Winter see an organization as combining ongoing behavior patterns producing stability and continuity with search activities for scouting new options. If an organization finds new possibilities, it tries them out. Those that work are kept; others are discarded. Change evolves over time, akin to the process of natural selection, through which an organization gradually evolves toward a better fit with its environment.

decide what. Clarity, predictability, and rationality give way to confusion, loss of control, and a sense that politics rather than policy rules. To minimize such difficulty, change efforts must anticipate structural issues and work to realign roles and relationships. In some situations, this can be done informally. In others, structural arrangements need to be renegotiated more formally (through some version of responsibility charting, discussed in Chapter Five).

CHANGE AND CONFLICT

Change invariably creates conflict. It spawns a hotly contested tug-of-war to determine winners and losers. Some individuals and groups support the change; others are dead set in opposition. Too often, conflicts submerge and smolder beneath the surface. Occasionally, they burst back into the open as outbreaks of unregulated warfare.

A case in point comes from a U.S. government initiative to improve America's rural schools. The Experimental Schools Project provided funds for comprehensive changes. It also carefully documented experiences of ten participating districts over a five-year period. The first year—the planning period—was free of conflict. But as plans became actions, hidden issues boiled to the surface. A Northwest school district illustrates a common pattern:

> In the high school, a teacher evaluator explained the evaluation process while emphasizing the elaborate precautions to insure the raters would be unable to connect specific evaluations with specific teachers. He also passed out copies of the check-list used to evaluate the [evaluation forms]. Because of the tension the subject aroused, he joked that teachers could use the list to "grade" their own [forms]. He got a few laughs; he got more laughs when he encouraged teachers to read the evaluation plan by suggesting, "If you have fifteen minutes to spare and are really bored, you should read this section." When another teacher pointed out that her anonymity could not be maintained because she was the only teacher in her subject, the whole room broke into laughter, followed by nervous and derisive questions and more laughter.
>
> When the superintendent got up to speak, shortly afterwards, he was furious. He cautioned teachers for making light of the teacher evaluators who, he said, were trying to protect

the staff. Several times he repeated that because teachers did not support the [project] they did not care for students. "Your attitude," he concluded, "is damn the children and full speed ahead!" He then rushed out of the room.

The superintendent's speech put the high school in turmoil. The woman who questioned the confidentiality of the procedure was in tears. Most teachers were incensed at the superintendent's outburst, and a couple said they came close to quitting. As word of the event spread through the system, it caused reverberations in other buildings as well. (Firestone, 1977, pp. 174–175)

After a heated exchange, conflict between the administration and teachers intensified. The school board got involved and reduced the superintendent's authority. Rumors he might be fired undermined his clout even more.

Such a scenario is predictable. As changes emerge, camps form: supporters, opponents, and fence-sitters. Conflict is avoided or smoothed over until eventually erupting in divisive battles. Coercive power may determine the winner. Often, the status quo prevails and change agents lose. From a political perspective, conflict is a natural part of life. It is managed through processes of negotiation and bargaining, where settlements and agreements can be hammered out. If ignored, disputes explode into street fights. Street fights have no rules. Anything goes. People get hurt, and scars last for years.

The alternative to street fights are arenas with rules, referees, and spectators. Arenas create opportunities to forge divisive issues into shared agreements. Through bargaining, compromises can be worked out between the status quo and innovative ideals. Welding new ideas onto existing practices is essential to successful change. One hospital administrator said, "The board and I had to learn how to wrestle in a public forum."

Mitroff describes a drug company facing competitive pressure to its branded, prescription drug from generic substitutes. Management was split into three factions: one group wanted to raise the price of the drug, another wanted to lower it, and still another wanted to keep it the same but cut costs (Mitroff, 1983). Each group collected information, constructed models, and developed reports showing that its solution was correct. The process degenerated into a frustrating spiral. Mitroff intervened to get each group to identify major stakeholders and articulate respective assumptions about them. All agreed the most critical stakeholders were physicians prescribing the drug. Each group had its own suppositions about how physicians would respond to a price change. But no one really knew.

The three groups finally agreed to test their assumptions by implementing a price increase in selected markets.

The intervention worked through convening an arena with a more productive set of rules. Similarly, experimental school districts that created arenas for resolving conflict were more successful than others in bringing about comprehensive change. In the school district just cited, teachers reacted to administrative coercion with a power strategy of their own:

> Community members initiated a group called Concerned Citizens for Education in response to a phone call from a teacher who noted that parents should be worried about what the [administrators] were doing to their children. The superintendent became increasingly occupied with responding to demands and concerns of the community group. Over time, the group joined in a coalition with teachers to defeat several of the superintendent's supporters on the school board and to elect members who were more supportive of their interests. The turnover in board membership reduced the administrator's power and authority, making it necessary to rely more and more on bargaining and negotiation strategies to promote the intended change. (Deal and Nutt, 1980, p. 20)

Changing always creates division and conflict among competing interest groups. Successful change requires an ability to frame issues, build coalitions, and establish arenas in which disagreements can be forged into workable pacts. One insightful executive remarked: "We need to confront, not duck, and face up to disagreements and differences of opinions and conflicting objectives. . . . All of us must make sure—day in and day out—that conflicts are aired and resolved before they lead to internecine war."

CHANGE AND LOSS

In the early 1980s, America's Cola wars—a battle between Coke and Pepsi—reached a fever pitch. The Pepsi Challenge—a head-to-head taste test—was making inroads in Coca-Cola's market share. In blind tests, even avowed Coke drinkers preferred Pepsi. In a Coke counterchallenge, held at its corporate headquarters in Atlanta, Pepsi again won by a slight margin. Later, Pepsi stunned the industry by signing Michael Jackson to a $5 million celebrity advertising campaign. Coca-Cola executives were getting nervous. They decided on a revolutionary strategy and struck back with one of the most important announcements in the company's ninety-nine-year history: Old Coke would be replaced with New Coke.

> Shortly before 11:00 A.M. [on Tuesday, April 23, 1985], the doors of the Vivian Beaumont The-ater at Lincoln Center opened to two hundred newspaper, magazine, and TV reporters. The stage was aglow with red. Three huge screens, each solid red and inscribed with the com-pany logo, rose behind the podium and a table draped in red. The lights were low: the music began. "We are. We will always be. Coca-Cola. All-American history." As the patriotic song filled the theater, slides of Americana flashed on the center screen—families and kids, Eisen-hower and JFK, the Grand Canyon and wheat fields, the Beatles and Bruce Springsteen, cowboys, athletes, and Statue of Liberty—and interspersed throughout, old commercials for Coke. Robert Goizueta [CEO of Coca-Cola] came to the podium. He first congratulated the reporters for their ingenuity in already having reported what he was about to say. And then he boasted, "The best has been made even better." Sidestepping the years of laboratory research that had gone into the program, Goizueta claimed that in the process of concocting Diet Coke, the company flavor chemists had "discovered" a new formula. And research had shown that consumers preferred this new one to old Coke. Management could then do one of two things: nothing, or buy the world a new Coke. Goizueta announced that the taste-test results made management's decisions "one of the easiest ever made." (Oliver, 1986, p. 132)

The rest is history. Coke drinkers rejected the new product. They felt betrayed, and many were outraged: "Duane Larson took down his collection of Coke bottles and outside of his restaurant hung a sign, 'They don't make Coke anymore' [. . . .] Dennis Overstreet of Beverly Hills hoarded 500 cases of old Coke and advertised them for $30 a case. He is almost sold out. . . . San Francisco *Examiner* columnist Bill Mandel called it 'Coke for wimps' [. . . .] Finally, Guy Mullins exclaimed, 'When they took old Coke off the market, they violated my freedom of choice—baseball, hamburgers, Coke—they're all the fabric of America.'" (Morganthau, 1985, pp. 32–33).

Even bottlers and Coca-Cola employees were aghast: "By June the anger and resentment of the public was disrupting the personal lives of Coke employees, from the top executives to the company secretaries. Friends and acquaintances were quick to attack, and once proud employees now shrank from displaying to the world any association with the Coca-Cola company" (Oliver, 1986, pp. 166–167).

Coca-Cola rebounded quickly with Classic Coke. Indeed, the company's massive miscalculation led to one of the strangest, most serendipitous triumphs in marketing history. All the controversy, passion, and free publicity stirred up by the New Coke fiasco ultimately helped Coca-Cola regain its dominance in the soft drink industry. A brilliant stratagem, if anyone had planned it.

What led Coke's executives into such a quagmire? Several factors were at work. Pepsi was gaining market share. As the newly appointed CEO of Coca-Cola, Goizueta was determined to modernize the company. A previous innovation, Diet Coke, had been a huge success. Most important, Coca-Cola's revered, long-time "Boss," Robert Woodruff, had just passed away. On his deathbed, he reportedly gave Goizueta his blessing for the new recipe.

In their zeal to compete with Pepsi, Coke's executives overlooked a central tenet of the symbolic frame. The meaning of an object or event can be far more powerful than the reality. Strangely, Coke's leadership had lost touch with their product's significance to consumers. To many people, old Coke was a piece of Americana. It was linked to cherished memories. Coke represented something far deeper than just a soft drink.

In introducing New Coke, company executives unintentionally announced the passing of an important American symbol. Symbols create meaning, and when a symbol is destroyed or vanishes people experience emotions akin to those at the passing of a spouse, child, old friend, or pet. When a relative or close friend dies, we feel a deep sense of loss. We unconsciously harbor similar feelings when a computer replaces old procedures, a logo changes after a merger, or an old leader is replaced by a new one. When these transitions take place in the workplace rather than in a family, feelings of loss are often denied or attributed to other causes.

Any significant change in an organization triggers two conflicting responses. The first is to keep things as they were, to replay the past. The second is to ignore the loss and rush busily into the future. Individuals or groups can get stuck in either form of denial or bog down vacillating between the two. Nurses in one hospital's intensive care unit were caught in a loss cycle for ten years following their move from an old facility. Four years after AT&T was forced to divest its local phone operations, an executive remarked: "Some mornings I feel like I can set the world on fire. Other mornings I can hardly get out of bed to face another day." Loss is an unavoidable by-product of change. As change accelerates, executives and employees get caught in endless cycles of unresolved grief.

In our personal lives, the pathway from loss to healing is culturally prescribed. Every culture outlines a sequence for transition rituals following significant loss: always a collective experience in which pain is expressed, felt, and juxtaposed against humor and hope. (Think of Irish actor Malachy McCourt who, as his mother lay dying, said to the distressed physician, "Don't worry, Doctor, we come from a long line of dead people.") In many societies, the sequence of ritual steps involves a wake, a funeral, a period of mourning, and some form of commemoration.

From a symbolic perspective, ritual is an essential companion to significant change. A military change-of-command ceremony is formally scripted. A wake is held for the outgoing commander, and the torch is passed publicly to the new commander in full ceremony. After a period of time, the old commander's face or name is displayed in a picture or plaque. Transition rituals initiate a sequence of steps that help people let go of the past, deal with a painful present, and move into a meaningful future. The form of these rites varies widely, but without them people are blocked from facing loss. They then vacillate between hanging on to the past and plunging into a meaningless future. Disruption of attachment even to negative symbols or harmful symbolic activities needs to be marked by some form of expressive event. The occasion should help people let go of old ways and offer something new that they can grasp to move ahead.

Owen (1987) vividly documents these issues in his description of change at "Delta Corporation." An entrepreneur named Harry invented a product that created enough demand to support a company of thirty-five hundred people. After a successful initial public stock offering, the company soon experienced soaring costs, flattened sales, and a dearth of new products. Facing stockholder dissatisfaction and charges of mismanagement, Harry passed the torch to a new leader.

Harry's replacement was very clear about her vision: she wanted "engineers who could fly." But her vision was juxtaposed against a history of "going downhill." Another problem was that various parts of the company were governed by a complicated array of stories, each representing a different Delta theme. Finance division stories exemplified the new breed of executives brought in following Harry's departure. Research and development stories varied by organizational level. At the executive level, "Old Harry" stories extolled the creative accomplishments of the former CEO. Middle management stories focused on the Golden Fleece award given monthly behind the scenes to the researcher who developed the idea with the least bottom-line potential. On the production benches, workers told of Serendipity Sam, winner of more Golden Fleece awards than anyone else, exemplar of the excitement and innovation of Harry's regime.

Instead of a company sharing a common story, Delta was a collection of independent cells, each with its own story. Across the levels and divisions, the stories clustered into two competing themes: the newcomers' focus on management versus the company's tradition of innovation. The new CEO recognized the importance of blending old and new to build a company where "engineers could fly." She brought thirty-five people from across the company to a management retreat where she surprised everyone:

> She opened with some stories of the early days, describing the intensity of Old Harry and the Garage Gang (now known as the Leper Colony). She even had one of the early models of Harry's machine out on a table. Most people had never seen one. It looked primitive, but during the coffee break, members of the Leper Colony surrounded the ancient artifact, and began swapping tales of the blind alleys, the late nights, and the breakthroughs. That dusty old machine became a magnet. Young shop floor folks went up and touched it, sort of snickering as they compared this prototype with the sleek creations they were manufacturing now. But even as they snickered, they stopped to listen as the Leper Colony recounted tales of accomplishment. It may have been just a 'prototype,' but that's where it all began. (Owen, 1987, p. 172)

After coffee break, the CEO divided the group into subgroups to share their hopes for the company. When the participants returned, their chairs had been rearranged into a circle with Old Harry's prototype in the center. With everyone facing one another, the CEO led a discussion, linking the stories from the various subgroups. Serendipity Sam's account of a new product possibility came out in a torrent of technical jargon:

> The noise level was fierce, but the rest of the group was being left out. Taking Sam by the hand, the CEO led him to the center of the circle right next to the old prototype. There it was the old and the new—the past, present, and potential. She whispered in Sam's ear that he

ought to take a deep breath and start over in words of one syllable. He did so, and in ways less than elegant, the concept emerged. He guessed about applications, competitors, market shares, and before long the old VP for finance was drawn in. No longer was he thinking about selling [tax] losses, but rather thinking out loud about how he was going to develop the capital to support the new project. The group from the shop floor . . . began to spin a likely tale as to how they might transform the assembly lines in order to make Sam's new machine. Even the Golden Fleece crowd became excited, telling each other how they always knew that Serendipity Sam could pull it off. They conveniently forgot that Sam had been the recipient of a record number of their awards, to say nothing of the fact that this new idea had emerged in spite of all their rules. (Owen, 1987, pp. 173–174)

In one intense event, part of the past was buried, yet its spirit was resurrected and revised to fit the new circumstances. Disparaging themes and stories were merged into a company where "engineers could fly" profitably.

CHANGE STRATEGY

The frames constitute a comprehensive checklist of issues that change agents must recognize and respond to. But how can they be combined into an integrated model? How does the change process move through time? John Kotter, an influential student of leadership and change, has studied both successful and unsuccessful change efforts in organizations around the world. In his book *The Heart of Change* (2002, written with Dan S. Cohen), he summarizes what he has learned. His basic message is very much like ours. Too many change initiatives fail because they rely too much on "data gathering, analysis, report writing, and presentations" instead of a more creative approach aimed at grabbing the "feelings that motivate useful action." In other words, change agents fail when they rely almost entirely on reason and structure and neglect human, political, and symbolic elements.

Kotter describes eight stages that he repeatedly found in successful change initiatives:

1. Creating a sense of urgency
2. Pulling together a guiding team with the needed skills, credibility, connections, and authority to move things along

3. Creating an uplifting vision and strategy

4. Communicating the vision and strategy through a combination of words, deeds, and symbols

5. Removing obstacles, or empowering people to move ahead

6. Producing visible signs of progress through short-term victories

7. Sticking with the process and refusing to quit when things get tough

8. Nurturing and shaping a new culture to support the emerging innovative ways

Kotter's stages are a model of a change process moving through time, though not necessarily unfolding in a linear sequence. In the real world, stages overlap, and change agents sometimes need to cycle back to earlier phases.

Combining Kotter's stages with the four frames generates the model presented in Table 18.2 (pp. 386–87). The table lists each of Kotter's stages and illustrates possible actions that change agents might take. Not every frame is essential to each stage, but all are critical to success. Consider, for example, Kotter's first stage, developing a sense of urgency. Strategies from the human resource, political, and symbolic strategies all contribute. Symbolically, leaders can construct a persuasive story by painting a picture of the current challenge or crisis and why failure to act would be catastrophic. Human resource techniques of participation and open meetings would help to get the story out and gauge audience reaction. Behind the scenes, leaders could meet with key players, assess their interests, and negotiate or use power as necessary to get people on board.

As another example, Kotter's fifth step calls for removing obstacles and empowering people to move forward. Structurally, this is a matter of identifying rules, roles, procedures, and patterns blocking progress and then working to realign them. Meanwhile, the human resource frame counsels training and providing support and resources to enable people to master new behaviors. Symbolically, a few "public hangings" (for example, firing, demoting, or exiling prominent opponents) could reinforce the message.

Table 18.2 is intended to be illustrative and suggestive, not exhaustive. Every situation and change effort is unique. Creative change agents can use the ideas to stimulate thinking and spur imagination as they develop an approach that fits local circumstances.

TEAM ZEBRA: THE REST OF THE STORY

In Chapter Three, we examined the successful restructuring of Kodak's Black-and-White Film Division. The storyline there attributed much of the division's success to structural improvements: integrated flows, performance measures and standards, cross-functional teams, lateral coordination, local decision making. These changes contributed substantially to the division's ability to reduce inventory, cut waste, improve relations with suppliers, and speed delivery time. All improvements paved the way for the division's transformation and return to profitability.

There is more to the story. Structural changes were necessary but not sufficient. Reengineering guru Michael Hammer, noting the disappointing outcomes of many restructuring efforts, acknowledged that there is more to change than redesigning process and structure. Team Zebra exemplifies an integrated multiframe approach to change.

Top-down, Bottom-up Structural Design

The division's first structural overhaul in a century was announced at a meeting for all employees. The shock was lessened by assurances that the initial changes were experimental, and that more substantive changes would appear gradually over a six-month period. This gave employees an opportunity to shape the initiative to fit local working conditions. Reasons for the change were clearly explained and reinforced by management, which had earlier learned in very graphic terms of the division's poor performance record from Jim Frangos, the divisional manager:

> During a special meeting convened one warm day in September, I rattled off my list of performance shockers to the Zebra managers. The reaction was one of disbelief and anger. "How could we have been kept in the dark so long?" People demanded to know. During my talk I boiled the issue down to the bitter problems that deeply eroded profit margins and made us dinosaurs in the marketplace.
>
> "You know about all the waste problems," I said. "But did you know we can't sell one-third of everything we make? We load up 1,000 dump trucks with wasted products every year."
>
> A whistle of disbelief broke the ensuing silence.

TABLE 18.2. Reframing Kotter's Change Stages.

Kotter's Stage of Change	Structural Frame	Human Resource Frame	Political Frame	Symbolic Frame
1. *Sense of urgency*		Involve people throughout organization; solicit input	Network with key players; use power base	Tell a compelling story
2. *Guiding team*	Develop coordination strategy	Team building for guiding team	Stack team with credible, influential members	Put commanding officer on team
3. *Uplifting vision and strategy*	Implementation plan		Map political terrain; develop agenda	Craft a hopeful vision of future rooted in organization history
4. *Communicate vision and strategy through words, deeds, and symbols*	Create structures to support change process	Meetings to communicate direction, get feedback	Create arenas; build alliances; defuse opposition	Visible leadership involvement; kickoff ceremonies

5. *Remove obstacles and empower*	Remove or alter structures, procedures that support the old ways	Provide training, resources, and support		Public hangings of counterrevolutionaries
6. *Early wins*	Plan for short-term victories		Invest resources, power to ensure early wins	Celebrate and communicate early signs of progress
7. *Keep going when going gets tough*	Keep people on plan			Revival meetings
8. *New culture to support new ways*	Align structure to new culture	Create a "culture" team; broad involvement in developing culture		Mourn the past; celebrate heroes of the revolution; share stories of the journey

"Imagine a consumer product company or automobile manufacturer tossing out one-third of its product—they'd be out of business in no time flat! Can you think of *any* organization that can survive that level of waste?" "Yeah, the federal government," someone called out from the back of the room.

That started a spate of laughter, and took the edge off the meeting. I wanted people to feel concerned, but not personally threatened. (Frangos, 1996, pp. 65–66)

This opening round is a good example of the first stage in Kotter's model of change: building a sense of urgency. The managers learned that half their finished product sat in inventory, only 10 percent of their products were improved each year, the percentage of work performed during the manufacturing process was about one percent, and they were able to deliver products on time in only 66 percent of the cases. At the end of the meeting, some one asked angrily, "How have we managed to stay afloat so long?" (Frangos, 1996, p. 67).

The shared sense of crisis, combined with an opportunity for everyone to fine-tune and tinker with the radical new design, helped to realign roles and relationships so the new structure worked for, rather than against, people's efforts. Responsibility for shaping and implementing change was widely shared: "Mary Cutcliffe, an emulsion-making operator, went to have her foot x-rayed and discovered her physician was not using Kodak film. She asked him why. He said he didn't think a company the size of Kodak would care about a small town physician like himself. Upon returning to work she asked 'why not'? Her question led to a plan to focus aggressively on doctors with in-house labs (Frangos, 1996, p. 120).

Zack Potter, on a family vacation, overheard a photographer complain about Kodak's poor service. When he returned, he spent his morning break and lunch hour trying to find out who was responsible. That afternoon the photographer received a call with the needed information (Frangos, 1996, pp.120–121).

Learning and Training

The division made available several kinds of training. Technical training helped people master new skills needed for changing work patterns. Supervisors, the often overlooked linchpin in any transition from old to new, found ample opportunity to meet with colleagues for training and "peer learning": "In our case we had a hundred year heritage of the drill sergeant model, and many of our first-line supervisors were 20–25 year veterans of the company. We took into account that asking people to adopt new ways of doing their jobs is a threatening proposition, and asking them to relinquish the authority they have 'earned' can seem downright outrageous—unless you can offer them something better. In our case, the 'something better' was a set of unprecedented opportunities; the opportunity to have a greater influence over people through enlightened coaching and teaching" (Frangos, 1996, p. 200).

Supervisors and other employees were given the opportunity to learn new skills in a supportive, psychologically safe environment: "Peer learning is critical, because everyone makes faster gains when they learn from one another. There's also a critical mass phenomenon—when enough first-line supervisors are reporting about their acts of coaching and facilitating, others will feel safe trying the 'new style.'" (Frangos, 1996, p. 200).

First-time supervisors and other were included with the management team in Pecos River experimental learning—training in team building: "The Pecos course turned out to be an ingenious blend of talk, music, high energy exercises, offered in an upbeat and emotionally charged atmosphere. Through experiential learning, the Pecos program helps people to uncover buried layers of creativity, and to relate in new ways to others with whom they might have worked side by side for many years but never have really come to know" (Frangos, 1996, p. 169).

Apart from formal training, the idea that people can learn new skills from their own experience on the job and from others looms as one of Team Zebra's greatest human resource insights. Informal learning groups become unofficial resources anyone can turn to for suggestions on how to improve their performance. As people mastered a particular aspect of the new order of things, a premium was put on sharing (or even stealing) new ideas from others: "Our catch phrase for this sharing of knowledge was to 'steal shamelessly but to remember to say thank you.' Through B&W Views [a division newsletter] and informal seminars put on by [employees], the flow management made a concerted effort to broadcast our success stories. At the same time, people were encouraged to aggressively seek innovative solutions in one part of the flow and then employ them in their own" (Frangos, 1996, p. 182).

Arenas for Venting Conflict

From the early launching of the project, a variety of occasions created arenas or forums for airing people's concerns and grievances. The initiatives changed people's roles, relationships, titles, locations, and working conditions. They threatened a long Kodak tradition of job security. In 1989, even before anything became operational, Jim Frangos convened a series of town meetings to hear all employees' reactions to the planned changes:

> The first of the town meetings was closer to the terrible end of the spectrum than I had hoped. Although I had steeled myself for the worst, I was still taken by surprise by the amount of anger and hostility that erupted like a furious volcano. . . . In hindsight my straight talk sessions were the first opportunity for the shop floor folks to speak their minds since the company began taking a battering in the Spring. Many were suspicious and completely distrustful of another desperate attempt on management's part to save the company. Some were convinced that they were going to be scapegoats for top management's poor judgment. So for the first month of straight talks I just resigned myself to getting skinned alive as I tried to sell the flow and the improvements it would bring." (Frangos, 1996, pp. 68–69)

The employees' negativity continued even though they were encouraged to get everything off their chest. Reactions to Frangos after the meetings included "The dude is nuts." "What's he been smoking?" "Turnaround? He probably can't even parallel park." "Does he think we're drunk or something?" "What's this 'fun' crap he keeps talking about? Glad I don't have to spend *my* fun off with him" (Frangos, 1996, p. 69).

Later, in 1990, Frangos scheduled a second round of what were now officially labeled Straight Talks. His wife asked him if he was a glutton for punishment. But Frangos knew that, even though the changes were moving along, anger remained. He was putting Kotter's stage seven into practice: he kept going when the going got tough. In the twenty-five or so sessions for all fifteen hundred B&W employees, he found people far less concerned about venting and more interested in "how things were going and what they could do to become part of the solution to our problems" (Frangos, 1996, p. 130).

In the second round, sessions moved beyond politics to encompass the social value of B&W's efforts. As Frangos put it, "I worked hard to reinforce the theme that we were making products important to society. At one meeting, I described Kodak CFT Film, which is used to determine if a patient needs bypass surgery, and Kodak MIN-RH Film, used in the detection of breast cancer. . . . At another I talked about Kodak WL Surveillance Film. Guess what? Every time you use your ATM card, you're being photographed with a camera loaded with 2210 film. Same if you're robbing the bank. Smile for the cameras" (Frangos, 1996, p. 130).

Occasions for Letting Go and Celebrating

Frangos's appeal to the deep purpose of B&W's operation highlights another impressive aspect of the division's turnaround: attention to symbols and culture. A change in physical arrangements was used to symbolize the management team's openness to dialogue: "I think we'd send a strong message to everyone if we got rid of the planning walls and used partitions instead. . . . We've been talking about a cross functional team—why not make the office a symbol of an organization without walls?" (Frangos, 1996, p. 71).

A central symbolic challenge in any transformation is helping people let go of old ways. Team Zebra's mourning rituals centered on humor and fun. Yet the subtext of outwardly zany occasions allowed sadness as well as playfulness. Humor is a powerful tool in making transitions. The line between laughing and crying is often subtle. Frangos understood that people would not let go until they could attach themselves to other symbols. In the liminal state between release and capture, celebration can serve dual purposes: mourning and meaning making. Team Zebra presents several poignant examples of how symbols and symbolic activity ease the passage from old to new.

KEEPING AN EYE ON CORE VALUES. "Attitudes and morale can't change unless people believe what they're doing has intrinsic worth to the market place, and makes a contribution to other people's lives" (Frangos, 1996, p. 70).

ENCOURAGING RITUAL. Forum meetings, Breakfast Clubs, and other regular gatherings were opportunities for bonding: "The Breakfast Club had become one of the most exciting aspects of the flow. But Team Zebra still needed some kind of 'glue' that would bind the flow together and create a strong feeling of unity. That 'glue' came in the form of a shared vision and the articulation of a set of values and principles to live and work by" (Frangos, 1996, p. 84).

ANCHORING VISION EMBODIED IN METAPHOR AND SYMBOLS. In one meeting the management team chose animals as metaphoric representatives of B&W's unity. One manager chose the mongoose: "One of its claims to fame is being able to defeat and devour poisonous snakes. In fact, I've thrown a few of our competitors down here . . . those snakes in the corner . . . the mongoose is extremely quick . . . tenacious, too. They just keep chipping away at whatever they're working on, just like us" (Frangos, 1996, p. 86).

Visioning experiences led to development of a division logo, "Images of Excellence": a black diamond on one edge with lines passing throughout it. But the superglue, the galvanizing symbol that pulled B&W's fifteen hundred people together, was the zebra. The idea of making the zebra the division mascot crystallized in 1990 during a Secretary's Day excursion to the zoo. As the visitors were admiring two adults and a baby, the zoo director told them: "Every zebra is unique. No two zebras stripes are the same—kind of like fingerprints. They also run in herds. Being animals that are preyed upon, they understand that to the extent they can stay together, they can defend themselves from lions and other predators. In fact, predators probably have a hard time distinguishing the individuals from the mass of black and white stripes" (Frangos, 1996, p. 126).

The visitors picked up on the analogy, observing that each B&W employee brings something unique to the herd. "We need to band together as part of a team—when we're operating as such we 'baffle the competition'" (Frangos, 1996, p. 126). The B&W group became Team Zebra, and in following years the zebra was everywhere.

INVENTING CEREMONIES TO KEEP TEAM SPIRIT HIGH. Numerous skits and awards ceremonies were playful occasions featuring music and merriment. The Whirling Dervish award, for example, honored the group with the best success each month in reducing inventory. The award and trophy (a toy pinwheel mounted on a block of wood) were both invented by employees. "Each month, after reviewing the inventory figures, Bill would announce the team with the best improvement and present the pinwheel. After one group won it three times in a row, the group's managers decided not to 'hog the wheel.' He had the machine shop make a permanent, windmill-like whirling dervish, complete with a plaque. He then relinquished the award for others to enjoy (Frangos, 1996, p. 134).

Another example was a meeting of Zebra's leadership group to review the first year's progress: "The entire workshop was dotted with songs and skits commemorating the first year. Marty, Tim, and Chip had written a number of skits and songs, with Marty playing the keyboard and Rick accompanying her on the banjo. We poked fun at ourselves in a playful way about moving from being victims to being accountable for the results we generated. And as a cap for the event, we donned sweatshirts bearing our new logo and took a team picture. We then had a funeral for the ways of the past" (Frangos, 1996, p. 17).

CONCLUSION

Major organizational change inevitably generates four categories of issues. First, it affects individuals' ability to feel effective, valued, and in control. Without support, training, and a chance to participate in the process, people become a powerful anchor, making forward motion almost impossible. Second, change disrupts existing patterns of roles and relationships, producing confusion and uncertainty. Structural patterns need to be revised and realigned to support the new direction.

Third, change creates conflict between winners and losers—those who benefit from the new direction and those who do not. This conflict requires creation of arenas where the issues can be renegotiated and the political map redrawn. Finally, change creates loss of meaning for recipients rather than owners of the change. Transition rituals, mourning the past, and celebrating the future help people let go of old attachments and embrace new ways of doing things.

Kotter's model of successive change includes eight stages: (1) developing urgency; (2) creating a guiding team; (3) developing an inspirational vision and strategy; (4) communicating through words, deeds, and symbols; (5) removing obstacles and empowering change agents; (6) creating early wins; (7) persisting when things get tough; and (8) shaping a new and supportive culture. Integrated with the frames, Kotter's model offers a well-orchestrated, integrated design responding to needs for learning, realignment, negotiation, and grieving.

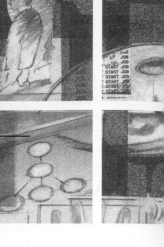

CHAPTER 19

Reframing Ethics and Spirit

What shall an organization profit if it should gain the world but lose its soul?[1] In the case of Enron, the answer was "not much"; the company eventually lost both its soul and what it hoped to gain. As noted earlier, Enron was America's largest gas pipeline company when Kenneth Lay took over as chief executive in 1985. At the time, it was a solid but not an exciting business. Its size and cost structure made it a strong competitor in its industry, but demand was flat, and gas had been in oversupply for several years (Bodily and Bruner, 2002). Deregulation loomed on the horizon, creating both threats and opportunities. Lay, as smart as he was genial, did what CEOs are expected to do: he looked for ways to grow the business and increase the share price. For more than fifteen years, he was remarkably successful. A once-sleepy company became the world's largest energy-trading business, and Enron's market value grew from \$2 billion in 1985 to \$70 billion in mid-2001.

Most of the excitement at Enron was generated by a new and very different business model. No longer content just to pump gas through pipes, the company redefined itself as a merchant, a deal maker in a variety of commodities. Initially, the focus was energy, but Enron gradually expanded into areas as diverse as broadband and an esoteric form of weather insurance. By 2000, the old pipelines represented only about a fifth of Enron's revenues and profits. Much of the rest came from the new "merchant" businesses, which attracted a new breed of Enron employees: bright, young fast-trackers with advanced degrees in business and finance.

The stable pipeline business was run by managers with years of industry experience. Reliability and operating efficiency were the keys to success. Pay was linked to seniority.

The new trading operations carried much higher risks, which brought Enron into the business equivalent of the Wild West. There were big rewards for aggressive gunslingers with the guts and smarts to grab whatever was there to be taken. Enron's old pay system gave way to big bonuses and stock options for high performers. This was topped off with corporate jets and lavish parties adorned by $500 bottles of champagne and strippers who cost even more (Roberts and Thomas, 2002). As James O'Toole, of the University of Southern California, put it, "At Enron, you had a bunch of kids running loose without adult supervision" (Byrne, France, and Zellner, 2002, p. 1).

It's easy to catch gold fever in a mining town during a boom, and many of Enron's aggressive young pioneers were stricken. One was Timothy Belden, the thirty-four-year-old head of Enron's energy trading office in Portland, Oregon. Belden earned bonuses totaling close to $5 million in 2001. A year later, he agreed to give some of it to the state of California, pleading guilty to illegal manipulation of California's energy crisis: "In the plea Belden admitted to working with others on trading tactics that effectively transformed California's complex system for buying and transmitting energy into a fictional world, complete with bogus transmission schedules, imaginary congestion on power lines and fraudulent sales of 'out of state' energy that in fact came from California itself" (Eichenwald and Richtel, 2002, p. C1).

When some of Enron's new mines produced only fool's gold, the company's financial wizards tried to keep the party going. Fancy financial maneuvers inflated revenue and hid debt, mostly by selling assets to supposedly independent partnerships controlled by Enron's chief financial officer, Andrew Fastow. The partnerships borrowed the money from banks or brokerages, and Enron guaranteed the loans (Eichenwald, 2002b). Moving money from one pocket to another made Enron's financial statements look good temporarily, but eventually the off-balance-sheet shenanigans came home to roost, and the company imploded.

At the heart of this tragedy is the company's loss of any sense of what it was and what it stood for. As Arie De Geus puts it, companies "need profits in the same way as any living being needs oxygen. It is a necessity to stay alive, but it is not the purpose of life" (De Geus, 1995, p. 29). Enron's story is far from unique. Over the years, corporate scandals have recurred in organizations around the world. What can managers and organizations do about this abysmal state of ethics in management? We argue in this chapter that ethics must rest in "soul," a sense of identity that defines an individual or an organization's core beliefs and values. We discuss why soul is important and how it sustains ethical behavior. Then we present a four-frame view of the ethics of leadership.

SOUL AND SPIRIT IN ORGANIZATIONS

What Enron lacked becomes obvious by comparing it to the pharmaceutical giant Merck, one of America's most successful firms. Merck states its core purpose as preserving and improving human life, not making a profit. A noble sentiment, but is it actually reflected in key decisions and everyday behavior? Merck can point to a number of instances of selling a drug at a loss, or giving it away, to fulfill the company's core value of putting patients first. In one famous example, Merck had to decide whether to develop and distribute a drug for river blindness, an affliction of the poor in many Third World countries. Cost-benefit analysis was clear: the drug had little chance of making money. For companies with an eye fixed on the bottom line, such a decision would be a no-brainer. Merck developed the drug, anyway, and then gave it away free. Merck's statement of purpose made the decision easy, the CEO said afterwards. In contrast, "the woods were filled with smart people at Enron, but there were really no wise people, or people who could say 'this is enough'" (Olson, cited in Eichenwald, 2002a, p. 26). Without foresight, Enron lost its soul in the race for innovation, growth, and a rising share price.

Many would scoff at the notion that organizations can have soul, but there is growing evidence that it is a critical element in long-run success. A dictionary definition of soul uses terms such as "animating force," "immaterial essence," and "spiritual nature." For an organization, group, or family, soul can also be viewed as a bedrock sense of identity, a deep confidence about who we are, what we care about, and what we deeply believe in. Merck had it. Enron did not.

Who cares? Why should a company, a school, or a public agency be concerned about soul? Many organizations and most management writers ignore the topic. As an example, two bestsellers on strategy, Treacy and Wiersema's *The Discipline of Market Leaders* (1995) and Hamel and Prahalad's *Competing for the Future* (1994), link the enormous success of Southwest Airlines to its strategic prowess. Southwest's results have certainly been impressive. From the mid-1980s until 2001, when founder Herb Kelleher retired as CEO, it was the most profitable company in the U.S. airline industry by a wide margin. It was the only major carrier that continued to be profitable in the brutal climate following the September 11 attacks; Southwest was still growing as United Airlines was declaring bankruptcy. Was strategy at the heart of the company's success?

Not in Herb Kelleher's mind. He offered a very different explanation for what makes Southwest work, one that features people, humor, love, and soul. "Simply put, Kelleher 'cherishes and respects' his 18,000 employees [now over twenty-five thousand], and his 'love' is returned in what he calls 'a spontaneous, voluntary overflowing of emotion'" (Farkas and De Backer, 1996, p. 87).

Kelleher's style was undoubtedly distinctive: "Kelleher has been known to sing 'Tea for Two' in front of 4,000 employees while wearing bloomers and a bonnet at a company picnic (featuring a chili cook-off). He regularly helps flight attendants serve drinks and peanuts when he flies. One Easter, he walked a plane's aisle clad in an Easter bunny outfit, and one St. Patrick's Day he dressed as a leprechaun. When Southwest started a new route to Sacramento, Kelleher sang a rap song at a press conference with two people in Teenage Mutant Ninja costumes and two others dressed as tomatoes" (Levering and Moskowitz, 1993, p. 413).

Kelleher claimed the most important group in the company was the "Culture Committee," a seventy-person cross-section of employees established to perpetuate the company's values and spirit. His charge to the committee was to "carry the spiritual message of Southwest Airlines" (Farkas and De Backer, 1996, p. 93).

Spiritual message? Love? From a CEO notorious for his addiction to cigarettes and bourbon? There are plenty of skeptics. A competing airline executive grumbled, "Southwest runs on Herb's bullshit" (Petzinger, 1995, p. 284). But there are many other successful leaders who embrace a philosophy much like Kelleher's. Ben Cohen, cofounder of the ice cream company Ben and Jerry's Homemade, observes: "Businesses tend to exploit communities and their workers, and that wasn't the way I thought the game should be played. I thought it should be the opposite—that because the business is allowed to be there in the first place, the business ought to support the community. What we're finding is that when you support the community, the community supports you back. When you give love, you receive love. I maintain that there is a spiritual dimension to business just as there is to the lives of individuals" (Levering and Moskowitz, 1993, p. 47).

Granted, Herb Kelleher and Ben Cohen are colorful, but organizational success may not require the CEO to dress up as the Easter Bunny or an Eastern mystic. (Cohen occasionally appeared at company celebrations in the person of Habeeni Ben Coheeni—whose stomach was the "mound of round" on which partner Jerry Greenfield broke cinder blocks with a sledge hammer.) An understated counterpoint to such high jinks is Aaron Feuerstein, president of the textile manufacturer Malden Mills in Massachusetts. Feuerstein astounded everyone, most of all his workforce, after fire wiped out most of his plant in December 1995. The next day, he announced that all three thousand of his workers would remain on the payroll for the following month. In January, he announced he would pay them for another month, and he extended the offer again in February. "The second time was a shock. It was the third time that brought tears to everyone's eyes" (Ryan, 1996, p. 4). By March, most employees were back on the job.

Feuerstein's generosity went against the advice of members of his board and cost him several million dollars. But he felt a responsibility to both workers and community. He quoted Hillel, a first-century Talmudic scholar: "Not all who increase their wealth are wise." Said Feuerstein, "If you think the only function of a CEO is to increase the wealth of shareholders, then any time he spends on Scripture or Shakespeare or the arts is wasteful. But if you think the CEO must balance responsibilities, then he should be involved with ideas that connect him with the past, the present and the future" (Ryan, 1996, p. 5).

Growing evidence suggests that tapping a deeper level of human energy pays off. Malden Mills was back in production faster than anyone expected, despite unusually bad winter weather. "Our people became very creative," said Feuerstein. "They were willing to work 25 hours a day." Collins and Porras (1994) and De Geus (1995) both found that a central characteristic of corporations that achieved outstanding, long-term success was a core ideology emphasizing "more than profits" (Collins and Porras, 1994, p. 48) and offering "guidance and inspiration to people inside the company" (Collins and Porras, 1994, p. 88). When they are authentic and lived, such core ideologies—love at Southwest, preserving human life at Merck—give a company soul.

Soul and ethics are inextricably intertwined. Recent decades have regularly produced scandals in which major corporations were found to have engaged in unethical, if not illegal, conduct. It happened in the 1980s, often characterized at the time as a decade of remarkable greed and corruption in business. It happened again with the spate of scandals in 2001 and 2002. Efforts to do something about the apparently abysmal state of "ethics" in management have ebbed and flowed as scandals come and go. One strand of such initiatives has spotlighted ethics as a topic in professional training programs. A second strand has emphasized corporate ethics statements. A third has pushed for stronger legal and regulatory requirements, such as the Foreign Corrupt Practices Act, which forbids U.S. corporations from bribing foreign officials to get business or retain it.

All these are important initiatives, but they do not go deep enough. Solomon (1993) calls for an "Aristotelian ethic":

> There is too little sense of business as itself enjoyable (the main virtue of the "game" metaphor), that business is not a matter of vulgar self-interest but of vital community interest, that the virtues on which one prides oneself in personal life are essentially the same as those essential to good business—honesty, dependability, courage, loyalty, integrity. Aristotle's central ethical concept, accordingly, is a unified, all-embracing notion of "happiness" (or, more accurately, *eudaimonia,* perhaps better translated as "flourishing" or "doing well"). The point is to view one's life as a whole and not separate the personal and the public or professional, or duty and pleasure. (p. 105)

Solomon chose the term *Aristotelian* in part "because it makes no pretensions of presenting something very new, the latest 'cutting-edge' theory or technique of management, but rather reminds us of something very old, a perspective and a debate going all the way back to ancient times. The idea is not to infuse corporate life with one more excuse for brutal changes, a new wave of experts and seminars and yet another downsizing bloodbath. It is to emphasize the importance of continuity and stability, clearness of vision and constancy of purpose, corporate loyalty and individual integrity" (Solomon, 1993, p. 104).

Solomon reminds us that ethics and soul are central to both the good life and the good organization. The world's philosophical and spiritual traditions offer much wisdom to guide us in our search for better ways to live life and conduct business. We have presented the four frames as lenses for understanding and tools for influencing organizations. The heads and hands of leaders are vitally important. But so are their hearts and souls. In this chapter, we examine the implications of the frames for organizations as ethical communities and for the moral responsibilities of leadership. Table 19.1 summarizes our view.

TABLE 19.1. Reframing Ethics.

Metaphor	Organizational Ethic	Leadership Contribution
Factory	Excellence	Authorship
Extended family	Caring	Love
Jungle	Justice	Power
Temple	Faith	Significance

THE FACTORY: EXCELLENCE AND AUTHORSHIP

One of our oldest images of organizations is that of factories engaged in a production process. Raw materials (steel, peanuts, or five-year-olds) come in the door and leave as finished products (refrigerators, peanut butter, or educated citizens). The ethical imperative of the factory is excellence: ensuring work is done as well and efficiently as possible to produce high-quality output. Since the publication of Peters and Waterman's famous book, almost everyone has claimed to be searching for excellence, though there are more than enough flawed products and mediocre services to make it clear that not everyone's quest has been successful.

One cause of disappointment is failure to recognize that excellence requires much more than sermons from top management; it requires commitment and autonomy at all levels of the organization. How do leaders foster such commitment? Bolman and Deal (2001, p. 106) maintain that "leading is giving. Leadership is an ethic, a gift of oneself." Critical for creating and maintaining excellence is the gift of authorship:

> Giving authorship provides space within boundaries. In an orchestra, musicians develop individual parts within the parameters of a particular musical score and the interpretative challenges posed by the conductor. Authorship turns the pyramid on its side. Leaders increase their influence and build more productive organizations. Workers experience the satisfactions of creativity, craftsmanship and a job well done. Gone is the traditional adversarial relationship in which superiors try to increase control while subordinates resist them at every turn.

Trusting people to solve problems generates higher levels of motivation and better solutions. The leader's responsibility is to create conditions that promote authorship. Individuals need to see their work as meaningful and worthwhile, to feel personally accountable for the consequences of their efforts, and to get feedback that lets them know the results. (Bolman and Deal, 2001, pp. 111–112)

We can see authorship in an example from Motorola. Stung by a comment from one of its officers that "Our quality stinks!" the company embarked on one of the world's most ambitious and successful quality improvement efforts. The successful initiative added some $3.2 billion to Motorola's bottom line between 1987 and 1992 (Waterman, 1994, p. 229). Central to the effort was extensive training and empowerment for front-line workers. One of them was Hossain Rasoli, a technician who worked on power transformers. Before the quality program, he wondered how the product was doing in the field but never knew. As part of the new initiative, he was given a level of responsibility he never had before: a charge to improve product quality. "I call it my baby," he says, pointing to the power amplifier. "I take pride in this product. If it fails in the field, I feel hurt, or I get depressed" (Waterman, 1994, p. 245). Rasoli used his training in problem solving and statistical process control to determine the power amplifier's weakest components. He then went to development engineering and asked them to redesign the parts. The result was a 400 percent improvement in reliability. One manager said of Rasoli, "He is now recognized as Mr. PA (power amplifier). He knows more about this product than any designer, any vendor, any manager, anyone else" (Waterman, 1994, p. 246).

Southwest Airlines offers another unique image of authorship. Its associates are encouraged to be themselves; have fun; and, above all, use their sense of humor. Only on Southwest are you likely to hear required FAA safety briefings sung to the music of a popular song or delivered as a stand-up comedy routine. ("Those of you who wish to smoke will please file out to our lounge on the wing, where you can enjoy our feature film, *Gone with the Wind*.") Too frivolous for something as weighty as a safety announcement? Just the opposite: it's a way to get passengers to pay attention to an announcement they usually ignore. Surely, it's also a way for flight attendants to have fun and feel some authorship.

One of Saturn's greatest accomplishments has been giving autoworkers a feeling they put a signature as well as a fender or windshield wiper on a new car. Saturn employees frequently telephone customers to ask how they enjoy their car. If they see a Saturn stopped along a road, they volunteer assistance. Said one Saturn worker, "When given a chance, everyone would prefer to build a superior automobile. At Saturn, they give us that chance."

THE FAMILY: CARING AND LOVE

Caring—one person's compassion and concern for another—is both the purpose and the ethical glue that holds a family together. Parents care for children and, eventually, children care for their parents. A caring family or community requires servant leaders who serve the best interests of its members and stakeholders. This implies a profound and challenging responsibility for leaders to understand the needs and concerns of community members so as to serve the best interests of individuals and the community as a whole. The gift of the servant leader is love.

Love is largely absent from the modern corporation. Most managers would never use the word in any context more profound than their feelings about food, films, or games. They shy away from love's deeper meanings, fearing both its power and its risks. Caring begins with knowing; it requires listening, understanding, and accepting. It progresses through a deepening sense of appreciation, respect, and ultimately love. Love is a willingness to reach out and open one's heart. An open heart is vulnerable. Confronting vulnerability allows us to drop our mask, meet heart to heart and be present for one another. We experience a sense of unity and delight in those voluntary, human exchanges that mold "the soul of community" (Whitmyer, 1993, p. 81).

They talk openly about love at Southwest Airlines. They fly out of Love Field in Dallas; their symbol on the New York Stock Exchange is LUV; the employee newsletter is called *Luv Lines*; and their twentieth anniversary slogan was "20 Years of Loving You" (Levering and Moskowitz, 1993). As described in an earlier chapter, they hold an annual "Heroes of the Heart" ceremony to honor members of the Southwest family who have gone above and beyond even Southwest's high standards of duty. There are, of course, ups and downs in any family, and the airline industry certainly brings both good days and bad. Through life's peaks and valleys, love holds people together in a caring community. A Southwest employee said, "Herb loves us. We love Herb. We love one another. We love the company. One of the primary beneficiaries of our collective caring is our passengers."

For Levi Strauss, the issue of caring came to a head in trying to apply the company's ethical principles (honesty, fairness, respect for others, compassion, promise keeping, and integrity) to the thorny dilemmas of working with foreign subcontractors. How should the company balance concern for domestic employees with concern for overseas workers? Even if pay and working conditions at foreign subcontractors are below those in the United States, are inferior jobs better than no jobs? A task force set to work to collect data and formulate guidelines for ethical practice. Ultimately, the company wound up making some tough decisions. It pulled out of China because of human rights abuses, despite the huge long-term market potential there. In a factory in Bangladesh employing underage children, Levi's arranged for the children to go back to school while the contractor continued to pay their salaries (Waterman, 1994).

THE JUNGLE: JUSTICE AND POWER

We turn now to a third image: the organization as jungle. Woody Allen captured the competitive, predator-prey imagery succinctly with the observation that "The lion and the calf shall lie down together, but the calf won't get much sleep." As the image implies, the jungle is a politically charged world of conflict and underregulated pursuit of self-interest. Politics and politicians are routinely viewed as objects of scorn. Is there any ethical obligation associated with the political frame? We believe there is: the duty of justice. In a world of competing interests and scarce resources, we are continually compelled to make trade-offs. We cannot give everyone everything they want, but we can honor a value of fairness in making decisions about who gets what. Solomon (1993, p. 231) sees justice as the ultimate virtue in corporations, because fairness—the perception that employees, customers, and investors are all getting their due—is the glue that holds things together.

In a world of people and groups with divergent interests and worldviews, justice is never easy to define, and disagreement about criteria is inevitable. The key gift that leaders can offer is power. People with a voice in key decisions are far more likely to feel a sense of justice than those with no seat at the table. Leaders who hoard power produce powerless organizations. People stripped of power look for ways to fight back: sabotage, passive resistance, withdrawal, or angry militancy. Giving power liberates energy for more productive use. If people have a sense of efficacy and an ability to influence their world, they seek to be productive. They direct their energy and intelligence toward making a contribution rather than making trouble.

The gift of power enrolls people in working toward a common cause. It also creates difficult choice points. If leaders clutch power too tightly, they activate old patterns of antagonism. But if they cave in and say yes to anything, they put the organizational mission at risk (Bolman and Deal, 2001).

Authorship and power are related; autonomy, space, and freedom are important in both. Yet there is an important difference. Artists, authors, and craftspeople can experience authorship even working alone. Power, in contrast, is meaningful only in relation to others. It is the capacity to influence others and get things to happen on a broader scale. Authorship without power is isolating and splintering; power without authorship can be dysfunctional and oppressive.

The gift of power is important at multiple levels: the individual, the group, and the organization. At the individual level, people want power to influence their immediate work environment and the factors that impinge on them. Many traditional workplaces still suffocate their employees with time clocks, rigid rules, and authoritarian bosses. Consider again Hossain Rasoli, Motorola's Mr. Power Amplifier. Putting his own signature on the product gave him a sense of authorship. His ability to persuade others in the organization gave him power as well. In one case, Rasoli was so distressed that he went to a vice president to complain because the purchasing department planned to bring in a new vendor on a particular component. Rasoli was very firm: "You're not going to put this in my product" (Waterman, 1994, p. 246). He won.

At Saturn, workers' power is symbolized by "the rope," which is actually a chain with a handle, hanging at regular intervals along the assembly line. Anyone who sees a deviation from Saturn's high standards is authorized to pull the rope and stop the line. One Saturn worker remembered with pride the day he pulled the rope: "It wasn't a major thing. Just a broken retainer clip. In the old (GM) world it had to be a life or death issue. At Saturn, they've given us the rope to do the job right, to build a car we can all be proud of."

At the group level, a challenge in organizations and societies around the world is responding to ethnic, racial, and gender diversity. Gallos and Ramsey (1997, pp. 215) get to the heart of the complexity: "Institutional, structural and systemic issues are very difficult for members of dominant groups to understand. Systems are most often designed by dominant group members to meet their own needs. It is then difficult to see the ways in which our institutions and structures systematically exclude others who are not 'like us.' It is hard to see and question what we have always taken for granted and painful to confront personal complicity in maintaining the status quo. Privilege enables us to remain unaware of institutional and social forces and their impact."

Justice requires that leaders systematically enhance the power of subdominant groups—ensuring access to decision making, creating internal advocacy groups, building diversity into information and incentive systems, and strengthening career opportunities (Cox, 1994; Gallos and Ramsey, 1997; Morrison, 1992). All this happens only if there is a rock-solid commitment from top management; this is the one condition that Morrison (1992) found to be universal in organizations that were leaders in responding to diversity.

Another version of the justice/power issue can be seen in Southwest's relationship with its unions. A labor union's central purpose is to give employees power—a voice in decisions affecting them—but this process is regularly distorted by unproductive labor-management conflict. Kelleher believed in starting with the premise that the purpose of bargaining is to give workers not as little as possible but as much as possible, while still enabling the company to prosper in the long run. After all, he said, they help make the company work. They should share in the profits.

THE TEMPLE: FAITH AND SIGNIFICANCE

An organization, like a temple, can be seen as a sacred place, an expression of human aspirations, a monument to faith in human possibility. A temple is a gathering place for a community of people with shared traditions, values, and beliefs. Members of a community may be diverse in many ways (age, background, economic status, personal interests), but they are held together by shared faith and a spiritual commitment to one another. In work organizations, faith is strengthened if individuals feel the organization is characterized by excellence, caring, and justice. Above all, they must feel that the organization is doing something worth doing—the work is a calling that adds something of value to the world. Significance is partly about work itself, but even more about how the work is understood. This point is made by an old story about three stonemasons giving an account of their work. The first said he was "cutting stone." The second reported that he was "building a cathedral." The third said simply that he was "serving God."

Temples need spiritual leaders. This does not mean promoting religion or a particular theology, but bringing a genuine concern for the human spirit. The dictionary defines *spirit* as "the intelligent or immaterial part of man," "the animating or vital principal in living things," and "the moral nature of humanity." Spiritual leaders help people find meaning and faith in work and help them answer fundamental questions that have confronted humans of every time and place: Who am I as an individual? Who are we as a people? What is the purpose of my life, of our collective life? What ethical principles should we follow? What legacy will we leave?

Spiritual leaders offer the gift of significance, rooted in confidence that the work is worthy of one's efforts and the institution deserves one's commitment and loyalty. Work is exhilarating and joyful at its best; arduous, frustrating, and exhausting in less happy moments. Many adults embark on their careers with enthusiasm, confidence, and a desire to make a contribution. Some never lose that spark, but many do. They become frustrated with working conditions and discouraged by how hard it is to make a difference, or even to know if they have made one. Tracy Kidder puts it well in writing about teachers: "Good teachers put snags in the river of children passing by, and over time, they redirect hundreds of lives. There is an innocence that conspires to hold humanity together, and it is made up of people who can never fully know the good they have done" (Kidder, 1989, p. 313). The gift of significance helps people sustain their faith rather than burn out and retire on the job.

Significance is built through the use of many expressive and symbolic forms: rituals, ceremonies, icons, music, and stories. An organization without a rich symbolic life grows empty and sterile. The magic of special occasions is vital in building significance into collective life. Moments of ecstasy are parentheses that mark life's major passages. Without ritual and ceremony, transition remains incomplete, a clutter of comings and goings; "life becomes an endless set of Wednesdays" (Campbell, 1983, p. 5).

When ritual and ceremony are authentic and attuned, they fire the imagination, evoke insight, and touch the heart. Ceremony weaves past, present, and future into life's ongoing tapestry. Ritual helps us face and comprehend life's everyday shocks, triumphs, and mysteries. Both help us experience the unseen web of significance that ties a community together. When inauthentic, such occasions become meaningless, repetitious, and alienating—wasting our time, disconnecting us from work, and splintering us from one another. "Community must become more than just gathering the troops, telling the stories, and remembering things past. Community must also be rooted in values that do not fail, values that go beyond the self-aggrandizement of human leaders" (Griffin, 1993, p. 178).

Stories give flesh to shared values and sacred beliefs. Everyday life in organizations brings many heartwarming moments and dramatic encounters. Turned into stories, these events fill an organization's treasure chest with lore and legend. Told and retold, they draw people together and connect them with the significance of their work.

Music captures and expresses life's deeper meaning. When people sing or dance together, they bond to one another and experience emotional connections otherwise hard to express. The late Harry Quadracci, chief executive officer of the printing company Quadgraphics, convened employees once a year for an annual gathering. A management chorus sang the year's themes. Quadracci himself voiced the company philosophy in a solo serenade.

Max De Pree, famed both as both a business leader and an author of elegant books on leadership, is clear about the role of faith in business: "Being faithful is more important than being successful. Corporations can and should have a redemptive purpose. We need to weigh the pragmatic in the clarifying light of the moral. We must understand that reaching our potential is more important than reaching our goals" (De Pree, 1989, p. 69). Spiritual leaders have the responsibility of sustaining and encouraging faith in themselves and in recalling others to the faith when they have lost it.

CONCLUSION

Ethics ultimately must be rooted in soul: an organization's understanding of its deeply held identity, beliefs, and values. Each frame offers a perspective on the ethical responsibilities of organizations and the role of leaders. Every organization needs to evolve for itself a sense of its own ethical and spiritual core. The frames offer guidelines for this process.

Signs are everywhere that institutions in many developed nations suffer from a crisis of meaning and moral authority. Rapid change, high mobility, globalization, and racial and ethnic conflict tear at the fabric of community. The most important responsibility of managers is not to answer every question or always make the right decision. They cannot escape their responsibility to track budgets, motivate people, respond to political pressures, and attend to symbols. As leaders, managers serve a deeper, more powerful, and more durable function if they are models and catalysts for such values as excellence, caring, justice, and faith.

NOTE

1. The query paraphrases Matthew 16:26: "For what is a man profited, if he shall gain the whole world, and lose his own soul?" (King James version).

CHAPTER **20**

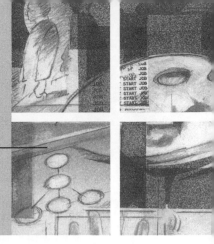

Bringing It All Together
Change and Leadership in Action

Life's daily challenges rarely arrive neatly packaged or clearly labeled. Instead, they envelop us in a murky, turbulent, and unrelenting river. The art of reframing uses knowledge and intuition to make sense of the flow and to find sensible and effective ways to channel the current.

In this chapter, we illustrate the process by following a new principal through his first week in a deeply troubled urban high school. Had this been a corporation in crisis, a struggling hospital, or an embattled public agency, the basic leadership issues would have been much the same. We assume that he is familiar with the frames and reframing and is committed to the view of leadership and ethics described in Chapter Nineteen. How might he mine his experience to figure out what's going on? What strategies can he consider? What will he do?

Read the case thoughtfully. Ask yourself what you think is going on and what options you would consider. Then compare your reflections with his.[1]

Robert F. Kennedy High School

On July 15, David King became principal of Robert F. Kennedy High School, the newest of six high schools in Great Ridge, Illinois. The school had opened two years earlier amid national acclaim as one of the first schools in the country designed and built on the "house system" concept. Kennedy High was organized into four "houses," each with three hundred students, eighteen faculty, and a housemaster. Each house was in a separate building connected to the "core facilities"—cafeteria, nurse's room, guidance offices, boys' and girls' gyms, offices, shops, and auditorium—and other houses by an enclosed outside passageway. Each had its own entrance, classrooms, toilets, conference rooms, and housemaster's office.

Hailed as a major innovation in inner-city education, Kennedy High was featured during its first year in a documentary on a Chicago television station. The school opened with a carefully selected staff of teachers, many chosen from other Great Ridge schools. At least a dozen were specially recruited from out of state. King knew that his faculty included graduates from several elite East Coast and West Coast schools, such as Yale, Princeton, and Stanford, as well as several of the very best midwestern schools. Even the racial mix of students had been carefully balanced so that blacks, whites, and Latinos each comprised a third of the student body (although King also knew—perhaps better than its planners—that Kennedy's students were drawn from the toughest and poorest areas of the city). The building itself was also widely admired for its beauty and functionality and had won several national architectural awards.

Despite careful and elaborate preparations, Kennedy High School was in serious trouble by the time King arrived. It had been racked by violence the preceding year—closed twice by student disturbances and once by a teacher walkout. It was also widely reported (although King did not know for sure) that achievement scores of its ninth- and tenth-grade students had declined during the last two years, and no significant improvement could be seen in the scores of the eleventh and twelfth graders' tests. So far, Kennedy High School had fallen far short of its planners' hopes and expectations.

David King

David King was born and raised in Great Ridge, Illinois. His father was one of the city's first black principals. King knew the city and its school system well. After two years of military service, King followed in his father's footsteps by going to Great Ridge State Teachers College, where he received B.Ed. and M.Ed. degrees. King taught English and coached in a predominantly black middle school for several years until he was asked to become the school's assistant principal. He remained in that post for five years, when he was asked to take over a large middle school of nine hundred pupils—believed at the time to be the most "difficult" middle school in the city. While there, King gained a citywide reputation as a gifted and popular administrator. He was credited with changing the worst middle school in the system into one of the best. He had been very effective in building community support, recruiting new faculty, and raising academic standards. He was also credited with turning out basketball and base-ball teams that had won state and county championships.

The superintendent made it clear that King had been selected for the Kennedy job over several more senior candidates because of his ability to handle tough situations. The superin-tendent had also told him that he would need every bit of skill and luck he could muster. King knew of the formidable credentials of Jack Weis, his predecessor at Kennedy High. Weis, a white man, had been the superintendent of a small, local township school system before becoming Kennedy's first principal. He had written one book on the house system concept and another on inner-city education. Weis held a Ph.D. from the University of Chicago and a divinity degree from Harvard. Yet despite his impressive background and ability, Weis had resigned in disillusionment. He was described by many as a "broken man." King remembered seeing the physical change in Weis over that two-year period. Weis's appearance had become progressively more fatigued and strained until he developed what appeared to be permanent dark rings under his eyes and a perpetual stoop. King remembered how he had pitied the man and wondered how Weis could find the job worth the obvious personal toll it was taking on him.

History of the School

The First Year

The school's troubles began to manifest themselves in its first year. Rumors of conflicts between the housemasters and the six subject-area department heads spread throughout the system by the middle of the year. The conflicts stemmed from differences in interpretations of curriculum policy on required learning and course content. In response, Weis had instituted a "free market" policy: subject-area department heads were supposed to convince housemas-ters why they should offer certain courses, and housemasters were supposed to convince department heads which teachers they wanted assigned to their houses. Many felt that this policy exacerbated the conflicts.

To add to the tension, a teacher was assaulted in her classroom in February. The beating frightened many of the staff, particularly older teachers. A week later, eight teachers asked

Weis to hire security guards. This request precipitated a debate in the faculty about the desirability of guards in the school. One group felt that the guards would instill a sense of safety and promote a better learning climate. The other faction felt that the presence of guards in the school would be repressive and would destroy the sense of community and trust that was developing. Weis refused the request for security guards because he believed they would symbolize everything the school was trying to change. In April, a second teacher was robbed and beaten in her classroom after school hours, and the debate was rekindled. This time, a group of Latino parents threatened to boycott the school unless better security measures were implemented. Again, Weis refused the request for security guards.

The Second Year

The school's second year was even more troubled than the first. Financial cutbacks ordered during the summer prevented Weis from replacing eight teachers who resigned. Since it was no longer possible for each house to staff all of its courses with its own faculty, Weis instituted a "flexible staffing" policy. Some teachers were asked to teach a course outside their assigned house, and students in the eleventh and twelfth grades were able to take elective and required courses in other houses. Chauncey Carver, one of the housemasters, publicly attacked the new policy as a step toward destroying the house system. In a letter to the *Great Ridge Times,* he accused the board of education of trying to subvert the house concept by cutting back funds.

The debate over the flexible staffing policy was heightened when two of the other housemasters joined a group of faculty and department heads in opposing Carver's criticisms. This group argued that interhouse cross-registration should be encouraged because the fifteen to eighteen teachers in each house could never offer the variety of courses that the schoolwide faculty of sixty-five to seventy could.

Further expansion of the flexible staffing policy was halted, however, because of difficulties in scheduling fall classes. Errors cropped up in the master schedule developed during the preceding summer. Scheduling problems persisted until November, when the vice principal responsible for developing the schedule resigned. Burtram Perkins, a Kennedy housemaster who had formerly planned the schedule at Central High, assumed the function on top of his duties as housemaster. Scheduling took most of Perkins's time until February.

Security again became an issue when three sophomores were assaulted because they refused to give up their lunch money during a "shakedown." The assailants were believed to be outsiders. Several teachers approached Weis and asked him to request the board of education to provide security guards. Again, Weis declined, but he asked Bill Smith, a vice principal at the school, to secure all doors except for the entrances to each of the four houses, the main entrance to the school, and the cafeteria. This move seemed to reduce the number of outsiders roaming through the school.

In May of the second year, a fight in the cafeteria spread and resulted in considerable damage, including broken classroom windows and desks. The disturbance was severe enough for Weis to close the school. A number of teachers and students reported that outsiders were involved in the fight and in damaging the classrooms. Several students were taken to the hospital for minor injuries, but all were released. A similar disturbance occurred two weeks later, and again the school was closed. The board of education ordered a temporary detail of municipal police to the school against Weis's advice. In protest to the assignment of police, thirty of Kennedy's sixty-eight teachers staged a walkout, joined by over half the student body. The police detail was removed, and an agreement was worked out by an ad hoc subcommittee composed of board members and informal representatives of teachers who were for and against a police detail. The compromise called for the temporary stationing of a police cruiser near the school.

King's First Week at Kennedy High

King arrived at Kennedy High on Monday, July 15, and spent most of his first week individually interviewing key administrators (see Exhibit 20.1). On Friday, he held a meeting with all administrators and department heads. King's purpose in these meetings was to familiarize himself with the school, its problems, and its key people.

His first interview was with Bill Smith, a vice principal. Smith was black and had worked as a counselor and then vice principal of a middle school before coming to Kennedy. King knew Smith's reputation as a tough disciplinarian who was very much disliked by many of the younger faculty and students. King had also heard from several teachers whose judgment he respected that Smith had been instrumental in keeping the school from "blowing apart" the preceding year. It became clear early in the interview that Smith felt that more stringent steps were needed to keep outsiders from wandering into the buildings. Smith urged King to consider locking all the school's thirty doors except for the front entrance so that everyone would enter and leave through one set of doors. Smith also told him that many of the teachers and pupils were scared and that "no learning will ever begin to take place until we make it so

EXHIBIT 20.1. Administrative Organization of Robert F. Kennedy High School.

Principal:	David King, 42 (black) B.Ed., M.Ed., Great Ridge State Teachers College
Vice principal:	William Smith, 44 (black) B.Ed., Breakwater State College; M.Ed., Great Ridge State Teachers College
Vice principal:	Vacant
Housemaster, A House:	Burtram Perkins, 47 (black) B.S., M.Ed., University of Illinois
Housemaster, B House:	Frank Czepak, 36 (white) B.S., University of Illinois; M.Ed., Great Ridge State Teachers College
Housemaster, C House:	Chauncey Carver, 32 (black) A.B., Wesleyan University; B.F.A., Pratt Institute; M.A.T., Yale University
Housemaster, D House:	John Bonavota, 26 (white) B.Ed., Great Ridge State Teachers College; M.Ed., Ohio State University
Assistant to the principal:	Vacant
Assistant to the principal for community affairs:	Vacant

people don't have to be afraid anymore." At the end of the interview, Smith said he had been approached by a nearby school system to become its director of counseling but that he had not yet made up his mind. He said he was committed enough to Kennedy High that he did not want to leave, but his decision depended on how hopeful he felt about the school's future.

As King talked with others, he discovered that the "door question" was highly controversial within the faculty and that feelings ran high on both sides of the issue. Two housemasters in particular, Chauncey Carver, who was black, and Frank Czepak, who was white, were strongly against closing the house entrances. The two men felt such an action would symbolically reduce house "autonomy" and the feeling of distinctness that was a central aspect of the house concept.

Carver, master of House C, was particularly vehement on this issue and on his opposition to allowing students in one house to take classes in another house. Carver contended that the flexible staffing program had nearly destroyed the house concept. He threatened to resign if King intended to expand cross-house enrollment. Carver also complained about what he described as "interference" from department heads that undermined his teachers' autonomy.

Carver appeared to be an outstanding housemaster from everything King had heard about him—even from his many enemies. Carver had an abrasive personality but seemed to have the best-operating house in the school and was well liked by most of his teachers and pupils. His program appeared to be the most innovative, but it was also the one most frequently attacked by department heads for lacking substance and ignoring requirements in the system's curriculum guide. Even with these criticisms, King imagined how much easier it would be if he had four housemasters like Chauncey Carver.

During his interviews with the other three housemasters, King discovered that they all felt infringed upon by the department heads, but only Carver and Czepak were strongly against locking the doors. The other two housemasters actively favored cross-house course enrollments. King's fourth interview was with Burtram Perkins, also a housemaster. Perkins, mentioned earlier, was a black man in his late forties who had served as assistant to the principal of Central High before coming to Kennedy. Perkins spent most of the interview discussing how schedule pressures could be relieved. Perkins was currently developing the schedule for the coming school year until a vice principal could be appointed to perform that job (Kennedy High had allocations for two vice principals and two assistants in addition to the housemasters).

Two bits of information concerning Perkins came to King during his first week at the school. The first was that several teachers were circulating a letter requesting Perkins's removal as a housemaster. They felt that he could not control the house or direct the faculty. This surprised King because he had heard that Perkins was widely respected within the faculty and had earned a reputation for supporting high academic standards and for working tirelessly with new teachers. As King inquired further, he discovered that Perkins was genuinely liked but was also widely acknowledged as a poor housemaster. The second piece of information concerned how Perkins's house compared with the others. Although students had been randomly assigned to each house, Perkins's house had the highest absence rate and the greatest number of disciplinary problems. Smith had told him that Perkins's dropout rate the previous year was three times that of the next highest house.

While King was in the process of interviewing his staff, he was called on by David Crimmins, chairman of the history department. Crimmins was a native of Great Ridge, white, and in his late forties. Though scheduled for an appointment the following week, he had asked King if he could see him immediately. Crimmins had heard about the letter asking for Perkins's removal and wanted to present the other side. He became very emotional, saying that Perkins was viewed by many of the teachers and department chairmen as the only housemaster trying to maintain high academic standards; his transfer would be seen as a blow to those concerned with quality education. Crimmins also described in detail Perkins's devotion and commitment to the school. He emphasized that Perkins was the only administrator with the ability to straighten out the schedule, which he had done in addition to all his other duties. Crimmins departed by threatening, if Perkins were transferred, to write a letter to the regional accreditation council decrying the level to which standards had sunk at Kennedy. King assured Crimmins that such a drastic measure was unnecessary and offered assurance that a cooperative resolution would be found. King knew that Kennedy High faced an accreditation review the following April and did not wish to complicate the process unnecessarily.

Within twenty minutes of Crimmins's departure, King was visited by Tim Shea, a young white teacher. He said he had heard that Crimmins had come in to see King. Shea identified himself as one of the teachers who had organized the movement to get rid of Perkins. He said that he liked and admired Perkins because of the man's devotion to the school but that Perkins's house was so disorganized and that discipline there was so bad that it was nearly impossible to do any good teaching. Shea added, "It's a shame to lock the school up when stronger leadership is all that's needed."

King's impressions of his administrators generally matched what he had heard before arriving at the school. Carver seemed to be a very bright, innovative, and charismatic leader whose mere presence generated excitement. Czepak came across as a highly competent though not very imaginative administrator who had earned the respect of his faculty and students. Bonavota, at twenty-six, seemed smart and earnest but unseasoned and unsure of himself. King felt that with a little guidance and training, Bonavota might have the greatest promise of all; at the moment, however, the young housemaster seemed confused and somewhat overwhelmed. Perkins impressed King as a sincere and devoted person with a good mind for administrative details but an incapacity for leadership.

King knew that he had the opportunity to make several administrative appointments because of the three vacancies that existed. Indeed, should Smith resign as vice principal,

King could fill both vice principal positions. He also knew that his recommendations for these positions would carry a great deal of weight with the central office. The only constraint King felt was the need to achieve some kind of racial balance among the Kennedy administrative group. With his own appointment as principal, the number of black administrators exceeded the number of white administrators by a ratio of two to one, and Kennedy did not have a single Latino administrator, even though a third of its pupils were Hispanic.

The Friday Afternoon Meeting

In contrast to the individual interviews, King was surprised to find how quiet and conflict-free these same people seemed in the staff meeting he called on Friday. He was amazed at how slow, polite, and friendly the conversation was among people who had so vehemently expressed negative opinions of each other in private. After about forty-five minutes of discussion about the upcoming accreditation review, King broached the subject of housemaster–department head relations. There was silence until Czepak made a joke about the uselessness of discussing the topic. King probed further by asking if everyone was happy with the current practices. Crimmins suggested that the topic might be better discussed in a smaller group. Everyone seemed to agree—except for Betsy Dula, a white woman in her late twenties who chaired the English department. She said that one of the problems with the school was that no one was willing to tackle tough issues until they exploded. She added that relations between housemasters and department heads were terrible, and that made her job very difficult. She then attacked Chauncey Carver for impeding her evaluation of a nontenured teacher in Carver's house. The two argued for several minutes about the teacher and the quality of an experimental sophomore English course the teacher was offering. Finally, Carver, by now quite angry, coldly warned Dula that he would "break her neck" if she stepped into his house again. King intervened in an attempt to cool both their tempers, and the meeting ended shortly thereafter.

The following morning, Dula called King at home and told him that unless Carver publicly apologized for his threat, she would file a grievance with the teachers' union and take it to court if necessary. King assured Dula that he would talk with Carver on Monday. King then called Eleanor Debbs, a Kennedy High math teacher whom he had known well for many years and whose judgment he respected. Debbs was a close friend of both Carver and Dula and was also vice president of the city's teachers' union. Debbs said that the two were long-time adversaries but both were excellent professionals.

She also reported that Dula would be a formidable opponent and could muster considerable support among the faculty. Debbs, who was black, feared that a confrontation between

Dula and Carver might stoke racial tensions in the school, even though both Dula and Carver were generally popular with students of all races. Debbs strongly urged King not to let the matter drop. She also told him that she had overheard Bill Smith, the vice principal, say at a party the night before that he felt King didn't have the stomach or the forcefulness to survive at Kennedy. Smith said that the only reason he was staying was that he did not expect King to last the year, in which case Smith would be in a good position to be appointed principal.

David King inherited a job that had broken his predecessor and could easily destroy him as well. His new staff greeted him with a jumble of problems, demands, maneuvers, and threats. His first staff meeting began with an undercurrent of tension and ended in outright hostility. Sooner or later, almost every manager will encounter situations this bad— or worse. The results are often devastating, leaving the manager feeling confused, overwhelmed, and helpless. Nothing makes any sense, and nothing seems to work. Can King escape such a dismal fate?

There is one potential bright spot. As the case ends, King is talking to Eleanor Debbs on a Saturday morning. He has a supportive colleague. He also has some slack—the rest of the weekend to regroup. Where should he begin? We suggest that he start by active reflection and reframing. A straightforward way to do that is to examine the situation one frame at a time and ask two simple questions: From this perspective, what's going on? And what options does this viewpoint suggest? This reflective process deserves time and careful thought. It requires "going to the balcony" (see Heifetz, 1994) to get a fuller perspective on the scene below. Ideally, King would include one or more other people— a valued mentor, principals in other schools, close friends, his spouse—for alternative perspectives in the diagnostic process. We present a streamlined version of the kind of thinking that David King might entertain.

STRUCTURAL ISSUES AND OPTIONS

King sits down at his kitchen table with a cup of coffee, a pen, and a fresh yellow pad. He starts to review structural issues at Kennedy High. He recalls the "people-blaming" approach (Chapter Two), in which individuals are blamed for everything that goes wrong. He smiles and nods his head. That's it! Everyone at Kennedy High School is blaming everyone else. He recalls the lesson of the structural frame: we blame individuals when the real problems are systemic.

So what structural problems does Kennedy High have? King thinks about the two cornerstones of structure, differentiation and integration. In a flash of insight, he sees that Kennedy High School has an ample division of labor but very little coordination. He scribbles on his pad, trying to draw the school's organization chart. He gradually realizes that the school has a matrix structure—teachers have an ill-defined dual reporting relationship to both department chairs and housemasters. He remembers the downside of the matrix structure; it's built for conflict (teachers wonder whom they're supposed to be loyal to, and administrators bicker about who's in charge). There are no integrating devices to link the concerns of housemasters like Chauncey Carver (who wants a coherent, effective program for his house) with those of department chairs like Betsy Dula (who is concerned about the schoolwide English curriculum and adherence to district guidelines). It's not just personalities; the structure is pushing Carver and Dula toward each other's throat. Goals, roles, and responsibilities are all vaguely defined. Nor is there a workable structural device (a task force, or standing committee) to diagnose and resolve such problems. If King had been in the job longer, he might have been able to rely more heavily on the authority of the principal's office. It helps that he's been authorized by the superintendent to fix the school. But so far, there is little evidence that Kennedy High staff are endorsing his authority with much enthusiasm.

King's musings are making sense, but it isn't clear what to do about the structural gaps. Is there any way to get the school back under control when it is teetering on the edge of chaos? Particularly when his authority is shaky? He is having trouble controlling the staff, and they are having the same problem with the students. The school is an underbounded system screaming for structure and boundaries.

King notes, ruefully, that he made things worse in the Friday meeting. "I knew how these people felt about one another," he thinks. "Why did I push them to talk about something they were trying to avoid? We hadn't done any homework. I didn't give them a clear goal for the conversation. I didn't set any ground rules for how to talk about it. When it started to heat up, I just watched. Why didn't I step in before it exploded?" He stops and shakes his head. "Live and learn, I guess. But I learned these lessons a long time ago—they served me well in turning the middle school around. In all the confusion, I forgot that even good people can't function very well without some structure. What did I do the last time around?"

King begins to brainstorm options. One possibility is responsibility charting (Chapter Five): bring people together to define tasks and responsibilities. It has worked before. Would it work here? He reviews the language of responsibility charting. Who's responsible? Who has to approve? Who needs to be consulted? Who should be informed? As he applies these questions to Kennedy High, the overlap between the housemasters and the department chairs is an obvious problem. Without a clear definition of roles and relationships, conflict and confusion are inevitable. He wonders about a total overhaul of the structure: "Is the house system viable in its current form? If not, is it fixable? Maybe we need a process to look at the structure: What if I chaired a small task force to examine it and develop recommendations? I could put Dula and Carver on it—let them see first-hand what's causing their conflict. Get them involved in working out a new design. Give each authority over specific areas. Develop some policies and procedures."

It is clear even from a few minutes' reflection that Kennedy High School has major structural problems that have to be addressed. But what to do about the immediate crisis between Dula and Carver? The structure helped create the problem in the first place, and fixing it might prevent stuff like this in the future. But Dula's demand for an apology didn't sound like something a rational approach would easily fix. King would prefer to try another angle. He turns to the human resource frame for counsel.

HUMAN RESOURCE ISSUES AND OPTIONS

"How ironic," King muses. "The original idea behind the school was to respond better to students. Break down the big, bureaucratic high school. Make the house a community, a family even, where people know each other and care about each other. But it's not going that way. Everyone's stuck at the bottom of Maslow's needs hierarchy: no one even feels safe. Until they do, they'll never focus on caring. The problem isn't personalities. Everyone's frustrated because no one is getting needs met. Not me, not Carver, not Dula. We're all so needy, we don't realize everyone else has the same problem."

King shifts from individual needs to interpersonal relationships. It's hard not to, with the Dula-Carver mess staring him in the face. Tense relationships everywhere. People talking only to people who agree with them. Why? How to get a handle on it? He remembers reading, "Lurking in Model I is the core assumption that an organization is a dangerous place where you have to look out for yourself or someone else will do you in" (Chapter Eight). "That's it!" he says. "That's us. Too bad they don't give a prize for the most Model I school in America. We'd win hands down. Everything here is win-lose. Nothing is discussed openly, and if it is, people just attack each other. If anything goes wrong, we blame others and try to straighten them out. They get defensive, which proves we were right. But we never test our assumptions. We don't ask questions. We just harbor suspicions and wait for people to prove us right. Then we hit them over the head. We've got to find better ways to deal with one another.

"How do you get better people management?" King wonders. "Successful organizations start with a clear human resource philosophy. We don't have one, but it might help. Invest in people? We've got good people. They're paid pretty well. They've got job security. We're probably OK there. Job enrichment? Jobs here are plenty challenging. Empowerment? That's a big problem. Everyone claims to be powerless, yet somehow everyone expects me to fix everything. Is there something we could do to get people's participation? Get them to own more of the problem? Convince them we've got to work together to make things better? The trouble is, if we go that way, people probably don't have the group skills they'd need. Staff development? With all the conflict, mediation skills might be a place to start." Conflict. Politics. Politics is normal in an organization. He's read it, and he knows it's true. "But we don't seem to have a midpoint between getting along and getting even."

POLITICAL ISSUES AND OPTIONS

King reluctantly turns his attention to the political frame. It isn't easy for him. He knows it's relevant; he's never seen a school with more intense political strife. His old school is beginning to seem tame by comparison; he tackled some things head on there. But Kennedy is a lot more volatile, with a history of explosions. Coercive force seems to be the power tactic of choice.

Things might get even more vicious if he tackles the conflict openly. He mulls over the basic elements of the political frame: enduring differences, scarce resources, conflict, power. "Bingo! We've got 'em all—in spades. We've got factions for and against the house concept. Housemasters want to run their houses and guard their turf. Department chairs want to run the faculty and expand their territory. One group wants to close the doors and bring in guards. Another wants to keep out the guards and throw open the doors. We've got race issues simmering under the surface. No Latino administrators. This Carver-Dula thing could blow up the school. Black male says he'll break white female's neck. A recipe for disaster. We need some damage control.

"Then we've got all those outside folks looking over our shoulder. Parents worry about safety. The school board doesn't trust us. The media are looking for a story. Accreditation is coming in the spring. Maybe there's some way to get people thinking about the enemies outside instead of inside. A common devil might pull people together—for a little while anyway.

"Scarce resources? They're getting scarcer. We lost 10 percent of our teachers—that got us into the flexible staffing mess. Housemasters and department chairs are fighting over turf. Bill Smith wants my job. It's a war zone. We need some kind of peace settlement. But who's going to take the diplomatic lead? We don't seem to have any neutral parties. Eleanor Debbs would respond to the call. People respect her. But she's not an administrator."

King's attention turns to the two faces of power. "Power can be used to do people in. That's what we're doing right now. But you can also use power to get things done. That's the constructive side of politics. Too bad no one here seems to have a clue about it. If I'm going to be a constructive politician, what can I do? First, I need an agenda. Without that, I'm dead in the water. Basically, I want everyone working in tandem to make the school better for kids. Most people could rally behind that. I also need a strategy. Networking— I need good relationships with key folks—like Smith, Carver, and Dula. The interviews were a good start. I learned a lot about who wants what. The Friday meeting was a mistake, a collision of special interests with no common ground. It's going to take some horse trading. We need a deal the housemasters and the department chairs can both buy into. And I need some allies—badly."

He smiles as he remembers all the times he's railed against analysis paralysis. But he feels he's getting somewhere. He turns to a clean sheet on his pad. "Let's lay this thing out," he says to the quiet, empty kitchen. Across the top he labels three columns: allies, fence-sitters, and opponents. At the top left, he writes "High power." At the bottom left, "Low power." Over the next half-hour, he creates a political map of Kennedy High School, arranging individuals and groups in terms of their interests and their power. When he finishes, he winces. Too many powerful opponents. Too few supportive allies. A bunch of people waiting to choose sides. He begins to think about how to build a coalition and reshape the school's political map.

"No doubt about it," King says, "I have to get on top of the political mess. Otherwise they'll carry me out the same way they did Weis. But it's a little depressing. Where's the ray of hope?" He smiles. He's ready to think about symbols and culture. "Where's Dr. King when I need him?" He recalls the famous words from 1963: "For even though we face the difficulties of today and tomorrow, I still have a dream." What happened to Kennedy High's dream?

He decides to take a break, get some fresh air. Moonlit night. Crowded sidewalks. Young and old, poor and affluent, black, white, and Latino. Merchandise pours out of stores into sidewalk bins: clothes, toys, electronic gear, fruits, vegetables—you name it. King runs into some students from his old school. They're at Kennedy now. "We're tellin' our friends we got a *good* principal now," they say. He thanks them, hoping they're right.

SYMBOLIC ISSUES AND OPTIONS

Back to the kitchen and the yellow pad. Fortified by the walk and another cup of coffee, he reviews the school's history. "Interesting," he observes. "That's one of the problems: the school's too new to have much history. What we have is mostly bad. We've got a hodge-podge of individual histories people brought from someplace else. Deep down, everyone is telling a different story. Maybe that's why Carver is so attached to his house and Dula to her English department. There's nothing schoolwide for people to bond to. Just little pockets of meaning."

He starts to think about symbols that might create common ground. Robert Kennedy, the school's namesake. He has only vague recollection of Bobby Kennedy's speeches. Anything there? He remembers the man. What was he like? What did he stand for? What were the founders thinking when they chose his name for the school? What signals were they trying to send? Any unifying theme? Then it comes to him—words from Bobby Kennedy's eulogy for his brother: "Some people see things as they are, and say why? I dream things that never were, and say why not?"

"That's the kind of thinking we need at Kennedy High," King realizes. "We need to get beyond all the factions and divisions. We need a banner that we all can rally around. Celebrate Kennedy now? Can we have a ceremony in the midst of chaos? It could backfire, make things worse. But it seems the school never had any special occasions—even at the start. No rituals, no traditions. The only stories are bad ones. The high road might work. We've got to get back to the values that launched the school in the first place. Rekindle the spark. What if I pull some people together? Start from scratch—this time with more sensitivity to symbols and ceremony? We need some glue to weld this thing together."

Meaning. Faith. He rolls the words around in his mind. Haunting images. Ideas start to tumble out. "We're supposed to be pioneers, but somehow we got lost. A lighthouse where the bulb burned out. Not a beacon anymore. We're on the rocks ourselves. A dream became a nightmare. People's faith is pretty shaky. There's a schism—folks splitting into two different faiths. Like a holy war between the church of the one true house system and the temple of academic excellence. We need something to pull both sides together. Why did people join up in the first place? How can we get them to sign up again—renew their vows?" He smiles at the religious overtones in his thoughts. His mother and father would be proud.

He catches himself. "We're not a church; we're a school, in a country that separates religion and state. But maybe the symbolic frame bridges the gap. Organization as temple. A lot of it is about meaning. What's Kennedy High School really about? Who are we? What happened to our spirit? What's our soul, our values? That's what folks are fighting over! Deep down, we're split over two versions of what we stand for. Department chairs promoting excellence. Housemasters pushing for caring. We need both. That was the original dream. Bring excellence and caring together. We'll never get either if we're always at war with one another."

He thinks about why he got into public education in the first place. It was his calling. Why? Growing up in a racist society was tough, but his father had it a lot tougher—he was a principal when it was something black men didn't do. King had always admired his dad's courage and discipline. More than anything, he remembered his father's passion about education. The man was a real champion for kids—high standards, deep compassion. Growing up with this man as a role model, there was never much question in King's mind. As far back as he could remember, he wanted to be a principal too. It was a way to give to the community and to help young people who really needed it. To give everyone a chance. In the midst of a firefight, it was easy to forget this. It felt good to remember.

Before going further, King senses that it is a good time for a review. Over another cup of coffee, he goes back over his notes. They strike him as stream of consciousness, with some good stuff and a little self-pity. He smiles as he remembers himself in graduate school, fighting against all that theory. "Don't think; do! Be a leader!" Now, here he is, thinking, reflecting, trying to pull things together. In a strange way, it feels natural.

He organizes his ideas into a chart (see Table 20.1). He's starting to feel better now. The picture is coming into focus. He feels he has a better sense of what he's up against. It's reassuring to see he has lots of options. There are lots of pitfalls, too, but some real possibilities. He knows he can't do everything at once; he needs to set priorities. He needs a plan of action, an agenda anchored in basic values. Where to begin? Soul? Values? He has to find a rallying point somewhere.

He has already embraced two values: excellence and caring. He turns his attention to leadership as gift-giving. "I've mostly been waiting for others to initiate. What about me? What are my gifts? If I want excellence, the gift I have to offer is authorship. That's what people want. They don't want to be told what to do. They want to put their signature on this place. Make a contribution. They're fighting so hard because they care so much. That's what brought them to Kennedy in the first place. They wanted to be a part of something better. Create something special. They all want to do a good job. How can I help them do it without tripping over each other?

"What about caring? The leadership gift is love. No one's getting much of that around here." (He smiles as a song fragment comes to mind: "Looking for love in all the wrong places.") "I've been waiting for someone else to show caring and compassion," he realizes. "I've been holding back."

The thought leads him to pick up the phone. He calls Betsy Dula. She is out, but he leaves a message on the machine: "Betsy, Dave King. I've been thinking a lot about our conversation. One thing I want you to know is that I'm really glad you're part of the Kennedy High team. You bring a lot, and I sure hope I can count on your help. We can't do it without you. We need to finish what we started out to do. I care. I know you do, too. I'll see you Monday."

He senses he's on a roll. But it's one thing to leave a message on someone's machine and another to deliver it in person—particularly if you don't know how receptive the other person will be.

TABLE 20.1. Reframing Robert F. Kennedy High School.

Frame	What's Going On?	What Options Are Available?
Structural	Weak integration-goals, roles, responsibilities, linkages undefined; ill-defined matrix structure; weak authority; underbounded structure	Responsibility charting; task force to look at structure
Human resource	Basic needs not met (safety, etc.); win-lose interpersonal dynamics; ineffective conflict management; feelings of disempowerment	Improve safety, security; training in communication, conflict management; participation, teaming
Political	House-department conflict; doors and guards issue; Carver-Dula and racial tensions; outside constituents-parents, board, media, etc.	Arenas for negotiating; damage control; unite against external threats; network, build coalitions; negotiate
Symbolic	No shared symbols (history, ceremony, ritual); loss of faith-religious schism; lack of identity (What is RFK's soul?)	Hoist a banner (common symbol: RFK?); develop symbols, ceremony, stories; gifts

On his next call, to Chauncey Carver, he gets through immediately. "Chauncey? Dave King. Sorry to bother you at home, but Betsy Dula called me this morning. She's upset about what you said yesterday. Particularly the part about breaking her neck."

King listens patiently as Carver makes it clear that he was only defending himself against Dula's unprovoked and inappropriate public attack. "Chauncey, I hear you. . . . Yeah, I know you're mad. So is she." King listens patiently through another one-sided tirade. "Yes, Chauncey, I understand. But look, you're a key to making this school work. I know how much you care about your house and the school. The word on the street is clear—you're a terrific housemaster. You know it, too. I need your help, man. If this thing with Betsy blows up and goes public, what's it going to do to the school? . . . You're right, we don't need it. Think about it. Betsy's pushing hard for an apology."

He feared that the word *apology* might set Carver off again, and it does. This is getting tough. He reminds himself why he made the call. He shifts back into listening mode. After several minutes of venting, Chauncey pauses. Softly, King tries to make his point. "Chauncey, I'm not telling you what to do. I'm just asking you to think about it. I don't know the answer. Two heads might be better than one. Let me know what you come up with. Can we meet first thing Monday? . . . Thanks for your time. Have a good weekend."

King puts down the phone. This is even harder than he expected. Things are still tense, but maybe he's made a start. Carver is a loose cannon with a short fuse. But he's also smart, and he cares deeply about the school. Get him thinking, King figures, and he'll see the enormous risks in his comment to Dula. Push him too hard, and he'll fight like a cornered badger. Give him some space; he might just figure out something on his own. The gift of authorship. Would Chauncey bite? Or would the problem wind up back on the principal's doorstep—with prejudice?

After the conversation with Chauncey, King needs another breather. He goes back to his yellow pad, which has become something of a security blanket. More than that, it's helping him find his way to the balcony. It has given him a better view of the situation. He's made notes about excellence and caring. Is he making progress or just musing? It doesn't matter. He feels better, and the situation seems to be getting clearer.

King's thoughts move on to justice. "Do people feel the school is fair?" he asks. "I'm not hearing a lot of complaints about injustice. But it wouldn't take much to set off another war. The Chauncey-Betsy thing is scary. A man physically threatening a woman could send a terrible message. There's too much male violence in the community already. Make it a black man and a white woman, and it's really heavy. The fact that Chauncey and I are black men is good and bad: it makes for a better chance of getting Chauncey's help—brothers united and all that. But it could be devastating if people think I'm siding with Chauncey against Betsy—sisters in defiance. It's like being on a tightrope: one false step and I'll be history. So would the school—a dismal prospect. All the more reason to encourage Chauncey and Betsy to work this out. If I could get the two together, what a symbol of unity that would be! Maybe just what we need. A positive step at least."

Finally, King thinks about the ethic of faith and the gift of significance. Symbols again, revisited in a deeper way. "How did Kennedy High go from high hopes to no hope in two years? How do we rekindle the original faith? How do we recapture the dream that launched the school? Well," he sighs, "I've been around this track before. My last school was a snakepit when I got there. Not as bad as Kennedy, but pretty awful. We turned that one around, and I learned some things in the process—including to be patient, but hang tough. It's gonna be hard. But fun, too. And it *will* happen. That's why I took this job in the first place. So what am I moaning about? I knew what I was getting into. It's just that knowing it in my head is one thing. Feeling it in my gut is another."

By Sunday night, King has twenty-five pages of notes. They help—but not as much as his conversation with himself in an empty kitchen. Going to the balcony, getting a fresh look, reflecting instead of just fretting. The inner dialogue has led to new conversations with others, on a deeper level. He's made a lot of phone calls, talked to almost every administrator in the building. A lot of them have been surprised—a principal who calls on the weekend is something new.

He is making headway. He needs to hear from Betsy but has some volunteers for a task force on structural issues. He's done some relationship building. A second call to Chauncey to commend him for devotion to the mission. A deeper connection. Crediting Frank Czepak for excellent counsel, even if the principal isn't smart enough to pay attention—a frank admission.

Some has been pure politics. Negotiating a deal with Bill Smith: "I *could* help you Bill, next time the district needs a principal, but only if you help me. You scratch my back, I'll scratch yours." Gently persuading Burt Perkins that his calling was scheduling, not running a house. A call to Dave Crimmins to tell him Perkins has decided to make a change. An encouraging conversation with Luz Hernandez, a stalwart in his previous school. She is at least willing to think about coming to Kennedy High as a housemaster. Planting seeds with everyone about ways to resolve the door problem.

Above all, King has worked on creating symbolic glue, renewing the hopes and dreams people felt at the time the school was founded. A cohesive group pulling together for a school everyone can feel proud of. His to-do list is ambitious. But at least he has some options. A month and a half until the first day of school and a lot to accomplish. He isn't sure what the future will bring, but he feels just a little more hope in the air. The knot in his stomach is pretty much gone. So are the images of being carried off like his predecessor, a broken man with a shattered career.

The phone rings. It's Betsy Dula. She's been away for the weekend but wants to thank King for his message. It was important to know he cared, she told him. "By the way," she says, "Chauncey Carver called me. Said he felt bad about Friday. Told me he'd lost his temper and said some things he didn't really mean. He invited me to breakfast tomorrow."

"Are you going?" King asks, as nonchalantly as possible. He holds his breath, thinking, *If she declines, we could be back to square one.*

"Yes," she says. "Even a phone call is a big step for Chauncey. He's a proud and stubborn man. But we're both professionals. It's worth a try."

A sigh of relief. "One more question," King says. "When you came to the school, you knew it wouldn't be easy. Why did you sign up for this trip in the first place?"

She is silent for a long time. He can almost hear her thinking.

"I love English and I love kids," she says. "And I want kids to love English."

"And now?" he asks.

"Can't we get past all the bickering and fighting? That's not why we launched this noble experiment. Let's get back to why we're here. Work together to make this a good school for our kids. They really need us."

"How about a great school we can all be proud of?" he asks.

"Sounds even better," she says. Maybe she doesn't grasp what he means. But they are beginning to read from the same page. It will take time, but they can work it out.

At the end of a very busy weekend, David King is still a long way from solving all the problems of Kennedy High. "But," he tells himself, "I made it through the valley of confusion and I'm feeling more like my old self. The picture of what I'm up against is a lot clearer. I'm seeing a lot more possibilities than I was seeing on Friday. In fact, I've got some exciting things to try. Some may work; some may not. But deep down, I think I know what's going on. And I know which way is west. We're now moving roughly in that direction."

He can't wait for Monday morning.

CONCLUSION: THE REFRAMING PROCESS

A different David King would likely raise other questions and see other choices. Reframing, like management and leadership, is much more art than science. Every artist brings a distinctive optic and produces unique works. King's reframing process necessarily builds on a lifetime of skill, knowledge, intuition, and wisdom. Reframing guides him in accessing what he already knows. It helps him feel less confused and overwhelmed by the uncertainty and disorder around him. A cluttered jumble of impressions and experiences gradually evolve into a manageable picture. His reflections help him see that he is far from helpless—he has a rich array of actions that he might take. He has also rediscovered a very old truth: reflection is a spiritual discipline, much like meditation or prayer. A path to faith and heart. He knows the road ahead is still long and difficult. There is no guarantee of success. But he feels far more confident and more energized than when he started. He is starting to dream things that never were and saying, "Why not?"

NOTE

1. Adapted from case no. 9–474–183, *Robert F. Kennedy High School*, ©1974 by the President and Fellows of Harvard College. Used by permission of the Harvard Business School. The case was prepared by John J. Gabarro as a basis for class discussion rather than to illustrate the effective or ineffective handling of an administrative situation.

CHAPTER 21

Epilogue

We hope *Reframing Organizations* continues to inspire inventive management and wise leadership. Both managers and leaders require a high level of personal artistry in response to today's challenges, ambiguities, and paradoxes. They need a sense of choice and personal freedom to find new patterns and possibilities in everyday life at work. They need versatility in thinking that fosters flexibility in action. They need the capacity to act inconsistently when uniformity fails, diplomatically when emotions are raw, nonrationally when reason flags, politically in the face of parochial self-interest, and playfully when fixating on task and purpose backfires.

Managers face a leadership paradox: maintaining integrity and mission without making organizations rigid and intractable. Leading means walking a tightrope between rigidity and spinelessness. Rigidity saps energy, stifles initiative, misdirects resources, and leads ultimately to catastrophe. These outcomes can be seen equally in the decline of great corporations and the growth of chronic ethnic violence. In a world of "permanent white water" (Vaill, 1989), nothing is solid and everything is in flux. It is tempting to follow a familiar path and rely on timeworn solutions, regardless of how much the problems have changed. Doing what's familiar is comforting; it lets us feel our world is orderly and we are in control. But when old ways fail, as they eventually must, managers often flip to the opposite extreme: they agree to anything and try to appease everyone. The result is aimlessness, anarchy, and disorganized systems that maim or kill concerted, purposeful action. Collins and Porras (1994) made it very clear: visionary companies have the paradoxical capacity to stimulate change and pursue high-risk new ventures while simultaneously maintaining their commitment to core ideology and values.

Good managers and leaders sustain a tension-filled balance between extremes. They combine core values with elastic strategies. They get things done without being done in. They know what they stand for and what they want and communicate their vision with clarity and power. But they also understand and respond to the complex forces that push and pull an organization in many conflicting directions. They think creatively about how to make things happen. They develop strategies with enough give to respond to the twists, turns, and potholes on the way to a better future.

There is a common, misguided notion that a leader takes risks and moves into uncharted terrain with omniscient foresight and unlimited power. Keller (1990) comes closer to the reality: "The greatest leaders are often, in reality, skillful followers. They do not control the flow of history, but by having the good sense not to stand in its way, they seem to. So it is with Mikhail S. Gorbachev. Mr. Gorbachev's achievement was having the vision to see the inevitable, and adopting it as his program rather than applying the repressive apparatus at his command to suppress it" (p. 1).

Gorbachev's extraordinary rise to world leadership and his stunningly rapid fall illustrate many of the complexities that all leaders face. Leaders need confidence to confront tangled problems and deep divisions. They must anticipate conflict knowing their action may unleash forces they cannot fully control. They need the courage to follow uncharted paths, expecting surprise, knowing events will sometimes outrun them, and pushing ahead even though the ultimate destination is only dimly foreseeable.

COMMITMENT TO CORE BELIEFS

Poetry and philosophy are rarely included in managerial training, and business schools rarely ask themselves if spiritual development is central to their mission. It is no wonder that managers are often viewed as chameleons who can adapt to any setting, or as dispassionate maneuverers guided only by expediency. Analysis and agility are necessary but are not enough. Organizations need leaders who can impart a persuasive and durable sense of purpose and direction, rooted deeply in values and the human spirit. "We have a revolution to make, and this revolution is not political, but spiritual" (Guéhenno, 1993, p. 167).

Leaders must be deeply reflective, actively thoughtful, and dramatically explicit about core values and beliefs. Many of the world's legendary corporate heroes articulated their philosophy and values in such a striking way that they are still visible in today's behavior and operations. In government, Franklin Delano Roosevelt, Charles de Gaulle, Margaret Thatcher, and Singapore's Lee Kuan Yew were as controversial as they were durable, but each espoused a stable and coherent set of values and beliefs. These in turn served as a means of formulating a vision for the direction of their respective nations.

MULTIFRAME THINKING

Commitment to both durable values and elastic strategy involves a paradox. Franklin Roosevelt's image as lion and fox and Mao's reputation as tiger and monkey were not so much contradictions as signs that they could embrace contradiction. They intuitively recognized the multiple dimensions of society and moved flexibly to implement their vision. The use of multiple frames permits leaders to see and understand more—*if* they are able to employ the logics that accompany different frames.

Leaders fail when they take too narrow a view. Unless they can think flexibly about organizations and see them from multiple angles, they will be unable to deal with the full range of issues they inevitably encounter. Jimmy Carter's preoccupation with details and rationality made it hard for him to marshal support for his programs or to capture the hearts of most Americans. After his presidency, his caring for people became a dominant theme—and won him the Nobel Prize. Even FDR's multifaceted approach to the presidency—he was a superb observer of human needs, a charming persuader, a solid administrator, a political manipulator, and a master of ritual and ceremony—miscarried when he underestimated the public reaction to his plan to enlarge the Supreme Court.

Multiframe thinking is challenging and often counterintuitive. To see the same organization *simultaneously* as machine, family, jungle, and theater requires the capacity to think in several ways at the same time about the same thing. Like surfers, leaders must ride the waves of change. If they move too far ahead, they will be crushed. If they fall behind, they will become irrelevant. Success requires artistry, skill, and the ability to see organizations as organic forms in which needs, roles, power, and symbols must be integrated to provide direction and shape behavior. The power to reframe is vital for modern leaders. The ability to see new possibilities and to create new opportunities enables leaders to discover alternatives when options seem severely constrained. It helps them find hope and faith amid fear and despair. Choice is at the heart of freedom, and freedom is essential to achieving the twin goals of commitment and flexibility.

Organizations everywhere are struggling to cope with a shrinking planet and a global economy. The accelerating pace of change continues to produce grave political, economic, and social discontinuity. A world ever more dependent on organizations now finds them evolving too slowly to meet pressing social demands. Without wise leaders and artistic managers to help close the gap, we will continue to see misdirected resources, massive ineffectiveness, and unnecessary human pain and suffering. All these afflictions are already here, and there is no guarantee that they will not get worse.

We see prodigious challenges ahead for organizations and those who guide them, yet we remain optimistic. We want this volume to lay the groundwork for a new generation of managers and leaders who recognize the importance of poetry and philosophy as well as analysis and technique. We need pioneers who embrace the fundamental values of human life and the human spirit. Such leaders and managers are playful theorists who can see an organization through a complex prism. They are negotiators able to design elastic strategies that simultaneously shape events and adapt to changing circumstances. They understand the importance of knowing and caring for themselves and the people with whom they work. They are architects, catalysts, advocates, and prophets who lead with soul.

APPENDIX

The Best of Organizational Studies: Scholars' Hits and Popular Best-Sellers

As we worked on this edition of *Reframing Organizations,* we sought a way to ensure that we did not overlook important works in the field, and that we cited or summarized them where appropriate. There is no perfect way to determine the best or most important books and articles, but we can at least determine which ones seem most often read by scholars and by the general public. We developed two lists: (1) the "greatest hits" as rated by scholars and (2) best-sellers as represented in *Business Week*'s annual list.

SCHOLARS' HITS

Our list of scholars' greatest hits relies on citation analysis, that is, how often a work is cited in the scholarly literature. This method is often used to measure scholarly impact. We began by conducting a citation analysis of two journals cited by Trieschmann, Dennis, and Northcraft (2000) as the most visible and influential in the field of management: *Administrative Science Quarterly* (for the years 1993 to 2000) and the *Academy of Management Journal* (for the years 1996 to 2001). We combined analyses from these two to construct a list of the top twenty-five articles and books on the basis of citation frequency. (In getting to our top twenty-five, we eliminated purely methodological works dealing with statistical analysis or research methods.) We then conducted an additional analysis using the ISI (Institute for Scientific Information) Web of Science. This includes citation data from articles published in approximately eighty-five hundred scholarly journals. This gave us three separate rankings: AMJ, ASQ, and ISI. The first two are specific to the field of organization studies; the ISI data give a broader indication of influence both within and beyond the management field. For the items in our top twenty-five, the correlations among AMJ, ASQ, and ISI are positive but fairly low (ranging between .09 for AMJ/ASQ to .16 for ASQ/ISI). We believe this reflects reality. Scholars who publish in different journals or come from disparate disciplines have differing tastes and preferences for sources. It also suggests that our results are partly arbitrary, since another set of journals might have produced contrasting results. The results for the top fifteen are shown in Table A.1.

The results are not definitive but do broadly estimate works with greatest influence on scholars. To reduce our list to a single rank order, we averaged the rankings across the three databases. For example, our highest ranking went to a book by Pfeffer and Salancik (1976), which ranked first in AMJ, second in ASQ, and seventh in ISI.

Though the citation analysis is based on recent articles, works that appear at the high end were published much earlier, in the 1960s, 1970s, and 1980s. The oldest item in the top fifteen was published in 1958, the newest in 1983. The results suggest that there is typically a lag of a decade or more before a new work can become a widely cited "classic."

TABLE A.1. Top Fifteen "Scholars' Hits" from Citation Analysis.

AMJ Rank	ASQ Rank	ISI Rank	Overall Rank	Author	Year	Title
1	2	7	1	Pfeffer, J., and Salancik, G.	1978	*The External Control of Organizations: A Resource Dependence Perspective*
3	3	6	2	Cyert, R. M., and March, J. G.	1963	*A Behavioral Theory of the Firm*
5	1	12	3	Dimaggio, P. J., and Powell, W. W.	1983	"The Iron Cage Revisited: Institutional Isomorphism and Collective Rationality in Organizational Fields"
8	11	5	4	Jensen, M. C., and Meckling W. H.	1976	"Theory of the Firm: Managerial Behavior, Agency Costs, and Ownership Structure"

12	14	2	5	March, J. G., and Simon, H. A.	1958	*Organizations*
8	11	9	5	Nelson, R. R., and Winter, S. G.	1982	*An Evolutionary Theory of Economic Change*
2	21	8	7	Hofstede, G.	1980	*Culture's Consequences: International Differences in Work-Related Values*
24	9	1	8	Thompson, J. D.	1967	*Organizations in Action: Social Science Bases of Administrative Theory*
20	4	11	9	Meyer, J., and Rowan, B.	1977	"Institutionalized Organizations: Formal Structure as Myth and Ceremony"
17	5	13	9	Pfeffer, J.	1981	*Power in Organizations*
12	20	4	11	Porter, M. E.	1980	*Competitive Strategy: Techniques for Analyzing Industries and Competitors*
17	17	3	12	Williamson, O. E.	1985	*The Economic Institutions of Capitalism: Firms, Markets, Relational Contracting*
19	8	10	12	Granovetter, M. S.	1985	*Economic Action and Social Structure: The Problem of Social Embeddedness*
7	18	14	14	Child, J.	1972	*Organizational Structure, Environment and Performance: The Role of Strategic Choice*
5	15	19	14	Hambrick, D. C., and Mason, P. A.	1984	"Upper Echelons: The Organization as a Reflection of Its Top Managers"

Note: Italicized titles are books; titles in quotation marks are journal articles. *AMJ = Academy of Management Journal*; *ASQ = Administrative Science Quarterly*; *ISI* = Institute for Scientific Information Web of Science.

POPULAR BEST-SELLERS

Scholars and the public have very different tastes. For each of the years 1996 to 2000, we have identified a book near or at the top of the *Business Week* best-sellers list (see Table A.2). Normally, we chose a book occupying the number-one position on the hardcover or softcover list. But we chose books lower in the rankings under two conditions: (1) top book(s) focused on topics outside the field of management and organizations (for example, works on personal finance), and (2) a book remaining in the top position for more than one year (particularly the case with Spenser Johnson's *Who Moved My Cheese?*).

Not surprisingly, popular best-sellers tend to be shorter and simpler than the scholars' picks. They usually emphasize people issues falling within the human resource or symbolic frames, whereas the scholars' top choices emphasized symbolic, political, and structural issues. Typically, the popular best-sellers are upbeat. The message is, "You can make a difference." The scholars often prefer the opposite message: "You probably won't make much difference because you and your organization are controlled by much larger social and economic forces."

TABLE A.2. *Business Week* Best-Sellers.

Year	Business Best-Seller	Rank on *Business Week* List
2002	Collins, *Good to Great*	No. 2 on hardcover list at press time (behind *Who Moved My Cheese?*)
2001	Welch, *Jack: Straight from the Gut*	No. 2 on hardcover list (behind *Who Moved My Cheese?*)
2000	Lewis, *The New New Thing*	No. 4 on hardcover list (behind *Who Moved My Cheese?*, *The Millionaire Mind*, and *The Tipping Point*)
1999	Johnson, *Who Moved My Cheese?*	No. 1 on hardcover list (for 1999, 2000, and 2001
1998	Chernow, *Titan*	No. 3 on hardcover list (behind two personal finance titles)
1997	Covey, *The 7 Habits of Highly Effective People*	No. 1 on paperback list for many years
1996	Adams, *The Dilbert Principle*	No. 1 on hardcover list

REFERENCES

"The ABB of Management." *Economist,* Jan. 6, 1996, p. 56.

Ackman, D. "Pay Madness at Enron." *Forbes,* Mar. 22, 2002. (www.forbes.com/2002/03/22/0322enronpay.html)

Adams, S. *The Dilbert Principle.* New York: HarperBusiness, 1996.

Adler, P. S., and Borys, B. "Two Types of Bureaucracy: Enabling and Coercive." *Administrative Science Quarterly,* 1996, *41,* 61–89.

Alderfer, C. P. *Existence, Relatedness, and Growth.* New York: Free Press, 1972.

Alderfer, C. P. "Consulting to Underbounded Systems." In C. P. Alderfer and C. Cooper (eds.), *Advances in Experiential Social Processes.* Vol. 2. New York: Wiley, 1979.

Alford, C. F. *Whistleblowers: Broken Lives and Organizational Power.* Ithaca, N.Y.: Cornell University Press, 2001.

Allison, G. *Essence of Decision: Explaining the Cuban Missile Crisis.* New York: Little, Brown, 1971.

Alterman, E. "Wrong on the Wall, and Most Else." *New York Times,* Nov. 12, 1989, p. E-23.

American Customer Satisfaction Index, 2002. (www.theacsi.org/third_quarter.htm#app)

Anderson, S., Cavanagh, J., Hartman, C., and Leondar-Wright, B. "Executive Excess 2001." Washington, D.C.: Institute for Policy Studies, 2001. (http://ufenet.org/press/2001/EE2001.pdf)

Appelbaum, E., Bailey, T., Berg, P., and Kalleberg, A. L. *Manufacturing Advantage: Why High-Performance Work Systems Pay Off.* New York: Cornell University Press, 2000.

Argyris, C. *Personality and Organization.* New York: HarperCollins, 1957.

Argyris, C. *Interpersonal Competence and Organizational Effectiveness.* Homewood, Ill.: Irwin, 1962.

Argyris, C. *Integrating the Individual and the Organization.* New York: Wiley, 1964.

Argyris, C. "Empowerment: The Emperor's New Clothes." *Harvard Business Review,* May/June 1998, *76*(3).

Argyris, C., and Schön, D. A. *Theory in Practice: Increasing Professional Effectiveness.* San Francisco: Jossey-Bass, 1974.

Argyris, C., and Schön, D. A. *Organizational Learning: A Theory of Action Perspective.* Reading, Mass.: Addison-Wesley, 1978.

Argyris, C., and Schön, D. A. *Organizational Learning II: Theory, Method, and Practice.* Reading, Mass.: Addison-Wesley, 1996.

Armstrong, D. *Managing by Storying Around.* New York: Doubleday, 1992.

Associated Press. "McDonald's Opens up in India." *Kansas City Star,* Oct. 14, 1996, p. A-4.

Aubrey, B., and Tilliette, B. *Savoir faire savoir: L'apprentissage de l'action en entreprise* [Knowing and teaching: Action learning in the enterprise]. Paris: InterÉditions, 1990.

"Average Sales Per Store." *Bizstats.com,* 2002. (www.bizstats.com/realworld.htm)

Axelrod, R. "More Effective Choice in the Prisoner's Dilemma." *Journal of Conflict Resolution,* 1980, *24,* 379–403.

Babineck, M. "Empire Strikes Back over Use of 'Star Wars' Names." *Houston Chronicle,* Feb. 7, 2002. (www.chron.com/cs/CDA/story.hts/special/enron/1246185)

Baldridge, J. V. *Power and Conflict in the University.* New York: Wiley, 1971.

Baldridge, J. V., and Deal, T. E. (eds.). *Managing Change in Educational Organizations.* Berkeley, Calif.: McCutchan, 1975.

Bales, F. *Personality and Interpersonal Behavior.* Austin, Tex.: Holt, Rinehart and Winston, 1970.

Barber, B. R. *Jihad vs. McWorld: How the Planet Is Both Falling Apart and Coming Together—and What This Means for Democracy.* New York: Times Books, 1995.

Bardach, E. *The Implementation Game: What Happens After a Bill Becomes Law.* Cambridge, Mass.: MIT Press, 1977.

Barley, S. R. "The Alignment of Technology and Structure Through Roles and Networks." *Administrative Science Quarterly,* 1990, *35,* 61–103.

Barnes, L. B., and Kriger, M. P. "The Hidden Side of Organizational Leadership." *Sloan Management Review,* Fall 1986, pp. 15–25.

Barry, D. "A Man Who Became More Than a Mayor." *New York Times,* Dec. 31, 2001.

Barstow, D., and Bergman, L. "At a Texas Foundry, an Indifference to Life." *New York Times,* Jan. 8, 2003(a), pp. A1 & A14-A15.

Barstow, D., and Bergman, L. "Deaths on the Job, Slaps on the Wrist." *New York Times,* Jan. 10, 2003(b), pp. A1, A14-A15.

Barstow, D., and Bergman, L. "Family's Profit, Wrung from Blood and Sweat." *New York Times,* Jan. 9, 2003(c), pp. A1, A14-A15.

Bartlett, C. A., and Elderkin, K. W. "General Electric: Reg Jones and Jack Welch." Case no. 9–391–144. Boston: Harvard Business School Case Services, 1991.

Barton, L. *Crisis in Organizations.* Cincinnati: Southwest, 2001.

Bass, B. M. *Stogdill's Handbook of Leadership: A Survey of Theory and Research.* New York: Free Press, 1981.

Bass, B. M. *Leadership and Performance Beyond Expectations.* New York: Free Press, 1985.

Bass, B. M. *Bass & Stogdill's Handbook of Leadership: Theory, Research, and Managerial Application.* (3rd ed.) New York: Free Press, 1990.

Bass, B., Avolio, B., and Atwater, L. "The Transformational and Transactional Leadership of Men and Women." *Applied Psychology: An International Review,* 1996, *45,* 5–34.

Bateson, G. *Steps to an Ecology of Mind.* New York: Ballantine, 1972.

Beam, A. "Michael Porter vs. McGraw-Hill." *Boston Globe,* Sept. 20, 1989, p. 40.

Bell, T. E., and Esch, K. "The Fatal Flaw in Flight 51-L." *IEEE Spectrum,* Feb. 1987, pp. 36–51.

Bellow, G., and Moulton, B. *The Lawyering Process: Cases and Materials.* Mineola, N.Y.: Foundation Press, 1978.

Bennis, W. G. *Why Leaders Can't Lead: The Unconscious Conspiracy Continues.* San Francisco: Jossey-Bass, 1989.

Bennis, W. G., and Nanus, B. *Leaders: Strategies for Taking Charge.* New York: HarperCollins, 1985.

Bensimon, E. M. "The Meaning of 'Good Presidential Leadership': A Frame Analysis." *Review of Higher Education,* 1989, *12,* 107–123.

Bensimon, E. M. "Viewing the Presidency: Perceptual Congruence Between Presidents and Leaders on Their Campuses." *Leadership Quarterly,* 1990, *1,* 71–90.

Bergquist, W. H. *The Four Cultures of the Academy: Insights and Strategies for Improving Leadership in Collegiate Organizations.* San Francisco: Jossey-Bass, 1992.

Bernstein, A. "Why ESOP Deals Have Slowed to a Crawl." *Business Week,* Mar. 18, 1996, pp. 101–102.

"The Best Places to Work in America." *Fortune,* 2002. (www.fortune.com/fortune/bestcompanies)

Bethune, G., and Huler, S. *From Worst to First: Behind the Scenes of Continental's Remarkable Comeback.* New York: Wiley, 1999.

Bettelheim, B. *The Uses of Enchantment.* New York: Vintage Books, 1977.

Bing, S. *What Would Machiavelli Do? The Ends Justify the Meanness.* New York: HarperBusiness, 2000.

Bion, W. R. *Experiences in Groups.* London: Tavistock, 1961.

Birnbaum, R. *How Colleges Work: The Cybernetics of Academic Organization and Leadership.* San Francisco: Jossey-Bass, 1988.

Birnbaum, R. *How Academic Leadership Works: Understanding Success and Failure in the College Presidency.* San Francisco: Jossey-Bass, 1992.

Blake, R., and Mouton, J. S. *Building a Dynamic Corporation Through Grid Organizational Development.* Reading, Mass.: Addison-Wesley, 1969.

Blake, R., and Mouton, J. S. "A Comparative Analysis of Situationalism and 9,9 Management by Principle." *Organizational Dynamics,* Spring 1982, pp. 20–42.

Blake, R., and Mouton, J. S. *Managerial Grid III.* Houston, Tex.: Gulf, 1985.

Blanchard, K., and Johnson, S. *The One-Minute Manager.* New York: Morrow, 1982.

Blank, W., Weitzel, J. R., and Green, S. G. "A Test of the Situational Leadership Theory." *Personnel Psychology,* 1990, *43,* 579–597.

Blau, P. M., and Scott, W. R. *Formal Organizations: A Comparative Approach.* Novato, Calif.: Chandler & Sharp, 1962.

Block, P. *The Empowered Manager: Positive Political Skills at Work.* San Francisco: Jossey-Bass, 1987.

Blum, A. "Collective Bargaining: Ritual or Reality." *Harvard Business Review,* Nov.-Dec. 1961, pp. 63–69.

Blumberg, P. *Industrial Democracy: The Sociology of Participation.* New York: Schocken Books, 1968.

Blumer, H. *Symbolic Interaction: Perspective and Method.* Upper Saddle River, N.J.: Prentice Hall, 1969.

Bodily, S., and Bruner, S. "Transformation of Enron 1986—2000." Multimedia Case, Darden School, University of Virginia, 2002.

Bok, S. *Lying: Moral Choice in Public and Private Life.* New York: Vintage Books, 1978.

Bolman, L. "The Client as Theorist." In J. Adams (ed.), *New Technologies in Organization Development.* La Jolla, Calif.: University Associates, 1975.

Bolman, L. G., and Deal, T. E. *Modern Approaches to Understanding and Managing Organizations.* San Francisco: Jossey-Bass, 1984.

Bolman, L. G., and Deal, T. E. "Leadership and Management Effectiveness: A Multi-Frame, Multi-Sector Analysis." *Human Resource Management,* 1991, *30,* 509–534.

Bolman, L. G., and Deal, T. E. "Leading and Managing: Effects of Context, Culture, and Gender." *Education Administration Quarterly,* 1992(a), *28,* 314–329.

Bolman, L. G., and Deal, T. E. "Reframing Leadership: The Effects of Leaders' Images of Leadership." In K. E. Clark, M. B. Clark, and D. Campbell (eds.), *Impact of Leadership.* Greensboro, N.C.: Center for Creative Leadership, 1992(b).

Bolman, L. G., and Deal, T. E. *Leading with Soul: An Uncommon Journey of Spirit.* (2nd ed.) San Francisco: Jossey-Bass, 2001.

Bolman, L. G., and Granell, E. "Versatile Leadership: A Comparative Analysis of Reframing in Venezuelan Managers." Paper presented at the World Conference of the Ibero-American Academy of Management, Madrid, Dec. 1999.

Bower, J. L. *Managing the Response Allocation Process.* Boston: Division of Research, Harvard Business School, 1970.

Bower, M. *The Will to Manage: Corporate Success Through Programmed Management.* New York: McGraw-Hill, 1966.

Bradford, D. L., and Cohen, A. R. *Managing for Excellence.* New York: Wiley, 1984.

Briand, M. "People, Lead Thyself." *Kettering Review,* Summer 1993, pp. 38–46.

Brief, A. P., and Downey, H. K. "Cognitive and Organizational Structure: A Conceptual Analysis of Implicit Organizing Theories." *Human Relations,* 1983, *36*(12), 1065–1090.

Broder, J. M., and Schmitt, E. "U.S. Attacks on Holdouts Dealt Iraqis Final Blow." *New York Times,* Apr. 13, 2003, p. B1.

Broughton, I. *Hangar Talk: Interview with Fliers 1920s to 1990s.* Cheney, Wash.: Eastern Washington University Press, 1988.

Brown, L. D. *Managing Conflict at Organizational Interfaces.* Reading, Mass.: Addison-Wesley, 1983.

Brown, L. D. "Power Outside Organizational Paradigms: Lessons from Community Partnerships." In S. Srivastva and Associates, *The Functioning of Executive Power: How Executives Influence People and Organizations.* San Francisco: Jossey-Bass, 1986.

Bunker, B. B., and Alban, B. T. *Large Group Interventions: Engaging the Whole System for Rapid Change.* San Francisco: Jossey-Bass, 1996.

Burns, J. M. *Leadership*. New York: HarperCollins, 1978.

Burrough, B., and Helyar, J. *Barbarians at the Gate: The Fall of RJR Nabisco*. New York: HarperCollins, 1990.

Burrows, P. "Carly's Last Stand?" *Business Week*, Dec. 24, 2001.
(www.businessweek.com/magazine/content/01_52/b3763001.htm)

Burrows, P., and Elstrom, P. "HP's Carly Fiorina: The Boss." *Business Week*, Aug. 2, 1999, pp. 76–84.

Byrne, J. A. "The Shredder: Did CEO Dunlap Save Scott Paper—or Just Pretty It Up?" *Business Week*, Jan. 15, 1996, pp. 56–61.

Byrne, J. A. "Inside McKinsey." *Business Week*, July 8, 2002(a), pp. 66–76.

Byrne, J. A. "Joe Berardino's Fall from Grace." *Business Week*, Aug. 12, 2002(b), pp. 50–56.

Byrne, J. A., France, M., and Zellner, W. "At Enron, the Environment Was Ripe for Abuse." *Business Week*, Feb. 25, 2002.
(www.businessweek.com/magazine/content/02_08/b3771092.htm)

Byrne, J. A., Lavelle, L., Byrnes, N., and Vickers, M. "How to Fix Corporate Governance." *Business Week*, May 6, 2002, pp. 69–78.

Byrnes, N., Byrne, J. A., Edwards, C., and Lee, L. "The Good CEO." *Business Week*, Sept. 23, 2002, pp. 80–88.

Cahlink, G. "Federal Aviation Administration: Cruising Altitude." *GovExec.Com*, May 15, 2002.
(www.govexec.com/features/fpp/fpp02/faa.htm)

Campbell, D. "If I'm in Charge, Why Is Everyone Laughing?" Paper presented at the Center for Creative Leadership, Greensboro, N.C., 1983.

Campbell, J. *The Power of Myth*. New York: Doubleday, 1988.

Carless, S. A. "Gender Differences in Transformational Leadership: An Examination of Superior, Leader, and Subordinate Perspectives." *Sex Roles: A Journal of Research*, Dec. 1998, pp. 1–10.
(www.findarticles.com/cf_dls/m2294/11–12_39/53590324/p1/article.jhtml?term=)

Carlson, S. *Executive Behavior*. Stockholm: Strombergs, 1951.

Carlzon, J. *Moments of Truth*. New York: Ballinger, 1987.

Case, J. *Open Book Management: The Coming Business Revolution*. New York: HarperBusiness, 1995.

Chaize, J. *La porte du changement s'ouvre de l'interieur: Les trois mutations de l'entreprise* [The door to change opens from the inside: The three transformations of the corporation]. Paris: Calmann-Lévy, 1992.

Chandler, A. D., Jr. *Strategy and Market Structure*. Cambridge, Mass.: MIT Press, 1962.

Chandler, A. D., Jr. *The Visible Hand: The Managerial Revolution in American Business*. Cambridge, Mass.: Harvard University Press, 1977.

Chandler, S. "United We Own." *Business Week*, Mar. 18, 1996, pp. 96-100.

Charan, R., and Useem, J. "Why Companies Fail." *Fortune*, May 27, 2002, pp. 50–62.

Cherniss, C. "Emotional Intelligence: What It Is and Why It Matters." Paper presented at Annual Meeting of the Society for Industrial and Organizational Psychology, New Orleans, 2000.

"China Issues White Paper on Labor, Social Security." *People's Daily*, Apr. 30, 2002.
(http://english.peopledaily.com.cn/200204/29/eng20020429_94943.shtml)

"China Says 'No' to Pirated Software." *People's Daily*, Apr. 5, 2002.
(http://english.peopledaily.com.cn/200204/05/eng20020405_93534.shtml

Clark, B. R. "The Organizational Saga in Higher Education." In J. V. Baldridge and T. E. Deal (eds.), *Managing Change in Educational Organizations*. Berkeley, Calif.: McCutchan, 1975.

Cleveland, H. *The Knowledge Executive: Leadership in an Information Society*. New York: Dutton, 1985.

Clifford, D. K., and Cavanagh, R. E. *The Winning Performance*. New York: Bantam Books, 1985.

Cohen, M., and March, J. G. *Leadership and Ambiguity*. New York: McGraw-Hill, 1974.

Cohen, P. S. "Theories of Myth." *Man*, 1969, *4*, 337–353.

Coleman, J. S. *Equality of Educational Opportunity*. Washington, D.C.: National Center for Educational Statistics, U. S. Department of Health, Education, and Welfare, 1966.

Coles, T. "How Rudy Rallied Us." *New York Post*, Sept. 9, 2002. (www.nypost.com/postopinion/opedcolumnists/56550.htm)

Collins, B. E., and Guetzkow, H. *A Social Psychology of Group Processes for Decision Making.* New York: Wiley, 1964.

Collins, J. C. *Good to Great: Why Some Companies Make the Leap and Others Don't.* New York: HarperCollins, 2001.

Collins, J. C., and Porras, J. I. *Built to Last: Successful Habits of Visionary Companies.* New York: HarperBusiness, 1994.

Collinson, D. L., and Collinson, M. "Sexuality in the Workplace: The Domination of Men's Sexuality." In J. Hearn, D. L. Sheppard, P. Tancred-Sheriff, and G. Burrell (eds.), *The Sexuality of Organization.* London: Sage, 1989.

Colvin, G. "The 50 Best Companies for Asians, Blacks, and Hispanics." *Fortune,* July 19, 1999, pp. 53–58.

Conger, J. A. *The Charismatic Leader: Behind the Mystique of Exceptional Leadership.* San Francisco: Jossey-Bass, 1989.

Corwin, R. "Organizations as Loosely Coupled Systems: Evolution of a Perspective." Paper presented at the Conference on Schools as Loosely Coupled Organizations, Stanford University, Nov. 1976.

Cox, H. *The Feast of Fools.* Cambridge, Mass.: Harvard University Press, 1969.

Cox, T., Jr. *Cultural Diversity in Organizations: Theory, Research, and Practice.* San Francisco: Berrett-Koehler, 1994.

Cronshaw, S. F. "Effects of Categorization, Attribution, and Encoding Processes on Leadership Perspectives." *Journal of Applied Psychology,* 1987, *72*(1), 91–106.

Crosby, P. *Let's Talk Quality.* New York: McGraw-Hill, 1989.

Crozier, M., and Friedberg, E. *L'acteur et le système* [The actor and the system]. Paris: Points/Politique Seuil, 1977.

Cusumano, M. A., and Selby, R. W. *Microsoft Secrets: How the World's Most Powerful Software Company Creates Technology, Shapes Markets, and Manages People.* New York: Free Press, 1995.

Cyert, R. M., and March, J. G. *A Behavioral Theory of the Firm.* Upper Saddle River, N.J.: Prentice Hall, 1963.

Dalton, M. *Men Who Manage.* New York: Wiley, 1959.

David, G. "Can McDonald's Cook Again?" *Fortune,* Apr. 14, 2003, pp. 120–29.

Davis, M., and others. "The Structure of Educational Systems." Paper presented at the Conference on Schools as Loosely Coupled Organizations, Stanford University, Nov. 1976.

Deal, T. E., and Jenkins, W. A. *Managing the Hidden Organization: Strategies for Empowering Your Behind-the-Scenes Employees.* New York: Warner Books, 1994.

Deal, T. E., and Kennedy, A. A. *Corporate Cultures.* Reading, Mass.: Addison-Wesley, 1982.

Deal, T. E., and Key, M. K. *Corporate Celebration.* San Francisco: Berrett-Koehler, 1998.

Deal, T. E., and Nutt, S. C. *Promoting, Guiding, and Surviving Change in School Districts.* Cambridge, Mass.: Abt Associates, 1980.

De Geus, A. "Companies: What Are They?" *RSA Journal,* June 1995, pp. 26–35.

Delbanco, A. "Scholarships for the Rich." *New York Times Magazine,* Sept. 1, 1996, pp. 36–39.

Deming, W. E. *Out of the Crisis.* Cambridge, Mass.: MIT Center for Advanced Engineering Study, 1986.

De Pree, M. *Leadership Is an Art.* New York: Dell, 1989.

De Pree, M. *Leadership Jazz.* New York: Dell, 1992.

Dewan, S. K. "A Video Study of Enron Offers a Picture of Life Before the Fall." *New York Times,* Jan. 31, 2002, pp. C1 & C7.

DiMaggio, P. J., and Powell, W. W. "The Iron Cage Revisited: Institutional Isomorphism and Collective Rationality in Organizational Fields." *American Sociological Review,* Apr. 1983, *48,* 147–160.

Dittmer, L. "Political Culture and Political Symbolism: Toward a Theoretical Synthesis." *World Politics,* 1977, *29,* 552–583.

Doktor, J. "The Early Implementation of the Family Resource and Youth Services Centers of Kentucky: Multi-Frame Perspective." Unpublished doctoral dissertation, Vanderbilt University, 1993.

Dornbusch, S., and Scott, W. R. *Evaluation and the Exercise of Authority.* San Francisco: Jossey-Bass, 1975.

Downer, L. *The Brothers: The Hidden World of Japan's Richest Family.* New York: Random House, 1994.

Drucker, P. F. "Peter Drucker's 1990s: The Futures That Have Already Happened." *Economist,* Oct. 21, 1989, pp. 19–20, 24.

Drucker, P. F. *Managing the Future: The 1990s and Beyond.* New York: Plume, 1993.

Dunford, R. W. *Organizational Behavior: An Organizational Analysis Perspective.* Sydney: Addison-Wesley, 1992.

Dunford, R. W., and Palmer, I. C. "Claims About Frames: Practitioners' Assessment of the Utility of Reframing." *Journal of Management Education,* 1995, *19,* 96–105.

Dwyer, J., Flynn, K. and Fessenden, F. "9/11 Exposed Deadly Flaws in Rescue Plan." *New York Times,* July 7, 2002, pp. A1 & A10–11.

Dwyer, P., Engardio, P., Schiller, Z., and Reed, S. "Tearing Up Today's Organization Chart." *Business Week,* 1994 (21st Century Capitalism Special Issue), pp. 80–90.

Eagly, A. H., and Johnson, B. T. "Gender and Leadership Style: A Meta-Analysis." *Psychological Bulletin,* 1990, *111,* 233–256.

Eckholm, E. "China's New Leader Works to Set Himself Apart." *New York Times,* Jan. 12, 2003, p. A6.

Edelfson, C., Johnson, R., and Stromquist, N. *Participatory Planning in a School District.* Washington, D.C.: National Institute of Education, 1977.

Edelman, M. J. *Politics as Symbolic Interaction: Mass Arousal and Quiescence.* Orlando: Academic Press, 1971.

Edelman, M. J. *The Symbolic Uses of Politics.* Madison: University of Wisconsin Press, 1977.

Edwards, M. R. "In-Situ Team Evaluation: A New Paradigm for Measuring and Developing Leadership at Work." Paper presented at conference "The Impact of Leadership," Center for Creative Leadership, Colorado Springs, 1991.

Eichenwald, K. "Audacious Climb to Success Ended in a Dizzying Plunge." *New York Times,* Jan. 13, 2002(a), pp. 1, 26–27.

Eichenwald, K. "Flinging Billions of Dollars to Buy Assets No One Else Would Touch." *New York Times,* Oct. 3, 2002(b), p. C-4.

Eichenwald, K. "For WorldCom, Acquisitions Were Behind Its Rise and Fall.(*New York Times,* Aug. 8, 2002(c), pp. A-1, C-6.

Eichenwald, K., and Richtel, M. "Enron Trader Pleads Guilty to Conspiracy." *New York Times,* Oct. 18, 2002, pp. C1 & C9.

Elden, M. "Client as Consultant: Work Reform Through Participative Research." *National Productivity Review,* Spring 1983, pp. 136–147.

Elden, M. "Sociotechnical Systems Ideas as Public Policy in Norway: Empowering Participation Through Worker-Managed Change." *Journal of Applied Behavioral Science,* 1986, *22,* 239–255.

Elmore, R. F. "Organizational Models of Social Program Implementation." *Public Policy,* 1978, *26,* 185–228.

Enderud, H. G. "The Perception of Power." In J. G. March and J. Olsen (eds.), *Ambiguity and Choice in Organizations.* Bergen, Norway: Universitetsforlaget, 1976.

Engardio, P., and DeGeorge, G. "Importing Enthusiasm." *Business Week,* 1994 (21st Century Capitalism Special Issue), pp. 122–123.

Esposito, F., and others. "America's 50 Best Companies for Minorities." *Fortune,* July 9, 2002, pp. 122–128.

Ewing, J., Baker, S., Echikson, W., and Capell, K. "Eager Europeans Press Their Noses to the Glass." *Business Week International Edition,* Apr. 19, 1999. (www.businessweek.com/1999/99_16/b3625014.htm)

Farkas, C. M., and De Backer, P. *Maximum Leadership: The World's Leading CEOs Share Their Five Strategies for Success.* New York: Henry Holt, 1996.

Fayol, H. *General and Industrial Management.* (C. Stours, trans.) London: Pitman, 1949. (Originally published 1919)

Feinberg, M., and Tarrant, J. J. *Why Smart People Do Dumb Things.* New York: Simon & Schuster, 1995.

Fiedler, F. E. *A Theory of Leadership Effectiveness.* New York: McGraw-Hill, 1967.

Fiedler, F. E., and Chemers, M. *Leadership and Effective Management.* Glenview, Ill.: Scott, Foresman, 1974.

Fiedler, K. "Casual Schemata: Review and Criticism of Research on a Popular Construct." *Journal of Personality and Social Psychology,* 1982, *42,* 1001–1013.

Fine, G. A. "Justifying Work: Occupational Rhetorics as Resources in Restaurant Kitchens." *Administrative Science Quarterly,* 1996, *41,* 90–115.

"Fire and Forget." *Economist,* Apr. 20, 1996, pp. 51–52.

Firestone, D. "Senate Votes, 90–9, to Set Up Homeland Security Department Geared to Fight Terrorism." *New York Times,* Nov. 20, 2002, pp. A-1 and A-12.

Firestone, W. A. "Butte-Angels Camp: Conflict and Transformation." In R. Herriot and N. Gross (eds.), *The Dynamics of Planned Educational Change.* Berkeley, Calif.: McCutchan, 1977.

Fisher, R., and Ury, W. *Getting to Yes.* Boston: Houghton Mifflin, 1981.

Fiske, S. T., and Dyer, L. M. "Structure and Development of Social Schemata: Evidence from Positive and Negative Transfer Effects." *Journal of Personality and Social Psychology,* 1985, *48*(4), 839–852.

Fleishman, E. A., and Harris, E. F. "Patterns of Leadership Behavior Related to Employee Grievances and Turnover." *Personnel Psychology,* 1962, *15,* 43–56.

Floden, R. E., and Weiner, S. S. "Rationality to Ritual." *Policy Sciences,* 1978, *9,* 9–18.

Follett, M. P. *The New State: Group Organization and the Solution of Popular Government.* London: Longmans, 1918.

Foucault, M. *Surveiller et punir* [Supervise and punish]. Paris: NRF-Gallimard, 1975.

Frangos, S. *Team Zebra.* New York: Wiley, 1996.

Freiberg, K., and Freiberg, J. *Nuts: Southwest Airlines' Crazy Recipe for Business and Personal Success.* New York: Bantam Doubleday, 1998.

French, J.R.P., and Raven, B. H. "The Bases of Social Power." In D. Cartwright (ed.), *Studies in Social Power.* Ann Arbor, Mich.: Institute for Social Research, 1959.

Frensch, P. A., and Sternberg, R. J. "Skill-Related Differences in Chess Playing." In R. J. Sternberg and P. A. Frensch (eds.), *Complex Problem Solving.* Hillsdale, N.J.: Erlbaum, 1991.

Freudenberg, W. R., and Gramling, R. "Bureaucratic Slippage and Failures of Agency Vigilance." *Social Problems,* 1994, *4(1),* 214–239.

Fried, I. "HP Board Slams Walter Hewlett." *CNet News.Com,* Jan. 18, 2002. (http://news.com.com/2100–1001–818687.html?tag=bplst)

Friedman, R. *Front Stage, Backstage: The Dramatic Structure of Labor Negotiations.* Cambridge, Mass.: MIT Press, 1994.

Frost, P. J. *Organizational Culture.* Thousand Oaks, Calif.: Sage, 1985.

Frost, P. J. "Power, Politics, and Influence." In L. W. Porter and others (eds.), *The Handbook of Organizational Communication.* Thousand Oaks, Calif.: Sage, 1986.

Fulghum, R. *From Beginning to End: The Rituals of Our Lives.* New York: Villard Books, 1995.

Galbraith, J. R. *Designing Complex Organizations.* Reading, Mass.: Addison-Wesley, 1973.

Galbraith, J. R. *Organization Design.* Reading, Mass.: Addison-Wesley, 1977.

Galbraith, J. R. *Designing Organizations: An Executive Briefing on Strategy, Structure, and Process.* San Francisco: Jossey-Bass, 1993.

Gallos, J. V., Ramsey, V. J., and Associates. *Teaching Diversity: Listening to the Soul, Speaking from the Heart.* San Francisco: Jossey-Bass, 1997.

Gamson, W. A. *Power and Discontent.* Florence, Ky.: Dorsey Press, 1968.

Ganitsky, J., and Sancho, A. "Martín Varsavsky (A)." *Revista de Empresa,* July—Sept. 2002, *1*(1), 97–126. (www.revistadeempresa.com/REVISTA/Public.nsf/index?OpenFrameSet)

Gardner, H. *Frames of Mind: The Theory of Multiple Intelligences.* (10th anniversary ed.) New York: Basic Books, 1993.

Gardner, J. W. *Handbook of Strategic Planning.* New York: Wiley, 1986.

Gardner, J. W. *The Moral Aspects of Leadership.* Washington, D.C.: Independent Sector, 1987.

Gardner, J. W. *On Leadership.* New York: Free Press, 1989.

Garland, H. "Throwing Good Money After Bad: The Effect of Sunk Costs on the Decision to Escalate." *Journal of Applied Psychology,* 1990, *75,* 728–731.

Gaventa, J. *Power and Powerlessness: Quiescence and Rebellion in an Appalachian Valley.* Urbana: University of Illinois Press, 1980.

Gegerenzer, G., Hoffrage, U., and Kleinbölting, H. "Probabilistic Mental Models: A Brunswikian Theory of Confidence." *Psychological Review,* 1991, *98,* 506–528.

Gertz, D., and Baptista, J.P.A. *Grow to Be Great: Breaking the Downsizing Cycle.* New York: Free Press, 1995.

Ghoshal, S., and Bartlett, C. A. "The Multinational Corporation as an Interorganizational Network." *Academy of Management Review,* 1990, *15,* 603–625.

Giuliani, R., and Kurson, K. *Leadership.* New York: Miramax, 2002.

Goffman, E. *Frame Analysis*. Cambridge, Mass.: Harvard University Press, 1974.

Goldberg, L. R. "The Development of Markers for the Big-Five Factor Structure." *Psychological Assessment*, 1992, *4*, 26–42.

Goleman, D. *Emotional Intelligence*. New York: Bantam, 1995.

Goleman, D. *Working with Emotional Intelligence*. New York: Bantam Doubleday, 2000.

Goleman, D., McKee, A., and Boyatzis, R. E. *Primal Leadership: Realizing the Power of Emotional Intelligence*. Boston: Harvard Business School Press, 2002.

Goodman, D. "Doctor Fights Order to Quit Maine Island." *Boston Globe*, Oct. 15, 1983, pp. 1, 8.

Gordon, M. R. "Ex-Soviet Pilot Still Insists KAL 007 Was Spying." *New York Times*, Dec. 9, 1996, p. A6.

Graeff, C. L. "The Situational Leadership Theory: A Critical View." *Academy of Management Review*, Apr. 1983, pp. 321–338.

Greenleaf, R. K. *The Servant as Leader*. Newton Center, Mass.: Robert K. Greenleaf Center, 1973.

Gregory, K. L. "Native View Paradigms: Multiple Cultures and Cultural Conflict in Organizations." *Administrative Science Quarterly*, 1983, *28*, 359–376.

Greiner, L. E. "Evolution and Revolution as Organizations Grow." *Harvard Business Review*, July-Aug. 1972, pp. 37–46.

Greising, D. "Quality: How to Make It Pay." *Business Week*, Aug. 8, 1994, pp. 54–59.

Griffin, E. *The Reflective Executive: A Spirituality of Business and Enterprise*. New York: Crossroad, 1993.

Guéhenno, J.-M. *La fin de la démocratie* [The end of democracy]. Paris: Flammarion, 1993.

Gulick, L., and Urwick, L. (eds.). *Papers on the Science of Administration*. New York: Columbia University Press, 1937.

Hackman, J. R. (ed.). *Groups That Work (and Those That Don't): Creating Conditions for Effective Teamwork*. San Francisco: Jossey-Bass, 1989.

Hackman, J. R., and Oldham, G. R. *Work Redesign*. Reading, Mass.: Addison-Wesley, 1980.

Hackman, J. R., Oldham, G. R., Janson, R., and Purdy, K. "A New Strategy for Job Enrichment." In L. E. Boone and D. D. Bowen (eds.), *The Great Writings in Management and Organizational Behavior*. New York: Random House, 1987.

Hackman, J. R., and Wageman, R. "Total Quality Management: Empirical, Conceptual, and Practical Issues." *Administrative Science Quarterly*, 1995, *40*, 309–342.

Hakim, C. *We Are All Self-Employed*. San Francisco: Berrett-Koehler, 1994.

Hall, R. H. "The Concept of Bureaucracy: An Empirical Assessment." *American Journal of Sociology*, 1963, *49*, 32–40.

Hall, R. H. *Organizations: Structures, Processes, and Outcomes*. (4th ed.) Upper Saddle River, N.J.: Prentice Hall, 1987.

Hallinger, P., Bickman, L., and Davis, K. *What Makes a Difference? School Context, Principal Leadership, and Student Achievement*. Occasional Paper no. 3, National Center for Educational Leadership, Harvard University, 1990.

Hambleton, R. K., and Gumpert, R. "The Validity of Hersey and Blanchard's Theory of Leader Effectiveness." *Group and Organization Studies*, June 1982, pp. 225–242.

Hamel, G., and Prahalad, C. K. *Competing for the Future: Breakthrough Strategies for Seizing Control of Your Industry and Creating the Markets of Tomorrow*. Boston: Harvard Business School Press, 1994.

Hammer, M., and Champy, J. *Reengineering the Corporation*. New York: HarperCollins, 1993.

Hammonds, K. H. "Size Is Not a Strategy." *Fast Company*, Sept. 2002, pp. 78–86.

Hampden-Turner, C. *Creating Corporate Culture: From Discord to Harmony*. Reading, Mass.: Addison-Wesley, 1992.

Hamper, B. *Rivethead: Tales from the Assembly Line*. New York: Warner Books, 1992.

Hampton, W. J., and Norman, J. R. "General Motors: What Went Wrong—Eight Years and Billions of Dollars Haven't Made Its Strategy Succeed." *Business Week*, Mar. 16, 1987, p. 102.

Handy, C. *The Age of Unreason*. Boston: Harvard Business School Press, 1989.

Handy, C. *Understanding Organizations*. New York: Oxford University Press, 1993.

Handy, C. *The Age of Paradox*. Boston: Harvard Business School Press, 1995.

Hansell, S. "Citibank: The Ante Rises in East Asia." *New York Times*, July 14, 1996, sec. 3, pp. 1, 12–13.

Hansot, E. "Some Functions of Humor in Organizations." Unpublished paper, Kenyon College, 1979.

Heath, C., and Gonzalez, R. "Interaction with Others Increases Decision Confidence But Not Decision Quality." *Organizational Behavior and Human Decision Processes*, 1995, *61*, 305–326.

Hedberg, B.L.T., Nystrom, P. C., and Starbuck, W. H. "Camping on Seesaws: Prescriptions for a Self-Designing Organization." *Administrative Science Quarterly*, 1976, *21*, 41–65.

Heffernan, M. "The Female CEO." *Fast Company*, Aug. 2002, pp. 58–66.

Heffron, F. *Organization Theory and Public Organizations: The Political Connection.* Upper Saddle River, N.J.: Prentice Hall, 1989.

Heifetz, R. A. *Leadership Without Easy Answers.* Cambridge, Mass.: Belknap Press, 1994.

Heimovics, R. D., Herman, R. D., and Jurkiewicz Coughlin, C. L. "Executive Leadership and Resource Dependence in Nonprofit Organizations: A Frame Analysis." *Public Administration Review*, 1993, *53*, 419–427.

Heimovics, R. D., Herman, R. D., and Jurkiewicz Coughlin, C. L. "The Political Dimension of Effective Nonprofit Executive Leadership." *Nonprofit Management and Leadership*, 1995, *5*, 233–248.

Helgesen, S. *The Female Advantage: Women(s Ways of Leadership.* New York: Doubleday, 1990.

Helgesen, S. *The Web of Inclusion: A New Architecture for Building Great Organizations.* New York: Currency/Doubleday, 1995.

Henderson, R. M., and Clark, K. B. "Architectural Innovation: The Reconfiguration of Existing Product Technologies and the Failure of Established Firms." *Administrative Science Quarterly*, 1990, *35*, 9–30.

Hersch, S. M. *The Target Is Destroyed: What Really Happened to Flight 007 and What America Knew About It.* New York: Random House, 1986.

Hersey, P. *The Situational Leader.* New York: Warner Books, 1984.

Hersey, P., and Blanchard, K. H. *The Management of Organizational Behavior.* (3rd ed.) Upper Saddle River, N.J.: Prentice Hall, 1977.

Herzberg, F. *Work and the Nature of Man.* Cleveland: World, 1966.

"Hewlett-Packard Merger Pitch Awarded Top Honor." *Corporate Financing Week*, June 16, 2002. (www.corporatefinancingweek.com/current+news/best+deal+pitch.asp)

Hill, L. A., and Farkas, M. T. *Meg Whitman at eBay, Inc.* Boston: Harvard Business School, 2000.

Hofstede, G. *Culture's Consequences: International Differences in Work-Related Values.* Newbury Park, Calif.: Sage, 1984.

Hogan, R., Curphy, G. J., and Hogan, J. "What We Know About Leadership." *American Psychologist*, 1994, *49*, 493–504.

Hoge, W. "Crashing, and Saving, the Old Lads' Front Office." *New York Times*, Sept. 14, 2002, p. A14.

Holland, J. H. *Hidden Order.* Reading, Mass.: Addison-Wesley, 1995.

Hollander, E. P. *Leadership Dynamics.* New York: Free Press, 1978.

Holusha, J. "No Utopia, But to Workers, It's a Job." *New York Times*, Jan. 29, 1989, sec. 3, p. 1.

Hoskisson, R. E., Hitt, M. A., Johnson, R. A., and Grossman, W. "Conflicting Voices: The Effects of Institutional Ownership Heterogeneity and Internal Governance on Corporate Innovation Strategies." *Academy of Management Journal*, 2002, *45(4)*, 697–716.

House, R. J. "The Path-Goal Theory of Effectiveness." *Administrative Science Quarterly*, 1971, *16*, 321–338.

Iacocca, L., and Novak, W. *Iacocca.* New York: Bantam Books, 1984.

"An Interview with Kevin Rollins." *Austin American Statesman*, May 26, 2002. (www.austin360.com/aas/business/052602/0526rollinsqna.html)

Ishikawa, K. *What Is Total Quality Control? The Japanese Way.* Upper Saddle River, N.J.: Prentice Hall, 1985.

"It's 'More Than Any of Us Can Bear.'" *CBS News*, Sept. 26, 2001. (www.cbsnews.com/stories/2001/09/11/archive/main310811.shtml)

Jackall, R. *Moral Mazes: The World of Corporate Managers.* New York: Oxford University Press, 1988.

Jacobson, J. "Parity and the Presidency." *Chronicle of Higher Education*, June 27, 2002.

Jehn, K. A. "A Multimethod Examination of the Benefits and Detriments of Intragroup Conflict." *Administrative Science Quarterly*, 1995, *40*, 256–282.

Jensen, C. *No Downlink: A Dramatic Narrative About the* Challenger *Accident and Our Time.* New York: Farrar, Straus & Giroux, 1995.

Jensen, M. C. and Meckling, W. H. "The Nature of Man." *Journal of Applied Corporate Finance*, 1994, *7(2)*, 4–19.

John, O. P. "The 'Big Five' Factor Taxonomy: Dimensions of Personality in the Natural Language and in Questionnaires." In L. Pervin (ed.), *Handbook of Personality: Theory and Research.* New York: Guilford, 1990.

Johnson, K. "Divorced from the Job, Still Wedded to the Culture." *New York Times,* June 16, 1996, p. F-11.

Johnson, S. *Who Moved My Cheese?* New York: Putnam, 1998.

Juran, J. M. *Juran on Leadership for Quality: An Executive Handbook.* New York: Free Press, 1989.

Kahn, J. "Diversity Trumps the Downturn." *Fortune,* July 9, 2001, pp. 114–115.

Kahn, J. "China's Congress of Crony Capitalists." *New York Times,* Nov. 10, 2002, pp. 4–1 & 4. (www.nytimes.com/2002/11/10/weekinreview/10KAHN.html)

Kahneman, D., and Tversky, A. "Prospect Theory: An Analysis of Decisions Under Risk." *Econometrica,* 1979, *47,* 263–291.

Kamens, D. H. "Legitimating Myths and Education Organizations: Relationship Between Organizational Ideology and Formal Structure." *American Sociological Review,* 1977, *42,* 208–219.

Kanter, R. M. *Men and Women of the Corporation.* New York: Basic Books, 1977.

Kanter, R. M. *The Change Masters: Innovations for Productivity in the American Corporation.* New York: Simon & Schuster, 1983.

Kanter, R. M. *When Giants Learn to Dance.* New York: Simon & Schuster, 1989.

Katzell, R. A., and Yankelovich, D. *Work, Productivity, and Job Satisfaction.* New York: Psychological Corporation, 1975.

Katzenbach, J. R., and Smith, D. K. *The Wisdom of Teams: Creating the High-Performance Organization.* Boston: Harvard Business School Press, 1993.

Kaufer, N., and Leader, G. C. "Diana Lam (A)." Case. Boston University, 1987(a).

Kaufer, N., and Leader, G. C. "Diana Lam (B)." Case. Boston University, 1987(b).

Kauffman, E. M. "Creating the Uncommon Company." In R. W. Smilor and D. L. Sexton (eds.), *Leadership and Entrepreneurship: Personal and Organizational Development in Entrepreneurial Values.* Westport, Conn.: Quorum/Greenwood, 1996.

Keidel, R. W. "Baseball, Football, and Basketball: Models for Business." *Organizational Dynamics,* Winter 1984, pp. 5–18.

Keller, B. "While Gorbachev Gives In, the World Marvels at His Power." *New York Times,* Feb. 11, 1990, sec. 4, p. 1.

Keller, B. "Women Superintendents: Few and Far Between." *Education Week,* Nov. 10, 1999. (www.edweek.org/ew/ewstory.cfm?slug=11women.h19)

Kidder, T. *The Soul of a New Machine.* New York: Little, Brown, 1981.

Kidder, T. *Among School Children.* Boston: Houghton Mifflin, 1989.

Killian, K., Perez, F., and Siehl, C. "Ricardo Semler and Semco, S. A." Glendale, Ariz.: Thunderbird, American Graduate School of International Management, 1998.

Kleinfeld, N. R. "The Company as Family No More." *New York Times,* Mar. 4, 1996, sec. A, pp. 1, 8–10.

Kohlberg, L. "The Claim to Moral Adequacy of a Highest Stage of Moral Judgment." *Journal of Philosophy,* 1973, *70,* 630–646.

Komives, S. R. "Gender Differences in the Relationship and Hall Directors' Transformational and Transactional Leadership and Achieving Styles." *Journal of College Student Development,* 1991, *32,* 155–164.

Kopelman, R. E. "Job Redesign and Productivity: A Review of the Evidence." *National Productivity Review,* 1985, *4,* 237–255.

Korten, D. C. *When Corporations Rule the World.* San Francisco: Berrett-Koehler, 1995.

Kotter, J. P. *The General Managers.* New York: Free Press, 1982.

Kotter, J. P. *Power and Influence: Beyond Formal Authority.* New York: Free Press, 1985.

Kotter, J. P. *The Leadership Factor.* New York: Free Press, 1988.

Kotter, J. P., and Cohen, D. S. *The Heart of Change: Real Life Stories of How People Change Their Organizations.* Boston: Harvard Business School Press, 2002.

Kotter, J. P., and Heskett, J. L. *Corporate Culture and Performance.* New York: Free Press, 1992.

Kouzes, J. M., and Posner, B. Z. *The Leadership Challenge: How to Get Extraordinary Things Done in Organizations.* San Francisco: Jossey-Bass, 1987.

KPMG. "Mergers and Acquisitions: A Global Research Report." KPMG, 2000. (www.kpmg.co.uk/kpmg/uk/image/m&a_99.pdf)

Kühberger, A. "The Framing of Decisions: A New Look at Old Problems." *Organizational Behavior and Human Decision Processes,* 1995, *62,* 230–240.

Kuhn, T. S. *The Structure of Scientific Revolutions.* (2nd ed.) Chicago: University of Chicago Press, 1970.

Labaton, S. "Downturn and Shift in the Population Feed Boom in White Collar Crime." *New York Times,* June 2, 2002. (www.nytimes.com/2002/06/02/business/02CRIM.html?)

Labich, K. "Is Herb Kelleher America's Best CEO?" *Fortune,* May 2, 1994, pp. 44–52.

Lamb, D. "He Wages War-on Reality." *Los Angeles Times,* Apr. 8, 2003. (www.latimes.com/news/printedition/la-war-sahaf8apr08010418,1,1881104.story)

Landler, M. "Their Watchword Efficiency, Swiss Recoil at Air Disasters." *New York Times,* July 13, 2002, p. A1.

Langer, E. *Mindfulness.* Reading, Mass.: Addison-Wesley, 1989.

Lawler, E. E., III. *High-Involvement Management: Participative Strategies for Improving Organizational Performance.* San Francisco: Jossey-Bass, 1986.

Lawler, E. E., III. *From the Ground up: Six Principles for Building the New Logic Corporation.* San Francisco: Jossey-Bass, 1996.

Lawler, E. E., III, and Shuttle, J. L. "A Causal Correlation Test of the Need Hierarchy Concept." *Organizational Behavior and Human Performance,* 1973, *7,* 265–287.

Lawrence, A. T., and Weckler, D. A. "Can NUMMI's Team Concept Work for You? Part I: A Bicultural Experiment." *Northern California Executive Review,* Spring 1990, pp. 12–17.

Lawrence, P., and Lorsch, J. *Organization and Environment.* Boston: Division of Research, Harvard Business School, 1967.

Lax, D. A., and Sebenius, J. K. *The Manager as Negotiator.* New York: Free Press, 1986.

Leavitt, H. J. *Managerial Psychology.* (4th ed.) Chicago: University of Chicago Press, 1978.

Leavitt, H. J. "The Old Days, Hot Groups, and Managers' Lib." *Administrative Science Quarterly,* 1996, *41,* 288–300.

Ledford, G. E. "Employee Involvement: Lessons and Predictions." In J. R. Galbraith, E. E. Lawler III, and Associates (eds.), *Organizing for the Future: The New Logic of Managing Complex Organizations.* San Francisco: Jossey-Bass, 1993.

Lee, A. *Call Me Roger.* Chicago: Contemporary Books, 1988.

Lesgold, A., and Lajoie, S. "Complex Problem Solving in Electronics." In R. J. Sternberg and P. A. Frensch (eds.), *Complex Problem Solving.* Hillsdale, N.J.: Erlbaum, 1991.

Levering, R. "Going Places." *Fortune,* Jan. 8, 2001. (www.fortune.com/indexw.jhtml?doc_id=00003099&channel=artcol.jhtml&_DARGS=%2Ffragments%2Ffrg_top_story_body.jhtml.2_A&_DAV=artcol.jhtml)

Levering, R., and Moskowitz, M. *The 100 Best Companies to Work for in America.* New York: Plume, 1993.

Levering, R., and Moskowitz, M. "The 100 Best Companies to Work For." *Fortune,* Jan. 20, 2003, pp. 127–152.

Levine, D. I., and Tyson, L. D. "Participation, Productivity, and the Firm's Environment." In A. S. Blinder (ed.), *Paying for Productivity: A Look at the Evidence.* Washington, D.C.: Brookings Institution, 1990.

Levinson, H. *The Exceptional Executive.* Cambridge, Mass.: Harvard University Press, 1968.

Levinson, H., and Rosenthal, S. *CEO: Corporate Leadership in Action.* New York: Basic Books, 1984.

Lewin, K., Lippitt, R., and White, R. "Patterns of Aggressive Behavior in Experimentally Created Social Climates." *Journal of Social Psychology,* 1939, *10,* 271–299.

Lewis, N. A. "This Mr. Smith Gets His Way in Washington." *New York Times,* Oct. 12, 1996, pp. 17, 30.

Lifson, T., and Takagi, H. *Mitsubishi Corporation: Organizational Overview.* Boston: Harvard Business School Case Services, 1981.

Likert, R. *New Patterns of Management.* New York: McGraw-Hill, 1961.

Likert, R. *The Human Organization.* New York: McGraw-Hill, 1967.

Lingle, C. "China's Economy Faces Severe Pain." *Taipei Times,* Feb. 3, 2002. (www.taipeitimes.com/news/2002/02/03/story/0000122610)

Lipsky, M. *Street-Level Bureaucracy.* New York: Russell Sage Foundation, 1980.

Longworth, R. C. "Old Rules of Economics Don't Work the Way Textbooks Say They Should." *Kansas City Star,* Oct. 27, 1996, sec. K, pp. 1, 4.

Loomis, C. J. "Dinosaurs?" *Fortune,* May 3, 1993, pp. 36–42.

Lopez, B. *Crow and Weasel.* New York: North Point, 1998.

Lord, R. G., and Foti, R. J. "Schema Theories, Information Processing, and Organizational Behavior." In H. P. Sims, Jr., D. A. Gioia, and Associates (eds.), *The Thinking Organization.* San Francisco: Jossey-Bass, 1986.

Love, J. F. *McDonald's: Behind the Arches.* New York: Bantam Books, 1986.

Lubans, J. "More Than a Game." (www.lubans.org/morethanagame.html, 2001)

Lukes, S. *Power: A Radical View.* New York: Macmillan, 1974.

Lundin, W., and Lundin, K. *When Smart People Work for Dumb Bosses.* New York: McGraw-Hill, 1998.

Luthans, F. "Successful vs. Effective Real Managers." *Academy of Management Executive,* 1988, *2*(2), 127–132.

Luthans, F., Yodgetts, R. M., and Rosenkrantz, S. A. *Real Managers.* Cambridge, Mass.: Ballinger, 1988.

Lynch, P. "In Defense of the Invisible Hand." *Worth,* June 1996, pp. 86–92.

Lynn, L. E., Jr. *Managing Public Policy.* New York: Little, Brown, 1987.

Maccoby, M. *The Leader.* New York: Ballantine, 1981.

Machan, D. "DEC's Democracy." *Forbes,* Mar. 23, 1987, pp. 154, 156.

Machiavelli, N. *The Prince.* New York: Penguin Books, 1961. (Originally published 1514)

Maier, N. "Assets and Liabilities in Group Problem Solving." *Psychological Review,* 1967, *74,* 239–249.

Malavé, J. *Gerencia en salud: Un modelo innovador* [Health management: An innovative model]. Caracas: Ediciones IESA, 1995.

Manes, S., and Andrews, P. *Gates.* New York: Touchstone, 1994.

Mangham, I. L., and Overington, M. A. *Organizations as Theater: A Social Psychology of Dramatic Appearances.* New York: Wiley, 1987.

Manning, P. *Police Work: The Social Organization of Policing.* Cambridge, Mass.: MIT Press, 1979.

March, J. G. "The Technology of Foolishness." In J. G. March and J. Olsen (eds.), *Ambiguity and Choice in Organizations.* Bergen, Norway: Universitetsforlaget, 1976.

March, J. G., and Olsen, J. (eds.), *Ambiguity and Choice in Organizations.* Bergen, Norway: Universitetsforlaget, 1976.

March, J. G., and Simon, H. A. *Organizations.* New York: Wiley, 1958.

Markels, A., and Murray, M. "Call It Dumbsizing: Why Some Companies Regret Cost-Cutting." *Wall Street Journal,* May 14, 1996, p. 1.

Marshall, M. V. "An Introduction to the Marketing Concept of Managing an Institution's Future." Cambridge, Mass.: Institute for Educational Management, 1984.

Marx, K. *Capital: A Critique of Political Economy.* (S. Moore and E. Aveling, trans.) London, 1887.

Marx, R., Stubbart, C., Traub, V., and Cavanaugh, M. "The NASA Space Shuttle Disaster: A Case Study." *Journal of Management Case Studies,* 1987, *3,* 300–318.

Maslow, A. H. *Motivation and Personality.* New York: HarperCollins, 1954.

Mayo, E. *The Human Problems of an Industrial Civilisation.* New York: Macmillan, 1933.

Mayo, E. *The Social Problems of an Industrial Civilisation.* Boston: Division of Research, Graduate School of Business Administration, Harvard University, 1945.

McCaskey, M. B. *The Executive Challenge: Managing Change and Ambiguity.* Marshfield, Mass.: Pitman, 1982.

McClean, B. "Why Enron Went Bust." *Fortune,* Dec. 24, 2001, pp. 58–68.

McClelland, D. C. *Human Motivation.* Glenview, Ill.: Scott, Foresman, 1985.

McConnell, M. *Into the Mouth of the Cat: The Story of Lance Sijan, Hero of Vietnam.* New York: New American Library, 1986.

McConnell, M. *Challenger: A Major Malfunction.* New York: Doubleday, 1987.

McGrath, J. E. *Groups: Interaction and Performance.* Upper Saddle River, N.J.: Prentice Hall, 1984.

McGregor, D. *The Human Side of Enterprise.* New York: McGraw-Hill, 1960.

McLean, B. "Why Enron Went Bust." *Fortune,* Dec. 24, 2001, pp. 58–68.

McLennan, R. *Managing Organizational Change.* Upper Saddle River, N.J.: Prentice Hall, 1989.

McNamee, M., and Borrus, A. "Out of Control at Enron." *Business Week,* Apr. 8, 2002, pp. 32-33.

Mendelson, H., and Korin, A. "The Computer Industry: A Brief History." Palo Alto, Calif.: Stanford Business School, n.d. (http://wesley.stanford.edu/computer_history/)

Meredith, R. "New Blood for the Big Three's Plants: This Hiring Spree Is Rewarding Brains, Not Brawn." *New York Times,* Apr. 21, 1996, sec. 3, pp. 1, 3.

"Mergers and Acquisitions: A Global Research Report." KPMG, 2000. (www.kpmg.co.uk/kpmg/uk/image/m&a_99.pdf)

Meyer, J. W., and Rowan, B. "The Structure of Educational Organizations." In M. W. Meyer and Associates, *Environments and Organizations: Theoretical and Empirical Perspectives.* San Francisco: Jossey-Bass, 1978.

Meyer, J. W., and Rowan, B. "Institutionalized Organizations: Formal Structure as Myth and Ceremony." In J. W. Meyer and W. R. Scott (eds.), *Organizational Environments: Ritual and Rationality.* Thousand Oaks, Calif.: Sage, 1983(a).

Meyer, J. W., and Rowan, B. "The Structure of Educational Organizations." In J. W. Meyer and W. R. Scott (eds.), *Organizational Environments: Ritual and Rationality.* Thousand Oaks, Calif.: Sage, 1983(b).

Miller, D., and Friesen, P. H. *Organizations: A Quantum View.* Upper Saddle River, N.J.: Prentice Hall, 1984.

Mintzberg, H. *The Nature of Managerial Work.* New York: HarperCollins, 1973.

Mintzberg, H. *The Structuring of Organizations.* Upper Saddle River, N.J.: Prentice Hall, 1979.

Mintzberg, H. *The Rise and Fall of Strategic Planning: Reconceiving Roles for Planning, Plans, Planners.* New York: Free Press, 1994.

Mirvis, P. H. "Organization Development, Part I: An Evolutionary Perspective." *Research in Organizational Change and Development,* 1988, *2,* 1–57.

Mirvis, P. H. "Organization Development, Part II: A Revolutionary Perspective." In W. A. Passmore and R. W. Woodman (eds.), *Research in Organizational Change and Development,* Vol. 2. Greenwich, Conn.: JAI Press, 1990.

Mirvis, P. H., and Hall, D. T. "New Organizational Forms and the New Career." In D. T. Hall and Associates, *The Career Is Dead: Long Live the Career.* San Francisco: Jossey-Bass, 1996.

Mishel, L., Bernstein, J., and Schmitt, J. *The State of Working America, 2000/2001.* Ithaca, N.Y.: ILR Press, 2001.

Mitroff, I. I. *Stakeholders of the Organizational Mind: Toward a New View of Organizational Policy Making.* San Francisco: Jossey-Bass, 1983.

Mitroff, I. I., and Kilmann, R. H. "Stories Managers Tell: A New Tool for Organizational Problem Solving." *Management Review,* July 1975, pp. 18–28.

Moeller, J. "Bureaucracy and Teachers' Sense of Power." In N. R. Bell and H. R. Stub (eds.), *Sociology of Education.* Florence, Ky.: Dorsey Press, 1968.

Montgomery, L. "Earning Loyalty: Pay Is Only One Issue When It Comes to Retaining Employees." *Insidebiz.com,* 2000. (www.insidebiz.com/hamptonroads/special_report/special091800.htm)

Moore, J. F. "Predators and Prey: A New Ecology of Competition." *Harvard Business Review,* May-June 1993, pp. 75–86.

Morgan, A. *Prescription for Success: The Life and Values of Ewing Marion Kauffman.* Kansas City, Mo.: Andrews & McMeel, 1995.

Morgan, G. *Images of Organization.* Thousand Oaks, Calif.: Sage, 1986.

Morgan, G. *Imaginization: The Art of Creative Management.* Thousand Oaks, Calif.: Sage, 1993.

Morganthau, T. "Saying 'No' to New Coke." *Newsweek,* June 23, 1985, pp. 32–33.

Morris, B. "The Wealth Builders." *Fortune,* Dec. 11, 1995, pp. 80–94.

Morris, B. "Trophy Husbands." *Fortune,* Oct. 14, 2002, pp. 79–98.

Morrison, A. M. *The New Leaders: Guidelines on Leadership Diversity in America.* San Francisco: Jossey-Bass, 1992.

Morrison, A. M., White, R. P., and Van Velsor, E. *Breaking the Glass Ceiling*. Reading, Mass.: Addison-Wesley, 1987.

Mosser, N. R., and Walls, R. T. "Leadership Frames of Nursing Chairpersons and the Organizational Climate in Baccalaureate Nursing Programs." *Southern Online Journal of Nursing Research,* 2002, *3*(2). (www.snrs.org/members/SOJNR_articles/iss02vol03.htm)

Murphy, J. T. *Managing Matters: Reflections from Practice.* (Monograph.) Cambridge, Mass.: Graduate School of Education, Harvard University, 1985.

Myers, I. *Introduction to Type.* Palo Alto, Calif.: Consulting Psychologists Press, 1980.

Nadler, D. A., Gerstein, M. S., and Shaw, R. B. *Organizational Architecture: Designs for Changing Organizations.* San Francisco: Jossey-Bass, 1992.

Norris, F. K. "A Tale Told to Congress, Full of Sound, But Blurry." *New York Times,* Feb. 8, 2002, p. C-1.

Nussbaum, B., and Dobrzynski, J. H. "The Battle for Corporate Control." *Business Week,* May 18, 1987, pp. 102–109.

O'Grady, S. *Basher Five-Two: The True Story of F-16 Pilot Captain Scott O'Grady.* New York: Bantam Doubleday Dell, 1997.

Ohmae, K. *The Borderless World: Power and Strategy in the Interlinked Economy.* New York: HarperBusiness, 1990.

Oliver, T. *The Real Coke, the Real Story.* New York: Random House, 1986.

Olsen, J. "The Process of Interpreting Organizational History." In J. G. March and J. Olsen (eds.), *Ambiguity and Choice in Organizations.* Bergen, Norway: Universitetsforlaget, 1976(a).

Olsen, J. "Reorganization as a Garbage Can." In J. G. March and J. Olsen (eds.), *Ambiguity and Choice in Organizations.* Bergen, Norway: Universitetsforlaget, 1976(b).

"On a Clear Day You Can Still See General Motors." *Economist,* Dec. 2, 1989, pp. 77–78, 80.

Oppel, R. A. "How Enron Got California to Buy Power It Didn't Need." *New York Times,* May 8, 2002, p. A1.

O'Reilly, C. A., III, and Chatman, J. A. "Working Smarter and Harder: A Longitudinal Study of Managerial Success." *Administrative Science Quarterly,* 1994, *39,* 603–627.

Orgogozo, I. *Les paradoxes du management* [The paradoxes of management]. Paris: Les Éditions d'Organisation, 1991.

Ortner, S. "On Key Symbols." *American Anthropologist,* 1973, *75,* 1338–1346.

Oshry, B. *Seeing Systems: Unlocking the Mysteries of Organizational Life.* San Francisco: Berrett-Koehler, 1995.

Osterman, P. "Work-Family Programs and the Employment Relationship." *Administrative Science Quarterly,* 1995, *40,* 681–700.

O'Toole, J. *Leading Change: Overcoming the Ideology of Comfort and the Tyranny of Custom.* San Francisco: Jossey-Bass, 1995.

O'Toole, J. *Forming the Future.* New York: Blackwell, 1996.

O'Toole, P. *Corporate Messiah: The Hiring and Firing of Million-Dollar Managers.* New York: Morrow, 1984.

Owen, H. *Spirit: Transformation and Development in Organizations.* Potomac, Md.: Abbott, 1987.

Owen, H. *Open Space Technology.* Potomac, Md.: Abbott, 1993.

Owen, H. *Tales from Open Space.* Potomac, Md.: Abbott, 1995.

Palumbo, G. *Gerencia participativa: Un caso exito en el sector salud* [Participative management: A successful case in the health sector]. Caracas: Fundación Antonio Cisneros Bermudez, 1991.

Pande, P. S., Neuman, R. P., and Cavanagh, R. R. *The Six Sigma Way: How GE, Motorola and Other Top Companies Are Honing Their Performance.* New York: McGraw-Hill, 2000.

Paré, T. P. "Jack Welch's Nightmare on Wall Street." *Fortune,* Sept. 5, 1994, pp. 40–48.

Parker, S., and Wall, T. D. *Job and Work Design: Organizing Work to Promote Well-Being and Effectiveness.* Thousand Oaks, Calif.: Sage, 1998.

Paulson, E. *Inside Cisco: The Real Story of Sustained M&A Growth.* New York: Wiley, 2001.

Pennar, K. "Economic Anxiety." *Business Week,* Mar. 11, 1996, pp. 50–52.

Perrow, C. *Complex Organizations: A Critical Essay.* (2nd ed.) Glenview, Ill.: Scott, Foresman, 1979.

Perrow, C. *Complex Organizations: A Critical Essay.* (3rd ed.) New York: Random House, 1986.

Peters, B. G. *American Public Policy: Promise and Performance.* New York: Chatham House, 1999.

Peters, T. J., and Austin, N. *A Passion for Excellence.* New York: Random House, 1985.

Peters, T. J., and Waterman, R. H. *In Search of Excellence.* New York: HarperCollins, 1982.

Petzinger, T. *Hard Landing: The Epic Contest for Power and Profits That Plunged the Airlines into Chaos.* New York: Times Business, 1995.

Pfeffer, J. *Organizational Design.* Arlington Heights, Ill.: AHM, 1978.

Pfeffer, J. *Power in Organizations.* Boston: Pitman, 1981.

Pfeffer, J. *Managing with Power: Politics and Influence in Organizations.* Boston: Harvard Business School Press, 1992.

Pfeffer, J. *Competitive Advantage Through People: Unleashing the Power of the Work Force.* Boston: Harvard Business School Press, 1994.

Pfeffer, J. *The Human Equation: Building Profits by Putting People First.* Boston: Harvard Business School Press, 1998.

Pfeffer, J., and Salancik, G. *The External Control of Organizations.* New York: Harper & Row, 1978.

Pichault, F. *Ressources humaines et changement stratégique: Vers un management politique* [Human Resources and Strategic Change: Toward a Political Approach to Management]. Brussels, Belgium: DeBoeck, 1993.

Port, O. "Quality." *Business Week,* Nov. 30, 1992, pp. 66–72.

Porter, E. "Notes for the Looking for Leadership Conference." Paper presented at the Looking for Leadership Conference, Graduate School of Education, Harvard University, Dec. 1989.

Powell, W. W., Koput, K. W., and Smith-Doerr, L. "Interorganizational Collaboration and the Locus of Innovation: Networks of Learning in Biotechnology." *Administrative Science Quarterly,* 1996, *41,* 116–145.

Pressman, J. L., and Wildavsky, A. B. *Implementation.* Berkeley: University of California Press, 1973.

Quinn, R. E. *Beyond Rational Management: Mastering the Paradoxes and Competing Demands of High Performance.* San Francisco: Jossey-Bass, 1988.

Quinn, R. E., and Cameron, K. "Organizational Life Cycles and Shifting Criteria of Effectiveness." *Management Science,* 1983, *29,* 33–51.

Quinn, R. E., Faerman, S. R., Thompson, M. P., and McGrath, M. R. *Becoming a Master Manager: A Competency Framework.* New York: Wiley, 1996.

Ragins, B., Townsend, B., and Mattis, M. "Gender Gap in the Executive Suite: CEOs and Female Executives Report on Breaking the Glass Ceiling." *Academy of Management Executive,* 1998, *12*(1), 28–42.

Rallis, S. "Different Views of Knowledge Use by Practitioners." Unpublished paper, Graduate School of Education, Harvard University, 1980.

Rappaport, C. "A Tough Swede Invades the U.S." *Fortune,* Jan. 29, 1992, pp. 76–79.

Reddin, W. J. *Managerial Effectiveness.* New York: McGraw-Hill, 1970.

Reed, K. "Rituals of Combat: Air War." Unpublished manuscript, University of Southern California, 2001.

Reed, S., and Sains, A. "Outraged in Europe over ABB." *Business Week,* Mar. 4, 2002. (www.businessweek.com/magazine/content/02_09/b3772140.htm)

Reichheld, F. F. "Loyalty-Based Management." *Harvard Business Review,* Mar.-Apr. 1993, pp. 64–73.

Reichheld, F. F. *The Loyalty Effect: The Hidden Force Behind Growth, Profits, and Lasting Value.* Boston: Harvard Business School Press, 1996.

Reid, P. C. *Well Made in America: Lessons from Harley-Davidson on Being the Best.* New York: McGraw-Hill, 1989.

Renner, M. "Corporate Mergers Skyrocket." Worldwatch Institute, 2000. (www.globalpolicy.org/socecon/tncs/mergers/renner.htm)

Rice, A. K. *The Enterprise and Its Environment.* London: Tavistock, 1953.

Ricks, T. E. *Making the Corps.* New York: Scribner, 1997.

Ridout, C. F., and Fenn, D. H. "Job Corps." Boston: Harvard Business School Case Services, 1974.

Riebling, M. *Wedge: From Pearl Harbor to 9/11—How the Secret War Between the FBI and CIA Has Endangered National Security.* New York: Touchstone, 2002.

Rifkin, J. *The End of Work: The Decline of the Global Labor Force and the Dawn of the Post-Market Era.* Los Angeles: Tarcher/Putnam, 1995.

Rising, D. "Pilot Got Bad Information." *San Francisco Examiner,* July 9, 2002. (www.examiner.com/headlines/default.jsp?story=n.crash.0709w)

Ritti, R. R., and Funkhouser, G. R. *The Ropes to Skip and the Ropes to Know.* (2nd ed.) Columbus, Ohio: Grid, 1982.

Roberts, J. L., and Thomas, E. "Enron's Dirty Laundry." *Newsweek,* Mar. 11, 2002.

Rosener, J. B. "Ways Women Lead." *Harvard Business Review,* 1990, *68,* 119–125.

Rosenthal, E. "China's Communists Try to Decide What They Stand For." *New York Times,* May 1, 2002, p. A-3.

Rosenthal, R., and Jacobson, L. *Pygmalion in the Classroom: Teacher Expectations and Pupils' Intellectual Development.* Austin, Tex.: Holt, Rinehart and Winston, 1968.

Rossiter, C. *1787: The Grand Convention.* New York: New American Library, 1966.

Roush, C. *Inside Home Depot.* New York: McGraw-Hill, 1999.

Russ, J. *Les théories du pouvoir* [Theories of power]. Paris: Librairie Générale Française, 1994.

Ryan, M. "They Call Their Boss a Hero." *Parade,* Sept. 8, 1996, pp. 4–5.

Salancik, G. R., and Pfeffer, J. "An Examination of Need-Satisfaction Models of Job Attitudes." *Administrative Science Quarterly,* 1977, *22,* 427–456.

Salovey, P., Bedell, B., Detweiler, J. B., and Mayer, J. D. "Coping Intelligently: Emotional Intelligence and the Coping Process." In C. R. Snyder (Ed.), *Coping: The Psychology of What Works.* New York: Oxford University Press, 1999.

Salovey, P., and Mayer, J. "Emotional Intelligence." *Imagination, Cognition, and Personality,* 1990, *9*(3), 185–211.

Sapolsky, H. *The Polaris System Development.* Cambridge, Mass.: Harvard University Press, 1972.

Schein, E. H. *Process Consultation.* Reading, Mass.: Addison-Wesley, 1969.

Schein, E. H. *Organizational Culture and Leadership.* (2nd ed.) San Francisco: Jossey-Bass, 1992.

Schein, V. E. "Relationships Between Sex Role Stereotypes and Requisite Management Characteristics Among Female Managers." *Journal of Applied Psychology,* 1975, *75,* 340–344.

Schein, V. E. "The Relationship Between Sex Role Stereotypes and Requisite Management Characteristics: A Cross-Cultural Look." Paper presented at the 22d International Congress of Applied Psychology, Kyoto, Japan, July 1990.

Schelling, T. *The Strategy of Conflict.* Cambridge, Mass.: Harvard University Press, 1960.

Schemo, D. J. "Is VW's New Plant Lean, or Just Mean?" *New York Times,* Nov. 19, 1996, p. C1.

Schlesinger, J. M. "NUMMI Keeps Promise of No Layoffs by Setting Nonproduction Workdays." *Wall Street Journal,* Oct. 29, 1987, p. 30.

Schlesinger, L., Eccles, R., and Gabarro, J. *Managerial Behavior in Organizations.* New York: McGraw-Hill, 1983.

Schneider, B., and Alderfer, C. "Three Studies of Measures of Need Satisfaction in Organizations." *Administrative Science Quarterly,* 1973, *18,* 498–505.

Schuler, D. A., Rehbein, K., and Cramer, R. D. "Pursuing Strategic Advantage Through Political Means: A Multivariate Approach." *Academy of Management Journal,* 2002, *45(4),* 659–672.

Schwartz, H. S. "The Clockwork or the Snakepit: An Essay on the Meaning of Teaching Organizational Behavior." *Organizational Behavior Teaching Review,* 1986, *11,* 19–26.

Schwartz, J. "The Former C.E.O.: Darth Vader. Machiavelli. Skilling Set Intense Pace." *New York Times,* Feb. 7, 2002, pp. C-1 & C-7.

Schwartz, J., with Wald, M. L. "Like Jigsaw Puzzle, Pieces of Data Are Forming Picture of Shuttle Disaster." *New York Times,* Apr. 3, 2003, p. A-14.

Scott, W. R. *Organizations: Rational, Natural, and Open Systems.* Upper Saddle River, N.J.: Prentice Hall, 1981.

Scott, W. R. "The Organization of Environments: Network, Cultural, and Historical Elements." In J. W. Meyer and W. R. Scott (eds.), *Organizational Environments: Ritual and Rationality.* Thousand Oaks, Calif.: Sage, 1983.

Seeger, J. A., Lorsch, J. W., and Gibson, C. F. "First National City Bank Operating Group (A) and (B)." Boston: Harvard Business School Case Services, 1975.

Sellers, P. "True Grit." *Fortune,* Oct. 14, 2002, pp. 107–110.

Selznick, P. *Leadership and Administration.* New York: HarperCollins, 1957.

Semler, R. *Maverick: The Success Story Behind the World's Most Unusual Workplace.* New York: Warner Books, 1993.

Senge, P. M. *The Fifth Discipline: The Art and Practice of the Learning Organization.* New York: Doubleday/Currency, 1990.

Sennett, R. *Authority.* New York: Knopf, 1980.

Sérieyx, H. *Le big bang des organisations* [The organizational big bang]. Paris: Calmann-Lévy, 1993.

Shu, L., and Adams, A. S. "Is There Something More Important Behind Framing?" *Organizational Behavior and Human Decision Processes,* 1995, *62,* 216–219.

Simmel, G. *The Sociology of Georg Simmel.* New York: Free Press, 1950.

Simon, H. *Hidden Champions: Lessons from 500 of the World's Best Unknown Companies.* Boston: Harvard Business School Press, 1996.

Simon, H. A. *Administrative Behavior.* New York: Macmillan, 1947.

Sirianni, C. "Tavistock Institute Develops Practices of Contemporary Work Reform." Civic Practices Network, Brandeis University, 1995. (www.cpn.org/cpn/sections/topics/work/stories-studies/tavistock_institute.html)

Sloan, A. P., Jr. *My Years with General Motors.* New York: Macfadden, 1965.

Smith, C. S. "China Faces Problems Creating Jobs, Officials Say." *New York Times,* Apr. 30, 2002, p. A8.

Smith, H. *The Power Game.* New York: Random House, 1988.

Smith, R. "It's No Fun Running No. 1 When You're Taking the Heat." *Fortune,* Aug. 3, 1987, pp. 26–27.

Snook, S. *Friendly Fire: The Accidental Shootdown of U.S. Black Hawks over Northern Iraq.* Princeton: Princeton University Press, 2000.

Solomon, R. C. *Ethics and Excellence: Cooperation and Integrity in Business.* Oxford, England: Oxford University Press, 1993.

Sorkin, A. R. "Tyco Details Lavish Lives of Executives." *New York Times,* Sept. 18, 2002, p. C-1.

Spector, R., and McCarthy, D. *The Nordstrom Way: The Inside Story of America's #1 Customer Service Company.* New York: Wiley, 1995.

Stack, J., and Burlingham, B. *The Great Game of Business.* New York: Doubleday/Currency, 1994.

Stack, J., and Burlingham, B. *A Stake in the Outcome: Building a Culture of Ownership for the Long-Term Success of Your Business.* New York: Doubleday, 2002.

Staw, B. M., and Epstein. "What Bandwagons Bring: Effects of Popular Management Techniques on Corporate Performance, Reputation, and CEO Pay." *Administrative Science Quarterly,* 2000, *45(3),* 523–556.

Staw, B. M., and Hoang, H. "Sunk Costs in the NBA: Why Draft Order Affects Playing Time and Survival in Professional Basketball." *Administrative Science Quarterly,* 1995, *40,* 474–494.

Stein, N. "Winning the War to Keep Top Talent." *Fortune,* May 29, 2000.

Stern, R. N., and Barley, S. R. "Organizations and Social Systems: Organization Theory's Neglected Mandate." *Administrative Science Quarterly,* 1996, *41,* 146–162.

Sternberg, R. J. *Beyond IQ: A Triarchic Theory of Human Intelligence.* New York: Cambridge University Press, 1985.

Steward, T. A. "Managing in a Wired Company." *Fortune,* July 11, 1994, pp. 44–56.

Stires, D. "Fallen Arches." *Fortune,* Apr. 29, 2002, pp. 74–76.

Stogdill, R. *Handbook of Leadership.* New York: Free Press, 1974.

Stross, R. E. "Microsoft's Big Advantage—Hiring Only the Supersmart." *Fortune,* Nov. 25, 1996, pp. 159–162.

Taylor, F. W. *The Principles of Scientific Management.* New York, 1911.

Taylor, M., Ramaya, K., and Puia, G. "Outback Steakhouse, Inc." Kansas City: Bloch School of Business and Public Administration, University of Missouri-Kansas City, 1999.

Tetlock, P. E. "Cognitive Biases and Organizational Correctives: Do Both Disease and Cure Depend on the Politics of the Beholder?" *Administrative Science Quarterly,* 2000, *45,* 293–326.

Thompson, J. D. *Organizations in Action.* New York: McGraw-Hill, 1967.

Thorndike, E. L. "Intelligence and Its Uses." *Harper's,* 1920, *140,* 227–235.

Tichy, G. " Fusionen und Übernehmen: Erfolgsaussichten der Fusionen" [Mergers and Takeovers: Prospects for Success]. Beiträge zur Wirtschaftspolitik Nr. 6—Studie im Auftrag der Kammer für Arbeiter und Angestellte für Wien, Vienna, 2000.

Tichy, G. "What Do We Know About Success and Failure of Mergers." *Journal of Industry, Competition and Trade,* forthcoming.

Toffler, B. L., and Reingold, J. *Final Accounting: Ambition, Greed and the Fall of Arthur Andersen.* New York: Broadway, 2003.

Tomsho, R. "How Greyhound Lines Re-Engineered Itself Right into a Deep Hole." *Wall Street Journal,* Oct. 20, 1994, p. A1.

Topoff, H. R. "The Social Behavior of Army Ants." *Scientific American,* Nov. 1972, pp. 71–79.

Trahair, R.C.S. "George Elton Mayo." Bristol, England: Thoemmes, 2001. (www.thoemmes.com/encyclopedia/mayo.htm)

Treacy, M., and Wiersema, F. *The Discipline of Market Leaders: Choose Your Customers, Narrow Your Focus, Dominate Your Market.* Reading, Mass.: Addison-Wesley, 1995.

Trieschmann, J. S., Dennis, A. R., and Northcraft, G. B. "Serving Multiple Constituencies in the Business School: MBA Program vs. Research Performance." *Academy of Management Journal,* 2000, *43,* 1130–1142. (www.aom.pace.edu/amj/december2000/Trieschmann.pdf)

Trist, E., and Bamforth, K. "Some Social and Psychological Consequences of the Longwall Method of Coal Getting." *Human Relations,* 1951, *4,* 3–38.

Trost, A. H. "Leadership Is Flesh and Blood." In L. Atwater and R. Penn (eds.), *Military Leadership: Traditions and Future Trends.* Annapolis, Md.: Naval Institute Press, 1989.

Uchitelle, L. "We're Leaner, Meaner and Going Nowhere Faster." *New York Times,* May 12, 1996, sec. 4, pp. 1, 4.

Uchitelle, L., and Kleinfeld, N. R. "On the Battlefields of Business: Millions of Casualties." *New York Times,* Mar. 3, 1996, pp. 1, 13–15.

Urwick, L. "Organization as a Technical Problem." In L. H. Gulick and L. Urwick (eds.), *Papers on the Science of Administration.* New York: Columbia University Press, 1937.

Useem, M. *Investor Capitalism: How Money Managers Are Changing the Face of Corporate America.* New York: Basic Books, 1996.

Vaill, P. B. "The Purposing of High-Performance Systems." *Organizational Dynamics,* Autumn 1982, pp. 23–39.

Vaill, P. B. *Managing as a Performing Art: New Ideas for a World of Chaotic Change.* San Francisco: Jossey-Bass, 1989.

Valian, V. *Why So Slow? The Advancement of Women.* Cambridge, Mass.: MIT Press, 1999.

Varin, A. "The Royal Family A.D. (After Diana)." ABC News, Aug. 31, 2002. (http://abcnews.go.com/sections/world/DailyNews/diana020828_aftermath.html)

Vaughan, D. "Autonomy, Interdependence, and Social Control: NASA and the Space Shuttle *Challenger.*" *Administrative Science Quarterly,* 1990, *35,* 225–257.

Vaughan, D. *The* Challenger *Launch Decision: Risky Technology, Culture, and Deviance at NASA.* Chicago: University of Chicago, 1995.

Voss, J. F., Wolfe, C. R., Lawrence, J. A., and Engle, R. A. "From Representation to Decision: An Analysis of Problem Solving in International Relations." In R. J. Sternberg and P. A. Frensch (eds.), *Complex Problem Solving.* Hillsdale, N.J.: Erlbaum, 1991.

Vroom, V. H., and Yetton, P. W. *Leadership and Decision Making.* Pittsburgh: University of Pittsburgh Press, 1973.

Wald, M. L. "Panel Examines Whether NASA Was Out of Touch with Safety Problems." *New York Times,* Mar. 25, 2003, p. A-12.

Waldrop, M. M. *Complexity: The Emerging Science at the Edge of Order and Chaos.* New York: Simon & Schuster, 1992.

Waterman, R. H., Jr. *What America Does Right: Learning from Companies That Put People First.* New York: Norton, 1994.

Weatherford, J. M. *Tribes on the Hill: The United States Congress—Rituals and Realities.* Westport, Conn.: Bergin & Garvey, 1985.

Weber, M. *The Theory of Social and Economic Organization.* (T. Parsons, trans.) New York: Free Press, 1947.

Weddle, C. J. "A Study of Leadership Styles and Personality of Successful Women Administrators in Higher Education: Implications for Organizations and Training." Paper presented at conference "The Impact of Leadership," Center for Creative Leadership, Colorado Springs, 1991.

Weick, K. E. "Educational Organizations as Loosely Coupled Systems." *Administrative Science Quarterly,* 1976, *21,* 1–19.

Weick, K. E. "Cognitive Processes in Organizations." In B. E. Staw (ed.), *Research in Organizational Behavior.* Greenwich, Conn.: JAI Press, 1981.

Weick, K. E., and Bougon, M. G. "Organizations as Cognitive Maps." In H. P. Sims, Jr., D. A. Gioia, and Associates (eds.), *The Thinking Organization.* San Francisco: Jossey-Bass, 1986.

Weiner, S. S. "Participation, Deadlines, and Choice." In J. G. March and J. Olsen (eds.), *Ambiguity and Choice in Organizations.* Bergen, Norway: Universitetsforlaget, 1976.

Weisbord, M. R., and Janoff, S. *Future Search: An Action Guide to Finding Common Ground in Organizations and Communities.* San Francisco: Berrett-Koehler, 1995.

Weiss, C. H. *Social Science Research and Decision Making.* New York: Columbia University Press, 1980.

Westerlund, G., and Sjostrand, S. *Organizational Myths.* New York: HarperCollins, 1979.

White, R. W. "Competence and the Psychosexual Stages of Development." In M. R. Jones (ed.), *Nebraska Symposium on Motivation, 1960.* Lincoln: University of Nebraska Press, 1960.

Whitmyer, C. *In the Company of Others.* New York: Putnam, 1993.

Whyte, W. F. *Money and Motivation.* New York: HarperCollins, 1955.

Wilson, C., and Wilson, J. "The Impact of Personality, Gender and International Location on Multi-Level Management Ratings." Paper presented at conference "The Impact of Leadership," Center for Creative Leadership, Colorado Springs, 1991.

Wimpelberg, R. K. "Managerial Images and School Effectiveness." *Administrators' Notebook,* 1987, *32,* 1–4.

Witkin, R. "Downing of KAL 007 Laid to Russian Error." *New York Times,* June 6, 1993, p. A7.

Woodward, J. (ed.). *Industrial Organizations: Behavior and Control.* Oxford, England: Oxford University Press, 1970.

WuDunn, S. "When Lifetime Jobs Die Prematurely." *New York Times,* June 12, 1996, sec. D, pp. 1, 8.

Yorks, L., and Whitsett, D. A. *Scenarios of Change: Advocacy and the Diffusion of Job Redesign in Organizations.* New York: Praeger, 1989.

Yukl, G. *Leadership in Organizations.* (5th ed.) Upper Saddle River, N.J.: Prentice Hall, 2001.

Zachary, G. P. "Climbing the Peak: Agony and Ecstasy of 200 Code Writers Beget Windows NT." *Wall Street Journal,* May 26, 1993, pp. A1, A6.

Zachary, G. P. *Showstopper! The Breakneck Race to Create Windows NT and the Next Generation at Microsoft.* New York: Free Press, 1994.

NAME INDEX

Lo, T., 368–369
Lombardi, V., 102
Longworth, R. C., 234
Loomis, C. J., 4, 230, 231
Lopez, B., 257
Lorsch, J. W., 86, 87, 275
Love, J. F., 59
Lubans, J., 103
Lukes, S., 195
Lundin, K., 6
Lundin, W., 6
Luthans, F., 304, 313, 315, 316, 317
Lynch, P., 127
Lynn, L. E., Jr., 313, 315–317

M

Maccoby, M., 131, 339, 340
Machan, D., 79
Machiavelli, N., 15, 370
Maier, N., 173, 179
Malavé, J., 146
Mandel, B., 379
Manes, S., 202
Mangham, I. L., 270, 274
Mao Zedong, 365, 433
March, J. G., 28, 36–37, 190, 191, 235, 242, 268, 274, 278, 280–281, 284, 285
Marcus, B., 254
Maritz, P., 203, 204, 206, 213
Mark, R., 22, 38, 39, 254
Markels, A., 128
Marriott, J. W., Sr., 258
Marshall, C., 320–333
Marshall, M. V., 234
Marx, K., 132n1, 134
Marx, R., 185
Maslow, A. H., 116, 117, 118, 217
Mattis, M., 347
Mayer, J. D., 168, 169
Mayo, E., 113, 134
McAuliffe, C., 183, 187
McCarthy, D., 244–246
McCaskey, M. B., 27
McClelland, D. C., 116
McConnell, M., 184, 185, 256, 263

McCourt, M., 381
McGrath, J. E., 173
McGregor, D., 113, 118–119, 123
McKee, A., 11, 169
McLean, B., 3, 143, 219
McLennan, R., 374
McNamee, M., 71
Meckling, W. H., 48, 116
Meese, E., 211
Mendelson, H., 214
Meredith, R., 126
Messier, J.-M., 196
Meyer, J. W., 242, 272, 274, 275
Miller, D., 84, 85
Minich, P., 93, 94
Mintzberg, H., 10, 49, 52, 53, 73–80, 82–83, 92, 161, 279, 280, 304
Mirvis, P. H., 124, 159
Mishel, L., 152
Mitroff, I. I., 257, 377
Moeller, J., 46
Mola, R., 264
Moliere, 211
Montgomery, L., 138
Moore, J. F., 228, 229
Morgan, G., 10, 129
Morganthau, T., 379
Morris, B., 230, 348
Morrison, A. M., 333, 346, 405
Moskowitz, M., 134, 137, 333, 397, 402
Moulton, B., 205
Mouton, J. S., 171, 340–341
Mullins, G., 379
Murphy, J. T., 338
Murray, M., 128
Myers, I., 171

N

Nadler, D. A., 47, 49
Nanus, B., 192, 337, 339, 340, 354, 362
Nelson, R. R., 375
Neuman, R. P., 11
Nicklaus, J., 223
Nickles, D., 262
Nixon, R., 6

SUBJECT INDEX

Benefits, employee, 138–139
Berwind Company, 77–78
Beth Israel Hospital, 90–91
Big 5 model of personality, 172
Black Hawk helicopters, accidental shooting
 down of, 31–32, 175, 185
Blame, 35, 37–39, 164–165, 185–186
Boeing, 84, 267, 313
Books on management, 11–12, 435–438
British Airways, 28
Built to Last (Collins and Porras), 246, 253,
 313–315, 317–318
Bureaucracies: blaming, 37–39; ethics in, 200;
 machine, 47, 75–77, 83, 86–88; professional,
 77, 78, 83; stagnant, 84; Weber's model of, 46
Business ecosystems, 230–231
Business-government ecosystems, 232–233

C

Camp David treaty (1978), 213
Caring, 219, 398, 400, 402
Carnaud et Metal Box, 10, 142
Caterpillar, 313
Catholic Church, ritual in, 260
Central Intelligence Agency (CIA), conflict
 between FBI and, 14, 15
Ceremony: in groups, 295–296; and organizational change, 381; significance built by,
 406–407; and spirit, 298; as symbolic form,
 251, 264–267
Challenger space shuttle disaster, 6–7, 183–185;
 political frame applied to, 185–186, 187–188,
 190, 199, 204, 208
Change: and conflict, 376–378, 389–391; failed
 implementation of, 367, 368–370; and
 human resource frame, 370, 372–373,
 386–387; integrated multiframe approach to,
 385, 388–393; and loss, 378–383; model of,
 383–384, 386–387, 393; parable about, 371;
 and political frame, 372, 376–378, 386–387;
 reframing, 370–383; resistance to, 373,
 376–377, 379–380; slow response to, 77;
 and structural frame, 372, 373–376, 386–387;
 and symbolic frame, 285–286, 372, 378–383,
 386–387, 391–393; and training, 370,

372–373, 388–389. *See also*
 Restructuring
Chase Manhattan, 128, 313
Chemical Bank, 128
Chernobyl nuclear accident, 22
China: antipiracy efforts in, 188–189;
 Community Party in, 28, 194; downsizing in,
 139; myth about Communist rule in, 195;
 skill gap in, 126; social control in, 193; sym-
 bolic leadership in, 365
"China Issues White Paper.," 189
"China Says 'No'.," 139
Chrysler Corporation, 127, 153, 356–360
Cin-Made, 144
Circle network team design, 97, 100
Cisco Systems, 7, 288
Citibank, 66, 86–88, 313
Civil rights movement, 226–227
Cluelessness, 4, 6–8
Coalitions: building, 210–211; organizations as,
 189–191; and political frame, 186, 187, 188
Coca-Cola, 153, 189, 378–380
Coercive isomorphism, 273
Coercive power, 195
Collective bargaining, 282–283, 405
Columbia space shuttle disaster, 183
Commitment: and choice of frame, 309, 312;
 to core values, 432–433
Communication: with lateral coordination,
 53; in Model II theory-in-use, 166; multiple
 frame view of, 307; in web of inclusion
 model, 81–82
Companies. *See* Organizations
Compaq, 56, 359–360
Compensation. *See* Pay
Competing for the Future (Hamel and
 Prahalad), 396
Complexity: coping with, 30–35; and
 environment, 61; of organizations, 25, 69
Computer operating systems, 202–203
Conflict: and change, 376–378, 389–391;
 and choice of frame, 311; interpersonal,
 in groups, 176–178; multiple frame view of
 approaching, 307; between personality and
 organizations, 119–124, 132n1; and political

Employees (*continued*)
downsizing's effect on, 128–129; participation by, 144–146; pay and benefits for, 138–139; promoting from within, 140; rest breaks for, 134; sharing wealth with, 136, 140–142; strategies for keeping, 136, 137–142; training, 142; trends affecting relationship between organizations and, 124–126; workload of, 70. *See also* Workforce

Empowerment: of employees, 136, 143–153; by human resource leaders, 356

Enron Corporation: blame at, 37, 38; cluelessness of leadership at, 7; competing strategies at, 22–23; deception at, 26, 30; executive compensation at, 152; fall of, 3–4, 19n1, 25; instrumental values ignored at, 218, 219; lack of financial clarity at, 143; loss of soul at, 394–395; managerial self-protection at, 167–168; performance assessment at, 199

Enterprise Rent-a-Car, 137

Environment: as reason for restructuring, 84; structural implications of, 61

Environmental Protection Agency, 277

Espoused theories, 163

Ethics: leadership's contributions to, 400–407; and political frame, 198–200; and politics, 216–219; reframing, 400; and soul, 395–396, 398–399

Evaluation: conflict over implementation of, 376–377; multiple frame view of, 306; as theater, 281–282

An Evolutionary Theory of Economic Change (Nelson and Winter), 375

Example, leadership by, 291–292, 361

Excellence, organizational, 313–315, 317–318, 400–402

Executives, pay for, 152–153

Expectations: perception as influenced by, 31–35; of women as leaders, 347

Experimental Schools Project, 376–377

Expertise: mix of, high-performing teams, 105; as source of power, 194

The External Control of Organizations (Pfeffer and Salancik), 235

Exxon, 159, 313

F

Factory metaphor, 400–402

Fairy tales, 251, 256–259

Faith, as organizational ethic, 400, 405–407

Fallacies, in organizational diagnosis, 35–39

Family metaphor, 400, 402–403

The Feast of Fools (Cox), 269

Federal Aviation Administration (FAA), 231, 277

Federal Bureau of Investigation (FBI), 199; conflict between CIA and, 14, 15

Federal Express (FedEx), 118, 135–136, 139, 140, 232–233, 355

Food and Drug Administration, 277

Football teams, 101–102

Ford Motor Company, 350

Four-frame model, overview of, 15, 16

Frames: choosing, 309–312; defined, 12–13; effective managers' use of, 315–318; functions of, 18; Giuliani's use of, 303–304; managers' preferences for, 318–319; model of four, overview of, 15, 16; and multiframe thinking, 15–18, 19n3, 306–307, 433–434; organizational decision making as influenced by, 36–37; and organizational excellence, 313–315, 317–318; reality determined by, 305–309; terms for, 12, 19n2. *See also* Human resource frame; Political frame; Reframing; Structural frame; Symbolic frame

Framing, as source of power, 195

"Framing effect," 35

Friendly-fire incident, 31–32, 175, 185

From Good to Great (Collins), 313–315, 317–318

From Worst to First: Behind the Scenes of Continental's Remarkable Comeback (Bethune and Huler), 11–12, 15

Future search programs, 158

G

Gain-sharing plans, 141

Gender: and leadership, 344–348; and masculinity-femininity as cultural dimension, 249

General Electric (GE), 74, 127, 230–231, 313, 351

General Foods, 150

The General Managers (Kotter), 313, 315–318

General Motors (GM), 159; as business eco-system, 230; challenge to leadership at, 4; "management by wandering around" at, 355–356; NUMMI venture of, 155–157, 353; quality of work life at, 130–131; restructuring of, 88; structural leadership of, 349–353. *See also* Saturn Corporation

Generality, as ethical value, 218

Geography, as basis of groups, 49

Getting to Yes (Fisher and Ury), 212–213

Glasnost, 197

Glass ceiling, 346–348

Global capitalism, vs. tribalism, 237–238

Globalization: interorganizational networks with, 55; new organization-employee relationship with, 124–126; and society as ecosystem, 233–238; structural implications of, 47, 51, 54–55, 66

Goal setting: multiple frame view of, 307; negotiation for, 186, 187–189

Goals: of high-performing teams, 105; structural implications of, 62–63, 72; structural vs. political, 190; types of, 62

Government: organizational improvement initiatives of, 9; regulatory agencies of, as theater, 277–278

Government-business ecosystems, 232–233

Greyhound Lines, 86

Groups, 93–109; advantages and disadvantages of, 172–173; autonomy vs. interdependence of, 71; identity of, and stories, 292–293; implementing human relations management in, 157–158; informal cultural players in, 296–297; informal norms in, 175–176; informal roles in, 173–175; interpersonal conflict in, 176–178; interpersonal dynamics in, 172–179; leadership in, 178–179; structural design options for, 49–50, 96–101; symbolic frame applied to, 289–298; T-groups, 157–158. *See also* Teams

H

Harley-Davidson, 241

Harvard University: as professional bureau-cracy, 77; restructuring of, 68, 69; structure of, 57–58, 60, 61, 62, 65, 66; symbols used by, 246

The Heart of Change (Cohen), 383

Heroes and heroines: leaders as, 338; as organizational symbols, 251, 254–256

Hewlett-Packard, 56, 71, 74, 313, 355, 356–360

"Hewlett-Packard Merger Pitch.," 359

Hierarchical structure: of McDonald's, 56–57, 58; for teams, 96–97, 98, 99. *See also* Vertical coordination

Hillcrest Corporation, 160–161

Hiring practices, 136, 137, 140

Home Depot, 254–255, 256

Homeland Security Department, 277

Horizontal coordination. *See* Lateral coordination

Hospital Corporation of America (HCA), 258

Human needs. *See* Needs

Human resource frame, 111–112, 132; assumptions of, 115; and change, 370, 372–373, 386–387; organizational process as viewed by, 306–307; overview of, 14, 16, 18; and political frame, 185; power as viewed by, 192; reframing in, 324–326, 420–421; and relationship between people and organizations, 113–132; shortcomings of, 332; theories underlying, 113–114; when to choose, 309–312. *See also* Human resource management; Interpersonal dynamics

Human resource leadership, 349, 354–356, 365

Human resource management, 133–159; barriers to successful, 134–135; diversity-promotion strategies for, 136, 153–154; early efforts to improve, 133–134; employee-empowerment strategies for, 136, 143–153; hiring strategies for, 136, 137, 140; investing-in-employees strategy for, 136, 142; keeping employees as strategy for, 136, 137–142; philosophy for, 135–136; techniques for implementing, 157–159; TQM strategy for, 154–157

Humor: in groups, 293–294; at Southwest Airlines, 137, 397, 401; as symbolic form, 268

Hygiene factors, and job redesign, 147–148

ership and, 337–338; improving, 8–9; in
Mintzberg's structural model, 73, 74; open-
book, 143–144; Theory X vs. Theory Y of,
118–119, 135. *See also* Human resource management; Leadership; Managers

Management styles, 170–172, 318, 319, 342–344

Managerial grid, 340–341, 344

Managers: agenda setting by, 205–207; bargaining and negotiation by, 211–216; effectiveness
of, 315–319; ethics of, 216–219; expanding
thinking of, 16–17; frames preferred by,
318–319; image vs. reality of, 304–305;
inevitability of politics for, 204–205, 220; network and coalition building by, 208, 210–211;
new or outside, reframing for, 332–333; perception of situation by, 24, 33, 34; political
mapping by, 207–208, 209; political skills of,
205–219; as politicians, 202–220; promoted
from within, 140; roles for, 235; self-
protection by, 167. *See also* Leadership;
Management

Managing by Storying Around (Armstrong),
257–258

Managing Public Policy (Lynn), 313, 315–318

Maps: mental, 12, 35; political, 207–208, 209,
422–423; system, 28

March of Dimes, 72

Marion Laboratories, 129–130

Marketing concept, 234, 236

Mary Kay Cosmetics, 265

Masculinity-femininity, as cultural dimension,
249

Maslow's hierarchy of needs, 117–118, 217

Matrix structures, 54–55, 56

Matsushita, 149

Mazda, 140

McDonald's, 313; action planning by, 53;
as machine bureaucracy, 75–76; structure of,
56–57, 58, 59–60, 62, 65, 66; symbols used by,
246

McGraw-Hill, 68–69

MCI, 85

McKinsey & Co., 9

McWane, 114, 131

McWorld, vs. jihad, 237–238

Meaning, 240. *See also* Symbolic frame

Meetings: with lateral coordination, 53, 55;
multiple frame view of, 307; as theater,
278–279; in web of inclusion model, 81–82

Mental maps, 12, 35

Mental models, 6–7, 13. *See also* Frames

Merck, 313, 396

Mergers, corporate, 8

Metaphors, 267–268, 391–392, 400

Metric system, 367

Microsoft, 28, 137, 202–203, 214–215

Mimetic isomorphism, 273

Minorities. *See* Diversity

The Misanthrope (Molière), 211

Mitsubishi, 298

Model I theory-in-use, 163–165, 176–177, 421

Model II theory-in-use, 165–167

Modern Times, 119–120

Moral reasoning, 217

Morale: with employee participation, 145;
organizational structure's effect on, 46–47

Morality. *See* Ethics

Morton Thiokol Corporation, 184–185,
187–188, 199, 208

Motivation: and choice of frame, 309, 312;
and job redesign, 147–148; multiple frame
view of, 307

Motorola, 401, 404

Multiframe thinking, 15–18, 19n3, 306–307,
433–434

Music, 407

Mutuality, 218

Myers-Briggs Type Indicator, 171–172

Myths, 251–252, 253–254, 259

N

Nabisco, 222–223. *See also* RJR Nabisco

National Aeronautics and Space Administration
(NASA), 6–7, 183–185, 187–188, 208

National Health Service Corps (NHSC),
308–309

National labor Relations Board, 277

Needs: human, 115–117; Maslow's hierarchy
of, 117–118, 217; workers', aligning jobs with,
113. *See also* Motivation

Negotiation: as managerial skill, 211–216; and political frame, 186, 187–189

Nepotism policy, 25–26

Networks: all-channel (star), 98, 101; building, 210–211; circle, 97, 100; electronic, 64; for lateral coordination, 55; as source of power, 195

New Lanark, Scotland knitting mills, 133–134

New Patterns of Management (Likert), 158

New United Motors Manufacturing, Inc. (NUMMI), 155–157, 353

Newsweek, 256

Nordstrom department stores, 47, 244–246

Normative isomorphism, 273

Norms, informal group, 175–176

Norway, 147, 151

Novo-Nordisk, 10

O

"On a Clear Day.," 353

One-boss team design, 96, 97

Open space programs, 158

Open systems, 113

Open-book management, 143–144

Openness, 167, 197, 218–219

Operating core, 73, 74

Organization charts, 14, 41

Organization development (OD), 159

Organizational change. *See* Change

Organizational culture: defined, 243; Harley-Davidson, 241; and leadership, 244; of Nordstrom department stores, 244–246; relationship between national culture and, 249; and symbolic frame, 287–299. *See also* Symbols

Organizational diagnosis, common fallacies in, 35–39

Organizational excellence, 313–315, 317–318, 400–402

Organizational learning, 27–30, 191

Organizational process: multiple frame perspective on, 306–307; as theater, 278–285

Organizational structure. *See* Structure

Organizations: advantages and disadvantages of, 5–6; characteristics of, affecting structural design, 58–66; as coalitions, 189–191; com-plexity of, 25, 69; conflict between people and, 119–124, 132n1; conflict in, 186, 187, 197–198; as cultures, 243–246; growth of, and restructuring, 84; high-performing, investment in workforce by, 129–131; improving, 8–12; inhuman treatment of workers in, 113–115, 119–124; mergers of, 8; as multiple realities, 305–309; as political agents, 224–225, 228–238; as political arenas, 224, 225–228, 238; properties of, 24–27; relationship between society and, 233–238; soul and spirit in, 396–399; symbols used by, 246–269; trends in relationship between workers and, 124–126. *See also* Organizational culture

Organizations (March and Simon), 36–37

Outback Steakhouse, 298

Overbounded systems, 196–197

P

Participation: employee, 144–146; and employee morale, 46–47

Partisans, 193–194, 226

Pay: for employees, 138; executive, 152–153; for skills, 150

People's Express, 47

Pepsi, 378–380

Perception: expectations' effect on, 31–35; as leadership task, 24, 33–34; personal theories' effect on, 34–35

Performance, and team structure, 104–106

Performance assessment. *See* Evaluation

Performance control, 52

Personal power, 195

Personality: and management styles, 171–172; and organizations, 119–124, 132n1

Pfizer, 313

Pharmaceutical companies, 232, 377–378

Planning: action, 53; strategic, 279, 306; as theater, 279–281; with vertical coordination, 52–53

Play, 268–269, 293–294

Polaris missile system, 270–271

Policies: flexibility in following, 72; with vertical coordination, 51–52

Political action: bottom-up, 226–227; top-down, 227–228

Political agents, organizations as, 224–225, 228–238

Political arenas, organizations as, 224, 225–228, 238

Political frame, 181–182; applied to *Challenger* disaster, 185–186, 187–188, 190, 199, 204, 208; assumptions of, 186–189; and authorities, 193–194, 200–201; and bargaining/negotiation, 186, 187–189; and change, 372, 376–378, 386–387; and conflict, 186, 187, 197–198; and ethics, 198–200; and human resource frame, 185; and organizational excellence, 314, 315; organizational process as viewed by, 306–307; overview of, 14–15, 16, 18; politics as viewed by, 185–186; and power, 186, 187, 188, 192–197, 201;reframing in, 326–328, 421–423; shortcomings of, 332; when to choose, 309–312

Political influence, steps for exercising, 208, 210

Political leadership, 349, 356–360

Political maps, 207–208, 209, 422–423

Politicians, managers as, 202–220

Politics: in development of computer operating system, 202–203; and ethics, 216–219; inevitability of, for managers, 204–205, 220; negative image of, 181; political frame's view of, 185–186

Power: of authorities and partisans, 193–194; destructive vs. constructive, 422; distribution of, 196–197, 358; gift of, 403–405; of organizations in society, 234, 236–237, 238; and political frame, 186, 187, 188, 192, 201; of reframing, 15–18, 19, 40, 331–332; sources of, 194–196; and theater, 283–285; thirst for, 38, 39

Power distance, 248–249

The Power of Myth (Campbell), 242

POWs, 256

Pret à Manger, 10

Primal Leadership (Goleman, McKee, and Boyatzis), 11, 14, 169

The Prince (Machiavelli), 15, 370

Princeton University, 348

Processes: as basis of groups, 49; core, 60–61;

group, 173–179; organizational, 278–285, 306–307

Procter & Gamble (P&G), 113, 149, 313

Productivity, with employee participation, 145, 146

Products, as basis of groups, 49

Professional bureaucracies, 77, 78, 83

Profit-sharing plans, 141–142

Promotion from within, 140

Public policy ecosystems, 231–232

Publix, 139

Pygmalion effect, 35

R

Rashomon (Kurosawa), 17

Real Managers (Luthans, Yodgetts, and Rosenkrantz), 313, 315–318

Realities: for managers, 304–305; multiple, organizations as, 305–309

Redesigning jobs, 146–149

Reengineering: case examples of, 85–92; goals unmet by, 8. *See also* Restructuring

Reframing: artistry in, 429–430, 433–434; case example of scenarios in, 320–333; change, 370–383; ethics, 400; in human resource frame, 324–326, 420–421; leadership, 348–366; for newcomers and outsiders, 332–333; in political frame, 326–328, 421–423; power of, 15–18, 19, 40, 331–332; rap about, 40; risks of, 331–332; in structural frame, 321–324, 418–420; in symbolic frame, 328–331, 423–425

Reorganization. *See* Restructuring

Reorganizing, multiple frame view of, 306

Resistance: by assembly-line workers, 120–123, 130–131; to change, 373, 376–377, 379–380

Resources. *See* Scarce resources

Responsibility charting, 106, 420

Restructuring: case examples of, 68–69, 85–92; and choice of frame, 311–312; and information technology, 64–65; issues in, 82–83; of McGraw-Hill, 68–69; principles for successful, 91–92; reasons for, 83–85. *See also* Reengineering

Rewards, control of, 194

The Rise and Fall of Strategic Planning (Mintzberg), 279

Rituals: with change, 381, 391; in groups, 295–296; significance built by, 406–407; and spirit, 298; as symbolic form, 251, 259–264, 266–267

Ritz-Carlton, 137, 142, 258–259

RJR Nabisco, 223–224, 226, 229, 310, 311

Robert F. Kennedy High School: case study of, 409–418; reframing applied to, 418–430

Roles: informal, in groups, 173–175; for managers, 235

Romania, 193

Rules: flexibility in following, 72; with vertical coordination, 51–52

Russian passenger jet disaster, 65

S

Salaries. *See* Pay

SAP, 149

SAS Institute, 10, 138–139

Saturn Corporation, 10, 47, 152, 353; authorship at, 401–402; ceremony at, 266–267; symbol of power at, 404; teams at, 106–108, 149

Scandals, corporate, 219, 398–399

Scandinavian Air System (SAS), 298, 356

Scanlon plans, 141

Scarce resources, 422; and choice of frame, 311; and political frame, 186, 187, 188

Scientific management, 45

Scott Paper, 28–29, 127

Securities and Exchange Commission (SEC), 277

Self-actualization, as human need, 117, 119

Self-destructive intelligence syndrome, 6

Self-protection, 167–168

Semco, 151, 152

Sensitivity training, 157–158

Seoul department store collapse, 22

September 11. *See* Terrorist attacks

Shearson Lehman Hutton, 224

Shoney's restaurants, 153

Significance, 400, 405–407

Simple hierarchy team design, 97, 99

Simple structures, 73–74, 75, 83

Situational model of leadership, 342–344

The Six Sigma Way (Pande, Neuman, and Cavanagh), 11, 14

Size: of high-performing teams, 105; organizational, structural implications of, 58–60

Skills: as basis of groups, 49; changing requirements for, 125–126; pay for, 150; political, of managers, 205–219

Social control, 193–194

Social intelligence, 168

Society, relationship between organizations and, 233–238

Sony Corporation, 313

Soul, 297–298; Enron's loss of, 394–395; and ethics, 395–396, 398–399; in organizations, 396–399

The Soul of a New Machine (Kidder), 288

Southwest Airlines: CEO pay at, 152; commitment of employees at, 129; heroes at, 255; humor at, 137, 397, 401; labor bargaining at, 405; love at, 402; myths at, 251–252; spirit at, 396–397

Soviet Union, 197

Specialization, 49, 105, 120

Spirit: and leadership, 406; in organizations, 396–399; of successful groups, 297–298; team building centered on, 298–299

Sports teams, 100–103

Springfield Remanufacturing. *See* SRC Holdings

SRC Holdings (formerly Springfield Remanufacturing), 143–144

Standard Brands, 221–222

Standard operating procedures (SOPs), 52

Standards, 51

Star networks, 98, 100

Stories, 251, 256–259; and group identity, 292–293; significance built by, 407; symbolic leaders' telling of, 363–364

Strategic apex, 73, 74, 82

Strategic planning, 279, 306

Strategy, structural implications of, 62–63

The Strategy of Conflict (Schelling), 214–215

Structural frame, 41–42, 66–67; assumptions of, 44–45; and change, 372, 373–376,

386–387; organizational process as viewed by, 306–307; overview of, 14, 16, 18; reframing in, 321–324, 418–420; shortcomings of, 332; theoretical roots of, 45–46; when to choose, 309–312. *See also* Structure

Structural leadership, 349–353

Structure: ad hoc, 79–80, 83; and agency problem, 48; of aircraft carrier, 43–44; of Citibank International, 66; configurations of, 72–82; considerations when designing, 58–66; differentiation in, 49, 50; dilemmas resolved by, 69–72; of Harvard University, 57–58, 60, 61, 62, 65, 66, 68; impact on workplace activities, 46–49; integration in, 49–50; lateral coordination in, 53–56; loose vs. tight, 71–72; matrix, 54–55; of McDonald's, 56–57, 58, 59–60, 62, 65, 66; Mintzberg's model of, 73–80, 82–83, 92; and response to terrorist attacks, 44; of successful teams, 93–95; as theater, 275–278; vertical coordination in, 50–53; web of inclusion model of, 80–82. *See also* Restructuring

Students for a Democratic Society (SDS), 195

Suboptimization, 50

Support staff, 73, 74, 83

Surprise, in organizations, 25–26

Surveys, and human resource management, 158–159

Sweden, 151

Symbolic egalitarianism, 152, 155

Symbolic frame, 239–240; applied to groups/teams, 289–298; assumptions of, 242–243; and change, 285–286, 372, 378–383, 386–387, 391–393; and organizational culture, 287–299; organizational process as viewed by, 306–307; overview of, 15, 16, 19; reframing in, 328–331, 423–425; shortcomings of, 332; theoretical roots of, 242; when to choose, 309–312. *See also* Symbols

Symbolic leadership, 349, 360–365

Symbols, 240, 246–269; after terrorist attacks, 241–242; "as if" quality of, 267–268; Continental Airline's use of, 250–251; forms of, 251–269; of Harley-Davidson culture, 241;

plans as, 280; significance built by, 406–407; in successful teams, 288–298; Volvo France's use of, 246–248. *See also specific symbolic forms*

System dynamics, 29–30

System maps, 28

Systems: open, 113; overbounded vs. underbounded, 196–197

Systems models, 28–29

T

T-groups, 157–158

Task forces, 53–54, 55

Tasks: impact on teamwork, 99–103, 108–109; as level of operation of groups, 173

Team building, 158, 298–299

Team Zebra, 385, 388–393

Teams, 93–109; diversity on, 290–291; high-performing, 104–106; interpersonal dynamics in, 172–179; language of, 292; at Saturn Corporation, 106–108; self-managing, 149–150; sports, 100–103; structural design options for, 95–101; structure of successful, 93–95; symbolic frame applied to, 289–298; teamwork and interdependence on, 99–103. *See also* Groups

Teamwork: determinants of successful, 103–104; task's impact on, 99–103, 108–109

Technical quality, and choice of frame, 309–310

Technology: new, structural implications of, 60–61; as reason for restructuring, 84; structural implications of, 63–65

Technostructure, 73, 74, 83

Temple metaphor, 400, 405–407

Terrorist attacks: and airline standard operating procedures (SOPs), 52; heroic response to, 255–256; structure of organizations responding to, 44; suboptimization in response to, 50; symbols after, 241–242

Texaco, 153

Texas Instruments, 159, 313

Theater, 270–286; institutional theory on organizations as, 271–275; organizational process as, 278–285; organizational structure as, 275–278; Polaris missile system as, 270–271

Theories: of change, 383–384, 386–387, 393; espoused vs. in-use, 163; of leadership, 339–344; on organizations as theater, 271–275; personal, 34–35, 163–167; total quality management (TQM), 154–155; underlying human resource frame, 113–114; underlying structural frame, 45–46; underlying symbolic frame, 242; value of pluralism of, 39–40

Theories-in-use: defined, 163; Model I, 163–165, 176–177, 421; Model II, 165–167

"Theory of the Firm: Managerial Behavior, Agency Costs, and Ownership Structure" (Jensen and Meckling), 48

Theory X, 118, 119, 135

Theory Y, 118–119

Thiokol. *See* Morton Thiokol Corporation

Three Mile Island nuclear accident, 22

3M, 253, 313

Time, as basis of groups, 49

Time magazine, Person of the Year award, 199

Total quality management (TQM): NUMMI example of, 155–157; theoretical basis of, 154–155

Toyota, 28, 149; NUMMI venture of, 155–157, 353

Training: and change, 370, 372–373, 388–389; employee, 142; group techniques for, 157–158; for teams, 150. *See also* Learning

Transforming vs. transactional leadership, 361

Tribalism, vs. global capitalism, 237–238

Twin Towers tragedy. *See* Terrorist attacks

Tyco, 48

Tyler Pipe, 114

U

Uncertainty: avoidance of, 249; and choice of frame, 310–311

Underbounded systems, 196–197

Understanding the situation. *See* Perception

Unions: as bottom-up political action, 226–227; justice/power issue with, 405; at NUMMI plant, 156

United Airlines, 141, 142

United Automobile Workers (UAW), 107, 131, 152

U.S. Air Force, 262–264, 298

U.S. Army, 52

U.S. Congress: ceremony in, 265–266; ritual in, 260–261

U.S. Department of Homeland Security, 50, 70

U.S. Marine Corps, 252

U.S. Navy, 159, 270–271

U.S. Postal Service, 159

USS Kennedy, 43–44, 51

USS Stark, 32, 33

USS Vincennes, 32–33

V

Value creating vs. claiming, 212, 213–215

Values: commitment to core, 432–433; as symbolic form, 252, 253

Venezuelan health care system, 145–146

Vertical coordination, 50–53, 56

Village Voice, 81

Vision: and change, 391–392; as symbolic form, 252–253; symbolic leaders' communication of, 362–363

Volkswagen, 125

Volvo, 13, 151

Volvo France, 246–248

W

War in Iraq (2003), 63, 364

Web of inclusion, 80–82

Westinghouse, 313

What Would Machiavelli Do? The Ends Justify the Meanness (Bing), 11, 14–15

Who Moved My Cheese? An A-Mazing Way to Deal with Change in Your Work and Your Life (Johnson), 371

Whole Foods Markets, 149–150, 152–153

The Wisdom of Teams (Katzenbach and Smith), 104

Women: glass ceiling for, 346–348; leadership by, 344–346, 348; and web of inclusion, 80–82. *See also* Diversity

Work-out conferences, 158

Workforce: diversity of, 153–154; skill requirements in, 125–126; structural implications
of, 65. *See also* Employees

Working with Emotional Intelligence (Goleman),
169

Workplace, democracy in, 150–153

World Trade Center. *See* Terrorist attacks

WorldCom, 19n1, 30, 85, 199, 218

Y

Yale University, 311

Yugoslavia, 150–15